THE HOOVER
POLICIES

THE
HOOVER
POLICIES

BY

RAY LYMAN WILBUR

President of Stanford University
Former Secretary of the Interior

AND

ARTHUR MASTICK HYDE

Former Governor of Missouri
Former Secretary of Agriculture

NEW YORK
CHARLES SCRIBNER'S SONS
1937

CONTENTS

v

CONTENTS

PREFACE

PREFACE

The world is enveloped in sweeping economic, social and political forces unleashed by the Great War, by tremendous advances in productive technology, by the failure of an economic system to advance apace with a growing sense of humanitarianism.

In the solution of these immense problems we are face to face with two clashing philosophies of government. Both have as their objective the advancement of the welfare of a great people.

The first proposes to find solutions through a vast turn toward centralization of government, "economic planning" with its strong measures of coercion of individuals. The second proposes to accomplish the same ends within the framework of strong local as well as Federal Government and the development of understanding and voluntary co-operative action among free men. The one drives toward personal government where the state is the master of men. The other drives toward a government of laws where men are masters of the state. The one drives toward Collectivism. The other drives toward American Individualism. The one attempts a revolution; the other moves forward by evolution.

Neither American form runs to European extremes, but the concepts of a system that seeks its ends through freedom and one that seeks them through coercion are as wide apart as the poles. The one represents progress in the spirit of the Constitution, the other insists in fundamental changes in authority under it.

One of these philosophies is represented in the "New Deal" under Franklin Roosevelt's leadership; the other is represented in traditional American principles, courageously and ably led by Herbert Hoover.

The purpose of this volume is to present Hoover's principles and policies both in philosophy of government and in action. It is not an attempt to write a history of the times.

Hoover had a dual and often conflicting job as President. He had to meet the surge of imperative social and economic forces demanding solution, and at the same time, he had to deal with an unparalleled economic emergency.

To best present these policies, they have been divided under the special problems of the times, yet those policies and actions dealing with the emergency of the depression are so connected with current events that a rough historic sequence has been followed. As his philosophy of government had roots deep in his public service long before he became President and as many of his policies were of long-standing use, we have in some cases gone back beyond his Presidency.

We present this philosophy and these policies mainly through quotations and actions of Hoover himself. Our contribution is to connect and to arrange them.

As members of a national administration that had both purpose and ideals, we have considered it a duty to present this volume not out of our affection for a leader but out of the need of understanding of these questions.

We not only struggled with the early stages of a great world depression, but in the midst of our work an election brought a Democratic Congress to Washington, more intent upon turning us out and winning places for themselves than in co-operating to bring the country out of the depression.

History will record that despite many handicaps President Hoover guided the Nation safely through perilous times and placed it on the road to recovery in 1932. It will also record the effective care of distress, the unparalleled industrial peace of the times, and the fidelity to national obligations.

It will record that Hoover originated and developed more new governmental policies for the correction of business abuse and the advancement of economic life than any President up to his time. It will record that it was Hoover who laid the foundations for an era of social progress in this country. It will record that with these great accomplishments he held to Constitutional Government and to the fundamental ideals of free men. Above all, it will record him as the American leader of these principles in his times.

THE HOOVER
POLICIES

SOCIAL–ECONOMIC AND GOVERNMENTAL POLICIES

PROBLEMS AND OBJECTIVES

Hoover has many times stated his conception of the objectives of American life.

Only a few of his many statements of deep humanitarian feeling can be reproduced here. (See also *Social Policies in Action,* pp. 48 ff.)

In an address before the Federated American Engineering Societies at Washington on November 19, 1920, he said:

". . . Our economic system under which it has been accomplished has given stimulation to invention, to enterprise, to individual improvement of the highest order, yet it presents a series of human and social difficulties to the solution of which we are groping. The congestion of population is producing subnormal conditions of life. The vast repetitive operations are dulling the human mind. The intermittency of employment due to the bad co-ordination of industry, the great waves of unemployment in the ebb and flow of economic tides, the ever present industrial conflicts by strike and lockout, produce infinite wastes and great suffering. Our business enterprises have become so large and complex that the old pleasant relationship between employer and worker has, to a great extent, disappeared. The aggregation of great wealth with its power to economic domination presents social and economic ills which we are constantly struggling to remedy."

Speaking in New York, October 16, 1926, he said:

". . . intellectual, moral and spiritual progress is not the product of poverty. . . . Of all human ideals, one of the most important is the achievement for men and women of freedom from anxiety about to-morrow's food. Only in peace of mind can man's spirit flower and his humanity expand toward others. Another ideal is that every parent should have confidence that he can give his children the highest education. That confidence must rest upon confidence in continued and stable

I

employment. . . . Further than that, educational institutions, colleges and public school, can only be erected and kept running by previous accumulations of material prosperity. Absence of poverty on the part of the individual and of the nation is one of the most important ideals, one of the most early sought. The abolition of poverty has been the dream of idealists since the beginning of time. That condition has been more nearly achieved in the United States today than ever before in any other country or in any other time. . . ."

Speaking at Palo Alto, on August 11, 1928, he said:

"One of the oldest and perhaps the noblest of human aspirations has been abolition of poverty. By poverty I mean the grinding by under-nourishment, cold and ignorance, and fear of old age of those who have the will to work. We in America today are nearer to the final triumph over poverty than ever before in the history of any land. The poorhouse is vanishing from among us. We have not yet reached the goal . . . but . . . we shall soon with the help of God be within sight of the day when poverty will be banished from this nation. There is no guarantee against poverty equal to a job for every man. That is the primary purpose of the economic policies we advocate."

"To me the foundation of American life rests upon the home and the family. I read into these great economic forces, these intricate and delicate relations of the government with business and with our political and social life, but one supreme end . . . that we strengthen the security, the happiness, and the independence of every home."

"My conception of America is a land where men and women may walk in ordered freedom in the independent conduct of their occupations; where they may enjoy the advantages of wealth, not concentrated in the hands of the few but spread through the lives of all; where they build and safeguard their homes, and give to their children the fullest advantages and opportunities of American life; where every man shall be respected in the faith that his conscience and his heart direct him to follow; where a contented and happy people, secure in their liberties, free from poverty and fear, shall have the leisure and impulse to seek a fuller life."

"Some may ask where all this may lead beyond mere material progress. It leads to a release of the energies of men and women from the dull drudgery of life to a wider vision and a higher hope. It leads to the opportunity for greater and greater service, not alone from man to man in our own land, but from our country to the whole world. It leads to an

America, healthy in body, healthy in spirit, unfettered, youthful, eager—
with a vision searching beyond the farthest horizons, with an open mind,
sympathetic and generous."   [*The New Day, pp. 16 ff.*]

He touched upon this subject in his Inaugural Address:

"The larger purpose of our economic thought should be to establish
more firmly stability and security of business and employment and
thereby remove poverty still further from our borders. . . . We have
need further to perfect the means by which Government can be adapted
to human service."

". . . Superficial observers fail to see that the American people are
engrossed in the building for themselves of a new economic system, a new
social system, a new political system. . . . The Government must, so far
as lies within its proper powers, give leadership to the realization of
these ideals and to the fruition of these aspirations. No one can adequately reduce these things of the spirit to phrases or to a catalogue of
definitions. We do know what the attainments of these ideals should be:
The preservation of self-government and its full foundations in local
government; the perfection of justice whether in economic or in social
fields; the maintenance of ordered liberty; the denial of domination by
any group or class; the building up and preservation of equality of opportunity; the stimulation of initiative and individuality; absolute integrity in public affairs; the choice of officials for fitness to office; the
direction of economic progress toward prosperity and the further lessening of poverty; the freedom of public opinion; the sustaining of education and of the advancement of knowledge; the growth of religious spirit
and the tolerance of all faiths; the strengthening of the home; the advancement of peace."

"There is no short road to the realization of these aspirations. Ours
is a progressive people, but with a determination that progress must be
based upon the foundation of experience. Ill-considered remedies for our
faults bring only penalties after them. But if we hold the faith of the
men in our mighty past who created these ideals, we shall leave them
heightened and strengthened for our children."

[*State Papers, Vol. I, pp. 6 ff.*]

In a communication to a meeting at Sacramento, California,
two years after the end of his Administration, on March 22,
1935, he said:

"It is well that we pause a moment to examine what objectives we wish to secure from the vast complex of invisible governmental, economic and social forces which dominate our civilization. The objective of American life must be to upbuild and protect the family and the home, whether farmer, worker, or business man. That is the unit of American life. It is the moral and spiritual as well as the economic unit. With its independence and security come the spiritual blessings of the nation. The fundamental protection of these homes is the spirit as well as the letter of the Bill of Rights, with the supports from the framework of the Constitution. They must be given peace with the world. There must be confidence in the security of the job, of the business, of the savings which sustain these homes. Increased standards of living, leisure, and security can come to that home through unshackling the productive genius of our people. The advancement of knowledge must be translated into increasing health and education for the children. There must be constantly improved safeguards to the family from the dislocations of economic life and of old age. With the growth of great industrial forces we must continue to add unceasing protections from abuse and exploitation. We must be liberal in reward to those who add service, material or spiritual wealth to these homes. Those deserve no reward who do not contribute or who gain from exploitation of them. The windows of these homes must be bright with hope. Their doors must be open outward to initiative, enterprise, opportunity, unbounded by regimentation and socialism. Today there must be restoration of faith, the removal of fear and uncertainty that these ideals and these hopes will be open to those who strive."

"To the young men and women it is vital that their opportunity in life shall be preserved; that the frontiers of initiative and enterprise shall not be closed; that their future shall not be burdened by unbearable debt for our follies; that their lives and opportunities shall not be circumscribed and limited; that they shall have the right to make their homes and careers and achieve their own position in the world. There are a host of problems to solve if we attain these ideals; but again I repeat, that the first condition in their solution is orderly individual liberty and responsible constitutional government as opposed to un-American regimentation and bureaucratic domination."

In the practical methods to attain these objectives, Hoover envisaged America as 25,000,000 families, some 80 per cent of whom in ordinary times enjoyed a high degree of freedom of comfort, of economic security, intellectual and recreational opportunity. Both the degree of these standards and the diffusion of them through the people are greater than in any other country or at any time in the history of the world.

The national problem to Hoover, therefore, separated itself into a series of marginal problems, on one hand to attain economic stability so that the high standards of the 80 per cent should not be interrupted by war and depressions, and on the other hand to extend these standards out over the remaining 20 per cent. He held that the American system of self-government, of spiritual freedoms, of free initiative, free enterprise, had produced this unparalleled human development, that it was the only sure basis of progress, that it had weaknesses which must be cured, but that all hope lay in building upon it, not in crippling or destroying it.

His economic policies were therefore absolute fidelity to American tradition of free initiative, free enterprise, open opportunity, and freedom from any attempt by either private or governmental interference with these freedoms. He supported a free economy not from any belief that property rights overrode other rights, but from the deeper philosophical foundation that the spiritual freedoms of the race—free speech, free press, free worship, self-government and all the other essentials of a free people—cannot exist without a free economic system. But freedom to him was not freedom at all if it permitted domination by economic groups through monopoly, exploitation or abuse—there was no *laissez faire* in the Hoover philosophy. His was a philosophy of equal opportunity, not privilege.

He was wholly opposed to pseudo-liberalism with its Collectivist doctrines, and its encroachment upon freedom, with its coercion and regimentalism of the individual and its inevitable destruction of democracy by increasing bureaucracy with all its autocratic spirit. He expressed that opposition in a hundred ways a hundred times. He held that the progress of humanity had been made in three great periods and that those were the periods of free men. They were the period of freedom and democracy in Greece which produced logic, art and our philosophical foundations, the period of freedom and democracy in Rome which produced and developed self-government, law and peace, and the modern period of freedom and democracy which had produced scientific discovery, invention, and the recognition of humanitarianism in government.

Hoover fully recognized the new ferments and dislocations in the world due to the World War and the growth of new social philosophies out of its miseries. He recognized, perhaps more than any other American, that our economic system had lagged behind advancing humanitarian and ethical ideas; that the major problem of statesmen was to secure a harmony of economic life with these ideas and at the same time not to sacrifice the greatest fundamental of all—free men and women. He held that the community as a whole had a definite obligation to the marginal groups of unemployed, and those of sub-standards of living or undeserved poverty and that it must perfect social and economic measures which would bring them over to the standards of the majority. He held there was a positive community obligation to children, aged, sick, disabled, unemployed, or poverty-stricken to assure their subsistence and improvement. He held that the first method in all these questions was to summon the co-operative action of the community and the responsibility of local government. To him this was an infinitely greater contribution to real progress than impositions from the Federal Government above, since the former would stick, that it represented permanent human advancement; and the latter was mostly either a mustard plaster or was coercion of some kind. It did not represent the real impulses of progress. His first step was always to stimulate action in this way. His final step, in failure of all else, was "government."

His Administration was, of course, enormously hampered in economic and social objectives by the financial collapse of the world in the depression. Nevertheless, he formulated and vigorously advanced programs and policies in vital directions despite the burdens of the depression. And he initiated the first nation-wide scientific survey of all these problems as a basis of national action. (See page 6.)

THE AMERICAN SYSTEM

On the philosophical side of government no statesman in American life has made a greater contribution to leadership in thought. In the conflict of rival philosophies, Hoover has made one great contribution, that is, to impress the American people with the fact that we have a defined social philosophy of our own. In these discussions, Hoover was, we believe, the first to use the expressions "American Individualism," "The American System," "The American way of life," which have now become part of the social vocabulary. He spoke upon the subject many times, and first formulated his views of it extensively in a small book in 1922 (*American Individualism*) and again in 1934 (*The Challenge to Liberty*).

"Five or six great social philosophies are at struggle in the world for ascendancy. There is the Individualism of America. There is the Individualism of the more democratic states of Europe with its careful reservations of castes and classes. There are Communism, Socialism, Syndicalism, Capitalism, and finally there is Autocracy—whether by birth, by possessions, militarism, or divine right of kings."

"All these thoughts are in ferment today in every country in the world. They fluctuate in ascendancy with times and places. They compromise with each other in daily reaction on governments and peoples. Some of these ideas are perhaps more adapted to one race than another. Some are false, some are true. What we are interested in is their challenge to the physical and spiritual forces of America."

"The partisans of some of these other brands of social schemes challenge us to comparison; and some of their partisans even among our own people are increasing in their agitation that we adopt one or another or parts of their devices in place of our tried individualism. They insist that our social foundations are exhausted, that like feudalism and autocracy America's plan has served its purpose—that it must be abandoned."

"No doubt, individualism run riot, with no tempering principle, would provide a long category of inequalities, of tyrannies, dominations, and injustices. America, however, has tempered the whole conecption of individualism by the injection of a definite principle, and from this principle it follows that attempts at domination, whether in government or in the processes of industry and commerce, are under an insistent curb . . . must be tempered with that firm and fixed ideal of American individualism—*an equality of opportunity.* . . . It is not the individualism of other countries for which I would speak, but the individualism of America. . . ."

"Individualism cannot be maintained as the foundation of a society if it looks to only legalistic justice based upon contracts, property, and political equality. Such legalistic safeguards are themselves not enough. In our individualism we have long since abandoned the *laissez faire* of the eighteenth century—the notion that it is "every man for himself and the devil take the hindmost." We abandoned that when we adopted the ideal of equality of opportunity—the fair chance of Abraham Lincoln. We have confirmed its abandonment in terms of legislation, of social and economic justice,—in part because we have learned that it is the hindmost who throws the bricks at our social edifice, in part because we have learned

that the foremost are not always the best nor the hindmost the worst—
and in part because we have learned that social injustice is the destruction
of justice itself. We have learned that the impulse to production can only
be maintained at a high pitch if there is a fair division of the product.
We have also learned that fair division can only be obtained by certain
restrictions on the strong and the dominant."

"The truth that is important for us to grasp today is that there is a
world of difference between the principles of the Old World and that
which we have developed in our own country."

"We have, in fact, a special social system of our own. We have made
it ourselves from materials brought in revolt from conditions in Europe.
We have lived it; we constantly improve it; we have seldom tried to define
it. It abhors autocracy and does not argue with it, but fights it. It is not
capitalism, or socialism, or syndicalism, nor a cross breed of them. Like
most Americans, I refuse to be damned by anybody's word-classification
of it, such as 'capitalism,' 'plutocracy,' 'proletariat' or 'middle class,' or
any other, or to any kind of compartment that is based on the assumption
of some group dominating somebody else."

"The social force in which I am interested is far higher and far more
precious a thing than all these. It springs from something infinitely more
enduring; it springs from the one source of human progress—that each
individual shall be given the chance and stimulation for development of
the best with which he has been endowed in heart and mind; it is the sole
source of progress; it is American individualism."

"The rightfulness of our individualism can rest either on philosophic,
political, economic, or spiritual grounds. It can rest on the ground of
being the only safe avenue to further human progress."

". . . To curb the forces in business which would destroy equality of
opportunity and yet to maintain the initiative and creative faculties of
our people are the twin objects we must attain. To preserve the former
we must regulate that type of activity that would dominate. To preserve
the latter, the Government must keep out of production and distribution
of commodities and services. This the deadline between our system and
socialism. Regulation to prevent domination and unfair practices, yet
preserving rightful initiative, is in keeping with our social foundations.
Nationalization of industry or business is their negation. . . ."

"One of the difficulties in social thought is to find the balance of perspective. A single crime does not mean a criminal community. It is easy
to point out undernourished, overworked, uneducated children, children
barred from the equality of opportunity that our ideals stand for. It is

easy to point out the luxurious petted and spoiled children with favored opportunity in every community. But if we take the whole 35,000,000 of children of the United States, it would be a gross exaggeration to say that 1,000,000 of them suffer from any of these injustices. This is indeed 1,000,000 too many, but it is the 34,000,000 that tests the system with the additional touchstone of whether there are forces in motivation which are insistently and carefully working for the amelioration of the 1,000,000. Its by-products of endowed loafers, or hoodlums, at respective ends of the economic scale, are indeed spectacular faults. Yet any analysis of the 105,000,000 of us would show that we harbor less than 1,000,000 of either rich or impecunious loafers. If we measure our people by scales of other civilized peoples, we also find consolation. We have a distaste for the very expression of "class," but if we would use European scales of "classes" we would find that above their scale of "lower classes" we have in equivalent comfort, morality, understanding, and intelligence fully eighty per cent of our native-born whites. No European state will lay claim to thirty per cent of this order. Does this not mean that we have been gaining something?"

"Instincts, character, and the divine spark in the human soul are the property alone of the individual. There can be no human thought, no impulse to action, which does not arise from the individual. A free people maintains as many potential centers of enterprise, leadership, and intellectual and spiritual progress as there are individuals. We might as well talk of abolishing the sun's rays if we would secure our food, as to talk of abolishing individualism as a basis of successful society."

[*American Individualism, Hoover, Doubleday, Page, 1922, pp. 4–9, and 60–1*]

He again formulated his views in 1934:

"Economic laws may be said to be the deduction from human experience of the average response of these varied selfish and altruistic raw materials of the human animal when applied in the mass. These cannot be repealed by official fiat. It is precisely upon this rock of human behavior that the most perfect academic hopes and panaceas are wrecked. Those amateur sociologists who are misleading this nation by ignoring the biological foundations of human action are as far from common sense as an engineer who ignores physics in bridge building. No economic equality can survive the working of biological inequality. This is a hard commonplace truth, disappointing as it may be to those who ride upon plans of Utopia. For at least the next several generations we dare not wholly abandon self-interest as a component of motive forces to initiative, to enterprise, to leadership."

". . . human experience over generations has developed an economic system which we may define as one of private property, competitive production and distribution of goods and services in hope of a profit, the payment of differential wages and salaries based upon abilities and services, the savings of earnings and profits, the lending of them at interest through their investment in our productive plant."

"This system of rewards to stimulate the creative instincts and impulses which motivate men secures the application of all their infinitely varied energies. Therefrom comes the transformation of the products of nature and their distribution as the goods and services which provide for the nation. It also secures the self-denial, thrift, and savings of a multitude of people which provide the productive capital from which we build our tools and equipment."

"Through competition we secure the most potent stimulant to improvement and progress. The manager's restless pillow has done more to advance the practical arts than all the legislation upon the statute books. Competition curbs rapacity and attempts at economic domination. Ours is a system of losses to the least intelligent producers as well as profits to the more intelligent . . . in the end it is the consumer that wins through the production of plenty of goods and services . . . increasing production at constantly lower costs which we require to reach our social objective —in constantly increasing standards of living. This system is greatly modified from the raw by the increasing knowledge of what constitutes self-interest, but more importantly by the ideals and standards vital to secure ordered liberty."

"Any hope of conducting this vast complex of civilization and of assuring progress for the future must lie in the development of millions of individuals for leadership in every agency of life, great or small. Leadership cannot be discovered by birth, nor bred like queen bees, nor assured by the appointment of autocrats or bureaucrats. This immense necessity of society can be supplied only from a full recruiting, out of the whole mass of the people, through the sifting test of competition among free men and women. If there were no other reason, this is the justification of the competitive system, for without its constant renewal of leadership our increasingly complex civilization will cease properly to function. . . ."

"No civilization could be built to endure solely upon a groundwork of greed or even upon the enlightened self-interest of the individual. It is out of the altruistic and constructive impulses that the standards and the ideals of the nation are molded and sustained."

"Our American System is not alone an economic method, a definition of rights, a scheme of representative government, an organization to maintain order and justice, a release of constructive instincts and desires. It is far more than that, for it is a system of stimulation to higher standards, to higher aspirations and ideals."

"While we have built a gigantic organized society upon the attainment of the individual, we should not have raised a brick of it but by the stimulation to self-restraint and by drawing upon those high aspirations of men and women expressed in their standards of truth and justice and in their spiritual yearnings."

"These ideals are never wholly realized. Not a single human being personifies their complete realization. It is therefore not surprising that society, a collection of persons, a necessary maze of instincts of individuals, cannot realize its ideals wholly."

"We may well examine what some of these ideals are. The first concern of the American System is for spiritual health and growth of men. It does not accept that the end and object of civilization or the pursuit of happiness lies in being well-fed or growing fat. It denies the economic concept of history, or that blind materialism can long engage the loyalties of mankind. Its faith is that the divine spark, the ideals, the conscience, the courage, the patriotism, the heroism, and the humanism of men make human destiny. It holds that freedom is a prize to be sought for itself, for from it come the infinite satisfactions of the spirit, far more important than all the goods and gadgets of life."

"American Liberalism holds that moral and spiritual advancement among men can come only through the freedom of individual conscience and opinion, and the responsibilities which of themselves come only in freedom. The very basis of freedom is justice, and our philosophy holds that justice extends further than protection of legal rights; that it extends into those fields of social relations which are outside the law; that every individual shall be given a fair chance—an equality of opportunity. It holds that there should be a just diffusion of national income which will give protection and security to those who have the will to work."

"American Liberty denies that special privileges come to men by birth; it denies the whole concept of frozen class and of class conflict, for these stratifications are barriers to the free spirit and the free rise of the individual by his own effort."

"The humanism of our system demands the protection of the suffering and the unfortunate. It places that prime responsibility upon the individual for the welfare of his neighbor, but it insists also that in necessity the local community, the State government, and in the last resort, the National government shall give protection to them. But it also insists that the full exercise of this responsibility by every individual and institution is an essential of sustained Liberty."

"It holds that the very sustenance of Liberty and the hope of humanity is in co-operation. It holds that this co-operation may be promoted by government, but to Liberty co-operation is a concept of consent among free men, not the compulsion of regimented men."

"It holds that the other freedoms cannot be maintained if economic freedom be impaired—not alone because the most insidious mastery of men's minds and lives is through economic domination, but because the maximum possible economic freedom is the most nearly universal field for release of the creative spirit of men. It has ever held that injury to others is an encroachment upon Liberty; and that restraints as well as freedoms are the very rights of men. Therefore, in fashioning its economic system, it does not hold that there is a license of business to exploit; on the contrary, it holds that economic oppression is servitude. The American System holds equally that monopoly, group or class advantage, economic domination, Regimentation, Fascism, Socialism, Communism, or any other form of tyranny, small or great, are violations of the basis of Liberty."

"True Liberty requires that all claims to human power must be subject to live criticism and the common judgment. The primary protections of humanity from oppressions either by private action or by government are the liberties of expression and protest. Ours is the sole system which maintains within itself the forces of corrective antagonism to oppression of any kind whether they come from the 'right' or the 'left.'"

"We may justifiably say that our system builded on Liberty stimulates those constructive instincts and aspirations through which men and women develop their individual capabilities to the maximum achievement; and that the sum of such achievements is far greater than that possible under any system which stultifies these desires and aspirations. Its essence is justice, self-restraint, obligation to fellowmen. Its practice is a sensitive adjustment of conflicting rights and interests through a spirit of decency and co-operation in human relationships, reinforced by governmental restraints, to the end that men may enjoy equal opportunities."

[*The Challenge to Liberty, Scribners, 1934, pp. 27 ff.*]

THE AMERICAN SYSTEM VS. COLLECTIVISM

Hoover's opposition to *laissez faire* or any form of Regimentation or Socialism or Fascism was insistent. It was founded on world-wide experience and broad philosophic understanding of freedom itself. In reviewing the subject, he said:

". . . the other social philosophies which are today offered as a challenge to our American System are Socialism, Communism, Fascism, Nazism, and National Regimentation. They all have in common the idea of the servitude of the individual to the state, and the denial of liberties unassailable by the state. . . ."

"It is rather a remarkable fact that while the alternative systems of society which are proposed to us have organized exponents who expound their philosophy, their ideals, their patterns, their methods, their promises, and their superiorities, we have little definite exposition of the philosophy, purpose, attainments, and the objectives of true American Liberalism. . . ."

"Before I proceed to discuss these alternate philosophies of society and government I shall, in order to clear some underbrush, take a moment to discuss one of the older economic systems, the ghost of which seems to walk the minds of some of our contemporary essayists. That is *laissez faire*."

"This old economic theory of the French Physiocrats of the eighteenth century and of its exponent in modified form, Adam Smith, has been lately revived as a vivid slogan, mostly for political defamation. It is the theory of economic 'let do,' 'go as you please,' or 'let nature rule.' It may thrive as an economic or social philosophy in some country today, but it has been dead in America for generations—except in books of economic history. It is now, however, trotted out and forms a comforting political invective for use by a long list of collectivist writers who infer that it dominated and directed the policies of the United States up to some recent date, when it was suddenly vanquished—and abandoned."

"The American economic system is hardly one of 'let do' or 'go as you please.' Ever since the Industrial Age began we have devised and enforced thousands of regulations in prevention of economic domination or abuse of our liberties through the growing instruments of business. Furthermore, the sense of public responsibility for the general welfare has successively produced public education, public health, public works, public stimulation of scientific research, and in 1929 for the first time embraced the responsibility for public action in the battle against depression. This is hardly *laissez faire.*"

"Every decent American and every sincere defender of the accomplishments of our people and the inherent soundness of their character and beliefs resents the charge that every wickedness in high place is because of our devotion to *laissez faire.* These horrid examples quoted to us daily are mostly violations of simple honesty or actions through the loopholes of law and the Ten Commandments and are not the bases of our economic or social system. If they were we should have perished some generations ago."

"While discussing defamation of economic or social ideas, I might also spend a few lines upon the term 'rugged individualism.' This term is lately clothed in false habiliments of heartless disregard of public welfare and daily demolished with hot invective. Yet to maintain the varied individuality and personality of men and women is one of the assurances of progress. We have predicated our entire educational system and our entire social advancement upon the development of the special qualities of individuals, their personality and character. While I can make no claim for having introduced the term 'rugged indiivdualism,' I should be proud to have invented it. It has been used by American leaders for over a half-century in eulogy of those God-fearing men and women of honesty whose stamina and character and fearless assertion of rights led them to make their own way in life."

"True American Liberalism utterly denies the whole creed of Socialism. The disguised or open objective of Socialism is equality in income, wages or economic rewards. The tenet of equality in true Liberalism is a tenet of equality in birth, equality before the law, and equality of opportunity as distinguished from equality of reward for services. True Liberalism insists that to equalize rewards and possession of material things robs the individual of free imagination, inventiveness, risk, adventure, and individual attainment, development of personality, and independence from a monotony that would sentence the soul to imprisonment. It denies the Socialist contention that men will be more free when compelled to work under, and to work for, only one employer—the government."

"It is important here to repeat that Liberty denies that the materials of life adequate to meet the needs of society can be obtained without reward proportionate to ability and service. It rejects the theory that men will strive to the utmost and will deny themselves from enjoying immediately the whole of the daily income unless they have confidence in the protection of their honestly acquired savings, and thus may protect themselves and their children by their own means and possessions against a rainy day. It holds that ample leadership and improvement cannot be found except by competition, that it cannot be found under the bushel of governmental bureaucracy. It denies that politicians can manage the economic system as well as the people who have risen in it and whose hopes and security of living rest in advancing it."

"The American System can point not only to theory but to practice. We have already seen our government try to operate railroads and ships. We know the results. The Socialists are fond of eulogizing the post office as a great example of successful Socialism. That the government should control the mails for reasons of confidence is not denied, but that private enterprise could collect and deliver the mail for three-quarters of the present cost is obvious to any one competent to study the subject. One thing is a certainty: that if all industry, through the inescapable play of political and bureaucratic action, were reduced to the efficiency of the post office, we should fail within a few years to produce sufficient to feed, clothe, and care for our people."

"These arguments are limited to the workability and utility of the Socialist system. There is a much larger aspect. The Socialists claim they would maintain democratic institutions and all other freedoms except economic freedom. Democratic institutions would not last long. Producing economic equality by regimenting of the whole population into government employees scarcely assures the election of an independent legislative body or any other independent official. Nor can such administration be conducted during the existence of legislative bodies, with all their inevitable interferences, with all their necessary sectionalism, party criticism, and their perennial pull and haul for advancement of individual constituents. Legislative bodies cannot exist if they delegate their authority to any dictator, but without such delegation every member of these bodies in such a scene is impelled by the interest of his constituents constantly to seek privilege and to interfere in the administering of economic agencies."

"For Socialism to maintain its hold against those who still aspire to liberty every guaranty of freedom—free speech, free press, assembly or a free legislative body, a free judiciary—ultimately must be suppressed. In order to give Socialism a fighting chance the whole structure of our government—constitution, courts, legislative and executive arms—must first be merged under despotism. While I shall deal with these effects more fully later on, I may mention here that the attempt to foist Socialism onto democratic institutions was a large part of the cause of the collapse of these institutions in Italy, Germany, Austria, Poland, and in other places, with the inevitable leap of dictatorship to their place."

"And I may add a word to that group of people in and out of government who are playing with Socialist fire without expecting it really to burn. The penetration of Socialist methods even to a partial degree will demoralize the economic system, the legislative bodies, and in fact the whole system of ordered Liberty. No people will for long permit demoralization. In the United States the reaction from such chaos will not be more Socialism but will be toward Fascism. That inevitability is not only establishable from internal study of the forces in the United States but it has been the invariable turn in foreign countries where there is a considerable economic middle class. And this group is proportionately larger in the United States than in any other country in the world. The path of Socialism leads straight to its downfall together with the pillars of Liberty."

"The whole openly represents a regimented economy dictated by government through bureaucracy. The Italian leaders frankly and realistically state that such is the case and that it is incompatible with and unworkable in a liberal state, because its operation necessitates the sacrifice to the state of fundamental rights of personal liberty. As independent legislative action, investigation, free speech, free press, free assembly, free elections—every form of political life except Fascism—have all been forbidden and rigorously suppressed by imprisonment and banishment, it is natural to conclude that Fascist experience has demonstrated what our deductions must be, that such an organization of society can only be held and administered by the extinction of the agencies of criticism and correction, and by the destruction of personal liberties through suppression and terrorization."

". . . Fascism is the flat contradiction of the Declaration of Independence, the Bill of Rights, the Liberal insistence that progress moves in freedom with the help of doubt and criticism. It means the destruction of self-government and of all checks upon incompetent or ruthless tyranny. Americans, unfamiliar with Italy today, do not know how safe a thing Liberty is both for soul and body."

[*The Challenge to Liberty, pp. 49–58*]

The most effective Hoover discussion of this fundamental issue was in public debate of national questions. The first time it broke into an issue in Hoover's public life was in the Presidential campaign of 1924 when he delivered a considerable blow against Government ownership and operation of railways and utilities then being advocated by Mr. La Follette. Hoover said in part:

"Our form of government has assured us a measure of freedom and progress hitherto unparalleled in political history. The more we cherish it the less ready we should be to load it with a burden for which it was not built. To bear this load the Constitution would need to be rewritten in a score of places, until it was no longer our democracy."

"The very first fundamental obstacle to government ownership that our form of government presents is the relationship of the States to the Federal Government. For in our plan we conceive that liberty requires a great measure of decentralization in authority. If these public utilities are to be operated by the Federal Government we at once deprive the States of their measure of authority and control over railway, power, light and communication companies—we make the service in these States dependent upon the will of Washington, thousands of miles away. Are we to give the States the power to regulate the business of the Federal Government as they now regulate these services? Or are we going to divide the railways and power and communications in forty-eight systems, each ending at the boundary of its own State? Whichever we do will crack the timbers of our government."

"If we pile these $40,000,000 of business and 2,700,000 employees upon the government, one of two things happens. Either the 530 members of Congress or the hundreds of members of State legislatures become their real boards of directors, or, as it has been claimed, these great businesses could be placed in the hands of non-partisan commissions or government corporations, somehow free from politics and the dead hand of bureaucracy. Neither alternative will work. If we were to set up such agencies, so free from restraint of the Congress and legislatures as to accomplish these objects, we would have created gigantic despotisms controlling the well-being of our whole people—and incidentally controlling the very election of our officials."

"As a matter of fact, we can do nothing of this kind if we are to maintain a democracy. We cannot have a democracy and deprive our elected representatives of their control of government investment, their power to fix salaries and wages, their independence in the investigation of the conduct of public officials. . . . The members of our legislative bodies represent districts, States, parties, and groups of opinion. Each member is expected by his constituents to look out for their local or group interests first. They have to be elected upon the results they obtain. Under government ownership, partisanship, 'log-rolling,' and politics would be the inseparable accompaniments of administration. No great business can be efficiently administered by such a board or such a basis of choice. We shall convert business into politics, and surrender efficiency for spoils. If we distribute railway extensions as we distribute public buildings; if we locate electric power plants as we locate reclamation projects; if we divide up public industries generally as we share river and harbor improvements and army and navy stations—then, as surely as night follows the day, facilities will be wastefully provided for those districts or groups which are politically strong, and they will not be adequately provided for the districts or groups that are politically weak."

"Also, under a régime of government ownership, these legislative bodies would have to deal with group pressures striving for favors in rates. The relative rates will affect the prosperity of every city and every section, every group and every industry. States, counties, farmers, town dwellers, every group of manufacturers will press their representatives to secure an advantage, and legislators will inevitably honestly favor their constituents. Every experience to date indicates that the taxpayer will pay for the resulting concessions. . . ."

"If we embark on this vast venture we snall at once increase the total of national and local officeholders up to about six millions. The rightful interest of this group is in higher pay, constantly better conditions of service, and better standards of living. The rightful public interest will be to hold down rates and taxes. These interests will clash, and their clash must fight itself out, not on grounds of economic bargaining between labor and employer, but in the political arena. The voting strength of this mass of officeholders, their wives and dependents, will be over twenty-five per cent of the whole. It is the balance of political power between parties in every district. Either every member of the legislative bodies will be elected to do the bidding of this bureaucracy or will be elected by a public in rebellion against it."

"No commission or any body of administrators can carry on these vast operations efficiently in this political maelstrom. We shall lose most of our democracy in the storm."

"Nor can the government operate as economically as private enterprise. If we take over nearly three million new employees into public service we must put them under an air-tight civil service, to be hired by a separate commission and promoted by seniority. At once we have created a bureaucracy. Otherwise, we would have nearly three million jobs to be given out and a political debauchery unparalleled in all history. There are certain inherent qualities of bureaucracy in its deliberate action, the necessity to maintain joint responsibility, its enlargement of 'red tape' designed to prevent error in judgment and conduct, all of which are perhaps an advantage in purely governing functions, but they become disaster when applied to the rapidity of movement vital to business and service. Numbers increase for every task. The alternative is political favoritism. And at the top where exceptional talent and genius must be had, neither seniority, nor competitive examination, nor politics will secure or find it. It is one thing to choose a postmaster but another to choose a railway president. These things are the actual and daily experiences of our public life; and if a hundred years of this experience is not proof that the efficiency of government operation must always be below the efficiency of private enterprise, then the public is incapable of conviction."

"But there lies even a broader issue of the ultimate results to the freedom of labor. Upon it I can do no better than to quote from Mr. Gompers in a speech at Montreal in June, 1920:

" 'I believe there is no man to whom I would take second position in my loyalty to the Republic of the United States, and yet I would not give it more power over the individual citizenship of our country. . . .' "

" 'It is a question of whether it shall be government ownership or private ownership under control. . . . If I were in the minority of one in this convention, I would want to cast my vote so that the men of labor shall not willingly enslave themselves to government authority in their industrial effort for freedom. . . . Let the future tell the story of who is right or who is wrong, who has stood for freedom and who has been willing to submit their fate industrially to the government.' "

Speaking in the Presidential Campaign of 1928 (Oct. 22) in New York, he said:

"You cannot extend the mastery of the government over the daily working life of a people without at the same time making it the master of the people's souls and thoughts. Every expansion of government in business means that government in order to protect itself from the political consequences of its errors and wrongs is driven irresistibly without peace to greater and greater control of the nation's press and platform. Free speech does not live many hours after free industry and free commerce die."

"It is a false liberalism that interprets itself into the government operation of commercial business. Every step of bureaucratizing of the business of our country poisons the very roots of liberalism—that is, political equality, free speech, free assembly, free press, and equality of opportunity. It is the road not to more liberty, but to less liberty. Liberalism should be found not striving to spread bureaucracy but striving to set bounds to it. True liberalism seeks all legitimate freedom first in the confident belief that without such freedom the pursuit of all other blessings and benefits is vain. That belief is the foundation of all American progress, political as well as economic."

"Liberalism is a force truly of the spirit, a force proceeding from the realization that economic freedom cannot be sacrificed if political freedom is to be preserved. Even if governmental conduct of business could give us more efficiency instead of less efficiency, the fundamental objection to it would remain unaltered and unabated. It would destroy political equality. It would increase rather than decrease abuse and corruption. It would stifle initiative and invention. It would undermine the development of leadership. It would cramp and cripple the mental and spiritual energies of our people. It would extinguish equality and opportunity. It would dry up the spirit of liberty and progress. For these reasons primarily it must be resisted. For a hundred and fifty years liberalism has found its true spirit in the American System, not in the European systems."

"I do not wish to be misunderstood in this statement. I am defining a general policy. It does not mean that our government is to part with one iota of its national resources without complete protection to the public interest."

"Nor do I wish to be misinterpreted as believing that the United States is free-for-all and devil-take-the-hindmost. The very essence of equality of opportunity and of American individualism is that there shall be no domination by any group or combination in this republic, whether it be business or political. On the contrary, it demands economic justice as well as political and social justice. It is no system of *laissez faire*."

"I feel deeply on this subject because during the war I had some practical experience with governmental operation and control. I have witnessed not only at home but abroad the many failures of government in business. I have seen its tyrannies, its injustices, its destructions of self-government, its undermining of the very instincts which carry our people forward to progress. I have witnessed the lack of advance, the lowered standards of living, the depressed spirits of people working under such a system. My objection is based not upon theory or upon a failure to recognize wrong or abuse, but I know the adoption of such methods would strike at the very roots of American life and would destroy the very basis of American progress."

"Our people have the right to know whether we can continue to solve our great problems without abandonment of our American System. I know we can. We have demonstrated that our system is responsive enough to meet any new and intricate development in our economic and business life. We have demonstrated that we can meet any economic problem and still maintain our democracy as master in its own house, and that we can at the same time preserve equality of opportunity and individual freedom."

"In the last fifty years we have discovered that mass production will produce articles for us at half the cost they required previously. We have seen the resultant growth of large units of production and distribution. This is big business. Many businesses must be bigger, for our tools are bigger, our country is bigger. We now build a single dynamo of a hundred thousand horsepower. Even fifteen years ago that would have been a big business all by itself. Yet today advance in production requires that we set ten of these units together in a row."

"The American people from bitter experience have a rightful fear that great business units might be used to dominate our industrial life and by illegal and unethical practices destroy equality of opportunity."

"Years ago the Republican administration established the principle that such evils could be corrected by regulation. It developed methods by which abuses could be prevented while the full value of industrial progress could be retained for the public. It insisted upon the principle that when great public utilities were clothed with the security of partial monopoly, whether it be railways, power plants, telephones, or what not, then there must be the fullest and most complete control of rates, services, and finances by government or local agencies. It declared that these businesses must be conducted with glass pockets."

"As to our great manufacturing and distributing industries, the Republican Party insisted upon the enactment of laws that not only would maintain competition, but would destroy conspiracies to destroy the smaller units or dominate and limit the equality of opportunity amongst our people."

"One of the great problems of government is to determine to what extent the government shall regulate and control commerce and industry and how much it shall leave it alone. No system is perfect. We have had many abuses in the private conduct of business. That every good citizen resents. It is just as important that business keep out of government as that government keep out of business."

"Nor am I setting up the contention that our institutions are perfect. No human ideal is ever perfectly attained, since humanity itself is not perfect."   [*The New Day, p. 162*]

On October 7, 1930, President Hoover delivered an address at King's Mountain Battlefield. He said in part:

". . . My friends, I have lived among many peoples and have observed many governments. Each has its own institutions and its own ideals, its own spirit. Many of them I have learned to respect and to admire. It is from these contrasts and these experiences that I wish to speak today—to speak upon the institutions, the ideals, upon the spirit of America."

". . . But far more inspiring than its growth of numbers has been the unfolding of a great experiment in human society. Within this land there have been builded new and powerful institutions designed of new ideas and new ideals in a new vision of human relations. . . ."

"In the large sense we have maintained open the channels of opportunity, constantly refreshing the leadership of the nation by men of lowly beginnings. We have no class or caste or aristocracy whose privilege limits the hopes and opportunities of our people. . . ."

"This unparalleled rise of the American man and woman was not alone the result of riches in lands or forests or mines; it sprang from ideas and ideals, which liberated the mind and stimulated the exertion of a people. There were other parts of the world even more easily accessible to new invasion by man, whose natural resources were as great as those of the United States, yet their history over this one hundred and fifty years presents no achievement parallel to the mighty march of the United States. But the deadening poverty of the other lands was in the absence of the stirring ideas and ideals which have lightened the path of the whole American people. A score of nations have borrowed our philosophy from us, and they have tempered the course of history in yet a score of others. . . ."

"Our political system was a revolt from dictatorship, whether by individuals or classes. It was founded upon the conception that freedom was inalienable, and that liberty and freedom should rest upon law, and that law should spring from the expressed wisdom of the representatives of the majority of the people themselves. This self-government was not in itself a new human ideal, but the Constitution which provided its framework, with the checks and balances which gave it stability, was of marvelous genius. Yet of vastly more importance than even the machinery of government was the inspired charter of the rights of men which it guaranteed. . . ."

"No student of American history can fail to realize that these principles and ideals grew largely out of the religious origins and spiritual aspirations of our people. . . . They are the precious heritage of America, far more important, far more valuable, than all the riches in land and mines and factories that we possess. Never had these principles and ideals been assembled elsewhere and combined into government. This is the American System."

"We have lived and breathed it. We have seldom tried even to name it. Perhaps we might well abandon efforts to define it—for things of the spirit can be little defined. Some have called it liberalism, but that term has become corrupted by political use. Some have called it individualism, but it is not an individualism which permits men to over-ride the equal opportunity of others. By its enemies it has been called capitalism, and yet under its ideals capital is but an instrument, not a master. Some have called it democracy, yet democracy exists elsewhere under social ideals which do not embrace equality of opportunity."

"Ours is a system unique with America—an expression of the spirit and environment of our people—it is just American."

". . . I cannot conceive of a wholesome social order or a sound economic system that does not have its roots in religious faith. No blind materialism can for long engage the loyalties of mankind. Economic aspiration, though it strongly marks the American system, is not an end in itself, but is only one of many instruments to accomplish the profound purposes of the American people, which are largely religious in origin. This country is supremely dedicated, not to the pursuit of material riches, but to pursuit of a richer life for the individual."

"It would be foolish for me to stand here and say that our political and social system works perfectly. It does not. The human race is not perfect yet. There are disheartening occurrences every hour of the day. There are always malevolent or selfish forces at work which, unchecked, would destroy the very basis of our American life. These forces of destruction vary from generation to generation; and if we would hand on our great inheritance to our children, we must successfully contend with them. . . ."

". . . The world about us is tormented with the spiritual and economic struggles that attend changing ideals and systems. Old faiths are being shaken. But we must follow our own destiny. Our institutions are a growth. They come out of our history as a people. Our ideals are a binding spiritual heritage. We cannot abandon them without chaos. We can follow them with confidence. . . ."   [State Papers, Vol. I, p, 395]

On October 30, 1932, in the Presidential Campaign Hoover again debated these questions. We substitute, however, later addresses which deal with later developments.

Speaking on March 7, 1936, at Colorado Springs, Hoover said:

"For many years I have studied the tactics and techniques in European countries by which Liberty has been dethroned and dictatorship erected by men greedy for power."

"First they ascribed the tragic miseries of the times not to the Great War, where it belongs, but to some party or class. The great phrases born from the finest emotions of mankind were used to camouflage the greed for power. They made great promises. They demanded violent action against human ills that are only slowly curable. They claimed that sporadic wickedness in high places had permeated the whole system of liberty. They shouted new destructive slogans and phrases day by day to inflame the people. They implanted unreasoning hates in the souls of men. They first grasped at power through elections which Liberty provided. Then began the 'must emergency instruments of power,' 'to save the nation.' The first demands were powers of dictation over industry and agriculture and finance and labor. Legislatures were reduced to rubber stamps. Honest debate was shut off in the halls of deliberation. A powerful government propaganda was put on the taxpayers' bill, that hates and suspicion could be further inflamed. And all of these men insisted that civilization had begun all over again when they came into power."

"In the final stages of European degeneration Liberty died from the waters of her own well. That was when the waters of free speech were poisoned by untruth. Then have followed the last steps to dictatorship, with suppression of freedom of speech, freedom of worship, of the courts, and all other freedoms. Men were goose-stepped in a march back to the Middle Ages."

"Whether they know it or not, the New Deal has imitated the intellectual and vocal technique of the typical European revolution. In the talking and legislative stages they made some progress. You will recollect also the claim that even civilization came to a dead stop on March 4, 1933."

"I believe in the American System of Liberty. I believe in it from thousands of experiences. I believe that upon its foundation is the one hope of the common man. It has faults. But it contains the only real ferment of progress."

"There are other systems of Liberty. But at the heart of our American System is embedded a great ideal unique in the world. That is the ideal that there shall be an opportunity in life, and equal opportunity, for every boy and girl, every man and woman. It holds that they have the chance to rise to any position to which their character and ability may entitle them. That ideal is limited or ended if this nation is to be goose-stepped from Washington."

"About every outstanding advance which has promoted the welfare of mankind in the last century has been born in countries of free men and women. The steam engine, electricity, automobiles, telephones, airplanes, radio, free schooling, the great advances in biology, are but part of them. I might include the adding machine but its present use by the New Deal raises doubts as to its contribution to the welfare of mankind."

"On the other hand almost every one of the world's mistakes has its origin in personal government. Violation of treaties, great wars, persecution of the Jews and other religionists, and so on down to the fantastic laws by a Must Congress, and the slaughter of pigs."

Youth and American Liberty

"American young men and women should have the right to plan, to live their own lives with just one limitation—that they shall not injure their neighbors. What they want of government is to keep the channels of opportunity open and equal, not to block them and then charge them for doing it. They want rewards to the winners in the race. They do not want to be planed down to a pattern. To red-blooded men and women there is joy of work and joy in the battle of competition. There is the daily joy of doing something worth while, of proving one's own worth, of telling every evil person where he can go. There is the joy of championing justice to the weak and downtrodden. These are the battles which create the national fibre of self-reliance and self-respect. That is what made America. If you concentrate all adventure in the government it does not leave much constructive joy for the governed."

"In economic life there is but one hope of increased security and comfort for the common man, of opportunity for all. That is to adopt every labor-saving device, every discovery, every idea to reduce waste and the cost of producing goods. We must work our machines heartlessly but not our men. Thereby goods can be sold cheaper and more people can buy. That is the only sure road to a job for every man. It is the only road to restored employment. That production of a plenty can spring alone from the initiative and enterprise of free men. That is no system of robbery. It is action for the common service. That is destroyed at once by the grotesque notion that government shall limit production."

"We cannot operate this world of machines and men without leadership. Competent leadership can come only by the rise of men and women in a free society by the impulse of their own ambition, character, and abilities. That leadership cannot come by birth, or by wealth, or be nursed like queen bees. That leadership cannot be chosen by bureaucrats.

It comes from the ambition of free men and women against the polishing-wheels of competition. It comes in a system of rewards. America should not be divided into the 'haves' and 'have nots,' but into the 'doers' and the 'do nots.' "

"There are those who scoff at individual liberty as of no consequence to the poor or unemployed. Yet it is alone through the creative impulses of free and confident spirits that redemption of their suffering must come. It is through them alone that social security can be attained. Our job is not to pull down the great majority but to pull up those who lag behind."

Speaking at Cleveland, Ohio, on June 10, 1936, he said:

"There are principles which neither tricks of organization, nor the rigors of depression, nor the march of time, nor New Dealers, nor Socialists, nor Fascists can change. There are some principles which came into the universe along with the shooting stars of which worlds are made, and they have always been and ever will be true. Such are the laws of mathematics, the law of gravitation, the existence of God and the ceaseless struggle of humankind to be free."

"Throughout the centuries of history, man's vigil and his quest have been to be free. For this, the best and bravest of earth have fought and died. To embody human liberty in workable government, America was born. Shall we keep that faith? Must we condemn the unborn generations to fight again and to die for the right to be free?"

"There are some principles that cannot be compromised. Either we shall have a society based upon ordered liberty and the initiative of the individual, or we shall have a planned society that means dictation, no matter what you call it or who does it. There is no half-way ground. They cannot be mixed. Government must either release the powers of the individual for honest achievement or the very forces it creates will drive it inexorably to lay its paralyzing hand more and more heavily upon individual effort."

One of the great addresses of political debate was delivered upon this subject by Hoover at Denver, October 30, 1936.

". . . If the Republic is to head in the right direction we must get at the real issues. We must dismiss the shadow-boxing of a political campaign. We must dismiss secondary questions of governmental policy. We must strip our problems down to the great issue before the country."

"Speaking just four years ago tonight in closing the Presidential campaign of 1932, I said:

" 'This campaign is more than a contest between two men. It is more than a contest between two parties. It is a contest between two philosophies of government. . . .' "

" 'We must go deeper than platitudes and emotional appeals of the public platform in the campaign, if we will penetrate to the full significance of the changes which our opponents are attempting to float upon the wave of distress and discontent from the difficulties we are passing through.' "

"That night I spoke for the regeneration of the American System—the America plan of true liberalism in contrast with the philosophy of the New Deal—and I continued: . . . 'you cannot extend the mastery of government over the daily life of a people without somewhere making it master of people's souls and thoughts. . . . Every step in that direction poisons the very roots of liberalism. It poisons political equality, free speech, free press, and equality of opportunity. It is the road not to more liberty but to less liberty. True liberalism is found not in striving to spread bureaucracy, but in striving to set bounds to it. True liberalism seeks all legitimate freedom first in the confident belief that without such freedom the pursuit of other blessings is in vain.' "

"And in that address four years ago I said:

" 'The spirit of liberalism is to create free men; it is not the regimentation of men.' "

"Through four years of experience this New Deal attack upon free institutions has emerged as the transcendent issue in America."

"All the men who are seeking for mastery in the world today are using the same weapons. They sing the same songs. They all promise the joys of Elysium without effort. But their philosophy is founded on the coercion and compulsory organization of men. True liberal government is founded on the emancipation of men. This is the issue upon which men are imprisoned and dying in Europe right now."

"The rise of this issue has dissolved our old party lines. The New Deal repudiation of Democracy has left the Republican Party alone the guardian of the Ark of the Covenant with its charter of freedom. The tremendous import of this issue, the peril to our country has brought the support of the ablest leaders of the Democratic Party. It is no passing matter which enlists side by side the fighting men who have opposed each other over many years. It is the unity demanded by a grave danger to the Republic. Their sacrifice to join with us has no parallel in American history since the Civil War. There run through my mind great words from the Battle Hymn of the Republic: . . . 'in the watchfires of a hundred circling camps They have builded them an altar.' "

"I realize that this danger of centralized personal government disturbs only thinking men and women. But surely the NRA and the AAA, alone, should prove what the New Deal philosophy of government means even to those who don't think."

"In these instances the Supreme Court, true to their oaths to support the Constitution, saved us temporarily. But Congress in obedience to their oaths should never have passed these acts. The President should never have signed them. But far more important than that, if these men were devoted to the American system of liberty they never would have proposed acts based on the coercion and compulsory organization of men."

"Freedom does not die from frontal attack. It dies because men in power no longer believe in a system based upon Liberty. . . ."

"But their illegal invasions of the Constitution are but the minor artillery with which this New Deal philosophy of government is being forced upon us. They are now using a more subtle and far more effective method of substituting personal power and centralized government for the institutions of free men. It is not by violation of the Constitution that they are making headway today. It is through taking vast sums of the people's money and then manipulating its spending to build up personal power. By this route relief has been centralized in their hands. By this route government has entered into business in competition with the citizen. In this way a score of new instruments of public power have been created. By this route the ordinary functions of government have been uselessly expanded with a double bookkeeping to conceal it. Public funds are used right and left to subsidize special groups of our citizens and special regions of the country. At public expense there is a steady drip of propaganda to poison the public mind."

"Through this spending there grows a huge number of citizens with a selfish vested interest in continuing this centralization of power. It has also made millions of citizens dependent upon the government."

"Thus also have been built huge political bureaucracies hungry for more power. This use of money has enabled the independence of members of Congress to be sapped by the pork barrel. It has subtly undermined the rights and the responsibility of States and local governments. Out of all this we see government daily by executive orders instead of by open laws openly arrived at."

"The New Deal taxes are in forms which stifle the growth of small business and discourage new enterprise. By stifling private enterprise the field is tilled for further extension of government enterprise. Intricate taxes are interpreted by political bureaucrats who coerce and threaten our business men. By politically managed currency the President has seized the power to alter all wages, all prices, all debts, all savings at will. But that is not the worst. They are creating personal power over votes. That crushes the first safeguard of liberty."

"Does Mr. Roosevelt not admit all this in his last report on the state of the Union: 'We have built up new instruments of public power' which he admits could 'provide shackles for the liberties of the people'? Does freedom permit any man or any government any such power? Have the people ever voted for these shackles?"

"Is not this very increase in personal power the suicide road upon which every democratic government has died from the time of Greece and Rome down to the dozen liberal governments that have perished in Europe during this past twenty years?"

"I gave the warning against this philosophy of government four years ago from a heart heavy with anxiety for the future of our country. It was born from many years' experience of the forces moving in the world which would weaken the vitality of American freedom. It grew in four years of battle as President to uphold the banner of free men."

"And that warning was based on sure ground from my knowledge of the ideas that Mr. Roosevelt and his bosom colleagues had covertly embraced despite the Democratic Platform."

"Those ideas were not new. Most of them had been urged upon me."

"During my four years powerful groups thundered at the White House with these same ideas. Some were honest, some promising votes, most of them threatening reprisals, and all of them yelling 'reactionary' at us."

"I rejected the notion of great trade monopolies and price fixing through codes. That could only stifle the little business man by regimenting him under his big brother. That idea was born of certain American Big Business and grew up to be the NRA."

"I rejected the schemes of 'economic planning' to regiment and coerce the farmer. That was born of a Roman despot 1400 years ago and grew up into the AAA."

"I refused national plans to put the government into business in competition with its citizens. That was born of Karl Marx."

"I vetoed the idea of recovery through stupendous spending to prime the pump. That was born of a British professor."

"I threw out attempts to centralize relief in Washington for politics and social experimentation. I defeated other plans to invade State rights, to centralize power in Washington. Those ideas were born of American radicals."

"I stopped attempts at currency inflation and repudiation of government obligation. That was robbery of insurance policy holders, savings bank depositors and wage earners. That was born of the early Brain Trusters."

"I rejected all these things because they would not only delay recovery but because I knew that in the end they would shackle free men."

"Rejecting these ideas we Republicans had erected agencies of government which did start our country to prosperity without the loss of a single atom of American freedom."

"All the ardent peddlers of these Trojan horses received sympathetic hearings from Mr. Roosevelt and joined vociferously in his election. Men are to be judged by the company they keep."

"Our people did not recognize the gravity of the issue when I stated it four years ago. That is no wonder, for the day Mr. Roosevelt was elected recovery was in progress, the Constitution was untrampled, the integrity of the government and the institutions of freedom were intact. It was not until after the election that the people began to awake. Then the realization of intended tinkering with the currency drove bank depositors into the panic that greeted Mr. Roosevelt's inauguration. Recovery was set back for two years, and hysteria was used as the bridge to reach the goal of personal government."

"I am proud to have carried the banner of free men to the last hour of the term my countrymen entrusted it to me. It matters nothing in the history of a race what happens to those who in their time have carried the banner of free men. What matters is that the battle shall go on."

"The people know now the aims of this New Deal philosophy of government."

"We propose instead leadership and authority in government within the moral and economic framework of the American System."

"We propose to relieve men from fear, coercion and spite that are inevitable in personal government."

"We propose to demobilize and decentralize all this spending upon which vast personal power is being built. We propose to amend the tax laws so as not to defeat free men and free enterprise."

"We propose to turn the whole direction of this country toward liberty, not away from it."

"The New Dealers say that all this that we propose is a worn-out System; that this machine age requires new measures for which we must sacrifice some part of the freedom of men. Men have lost their way with a confused idea that governments should run machines. Man-made machines cannot be of more worth than men themselves. Free men made these machines. Only free spirits can master them to their proper use."

"The relation of our government with all these questions is complicated and difficult. They rise into the very highest ranges of economics, statesmanship, and morals."

"And do not mistake. Free government is the most difficult of all government. But it is everlastingly true that the plain people will make fewer mistakes than any group of men no matter how powerful. But free government implies vigilant thinking and courageous living and self reliance in a people."

"Let me say to you that any measure which breaks our dykes of freedom will flood the land with misery."

The Social Field

"In the field which is more largely social our first America objective should be the protection of the health, the assurance of the education and training of every child in our land. We want children kept out of our factories. We want them kept in school. We want every character-building agency to surround them, including good homes. Freedom can march only upon the feet of educated, healthy and happy children."

"We want a land of health, and greater recreation for everybody. We want more opportunity for the creation and care of beauty and those things which satisfy the spirit."

The Economic Field

"In the field which is more largely economic our first objective must be to provide security from poverty and want. We want security in living for every home. We want to see a nation built of home owners and farm owners."

"We want to see their savings protected. We want to see them in steady jobs."

"These are the first economic securities of human beings."

"We want to see more and more of them insured against death and accident, unemployment and old age. We want them all secure."

"The American system of liberty has driven toward these ideals for a century and a half. We realize that one-quarter of our people are not able today to have the standards we desire. But we are proud of a system that has given security and comfort to three-quarters of our families and in which even the under-quarter ranks higher than that of any nation in the world."

"National wisdom and national ideals require that we constantly develop the economic forces which will lift this one-quarter of our people. It requires that we at the same time attain greater stability to employment and to agriculture in the other three-quarters."

"This is no occasion to elaborate the details of a program. But surely we must dump the whole New Deal theory of restriction of production, of code monopolies, of constantly higher prices for manufactured goods. We must reject their currency and credit policies which will repeat our calamities of booms and depressions, with greater heights and depths. We must reduce spending and amend the forms of taxation which now destroy enterprise and employment. We hold over-swollen fortunes must be distributed through pressure of taxes."

"We hold the first essential is to improve constantly our machines and methods. That will create plenty and make it cheaper. That will enable the under-quarter of our people to obtain more goods. Thereby we give increasing employment to everybody. We hold that this can be done only by private industry and not by government. We hold it can be done only by rewarding men for skill and merit. We hold it can be done only through the energizing force of competition."

"We hold that we must direct the mind of the nation to the elimination of wastes. There is waste in this government. There is waste in natural resources. There is waste in production and distribution. There is waste in labor conflicts. There is the worst of all waste in human beings. If we turn national effort to this instead of listening to ways to get something for nothing, we will attain not only security, but we will also raise comfort to levels never before envisioned. And above all we can do it and be free."

"It may be that some super-mind can tell us what to do each day for our own good or can even force us to do it. But we haven't seen any indication of such mind among the New Dealers. This country moves forward because each individual of all these millions, each thinking for himself, using his own best judgment, using his own skill and experience, becomes expert in bettering his family and his community. To do that they must captain their own souls. No man will be the captain of his own soul if a Tugwell manages it for him."

"Doubtless some one will at once arise and shout wicked capitalism, laissez faire, special privilege, or wolfish individualism. These are the illuminated pumpkins of tomorrow night's New Deal Hallowe'en."

"We hold a rule of free men which overrides all such nonsense. That is, free men must have equal rights and equal opportunities. For that the government must be the vigorous umpire. But we want a Judge Landis, we do not want a Simon Legree."

"You might think that reform and change to meet new conditions of life are discoveries of the New Deal. Free men have always applied reform. We have been reforming and changing ever since George Washington. Democracy is not static. It is a living force. Every new idea, every new invention offers opportunity for both good and evil."

"We are in need of reform every day in the week as long as men are greedy for money or power. We need a whole list of reforms right now, including the reform of these people who have created a gigantic spoils system as a method of seizing political power."

"Many of the problems discussed in this campaign concern our material welfare. That is right. But there are things far more important to a nation than material welfare. It is possible to have a prosperous country under a dictatorship. It is not possible to have a free country. No great question will ever be settled in dollars and cents. Great questions must be settled on moral grounds and the tests of what makes free men. What is the nation profited if it shall gain the whole world and lose its own soul?"

"We want recovery. Not alone economic recovery. We must have moral recovery. And there are many elements in this."

"We must re-establish truth and morals in public life. No people will long remain a moral people under a government that repudiates its obligations, that uses public funds to corrupt the people, that conceals its actions by double bookkeeping."

"We must have government that builds stamina into communities and men. That makes men instead of mendicants. We must stop this softening of thrift, self-reliance and self-respect through dependence on government. We must stop telling youth that the country is going to the devil and they haven't a chance. We must stop this dissipating the initiative and aspirations of our people. We must revive the courage of men and women and their faith in American liberty. We must recover these spiritual heritages of America."

"All this clatter of class and class hate should end. Thieves will get into high places as well as low places and they should both be given economic security—in jail. But they are not a class. This is a classless country. If we hold to our unique American ideal of equal opportunity there can never be classes or masses in our country. To preach these class ideas from the White House is new in American life. There is no employing class, no working class, no farming class. You may pigeonhole a man or woman as a farmer or a worker or a professional men or an employer or even a banker. But the son of the farmer will be a doctor or a worker or even a banker, and his daughter a teacher. The son of a worker will be an employer—or maybe President. And certainly the sons of even economic royalists have a bad time holding the title of nobility."

"The glory of our country has been that every mother could look at the babe in her arms with confidence that the highest position in the world was open to it."

"The transcendent issue before us today is free men and women. How do we test freedom? It is not a catalogue of political rights. It is a thing of the spirit. Men must be free to worship, to think, to hold opinions, to speak without fear. They must be free to challenge wrong and oppression with surety of justice. Freedom conceives that the mind and spirit of man can be free only if he be free to pattern his own life, to develop his own talents, free to earn, to spend, to save, to acquire property as the security of his old age and his family."

"Freedom demands that these rights and ideals shall be protected from infringement by others, whether men or groups, corporations or governments."

"The conviction of our fathers was that all these freedoms come from the Creator and that they can be denied by no man or no government or no New Deal. They were spiritual rights of men. The prime purpose of liberal government is to enlarge and not to destroy these freedoms. It was for that purpose that the Constitution of the United States was enacted. For that reason we demand that the safeguards of freedom shall be upheld. It is for this reason that we demand that this country should turn its direction from a system of personal centralized government to the ideals of liberty."

"And again I repeat that statement of four years ago—'This campaign is more than a contest between two men. It is a contest between two philosophies of government.'"

"Whatever the outcome of this election that issue is set. We shall battle it out until the soul of America is saved."

POLITICAL LABELS

The attempt to force American political parties into European molds greatly irritated Hoover. He had never believed our people could be properly fitted into such pigeonholes and he held that to force them in must ultimately lead to destruction of free government because of the bitterness and class conflicts that would inflame the country.

Speaking in the campaign of 1924 (Los Angeles, October 29), he said:

"We have as the usual stage make-up of political campaigns a vast amount of clamor over who is a radical, who is progressive, who is conservative, who is a reactionary. A far more important test is who is constructive, for this nation grows by constructive statesmanship alone. The test of what men are is not what they claim but what they have done, that they propose. If we would choose rightly we must examine their history, their acts and their proposals solely as to whether they will safeguard these fundamentals and upbuild these forces that make this nation a better and a happier place for a great people to live in; whether they are building up the forces of material and spiritual welfare not of any special group but of all the people. These are the tests of progress—the tests of men."

"Constructive government is not conducted on slogans—it is built on sound statesmanship. As a matter of fact, the vast majority of America is progressive. We are progressive in business, progressive in the advancement of science and industry, progressive in the building up of our homes, progressive in the upbuilding of our cities and our states, progressive in social thought, progressive in political ideals. We all want to go ahead. Where do we want to go? As I see it, to greater security in living, greater comfort, greater education, greater social and political justice, greater moral fiber—for everybody who will work—and nobody else."

Speaking on August 11 in the 1928 campaign, he said:

"Conservative, progressive, and liberal thought and action have their only real test in whether they contribute to equal opportunity, whether they hold open the door of opportunity. If they do not they are false in their premise no matter what their name may be."   [*The New Day, p. 42*]

With his own clarity of thought, Hoover had little patience with intellectual dishonesty in the use of terms. In the 1932 campaign, on October 31, 1932, in New York City, he said:

"We have heard a great deal in this campaign about reactionaries, conservatives, progressives, liberals, and radicals. I have not yet heard an attempt by any one of the orators who mouth these phrases to define the principles upon which they base these classifications. There is one thing I can say without any question of doubt—that is, that the spirit of liberalism is to create free men; it is not the regimentation of men. It is not the extension of bureaucracy. I have said in this city before now that you can not extend the mastery of government over the daily life of a people without somewhere making it master of people's souls and thoughts. Expansion of government in business means that the Government in order to protect itself from the political consequences of its errors is driven irresistibly without peace to greater and greater control of the Nation's press and platform. Free speech does not live many hours after free industry and free commerce die. It is a false liberalism that interprets itself into Government operation of business. Every step in that direction poisons the very roots of liberalism. It poisons political equality, free speech, free press, and equality of opportunity. It is the road not to liberty but to less liberty. True liberalism is found not in striving to spread bureaucracy, but in striving to set bounds to it. True liberalism seeks all legitimate freedom first in the confident belief that without such freedom the pursuit of other blessings is in vain. Iiberalism is a force truly of the spirit proceeding from the deep realization that economic freedom cannot be sacrificed if political freedom is to be preserved."

"Even if the Government conduct of business could give us the maximum of efficiency instead of least efficiency, it would be purchased at the cost of freedom. It would increase rather than decrease abuse and corruption, stifle initiative and invention, undermine development of leadership, cripple mental and spiritual energies of our people, extinguish equality of opportunity, and dry up the spirit of liberty and progress. Men who are going about this country announcing that they are liberals because of their promises to extend the Government in business are not liberals, they are reactionaries of the United States."

[*State Papers, Vol. II, p. 425*]

Speaking at Colorado Springs on March 7, 1936, he said:

". . . We hear much as to who is a Tory, a Reactionary, a Conservative, a Liberal, or a Radical. These terms when used honestly reflect an attitude of mind. The political use of them was imported from England. They do not fit well in America. However, they have certain advantages. You can elect yourself to any one of these groups if you say it often enough. If you do not like anybody you can consign him to the one which is most hated by your listener."

"Taking a compound of definitions coming out of Washington, the impression would be that the Tories do the money-changing. The Reactionaries are members of well-warmed and well-stocked clubs. The Conservatives are greedily trying to keep their jobs and their savings. The Liberals have the exclusive right to define the opinions of others. The Radicals do not know what to do but do it in every direction."

"As a matter of serious fact, these terms have been used mostly for camouflage and for political assassination."

"The natural choice of youth is toward true liberalism. True liberalism seeks all legitimate freedom first, in the confident belief that without such freedom the pursuit of other blessings is in vain. Liberalism is a force true of the spirit, proceeding from the deep realization that economic freedom cannot be sacrificed if political freedom is to be preserved."

"It is a false liberalism that interprets itself into dictation by government. Every step in that direction crushes the very roots of liberalism. It is the road not to liberty but to less liberty. The spirit of liberalism is to create free men. It is not the regimentation of men. It is not the extension of bureaucracy. You cannot extend the mastery of government over the daily life of a people without somewhere making it master of people's souls and thoughts."

"Today, however, the term Liberal is claimed by every sect that would limit human freedom and stagnate the human soul—whether they be Fascists, Socialists, Communists, Epics, or New Dealers."

"This misuse of English political terms is used to cover the confusion of thought that pumps from the New Deal. Yet our American problems cut squarely across such muddy classifications."

"If an open mind, free to search for the truth and apply it in government, is liberal, then you should be liberal."

"If belief in open opportunity and equal opportunity has become conservative, then you should be conservative."

"If belief that this can be held only in a society of orderly individual initiative and enterprise is conservative, then you should be conservative."

"If opposition to those things which abuse and limit equal opportunity, such as privilege, monopolies, exploitation, or oppression whether in business or in government, is liberal, then you should be liberal."

"If opposition to managed economy whether of the Socialist, Fascist, or New Deal pattern is Tory, then you should be Tory."

"If the humane action to eliminate such abominations as slum squalor, child labor, and sweated labor, to give greater protection from unemployment and old age is radical, then you should be radical."

"If the use of all the powers of the government to relieve our people from hunger and cold in calamity is radical, then you should be radical."

"If belief in the old-fashioned virtues of self-reliance, thrift, government economy, of a balanced budget, of a stable currency, of fidelity of government to its obligations is reactionary, then you should be reactionary."

"If holding to the Bill of Rights with its safeguards of the balance of powers and local government is Tory, then you should be Tory."

"If demand that change in the Constitution be by open submission to the people and not by subterfuge constitutes reaction, then again you should be reactionary."

"If demand that we have a government of laws and not of bureaucrats is conservative, then you should be conservative."

"If you agree with all this, then you have shed yourselves of many 'isms' or you have melted them into plain Americanism."

"If you add to that a belief in decency of Americans, a conception of spiritual prosperity, and a faith in the greatness of America, you will have lifted these realities to the realms of idealism."

"But it all sums up to this—whether the choice of youth will be to carry on that liberty for which Americans have died upon a thousand battlefields."

No student of the Hoover policies or philosophy will fail to find a clear-cut fidelity to the historic liberalism which has made the civilization of the nineteenth and twentieth centuries. It may be the "conservatism" of today but it is the only road to liberty—which is true liberalism.

PARTY ORGANIZATION

The doctrine is not new that democracy can only function through organized political parties as the vehicles through whom the people may make effective expression of their will. This expression can only be given by sustaining major parties and these parties must carry out their promises. Hoover early called attention to the vivid proof of the dangers of multiple parties shown by European experience and the dangers of despotism that arise from such source.

In 1924, he remarked:

"In practically every government in Europe there are in these days from three to twenty parties in the legislative assembly with no single party in majority. In consequence, their cabinets . . . have been founded on temporary coalitions—or ephemeral cabinets representing minorities. . . ."

"Any coalition between groups of different political thought and object is bound to result in the abandonment of matters of important principle and the consequent adoption of largely negative policies. All virility and strength are lost, cabinets are but shortlived, and constructive and courageous policies in legislation or administrative action have been conspicuously absent. The problems in economic and social reconstruction have been enormous and in the face of the violent differences of opinion between the different factions the negative policies have resulted in little more than drift and paralysis of government."

". . . As a result the people in one country after another in exasperation have welcomed some form of dictatorship. . . . Practical democracy requires two-party government; otherwise there is unlikely to be any stable majority. . . ."

"I doubt whether any two thinking men will entirely agree in every particular of political philosophy or ever agree precisely on all the items of a legislative or administrative program . . . but the whole survival of our form of democracy will depend upon a willingness to adopt team play and to fight out the secondary contentions within the main ranks. Our political parties change their objectives with time and changing problems; or new parties are born which bury the old, but these are not very helpful periods. A crystallization of new objectives in old parties is the safest course for democracy; but this course has not always been possible—usually because a few extremists will not make the necessary compromises with new developments. . . ."

". . . it is a talent for tempering logic with compromise and common sense that has made our institutions workable."

[Emporia Gazette, January 4, 1924]

In an address at Los Angeles on September 7, 1926, Secretary Hoover said:

"There must be a method by which we find organized expression of the will of the people as a substitute for the violence of revolution. . . ."

"Democracy can have no such expression without organized political parties. . . . All successful democracies must in the practical consummation of government be based on parties. And it is just as fundamental that parties must maintain organization, discipline and cohesion as it is that they carry out their policies and promises upon which they have been elected in full good faith.

"But the further and outstanding lesson of Europe . . . is that if democracy is to sustain majority government, it can only do so with two dominant parties in the field. . . . The whole course of . . . European democracies in the past five years . . . possessed of from three to ten different political parties—has been one of shifting government, vacillating policies and defeat of orderly government. . . . Definite policies of strong and courageous action are nullified where multiple parties exist. They become governments of negative policies, compromising, compounding and intriguing in all directions to maintain office. Ultimately there is a breakdown of the whole political system and democracy turns to dictatorship to save the state."

In his Inaugural Address in 1929, he said:

"In our form of democracy the expression of the popular will can be effected only through the instrumentality of political parties. We maintain party government not to promote intolerant partisanship but because opportunity must be given for expression of the popular will, and organization provided for the execution of its mandates and for accountability of government to the people. It follows that the Government both in the executive and the legislative branches must carry out in good faith the platforms upon which the party was intrusted with power. But the government is that of the whole people; the party is the instrument through which policies are determined and men chosen to bring them into being. The animosities of elections should have no place in our Government, for government must concern itself alone with the common weal."

[*State Papers, Vol. I, p. 10*]

And this high purpose of political organization held to the end. President Hoover, on February 27, 1933, said:

"This work of party organization is a public duty often thankless . . . yet in the highest sense a public service, for organized political parties have become an absolute necessity for the functioning of popular government in so large a population as ours. Only through such organization can the people express their will. The nation would be a bedlam of wholly discordant voices without such organization, without loyalty to it. . . . A party deserves to exist only as it embodies the thought and conviction of earnest men and women who have the welfare of the nation at heart. It must be a party of ideals since only exalted purpose can bring great numbers of people together in united action. But the consummation of ideals must be organized. . . ."

"Political parties have great obligations of service whether the party be in power or not. . . . It is not less an obligation of the party to subject all proposals to the scrutiny of constructive debate and to oppose those which will hurt the progress and the welfare of the country. . . ."

METHOD OF APPROACH TO NATIONAL PROBLEMS

INVESTIGATION BEFORE ACTION

Herbert Hoover was an engineer. His mind therefore built with soundness and sincerity upon determined facts. That required that every problem must be adequately investigated as to fact and method before action. That is the method of science and engineering and the only method of sure action. Hoover insisted however that many human problems did not lend themselves to statistical solution.

Speaking at Johns Hopkins University, February 23, 1920, Hoover said:

"I sometimes feel that public problems can be divided into two classes. The first is that in which sufficient facts, figures, or concrete experience can be amassed to give certain indication of the course of constructive action. The second are those arising out of sheer complexes of political, economic and social currents, in which solution at best is more largely pure judgment guided by the adherence to national ideals. The common judgment must arise out of common discussion, the development of a common mind flowing from the common sense of our people. This latter type of problem seems to especially lend itself to destructive criticism. The greatness of this country, however, has not grown from the police court mind."

During his administration, the opposition became much exercised over his frequent commissions or investigations, and the President comforted them with the following words in an address on December 14, 1929:

"One of your anxieties this evening has been my appointment of commissions and committees. You have been misled into the impression that I shall soon appoint one every day. That is wrong—I shall probably need to appoint two a day. My conception of government leads me to the firm conviction that we have arrived at a time in our history, because of the increasing complexity of our civilization and the delicacy of its adjustments, when we must make doubly certain that we discover the truth. It is necessary that we make the fullest use of the best brains and the best judgment and the best leadership in our country before we determine upon policies which affect the welfare of a hundred and twenty million people. And I propose to do it."

"The President of the United States is obliged to determine a multitude of questions and policies. By the Constitution he must recommend to Congress such measures as he shall deem necessary and expedient, and he is required to finally pass upon every act of Congress. He is the Chief Executive of the greatest business in the world, which at some point touches upon every single activity of our people."

"By his position he must, within his capacities, give leadership to the development of moral, social, and economic forces outside of government which make for betterment of our country."

"The committees of Congress are themselves commissions for the investigation and the determination of legislative policies. But Congress cannot longer encompass the entire human field. Congress cannot determine administrative policies; it cannot inspire or lead voluntary forces."

"The most dangerous animal in the United States is the man with an emotion and a desire to pass a new law. He is prolific with drama and the headlines. His is not the road to the fundamental advance of the liberty and the progress of the American people at this time in our history. The greatest antidote for him is to set him upon a committee with a dozen people whose appetite is for facts. The greatest catastrophe that could come to our country is that administration policies or legislation or voluntary movements shall be encouraged or enacted upon the basis of emotion, not upon facts and reason."

"The President has open to him many governmental agencies in search for fact and for the determination of conclusion from them. He receives the largest measure of assistance from the executive departments and congressional committees. But over and beyond all these agencies there are a thousand problems; where the truth must be searched from a multitude of facts; where individual and regional experience must be had; where new ideas must be recruited from the kaleidoscope of a great shifting mass of humanity; where judgment must be distilled from many minds; where common agreement must be secured from conflicting forces; where assurance must be given to the people of the correctness of conclusions; and where their exposition must be secured."

"These subjects cover the whole range of human thought, and I do not arrogate to myself the combined knowledge or judgment of the technologists, the philosophers, the scientists, the social thinkers, the economists, and the thousand callings of our people."

"In these matters commissions and committees of our citizens can be made to add to the security of our steps and the certainty of acceptance of our policies. There is no worse agency of government than commissions and committees for executive action. Action requires undivided mind and undivided responsibility. But for the purpose of these special determinations I shall need more and more commissions, and more and more conferences, and I am grateful for the willingness our citizens have shown to give their time and service upon them."

"And it is my belief that this is a vital means of government by the people and for the people, now that the people have ceased to live the simple life."   [*Hoover After Dinner, Scribners, 1935, pp. 16–20*]

> Representative investigations of this type were: The Committees on Recent Economic Change, on Child Health and Protection, Bankruptcy Laws, Housing and Home Ownership, Conservation of the Public Domain, Colorado River Commission, Commission on Law Enforcement, on Veterans' Hospitalization, St. Lawrence Waterway, on Statistical Services, San Francisco Bay Ridge, Mississippi Flood Control, California Water Resources, Merchant Marine, Conference on Street and Highway Safety, Research Committee on Social Trends, etc., etc.

CO-OPERATION

Hoover constantly emphasized that self-government does not consist wholly of laws and courts, nor of county, municipal, State or Federal legislatures; nor of administrative officers or institutions. Vast processes of democracy must be carried on by co-operative action among the people. The multitude of spiritual, charitable and trade organizations are perhaps the largest part of American democracy. The settlement of problems, the advancement of ideas, the finding of solutions through these activities, constitute the most fundamental progress for they have values in flexibility and permanency far greater than the imposition of law or government.

Therefore, Hoover, more than any other American government official, insisted on at least a first reliance upon these agencies. He insisted that the government could properly give leadership to the mobilization of these forces.

Speaking at Oskaloosa, Iowa, on June 12, 1925, he said:

"This quality of co-operation . . . has shown . . . extraordinary growth of associational activities. . . . Farmers' organizations, trade associations, community conferences, chambers of commerce, employers' organizations, labor unions, banks, lawyers' and engineers' institutes, welfare and social organizations and scores of others for one purpose or another have become nation-wide . . . variable mixtures of self-interest and altruism, but they are steadily welding toward common action. . . . It represents the instinct of common action in barn-raising and mutual protection from the Indians, whether savage or in business. . . ."

"At times, these groups come into sharp conflict. . . . They do contain faults. If they are to dominate legislators and intimidate public officials, if they are to be a new setting for tyranny, if they are to develop the practice of dog-eat-dog between groups, then we are lost. We shall have developed into a vast syndicalism. . . . Neither our form of government nor this vast machine of production and distribution can withstand the shocks of class or group conflicts. . . ."

"Much of our fears for our democracy arise from these activities. . . ."

". . . The growth of these organized associations is not necessarily bad in itself. . . . Our industrial transformation to a national scale requires national thinking and planning. If we are wise, this spirit of associational action should offer us the way out. If we can summon the responsibilities of these groups to the nation. . . ."

"It is idle to argue that there are no conflicts of interest between groups. But the areas of common interest are infinitely greater . . . it is the part of statesmanship . . . to organize this identity of interest in order to limit the area of conflict. These groups must learn that progress will not come from crushing the individual into a shapeless mass, but in giving to him enlarged opportunity. . . ."

". . . co-operation and good will among groups are practicable things. We secured a magnificent degree of co-operation during the war. . . . I recollect with great satisfaction the fine co-operation of many groups when, four years ago, we were confronted with a great emergency from the great industrial slump when we had five million unemployed on our streets, drifting into great privation, when agriculture was confronted with complete bankruptcy because of the inability of our unemployed to buy farm products, when demoralized Europe was reduced in great areas to the point of starvation by loss of its buying power. The problem then confronting the Department of Commerce, over which I have the honor to preside, was not alone a problem of stagnated commerce and industry, with its heartbreaking waste of production but also a problem of agriculture. . . . On that occasion, the organized co-operation of our manufacturers, of our utilities and bankers, and of our labor organizations accomplished far more to restore employment than any action of legislation . . . we alone of all countries solved this with but little legislation; other war countries have depended on legislation and have failed."

"Through this enlarged sense of co-operation in industrial associations we have accomplished something in the reduction of abuse by unfair trade practices. By their co-operation we have accomplished something in the elimination of waste and the inauguration of improved methods of production and distribution. Through these organizations we have . . . better understanding of the responsibilities of both employers and employees. . . . We have at least demonstrated that the spirit of co-operation is within us. . . ."

"Nor will solutions be found in economic patent medicines of government action. We cannot cure foolishness by legislation. We cannot catch economic forces with bureaucracy. Yet we can influence economic forces by co-operation in the community. The national and local governments must cure abuse and fraud, and they can act as umpires. They can do many other things. But, above all, they can best serve the community by bringing about co-operation in the large sense between groups. It is the failure of groups to respond to their responsibilities to others that drives government more and more into the lives of our people. And every time the government is forced to act, we lose something in self-reliance, character, and initiative. Every time we find solution outside of government we have not only strengthened character but we have preserved our sense of real self-government."

Speaking at St. Louis, on November 2, 1928, he said:

"We have in the past quarter of a century evolved a higher sense of organized co-operation than has ever been known before. We have ten thousand examples of this conscious co-operative development in the enormous growth of associational activities."

". . . They represent every phase of our national life, both on the economic and on the welfare side. They constitute a vast ferment toward conscious co-operation. They have become a part of the very fabric of American life. While some of them engage in highly objectionable attempts to wrongly influence public opinion and the action of government . . . a large part of them are founded solely on public interest."

"Wherever these associations undertake high public purposes I wish to see active co-operation by the government with them. Without intrusion the government can serve to bring together discordant elements and to secure co-operation between different industries and groups. It gives great hope of a new basis of solution for many of our problems and progressive action in our people. It should be the response of government to our new economic conceptions. It is consonant with the American System. It is a method that reinforces our individualism by reducing, and not increasing, government interference in business and the life of our citizens."

"Such co-operation strengthens the whole foundation of self-government and serves to maintain equality of opportunity and constructive leadership."

"This co-operation can take two distinct directions. It can assist in the promotion of constructive projects of public interest on the one hand and it can assist in the cure of abuses by the voluntary establishment of a higher code of ethics and a stricter standard in the conduct of business."

"These are not theoretical proposals. Seven and one half years ago I introduced this relationship between the Department of Commerce and industrial, commercial and civic organizations of our country for the promotion of matters that were of public importance. We co-operate with these associational groups in promotion of foreign trade, in the elimination of waste, in furtherance of economic and scientific research, in improvement of homes and in scores of other activities. During this period hundreds of committees have been in active co-operation with the Department of Commerce not under compulsion and not even under solicitation from the Department, but merely because the government was willing and ready to assist in bringing together the elements of any movement that would promote public welfare. . . ."

[*The New Day, p. 196*]

In his Inaugural Address in March, 1929, President Hoover said:

"Our people have in recent years developed a newfound capacity for co-operation among themselves to effect high purposes in public welfare. It is an advance toward the highest conception of self-government. Self-government does not and should not imply the use of political agencies alone. Progress is born of co-operation in the community—not from governmental restraints. The Government should assist and encourage these movements of collective self-help by itself co-operating with them. Business has by co-operation made great progress in the advancement of service, in stability, in regularity of employment and in the correction of its own abuses. Such progress, however, can continue only so long as business manifests its respect for law."

"There is an equally important field of co-operation by the Federal Government with the multitude of agencies, State, municipal and private, in the systematic development of those processes which directly affect public health, recreation, education, and the home. We have need further to perfect the means by which Government can be adapted to human service."

[*State Papers, Vol. I, p. —*]

Notable instances of the Hoover leadership in public action of this type were: Unemployment relief—see pp. 361 ff.; maintenance of wages during the depression—see p. 129; elimination of national wastes—see p. 107; creation of financial supports—see p. 410; organization of codes of ethics in business—see p. 300; his extensive voluntary organization for better homes—see p. 80; the voluntary organization of child health and protection—see pp. 58 ff.; organization of voluntary radio regulation—see p. 207. Less successful were his attempts to reform voluntarily the New York Stock Exchange—see p. 343.

Only when voluntary action wholly failed was Hoover prepared to undertake governmental action.

SOCIAL POLICIES IN ACTION

SOCIAL SECURITY

To President Hoover the first step of social security or any other security was to get the people back to work from the depression and the nation into productivity. After social security became a popular catchword, he summed up his long standing views upon it. To him "social security" was a far more inclusive subject than the public health, unemployment insurance and old age pensions proposals of the New Deal. The whole problem is of course more "economic" than "social" and phases of the Hoover policies are discussed in the next chapter.

He summed up his views in a public address on June 16, 1935:

"The first of social securities is freedom—freedom of men to worship, to think, to speak, to direct their energies, to develop their own talents, and to be rewarded for their effort. Too often plans of social security ignore these, the primary forces which make for human progress, without which America as we know it could not exist. Freedom is a spiritual need and a spiritual right of man. We can get security in food, shelter, education, leisure, music, books, and what not, in some jails. But we don't get freedom. Those who scoff that individual liberty is of no consequence to the underprivileged and the unemployed are grossly ignorant of the primary fact that it is through the creative impulses of liberty that the redemption of these sufferings and that social security must come."

"The second of social securities is the capacity to produce a plenty of goods and services with which to give economic security to the whole of us. Scientific discovery, this vast technology and mechanical power, are the achievement of personal and intellectual freedom. Creativeness, intellectual accomplishment, initiative, and enterprise are the dynamic forces of civilization. They thrive alone among free men and women. It is these impulses which have built this capacity to produce a plenty that society must now learn to employ more effectively. This freedom and this plenty came into western civilization hand in hand—they are inseparable. This vastly complicated mechanism is not alone a mass of machines. These engines and machines are inert materials which require every hour of the day new human initiative, new enterprise, and new creative action, or they will not work. No other group of impulses would have produced this productivity. No other method but that of orderly personal liberty can operate or improve it. Economic security is lost the moment that freedom is sacrificed."

"Any system which curtails these freedoms or stimulants to men destroys the possibility of the production which we know we must have to attain economic security. Social security will never be attained by an economy of scarcity. That is the economy of fear. Not out of scarcity or restriction but out of abundance can society make provision for all its members and support the unemployed, the sick, the aged, and the orphan. That is the economy of hope."

"The safeguards of freedom lie in self-government. There never has been nor never will be freedom when powers of government are lodged in a man or a group of men. Moreover, all history teaches us that even majorities cannot be trusted with the ark of freedom without checks. Constitutional government, the division of powers, are the only successful protections the human race has devised. To transgress or to override them will weaken and finally destroy freedom itself."

"The hope of social security can be destroyed both from the right and the left. From the right come the abuses of monopoly, economic tyranny, exploitation of labor, or of consumers or investors. From the left come power-seeking, job-holding bureaucracies, which bleed our productive strength with taxes and destroy confidence and enterprise with their tyrannies and their interferences. The concentration of economic power and the concentration of political power are equally destructive. The weeds of abuse will always grow among the fine blossoms of free initiative and free enterprise. Evil as these weeds are, we can better spend the unceasing labor to dig them out than to have the blossoms killed by the blights of little and big governmental tyrannies."

"If we are to attain social security we must find remedy or mitigation of interruptions and dislocations in the economic system. Its stable functioning must be our first objective. War and its long dreadful aftermaths of instability are the first and worst of these interruptions. War in defense of our country and our rights is justified. But we should not blame the social and economic system for injuries produced by war. We should sacrifice until they are healed and cease passing the infection to the next generation."

"The next worst interruption is the business cycle with all its waste in booms and the vast miseries of slumps. We can never get wholly free from them because sometimes they sweep our borders from abroad. But depressions other than from war origins are capable of great mitigation by wiser use of our credit machinery."

"In any process of returning the machine to stable operation we must consider the problems arising from the dislocation of individuals. . . . It is the individual who suffers from these instabilities . . . it will be a slow and difficult job to bring stability to the system as a whole, . . . every interruption brings misfortune to individuals. Moreover, the rapid advance of labor-saving devices imposes upon us individual dislocations pending re-employment. Therefore, the foundations of individual security must in the end be strengthened beyond relief work. Over the century we have seen the vast development of insurance against the effect of fire, flood, sickness, accident, and death. The extension of these principles to the remaining fields of human accident—that is, to poverty in old age, to unemployment, must now be brought into action. While the aid of the government is necessary to overcome the initial risks yet the world has not yet developed a satisfactory system of doing it."

"Even if we attained as much economic and social security in these areas as could be expected of human endeavor, we still have the problem of distribution of our productivity so as to find security for the remaining 10 or 25 per cent, whatever it may be, who are not yet upon the ladder of social security."

"Having the vast majority economically secure when the system is stable, our job is not to pull down this great majority but to build up those who lag. And herein lies a great area of unclarified national thought. Here America has, however, developed one new idea—that wages are linked to ability to consume goods; that the highest possible real wage is the necessary accompaniment of mass production. No one denies today that the road to higher consumption of goods and services is lower costs, lower prices, and thus higher real wages and incomes."

"Theoretically, the end of that road would be complete economic security. But there is and will be a segment of the dislocated, the less fortunate, the misused, and the less wise. Herein we have vast problems of eliminating sweated labor, child labor, marginal farmers, slums, industrial conflicts, and a score of others. That is indeed a far-flung battle front in human welfare."

"Economic security and in fact social security can be greatly strengthened by wider-spread property ownership. The home, farm, business, savings, insurance, and investment are not only a reserve of economic security but by their wide distribution they become of vast social importance far beyond their monetary value. Here lies a sense of freedom from fear, a sense of independence, the accomplishment of personal endeavor and choice."

"Sometimes we can find our feet if we examine what sort of civilization we seek to secure from all this vast complex of visible and invisible forces which dominate our civilization. Surely our social objective must be to upbuild and protect the family and the home. The family is the unit of American life; it is the moral and spiritual unit as well as the economic unit. With the independence and the security of the family have come the spiritual blessings of the nation. In that home must be men and women of individuality and character. There must be security in education and health, safety from invasion and crime. There must be increasing protections from exploitation, whether from private economic tyranny or governmental tyranny. We must build security in the individual job, for the individual business, for the thrift and savings which sustain it. Fear of ruin, fear of poverty, fear of old age and dislocation must be removed from the individual and thus from the heart of the family. The doors of freedom must be kept open wide to initiative, to honest enterprise, to effort. The windows must be kept bright with hope and confidence in the future. These are the standards and tests which may be applied to every social proposal made to you."

"Upon all these . . . I should like to make these observations."

"Universal social security cannot be had by sudden inspiration of panaceas. There are no short cuts. Permanent social growth cannot be had by hothouse methods. The soil of human nature requires infinite patience in search for useful plants and equally in search for methods of elimination of weeds and pests. It requires experiment to develop the plants and to poison the pests. Just as we must be bold in experiment also it is doubly necessary that we use caution in experimenting with the welfare of human beings or we can produce infinite misery—not social security."

"The functioning of any economic system is peculiarly based upon faith in the future and confidence in certain constants in life. Without that faith all effort slackens. They are not only liberty in the broad sense but these constants include the detail of sanctity of contracts which are not unconscionable, the stability of the currency and credit, the maintenance of legitimate competition, government by specific laws, not by the uncertainties of administrative fiat. Without security in those constants, confidence and faith are impossible. Indeed, today our daily life and the whole world are seized with fears. There are within our ranks defeatists who in despair abandon all confidence in the race, in our accomplishment hitherto, and all hope that upon this rich experience we can further advance."

"Our sympathetic thought properly drives to consideration of the 25 per cent of the less fortunate. It is right that it should be so. But let us not forget that the 75 per cent need consideration also. They alone can carry the burden of the 25 per cent in these times until that minority per cent can begin their own upward climb. Through them is the sole hope of the 25 per cent. If they be harassed, coerced, intimidated, discouraged, unduly taxed, the whole fabric will fall. The times demand a determined spirit whose faith is not dulled by the mere aftermaths of a great war, a vicious business cycle, or the sudden triumphs of science."

"Social security must be builded upon a cult of work, not a cult of leisure. The judgment on Adam has not yet been reversed. That proscription was for his better health and life. Work fails without character, education, special training, the stimulation of intelligence and genius, the advance of knowledge. All these seem platitudes, but they are worth mentioning because some systems which pretend to social security forget them all or in part."

THE NATIONAL SOCIAL SURVEY

Hoover came to the Presidency resolute upon two needs: first the restoration of certain human rights which mechanization had infringed, and second, that a government lead in humanitarian fields. Therefore at the beginning of his Administration, in accord with his invariable demand for the facts by scientific methods of inquiry, he instituted a thorough and complete investigation into the whole field of social problems—the first time it had ever been undertaken. On September 19, 1929, he appointed a committee of leading economists and sociologists to undertake an exhaustive examination and report. The directing members of the inquiry were Wesley C. Mitchell, Charles E. Merriam, Doctor Alice Hamilton, William F. Ogburn, Howard W. Odum and Shelby M. Harrison, with Edward Eyre Hunt as secretary and French Strother as the liaison with the President. The Committee's own statement of their instructions were:

"In September, 1929, the Chief Executive of the Nation called upon the members of this Committee to examine and to report upon recent social trends in the United States with view to providing such a review as might supply the basis for the formulation of large national policies looking to the next phase of the national development. The summons was unique in history. . . . The first third of the Twentieth Century has been filled with epoch-making events and crowded with problems urgently demanding attention on many fronts. . . ."

The Committee secured the co-operation of several hundred specialists in different fields. The survey required three years. It formed the first thorough foundation of social fact ever presented as a guide to public action. The loss of the election prevented the President from offering a program of practical action based upon the facts.

On issuing the report on January 2, 1933, the President said:

". . . The significance of this report lies primarily in the fact that it is a co-operative effort on a very broad scale to project into the field of social thought the scientific mood and the scientific method as correctives to undiscriminating emotional approach and to secure factual basis in seeking for constructive remedies of great social problems. The second significance of the undertaking is that, so far as I can learn, it is the first attempt ever made to study simultaneously all of the fundamental social facts which underlie all our social problems. Much ineffective thinking and many impracticable proposals of remedy have in the past been due to unfamiliarity with facts in fields related to that in which a given problem lies. The effort here has been to relate all the facts and present them under a common standard of measurement." [State Papers, Vol. II, p. 559]

The work represented a cost, in paid and voluntary services, of fully a million dollars. The funds needed were supplied by private subscription. The reports embrace two volumes of summary and a number of special monographs.

The Committee's work covered: Utilization of Natural Resources, Influence of Invention and Discovery, The Agencies of Communication, Trends in Economic Organization, Education, Rural Life, the Vitality of the American People, the Family and its Functions, the Activities of Women outside the Home, Childhood and Youth, Labor Groups, the People as Consumers, Recreation, the Arts, Changes in Religious Organization, Health, Crime and Punishment, Public Welfare Activities, the Growth of Governmental Functions, Taxation and Public Finance, Public Administration, Law and Legal Institutions, Government and Society, and many other subjects. It entered into questions of national planning (not the New Deal plan of coercion), old age pensions, unemployment insurance, greater stability in the economic system and many other avenues of action.

The Committee's own modest summation was:

". . . We were not commissioned to lead the people into some new land of promise, but to retrace our recent wanderings, to indicate and interpret our ways and rates of change, to provide maps of progress, make observations of danger zones, point out hopeful roads of advance, helpful in finding a more intelligent course in the next phase of our progress. Our information has been laboriously gathered, our interpretations made with every effort toward accuracy and impartiality, our forecasts tentative rather than dogmatic in form and spirit, and we trust that our endeavors may contribute to the readier growth of the new ideals, ideas and emotional values of the next period, as well as the mechanisms, institutions, skills, techniques and ways of life through which these values will be expressed and fulfilled in the years to come."

Public interest in the report was well indicated by the fact that it was carried as news for several columns upon the first pages of the newspapers of the country. It has had a profound effect upon national thinking.

This report represented not only the President's interest and devotion to social development but also his resolution that, before even reform policies should be extended beyond those in course, full facts and judgment must be secured.

PARTICULAR SOCIAL POLICIES

Many of the President's particular social policies are discussed under *Agriculture*, p. 146; *Labor*, p. 116; *Relief*, p. 359, etc. In this section we deal with

Protection to Children.	Prohibition.
Public Health.	Prison Reform.
Housing.	Old Age Pensions.
Education.	Unemployment Insurance.
Indians	Diffusion of Property
Enforcement of Law.	Ownership.

PROTECTION OF CHILDREN

Hoover had shown his devotion to the interest of children all his life. The special care set up of 5,000,000 children in Belgium and Northern France which after four years of war found them to be in better health and strength than ever before; his organization which cared for 10,000,000 waifs, orphans and destitute children in Central Europe for two years after the Armistice; the special relief of 7,000,000 children during the Russian Famine of 1922, are evidence enough. But his devotion to American children was no less.

The moment he was released from war responsibility he applied his great experience to the welfare of the children of America. In 1921, he organized the American Child Health Association by consolidating some seven smaller organizations devoted to children's welfare. As chairman of the association for over twelve years, he raised over $400,000 annually for its work. The work of this association was primarily to develop public opinion to the public responsibilities, national, State and local, in protection of children. It pioneered and advanced methods for State and municipal and county health and welfare organization; for health education in schools, feeding of undernourished children at school, milk and food inspection, and a hundred different activities. The association furnished expert advice to public institutions. In this work it made detailed surveys of child conditions in eighty-seven cities, and by arousing public opinion in these cities, it brought about great reform.

The conversion of May Day in 1923 into a national Children's Health and Protection Day throughout the nation was but one of the Hoover inventions. "Civilization marches upon the feet of strong and healthy children" was one of his watchwords. May Day as "Children's Day" was an unofficial action of the American Child Health Association, but in 1928 the Association secured its enactment and thereafter it was proclaimed from the White House. President Hoover proclaimed it each year with a statement of its purpose.

Herbert Hoover was a determined crusader for the child. Characteristically he put it on the broad ground of the good of the race. But his tenderness for the individual child is shown by his enunciation of the Child's Bill of Rights:

"I might repeat that a Bill of Rights should be written for children, and I would compose it somewhat as follows:

" 'The ideal to which we should strive is that there shall be no child in America that has not been born under proper conditions, that does not live in hygienic surroundings, that ever suffers from undernutrition; that does not have prompt and efficient medical attention and inspection, that does not receive primary instruction in the elements of hygiene and good health, that there shall be no child that has not the complete birthright of a sound mind in a sound body and the encouragement to express the spirit within which is the final endowment of every human being.' "

[*McClure's Magazine, May, 1925*]

ABOLITION OF CHILD LABOR

Hoover, immediately after the war, joined the crusade against child labor. In a public statement in December, 1919, he said (*Saturday Evening Post*, December 29, 1919) :

"The use of children in labor with its attendant racial damage . . . is a most flagrant violation. . . ."

On October 11, 1920, in a public address at St. Louis, he said of child labor:

". . . It is absolutely critical that we have such Constitutional Amendment as permits the Federal Government to take direct action. . . . Certain States are so backward in their social development that they will sacrifice their children to industrial advantage . . . not only unfair to other States but is poisoning the springs of the nation at their source. . . . Every State has to bear the burden of shiftless poverty, criminality that spreads from such areas. . . ."

On December 8, 1921, in a published letter, Hoover wrote:

"It is infinitely better to prevent child labor and to compel and support education of our children today than to look after untrained, inefficient, unhealthy citizens tomorrow."

On June 27, 1922, in a public address at Providence, Rhode Island, discussing this evil he said:

". . . All of us would wish that . . . every State would advance itself to the forefront. . . . It would be far better for the future of the Republic. . . . The constant resort to Federal control for solution of difficulties will yet undermine the very basis of social progress by destruction of the sense of local responsibility. . . . However, if it is impossible to safeguard our people by local government. . . . I stand for amendment to the Constitution that will give power and authority to compel action. . . . Let us have our eyes open . . . that so doing is . . . undermining the autonomy of local government . . . the sacrifice that a few States are imposing . . . will open the gates of encroachment on the Constitution every time some local cesspool must be drained. . . . I suggest a final effort be made to bring all the States into line . . . if that is not accomplished quickly, I regretfully join with those in favor of public action."

The Child Labor Amendment to the Constitution was inaugurated by a Republican Congress and was warmly supported by Hoover as Secretary of Commerce, although he felt it was not as carefully worded as might be. He spoke for abolition of child labor on many occasions and emphasized it in the work of the White House Conference on Protection of Children mentioned later on.

After leaving the Presidency, Hoover continued to agitate for the abolition of child labor. Speaking at Philadelphia, on May 14, 1936, he said:

"Every decent American agrees upon the abolition of child labor. Republican Presidents have progressively mobilized opinion against it. We did in twenty years decrease the number of children under sixteen in industry—that is, outside of farming—from about 900,000 to less than 200,000 at the last census report in 1930. That was a decrease in proportion of about 70 per cent in twenty years. The President said that under the codes child labor went out in a flash. It was mostly a flash in the pan."

"The Republican Party must pledge that it will really be done. . . ."

On January 10, 1937, he issued the following statement in support of President Roosevelt on the Child Labor Amendment:

"The President is right. The Child Labor constitutional amendment should be passed now. It has already been ratified by states covering a majority of the country's population."

"While some of us have advocated this amendment from the beginning, I can say this to those who believe it should be done by the states rather than the Federal Government. You have through the years brought a fine accomplishment, for states comprising more than 80 per cent of the population now have some sort of regulatory laws, and thereby child labor outside of agriculture has diminished by 70 per cent in the twenty years between the census of 1910 and 1930. But surely the thirty years in which such state laws have been strongly urged should be enough opportunity for recalcitrant areas to have risen to their own responsibilities. Some of the states which have not ratified the amendment have set examples by the most progressive of laws, but their industries suffer from competition of those states which refuse to give up this hideous advantage."

"The major reason for its ratification is the rights of children to health and a fair chance. But it is also important that we have orderly constitutional change instead of pressure on the independence of the Supreme Court."

CHILDREN'S BUREAU

On coming to the White House his interest in the welfare of children was not diminished but his opportunity increased. In a letter to the Director of the Budget, under date of October 16, 1929, Hoover said:

"I would be obliged if you would treat with as liberal a hand as possible the applications of . . . the Children's and Women's Bureaus. I have great sympathy with the tasks they are undertaking."

In the first appropriations of his term he secured an increase for the Children's and Women's Bureaus, despite decreases in nearly every other bureau of the government.

THE WHITE HOUSE CONFERENCE ON CHILDREN IN 1930

The President determined to have all questions affecting the welfare of children sifted to the bottom by the best experts of the nation and a real program formulated for national action. On July 2, 1929, four months after coming into office, he announced:

"I have decided to call a White House conference on the health and protection of children. This conference will be composed of representatives of the great voluntary associations, together with the Federal and State and municipal authorities interested in these questions. Its purpose will be to determine the facts as to our present progress and our future needs. . . ."

"In order that these determinations may be effectively made and intelligent presentation given at the conference, a series of committees will be appointed. . . ."

"The subjects to be covered embrace problems of dependent children;

regular medical examination; school or public clinics for children; hospitalization; adequate milk supplies; community nurses; maternity instruction and nurses; teaching of health in the schools; facilities for playgrounds and recreation; voluntary organization of children; child labor and scores of allied subjects."

"To cover the expenses of the preliminary committees and the conference and follow-up work which will be required to carry out the conclusions of the conference, a sum of $500,000 has been placed at my disposal from private sources."

"This will be the first national conference held in review of this subject since the conference called by President Roosevelt in 1909. That conference resulted in a great impulse to social and protective activities in behalf of children." *[State Papers, Vol. I, pp. 73–74]*

The committee which directed the White House Child Conference and later was engaged in activities in child health and protection, was made up of the following: Secretary of the Interior Wilbur, chairman; Secretary of Labor Davis, vice chairman; H. E. Barnard, director; Edgar Rickard, treasurer; Grace Abbott, Washington, D. C.; Henry Breckenridge, New York; Frederick Cabot, Boston; Frank Cody, Detroit; Senator James Couzens, of Michigan; S. J. Crumbine, New York City; Hugh S. Cumming, Washington, D. C.; Lee Frankel, New York; William Green, Washington, D. C.; Samuel McC. Hammill, Philadelphia; William King, Indianapolis; Gertrude Lane, New York City; Julia C. Lathrop, Washington, D. C.; Mrs. William B. Meloney, New York City; Mrs. Bina West Miller, Port Huron, Michigan; Mrs. Raymond Robins, Florida; Mrs. F. Louis Slade, New York; Louise Stanley, Washington, D. C.; and French Strother, Administrative Assistant to the President.

On July 29, 1929, addressing this organizing committee for the conference, the President said:

"Through Secretary Wilbur and Secretary Davis, I have invited you here as the nuclei of a Planning Committee to inaugurate a most important movement to the nation as a whole. That is, that we should take national stock of the progress and present situation in the health and protection of childhood; that out of this investigation we should also develop common sense plans for the further advancement in these directions."

". . . in order that these investigations and recommendations may be brought about in the most effective manner, a number of committees . . . embracing the leadership in thought and knowledge of these subjects throughout the nation . . . that after these investigations . . . we should call a White House conference. Such of the policies that may be adopted by that conference should be followed up by definite organization throughout the country. . . . We may save years in national progress if we can secure some measure of unity as to view and unity as to program, more especially as these views and programs are to be based on searching examination of fact and experience."

"I need not urge upon you the fundamental importance of this undertaking. The greatest asset of a race is its children, that their bodily strength and development should prepare them to receive the heritage which each generation must bequeath to the next. These questions reach to the roots of democracy itself."   [State Papers, Vol. I, p. 83]

> The work of the conference was in the main to be the work of American women. In this connection Hoover had at one time said:

"These problems are not the sole responsibility of women, but in many phases they are problems with which no one else is so competent to deal as are women. The general endowment of women with suffrage during the last decade has greatly strengthened their ability to enforce recognition of these fundamentals. Many of us have welcomed the endowment of womanhood with political equality because of our feelings that their influence in moral and spiritual advancement of our people is more safe and certain."

> November 15, 1930, the President announced:

"We have next week the Conference on Child Health and Protection."

"The Governors have appointed their delegates and various mayors their delegates as well as delegates from muncipalities and associations interested."

"So far over 2500 delegates have been appointed. Some sixteen months ago I announced the convening of this Conference. A number of committees were appointed for research and investigation and now total over 1200 members covering every field and phase of child problems."

"The committees will be able to lay before this Conference the most complete survey ever placed before this country on all questions relating to children's health and protection covering all problems, including deficient and delinquent children, to enable the Conference to come to conclusions on the material gathered. Those conclusions will have a very important effect in the activities of States and municipalities on these problems."

"I do not think—I know—that there never has been so exhaustive an investigation and presentation of the subject as will be made at the Conference."

[*State Papers, Vol. I, p. 418*]

On November 19, 1930, President Hoover opened the Children's Conference with one of the most notable addresses of his career:

"I am satisfied that . . . your conference here will result in . . . a series of conclusions and judgments of unprecedented service in behalf of childhood, the benefits of which will be felt for a full generation."

"The reward that accrues to you is the consciousness of something done unselfishly to lighten the burdens of children, to set their feet upon surer paths to health, well-being and happiness. For many years I have hoped for such a national consideration as this. You comprise the delegates appointed by our Federal departments and by the governors of our States, the mayors of our cities, and the representatives of our great national associations, our medical and public health professions. In your hands rest the knowledge and authority outside of the home itself."

"I am mindful also of the unseen millions listening in their homes, who likewise are truly members of this conference, for these problems are theirs—it is their children whose welfare is involved, its helpful services are for them, and their co-operation is essential in carrying out a united and nation-wide effort in behalf of the children."

"We approach all problems of childhood with affection. Theirs is the province of joy and good humor. They are the most wholesome part of the race, the sweetest, for they are fresher from the hands of God. Whimsical, ingenious, mischievous, we live a life of apprehension as to what their opinion may be of us; a life of defense against their terrifying energy; we put them to bed with a sense of relief and a lingering of devotion. We envy them the freshness of adventure and discovery of life; we mourn over the disappointments they will meet. . . ."

"The fundamental purpose of this conference is to set forth an understanding of those safeguards which will assure to them health in mind and body. There are safeguards and services to childhood which can be provided by the community, the state, or the Nation—all of which are beyond the reach of the individual parent. We approach these problems in no spirit of diminishing the responsibilities and values or invading the sanctities of those primary safeguards to child life—their homes and their mothers. After we have determined every scientific fact, after we have erected every public safeguard, after we have constructed every edifice for education or training or hospitalization or play, yet all these things are but a tithe of the physical, moral, and spiritual gifts which motherhood gives and home confers. None of these things carry that affection, that devotion of soul, which is the great endowment from mothers. Our purpose here today is to consider and give our mite of help to strengthen her hand that her boy and girl may have a fair chance."

"These questions of child health and protection are a complicated problem requiring much learning and much action. And we need have great concern over this matter. Let no one believe that these are questions which should not stir a nation; that they are below the dignity of statesmen or governments. If we could have but one generation of properly born, trained, educated, and healthy children, a thousand other problems of government would vanish. We would assure ourselves of healthier minds in more vigorous bodies, to direct the energies of our Nation to yet greater heights of achievement. Moreover, one good community nurse will save a dozen future policemen."

"Our problem falls into three groups: First, the protection and stimulation of the normal child; second, aid to the physically defective and handicapped child; third, the problems of the delinquent child."

"Statistics can well be used to give emphasis to our problem. One of your committees reports that out of 45,000,000 children—

    35,000,000 are reasonably normal.

    6,000,000 are improperly nourished.

    1,000,000 have defective speech.

    1,000,000 have weak or damaged hearts.

    675,000 present behavior problems.

    450,000 are mentally retarded

    382,000 are tubercular.

    342,000 have impaired hearing.

    18,000 are totally deaf.

    300,000 are crippled.

    50,000 are partially blind.

    14,000 are wholly blind.

    200,000 are delinquent.

    500,000 are dependent."

"And so on, to a total of at least ten millions of deficients, more than eighty per cent of whom are not receiving the necessary attention, though our knowledge and experience show that these deficiencies can be prevented and remedied to a high degree. The reports you have before you are not only replete with information upon each of these groups, they are also vivid with recommendation for remedy. And if we do not perform our duty to these children, we leave them dependent, or we provide from them the major recruiting ground for the army of ne'er-do-wells and criminals."

"But that we be not discouraged let us bear in mind that there are 35,000,000 reasonably normal, cheerful human electrons radiating joy and mischief and hope and faith. Their faces are turned toward the light—theirs is the life of great adventure. These are the vivid, romping, every-day children, our own and our neighbors' with all their strongly marked differences—and the more differences the better. The more they charge us with their separate problems the more we know they are vitally and humanly alive."

"From what we know of foreign countries, I am convinced that we have a right to assume that we have a larger proportion of happy, normal children than any other country in the world. And also, on the bright side, your reports show that we have 1,500,000 specially gifted children. There lies the future leadership of the Nation if we devote ourselves to their guidance."

"Again, there are the problems of child labor. Industry must not rob our children of their rightful heritage. Any labor which stunts growth, either physical or mental, that limits education, that deprives children of right of comradeship, of joy and play, is sapping the next generation."

"Nor is our problem one solely of the city child. We have grave responsibilities to the rural child. Adequate expert service should be as available to him from maternity to maturity. Since science discovered the cause of communicable disease, protection from these diseases for the child of the farm is as much an obligation to them as to the child of the city. The child of the country is handicapped by lack of some cultural influences extended by the city. We must find ways and means of extending these influences to the children of rural districts."

"There has not been before the summation of knowledge and experience such as lies before this conference. There has been no period when it could be undertaken with so much experience and background. The Nation looks to you to derive from it positive, definite, guiding judgments. But greater than the facts and the judgments, more fundamental than all, we need the vision and inspired understanding to interpret these facts and put them into practice. It will rest with you to light the fires of that inspiration in the general public conscience, and from conscience lead it into action."

"In democracy our progress is the sum of progress of the individuals —that they each individually achieve to the full capacity of their abilities and character. Their varied personalities and abilities must be brought fully to bloom; they must not be mentally regimented to a single mold or the qualities of many will be stifled; the door of opportunity must be opened to each of them."

"May you who are meeting here find in your deliberations new fuel with which to light this flame of progress so that this occasion may be marked with a fresh luster that will set us anew on the road through the crowding complexities of modern life."

[*State Papers, Vol. I, pp. 419 ff.*]

On November 21, 1930, the conference concluded its deliberations with the adoption of the "Children's Charter." Its first outline was drafted by the President and it was put in final form by the conference. It was issued over his signature by request of the conference. This document was to have a powerful effect upon awakening the American people to the problems of childhood. It has been estimated that thirty millions of copies have been circulated by the press. And over a million copies were specially printed and distributed by various associations.

The conference completed its work as an investigating body with a series of special reports from the conference committees, which have been published and which form the foundation of our present knowledge of the problems.

The Charter is in fact the statement of the Hoover policies in respect to the Nation's responsibility toward children.

"THE CHILDREN'S CHARTER"

President Hoover's White House Conference on Child Health and Protection, recognizing the rights of the child as the first rights of citizenship, pledges itself to these aims for the children of America.

I

For every child spiritual and moral training to help him to stand firm under the pressure of life.

II

For every child understanding and the guarding of his personality as his most precious right.

III

For every child a home and that love and security which a home provides; and for that child who must receive foster care, the nearest substitute for his own home.

IV

For every child full preparation for his birth, his mother receiving parental, natal and postnatal care; and the establishment of such protective measures as will make childbearing safer.

V

For every child health protection from birth through adolescence including: periodical health examinations and where needed, care of specialists and hospital treatment; regular dental examinations and care of the teeth; protective and preventive measures against communicable diseases; the insuring of pure food, pure milk and pure water.

VI

For every child from birth, through adolescence, promotion of health, including health instruction and a health program, wholesome physical and mental recreation, with teachers and leaders adequately trained.

VII

For every child a dwelling-place safe, sanitary, and wholesome, with reasonable provisions for privacy; free from conditions which tend to thwart his development; and a home environment harmonious and enriching.

VIII

For every child a school which is safe from hazards, sanitary, properly equipped, lighted, and ventilated. For younger children nursery schools and kindergartens to supplement home care.

IX

For every child a community which recognizes and plans for his needs, protects him against physical dangers, moral hazards and disease; provides him with safe and wholesome places for play and recreation; and makes provision for his cultural and social needs.

X

For every child an education which, through the discovery and development of his individual abilities, prepares him for life; and through training and vocational guidance prepares him for a living which will yield him the maximum of satisfaction.

XI

For every child such teaching and training as will prepare him for successful parenthood, homemaking, and the rights of citizenship; and, for parents, supplementary training to fit them to deal wisely with the problems of parenthood.

XII

For every child education for safety and protection against accidents to which modern conditions subject him—those to which he is directly exposed and those which, through loss or maiming of his parents, affect him indirectly.

XIII

For every child who is blind, deaf, crippled, or otherwise physically handicapped, and for the child who is mentally handicapped, such measures as will early discover and diagnose his handicap, provide care and treatment, and so train him that he may become an asset to society rather than a liability. Expenses of these services should be borne publicly where they cannot be privately met.

XIV

For every child who is in conflict with society the right to be dealt with intelligently as society's charge, not society's outcast; with the home, the school, the church, the court and the institution when needed, shaped to return him whenever possible to the normal stream of life.

XV

For every child the right to grow up in a family with an adequate standard of living and the security of a stable income as the surest safeguard against social handicaps.

XVI

For every child protection against labor that stunts growth either physical or mental, that limits education, that deprives children of the right of comradeship, of play, and of joy.

XVII

For every rural child a satisfactory schooling and health services as for the city child, and an extension to rural families of social, recreational, and cultural facilities.

XVIII

To supplement the home and the school in the training of youth, and to return to them those interests of which modern life tends to cheat children, every stimulation and encouragement should be given to the extension and development of the voluntary youth organizations.

XIX

To make everywhere available these minimum protections of the health and welfare of children, there should be a district, county, or community organization for health, education and welfare, with full-time officials, co-ordinating with a state-wide program which will be responsive to a nation-wide service of general information, statistics, and scientific research. This should include:

(a) Trained full-time public health officials, with public health nurses, sanitary inspection and laboratory workers.

(b) Available hospital beds.

(c) Full-time public welfare service for the relief, aid and guidance of children, in special need due to poverty, misfortune or behavior difficulties, and for the protection of children from abuse, neglect, exploitation or moral hazard.

FOR EVERY CHILD THESE RIGHTS, REGARDLESS OF RACE, OR COLOR, OR SITUATION, WHEREVER HE MAY LIVE UNDER THE PROTECTION OF THE AMERICAN FLAG.

[*State Papers, Vol. II, p. 289*]

The work upon protection of children did not end with the conference. Steadily the President was building up public opinion to continued and concrete action. A permanent staff of the conference was set up. Special reports of committees were issued in thirty-five volumes on special subjects and given nation-wide distribution. State Child Protection Conferences were held in twenty States under the patronage of the governors. A large amount of State and municipal action flowed steadily from the movement. Scores of States and municipalities improved their laws and ordinances.

THE RURAL CHILD HEALTH BILL OF 1931

The President in his first Annual Message of December 3, 1929, recommended:

"I recommend to the Congress that the purpose of the Sheppard-Towner Act should be continued through the Children's Bureau for a limited period of years; and that the Congress should consider the desirability of . . . the building up of such county or other local units, and that such outlay should be positively coördinated with . . . the United States Public Health Service."

"All funds appropriated should of course be applied through the States, so that the public health program of the county or local unit will be efficiently coördinated with that of the whole state."

[*State Papers, Vol. I, p. 160*]

Congress not having acted on the President's rural health program, on December 2, 1930, in his Second Annual Message, he again returned to the charge.

"I urge further consideration by the Congress of the recommendations I made a year ago looking to the development through temporary Federal aid of adequate state and local services for the health of children and the further stamping out of communicable disease, particularly in the rural sections. The advance of scientific discovery, methods, and social thought imposes a new vision in these matters. The drain upon the Federal Treasury is comparatively small. The results both economic and moral are of the utmost importance." [*State Papers, Vol. I, p. 439*]

Secretary Wilbur and the President drafted and introduced in the Congress a comprehensive measure of Federal aid to States and counties to effectuate these purposes:

The bill provided for subsidies to the States and counties for the establishment of health units, provided for subsidies to the States and counties additional sums for promotion of child health and welfare including maternity.

The measure was passed by the House and reported upon favorably to the Senate; Messrs. Newton and Myers' comment is as follows:

"*March 4, 1931:* Congress adjourned. A filibuster by Senator Thomas of Oklahoma killed the President's rural health program for children, which otherwise would have passed."

"The President was disappointed. Some years before he had, as chairman of the American Child Health Association, carried forward experiments in developing more effective county organization with respect to the health and care of children. After the Mississippi flood, with private financial aid, he had established a health supervision in more than one hundred counties. The result had been practically to stamp out malaria, plague, typhoid, and other diseases in those areas, so long as the supervision was continued, and greatly to aid in better conditions of birth and nurture of children."

"The Federal administration was to be conducted jointly by the Public Health Service and the Children's Bureau. The failure of the passage of the bill postponed its benefits for many years. The succeeding Congress was so engrossed in legislation necessitated by meeting the problems of the depression, deepened by the European collapse, that it would not give attention to the subject."

[*Hoover Administration, p. 471*]

Despite the set-back in the last Congress, the President again returned to the charge in his Annual Message of December 8, 1931:

"I again call attention to my previous recommendations upon this subject, particularly in its relation to children. The moral results are of the utmost importance."

[*State Papers, Vol. II, p. 56*]

The President had the bill re-introduced but the House, by then under Democratic control, would have none of it.

A recommendation of the White House conference as to juvenile offenders was pushed through the Congress on June 11, 1932. It transferred Federal juvenile offenders from the Federal Courts to the State Juvenile Courts.

On September 29, 1932, in an address to the Herald-Tribune's Woman's Conference, the President said:

"Our most immediate question is the strain of the depression upon the children. In this depression as never before the American people have responded with a high sense of responsibility to safeguard and protect the children not only as the humane necessity of the day but that there may be no danger for the future. The devotion of voluntary effort, the solicitude being given throughout the Nation to the welfare of children through this trying distress is a stimulant to the spirit of every one of us. The continuous reports of the Public Health Service showing a less infant mortality, less infant disease than in prosperous times, can mark only one thing and that is the most extraordinary devotion to those who would be normally the most hard pressed. I know of no greater service than constant watchfulness of your groups that they shall continue to be safeguarded."

"There is another opportunity growing out of these times to advance the cause of children . . . that is the steady elimination of child labor."

"We should not forget . . . maintaining and supporting our schools as a first charge upon all of our resources in these times of emergency."

"We cannot afford to slacken one moment in the preparation of the new day of a generation of Americans stronger and better, not only physically and intellectually, but above all morally."

"We can do much to help the Nation and the children over the present emergencies. But the greatest service in the long view is the endowment we can give to the next generation in health and character."

"So much have I felt this to be an imperative responsibility, that I have given every weight of this office and much time in association with these efforts."   [*State Papers, Vol. II, pp. 290–291*]

The President's constant insistence that the care of children was the first obligation in the depression found a great response. Of these appeals a typical radio broadcast was on October 18, 1931:

"The possible misery of helpless people gives me more concern than any other trouble this depression has brought us."

". . . Every one who aids in this service will have lighted a beacon of help on the stormy coast of human adversity."

"The success and the character of nations are to be judged by the ideals and the spirit of its people. Time and again the American people have demonstrated a spiritual quality, a capacity for unity of action, of generosity, a certainty of results in time of emergency that have made them great in the annals of the history of all nations. This is the time and this is the occasion when we must arouse that idealism, that spirit, that determination, that unity of action, from which there can be no failure in this primary obligation of every man to his neighbor and of a nation to its citizens, that none who deserve shall suffer."

"I would that I possessed the art of words to fix the real issue with which the troubled world is faced into the mind and heart of every American man and woman. Our country and the world are today involved in more than a financial crisis. We are faced with the primary question of human relations, which reaches to the very depth of organized society and to the very depth of human conscience. This civilization and this great complex, which we call American life, is builded and can alone survive upon the translation into individual action of that fundamental philosophy announced by the Savior nineteen centuries ago. Part of our national suffering today is from failure to observe these primary yet inexorable laws of human relationship. Modern society cannot survive with the defense of Cain, "Am I my brother's keeper?"

"No governmental action, no economic doctrine, no economic plan or project can replace that God-imposed responsibility of the individual man and woman to their neighbors. That is a vital part of the very soul of the people. If we shall gain in this spirit from this painful time, we shall have created a greater and more glorious America. The trial of it is here now. It is a trial of the heart and conscience of individual men and women." [*State Papers, Vol. II, pp. 14–15*]

In his last important address of the campaign of 1932, Hoover paid the following tribute to American women for their care of children in the depression:

"Throughout the difficulties of the past two years there have stood out in high relief the courage and fortitude of the American people. Yet steadfast and brave as have been our men in the face of suffering and disaster, our women have been braver and more steadfast. Upon them the rigors of the world depression, as did the rigors of the World War, have borne most heavily. Untold anxiety, self-denial, and drudgery have been their lot that their loved ones might be assured of that care in mind and body that would equip them to meet the problems of the future. That the health of our people, both infants and adults, as evidenced by vital statistics, is now at its highest point, is a notable tribute to the loving care and devotion of our women. Today their hearts are gladdened by a well-founded hope of an early return to normal living conditions. They must not be disappointed." [*State Papers, Vol. II, p. 464*]

The subject of depression relief for children is discussed elsewhere, on page 377.[1]

[1] Under the Hoover system of local responsibility and administration of relief, that care was given far more efficiently than when local responsibility was displaced by the centralized government bureaucracy of the New Deal. The proof is complete.

1928..................6880 deaths per 100,000
1929..................6730 deaths per 100,000
1930..................6460 deaths per 100,000
1931..................6170 deaths per 100,000
1932..................5760 deaths per 100,000
1933..................5810 deaths per 100,000
1934..................5990 deaths per 100,000

The Roosevelt Administration having a majority of their own party in both Houses was able to legislate Federal aid to the health and protection for children. No one will say that Mr. Hoover's fifteen years of public agitation of his policy did not greatly contribute to bring this about.

PUBLIC HEALTH

For many years Hoover had been deeply interested in national public health policies. He constantly referred to the subject in the campaign of 1928. He felt it must have greater Federal guidance. In his Inaugural Address he emphasized the importance and gave as his policies "public health service should be as fully organized and as universally incorporated into our governmental system as is public education." His special policies in relation to children have already been discussed.

After the Mississippi flood of 1927 where he had directed the removal of 1,000,000 persons from the flood area, the dangerous health aftermaths of their return led him to organize a "Health Unit" in each of more than one hundred counties in the flood area. For maintenance of these units for eighteen months, he raised some $2,000,000 from private sources to aid the county governments. The results have already been mentioned.

The great results attained in that area caused the adoption of the plan in some four hundred rural counties. But the majority of rural counties were too poor to support it.

In his Message to the first regular Congress of his administration, the President urged:

"The advance in scientific discovery as to disease and health imposes new considerations upon us. The nation as a whole is vitally interested in the health of all the people; in protection from spread of contagious disease; in the relation of physical and mental disabilities to criminality; and in the economic and moral advancement which is fundamentally associated with sound body and mind. The organization of preventive measures and health education in its personal application is the province of public health service. Such organization should be as universal as public education. Its support is a proper burden upon the taxpayer. It cannot be organized with success, either in its sanitary or educational phases, except under public authority. It should be based upon local and state responsibility, but I consider that the Federal Government has an obligation of contribution to the establishment of such agencies."

"In the practical working out of organization, exhaustive experiment and trial have demonstrated that the base should be competent organization of the municipality, county, or other local unit. Most of our municipalities and some 400 rural counties out of 3000 now have some such unit organization. Where highly developed, a health unit comprises at least a physician, sanitary engineer, and community nurse with the addition, in some cases, of another nurse devoted to the problems of maternity and children. Such organization gives at once a fnduamental control of preventive measures and assists in community instruction. The Federal Government, through its interest in control of contagion, acting through the United States Public Health Service and the state agencies, has in the past and should in the future concern itself with this development, particularly in the many rural sections which are unfortunately far behind in progress. Some parts of the funds contributed under the Sheppard-Towner Act through the Children's Bureau of the Department of Labor have also found their way into these channels."

[*State Papers, Vol. I, p. 159*]

The President gave constant personal and financial help to the Federal Public Health Service. He and Secretary Wilbur drafted for the committees of Congress model legislation for a Federal subsidy for a county-unit health system combining it with the special legislation for child protection. Nothing having been done except committee hearings, the President returned to it at the next session. In his Message of December 2, 1930, he urged:

"I urge further consideration by the Congress of the recommendations I made a year ago looking to the development through temporary Federal aid of adequate state and local services for the health of children and the further stamping of out of communicable disease, particularly in the rural sections. The advance of scientific discovery, methods, and social thought imposes a new vision in these matters. The drain upon the Federal Treasury is comparatively small. The results both economic and moral are of the utmost importance." [*State Papers, Vol. I, p. 439*]

As already stated the bill was enacted in the House and passed the committee in the Senate but was killed by a filibuster by Senator Thomas of Oklahoma (Democrat). The bill was again introduced but the Democratic House refused to put it up for action.

In an address to the American Public Health Association on October 24, 1932, the President said:

"By every means within my reach I have ever since promoted the idea of establishing these units in every one of our 5000 counties in the United States. I have frequently helped the voluntary co-operating groups to raise the funds for such units by public subscription, and many times, through conferences and in other ways, have assisted in promoting legislation in the states by which state governments have supplemented these funds on the familiar basis of duplicating from the state treasury the sums raised locally by the county or municipal governments. I have gone farther than that. Although I am generally opposed to Federal subsidies to the states, yet I have regarded contagion as one interstate question and have recommended Federal contributions to such a universal service."

"I am in favor, as a constructive measure of public economy, of a program to be carried out on such wise lines, to reduce contagious disease with government encouragement. If communicable diseases could be reduced by even one-third, such a reduction would repay the country more than a thousandfold its cost, by its saving of the present losses in productive time of workers and its saving of the present losses to school funds by absences from classes. That is the sheer economics of it. But far beyond that, there would be the wealth of gain in human comfort and human happiness."

"Still beyond that, there is the gain of definite community action looking to the protection of the home—the co-operation of organized society in a great work of social well-being, with all its additions of assurance to men and women of a further security to their families against the menace of contagion and ill-health."

"And even beyond that in importance, there is the well-being of the future generations of our children, the building up of safeguards around the home and the health of the parents and of the growing family, which will contribute to the production of a healthier and more virile race and to the preservation not only of the treasures of childhood as a whole, but also to the preservation of those precious exceptional children, whose birth cannot be predicted of any class or moment and from whom comes the leadership of our democracy, to which they rise through the free channels of opportunity in our country." [*State Papers, Vol. II, pp. 386–387*]

EDUCATION

GENERAL POLICIES

To reproduce the Hoover addresses, statements and actions over twenty years in support of education would be a book in itself.

His support is sufficiently indicated by these two quotations:

"About one-fourth of the whole population of our country is always simultaneously engaged in the same occupation—the job of going to school. It is the largest group in any one employment. To use a term of the census, it is truly a "gainful occupation." Moreover, as nearly the whole people have worked at it at one time or another, no matter how diverse their later life may become, they all have a common memory of the schoolyard and the classroom, and they all have a lasting affection for some teacher."

"Not three other industries in our country can boast of so large a physical plant as yours. Hundreds of millions are invested in new construction every decade, and still, in commercial slang, you are behind your orders, as witness the unsatisfied demand for seats in the schools of every city in the country. Yours is a big business. And it is big in its responsibilities and bigger in its possibilities than any other business ever undertaken by our countrymen."

"Both as the cause and the effect the maintenance of our complex civilization now depends upon it. From generation to generation we hand on our vast material equipment, our knowledge of how to run it, and our stock of intellectual and spiritual ideas. If we were to suppress our educational system for a single generation the equipment would decay, the most of our people would die of starvation, and intellectually and spiritually we should slip back four thousand years in human progress. We could recover the loss of any other big business in a few years—but not this one. And unless our educational system keeps pace with the growth of our material equipment we will slip also."

"The spirit of democracy can survive only through universal education. All this has been said often enough before, but it seems to me it will always bear repetition. I may add that we don't expect you to teach the gamut of local, national, and international problems to children. What democracy requires is a basic training of mind which will permit an understanding of such problems, and the formation of a reasonable opinion upon them. That the resultant will in the long run be an enlightened public opinion is a hazard upon the intelligence of our race that we the believers in democracy are willing to take."

"But after all our schools do more than merely transmit knowledge and training; they are America itself in miniature, where, in a purer air and under wise guidance, a whole life of citizenship is levied experimentally with its social contacts, its recreations, its ethical problems, its political practice, its duties and its rewards. Ideals are developed that shape the whole adult life. Experience is gained that is valuable for all the years of maturity. I would be one of the last people in the world to belittle the importance of the exact knowledge that teachers impart to their pupils —as an engineer I set a high value upon precise information—but knowledge, however exact, is secondary to a trained mind and serves no useful purpose unless it is the servant of an ambitious mind, a sound character, and an idealistic spirit."

[*Address before the National Education Association, February 25, 1926*]

"The job of our universities extends even deeper than this in our national life. They have a vital duty in fostering new recruits for leadership in our States and our nation."

"Indeed one of the greatest problems of democracy—and civilization for that matter—is to provide sustained leadership in all avenues of life. If it can maintain virile, capable leadership, true to high moral standards and devoted to the ideals of democracy, there will not be degeneration within our nation. There will be continuous economic, social and moral progress. It is true that leadership founded upon birth or upon class has always decayed through degeneration. Certainly the supply of this leadership cannot be replenished each generation by selection like queen bees, or by divine right, or through bureaucracies."

"The great American experiment in democracy is based upon a new conception in selection of leadership, which the prophets of our impending decay oft overlook. This conception is, first, that in the great mass of our people there are plenty of individuals of intelligence from among whom leadership can be recruited; and second, that if we maintain for every individual an equality of opportunity to attain that position in the community to which his intelligence, character, ability, and ambition entitle him, and if we stimulate him to endeavor, then our supply of leadership will stream forward of its own initiative."

"A group of critics has informed us that as each succeeding generation elaborates its social and economic environment and thus increasingly complicates the problem of living and working, the time is likely to come when the structural overloading will be so great that civilization will collapse—either by inability to provide leadership or by revolt against the whole thing. All of which is based upon the hypothesis that we do not have in our country men of sufficient material for leadership and direction of the vast agencies of modern civilization. Here in America we have conclusively demonstrated that our nation possesses within its ranks a vast reservoir of leadership. Were we to consider 20,000 men who dominate our economic, political, educational and spiritual activities, I dare say you would find that 90 per cent of them have either themselves sometime earned their living by manual labor or had fathers who did."

"Now the only door to equal opportunity is education. All the other factors that make for equality of opportunity are insignificant compared to an equal chance to obtain the highest physical, moral, and intellectual equipment which our colleges and universities afford. Great administrators, engineers, lawyers, moral leaders cannot be made by birth and money. The creation of an efficient system of universal and free education, with its progress stage by stage from the lowest grade in our public schools to the highest training in our universities and colleges, has thus become a primary responsibility of every State. It is a right of every youth in the State."

"By building this open stair we set up a fundamental protection to our democracy itself, for it is the maintenance of leadership by the rise of the individual out of the mass which assures us against the crystallization of classes or special groups. No stratification or segregation of classes or castes can take place in a mass livened by the free stir of its particles. It is in this particular, this stressing equality of opportunity for the whole mass, that our national experiment has fundamentally departed from those of the democracies of the old world. We may not have clearly envisaged this ideal at the founding of our republic, but through the interaction of our laboratories in government we have gradually moulded it into our social system. We may not always be perfect in providing this equality of opportunity but the instinct and the ideal are strong within us." *[Address, Georgia University, June 16, 1926]*

His Inaugural Address included this paragraph:

"Although education is primarily a responsibility of the States and local communities, and rightly so, yet the Nation as a whole is vitally concerned in its development everywhere to the highest standards and to complete universality."

". . . We cannot hope to succeed in directing this increasingly complex civilization unless we can draw all the talent of leadership from the whole people. One civilization after another has been wrecked upon the attempt to secure sufficient leadership from a single group or class. If we would prevent the growth of class distinctions and would constantly refresh our leadership with the ideals of our people, we must draw constantly from the general mass. The full opportunity for every boy and girl to rise through the selective processes of education can alone secure to us this leadership." [*State Papers, Vol. I, p. 7*]

NEGRO EDUCATION

Hoover's interest in education extended to a special interest in the problems of the Negroes. In an address before the Tuskegee Institute on April 14, 1931, he said:

"I consider it a great privilege to take even a small part in this celebration of the fiftieth anniversary of Tuskegee Institute. . . ."

"It is now over sixty years since the Negro was released from slavery and given the status of a citizen in our country whose wealth and general prosperity his labor has helped create. The progress of the race within this period has surpassed the most sanguine hopes of the most ardent advocates. No group of people in history ever started from a more complete economic and cultural destitution. . . . Within that period the race has multiplied its wealth more than one hundred and thirty times, has reduced its illiteracy from 95 per cent to 20 per cent, and reduced its death rate by one-half. It has risen to the ownership of more than 750,000 homes, has accumulated property to the value of billions, has developed a far-reaching internal network of social, religious, and economic organizations for the continued advancement of its people, has produced leadership in all walks of life that for faith, courage, devotion, and patriotic loyalty ranks with all the other groups in our country."

"The greatest single factor in the progress of the Negro race has been the schools, private and public, established and conducted by high-minded self-sacrificing men and women of both races and all sections of our country, maintained by the states and by private philanthropy, covering the whole field of education from primary school through to college and university. These have been the most effective agents in solving the problems created by the admission to citizenship of 4,000,000 ex-slaves without preparation for their new responsibilities. . . ."

"The Nation owes a debt of gratitude to the wisdom and constructive vision of Booker T. Washington, . . . and Doctor R. R. Moton. . . ."

[*State Papers, Vol. I, pp. 545–547*]

In an address to Howard University, in Washington, D. C. on June 10, 1932, the President said:

". . . Nothing that the Federal Government has done reflects more credit upon it . . . than this institution . . . it brings . . . an equal opportunity to share in the full measures of citizenship with their brethren of other races . . . the colored people are being integrated fully into the broad stream of the national life, . . . and a share in the intellectual progress of mankind."

[*State Papers, Vol. II, p. 207*]

DEPARTMENT OF EDUCATION

The question of a Federal Department of Education had long been advocated. On June 6, 1929, the President and Secretary Wilbur appointed a citizens' committee of leading educators to consider the question. The committee reported on November 16, 1931. Its opinions on the Department question were divided, but it was emphatic that the Federal Government should not invade the public schools.

ABOLITION OF ADULT ILLITERACY

On November 17 the President appointed a committee of distinguished membership under Secretary Wilbur to organize, in co-operation with the Department of the Interior, a nation-wide movement for the abolition of illiteracy through immediate adult education. This committee set up a vigorous movement with important results. In an interim report on April 9, 1931, it said that the national percentage of illiteracy was 4.3 per cent of the population, showing also the percentage in each State. It announced that in forty-three States and districts there were active co-operating and civic organizations. It recommended further arousing of thoughtful people, working with private funds, since "people closest to their problems are regarded as best equipped to direct their own machinery and resources."

MAINTENANCE OF SCHOOLS IN THE DEPRESSION

In one of the last addresses of his administration, on January 5, 1933, the President said:

"Our Nation faces the acute responsibility of providing a right-of-way for the American child. In spite of our economic, social, and governmental difficulties, our future citizens must be built up now. We may delay other problems but we cannot delay the day to day care and instruction of our children."

"We are now forced to make decisions on the merits of the various expenditures. But in the rigid governmental economies that are requisite everywhere we must not encroach upon the schools or reduce the opportunity of the child through the school to develop adequate citizenship. There is no safety for our republic without the education of our youth. That is the first charge upon all citizens and local governments."

". . . May I ask that throughout your deliberations you bear in mind that the proper care and training of our children is more important than any other process that is carried on by our government. If we are to continue to educate our children, we must keep and sustain our teachers and our schools."   [*State Papers, Vol. II, pp. 564–565*]

HOUSING

Early in his public career Hoover started definite movement toward better housing for the lower income groups in the nation. His better housing policies, as developed over years, were:

First: To create a better public understanding of what constitutes good housing.

Second: To create an interest in home ownership by the individual.

Third: To make available, at nominal cost, plans and specifications of more practical and more attractive homes.

Fourth: To create a national interest and a sense of community responsibility for better homes and housing.

Fifth: To reduce the cost of housing by simplifying or removing cumbersome municipal and state regulations which added cost and impeded housing; to simplify and standardize building materials and thus contribute to reducing costs. By co-operation, to extend the seasonal period of building by voluntarily organization, and thus fundamentally reduce costs.

Sixth: To organize honest, abundant and reasonable credit facilities, both for homes and slum improvements.

His policies never included Federal Government construction of housing.

As a practical start toward all these aims, in 1921 Hoover established in the Department of Commerce a housing division to develop the whole problem of better housing in the country.

In his annual report as Secretary of Commerce for 1922 he said:

"Systematic measures of co-operation were set in motion [for housing] in trade and civic bodies. . . . Typical among the latter activities was the appointment of a committee . . . to formulate a standard building code, as . . . the varying regulations in force in hundreds of different municipalities . . . had imposed an unnecessary cost upon building of from 10 to 20 per cent. . . . A tentative draft was submitted to some 975 engineers, architects, municipal officials, and representatives of the building industry, whose useful criticisms were incorporated. . . . The code is already being adopted . . . elimination of unnecessary variation in dimensions of building material, and in the simplification of specifications have been undertaken by experts . . . with gratifying results."

On May 10, 1922, in a public statement the Secretary said:

"The enormous losses in human happiness and in money, which have resulted from lack of city plans which take into account the conditions of modern life, need little proof. The lack of adequate open spaces, of playgrounds and parks, the congestion of streets, the misery of tenement life and its repercussions upon each new generation, are an untold charge against our American life. Our cities do not produce their full contribution to the sinews of American life and national character. The moral and social issues can only be solved by a new conception of city building."

BETTER HOMES IN AMERICA

As a further step, during the year 1923, Hoover, with the aid of Mrs. William Brown Meloney, organized a voluntary association "Better Homes in America" of which he was chairman. Over a period of ten years Hoover raised from private sources upward of $200,000 annually to support this movement. The work was carried on by over 9000 active committees comprising some 30,000 men and women members.

The report of the Secretary of Commerce for 1925 says:

"Important progress in the science of small-house construction has been made as a result of the work of Better Homes in America. This organization for public service is supported by public contributions and is under the direction of the Secretary of Commerce as president. . . . 'Better Homes Week' was observed in more than 2000 communities last May— a large number have built, furnished, and equipped demonstration houses with the object of developing a better utilization of funds for household expenditures. . . ."

"Financing the home owner of a small home is in reality one of the great problems of the construction industry, and the department has endeavored to aid the best classes of home-financing agencies. . . ."

HOUSING DIVISION OF DEPARTMENT OF COMMERCE

Secretary of Commerce Hoover's Annual Report for 1923 reads:

". . . I referred in my last annual report to a new division created in this department to assist and co-operate with voluntary bodies . . . a movement sponsoring demonstration houses that have been equipped and opened to the public in several hundred cities, usually by women's organizations in co-operation with business and civic groups. The result has been to encourage wiser expenditure for household purposes. . . ."

". . . the small house service bureaus, . . . have been encouraged by this department, in providing at cost small-house plans designed by competent architects."

". . . a handbook for prospective home owners was prepared in the department. . . . Its value . . . is well indicated by the fact that its sales by the Superintendent of Documents immediately ran into the hundreds of thousands."

". . . the members of the department's staff, and its funds, have been pressed to the limit by request for co-operation in work on building codes, plumbing codes, simplification and elimination of dimensional varieties of building materials, research on the use of building materials, and studies of zoning and city planning problems."

[*Commerce Report, 1923, pp. 20–21*]

The department undertook to secure an extension of "Zoning" as the first step to city and community planning. In reporting upon this co-operative effort, Secretary Hoover said on February 15, 1924:

"The importance of this standard state zoning enabling act cannot well be overemphasized. When the advisory committee on zoning was formed in the Department of Commerce, the proposal to frame it received unanimous support from the public-spirited organizations represented on the committee, and other groups interested in zoning. The urgency of the need for such a standard act was at once demonstrated, when, within a year of its issuance, eleven states passed zoning enabling acts which were modelled either wholly or partly after it. Similar acts have been introduced in four other states, with the prospect of more to follow."

"The discovery that it is practical by city zoning to carry out reasonable neighborly agreements as to the use of land has made an almost instant appeal to the American people. When the advisory committee on zoning was formed in the Department of Commerce in September, 1921, only 48 cities and towns, with less than 11,000,000 inhabitants, had adopted zoning ordinances. By the end of 1923, a little more than two years later, zoning was in effect in 218 municipalities, with more than 22,000,-000 inhabitants, and new ones are being added to the list each month."

The report of the Secretary of Commerce for 1928 says:

"The past year has brought most gratifying results from the department's co-operation with business, civic, and labor groups, and local government officials toward solving various outstanding problems. . . . In addition to standardization and simplification of building materials, improved wood utilization, and scientific investigations of the manufacture, uses, and properties of building materials . . . distinct progress has been made along the following lines."

". . . At least 120 municipalities throughout the country have now made use of the recommendations prepared by the department's building code committee . . . more than $3,000,000,000 worth of construction is required to meet the provisions of local building codes, and savings up to 20 per cent of the cost are sometimes made by the revision of obsolete requirements. . . ."

". . . campaigns to put construction more nearly on a year-round basis were inaugurated in a number of cities during the past year and indicate a steady growth of the movement through the department. . . . These voluntary efforts have helped to stabilize employment among more than 1,000,000 men engaged in construction, and several times as many engaged in the manufacture and transportation of building materials. . . ."

"Now more than 640 cities, towns, and villages aim to minimize such occurrences through zoning ordinances . . . now number ten times more than when the . . . committee on city planning and zoning was created in the department seven years ago . . . the sound development and application of zoning principles."

WHITE HOUSE CONFERENCE ON HOUSING

After coming to the White House, the President announced a White House Conference on Home Building and Housing. He stated on August 1, 1930:

"I have decided to undertake the organization of an adequate investigation and study on a nation-wide scale of the problems presented in home ownership and home building. . . ."

"The conference will be organized by a Planning Committee comprised of representatives of the leading national groups interested in this field, under the direction of Secretary Wilbur and Doctor H. E. Barnard. . . ." [*State Papers, Vol. I, p. 362*]

The Planning Committee included the heads of twenty national associations interested in the subject, social students, labor, bankers and builders. Expert committees were organized to investigate and to make preparatory reports on every part of the subject and given resources and time to do an exhaustive job. The expenses of the investigation and the conference were paid from private subscription.

The Planning Committee of the conference comprised Secretary of Commerce Lamont, chairman; John M. Gries, Chief of the Division of Building and Housing, Department of Commerce, executive secretary; and the heads of the following associations—

American Civic Association
American Farm Bureau Federation
American Federation of Labor
American Home Economics Association
American Institute of Architects
Association of General Contractors
Association of Life Insurance Presidents
Better Homes in America
Chamber of Commerce of the United States
General Federation of Women's Clubs
National Association of Builders' Exchanges
National Association of Real Estate Boards
National Congress of Parents and Teachers
National Farmers' Union
National Grange

Russell Sage Foundation
Savings Bank Division—American Bankers' Association
United States League of Building and Loan Associations
Women's National Farm and Garden Association

On September 15, 1931, the President announced that the
committee work had so far progressed that the conference would
be convened in December. He said:

". . . About 400 persons have assisted in the preparatory work and
1000 representative citizens from the forty-eight states, associated with
building and housing activities, are expected to participate in the conference. . . ."

"The conference in December will be the first of its kind on this scale
in the United States. It will deal with the whole question. . . . It will
embrace finance, design, equipment, city planning, household management, and many other aspects. . . ."   [*State Papers, Vol. II, p. 614*]

On December 2, 1931, the President opened the Conference
on Housing, and said:

"You have come from every State in the Union to consider a matter
of basic national interest. Your purpose is to consider it in its long view
rather than its emergency aspects. Next to food and clothing the housing
of a nation is its most vital social and economic problem. This conference
has been called to facilitate the ownership of homes, and protect the
owners of homes. . . . the standards of tenement and apartment
dwellings. . . ."

"While the purpose of this conference is to study and advise upon the
very practical questions of home design, of materials, of building regulations, of zoning, of taxes, of transportation, of financing, of parks and
playgrounds and other topics, yet behind it all every one of you here is
impelled by the high ideal and aspiration that each family may pass their
days in the home which they own; that they may nurture it as theirs;
in all that exquisite sentiment which it surrounds with the sweetness of
family life. This aspiration penetrates the heart of our national well-
being. It makes for happier married life, it makes for better children, it
makes for confidence and security, it makes for courage to meet the
battle of life, it makes for better citizenship. . . ."

". . . Over thirty committees embracing the collective skill and experience of our country have been voluntarily engaged for the past year in

collecting the best of national experience from every part of the country, in collating it into definite recommendations for your consideration. Like the solution of all practical problems, the facts first must be discovered; they must be assembled in their true perspective; and the conclusions to be drawn from them must be the inexorable march of logic. . . ."

"It has long been my opinion that we have fairly creditably solved every other segment of our credit structure more effectively than we have solved this one. . . ."

". . . To find a way to meet the need is one of the problems that you have to consider; that is, how we can make a home available for installment purchase on terms that dignify the name credit and not upon terms comparable to the credit extended by a pawnbroker. . . ."

"I recently made a public proposal for the creation of a system of Home Loan Discount Banks. That proposal is familiar to you, and I will not traverse its details at the present time. . . ."

"And there are many other problems. . . ."

[State Papers, Vol. II, p. 36]

The conference presented a definite program of national action, with exhaustive reports giving the fact and reason for every recommendation. It laid the foundation for sound and progressive achievements.

Later on, the President, in thanking William Green of the American Federation of Labor for his co-operation in the Housing Conference, thus described its objectives:

"The conference . . . not only assembled in an orderly manner a great deal of material not heretofore so readily available, but it brought forth a number of new ideas, gave a new setting and a new relationship to principles previously well known. It marks the beginning of a new effort to raise the housing standards."

The conference established new standards, new methods of community co-operation and a renewed stimulus of community action. Its special volumes upon "Planning Residential Districts," "Slums and Decentralization," "Home Finance and Taxation," "Home Ownership," "House Design and Equipment," "Negro Housing," "Farm Housing," Home Furnishing," "Housing Objectives" have sold in thousands. They furnish today the standards of individual municipal and state action over the whole Union.

The Home Loan Banking System dealt with elsewhere was one of the results of the conference.

SLUM CLEARANCE

Another was the President's proposal in December, 1931, of loans from the Reconstruction Finance Corporation for slum clearance. This idea was not incorporated into the law until July, 1932, this being the provision:

"The Reconstruction Finance Corporation is authorized and empowered . . . to make loans to corporations formed wholly for the purpose of providing housing for families of low income or reconstruction of slum areas which are regulated by state or municipal laws as to rents, charges, etc."

On September 18, 1932, the President, in conference with Chairman Pomerene of the R. F. C., arranged to set up a committee of leading architects to consider and forward plans for slum clearance, which the Reconstruction Finance Corporation now had authority to inaugurate by "self-liquidating" loans. Such a double service to public health and welfare, and to employment, was a part of the President's original R. F. C. proposals of the year before, but it was delayed until the authority of the Corporation was expanded in July.

INDIANS

The President's policies on the Indian question were stated in his first Message to Congress of December 4, 1929:

"As wards of the Nation the Government has an obligation to the Indians which concerns not alone their present but their future welfare. To raise the standard of their living, to adequately provide for their health and education, and to advance their opportunity for profitable employment are the concern of the Government. In order that we may meet more fully our obligations to the Indians, I am asking for an increase of something more than $3,100,000 over the appropriations for the current year. This increase is requested so that we may more adequately meet the need for educational and health work among the Indians and for their industrial assistance and advancement. I do not feel, however, that we should wait until the next fiscal year to make a general improvement in our Indian affairs. Rather do I feel that we should commence this now. This will require additional funds for the current fiscal year for which an estimate will be presented to the Congress."

[*State Papers, Vol. I, pp. 171–2*]

Secretary Wilbur with Charles Rhoads and Henry Scattergood undertook the entire reorganization of the Indian service. On December 4, 1929, the President announced:

". . . I have emphasized the necessity for this reorganization by the appointment of Mr. Rhoads as the head of the Bureau and of Mr. Scattergood as his assistant, and Secretary Wilbur is giving it his very special attention."

"We have presented to Congress a request for an increased appropriation of some $3,000,000 for next year's budget. . . . The purposes of these increases are mainly to build up the education and health facilities, to change the direction of educational work and to develop the industrial improvement of the Indians. The support to the schools and health program has not been adjusted to meet the reduced post-war purchasing power of money. The result has been to ever pinch the allotments for food and clothing for Indian children. The present allowance is about twenty cents per day for each child for food, and it must be doubled if they are to be maintained in reasonable health. We have 338,000 Indians. The broad problem is to better train the Indian youth to take care of themselves and their property. It is the only course by which we can ultimately discharge this problem from the Nation, and blend them as a self-supporting people into the Nation as a whole."

"The Indian Bureau is recommending to the Congress a number of changes in the laws bearing on Indian affairs. The recommendations are designed to secure better administration of the very large properties owned by the Indians and to correct many things in the administration of these properties that will make for citizenship."

[*State Papers, Vol. I, pp. 201–2*]

On August 6, 1930, the President asked for and issued to the public a report by Secretary of the Interior Wilbur and Commissioner of Indian Affairs Rhoads on the plans and progress or reorganization of the Indian Bureau. The report stated that the new objective of the Administration was to make the Indian self-supporting and self-respecting American citizens. The Indians were to be no longer viewed as wards of the nation but as potential citizens.

Under the reorganization the protection to the Indians from exploitation was greatly extended, educational and health services improved; and other notable advances made in their development.

PRISON REFORM

Hoover had long held that current treatment of prisoners, Federal as well as local, was not socially constructive. On December 3, 1929, in his first Message to Congress he recommended:

"Closely related to crime conditions is the administration of the Federal prison system. Our Federal penal institutions are over-crowded, and this condition is daily becoming worse. The parole and probation systems are inadequate. These conditions make it impossible to perform the work of personal reconstruction of prisoners so as to prepare them for return to the duties of citizenship. In order to relieve the pressing evils I have directed the temporary transfer of the Army Disciplinary Barracks at Leavenworth to the Department of Justice for use as a Federal prison. Not only is this temporary but it is inadequate for present needs."

"We need some new Federal prisons and a reorganization of our probation and parole systems; and there should be established in the Department of Justice a Bureau of Prisons with a sufficient force to deal adequately with the growing activities of our prison institutions. Authorization for the improvements should be given speedily, with initial appropriations to allow the construction of the new institutions to be undertaken at once.　　　　　　　　　[State Papers, Vol. I, p. 160]

On April 28, 1930, President Hoover sent a further Message to the Congress:

". . . There must be extension of Federal prisons with more adequate parole system and other modern treatment of prisoners. We have already 11,985 prisoners in Federal establishments built for 6946. The number of Federal prisoners in Federal and state institutions increased 6277 in the nine months from June 30, 1929, to April 1, 1930. The Attorney General has stated that we cannot hope to enforce the laws unless we can have some point of reception for convicted persons. The overcrowding of the prisons themselves is inhumane and accentuates criminal tendencies. . . ."

"Our care and methods of handling prisoners are far from the standards that must be secured. These proposals, while they do not comprehend the whole which remains to be done in the Nation, are a step toward lifting the Federal standards which must have a general beneficial influence." [State Papers, Vol. I, pp. 273-4]

Draft legislation was furnished to the Committees for study.

On August 23, 1929, the President transferred the almost unoccupied army prison at Leavenworth, Kansas, to the Department of Justice, thus relieving the pressure on Federal criminal prisons.

On May 13, 1930, the President signed the first of a series of bills covering the Federal prison reforms which he had recommended to Congress. The Acts provided (a) the creation of a Bureau of Federal Prisons in the Department of Justice, under a director appointed by the Attorney General with complete authority over all United States prisons and prisoners; (b) a National Board of Parole; (c) medical services in all prisons placed under the Public Health Service; (d) the establishment of a boy's reformatory; (e) establishment of a new prison for vicious offenders; (f) a declaration of policy of classification and segregation of prisoners according to character, offense, etc.; (g) provision for instruction and industrial employment in prisons, the latter to be of non-competitive type, and the creation of temporary camps for prisoners in outside government work with reduction in sentences for faithful work; (h) increase in the number of Federal judges in a number of districts; (i) establishment of a probation system in the United States courts with probation officers under the direction of the Department of Justice; and (j) establishment of the Division of Identification and Information, in the Bureau of Investigation, in the Department of Justice. The acquiring and the exchanging of criminal records with State and municipal authorities was to constitute a major function of the division.

No such extensive or enlightened reform in dealing with criminals had been accomplished heretofore in the entire social history of the Federal Government.

OLD AGE PENSIONS

Hoover believed in old age pensions. His original belief was that they should be established by the states. After later study he felt that the subject must extend further than dependence upon the states.

Early in his Administration, the President took up the problem. As a preliminary step both for information and private action over a portion of the field, on September 28, 1929, he addressed to the heads of certain mutual life insurance companies the following letter:

"I am wondering whether it would be too much trouble for you to have your actuaries prepare a table for me, indicating what the cost of an old age pension would be, assuming that there are no repayments of any kind except the pension itself—that is, take some basis, say $1200 a year payable in two cases, one at 60 years of age and another at 70, and tabulate the annual payments the policy holders of different ages must make, say from 21 years onward."

"It would also be of great interest to know what sort of *lump sum payment* would need to be made at 21 and other ages in order to secure such pension."

The response showed that for a pension of $50 per month, beginning at sixty-five years, the following approximate lump sum payments would be required.

Age at which lump sum payment is made:

21	$ 775.00
31	1,010.00
41	1,540.00
51	2,450.00

If the payments were made annual, the yearly payment for persons of different ages would be:

21	$ 39.00
31	58.00
41	110.00
51	250.00

It was the Hoover view that both experience and public opinion could best be developed on the side of contributory insurance through a try-out of pension schemes by the mutual companies. He proposed to some of the leading companies that they should issue such a policy to the public, also that the industrial and commercial groups in the country should be organized to push the idea. His purpose was to build old age insurance through the normal insurance channels of the country and at some stage, after it was developed, to determine what steps might be necessary for the Government to supplement it or to assist the companies to care for certain groups. He succeeded in getting Mr. Samuel Crowther, a well-known economic writer, to interest himself in obtaining endorsement from commercial organizations to make the plan widely known. An interview with a prominent insurance president upon the plan was published in the *Ladies' Home Journal* in March, 1930.

However, with the economic crash every effort had to be concentrated on restoring jobs. The matter was deferred until times should improve.[1]

UNEMPLOYMENT INSURANCE

Hoover had long been interested in the subject of unemployment insurance. In an address in New York on January 27, 1923, he urged the insurance companies to take it up:

"There is one field of insurance not yet covered. You have covered the great range of accidents and disaster, but one great disaster that comes to our workfolk has yet been unguarded. In the ebb and flow of business, at irregular periods, we meet with great floods of unemployment. It is less than eighteen months ago when we had five millions of unemployed men in our streets, of men who wished to work but for whom no work could be found. There is nothing that leads to such despair and such decay of self-respect as the man who wants a job and wants to work, the support of whose family is in jeopardy. There is no field in which more thought should be devoted today than to the problem of insurance against unemployment."

"Unemployment insurance in the hands of a great mutual, non-gov-

---

[1]Hoover approved the New Deal provision of subsidy to the states for old age pensions. He believed the New Deal's contributory system while right in principle yet contained many unjust and unworkable features, and that it did not preserve the fundamental relationship of the Federal Government to the states. He felt that the whole problem would have to be and could be better worked out.

ernmental institution, built as your Association is, is not Socialism. It is the antithesis of Socialism, for Socialism is an attempt to do all things under the blighting hand of Government. Unemployment insurance in the hands of the Government would bring the disaster of incompetent and vicious encroachment of bureaucracy into the daily life of our people."

"There are many great employers who would today join in the cost of such insurance if it were undertaken by such a great institution as yours and it is not infeasible to develop great industrial groups whose joint action in such a matter would decrease the risks and establish a great measure securely to their employees. Some actual experience already exists in various countries and even upon our own statistics of unemployment it could be given sound, actuarial basis if applied to large groups."

"I do commend to your president and your officers and to you, that here remains the one great field where insurance can be newly developed, where if scientifically employed, founded on a basis of actual savings, contributed to by the employer, you would provide one of those great safeguards against suffering and add to our social stability."

The companies applied to the Legislature of the State of New York for change in the state law that would permit such action but were denied it.

With full employment of the later '20's, the public interest died out. With the depression at the beginning of the Hoover Administration, he felt its initiation would interfere with recovery, and that at the moment the problem had become one of relief.

DIFFUSION OF PROPERTY OWNERSHIP

Involved in all social security policies—and economic policies as well—is the intangible problem of the wider diffusion of property ownership, for here is the first reserve of social security.

Hoover regarded this as a major long view national policy and often expressed himself upon it. His approach was first that wider diffusion of property must take place by increase in national wealth; that increase in national wealth involved development of natural resources, elimination of industrial waste, and the improvement of industrial methods. From this, in turn, came consequent lower costs of production, lower prices and higher real income to all the people. The diffusion of wealth would become general and automatic through increased standards of living and wider savings.

He knew statistically that the current idea that an immediate distribution of large fortunes would give any consequential diffusion of property was an illusion. In proportion it was infinitesimal to what could be accomplished by building up the whole productive capacity of the country. On the other hand, he very definitely objected to overswollen fortunes, their flagrant display of gaudy extravagance and the economic power they bequeathed. To him the limits of action, however, were always at the point where socially useful initiative and enterprise might be reduced by interference.

He held steadily that the most effective method of such distribution is through inheritance or estate taxes, that it is the only method which will not so disrupt the economic system as to do great harm. His view was that overswollen fortunes must be reduced by the consistent and drastic pressure of such taxes.

He drew a sharp distinction between the economic and social effects of *income* taxes and *estate* taxes or *inheritance* taxes. His general position was that the former should be as light as government necessity permitted, that the latter should be as heavy as would not destroy wealth or initiative.

". . . We have in the United States today a better division of wealth and a greater equality of opportunity than any other nation in the world and we have thus a better foundation upon which to build. We have reason for discontent in the fact that our industrial development has outrun our social progress and we have reason to hasten those measures that lead to larger justice in distribution . . . strengthen our measures for the restraint of economic domination by the few and for the liquidation into the hands of the many of the larger industrial accumulations in the hands of the few that our rapid development has made possible."

In *The Saturday Evening Post* on December 27, 1919, he said:

"The price we must pay for the invaluable principle that stimulation of the initiative, ability and character of the individual requires free play in compensation is that some persons will gain much more than their service to the community warrants. . . . Often enough inherited economic power is misused. The line between the amounts needed to stimulate initiative and ability and the amounts of flagrant excess for services given is . . . hard to draw . . . there can be no equality of opportunity if the ownership of the tools of production and service is to become frozen to a narrow group of holders. . . ."

And again in the same journal on April 10, 1920:

"The inheritance tax field has not been fully exploited as yet, it cannot be deducted from either farmer or consumer, it does not affect the cost of living, it does not destroy initiative in the individual if it leaves large and proper residues for dependents. It does redistribute overswollen fortunes. It does make for equality of opportunity by freeing from the dead hand control of our tools of production. It reduces extravagance in the next generation and sends them to constructive service. It has a theoretic economic objection of being a dispersal of capital into income at the hands of the Government, but so long as the Government spends an equal amount on redemption of the debt or productive works even this argument no longer stands."

In a tax memorandum to President Harding on November 28, 1921, Hoover said:

"I present herewith for your consideration some notes on the necessity of revising some features of the new income tax provisions."

"Every one recognizes that the high brackets of the new income tax are intended to adjust taxation to proportionate wealth but this method of arriving at that end is costing the workers and the farmers more dollars for every dollar that we collect in this fashion. . . ."

"Any study of the commercial situation will show that the evasion of the high brackets of the income tax by investment in tax-free securities is increasing the interest rate on industrial and agricultural loans; is giving impulse to reckless municipal spending. It also serves to blockade the sale of property where this has been enhanced in value and thus tends to lift prices of stocks and real estate. . . ."

"I do not believe that any well-thinking person wishes to relieve concentrated wealth of its great share of the burden but accepting this we are in the present plan confusing property and production; and on the top of it we are allowing large property to escape. I am convinced we should make a distinction between income which is the result of individual earnings and income from property. . . ."

"If we are to lessen the stifling of initiative we should [make] lower schedules applicable to individual incomes from wages, salaries, professions, and business transactions, than to those from dividends and interest and rents. That the Government takes up to 50 per cent of the profits from professional earnings of business transactions, while the individual takes all the risks, is intensely discouraging to initiative. It is fundamentally wrong to charge at the same rate these two types of income, 'earnings' and 'property income,' because a person who possesses 'property income' has already the capital protection of his dependents while a part of 'earned' income must be put aside for such a purpose."

". . . decrease the income tax and transfer an equal load upon larger fortunes by increasing the estate taxes, thus shifting the load from income during life to capital at death."

"The tax-free securities would not escape taxation under such arrangement. It would not destroy the initiative of the living. It would effect a larger measure of distribution of concentrated property. Furthermore, it would place the tax squarely upon windfalls as distinguished from necessary support of dependents and not upon the reproductive earnings of the population."

"The primary criticisms brought against an increase in estate taxes are that they (a) invade the territory of state taxation; (b) tend to decrease the value of stocks, bonds and property by the pressure upon executors to liquidate the tax; (c) can be evaded by gifts prior to death; (d) are a tax on capital diverted to revenue purposes and thus a destruction of capital; and (e) where the estate is a private business buyers cannot be found for the proportion represented by the tax."

"All of these criticisms can be met by proper arrangement with regard to the tax."

"(a) The states will be no worse off . . . in any event an arrangement as to the division of this tax with the states needs settlement badly now."

"(b) and (e) The depreciation and difficulties in paying the Government suddenly such large sums can be avoided if the executors were allowed ten years in which to make such payments. It would also assist if the tax could be paid in Federal bonds at par."

"(c) The evasion through gifts can be sufficiently prevented. . . ."

"(d) The charge that capital by this tax is absorbed by the Government and used as revenue can be answered at once if the tax were devoted to the reduction of public debt."

"I am convinced [this] would give great comfort to the public at large in that this debt was being largely redeemed squarely by the great wealth of the country."

In 1922 he wrote:

"While there should be no minimizing of a certain fringe of injus-

tices in sharing the results of production or in the wasteful use made
by some of their share, yet there is vastly wider field for gains to all of
us through cheapening the costs of production and distribution through
the eliminating of their wastes, from increasing the volume of product
by each and every one doing his utmost, than will ever come to us even
if we can think out a method of abstract justice in sharing which did not
stifle production of the total product." [*American Individualism, p. 35*]

In a letter to Professor Samuel McCune Lindsey of April
4, 1924, discussing these questions, Hoover, then Secretary of
Commerce, said:

". . . I am convinced that for social reasons we need an entirely revised inheritance tax. In other words, I would like to see a steeply
graduated tax on legacies and gifts (except charitable gifts) for the
deliberate purpose of disintegrating large fortunes. If such an arrangement were set up it would result in gifts to great numbers of people."

"If the tax were authorized on a legacy or gift and graduated on the
sum thus involved, it would exert a great pressure in the direction of
dividing these fortunes in order to escape the effect of graduation. For
instance, a tax of 5 per cent on a million rising to 25 per cent on ten
million would have the result of taking two and one-half millions of tax
if the ten million were given to one beneficiary, whereas it would take
only $500,000 of tax if the sum were divided amongst ten beneficiaries."

". . . I am in thorough accord with reducing income taxes but I believe there is just the above amount of social right in those who are
contending for the higher brackets of income tax."

"If you think it is desirable that I should come up and express my
frank views on this whole question, I am not afraid to do it. I have no
belief in all of the argument made that there is any benefit to the community by large aggregations of wealth. The fundamental capital of the
country is provided by small savings, not by the big ones."

Speaking to the Academy of Political Science in New York
City, on March 9, 1925, he said:

". . . one of the continuous and underlying problems of sustained
democracy is the constant and wider diffusion of property ownership.
Indeed I should become fatalistic of ultimate destruction of democracy
itself if I believed that the result of all of our invention, all our dis-

covery, all our increasing economic efficiency and all our growing wealth would be toward the further and further concentration of ownership. In the large vision we have a wider diffusion of ownership today than any other nation in the world. It has been so since the beginning of the Republic. In our enormous growth in wealth there have been periods when the tendencies were toward concentration of ownership and greater diffusion. Certainly the forces of diffusion were dominant during the great migration which occupied the West. And again I have the impression that one of the by-products from the economic shift of the last war has been still another period of increasing diffusion of ownership of property. Our high real wages during the past three years, with consequent general expansion of savings, has, I believe, also marked another period of wider diffusion of property ownership."

". . . our public and private policies should be so directed that with our increasing wealth the tendencies of diffusion of ownership shall be greater than the tendencies of concentration . . . it is equally important that we shall maintain this . . . without destruction of the moral, spiritual, and economic impulses of production."

"We are woefully lacking in actual facts upon this most important question. . . ."

". . . The vast increase in numbers of savings banks and other distributed deposits, the great growth of industrial and life insurance, the large expansion of the building and loan associations, and the unprecedented absorption of all sorts of governmental securities in small sales all evidence this. In this direction there appears to be an undoubted increase in diffusion of ownership."

"The ownership of common stock, land, homes, current goods, and other forms which include the equity are . . . many indications of a movement toward diffusion in this field. . . ."

He stated this thesis more extensively in 1934:

"There enters into the problem of security also the just division and diffusion of the national product. (I here use 'diffusion' instead of 'distribution,' for that term so commonly connotes the purely business function of the delivery of goods.) That some individuals receive too little and some receive too much for the services they perform is a certainty. The contrast between poverty in a hard-working, thrifty home and the perverse extravagance of the willful drones is a blot. But we may point out that with the diffusion of income in normal times under our system among 25,000,000 American families, it cannot be justly claimed that more than a fringe of a few hundred thousand receive more than they deserve for the service they give the community and that there are not more than a few million on the other fringe who conscientiously work and strive and do not receive that to which they are justly entitled. In between lies the vast majority of our people. (There has been spread a vast amount of misinformation upon the whole subject of diffusion of income and wealth. That is the natural method of those who are anxious to destroy liberty. A competent study will show that over 90 per cent of the national income goes to persons receiving less than $10,000 per annum income and over 97 per cent to persons receiving less than $50,000 annually. These individuals in the higher brackets pay from 30 to 60 per cent of their income away in taxes. A study of the distribution of national wealth shows that about 74 per cent belongs to persons of less than $10,000 per annum income and 89 per cent to persons receiving less than $50,000 annual income.) Over the last half-century, except for the interruption of depressions, our standard of living, which is the real test of diffusion, has increased steadily and the proportion of families in the area of poverty has decreased constantly."

"The constant ideal of the whole American System has been thrift and the wider and wider diffusion of property. That makes for solution of many social questions including the whole problem of security in rainy days and old age. But there can be no incentive to acquire such security unless the right to honest possession is maintained."

"Distribution of national wealth and income must from any constructive point of view embrace the widest considerations of stimulation to effort. What the absolute gauge of payment for service may be, which will stimulate work, initiative, and enterprise, will never be completely determined on this earth, for there is no common currency between the several rewards for which men strive—whether they be money or power or mental or spiritual satisfactions. But society must have the maximum effective whole, and to get it, men must be given competitive rewards which inspire labor and enterprise. We can better afford to pay too much for creative enterprise than too little, for creative activity brings reward to the whole nation."

"The American System has long since realized the necessity of curbing the undue amassing and concentration of wealth. The denial of primogeniture, the constant drive to preserve competition, to control monopoly, the drastic taxes upon inheritance, all have shown evidence of this realization. A vast amount of so-called concentration of wealth of recent years is the concentration of 'stage money' created by war and boom inflation; and in this aspect the Great Depression has been a most drastic agent in its redistribution."

"Nothing is more certain than that we require a constantly wider diffusion of income. But this constantly wider diffusion which all thinking people desire comes slowly, for violent action distributes more poverty than wealth."

"And one of the solutions of this problem lies in devoting our energies to recovering and increasing the total income and wealth of the nation and thus having still more to diffuse. . . ."

[*The Challenge to Liberty, p. 180*]

In the first tax bill proposed by his Administration as President in December, 1931, he advocated a strong increase in estate taxes in the upper brackets. The upper brackets were increased from 20 per cent of the Coolidge Administration to 55 per cent. Speaking at Colorado Springs on March 7, 1936, he said:

"At one time we relied upon the theory of 'shirtsleeves to shirtsleeves in three generations' to regulate over-accumulations of wealth. This is now guaranteed by our income and inheritance taxes. Some people feel these taxes take the shirt also."

Speaking upon one phase of these policies at Denver, Colorado, on September 30, 1936, he said:

". . . My Administration having more than doubled the upper brackets of the income tax and the estate tax up to 55 per cent, no one will accuse me of wanting to give relief from the burden of government to those classes of the destitute. . . ."

"Let me say one thing about taxes in general. It has been a sort of theory that taxes should not be used to effect social or economic ends. That idea has been more honored in speech than in action, as witness the tariff ever since George Washington. Moreover all taxes are an economic and social burden no matter how light they may be. But when taxation rises to the volume of from 15 per cent to 20 per cent of the national income then the method of them may powerfully advance or retard social or economic forces no matter how they are levied. We might just as well frankly face the fact and try to direct them first into the least damage and second, into producing the most benevolent effects possible."

"Luck and genius create large fortunes. But the inheritance of great economic power by descendants is not consonant with a free people. We used to rely upon the incompetence of the descendants to dissolve these accumulations. But the old formula of shirtsleeve to shirtsleeve in three generations is impeded through the erection of two or three generation trusts which are about as bad as the old law of primogeniture. We abolished that long long ago."

"No doubt estate taxes do drive for the distribution of oversized fortunes, but they could be made to do a better job. I will not go into that intricate question. But we could amply protect widows and children."

"At the same time we could dissolve any inheritance of important economic power if we intelligently reform these taxes."

INCREASING STANDARDS OF LIVING

Hoover held that the Government could give leadership and organize action in economic life that would be beneficial to the people without projecting the Government into competition with its citizens. An instance of this was the campaign which he began as early as 1919 to bring into the economic consciousness of the country the premise that increased wages, decreased hours of labor, increased standard of living and increased employment were the fruit solely of decreased costs of production and decreased prices of old articles and the introduction of new articles into consumption. The corollaries to this premise were:

(*a*) That every possible national improvement, every labor-saving device, and every possible elimination of waste must be introduced in order to decrease costs of production;

(*b*) That labor must share in these savings made through increased wages or shortened hours—and in consequent buying power; that the highest possible wage is the absolutely necessary complement of production for thereby comes mass consumption.

(*c*) That the consumer must share by reduction of prices.

(*d*) That capital should have part of the increase as an inducement to savings and the undertaking of new enterprise.

(*e*) That this distribution of reduced costs to labor and the consumer would only take place if a free competitive system were rigorously maintained.

To Hoover these economic policies were the only road to the social objective of better diffusion of income, and of better distribution of wealth, to more stable employment, to social security. It was the real way to overcome poverty and to lift the fifth of our population who were underprivileged.

As this theory of economic action has been newly discovered and re-expounded periodically during recent years, we may cite from a few of the hundreds of Hoover statements and public addresses on this subject.

On October 9, 1919, he said:

"The very foundation of the maintenance and improvement in the standard of living lies in securing the maximum productivity of the human being . . . and the elimination of waste . . . conditions that protect and stimulate the well-being of the individual producer (*i.e.,* worker). . . ."

And in December, 1919:

"That the object of all national economic policy must be to maintain and improve the standard of living of the whole population. Upon this enhanced standard only can the higher opportunities of life be built. . . ."

"That the standard of living is the direct quotient of the amount of commodities and services that are available among the total population. Therefore the standard cannot be maintained or improved unless there is a maintenance and increase in the production of commodities and services up to the maximum need of the entire number. There is no equality of opportunity to the consumer with deficient production. The maximum production cannot be maintained unless there is . . . co-ordinated action in effort; . . . unless there is an elimination of waste . . . giving a participation in savings from decreased costs of production and increase in quality. . . . If the other sections of the community . . . take an undue toll from their services, then the farmer will be paying undue amounts for his supplies—he will be carrying an undue portion of the load of maintaining the standard of living. . . ."

On April 4, 1922, in a public address, he said:

"There can be no answer to the fundamental fact. . . . The more we cheapen the production of a commodity or service, the larger the number of people who can obtain it."

In speaking in Washington on April 12, 1922, Hoover said:

"It would be possible to demonstrate that these activities (co-operation in reducing waste) have resulted in great savings in costs of production and distribution amounting to enormous benefit to both the producer and consumer."

On April 29, 1922, he discussed disparities in after-war prices:

". . . unless we restore this relativity of price levels, the consumer must suffer through inability to buy . . . the manufacturer must suffer from decreased volume of business . . . unemployment . . . lowered standards of living to all. . . ."

Speaking on May 22, 1922, he said:

"Every time we can take a penny off the costs of distribution of any commodity we have made that much more of the commodity available to that many more persons. In other words, the whole standard of living of the American people rises directly with the cheapening of production and distribution costs of any commodity; more people can have that commodity, a wider area can be served with it, a larger number derive the benefits."

And speaking on October 5, 1922:

"The only way . . . industry can expand . . . standards of living be maintained . . . is by lower production costs . . . brought by elimination of waste. . . not by lowering of wages. . . ."

In the Annual Report of the Secretary of Commerce for June, 1924:

"The American standard of living is the product of high wages to producers and low prices to consumers. The road to national progress lies in increasing real wages through proportionally lower prices. The one and only way is to improve methods and processes and to eliminate waste."

In an address at Washington, D. C., on January 7, 1925:

"Some five years ago a body of engineers under my direction made an investigation into this problem of waste, and the conclusion of that body of eminent men who gave many months to a close investigation of our entire production and distribution machinery was that we were wasting somewhere between 20 and 30 per cent of our entire cost of production and distribution. In other words, that there is a margin of some 20 or 30 per cent of the prices of commodities, which could be saved without lowering the standards of living of our people, without lowering our wages, without lowering our returns, but by the sheer elimination of waste."

On January 19, 1925, he applied this to the farmer:

"The elimination of waste and increase in general economic efficiency directly helps the farmer in three directions. It reduces the cost of things he buys. It increases the return on what he sells. It increases the consumption of agricultural products. . . ."

"Whereas the standard of living of our farmers certainly shows no increase and in certain branches of the agricultural industry it has not even been maintained. Our job is to attack the national problem of how to lift the farmer up to this level. It is not to engage in policies that will drag down the standards of living of our workers and city people."

In an address at Washington on January 14, 1925, he discussed the consumer's side:

"It is the public who pays the bill (for increased production costs). It is either charged into the consumer's price of goods at one end or subtracted from wages . . . at the other . . . it means more goods for the same money . . . more time for recreation . . . no attack on wage levels . . . if we decrease these costs . . . it means enlarged consumption . . . a total asset. It has no liabilities."

". . . for it is through the elimination of waste and the increase in our national efficiency that we can hope to reduce the cost of living on one hand, and to increase the standards of living of our people on the other."

In an article in *Factory*, October, 1925, he wrote:

"And these efforts to reduce production costs are profoundly in the public interest, for every dollar by which we decrease the cost of production and distribution by just that much do we add to the total goods and services for the nation and thus to our standard of living. . . ."

He addressed the American Federation of Labor on October 6, 1930:

"Your chairman has spoken of my interest in the development of an American basis of wage. Both the directors of industry and your leaders have made great progress toward a new and common ground in economic conceptions, which, I am confident, has had a profound effect upon our economic progress during the last few years. That is the conception that industry must be constantly renovated by scientific research and invention; that labor welcomes these labor-saving devices; that labor gives its full and unrestricted effort to reduce costs by the use of these machines and methods; that the savings from these reduced costs shall be shared between labor, employer, and the consumer. It is a philosophy of mutual interest. It is a practice of co-operation for an advantage that is not only mutual but universal. Labor gains either through increase of wage or reduction of cost of living or shortened hours. Employers gain through enlarged consumption, and a wider spread distribution of their products, and more stable business. Consumers gain through lower cost of what they buy. Indeed, mass production must be accompanied by mass consumption through increased standards of living."

"A conception of this sort does not at once find universal application. We ought not to forget that it is something new in the world's economic life. And there are, of course, those who do not yet believe. It is as far apart as the two poles from the teachings of economists of one hundred years ago, who took it for granted that the well-being of the worker could be purchased only at the expense of the well-being of the employer or some other group in the community, and further that wages could never rise above subsistence or the number of workers would so increase as to pull the weaker back into the cesspool of poverty."

"No system is or can be free of difficulties or problems. The rapidity of our inventions and discoveries has intensified many problems in adjusting what we nowadays call technological unemployment. I am co-operating with President Green and representatives of employers' associations in an exhaustive inquiry into its various phases. If we stretch our vision over the last ten years, we shall find much to convince us that the problem is not at all insurmountable in the long run. It is estimated by some of our statisticians that in this period over 2,000,000 workers have been displaced from older industry due to labor-saving devices. Some way, somehow, most of these were re-established in new industry and new services. Nor is there any reason to believe that we cannot revolve our economic system in such fashion that further new discoveries and inventions will further increase our standard of living and thereby continue to absorb men who are displaced in the older industries. Nevertheless, there is a period of readjustment in each case of new discovery, and industry has need of a larger understanding of the facts."

[*State Papers, Vol. I, p. 392*]

It is of interest to note the reversal of this fundamental basis of economic life. Speaking in Philadelphia on May 14, 1936, Hoover said:

"Since I last discussed these questions the New Deal has brought forth another new magic formula to reach the millennium. On April 25, President Roosevelt said: 'Reduction of costs of manufacture does not mean more purchasing power and more goods consumed. It means just the opposite.' The President elaborates its benefits and implies it is the base of his slogan for '36. If this word 'opposite' means anything, then this statement says that 'increased costs of manufacturing means increased purchasing power and more goods consumed.' Most of the world has been under an illusion about this up to now. We had all thought that the way to enable the people to buy more was to use every art of technology and government to reduce costs and therefore prices, provided we held up wages and incomes to farmers and others. We had relied on such experiences as the automobile. We got about two-thirds of the world's automobiles because the production costs and, therefore, prices were brought down into reach of 20,000,000 families."

"At least we now know why the New Deal has imposed all their different devices of debts, taxes, restriction of production, juggling with currency, and a score of other methods of artificially forcing up costs and prices. The magic formula may also explain why we still have 12,000,000 unemployed. Certainly there is no joy for the consumer in this return again to Planned Scarcity."

ELIMINATION OF WASTE

This policy of lower costs, consequently lower prices, higher wages and higher standards of living, was not theory with Hoover. He early proceeded to put it into action on a nation-wide scale.

On February 14, 1921, just before taking the office of Secretary of Commerce, in an address to Engineers at Syracuse, New York, he said:

"The waste in our production is measured by the unemployment, the lost time due to labor conflict, the losses in labor turnover, the failure to secure maximum production of the individual due either to misfit or lack of interest. Beyond this again is a wide area of waste in the poor co-ordination of great industries, the failures in transportation, coal, and power supplies which re-echo daily to interrupt the steady operation of industry. There are again such other wastes due to lack of standardization, to speculation, to mismanagement, to inefficient national equipment, and a hundred other causes. There is a certain proof of deficient production by comparisons of our intense results in 1918, when, with 20 per cent of our man-power withdrawn into the army, we yet produced 20 per cent more commodities than we are doing today. We are probably not producing more than 60 or 70 per cent of our capacity; that is, if we could synchronize all national effort to maximum production, we could produce 30 or 40 per cent more commodities and service. Our national machine is today doing worse than usual, as witness the 3,000,000 idle men walking our streets. One part of the human measure of this . . . is their anxieties as to the future."

"No one will ever suppose that it is ever possible to bring national productivity up to the full 100, but the whole basis of national progress, of an increased standard of living, of better human relations, indeed of the advancement of civilization, depends upon the continuous improvement in productivity."

"The primary duty of organized society is to enlarge the lives and increase the standards of living of all the people—not of any special class whatever. We are therefore proposing to make a preliminary examination of the volume of waste in certain industries, the proportions that lie in each field of fault. And no engineering report is worth the paper it is written upon without constructive suggestions in remedy."

The investigation that he referred to was an exhaustive inquiry that he as chairman of the American Engineering Council (representing all the major engineering societies) instituted into the wastes in industry. The first comprehensive study of the subject resulted. In the foreword to publication of the findings, Hoover said:

"We have probably the highest ingenuity and efficiency in the operation of our industries of any nation. Yet our industrial machine is far from perfect. The wastes of unemployment during depressions; from speculation and over-production in booms; from labor turnover; from labor conflicts; from intermittent failure of transportation of supplies of fuel and power; from excessive seasonal operation; from lack of standardization; from loss in our processes and materials—all combine to represent a huge deduction from the goods and services that we might all enjoy if we could do a better job of it." *[Waste in Industry, 1921, p. ix]*

At once on becoming Secretary of Commerce, Hoover inaugurated a great crusade for the reduction of industrial wastes and for utilization of national resources which were going to waste. He organized a voluntary movement in industry with co-operation by the Government. The cry was at once raised that these activities would violate the Sherman Act and diminish competition. Hoover stoutly maintained they would decrease costs and prices and increase competition. Shortly afterwards, decisions of the Supreme Court supported this view. (See Monopolies, page 305.)

Speaking again on April 29, 1922, he said:

"The war has left us with certain economic conditions for which we must find systematic and constructive remedy if we would . . . sustain the high standard of living and of wages of the American people. . . ."

"We search for remedies to this situation and we find there is only one . . . that is, to increase our efficiency in production . . . and distribution . . . the elimination of great wastes. If we examine . . . further . . . the nature of these . . . wastes they include things that can only be corrected by co-operative action in some form . . . waste of unemployment . . . speculation . . . booms; . . . labor conflict turnover, jurisdictional quarrels, . . . restraint on effort; . . . car shortages, excessive seasonal operation, and lack of standardization in many things. . . . We need better developed transportation . . . electricity . . . water."

On October 5, 1922, at Washington, D. C., the Secretary explained his plans:

"Government co-operation with industry has never been attempted before. We are now trying to bring it about in a definite way."

"The cost of production in this country is higher than anywhere else, and the only way that American industry can expand, and American standards of living be maintained, is by lower production costs, brought about by elimination of waste in production, and not by the lowering of wages."

"It is not the intention of the Department of Commerce to enter into any compulsory methods. Industrial progress cannot be carried on by legislation . . . the Government can render very constructive service to industry, and to the country, by bringing groups of manufacturers, distributors and users together in conference, for the purpose of eliminating industrial waste."

"The necessity for large production at the lowest possible cost is generally recognized, but the way of doing it does not seem to receive the same degree of appreciation."

"Engineers, I think, agree that there is a great area of waste in American industry, that can only be corrected by the voluntary action of manufacturers and distributors."

This program of national co-operation extended over two thousand conferences and committees. It was continued vigorously to the end of the Secretary's service. The results attracted world-wide attention. The British, French and German Governments sent commissions to study it and to introduce it into their industrial fabric.

In a public address in Washington, Hoover said (January 14, 1925):

"Can we reduce the margin between our . . . producers on one side, and our consumers on the other?"

"I am convinced that we can. I believe it can be done without reduction of wages. I believe it can be done by voluntary co-operation in industry and commerce without Government regulation."

"I have hesitated to make so general a pronouncement until I felt that we could clearly demonstrate not only the existence of such great wastes but also demonstrate from actual experience the practicability of their elimination and the method of doing it."

"The Department of Commerce has . . . demonstrated in several score of different directions the practicability and success of a definite program. . . . There is today in actual motion effective organization co-operating with the Department in systematic and gradual elimination of such waste. Something over one hundred industries and trades. . . . They vary from a single commodity to such organization as that which we have set up for regional action of shippers and the railways."

"There is no room for soap-box oratory in this theme. It is necessary to get down into the dry economic fundamentals . . . for remedy lies in more tedious work of investigation and negotiation and decision. It is easy to be entertaining if we set up straw men and wail at their destruction of human liberty, to effect the discovery of wicked profiteers and leeches who are sucking out the blood of the nation, but there is little poetry and no recreation in working out these problems trade by trade."

After reviewing the various industrial wastes, he continued:

"These wastes are not the small change of industry and commerce. There is scarcely a step in this accomplishment of squeezing out waste which does not interpret itself in millions of dollars of annual savings."

"As these wastes are enumerated they may seem to be of main interest to manufacturers and distributors. But in the end the public pays the bill. It is either charged into the consumer's price of goods at one end, or subtracted from the wages . . . at the other."

"I am disposed to agree with a recent report of the Engineering Council that they amount in many lines to 25 or 30 per cent of the cost paid by the consumer or producer of raw materials. They cannot all be corrected and where progress can be made it is only through toilsome building step by step in a thousand places, and always and only through the co-operation of well-disposed trade and industry, and through a wider understanding of the problems involved, and of the co-ordination of effort necessary to secure results. This is not emergency work as new wastes will constantly arise, and permanent trade organizations are needed in each industry for their elimination."

"Others have searched for a miracle panacea that would overnight effect enormous cuts in the great margin between our farmers and our consumers, or between the manufacturers and their clientele. No such panacea has been found simply because there is none. There are no short cuts to progress."

"Nor are we here to worry on behalf of the lady who wishes to order a cake of yeast by telephone to be delivered by a gold-colored automobile. You and I are interested in this problem solely for a better service to our producers and consumers of the primary necessities and ordinary comforts of life."

"The reduction of waste means that a considerable part of our population who are busily employed in this unnecessary motion can be directed towards the production of other commodities and thus their addition to the national standard of living; it means a lowering in cost of living; or it means more goods for the same money. To our workers it means less labor, more time for recreation, and no attack upon wage levels; to our farmers it means an increased proportion of the consumers' dollar. . . . If we decrease these costs by the elimination of the waste . . . it also means enlarged domestic consumption. . . . To our industrial and commercial men there is an increase in stability in business and a sounder foundation under our entire business fabric. The elimination of waste is a total asset. It has no liabilities."

"These are the wastes which have grown naturally into our economic system. They can only be corrected by co-operate action."

"Nor am I talking about abrogating the Sherman Act. I have no patience with those who deliberately try to confuse these efforts at co-operation in waste elimination with price-fixing and restraint of trade. Any intelligent person who has the patience to read and think these problems through and the methods we have developed for their correction will find these efforts to be in the interest of public welfare, and free from trade restraint. They are, in fact, the foundations of real competition."

He addressed a labor group in New York on the subject on April 11, 1925:

"I have been asked to speak for a few moments on the elimination of industrial waste and its social implications."

"Any problem of this kind involves dry economic discussion, and the world, recollecting the 'economic man' of the last generation, ofttimes conceives economic thought as something devoid of human considerations These matters do not lend themselves to the oratorical joy of destructive criticism. Nevertheless, the establishment of better directed economic thought, the determination of economic policy, and stimulation to right economic action, have an interpretation into more human blessings than rivers of oratory."

"Although I know of no better term, I have never liked the use of the word 'waste' in this connection. It carries an implication of personal shortcoming or willful action which is not what we mean. Likewise, I find difficulty in the use of the term 'efficiency' in this connection because that term has come to imply in the public mind a certain ruthless inhuman point of view. What we are discussing are our economic wastes. They contain the paradox that if we save them collectively, we shall have more goods and services to expend individually. We do not by this process propose to abolish Easter bonnets; we propose more bonnets for the same money and effort."

After enumerating various wastes, he said:

"These savings are just as important as economy in Government. They mean just as much to the taxpayers' pocketbook as reduction in taxes. They are not brought about by personal self-denial or deprivation."

"I wish again to emphasize the fact that in this discussion I am not stressing the waste within the control of individuals. Nor are the wastes which I refer to to be corrected by the Ten Commandments or by any legislative extension thereof. You cannot catch an economic force with a policeman."

"Organization of labor and a growing sense of responsibility to the community by business have both contributed to these ends. And there has been a growth of interest by labor in its responsibilities in the functioning of the whole economic machine. I believe all will agree that the fund from which labor must expect its maintenance of real wage, or increase in real wage, must come from more and more efficient production and the elimination of waste. Labor deserves its participation in the gains made in these directions and this alone is the field from which advanced real wages can permanently come. Therefore, labor has a very large self-interest in these matters."

"To this I would like to add this further observation. Perhaps dimly, but no less certainly, there is looming up in the American industrial world a definitely new relationship in the whole setting of industry. The ownership of utilities and large manufacture has to a large degree been divorced from management. The capital ownership of great service and production is rapidly being diffused over millions of individuals. None is able to dictate management. The managers of older and settled industry are today rising out of the skill of the industry itself. And they are gradually coming into a new vision of their relationships. Those relationships have a tripartite responsibility; to the consumer on the one hand, to the worker on another, and a grudging regard for capital in the sense that it shall be assured no more than security, and thus given the lowest terms in the market. Under this regime the savings we can make through application of invention, through increase in skill, through elimination of collective waste, are bound to be shared with the consumer to attract business, to be shared with labor to secure service and contentment, and to be decreasingly shared with capital, because capital comes cheaper with increasing security."

"It is thus that we shall reach higher standards of living and the greater diffusion of these standards. These are the foundations upon which the finer reactions of life, recreation, and culture can be expanded and strengthened, and that is the end to be attained by economic discussions."

In review of his campaign to reduce waste, Hoover wrote in the Annual Report of the Secretary of Commerce for 1925:

"Great progress has been made during the year in the national movement for elimination of industrial waste. The Department of Commerce, in continuation of its work of the past five years, has devoted much of its activities to this end."

"While various divisions of the Department have been actively aiding in the campaign in many specific directions, it must be borne in mind that the whole program is one fundamentally to stimulate action among industries, trades, and consumers themselves. It is obviously not the function of Government to manage business, but to investigate economic questions, to survey economic phenomena and point out the remedy for economic failure or the road to progress, to inspire and assist co-operative action, and to stimulate forces to these ends—surely all these are well within the proper field of public service."

"It may be worth while repeating the major directions of this effort as they were outlined by the Department at the beginning of this undertaking four years ago."

"1. Elimination of waste in railway transportation by the provision of adequate facilities and better methods."

"2. Vigorous improvement of our natural interior water channels for cheaper transportation of bulk commodities."

"3. Enlarged electrification of the country for the saving in fuel, effort, and labor."

"4. Reduction of the periodic waves of unemployment due to the booms and slumps of the 'business cycle.'"

"5. Improved statistical service as to the production, distribution, stocks, and prices of commodities, both domestic and foreign, as a contribution to the elimination of hazard in business and therefore of wasteful speculation."

"6. Reduction of seasonal employment in construction and other industries, and intermittent employment in such industries as bituminous coal."

"7. Reduction of waste in manufacture and distribution through the establishment of grades, standards of quality, dimensions, and performance in non-style articles of commerce; through the simplification in dimensions of many articles of manufacture, and the reduction of unnecessary varieties; through more uniform business documents such as specifications, bills of lading, warehouse receipts, etc."

"8. Development of scientific industrial and economic research as the foundation of genuine labor-saving devices, better processes, and sounder methods."

"9. Development of co-operative marketing and better terminal facilities in agricultural products in order to reduce the waste in agricultural distribution."

"10. Stimulation of commercial arbitration in order to eliminate the wastes of litigation."

"11. Reduction of the waste arising from industrial strife between employers and employees."

"What the country as a whole has accomplished during the past five years in increased national efficiency in these directions is impossible of measurement. Nor does the Department of Commerce lay claim to credit for the great progress that has been made, save as we may have helped to organize a definite public movement. That movement is the result of a realization by every group—business men, industrial leaders, engineers, and workers—of the fundamental importance of this business of waste elimination. In addition to elimination of waste we have had the benefit of notable advances in science, improvement in methods of management, and prohibition."

"Thanks to elimination of waste and these other contributing factors, we can as a Nation show one of the most astonishing transformations in economic history, . . ."

"While wages are higher than in 1920, wholesale prices are lower. We have thus the highest real wage in our history, and we have had three years of remarkable price stability, which has reduced speculation in commodities to a minimum. We can hold that stability if we avoid speculation."

"A comparison with similar British indexes gives striking evidence that these results are peculiar to the United States. . . ."

"The activity of the Department of Commerce in this field of waste elimination is indicated by the fact that since the work was launched on a large scale in 1921 some 900 group conferences have been held, practically all at the request of the industries themselves, and 229 committees are now at work on various phases of the program."

This subject of reduction of costs and its broad effects is further exemplified under Conservation, Public Works, etc.

LABOR POLICIES

THE ELIMINATION AND SETTLEMENT OF INDUSTRIAL CONFLICT

Hoover's labor policies extended far back before he came into public life. As the engineer and director of large enterprise he had never had a strike. He believed in organized labor and recognized it in collective bargaining.

He became at once an important factor in formulating the public mind on labor policies when he became Secretary of Commerce although he did not have the direct responsibility in labor questions.

His policies extended to a wider field than wage negotiations. They covered the development of fundamentals of employer and employee relations. He held:

(a) That there was a great common ground of mutual interest between employer and employee which must be understood and that statesmanship required that it be builded upon. To him they were both producers, they were not classes. He urged that through labor-saving devices, increased efficiency, and elimination of waste, costs could be reduced; that the savings from reduction of costs should be divided between labor, the consumer and the employer; that thereby consumption would increase employment and through wide consumption, employment become more stable; that it was therein that real wages could be increased and hours shortened. He supported constantly the highest wages and shortest hours that increase of national production could afford. For his typical pronouncements upon this subject see pages 109 ff.

(b) He continuously supported the organization of labor and collective bargaining by representatives of labor's own choosing. He opposed all forms of compulsory settlement of disputes. He insisted at all times that there must be an equal responsibility upon labor organizations to the end that they give consideration to the economic effects of their actions and that their bargains were inviolable. (See also Social Policies, pages 48, 93.)

(c) He held the Government could help to bring about co-operation in industry to industrial peace.

He gave consistent leadership in all these directions from the time he first entered public life until the end of his term as President. They were not emergency policies but he used them in the emergency of depression. Under his leadership he conducted the country through the worst phase of the world depression—the downhill slide—with an industrial peace unparalleled in all American experience.

We may quote from a few of the Hoover statements upon these subjects beginning with 1919. In an address before the San Francisco Commercial Club, on October 9, 1919, he said:

". . . any solution (to industrial conflict) must go deeper than questions of strikes, lockouts, or arbitrations. . . . We have got to go, sooner or later, to the root of this difficulty. There is no solution short of community of interest. We must begin by creating, somehow and somewhere, a solidarity of interest in every section of the people conducting our industrial machine. The worker, the administrator, and the employer are absolutely interdependent on one another in this task of securing the maximum production and a better division of its results. It is hopeless to secure a solution if we are to set these people up as different classes fighting with each other. Maximum production must be founded on the maximum exertion of every individual within his physical ability, and upon the reduction of waste, not only individual but national. Unless we are going to secure this maximum production through the combined effort and intelligence of our entire economic machine, we will have destroyed the very foundations upon which we build the higher activities of life."

In a statement in April, 1920, he said:

". . . There is but one way out, and that is to again re-establish through organized representation that personal co-operation between employer and employee in production. . . . The attitude of refusal to participate in collective bargaining with representatives of the employees' own choosing is the negation of this bridge to better relationship. On the other hand, a complete sense of obligation to bargains entered upon is fundamental to the process itself. The interests of employee and employer are not necessarily antagonistic; they have a great common ground of mutuality, and if we could secure emphasis upon these common interests we would greatly mitigate conflict. Our Government can stimulate these forces, but the new relationship of employer and employee must be a matter of deliberate organization within industry itself."

". . . adopt the . . . gospel of maximum effort and skill of each individual worker and the sharing of its results . . . then the largest part of the friction . . . would disappear."

In an article in *System Magazine* in July, 1920, he wrote:

"We are . . . wasting our time if we think of the human relationships in industry only as matters of wages or hours or unwillingness to work as compared with a former willingness to work. In that view we are treating labor as a commodity. Instead of thinking of men we are thinking of the purchase of human force . . . for which sometimes we may have to pay a high price, or again a lower price."

"Now exactly what the worker is in process of refusing to be is a 'commodity'; your average man is no longer content to be merely a part of the 'labor supply.' By and large the employees of the country are looking for a position of right instead of a position of consideration; that is, they want their rights instead of benevolence."

"Exactly what those rights are is the question that we have to solve, not only from an economic, but a human, point of view. This is our largest national problem. In default of a better working relation we shall have decreased instead of increased production and hence a lowering standard of living. If our standard of living goes down it will hardly be worth while to consider our other national aspirations."

"The problem goes far beyond the mere settling of disputes. I have seen growing out of the masses of people in every country aspirations for a great economic change. That change broadly will be that those who work with their hands will obtain a large proportion of this world's goods and those who work with their brains will obtain less. Those who do not work will probably obtain nothing . . . any solution to this problem must go deeper than questions of strikes, lockouts, or arbitrations. We have got to go sooner or later to the root of this difficulty. We must begin by creating somehow and somewhere a solidarity of interest in every section of the people conducting our industrial machine."

"Before thinking of remedies let us consider causes, fully recognizing at once that there is no one single cause. . . . A strong factor is the growth of machine production in which the ownership of the tools of production—that is, capital—has not only grown more important but has also become more dependent upon labor and both have become wholly dependent upon the public. None are self-sustaining. They form an indivisible trinity—but each member at some time or other thinks that it may go on alone. . . . Capital has thought itself supreme; labor, now recognizing that capital without it is useless, is beginning to think that capital itself is useless and that labor is supreme. The public is demanding a service of both at a price neither can perform."

"These troubles have not arisen in a day. They were only intensified, not created, by the War. They will not be cured in a day. They will not be cured at all by legalistic process or repression, or by any quick, sure remedy patented, bottled and distributed by the Government. The difficulty with all legal process of a compulsory nature . . . is that thereby we substitute Government control for competition, for if a court may control wages it will in effect control industry and in the end stifle it. That is, we adopt socialism without its terminology."

"The problem must be solved step by step, and it will take time. It is certain that the relationship between labor and capital never can be settled by any form of legal repression, with the use of the jail as a means of enforcement."

"Public opinion and good will are the forces we must depend on for enforcement of the right sort of settlements. Repression leads to the border of martyrdom and tends to make for compulsory employment and a compulsory wage and also for compulsory profits."

"No one doubts that the modern consolidation of the employers over large units of employees gives every justification and right for the organization of the employees similarly into units for the exertion of equality in bargaining powers. Such organization has a right to present its own representatives in bargaining, but those representatives must truly represent the employees for whom they speak. On the other hand, there can be no legal compulsion to join or not to join such an organization."

THE INDUSTRIAL CONFERENCE OF 1920

Hoover was the vice-chairman of President Wilson's Second Industrial Conference. That Conference had been assembled by the President upon the failure of the First Industrial Conference to come to any constructive conclusions. The Second Industrial Conference produced a notable report. While the plan in that report was never fully adopted it placed national thinking on a new plane and great benefits came from it.

In speaking upon the proposals of this Conference, Hoover said:

"The President's Second Industrial Conference, whose report was published in March, 1920, made a serious effort to outline a comprehensive national policy as to industrial conflicts. Its members also agreed on certain machinery for making collective bargaining systematic and effective."

"The Conference had before it four possible alternative lines of action. First, . . . the development of the progressive forces at work for better understanding in industry under such conditions as would maintain self-government in industry itself; second, to adopt some current plan for an industrial court, . . . such as . . . in the State of Kansas; third, the nationalization of the services upon which the very life of the community depends; fourth, to do nothing."

"In a survey of the forces making for self-government in industry, the Conference considered that definite organization must be given to the principles of collective bargaining from which bargains, conciliation, and arbitration should flow automatically, but agreed that such forces could not develop in an atmosphere of legal repression."

"The real conflict in the adoption of collective bargaining has been over the methods of representation on both sides. Both employers and workers have long since agreed in the principle, but not on the method. The Conference, therefore, proposed that the Government should intervene to assist in the determination of the credentials of all representatives in case of disagreement, and to bring such pressure as would induce voluntary entry into collective bargaining. Furthermore, it was considered that the large development of conciliation and arbitration already current as part of such bargaining should be encouraged and organized under a broad national plan that would give liberty of action to all existing arrangements and stimulate their further development."

"The Conference therefore proposed to set up a small amount of governmental machinery comprising a chairman covering various regions in the United States, with a Central Board in Washington, as a definite organization for the promotion of these agencies. . . . No one is compelled to submit to the machinery established, but where the employer and employees refuse to enter into or fail in bargaining, then . . . the public stimulated them to come together under conditions of just determination of the credentials of their duly appointed representatives."

"The plan is a development of the principle of collective bargaining. It is not founded on the principle of arbitration or compulsion. It is designed to prevent the losses through cessation of production due to conflict."

". . . Therefore, under the plan of the Conference that mutual agreement is the best basis for prevention of conflict, the second proposal of the Conference was that there should be some penalty for failure to submit to such processes. That penalty is a public inquiry into the causes of the dispute and the exposure to public opinion of its rights and wrongs. The strength of the penalty is based upon the conviction that neither side can afford to lose public good will."

". . . They are given the alternative of investigation, or collective bargaining under persuasive circumstances to voluntary settlement. In order to increase the moral pressure surrounding the investigation, either one of the parties to the conflict may become a member of the board of investigation, provided he will have entered as a priori undertaking that he is prepared to submit his case to orderly and simple processes of adjustment. Thus his opponent will be put at more than usual disadvantage in the investigation. If both sides should agree to submit to normal processes of settlement, the board of investigation at once stages a collective bargain and the investigation ceases."

"In detail, the plan involves a great deal of consideration as to many difficult questions of selection of representatives, provision for action by umpires, for appeal to a board in certain contingencies, the character of questions to be considered, methods of enforcement, standards of labor, and so on. The point to be made clear here is that the Conference plan is fundamentally the promotion of collective bargaining under fair conditions of representation by both sides, and the definite organization of public opinion only as a pressure on the parties at conflict to secure it. It is . . . not a plan of arbitration nor is it an industrial court. It is stimulation of self-government in industry."

"The trade unions of the United States have conferred such essential services upon their membership and upon the community that their real values are not to be overlooked or destroyed. They can fairly claim great credit for the abolition of sweat shops, of recognition of fairer hours in industry, of reduction of overstrain, employment under more healthful conditions, and many other reforms. They have given great stability to our institutions in their fight against red radicalism."

"For years, trade unionism was dominated mainly by the economic theories of Adam Smith, and union labor adopted as one of its tenets that decrease of productive effort by workers below their actual capacity would result in more employment and better wages. During the past twenty-five or thirty years, however, this economic error has been gradually abandoned in American trade unions. It may be adhered to in isolated cases today, but it is not the economic conception of the majority. These have long since realized that an increased standard of living of the whole nation must depend upon a maximum production within the limits of proper conservation of the human machine."

"Attempts by governments to stop industrial war are not new. The public interest in continuous production and operation is so great that practically every civilized government has time and again ventured upon attempts at reduction of conflict. A great volume of experience exists to serve as a guide. The world is strewn with wrecks of labor conferences, conciliation boards, arbitration boards, and industrial courts."

". . . While it may be argued that the state may . . . substitute the protection of justice for the right of strike and lockout, the belief in the right to strike has become imbedded in the minds of the laboring community. Workers will not receive with confidence any alternative in driving their own bargains."

". . . There are some things worse in the development of democracy than strikes and lockouts . . . set up economic and social perils of worse character . . . Government control also hinders the real development of self-government in industry, and that is part of the growth of democracy itself. Courts and litigations are necessary to the preservation of life and property, but they are less effective as a stimulus to improved relations among men than is discussion and a system of voluntary settlement of differences."

"We must all agree that these deficiencies in our social, economic and political structure which find solution through education and voluntary action of our people themselves are the solutions that endure. The upbuilding of the sense of responsibility, of intelligence in each individual unit in the United States, with the intervention of Government only to promote better relations and prevent the domination by any one group over another, is the basis upon which democracy must progress."

The machinery proposed was never adopted as a whole largely

because labor conflicts died down with growing prosperity from 1922 to 1929. But the Railway Labor Board and the strengthening of the Labor Conciliation Division of the Department of Labor were direct results and today (1937) many of the ideas being advanced for peace in industry run parallel with this proposal of seventeen years ago.

One effect of the report was a great stimulus among employers to form shop councils so as to set up a form of collective bargaining. Whatever the other objections may be no one will deny that these councils by grievance elimination accomplished great good. Their greater effect may have been overlooked by certain types of employers—that they marked a stage in the evolution of labor organization, for these councils trained their men in the values of collective bargaining.

The report of the Second Industrial Conference having come up later for renewed discussion, Hoover explained in *Collier's Magazine* on November 27, 1925:

"The principle enunciated by the Second Industrial Conference was the general acceptance of collective bargaining as the basis of prevention of industrial conflict."

The method was:

"The creation of regional boards of investigation, drawn equally from employers and employees . . . not parties to the conflict, that would come into action if the parties to a threatened conflict refused to enter upon the processes of collective bargaining."

"In order to create a pressure upon them, it was proposed that if either of the parties to the conflict would give an a priori undertaking to enter upon the processes of collective bargaining and to accept the unanimous opinion of a Board of Appeal in case of failure to make a collective bargain, he could then have a seat upon the Investigation Board and somewhat prejudice the position of his opponent. If both sides made this undertaking, the Board of Investigation became automatically simply the stage for collective bargaining."

"The Board of Investigation, as proposed by the Conference, in case one or both parties refused to enter upon the process of collective bargaining, has the power to summon witnesses and publish the merits of the suit, but there are no penalities except public opinion. Elaborate provisions are made to secure fair presentation, expert ability, the prevention of political interference, etc., which are important details."

"The plan (except so far as the initial collective bargain might agree to it as a subsequent step) is not a plan of arbitration. It contains no force except the moral pressures arising from publicity and the exposure of wrong under investigation. It does not prohibit strikes. . . . It is a plan to stimulate universal collective bargaining under conditions of equitable representation of both the employer and the employee."

On April 11 in an address to a labor group in New York, he said:

"He would be a rash man who would state that we are finally entering the industrial millennium, but there is a great ray of hope that America is finding herself on the road to a solution of the greatest of all her problems; that is, a method by which social satisfaction is to be attained with the preservation of private industry, of initiative, and full development of the individual. It is idle to argue that there are at times no conflicts of interest between the employee and the employer. But there are wide areas of activity in which their interest should coincide, and it is the part of statesmanship on both sides to organize this identity of interest in order to limit the area of conflict. There is an identity of interest in waste elimination. It affords a wide field for co-operation in which the acerbities of other relations will be moderated, in which larger mutual respect will be established and actual increased living standards assured. In this setting it has become possible to deal with the problem of waste elimination more successfully than ever before in our history, for co-operative action is easier to summon today than ever before, and is more certain of action. To deal with waste by such action is to strengthen the very foundation of a better relationship between employer and employee."

REDUCING HOURS OF LABOR

In an address on November 19, 1920, Hoover gave his own policies as to hours of work.

". . . if we would build up character and abilities and standard of living in our people we must have regard to their leisure for citizenship, for recreation, for family life. These considerations together with protection against strain must be the fundamentals of determination of hours of labor. . . . It is certainty that the eighty-four hour week of some employment transgresses these fundamentals to a point of inhumanity."

As practical steps to bring these ideas about we may cite an incident soon after he became Secretary of Commerce.

In the winter of 1922 he started an investigation to determine by what method the twelve-hour day eighty-four-hour week in the steel industry could be reduced to an eight-hour day forty-eight-hour week. He concluded from his own inquiries and those of Doctor Samuel McCune Lindsey of New York that with some pressure and leadership this great step might be accomplished. Judge Gary, the president of the United States Steel Corporation, and a few other leaders gave a very qualified encouragement. In April Secretary Hoover recommended to President Harding that he invite the leading steel manufacturers to the White House to discuss the whole question frankly. This dinner was arranged for May 18, 1922. All of the principal steel men were present. President Harding presided. He warmly urged some steps should be taken to meet a real social necessity and asked the manufacturers to co-operate. Hoover was called upon by the President to present the subject fully, which he did. He urged its social and humane necessity; that the gain in efficiency would take up much or all of the cost; that the steady mechanization of the industry made it feasible to do it now. A number of manufacturers severely criticized Hoover's figures, the feasibility of the plan and his assertion of its social necessity. A spirited debate ensued, the final result being that President Harding requested Judge Gary to act as the chairman of a committee of nine to study the possibilities further. The situation at the end of the dinner seemed very discouraging. The press were informed that the subject of the dinner was the abolition of the twelve-hour day and the shift to an eight-hour basis. At once large public debate ensued. Ten days later on May 27, Doctor Lindsey wrote Secretary Hoover:

"The reception which was given by the press . . . shows how keen and widespread is the interest and public demand that something must be done to get rid of the twelve-hour day. . . . Certainly you and the President must feel gratified at the indications of widespread appreciation and support of your leadership in this matter."

As Hoover's estimates of the cost and the social benefits had been severely challenged by some of the manufacturers, he requested the Federated Engineering Societies (of which he had been president) to study and report upon the question. This report substantiated Hoover's position as did also certain manufacturers. On November 1 Hoover drafted a foreword to this report for President Harding's signature which served to give it much public attention. The President's fore-word said:

"It is a matter of very much gratification to me that the Federated American Engineering Societies, our foremost organization of American industrial skill, should have given two years of diligent inquiry, under competent experts, to a subject which is of very deep interest to me, and important to the country."

"I rejoice to note the conclusions of this great body of experts are identical with those which I have reached from a purely social viewpoint. It has seemed to me for a long time that the twelve-hour day and the type of worker it produces have outlived their usefulness and their part in American life in the interests of good citizenship, of good business, and of economic stability. The old order of the twelve-hour day must give way to a better and wiser form of organization of the productive forces of the nation, so that proper family life and citizenship may be enjoyed suitably by all of our people."

"This clear and convincing report of the engineers must prove exceedingly helpful in showing that this much-to-be-desired result can be achieved without either economic or financial disturbance to the progress of American industry."   "WARREN G. HARDING."

The Committee of the Industry under Judge Gary, however, on June 25, 1923, brought in and published a report which, although not entirely adverse, was very disappointing and among other things asserted that there was not at that time sufficient labor supply to make the change. Secretary Hoover was advised that certain of the lesser manufacturers did not agree and would be glad to co-operate to adopt the eight-hour shift.

He then drafted a letter for President Harding expressing disappointment at the result, which was made public. The manufacturers reconsidered and came to the conclusion that they should co-operate to end the matter. On June 27 they telegraphed President Harding (then en route to Alaska) their conclusions. The President announced the end of the twelve-hour day in a speech on the Fourth of July.

Speaking on this incident in an address at Denver on October 25, 1924, the Secretary said:

"Out of many instances of direct service to labor I may recount one other instance. One of the sorest spots in the whole annals of American labor was the twelve-hour day, the eighty-four-hour week, in a considerable portion of the steel industry. Labor had fought for thirty years for the eight-hour day in this industry. At the direction of the President I approached the steel manufacturers with the proposition that the twelve-hour day should not be continued in American life. Everywhere I met the statement that they could not do away with the twelve-hour day because competitors would have an advantage over us. It was contended that it would increase the price of steel, that it would wipe out the margin of profit. Nevertheless we got the whole of the steel manufacturers together and induced them to make an accurate investigation as to the method by which the twelve-hour day should be abolished. Finally, we secured an agreement with them that they would act together in this matter. And two years ago the eight-hour day reigned in the steel industry."

In a letter published on May 19, 1925, Hoover wrote:

"I believe every well-thinking business man hopes for the abolition of the seven-day work-week. Obviously we have a multitude of production processes and public services which require continuous operation. Nevertheless, our managers are steadily installing a larger proportion of 'one day off a week' out of seven."

One of the outstanding qualities of this action was characteristic of the Hoover policies—this great step had been accomplished by co-operative action and not by legislation or coercion.

The weekly hours of labor steadily diminished during Republican administrations as shown by the following table:

		1921	1929	1933
54 hours	(%)	25.8	6.3	4.3
54–60 hours	(%)	21.9	14.9	4.6
60 and over	(%)	26.9	7.4	4.6

ORGANIZED LABOR

Hoover's views on the importance of labor organization were given on many occasions.

In an address at Washington, D. C., on November 19, 1920, he said:

". . . the employer sometimes overlooks a fundamental fact in connection with organized labor in the United States. This is that the vast majority of its membership and its leaders are individualists in their attitude of mind and in their social outlook; that the expansion of Socialist doctrines finds its most fertile area in the ignorance of many workers, and yet the labor organizations, as they stand today, are the greatest bulwark against Socialism. On the other hand, some labor leaders overlook the fact that if we are to maintain our high standards of living, our productivity, it can only be in a society in which we maintain the utmost possible initiative on the part of the employee and through that, in the long run, we can only expand the standard of living by the steady increase of production and the creation of more goods for division over the same numbers."

And in an address at Washington, D. C., on September 5, 1925:

"It is my opinion that our nation is very fortunate in having the American Federation of Labor. It has exercised a powerful influence in stabilizing industry, and in maintaining an American standard of citizenship. Those forces of the old world that would destroy our institutions and our civilization have been met in the front line trenches by the Federation of Labor and routed at every turn."

Hoover summed up progress in fundamental improvements in labor questions, in a public address on May 12, 1926:

"There is a marked change during this last twenty-five years in the attitude of employers and employees. . . . It is not so many years ago that the employer considered it was in his interest to use the opportunities of unemployment and immigration to lower wages irrespective of other considerations. The lowest wages and longest hours were then conceived as the means to attain lowest production costs and largest profits. Nor is it many years ago that our labor unions considered that the maximum of jobs and the greatest security in a job were to be attained by restricting individual effort."

"But we are a long way on the road to new conceptions. The very essence of great production is high wages and low prices, because it depends upon a widening range of consumption only to be obtained from the purchasing power of high real wages and increasing standards of living. Today the majority of employers in time of desperation exhaust every device to make ends meet before resorting to wage reduction. They turn to labor-saving machinery, to constant research for better processes and better administrative methods."

"Parallel with this conception there has been an equal revolution in the views of labor."

"No one will doubt that labor has always accepted the dictum of the high wage, but labor has only gradually come to the view that unrestricted individual effort, driving of machinery to its utmost, and elimination of every waste in production, are the only secure foundations upon which a high real wage can be builded, because the greater the production the greater will be the quantity to divide."

". . . the enormous distance which our organized labor has travelled from the tenets of the old world needs no further proof than the new vision of wage crystallized by the American Federation of Labor at its last annual meeting. The background of those proposals is an urge for improved methods, elimination of waste, increase of production, and participation by labor in the resulting gains."

"The acceptance of these ideas is obviously not universal. Not all employers, not all businesses have these conceptions, nor has every union abandoned the fallacy of restricted effort as the basis of service. But the tendency for both employer and employee to think in terms of the mutual interest of increased production has gained greatly in strength. It is a long cry from the conceptions of the old economics. And it has all contributed profoundly to improvement in the whole basis of employer and employee relationship over a large area of industry, and to the constant growth of national efficiency."

LABOR IN THE DEPRESSION

The consistent Hoover position on labor was never more clearly demonstrated than at the conference of industrial leaders called on November 21, 1929, after the first crash of the depression, where he inaugurated the holding of wages during the depression, the spread of work and increase of construction work.

THE INDUSTRIAL CONFERENCE OF 1929

Mr. Newton, who was present, summarizes the President's statement to that meeting thus: "He outlined the situation. He said that he would not have called them were it not that he viewed the crisis more seriously than a mere stock market crash; that no one could measure the problem before us or the depth of the disaster; that the depression must last for some time; that there were two or three millions unemployed by the sudden suspension of many activities. He warned them that we could expect a long and difficult period at best; that there must be much liquidation of inflated values, debts and prices with heavy penalties on the Nation; that no one could at this time measure the destructive forces we must meet, since the stock boom and collapse were world-wide; that Europe was still under the influence of the destructive aftermath of the War."

"The President further proceeded to point out that our immediate duty was to consider the human problem of unemployment and distress; that our second problem was to maintain social order and industrial peace; the third was orderly liquidation and the prevention of panic, and the final readjustment of new concepts of living. He explained that immediate 'liquidation' of labor had been the industrial policy of previous depressions; that his every instinct was opposed to both the term and the policy, for labor was not a commodity. It represented human homes. Moreover, from an economic viewpoint such action would deepen the depression by suddenly reducing purchasing power and, as a still worse consequence, it would bring about industrial strife, bitterness, disorder, and fear. He put forward his own view that, in our modern economy and on account of the intensified competition from shrinkage in demand and the inevitable loss of profits due to a depression, the cost of living would fall even if wages were temporarily maintained. Hence if wages were reduced subsequently, and then no more and no faster than the cost of living had previously fallen, the burden would not fall primarily on labor, and values could be 'stepped down.' Thereby great hardships and economic and social difficulties would be avoided. In any event the first shock must fall on profits and not on wages."

"President Hoover held the fundamental view that wages should be maintained for the present; that planned construction work should be maintained by industry, and governmental agencies even should increase construction to give as much employment as possible; that the available work should be spread among all employees by temporarily shortening the work-week of individuals; and that each industry should look after distress among its own employees. By these means industry would help to 'cushion down' the situation."

"A discussion followed in which the industrial representatives expressed major agreement. The program was accepted subject to its approval by labor leaders and the agreement by them that they would initiate no strikes or demands for increased pay during the present situation. It was also agreed that those present would sponsor a larger meeting of industrial leaders in Washington on December 5 to further organize the program of cooperation by industry as a whole."

"The same afternoon (November 21) the President held conferences with the outstanding labor leaders and secured their adherence to the program. This co-operation required the patriotic withdrawal of some wage demands which already had been made. The labor leaders loyally carried out their part in these withdrawals."

The press announcement was as follows:

"The President was authorized by the employers who were present at this morning's conference to state on their individual behalf that they will not initiate any movement for wage reduction, and it was their strong recommendation that this attitude should be pursued by the country as a whole."

"They considered that aside from the human considerations involved, the consuming power of the country will thereby be maintained."

"The President was also authorized by the representatives of labor to state that in their individual views and as their strong recommendation to the country as a whole, no movement beyond those already in negotiation should be initiated for increase of wages, and that every co-operation should be given by labor to industry in the handling of its problems."

"The purpose of these declarations is to give assurance that conflicts should not occur during the present situation which will affect the continuity of work, and thus to maintain stability of employment."

[*State Papers, Vol. I, p. 136*]

The *Journal* of the American Federation of Labor wrote January 1, 1930: "The President's conference has given industrial leaders a new sense of their responsibilities. . . . Never before have they been called upon to act together . . . in earlier recessions they have acted individually to protect their own interests and . . . have intensified depression."

President Hoover, at Boston, on October 6, 1930, addressed the annual meeting of the American Federation of Labor on the same subject. He said:

"In his invitation that I should address you on this occasion President Green [of the American Federation of Labor] spoke in terms of high praise of the benefits to labor from the nation-wide co-operation initiated at the White House last November for mitigation of the effects of the present depression."

"At those White House conferences the leaders of business and industry undertook to do their utmost to maintain the rate of wages. They also undertook in case of shortened employment to distribute work as evenly as possible over their regular body of employees. The leaders of labor undertook to urge effort in production and to prevent conflict and dispute. . . ."

"We have now had nearly a year in which to observe the working of these arrangements. These, the first undertakings of this character in our history, have been carried out in astonishing degree. There are, of course, exceptions, but in the large sense our great manufacturing companies, the railways, utilities, and business houses have been able to maintain the established wages. Employers have spread their employment systematically. *For the first time in more than a century of these recurring depressions we have been practically free of bitter industrial conflict. . . .*"

". . . Our freedom from strike and lockout is well evidenced by the statement of the Department of Labor that in the last depression there were more than 2000 labor disputes, many of them of major character and accompanied by great public disorder, as compared with less than 300 disputes in this period, and these mostly of minor character. . . ."

"The undertakings made at that time represent a growing sense of mutual responsibility and a willingness to bend private interests to the general good."

"Your chairman has spoken of my interest in the development of an American basis of wage. Both the directors of industry and your leaders have made great progress toward a new and common ground in economic conceptions, which, I am confident, has had a profound effect upon our economic progress during the last few years. *That is the conception that industry must be constantly renovated by scientific research and invention; that labor welcomes these labor-saving devices; that labor gives its full and unrestricted effort to reduce costs by the use of these machines and methods;* that the savings from these reduced costs shall be shared between labor, employer, and the consumer. It is a philosophy of mutual interest. It is a practice of co-operation for an advantage that is not only mutual but universal. Labor gains either through increase of wage or reduction of cost of living or shortened hours. Employers gain through enlarged consumption, and a wider spread distribution of their products, and more stable business. Consumers gain through lower cost of what they buy. Indeed, mass production must be accompanied by mass consumption through increased standards of living."

"A conception of this sort does not at once find universal application. We ought not to forget that it is something new in the world's economic life. And there are, of course, those who do not yet believe. It is as far apart as the two poles from the teachings of the economists of one hundred years ago, who took it for granted tha the well-being of the worker could be purchased only at the expense of the well-being of the employer or some other group in the community, and further that wages could never rise above subsistence or the number of workers would so increase as to pull the weaker back in to the cesspool of poverty. . . ."

[*State Papers, Vol. I, p. 390*]

Speaking of the coal industry, on the same occasion, the President said:

"All these conditions have culminated in a demoralization of the coal industry and a depth of human misery in some sections which is wholly out of place in our American system. . . . One key to solution seems to me to lie in reduction of this destructive competition. It certainly is not the purpose of our competitive system that it should produce a competition which destroys stability in an industry and reduces to poverty all those within it. Its purpose is rather to maintain that degree of competition which induces progress and protects the consumer. If our regulatory laws be at fault they should be revised."

"But most of these problems are problems of stability. With the job secure, other questions can be solved with much more assurance. You, as workers, know best of all how much a man gains from security in his job. It is the insurance of his manliness, it upholds the personal valuation of himself and of his family. To establish a system that assures this security is the supreme challenge to our responsibility as representatives of millions of our fellow workers and fellow citizens. The discharge of that responsibility does not allow present difficulties to rob us of our clear vision or the wholesome faith and courageous aggressive character for which our country has been long the leader of the world. . . ."

[*State Papers, Vol. I, p. 394*]

The result of the President's campaign to maintain wages was commented on by Mr. William Green, president of the American Federation of Labor, in a speech on October 6, 1930:

"At that conference he suggested that peace be preserved in industry and that wages be maintained during the period of unemployment through which we are passing. The great influence which he exercised upon that occasion served to maintain wage standards and to prevent a general reduction of wages. As we emerge from this distressing period of unemployment we are permitted to understand and appreciate the value of the service which the President rendered the wage earners of the country and industry when he convened the White House conference to which I have just referred."

In the Convention of the same organization held at Vancouver in 1931, the executive council in its report expressed appreciation of the President's efforts and the substantial success attending them.

"Realization of the pernicious effects of wage reductions has prevented a widespread liquidation of wages such as we had in the depression of 1921. Growing adherence to the high-wage principle, strengthened by the President's stand against wage cuts, has brought effective support from the leading industrialists of the country."

"In the full year of 1921 there were ninety-two wage cuts per hundred firms reporting to the Bureau of Labor Statistics, while in the full year of 1930 there were only seven firms per hundred firms reporting."

"Although wage cuts have increased in 1931, there still has been no widespread tendency toward a liquidation of wages such as we experienced in 1921."

"In the first seven months of 1931 the number of cuts reported per hundred firms was twelve compared to fifty-four in 1921."

WAGES IN GOVERNMENT WORK

On December 23, 1930, Hoover established a policy of wages to men employed on Government work which has since been abandoned. He ruled that wages paid in Government work generally should be at the rate prevailing in the locality. He was fully convinced from his own observations that "made" work at low wages, as distinguished from a serious man's job at full pay and full effort, was even more deteriorating and damaging to men's self-respect than direct relief. He insisted that whatever the Federal Government did by way of employment upon needed public improvements should be at full pay, regular work, and no shirking.

LIMITING THE USE OF FEDERAL INJUNCTIONS
IN LABOR DISPUTES

Hoover opposed many of the uses of Federal injunctions in labor disputes. In the great strike of maintenance men on the railways in 1922 when the Attorney-General made use of sweeping injunctions, Secretary Hoover and others of the Cabinet protested vigorously. Most of the injunctions were withdrawn and the others allowed to die.

As President, Hoover was much interested in the passage of a bill limiting the use of injunctions in the Federal courts in labor disputes. That law also declared the so-called "Yellow Dog" contracts contrary to public policy. The President received many protests against his signing the law, some of which challenged its constitutionality. Attorney-General Mitchell however advised its constitutionality and the President signed it on March 13, 1932, with public expressions of satisfaction. The law has stood the test of the courts.

FIVE–DAY WEEK IN GOVERNMENT

During the winter of 1932 the Congress attempted to reduce the wages of Government employees. Hoover insisted upon substitution of part-time work so as to save the discharge of 50,000 Post Office employees. In fact, he established the five-day week in Government service.

In a public statement issued on April 16, 1932, he said:

"The following description of the effect of the 'five-day week staggered furlough plan' in substitution for the 'pay-cut plan' is given in reply to a great many telegraphic and other inquiries."

"This plan provides for one year:"

"1. Application of five-day week directly to per diem employees by eliminating the equivalent of Saturday half day employment; that is twenty-six days' furlough in the year without pay. The equivalent is reached with annual employees by one calendar month's furlough without pay, the month not necessarily to be continuous."

"2. Furlough to be mandatory and all holidays with pay are eliminated."

"3. The following groups are excepted: (a) all civil employees of income of $1200 per annum and less, (b) the enlisted forces of the military services, (c) special cases in continuous services where suitable substitute cannot be provided and public interest forbids the absence of regular employees, (d) rural mail carriers in respect to whom it is provided that their vehicle allowances are eliminated in lieu of the shortened time, (e) in cases where the plan would reduce employees between $1200 and $2500 income below the prevailing income of comparable occupations outside of the Government. An adjustment to reduced compulsory furloughs is provided through appeal to the Classification Board."

"The arguments in favor of the plan are:"

"*a.* It establishes the principle of the five-day week in the Government."

"*b.* It maintains present scale of salaries but each person takes holidays at his own expense."

"*c.* It is prorated to all officials, from Cabinet officers down to persons receiving $1200 per annum, and provides against hardship to those receiving between $1200 and $2500."

"*d.* It provides a saving of $80,000,000 to $82,000,000 as against $67,000,000 on the straight pay-cut basis."

[*State Papers, Vol. II, p. 165*]

Hoover's plan prevailed and was enacted into law.

FEDERAL EMPLOYMENT AGENCIES

Hoover believed in a Federal employment service. A bill that would have made it into a political machine met his prompt veto. His Message upon it on March 7, 1931, was as follows:

"I have given earnest study to the so-called Wagner Bill for improvement of public employment agencies, in an effort to find a method to make it of use in the present employment situation. I find upon study, however, that if I would prevent a serious blow to labor during this crisis, I should not approve the bill. I have repeatedly urged a proper extension of public employment agencies, but this bill, unfortunately, abolishes the whole of the present well-developed Federal Employment Service, and proposes, after certain requirements are complied with, to set up an entirely new plan by subsidies to the states from the Federal Treasury. And even were there no other objections to the plan, it cannot be made effective for many months or even years. It is not only changing horses while crossing a stream but the other horse would not arrive for many months. This situation alone required that legislation be deferred, as it will not help in emergency but will do great damage."

"The fundamental questions involved also require more consideration. This bill proposes, as I have said, to destroy the Federal Employment Service in the Department of Labor, which has developed out of many years of experience, and to substitute for it forty-eight practically independent agencies, each under state control, the Federal Government paying for them as to 50 per cent and based not upon economic need of the particular state but upon mathematical ratio to population. On the other hand, the existing Federal Employment Service is today finding places of employment for men and women at the rate of 1,300,000 per annum. It co-operates and co-ordinates with the service already established by some thirty states. It applies its energies to interstate movements and, being a mobile service, it concentrates upon the areas in need. Beyond this, however, the present Federal Service has special divisions devoted to the planting and harvest movement in agriculture and a special organization for veterans. There is no provision for the continuation of these two very important special services under the new plan, and the interstate quality of the Federal Service is destroyed. In any event, the bill requires effective action by the legislatures and governors of the various states at a minimum time requiring so long a period for its establishment as to be of no purpose in this emergency. And there is, therefore, ample time to consider the whole of the questions involved. There is no financial loss to labor in allowing this bill to lapse. While the bill provides for $1,500,000 expenditures over the next fifteen or sixteen months, one-half of it would be absorbed in relieving one-half the present expenditure of the states without any additional service on their part. On the other hand, the present Federal Service has available over the next fifteen or sixteen months nearly $1,000,000 for the conduct of its agencies, which are being rapidly expanded through the emergency appropriations."

"I am asking the Secretary of Labor to co-operate with the various interested organizations to draft a plan for presentation to the next session of Congress which will avoid the difficulties presented by this bill."

[State Papers, Vol. I, p. 530]

The President had himself already reorganized the service on sounder lines. On March 12, 1931, he announced the completion of this reorganization.

"In co-operation with Secretary Doak, I have appointed Mr. John R. Alpine of New York as Special Assistant to the Secretary of Labor in charge of the United States Employment Service activities to include the application at once of the emergency appropriation of $500,000 made, at my suggestion, at the end of the last session of Congress over and above the usual $380,000 per annum."

"Mr. Alpine comes to the service with a long successful record in the organized labor movement and large experience in employment management. He was International President of the United States Association of Plumbers and Steamfitters; Vice-President of the American Federation of Labor; was Acting President of the Federation in 1918 during the absence of President Gompers in Europe . . . was a delegate in the Labor Section of the Paris Peace Conference in 1918. He has had long

experience in employment problems and will take up his new duties at
once." [State Papers, Vol. I, p. 532]

The effect of the reorganization is shown by the increase in
placements through the Service's own employment offices and
those with whom it co-operated. Together with co-operating
state and municipal employment offices 1,104,136 persons were
placed in 1931 and 2,174,179 in 1932. The service to agricultural seasonal workers expanded from placing 559,571 persons in
1929 to 886,605 in 1932.

GENERAL LABOR POLICIES

The President spoke upon labor problems many times during
the campaign of 1932. At Cleveland on October 14, he said:

"I propose to review what the administration has done and the measures and policies it has in action together with the relation of these policies
to those of our opponents. As President of the United States, I have the
duty to speak to workers, but I have also a certain personal right to
speak."

"When I talk to you tonight about labor I speak not out of academic
imaginings but from sharp personal experience. I have looked at these
human problems, not only from the fireside of one who has returned from
a day's work with his own hands but I know the problem that haunts the
employer through the night, desperate to find the money with which to
meet the week's pay roll. In public service during years past I have had to
look at these problems from the point of view of the national welfare as
a whole."

"I have for many years advocated high wages as the economic basis
for the country. That is the road to economical production and high consumption of products of the farm and factory."

"Those who say that things could not be worse speak without knowledge of what has happened in other countries which have gone through
this cataclysm. In order to show you what the rates of wages are in the
United States compared with other countries I have this week secured
through the Department of Commerce a calculation on a basis which I
have used before for purposes of illustration. The actual wages in terms
of the currencies of other countries are difficult to compare. We must
find a common denominator."

"If we say that 5 per cent of butter and 95 per cent of flour form the basis of that useful mixture called 'bread and butter,' then the weekly earnings in each country would buy at retail in those countries the following totals of this useful compound:"

WEEKLY WAGES IF APPLIED TO THE PURCHASE OF "COMPOSITE POUNDS OF BREAD AND BUTTER" AS OF OCTOBER, 1932

	Railway Engineers	Carpenters	Electricians	Coal Miners	Weavers	Day Labor
United States........	1,069	1,064	1,300	734	565	393
United Kingdom.....	342	253	276	223	161	184
Germany............	271	176	169	162	120	106
France.............	246	183	164	123	86	86
Belgium............	288	228	240	180	199	160
Italy..............	275	118	149	70	67	85
Japan..............	131	86	90	57	31	55

"Let no man say it could not be worse."

". . . There is no measure in the whole economic gamut more vital to the American workingman and the farmer today than the maintenance of a protective tariff. I stand on that principle of protection. Our opponents are opposed to that principle. They propose 'a competitive tariff for revenue.' They propose to do this in the face of the fact that in the last year currencies of competing nations have depreciated by going off the gold standard and consequently wages have been lowered in thirty competing countries. This is a flat issue which every farmer and workman in the United States should consider from the point of view of his home and his living."

"That it is the intention of the Democratic candidate to reduce the tariffs—on all commodities—must be clear from these typical expressions in respect to the present tariff used in this campaign—'Wicked and exorbitant tariff,' 'its outrageous rates,' 'almost prohibitive tariffs,' 'the notorious and indefensible Smoot-Hawley tariff,' 'the excessive rates of that bill must come down,' 'until the tariff is lowered,' 'our policy calls for lower tariffs.' "

"Do you want to compete with laborers whose wages in his own money are only sufficient to buy from one-eighth to one-third of the amount of bread and butter which you can buy at the present rates of wages? That is a plain question. It does not require a great deal of ingenious argument to support its correct answer. It is true we have the most gigantic market in the world today, surrounded by nations clamoring to get in. But it has been my belief—and it is still my belief—that we should protect this market for our own labor; not surrender it to the labor of foreign countries as the Democratic Party proposes to do."

"In order to hold the jobs we have for our own people and to prevent further additions to our unemployed and thus prevent further burdens upon our communities, I have by administrative order practically prohibited all immigration from every quarter of the globe except the relatives of our residents. . . . Had the net immigration taken place since the date of that order which took place in the two years previous, we would have had 400,000 jobs taken from our people or had just that many persons added to our unemployed. That might have been worse."

"There is nothing in which the American workman is more concerned than in preserving the integrity of the American dollar. The Democratic Party has at various times, and specifically by the passage of the Patman bill by the Democratic House of Representatives on June 15 last, endeavored to undermine the integrity of the American currency through the issue of $2,300,000,000 of greenbacks—harking back to the disastrous experience of sixty years ago. If any of you will study what happened in Germany, or France, or Austria, or any other European country when they resorted to these measures in order to meet their immediate difficulties, you will find that the major hardship fell upon the working people. There was a time when the value of the German mark was five to the dollar. They tried this plan of relief. I have in my desk a 5,000,000 mark note which before the entrance into these processes would have been worth $1,000,000, and yet which I bought for actually one dollar. The effect of their experiment was a subtle and steady reduction of real wages, right and left."

"We have fought a great battle to maintain the stability of the American dollar, the stability of its exchange, in order that we might protect the working people of the United States."

"Over and above and of infinitely more importance than all these measures I have mentioned is the problem of restoring the great mass of normal jobs in the country. Emergency jobs have helped enormously, but the normal jobs are the permanent dependence of the worker. Emergency jobs will never heal the depression."

"Obviously, the normal jobs lie in the production and distribution of goods and services; in other words, the factories, the mills, the mines, the railways, the public utilities, the stores, the offices."

"And every part of this mechanism is lubricated by what we call credit. That is, the ability of the manager of a business to borrow money to buy his raw materials and to pay his labor. This credit is the very lifeblood of this whole structure. It is the lifeblood of jobs. If credit fails, the enterprise dries up; it withers or it dies. And jobs decrease or disappear."

"And what is the source of credit? The savings of the people themselves. These are gathered in a myriad of tiny rivulets of their deposits in the banks, their premiums to life-insurance companies, their dues to benevolent fraternal organizations, their payments to building and loan associations, and a score of other ways. These rivulets in total volume are a mighty river. Their waters are stored in credit reservoirs. These are the banks, the mortgage companies, the insurance companies, investments in the services of industry and business."

"Thus credit is born of the people themselves. What the people give, the people can take away. The reservoirs of credit are built upon the confidence of the people in them. Fear is death to credit."

"When the great economic earthquakes abroad struck directly at the credit structures of those foreign countries, the shocks reverberated to us. I have already said foreigners dumped their securities here at panic prices and demanded gold in payment. They claimed their deposits in American banks. They demanded cash for all goods they had sold us. Our own people in fear drew out $1,500,000,000 of their savings from our own banks."

"Thus credit began to dry up. The managers of business turned in vain for the accustomed loans to buy raw materials and to pay their labor."

"Beyond all this contraction of credit was the fear and panic through the world, spreading its destruction into the United States. It imperiled the institutions in which were the savings of every fireside—bank deposits or insurance policies or investments. In this contraction of credit lay dangers to every one who owed money, for upon demand for immediate payment he was compelled to sell his property in a limited and vastly depreciated market and so was threatened with ruin."

"Faced with these unprecedented perils, we took unprecedented steps. We refused to allow these destructive forces to run their course to chaos and ruin. We organized the co-operation of the community; we thrust the strength of the Government as a shield before the people as has never been done before in the history of all time."

"I have referred to these gigantic measures on other occasions. I will not take your time to again describe the weapons and instrumentalities we have brought to bear in this battle. We created them, and we created them to preserve your savings deposits, your insurance policies; to protect you from foreclosure on your homes. We did it to hold for you the jobs you have and, finally, to recover the ground lost in the battle and restore the jobs which have been lost. It has been a battle with inevitable casualties, but that battle is now being won. Credit is being expanded, and normal jobs are coming back."

"These agencies are working day and night. They are producing results. September alone shows an increase of 3.6 per cent in employment for the whole country. If these policies shall be uninterrupted, if we shall hold the financial integrity of the United States by maintaining a balance in our budget, these measures and the courage and industry of our people will bring back our economic system a long way toward its normal functioning and the restoration of our people to their jobs."

"Let no man say that things could not have been worse. Without these many measures, things would have been so much worse that today would look like prosperity in retrospect."

"It must be clear to you and clear to the country that a major part of the shocks and dislocations which have brought this destruction are of foreign origin. They are not of American making; but by the fact that we have suffered from them it is implied that labor and agriculture have a fundamental interest in securing greater stability abroad. Our self-containment is such that we can build back a long way on our own resources. But if it is possible to improve the internal stability of other nations, it would at once allow them to relax their emergency restrictions against exchange and the import of commodities; it would allow them to return to stable currencies and enable the world to be free from political shocks— all of which build for American markets for the American farmer and for American labor. It would protect the American worker and farmer and business man from the rising flood of goods due to depreciated currencies and lowered standards of living. To this major end, which means work for our unemployed and increased prices for our farmers, we have given great devotion over the past year." [*State Papers, Vol. II, p. 337*]

THE RESULT OF HOOVER LABOR POLICIES

President Hoover was ably seconded in his policies of co-operation and conciliation by Secretary of Labor Davis and by Secretary of Labor Doak who succeeded Mr. Davis in 1930.

Hoover's policies of long-built co-operation and ever ready sense of industrial responsibility to labor brought the country great benefits. Although his administration had to cope with the worst phases of the depression, the country enjoyed an unparalleled industrial peace. The tangible proof lies in the fact during the downhill slide of the depression when industrial conflict has hitherto in our history been the most acute, there was not a single disturbance where troops were needed to preserve order and there was no consequential conflict where men were injured.

The number of strikes and lockouts were reduced to the lowest levels of many years both before and after this period as can be seen by the number of man-days lost from strikes and lockouts as shown in the reports of the Department of Labor:

Under President Hoover	*Under President Roosevelt*
1929........9,975,213	1933........14,818,846
1930........2,730,368	1934........19,591,949
1931........6,386,183	1935........15,456,337
1932........6,462,973	1936........16,752,378

IMMIGRATION POLICIES

COOLIDGE QUOTA LIMITATION

Secretary Hoover had warmly supported President Coolidge's efforts to secure quota-limitation of immigration. A commission was set up, of which the Secretary was a member, to determine the base of quotas. Out of the alternatives a sharp dispute grew up, Hoover favoring quotas on the "census basis" as distinguished from the "national origins" basis. The Congress did not agree to Hoover's views and it became his duty as President on March 22, 1929, to promulgate the "national origins" plan.

"While I am strongly in favor of restricted and selected immigration, I have opposed the national origins basis. I therefore dislike the duty of issuing this proclamation . . . but the President of the United States must be the first to obey the law."

He believed the Coolidge immigration law could be improved. In his Message to Congress on December 3, 1929, the President said:

"I have been opposed to the basis of the quotas now in force and I have hoped that we could find some practical method to secure what I believe should be our real national objective; that is, fitness of the immigrant as to physique, character, training, and our need of service. Perhaps some system of priorities within the quotas could produce these results and at the same time enable some hardships in the present system to be cleared up. I recommend that the Congress should give the subject further study, in which the executive departments will gladly co-operate with the hope of discovering such method as will more fully secure our national necessities."

"Restriction of immigration has from every aspect proved a sound national policy. Our pressing problem is to formulate a method by which the limited number of immigrants whom we do welcome shall be adapted to our national setting and our national needs."

[*State Papers, Vol. I, p. 161*]

FURTHER LIMITATION OF IMMIGRATION

On September 9, 1930, the President in co-operation with Secretaries Doak and Stimson took a new step of policy in immigration of the most profound effect. The immigration law provided that persons likely to become public charges could be refused entrance. With the large amount of unemployment the President concluded that directly or indirectly all immigrants were a public charge—either by themselves going on relief or if they got jobs by forcing some one else on relief. He therefore stopped all immigration with some minor exceptions and made it include the non-quota countries as well.

In his public statement he said:

". . . the quota entrants amounted to about 150,000 per annum and the immigration from non-quota countries to about 100,000 per annum. . . . As shown later, this action prevented the addition of several hundred thousand persons to the unemployed within the next three years."

In reporting his action to the Congress, he said on December 2, 1930:

"There is need for revision of our immigration laws upon a more limited and more selective basis, flexible to the needs of the country."

"Under conditions of current unemployment it is obvious that persons coming to the United States seeking work would likely become either a direct or indirect public charge. As a temporary measure the officers issuing visas to immigrants have been, in pursuance of the law, instructed to refuse visas to applicants likely to fall into this class. As a result the visas issued have decreased from an average of about 24,000 per month prior to restrictions to a rate of about 7000 during the last month. These are largely preferred persons under the law. Visas from Mexico are about 250 per month compared to about 4000 previous to restrictions. The whole subject requires exhaustive consideration."

[*State Papers, Vol. I, p. 438*]

Reports issued from time to time showed that the persons deported exceeded the persons arriving by 100 per cent. This policy was held throughout the Hoover Administration.

The result of this order is shown by the following figures:

	Immigrants (inward)	Emigrants (outward)
1929	279,678	69,203
1930	241,700	50,661
1931	97,139	61,882
1932	35,576	103,295

DEPORTATIONS

The deportation of convicted aliens, illegal entries, and other undesirables, was rigidly enforced. The results were as follows:

DEPORTATIONS

	Fiscal Year	Number
Hoover Administration	1930	16,631
	1931	18,141
	1932	19,426
	1933	19,865
Roosevelt Administration	1934	8,879
	1935	8,319
	1936	9,195

AGRICULTURE

THE AGRICULTURAL PROBLEM

As Food Administrator during the War, Hoover had had a large experience in agricultural problems. Those problems concerned the farmer's interest as well as the consumer's and the War objectives. When the Armistice came in November, 1918, the American farmer had prepared at the request of our government for the benefit of the Allies the most gigantic surplus in all American history. With the Armistice the Allies sought to buy their supplies from the cheaper dammed-up surpluses of the Southern Hemisphere. Hoover's successful battle on behalf of the American farmer during the winter of 1918–19 finally disposed of these surpluses, partly to the Allies and partly to former enemy territory, at the prices which the American farmer had been promised.

Since the War no Agricultural policies of any administration have met with the satisfactions that were hoped of them—not even those of the New Deal.

The plain facts are that agricultural acreage was necessarily over-expanded, land values and prices were greatly inflated by the War. Add to this the mechanical improvements, which substituted gasoline for feed development in plant life, and better farm management, all of which still further increased productivity. Liquidation of this excessive production was inevitable. Other agricultural nations were in the same fix. But those with virgin and cheaper lands, and cheaper labor, were crowding American farmers from the world market.

Beyond all these special difficulties of the farmer, the industrial system had become inflexible by the fixity of wages and consequently prices. Agricultural prices respond to every wind that blows. When depression comes, the manufacturer quickly reduces production with decreased demands and thus tends to hold his prices; the farmer increases production hoping by increased quantities to maintain his gross income at lower prices. The farmer is thus the major sufferer in depression.

After the immediate adjustments from the War, the agricultural prices—from 1923 to 1929—were fairly stable and the gross income to agriculture was fairly satisfactory as compared with pre-war. But wages and the prices of the farmer's supplies and transportation remained high.

In reply to a request for his views on agricultural policies at that period, Hoover said in a press statement on December 1, 1920:

"My view of the major needs of American agriculture in the short view is:"

"First: Peace with Europe and participation of the United States in preserving peace in order the economic life there may revive and again restore a demand for our surplus. This includes the settlement of such world disturbing factors as the blockade on Russian imports and the fixing of the enemy indemnities that they too may return trade."

"Second: The erection of international credit machinery by which we can enable Europe to buy our surplus pending this recuperation."

"Third: An abolition of consolidated buying and thus control of our farm prices by European governments."

"My view of the major needs in the long view is:"

"First: A better marketing system that all impediments to the free flow of the law of supply and demand may be removed by constructive and not destructive control of the great agencies of distribution."

"Second: Better transportation system."

"Third: Better adjustment of taxation so that the burden may be better shifted to non-essential expenditure."

"Fourth: Development of a farm loan system in remedy of tenant problem."

"Fifth: Sane development of co-operative buying and selling among farmers."

"Sixth: A development of our credit system to one that distinguishes between credits for speculative purposes and those for production and marketing of essentials in favor of the latter."

During his years as Secretary of Commerce Hoover had devoted his energies largely to policies which would reduce manufacturing costs and thereby render lower prices of farmers' supplies possible.

(See Elimination of Waste, p. 107, Improvement of Waterways, p. 254.)

This period—1922 to 1929—showed an extraordinary growth in manufacturing and service efficiency, but the savings went more largely to labor in increased wages and shorter hours than to the farmer as consumer. Agricultural prices were fairly stable and the cost of the farmer's supplies diminished slightly but he made no such gain in living standards as did the wage earner.

The agricultural industry in 1929 was not in a satisfactory condition, entirely aside from the terrific dislocations which later on rose from the world depression. The subject had loomed large for many reasons.

President Coolidge on recommendation of leading farm groups had proposed a Farm Board for consideration and development of farmers' problems, of farmers' co-operative marketing—in fact, to be given authority in the solution of farm questions. The farmers' organizations advocated it at the Republican Convention. It was adopted as a primary part of the Republican platform. Hoover accepted it when he was nominated. It was the farm leaders' own plan. This, and increased tariff on farm products and the improvement of waterway transportation, were the farm proposals of the 1928 campaign.

FEDERAL FARM BOARD

In an address during the 1928 campaign at West Branch, Iowa, on August 21, he said:

". . . A Federal Farm Board is to be set up with the necessary powers and resources to assist the industry to meet not alone the varied problems of today, but those which may arise in the future. My fundamental concept of agriculture is one controlled by its own members, organized to fight its own economic battles and to determine its own destinies. Nor do I speak of organization in the narrow sense of traditional farm co-operatives or pools, but in the much wider sense of a sound marketing organization. It is not by these proposals intended to put the Government into the control of the business of agriculture, nor to subsidize the prices of farm products and pay the losses thereon either by the Federal Treasury or by a tax or fee on the farmer. We propose with governmental assistance and an initial advance of capital to enable the agricultural industry to reach a stature of modern business operations by which the farmer will attain his independence and maintain his individuality."

The agricultural policies of the Hoover Administration fall into four periods:

1. For about eight months from March 4, 1929, to October, 1929;

2. For about eighteen months covering essentially the local American stage of the depression during 1930 to the summer of 1931;

3. During the year of the world crash from the summer of 1931 to June, 1932, when the depression turned;

4. Policies proposed in the campaign of 1932.

Within thirty days of the beginning of the administration, President Hoover called a special session of the Congress to deal almost solely with the agricultural questions. His Message to the Congress on April 16, 1929, read in part:

"I have called this special session of Congress to redeem two pledges given in the last election—farm relief and limited changes in the tariff. . . ."

"The difficulties of the agricultural industry arise out of a multitude of causes. A heavy indebtedness . . . from . . . 1920 . . . wasteful methods of marketing . . . specialization . . . prices . . . depressed by congested marketing at the harvest or by the occasional climatic surpluses. Railway rates . . . increased . . . growth of competition in the world markets from countries that enjoy cheaper labor or more nearly virgin soils . . . expansion of . . . our marginal lands during the war, . . . taxes have doubled . . . work animals replaced by mechanical appliances . . . decreasing the consumption of farm products . . . agricultural industry has not kept pace . . . in standards of living with other lines of industry. . . ."

"Because of the multitude of causes and because agriculture is not one industry but a score of industries, we are confronted not with a single problem alone but a great number of problems. Therefore there is no single plan or principle that can be generally applied. Some of the forces working to the detriment of agriculture can be greatly mitigated by improving our waterway transportation; some of them by readjustment of the tariff; some by better understanding and adjustment of production needs; and some by improvement in the methods of marketing."

"An effective tariff upon agricultural products, that will compensate the farmer's higher costs and higher standards of living, has a dual purpose. Such a tariff not only protects the farmer in our domestic market but it also stimulates him to diversify his crops and to grow products that he could not otherwise produce, and thus lessens his dependence upon exports to foreign markets. The great expansion of production abroad under the conditions I have mentioned renders foreign competition in our export markets increasingly serious. It seems but natural, therefore, that the American farmer, having been greatly handicapped in his foreign market by such competition from the younger expanding countries, should ask that foreign access to our domestic market should be regulated by taking into account the differences in our costs of production."

"The Government has a special mandate from the recent election, not only to further develop our waterways and revise the agricultural tariff, but also to extend systematic relief in other directions."

"I have long held that the multiplicity of causes of agricultural depression could only be met by the creation of a great instrumentality clothed with sufficient authority and resources to assist our farmers to meet these problems, each upon its own merits. The creation of such an agency would at once transfer the agricultural question from the field of politics into the realm of economics and would result in constructive action. The administration is pledged to create an instrumentality that will investigate the causes, find sound remedies, and have the authority and resources to apply those remedies."

"The pledged purpose of such a Federal farm board is the reorganization of the marketing system on sounder and more stable and more economic lines."

"In addition to these special provisions in the direction of improved returns, the board should be organized to investigate every field of economic betterment for the farmer so as to funrnish guidance as to need in production, to devise methods for elimination of unprofitable marginal lands and their adaptation to other uses; to develop industrial by-products and to survey a score of other fields of helpfulness."

"Certain safeguards must naturally surround these activities and the instrumentalities that are created. Certain vital principles must be adhered to in order that we may not undermine the freedom of our farmers and of our people as a whole by bureaucratic and governmental domination and interference. We must not undermine initiative. There should be no fee or tax imposed upon the farmer. No governmental agency should engage in the buying and selling and price fixing of products, for such courses can lead only to bureaucracy and domination. Government funds should not be loaned or facilities duplicated where other services of credit and facilities are available at reasonable rates. No activities should be set in motion that will result in increasing the surplus production, as such will defeat any plans of relief."

"The most progressive movement in all agriculture has been the upbuilding of the farmer's own marketing organizations, which now embrace nearly 2,000,000 farmers in membership and annually distribute nearly $2,500,000,000 worth of farm products."

"The difficulties of agriculture cannot be cured in a day; they cannot all be cured by legislation; they cannot be cured by the Federal Government alone. But farmers and their organizations can be assisted to overcome these inequalities. Every effort of this character is an experiment, and we shall find from our experience the way to further advance. We must make a start. With the creation of a great instrumentality of this character, of a strength and importance equal to that of those which we have created for transportation and banking, we give immediate assurance of the determined purpose of the Government to meet the difficulties of which we are now aware, and to create an agency through which constructive action for the future will be assured."

"In this treatment of this problem we recognize the responsibility of the people as a whole, and we shall lay the foundations for a new day in agriculture, from which we shall preserve to the Nation the great values of its individuality and strengthen our whole national fabric. . . ."

[*State Papers, Vol. I, pp. 31–2*]

The Agricultural Marketing Act contained the provisions set out in the Presidential Message. Senator Borah and some Democratic allies endeavored to introduce an export bounty into the act. President Hoover was compelled to oppose this idea. It was certain to produce foreign reprisals upon the American farmer. In any event, the benefits would go less to the farmers than to intermediaries.[1]

The President on June 15, 1929, signed the Marketing Bill and made the following statement:

"After many years of contention we have at last made a constructive start at agricultural relief with the most important measure ever passed by Congress in aid of a single industry. . . . I am asking for a preliminary appropriation of $150,000,000 at once out of the $500,000,000 that has been authorized, and as Congress will be in session except for short periods, the Board will be able to present its further requirements at almost any time."

The President announced that he would canvass the several hundred farmers' organizations and agricultural colleges to get their views: first, on whether some outstanding business man should be placed upon the Board; second, on the persons whom these organization favored for appointment to the Board to represent the major branches of agriculture. These were to be men of actual experience in agriculture. As a result of this canvass, carried out through Secretary of Agriculture Hyde, the several hundred farm organizations recommended that a busi-

[1] It is to be noted that since the Democratic Party came into power, its leaders have not proposed this scheme again; obviously these were merely tactics to create prejudice against Hoover.

ness man of wide experience should be appointed chairman. They recommended a list of names for other members of the Board whom the President appointed. The farmers thus selected their own Board.

It consisted of Alexander Legge of Chicago, president of the International Harvester Company, chairman; James C. Stone, Kentucky, founder and former president of the Burley Tobacco Growers' Co-operative Association; Carl Williams, Oklahoma, of the Farmers' Co-operative Marketing Association; C. B. Denman, Missouri, of the National Livestock Producers' Association; Charles S. Wilson, New York, professor of agriculture, Cornell University; William F. Schilling, Minnesota, of the National Dairy Association; ex-Governor Samuel McKelvie, Nebraska, publisher of *The Nebraska Farmer;* and C. C. Teague, California, of the California Fruit Growers' Exchange.

EMERGENCY FARM POLICIES

The Board was hardly underway when the crash in October, 1929 struck the country. The long-view developmental plans for which the Board had been founded gradually went into the background as the Board was plunged into the unknown seas of the greatest economic emergency in history.

The crash in the stock markets quickly created panic conditions in the markets for farm products. These markets were in special peril at that time of year because the farmer as usual had produced the Nation's supply for the year on credit and had not sold all of it. He was therefore greatly indebted for loans against his products. Likewise merchants who had bought the crop were heavily indebted. A sudden drop in prices would result in calling loans and this in turn would force vast quantities of commodities into the markets through liquidation to pay the loans. Therein lay a panic in farm prices parallel with the stock market panic, with the difference that somebody would buy stocks but nobody would buy farm products.

Such a panic was prevented. The Farm Board had already organized cotton and wheat co-operatives into national marketing corporations. On October 24, the day after the stock crash, in view of the emergency and in order to prevent panic spreading to all these markets, the Farm Board under the chairmanship of Alexander Legge authorized these organizations to make loans upon wheat and cotton at certain prices and later to purchase some of these commodities. The cushioning of wheat and cotton helped the other agricultural markets. These commodities recovered most of their loss in prices by the end of December.

Two months later, on February 25, 1930, Legge, in defense of these policies, stated to the press:

"Some objection has developed in the grain trade against the action of the Farm Board in financing farm co-operatives in the purchase of wheat and cotton in the present situation. . . ."

"In connection with these objections I should like to make this statement as a conservative business man, addressed to the conservative business men of the country."

"The country as a whole was thrown into depression through the collapse of speculation on the New York Stock Exchange. The action of the President in securing co-operation of the business world absolutely prevented this collapse from developing into a panic and has enormously mitigated its effects upon employment and business, including agriculture."

"The co-operation of the great employers of the country in upholding wages, and therefore the buying power of the public, the action of the railways, the public utilities, the industries, the Federal Government, the states, the municipalities in undertaking great programs of construction, are greatly mitigating unemployment and giving protection to the workman and stability to business."

"The farmer also was the victim of this collapse. His products and his labor were jeopardized the same as the other workers through the currents started in considerable part from the same causes. His only direct support in this emergency is the Farm Board, through powers conferred upon it. The Board is endeavoring, through finance of the farmers' own organization, to help restore stability and expedite recovery from a crisis which the farmer did not create and for which he is not responsible."

"The measures taken are purely emergency measures on the par with those taken by other business agencies of the country, and I am confident that the Board deserves and will receive the support of all thinking business men in its endeavor to contribute its part toward the swift recovery of the country as a whole from this situation. . . ."

In reply to a letter from Legge suggesting further appropriations, the President was clear that this was no permanent policy. On March 15, 1930, he said:

". . . I note the reasons which induced the Board's decision to undertake a large operation in wheat under Section 9 of the Agricultural Marketing Act. A stabilization under this section is practically subject to the determination of the Board as to the circumstances under which it should be made use of. . . ."

"The major purpose of the Board, as you say, is to build up farmer-owned, farmer-controlled marketing organizations. . . . This will require years of steady building toward a reorganized marketing system, but without this foundation I see no permanent realization of our hopes of a new day for agriculture."

"The Board has unanimously determined that the collapse in the wheat market which arose from the boom and slump of the stock exchange presents a national emergency to agriculture of the first importance, which in its many ramifications through this and foreign countries has definitely interfered with the free flow of supply and demand in respect to wheat, and that the Board should in this emergency exert every power at its disposal not to fix prices, but to maintain and restore to the farmer a free market based upon the realities of supply and demand even though the prerequisites I have mentioned are not all of them present. I have accepted the views of the Board and have given it my support by recommending the appropriation asked for."

"I am glad to know from you that the operation has so far been successful in stemming a panic and slowing the fall in prices so that the grain farmer has realized prices much above the point he would otherwise have secured, and has thus saved many hundreds of millions directly and indirectly to them and contributed to re-establish stability in business in general. It is of course too early to see the final results of this action. The difficulties and dangers to the farmer which have already developed in it are indeed an indication that nothing but a most unusual emergency warrants its use. Whatever the results are it will have compensations in experience."

"But I am concerned with the necessity of drawing for the future a complete defined separation of the Government from stabilization activities and the building of a sound system of independent farmer-marketing institutions through other powers of the Board."

[*Hoover Administration, p. 38*]

Prices were supported during the panic months from October and November to the end of May, 1930. By this time the previous season's production had been marketed. In this time the farm co-operatives accumulated a net amount of about 8 per cent of the wheat crop and 10 per cent of the cotton crop with loans from the Farm Board. The dairy, wool and other products had been supported without accumulation. Prices of wheat had declined slowly from $1.29 per bushel at the time of the crash to $1.05 per bushel at the end of May. Cotton receded from 17.48 cents to about 15 cents per pound. Since the farmer by this time had marketed his crop which had been produced at the high costs of 1929, the Board considered the cushioning should end for the present to allow for readjustment. Panic had been prevented and the farmer had realized hundreds of millions more for his 1929 crop than otherwise would have been the case, and was thus enabled better to adjust himself. A more economical production of his new crop now was possible due to the fall in prices which he must pay for living and farming materials.

A new crisis arose in November, 1930, when the world's products began to move to the markets from the harvest of 1930. Grain prices collapsed in Europe to an equivalent abroad of about fifty cents per bushel in the American market. European trade restrictions, Soviet dumping and excessive world supplies had combined to produce such an outcome. The Farm Board authorized the farmers' grain co-operatives again to cushion our grain and cotton markets. This operation was continued until the following June, 1931. The new crop had been produced at less cost than the previous year. Wheat prices were held at from seventy-five to eighty cents per bushel, and cotton at nine and one-half to ten and one-half cents per pound for the period necessary to market the crop of 1930. The prices for wheat ranged from twenty-five to thirty-five cents per bushel above parity in Liverpool. All agricultural prices were steadied up. Through these activities the farmers received a great deal more for the 1930 crop than they otherwise would. Of the Government advances to the co-operatives to aid in marketing the 1929 and 1930 crops, probably less than $150,000,000 were lost. The benefits to the farmer were many times the amount of loss by the Government and represented the margin necessary to hold the agricultural industry from bankruptcy with all the consequent suffering and contagious disorganization. The solution was not perfect, but there is no complete solution in a world collapse which so severely reduces demand, following a tremendous world increase in supply.

In the spring of 1931 came the second stage of the depression through the collapse of the European financial structure. The whole picture was changed, but to what degree no mortal man could tell in advance. The immediate problem was to save the United States from financial collapse. The national house was on fire and the first thing to do was to put the fire out,

The agricultural difficulties were sensibly increased by the large harvests the world over and the increase in world stocks in addition to abrupt further shrinkage of world demand. No sort of agricultural policies could save the farmer from difficulty under these blows.

The financial collapse in Europe began in May, 1931, and culminated in October when the Bank of England defaulted gold payments. At one time (July, 1931), the action of President Hoover in bringing about the "Moratorium" and "Standstill" agreements, seemed to have transformed the whole international situation. Prices and business activity responded in every part of the world. In the United States wheat rose four to five cents per bushel, cotton almost 20 per cent.

The Farm Board continued purchases during the autumn and winter of 1931–2 and kept prices above foreign levels, but the farmers of the whole world including the United States swamped the world with supplies. The Board asked the farmers for voluntary reduction of crop acreage by 30 per cent as the whole world was accumulating enormous surpluses of farm products. From the public assurances of the farmers' organizations, from governors and others, it looked as if this would succeed. It did not prove to be the case. The American crop planted for 1932 was even larger. The President absolutely refused to accept proposals by which farmers would be forced to reduce production. To him this meant sheer Fascism. By the first of the year (1932), it was obvious that the larger problem was to prevent American financial collapse along with Europe.

The immediate battle now became one of tiding the farmer over financially until the chaos in world finances could be straightened out. The President brought about a great expansion of farm credit. (See Expansion Agricultural Credit, page 442.)

During the winter of 1932, the Government holdings and the collapse of foreign buyers left the Government holdings a weight over the market. The Board negotiated large special sales to China, Germany and Brazil. Hoover turned about one-half of the holdings over for relief. (See page 378.) Through the Farm Board, the whole of the farmers' co-operatives were carried through without bankruptcy—a better record than the private corporations.[1]

The economic tide turned sharply upward in June, 1932; the price of wheat, corn, and cotton rose by 20 per cent between July and October. With the election, all Republican poli-

[1]This policy has been continued by the Roosevelt Administration through the "Bank of Co-operatives."

cies came to an end. The advance notice of Democratic policies by raising fear created a panic in bank depositors which
overclouded everything. (See the Panic of 1933, page 527.)

The great service of the Hoover Administration for the farmers has not been challenged upon the upbuilding of co-operative
marketing, the organization of co-operative finance, the expansion and organization of agricultural credit, the tariff protections from foreign competition, or the development of sound
long-view economic and social program for agriculture.

The criticism arises from three policies of the Farm Board—
that is, their lending against crops for the purpose of holding
prices; their purchase of farm products to support markets;
and their request to farmers voluntarily to reduce the acreage
of export crops, such as wheat and cotton, for which there were
no foreign markets.

The farmers' real criticism of these Farm Board policies is
that they did not hold farm prices to the level of 1928. No
action of government could do that. If they had done so,
agriculture would have been ruined by the resulting over-production; the Government would have been ruined with the gigantic amassing of eventually perishable commodities which the
Government must have bought, and the cities would have had
price riots.

The criticism of the economist is that it was a self-destruc-
tive program, that in the end the Government accumulations of
wheat and cotton depressed heavily upon the price levels of the
farmer himself. That is true. The partial answer is that it
succeeded for two years, that the depression lasted too long.
It was made worse by a sequence of bumper crops. Under other
circumstances, it would have got by better.

There was at least a national lesson in economics to those
farm organizations who so ardently advocated it. Likewise
there have been national lessons in Hoover's opposition to the
plans known as "domestic allotment," "equalization fee," the
"one big farm," "the export bounty." He opposed them for being coercions and unworkable or unconstitutional.[1]

The objective student, to whom compromise in method with

[1] A further lesson lies in the fact that at last the New Deal has come to the Hyde-
Hoover concept of land use as a basis of national aid to the farmer.

The criticism of the New Dealer has no validity. Messrs. Wallace and Roosevelt, who
denounced the Farm Board policies so vigorously during the campaign, were destined to
prove either their faulty thinking or their intellectual dishonesty; for within six months
they had initiated every one of the policies they so bitterly denounced—buying of commodities, loaning and losing money on them; asking for reduction of production. But they
went further by actually destroying commodities and ultimately coercing the farmer to
reduce production.

necessity and emergency is an essential of human progress, would say the Farm Board did cushion the fall so as to save billions of dollars to the farmers. The 200,000,000 bushels of wheat and 2,000,000 bales of cotton bought were mostly liquidated or distributed for relief in 1931 and 1932.

The total expenditures of the Hoover Administration upon relief of agriculture were about $775,000,000 outside of the hundreds of millions of credits extended through the Intermediate Credit Banks, the Reconstruction Finance Corporation, the Agricultural Credit Banks and the Federal Land Banks, all of which bore a Federal responsibility. Of the $775,000,000 mentioned, $125,000,000 was recoverable from the Land Banks, and sundry advances for seed, etc., were or are recoverable to the extent of about $75,000,000. Of the $500,000,000 expended through the Farm Board, some $200,000,000 were loans to Farm Co-operatives since recovered. The remaining Farm Board expenditures have been much misrepresented. Of the commodities bought by Co-operatives which were ultimately taken over by the Farm Board, wheat and cotton costing over $125,000,000 were used for relief and were credited to the Farm Board at much lower prices. Moreover, wheat and cotton held by the Farm Board at the end of the Hoover Administration were at once thrown into the market at bottom prices. Ninety days later, prices of wheat and cotton were doubled by devaluation and thus some $50,000,000 were recklessly thrown away. The real loss to the Government on all these operations, had they been intelligently liquidated, would have been probably under $150,000,000 if relief commodities had been charged at cost including losses on recoverable loans.

LONG–VIEW AGRICULTURAL POLICIES

The problem of long-view agricultural policies was constantly before the administration. The Farm Board experiment was originally based on the expansion of farmer-controlled marketing machinery, 20 per cent of farm products being marketed this way. The idea was that if the large majority of any one crop could be marketed through one agency and that controlled by farmers, it could so regulate the flow to market and so increase the farmers' collective bargaining power as to bring about great improvement. The basis of these policies was cut off by the collapse before it could be properly organized and developed. The Farm Board had to turn to emergency action.

DEVELOPMENT OF LAND USE PROGRAM

In the meantime Secretary Hyde had undertaken to work out some more effective basis of agricultural action that would get the Government out of the markets and assure some permanent outlook for the farmer.

The Secretary developed a new dominant approach to the whole problem: *i.e.,* from the point of view not of marketing problems but of land use.

Secretary Arthur M. Hyde on Nov. 24, 1931 called a nation-wide conference on land utilization. In his address to that conference he outlined the tentative administration conclusions as follows:

"We have made, over the last ten years, a good many studies of the national problem of land use. The object of this conference is to get all these studies out in the open."

"Our research has been largely upon the problems of production. We know far too little about what to produce, how much to produce."

"The cure for overproduction is production balanced to market demand. This is our fundamental problem. If we decline to attempt to solve that problem by law, or by shotgun methods, what way is left to us? There is a way. It is not easy, but it will work—and work without a raid on our ideas of liberty, property rights, and common sense. That is the method of voluntary control of production through farmer-owned, farmer-controlled co-operative associations."

"The economic definition of submarginal land is a slippery, elusive thing. The definition from a social point of view is simple enough. It is land on which no farmer, however skillful, can support a decent standard of living. It is the old, old, tragic story of someone trying to get bread out of a stone."

"Such, stated in economic terms, is the hideous cycle. Stated in terms of human values, of high hopes and bitter disappointment, of unrequited labor, of wasted lives, of men and women broken against hard conditions, of children denied a chance in the world, it states a tragedy to the poignancy of which we have become calloused."

"In one Great Lake state, in 1927, 2,600,000 acres were sold for taxes. Two-thirds of the land thus sold reverted to the counties. In another state a few years back, three farms per day were falling into the hands of the state for unpaid taxes. In one Eastern state, farms have been abandoned at the annual rate of 272,000 acres since 1920."

"Within the past few years many millions of acres of farm lands have been abandoned or sold for taxes. Many more millions of acres have been sold under foreclosure of mortgages. Many irrigation and drainage districts have fallen into financial difficulty."

"A proper land policy would approach such problems sympathetically with a view to helping maintain the economic community life while pointing to such reorganization as would make it better."

"Such a policy will deal not alone with areas which lack in fertility, but also with the best farming areas we have. Even on good land, some farms are submarginal because conditions have produced a size and type of organization unsuited to economic conditions."

"High taxes, high rentals, and high wages, are, for the most part, passed on by industry to be paid by the consumer. They are elements of production cost which the consumer must pay. Farmers, along with others, pay a part of these charges in the form of higher prices for goods and services. Land is the principal part of the valuation of farm property. Unless the farmer can sell his products at a profit, he cannot pass the taxes on to the consumer."

"Thus the farmer has been caught between the upper and the nether millstones of mounting tax levies on the one hand and low income on the other. These have caused a serious decline in land values which has not only reduced the farmers' equity but also made it difficult in many instances to renew mortgage loans. Taxes, after all, are the first lien on the land."

"Any program, to be sound as well as humane, must be elastic. In that program, the problems of submarginal land and the closely allied taxation question must be considered. Whatever the solution may prove to be, it should approach helpfully the problems of both the farms and the local communities dependent upon them. No violent shift of the population or of land use is desirable or possible. No modern hegira is being planned. Yet some action is imperative, for there is nothing economically sound or socially desirable in producing crops to sell always at a loss. Such production exacts an enormous toll in living standards at the expense of helpless women and children."

"The answer to the problem of submarginal lands is purchase and reforestation by the Government. There probably are areas which possess so high a value for national uses that they should be acquired. National uses, under our present policy, include watershed protection, national forests, parks, and game preserves. Possibly sound policy would include acquisition to stop erosion and to conserve the soil for future generations. There are other areas in which the continuance of the economic life of whole communities depends upon the maintenance of some national resource, such as forests, which provides raw materials and employment to farmers and workmen in small towns."

"There is probably more hope of success in slamming shut a few doors through which expansion is flowing than there is in the recapture of acreage. Most of the expansion takes place in four directions—drainage, irrigation, clearing of forests, and dry-land farming. The extent of that expansion is not generally recognized. There are both dynamite and enlightenment in the statistics, taken from the Fifteenth Census, that there were 84,000 fewer farms in 1930 than in 1925, but there were 15,000,000 more acres in crops. This in five years, and the last five years at that. There are both pathos and problems in the fact that the 366,000,000 acres planted in crops in 1930 was 55,000,000 acres more than our cultivated area in 1909, and larger than the war-time peak of 1919."

"We must start sometime. No program which we can conceive will immediately cure the present emergency. A long-time land-use program cannot write an immediate answer to the present emergency, but the present emergency emphasizes the immediate need for a long-time program. If we had begun even so short a time as 20 years ago—before the expansion of our cultivated area by 55,000,000 acres—how much of tragedy and distress might have been prevented. If we could have prevented the entry of the submarginal portion of those 55,000,000 acres, or could have held in abeyance such portion as was not economically needed, what a different story we could write for American agriculture."

"But it is no less vital that the Nation, in the interest of a profitable agriculture and a balanced national life, shall promote a wise utilization of our resources. Our traditional national policy of planless agricultural development should be replaced without delay by a program based upon such a utilization of our land resources as will yield greater economic and social values, will stay erosion and soil depletion, will preserve and conserve our land inheritance, and limit our agricultural plant to such size as will supply the Nation's needs, without the ruinous blight of overproduction."

"We have come now to the time when we should write a new epic—the epic of adjustments, of regrouping, of retirement from cultivation of lands which the pioneer subdued, but which stub-

bornly refuse to yield to his grandchildren a reasonable stand-
dard of living, of developing parts of our great patrimony and
conserving other parts; in short, the epic of conserving a hard-
working, God-fearing, agricultural people—proud to be, as in
fact they always have been, the mainstay of a great people,
the nursery of a great race."

The conference reached conclusions as to retirement of marginal land, soil conservation, new crops and other vital problems of land utilization.

At the President's instance, the Republican Party's platform
of June, 1932, embraced the following statement upon land use:

"The fundamental problem of American agriculture is the control of
production to such volume as will balance supply with demand. In the
solution of this problem the co-operative organization of farmers to plan
production and the tariff, to hold the home market for American farmers,
are vital elements. A third element equally as vital is the control of the
acreage of land under cultivation, as an aid to the efforts of the farmer
to balance production."

"We favor a national policy of land utilization which looks to national
needs, such as the administration has already begun to formulate. Such
a policy must foster reorganization of taxing units in areas beset by tax
delinquency, and divert lands that are submarginal for crop production
to other uses. The national welfare plainly can be served by the acquisition of submarginal lands for water shed protection, grazing, forestry,
public parks, and game reserves. We favor such acquisitions."

THE PROGRAM OF 1932

At Des Moines on October 4, 1932, Hoover delivered an
address upon the agricultural policies of his administration:

"I am glad, a son of the soil of this state, to come back to where I
was born and where I spent the first ten years of my boyhood. My
parents and grandparents came to Iowa in the covered wagon—pioneers
in this community. They lie buried in your soil. They broke the prairie
into homes of independent living. They worshipped God, they did their
duty to their neighbors. They toiled to bring to their children greater
comfort, better education, and to open to them a wider opportunity than
theirs."

". . . Seldom in our history have we gone through greater dangers, or have the difficulties before the Nation been of such gravity. They attain this gravity not only because of the unprecedented dislocation in our domestic life but because our problems are world-wide."

". . . the result of a terrific eruption in civilization itself. Something infinitely deeper and of greater portent has happened to the world than any reaction from our own reckless speculation and exploitation. We are contending today with forces at home and abroad which still threaten the safety of civilization."

"You can test the part which the Great War played in the difficulties in your home and their relation to the gravity of the situation today right at your own doors."

"You will recollect that the values of your land doubled and trebled under the transitory demands of the Great War. You will recollect the expansion of mortgages, the collapse in values immediately thereafter, the doubling of taxation, the aftermaths of all which are still a part of your problems. You know the stifling of your markets from the collapse of other nations under the calamities they have inherited from the War."

"We have fought an unending war against the effect of these calamities upon our people. This is no time to recount the battles on a thousand fronts. We have fought the good fight to protect our people in a thousand cities from hunger and cold."

"We have carried on an unceasing campaign to protect the Nation from that unhealing class bitterness which arises from strikes and lock-outs and industrial conflict. We have accomplished this through the willing agreement of employer and labor which placed humanity before money through the sacrifice of profits and dividends before wages."

"We have defended millions from the tragic result of droughts."

"We have mobilized a vast expansion of public construction to make work for the unemployed."

"We fought the battle to balance the budget."

"We have defended the country from being forced off the gold standard, with its crushing effect upon all who are in debt."

"We have battled to provide a supply of credits to merchants and farmers and industries."

"We have fought to retard falling prices."

"We have struggled to save homes and farms from foreclosure of mortgages, battled to save millions of depositors and borrowers from the ruin caused by the failure of banks, fought to assure the safety of millions of policy holders from failure of their insurance companies,

and fought to save commerce and employment from the failure of railways."

"All these battles, related and unrelated, have had a single strategy
and a single purpose. That was to protect your living, your comfort,
and the safety of your fireside. They have been waged and have succeeded in protecting you from infinitely greater harm which could have
come to you."

"Thousands of our people in their bitter distress and losses today are
saying that 'things could not be worse.' No person who has any remote
understanding of the forces which confronted this country during these
last eighteen months ever utters that remark. Had it not been for the
immediate and unprecedented actions of our Government things would
be infinitely worse today."

"Let no man tell you that it could not be worse. It could be so much
worse that these days now, distressing as they are, would look like
veritable prosperity."

"Many of these battles have had to be fought in silence, without the
cheers of the limelight or the encouragement of public support, because
the very disclosure of the forces opposed to us would have undermined
the courage of the weak and induced panic in the timid, which would
have destroyed the very basis of success."

"Hideous misrepresentation and unjustified complaint had to be accepted in silence. It was as if a great battle in war should be fought
without public knowledge of any incident except the stream of dead and
wounded from the front. There has been much of tragedy, but there
has been but little public evidence of the dangers and enormous risks
from which a great national victory has been achieved."

"I have every confidence that the whole American people know in
their hearts that there has been but one test in my mind, one supreme
object in the measures and policies we have forged to win in this war
against depression: that test was the interest of the people in the homes
and at the firesides of our country. I have had before me but one vision:
that is, the vision of the millions of homes of the sort which I knew
as a boy in this state."   [*State Papers, Vol. II, p. 293*]

After sketching the great financial crisis that swept from
Europe and the measures taken to protect America, the President continued:

"Of vital concern to you are the difficulties of agriculture. They have been of vital concern to me for the whole of these difficult years. I have been at the post to which the first news of every disaster is delivered, to which no detail of human suffering is spared. I have heard the cries of distress, and not only as a sympathetic listener but as one oppressed by a deep sense of responsibility to do all that human ingenuity could devise."

"I wish to speak directly to those of my hearers who are farmers of what is on my mind, of what is in my heart, to tell you the conclusions I have reached from this bitter experience of the years in dealing with these problems which affect agriculture at home and their relations to foreign countries."

"That agriculture is prostrate needs no proof. You have saved and economized and worked to reduce costs, but with all this, yours is a story of distress and suffering."

"What the farmer wants and needs is higher prices, and in the meantime to keep from being dispossessed from his farm, to have a fighting chance to keep his home. The pressing question is how these two things are to be attained. Every decent citizen wants to see the farmer receive higher prices and wants to see him hold his home. Every citizen realizes that the general recovery of the country cannot be attained unless these things are secured to the farmer."

"Every thinking citizen knows that most of these low price levels and most of this distress, except in one or two commodities where there is an unwieldy surplus, are due to the decreased demand for farm products by our millions of unemployed and by foreign countries. Every citizen knows that part of this unemployment is due to the inability of the farmer to buy the products of the factory. Every thinking citizen knows that the farmer, the worker, and the business man are in the same boat and must all come to shore together."

"Every citizen who stretches his vision across the United States realizes that for the last three years we have been on this downward spiral owing to the destructive forces which I have already described. If he has this vision, he today takes courage and hope because he also knows that these destructive forces have been stopped; that the spiral is moving upward; that more men are being employed and are able to consume more agricultural products."

"The policies of the Republican Party and the unprecedented instrumentalities and measures which we have put in motion, many of which are designed directly for agriculture—they are winning out. If we continue to fight along these lines we shall win."

"1. The very basis of safety to American agriculture is the protective tariff on farm products."

"The Republican Party originated and proposes to maintain the protective tariff on agricultural products. We will even widen that tariff further where necessary to protect agriculture. Ninety per cent of your market is at home, and I propose to reserve this market to the American farmer."

"When you return to your homes you can compare prices with foreign countries and count up this proposed destruction at your own firesides. There are this minute 2,000,000 cattle in the northern states of Mexico seeking market. The price is about $2.50 per 100 pounds on the south bank of the Rio Grande. It is $4.50 on the north bank—and only the tariff wall between."

"Bad as our prices are, if we take comparable prices of farm products today in the United States and abroad, I am informed by the Department of Agriculture that you will find that except for the guardianship of the tariff, butter could be imported for 25 per cent below your prices, pork products for 30 per cent below your prices, lamb and beef products from 30 to 50 per cent below your prices, flaxseed for 35 per cent below your prices, beans for 40 per cent below your prices, and wool 30 per cent below your prices. Both corn and wheat could be sold in New York from the Argentine at prices below yours at this moment were it not for the tariff. . . ."

"The removal of or reduction of the tariff on farm products means a flood of them into the United States from every direction, and either you would be forced to still further reduce your prices, or your products would rot on your farms."

"The main thing these foreign countries want is entrance for their surplus agricultural products into our markets. Many of these countries would decrease their tariffs against our industrial goods tomorrow in exchange for reduction on their farm products, but that is no help to our farmers."

"The Democratic Party proposes that they would enter into bargaining tariffs to secure special concessions from other countries. They represent this to be in the farmer's interest. But I may tell you here and now that the largest part of the whole world desires to make only one bargain with the United States. The bargain these countries wish to make is to lower our tariff on agricultural products in exchange for lowering their tariffs on our industrial goods. . . ."

"All tariff acts contain injustices and inequities. That is the case with the last tariff bill. Some people get too much and some too little. . . . I secured in the last tariff act, twenty-five years after it had originally been advocated by President Theodore Roosevelt, the adoption of effective flexible tariff provisions to be administered by a bipartisan body. . . ."

"By maintaining that reform the country need no longer be faced with heartbreaking, log-rolling selfishness and greed which come to the surface on every occasion when Congress revises the tariff. . . ."

"What the Democratic Party proposes is to reduce your farm tariffs. Aside from ruin to agriculture, such an undertaking in the midst of this depression will disturb every possibility of recovery."

"2. Four years ago organized agriculture requested the passage of an agricultural marketing act. I called a special session of Congress to pass such an act and increase tariffs on farm products. A distinguished board of men recommended by organized agriculture was appointed to administer the act. Those portions of the board's activities which directed themselves to the support and expansion of co-operative marketing organizations have proved of great benefit to the farmer. Today over a million farm families participate in the benefits which flow from it."

"I wish to state frankly the difficulties that have arisen under some other portions of the act. They arise mostly from the so-called stabilization provisions, which never were and are not now the major purpose of the Farm Board. Even indirect purchase and sale of commodities is absolutely opposed to my theory of government."

"When the panic struck agricultural prices the Board determined that unless the markets were supported hundreds of thousands of farmers would be bankrupt by the sale of their products at less than the money they had already borrowed upon them, that a thousand country banks would likely be closed, and that a general panic was possible."

"As a result of these emergency purchases the prices of farm commodities were temporarily held and their fall cushioned. The farmers secured hundreds of millions of dollars of income which they would not otherwise have received."

"3. For several years the United States Department of Agriculture has studied the complex social and economic problems which lie embedded in the general problem of land use. About a year ago these studies had reached such a point that the Secretary of Agriculture felt justified in calling a conference of economists, farm leaders, agricultural college authorities, to formulate practical means of action. The broad objective of such a program is to promote the reorganization of agriculture so as to divert lands from unprofitable to profitable use, and to avoid the cultivation of lands the chief return of which is the poverty and misery of those who live upon them. The Republican platform contains a plank which constitutes the first declaration upon this subject. I shall be happy to support a sound program."

"4. Four years ago, in this state, I gave assurance to the farmers that one of the first policies of my administration would be the vigorous prosecution and completion of the inland waterway system and advancement of the Great Lakes-St. Lawrence seaway as a fundamental relief to agriculture by cheaper transportation. I am glad to report to you that more than twice the amount of work has been done on the waterways in the last three years than in any similar period in the history of the United States. I am also glad to report that after twenty years of discussion, examination and intermittent negotiation a treaty has been signed with Canada which only awaits ratification of the United States Senate and the Dominion Parliament for us to undertake that great contribution to the strengthening of Midwest agriculture in reaching out to world markets."

"5. We have suffered from unprecedented droughts both to the north and south of you. Some other sections were unable to obtain credit for seed and feed for live stock. Through various Government agencies loans to the amount of $120,000,000 have been made to 900,000 of our families to rehabilitate their production and ameliorate these conditions. Some of these families are in difficulties in making immediate repayment because of demoralized prices. I have seen to it that they are not unduly pressed."

"6. Last April I delivered an address to the conference of the governors of the various states. I stated in effect that the most inflexible tax in our country is the tax on land and on real property. It is the least adaptable to the varying income of the taxpayers. I stated that in the present situation the taxes upon farms and homes have become almost unbearable, that such taxes are wholly out of proportion to other forms of taxes."

"I stated then emphatically that there is no farm relief more needed today than readjustment of land taxes."

"I announced last April that I would call tax experts of the Nation together to determine methods we should pursue. I shall do so as soon as the national election is out of the way, and I shall then recommend methods to Congress."

"7. The very first necessity to prevent collapse and secure recovery in agriculture has been to keep open to the farmer the banking and other sources from which to make short-term loans for planting, harvesting, feeding live stock, and other production necessities. That has been accomplished indirectly in a large measure through the increased authority to the Federal Reserve system and its expansion of credits, and indirectly through the Reconstruction Corporation loans to your banks. It has been aided directly through the Intermediate Credit banks and through the ten new Agricultural Credit institutions which alone can command over $300,000,000 credit and which are now being erected in all parts of the country."

"We are thus rapidly everywhere restoring normal short-term credits to agriculture."

"8. In another direction upon my recommendation the Reconstruction Corporation has been authorized to make credit available to processors to purchase and carry their usual stocks of agricultural products and thus relieve a burden which was resting upon farm prices because the farmer was forced to carry these stocks. But even more important than this, at my recommendation the Reconstruction Corporation has been authorized to make credits available for sales of farm products in new markets abroad. This is today and will, with increasing activity, extend immediate markets in relief of farmers and the prices of products."

"9. The mortgage situation—that is, long-term credits—is one of our most difficult problems. On October 6 a year ago, I secured and published an undertaking from the leaders of both political parties that we should extend aid to this situation. In December we appropriated $125,-000,000 directly to increase the capital of the Federal land banks, and we provided further capital through authority that the Reconstruction Corporation should purchase the bonds of these banks. The purpose was to enable the Federal land banks to expand their activities and to give humane and constructive consideration to those indebted to them who were in difficulties. In the large sense it has pursued this policy. A little over 1 per cent of the farms held under mortgage by the Federal land bank system today are under foreclosure, and these are mostly cases where men wished to give up."

"The character of the organization of the Joint Stock land banks whose business methods are not controlled by the Federal Farm Loan

Board has resulted in disastrous and unjust pressure for payments in some of these banks. The basis of that organization should be remedied. We have sought to further aid the whole mortgage situation by loans from the Reconstruction Corporation to banks, mortgage companies, and insurance companies to enable them to show consideration to their farmer borrowers. As a result of these actions hundreds of thousands of foreclosures have been prevented."

"But despite the relief afforded by these measures, the mortgage situation has become more acute. There must be more effective relief. In it lies a primary social problem."

"I conceive that in this civilization of ours, and more particularly under our distinctive American system, there is one primary necessity to its permanent success. That is, we must build up men and women in their own homes, on their own farms, where they may find their own security and express their own individuality."

". . . And for prompt and practical action I have, during the last month, secured definite and positive steps in co-ordination of the policies not only of the Federal agencies but of the important private mortgage agencies as well. These agencies have undertaken to give their help."

"But further and more definitely than this I shall propose to Congress at the next session that we further reorganize the Federal land banks and give to them the resources and liberty of action necessary to enable them definitely and positively to expand in the refinancing of the farm-mortgage situation where it is necessary to give men who want to fight for it a chance to hold their homes."

"10. I cannot overemphasize the importance of the element of world stability in the recovery and expansion of our agricultural markets. This involves the promotion of good will, of disarmament, and of maintained peace. It requires the rebuilding of the credit structure within nations which have been forced off the gold standard or compelled to restrict exchange. Until that is done there is a definite blockade upon the movement of commodities and upon the market for your products. We have given aid in these things. That we may get to grips with these questions in the interest of our agriculture and our industry and in the interest of world progress, I am participating in the organization of a world economic conference to be held late this year. Every intelligence the world can command will be concentrated on the rehabilitation of economic stability."

"I shall send a representative of agriculture as a member of that world economic conference."

"11. And in connection with agriculture, I may mention the question of war debts. I do not approve cancellation of these debts. I certainly do not approve the proposal of our opponents to lower our tariffs in order that by profits gained from a flood of goods into the United States this debt should be transferred to our workers by putting them out of employment and to our farmers by forcing their produce to rot in their barns."

"In my acceptance address I stated the exact reverse of this proposal. I said:

"'If for some particular annual payment we are offered some other tangible form of compensation such as the expansion of markets for American agriculture, and labor, and the restoration and maintenance of our prosperity, then I am sure our citizens would consider such a proposal.'"

"I am prepared to go farther. I am prepared to recommend that any annual payment on the foreign debt be used for the specific purpose of securing an expansion of the foreign markets for American agricultural products. There is justice in that for the difficulties inherited from the War are part of your difficulties today. That is a proposal of more importance to the farmer than any panacea."

"12. In the advancement of agricultural prices from the depression the first fortress to take and hold was the increased tariffs on farm products. There will be an immediate decrease in prices if these tariffs are reduced as our opponents propose. The next move in the battle for improved prices was to stop the general deflation. By deflation I mean the lessening of market values and prices for land, products of the land, manufacturers and all securities. That battle has been won. The next attack on this front is to reverse these processes of deflation and bring things back to their real values. That battle is in progress."

"The Government is giving aid by its vast constructive program for agriculture, for commerce, and for industry. Through the renewed flow of credit for industry and by direct measures of employment, by the great co-operative movements which we have instituted in commerce and industry, for attacks all along the line, we are returning men to work. Every new man re-employed is a greater purchaser of farm products. Wherever we properly can, without entangling ourselves in political difficulties abroad, we are joining for the rehabilitation of the world and thereby the foreign markets for agricultural products. I come to you with no economic patent medicine especially compounded for farmers. I refuse to offer counterfeit currency or false hopes. I will not make any pledge to you which I cannot fulfill."

"As I have stated before, in the shifting battle against depression, we shall need to adopt new measures and new tactics as the battle moves on. The essential thing is that we should build soundly and solidly for the future. My solicitude and willingness to advance and protect the interests of agriculture is shown by the record. Protection and advancement of this industry will have my continued deepest concern, for in it lies the progress of all America. It was in this industry that I was born."

"The battle against depression is making progress. We are still faced with forces which render 10,000,000 men idle and agriculture prostrate. We have forged new weapons, we have turned the tide from defense to attack. I shall continue the fight. It calls for that co-operation, that courage, that patience and fortitude with which our fathers conquered these prairies."

"In conclusion, my friends, there are many other subjects of vast importance to our country. The farmers of America are not selfishly interested in their own industry alone. They are Americans with the same concern for the welfare of the Nation in its multitude of other problems, both at home and abroad. Time does not permit of their exposition tonight. The issues are grave, the stake is great."

"These issues rise above the concern of an ordinary campaign. Our cause is not alone the restoration of prosperity. It is to soundly and sanely correct the weaknesses in our system which this depression has brought to the surface. It is the maintenance of courageous integrity in political action and in Government. It is the holding of this Nation to the principles and ideals which it has had from the beginning. It is to make free men and women."

"Finally, let me deal for a moment with the ultimate realities. I have had to describe the complicated processes of currencies and taxation and other such dreary things. They are but the tools we use to manage the processes by which we answer the old, old question, wherewithal shall we live? They are necessary tools, but they are not an end in themselves. Our toils and cares are for a higher purpose."

"We are not a nation of 120,000,000 solitary individuals, we are a nation of 25,000,000 families dwelling in 25,000,000 homes, each warmed by the fires of affection and cherishing within it a mutual solicitude for kinfolk and children. Their safety is what we are really striving for. Their happiness is our true concern. Our most solemn hope for them is that they may share richly in a spiritual life as well, that puts them not only at peace with their fellows but also in harmony with the will of a beneficent Providence."

"Out of our strivings for material blessings must come safety for homes and schools and churches and holding of national ideals, the forming of national character. These are the real aspirations of our people. These are the promises of America, and those promises must be fulfilled."

[*State Papers, Vol. II, pp. 307–17*]

After the election, the President tried to get the immediate application of some parts of the Land Use program. In a Message to the Congress on February 20, 1933, he said:

"Pending the return of the great commercial countries to the gold standard and the consequent increase in world consumption and thus rise in world prices, it is essential temporarily to reduce farm production so as to remove the backbreaking surpluses of agricultural products and thus to raise agricultural income. The plan proposed by the Secretary of Agriculture some time since for temporary leasing of marginal lands is the least harmful and the most hopeful of all the plans which have been proposed. It has the merit of direct action in reducing supply to demand and thus unquestionably increasing prices; it would affect all farm products; give equal benefits to all farmers; is free of increased bureaucracy; very much less costly; and could be covered by a manufacturers' excise tax of probably 1 per cent to 2 per cent upon these commodities. It would also largely eliminate the tax and interest problems which the Congress is seeking to solve at much greater cost."

[*State Papers, Vol. II, p. 598*]

On January 16, 1936, Hoover spoke at Lincoln, Nebraska, in a general review of his own agricultural policies and those of the New Deal:

"The causes of the farmer's troubles must be honestly faced if we are to have common-sense remedy. Economic patent medicines require no diagnosis except decision that the patient is in pain."

"The difficulties of our agriculture came mainly from the War and its hectic aftermaths. Wars always do that to the farmer. Demoralization lasted twenty years after the Napoleonic Wars and a dozen years after our own Civil War."

"I am glad that the President at last admits that the War had something to do with the farm depression. At Chicago, on December 9, 1935, he says, in referring to farm prosperity in the period before the War: 'They were the last years before the world-wide disturbance, caused by the World War, took place in our economic life.' I had been told so often by the New Deal that I did it that I had given up hope of salvation. I feel better."

"The dislocation of wars and slumps hits the farmer harder than any other group. Farm prices are more sensitive to these shocks than wages and industrial prices. All parts of the economic system inevitably come back into balance with time. But farm recovery is longer drawn out. That is the higher economics of it."

"The painful symptom of it appears in the farmer's pocket in the slump of purchasing power of his dollar. Many farmers cannot hold on against these delays in readjustment. I have held that we cannot see the capable and industrious driven from their homes during these periods if they want to make a fight for them. That is the humanity of it."

"There is at least one hopeful aspect of these war causes of the farmer's difficulties. They do not last forever. Many of our measures can be of emergency character. Recovery will cure many difficulties—that is, if it is allowed by the New Deal to come."

"When the world depression was turned, in June and July, 1932, agricultural prices rose in a start toward equality with industrial prices. The farmer's dollar improved more than 20 per cent. Prices were moving into a natural relation again. Then came the era of the Great Fear. Fright over the coming of the New Deal skidded the country into the money and bank panic. The President said 'the mechanics of civilization had come to a dead stop.' Many a driver who has had a bad skid thinks that. Then began the magic of the New Deal. And they repeated each mistake of the Farm Board and added a big idea. That big idea is that you can catch an economic force with a policeman."

"Incidentally the culmination of that era of Great Fear is the convenient starting point for all the President's comparative statistics. He chooses the low point of quotation induced by their own actions. If he would go back a few months into 1932, before the Great Fear started, he would find the prices were 80 to 100 per cent higher than those he quotes. And they were in 100-cent dollars. And even then they were only at the turning of the greatest depression in history. His quotations look like an effort to warm the Nation over cold glass chunks in an illuminated grate."

"Things have been done to the farmer by the New Deal which do not relate alone to agriculture."

"Firstly, this torrent of wasteful spending, unbalanced budget and debt will be paid by the farmer as well as all others. It will blight all his days with anxiety. The farmer pays for it not alone in direct taxes, but hidden taxes are wrapped in everything he buys. The farmer in fact pays in larger measure than any other group because he buys not alone for his family but also for his farm and is less able than any other production group to mark up the prices of his products and pass these taxes on to the consumer. Moreover, about one-quarter of the $14,000,000,000 of probable increased New Deal debt will rest on the farm as a super-mortgage. Blessed are the young, for they shall inherit the national debt."

"Secondly, the present policies of paying for the New Deal by credit inflation produce stock booms that are a great dole for the 'money changers.' President Roosevelt, on July 24, 1933, stated that we cannot attain prosperity 'in a nation half-boom and half-broke.' The New Deal has attained just that. That half-boom is on in the Stock Exchange, the farmers are half-broke—and the 20,000,000 on relief are fully broke. These credit booms add little to farm prices. When they crack they throw the farmer in the ditch."

"There is a thirdly, on currency policies. There is a fourthly, on making the farmers pay for a large part of the Social Security Act and receiving little benefits. There is a fifthly, on relief policies which make it impossible for farmers to get labor in the midst of unemployment. There is a sixthly and a seventhly, on some other white rabbits. All of them make farm thinking difficult and intense. I do not have the time to discuss them all now."

"If we are now to deal competently with farm relief we must examine the experience with the New Deal farm masures. There are proved dangrs which must be avoided. I nother words, what have these New Deal principles done to the farmer?"

"President Roosevelt on one occasion said: 'I like to think of the AAA not as a temporary means . . . but as an expression of principle.' From their practical works, irrespective of their words, the main principle is the economy of scarcity based on control of production enforced by telling the farmer what he can plant."

"The largest justification has been that it has raised prices. Prices have improved. I leave you three thoughts on that subject: First: The inflation of the dollar, the drought, and world recovery would have made higher prices in any event. Second: *The Chicago Tribune* is authority for the statement that the farmer's income from many uncontrolled commodities has been greater in proportion than from those which have had the attention of the New Deal. President Roosevelt on May 30, 1935, prophesied that 'if we abandon crop control wheat will immediately drop to 36 cents a bushel and cotton to 5 cents a pound.' He felt the same about hogs. I do not know how long a time there is in 'immediately.' It is more than a week. Third: At the same time another principle of the New Deal was to lift wages and industrial prices. The sum of these two principles is that the farmer has less to sell and pays more for what he buys. Labor pays for it in increased cost of living. By this device we have got the Economic Dog running around in circles chasing his tail."

"We may explore the effect of the processing tax in case some one might suggest we try it again. In early 1933 President-elect Roosevelt expressed himself as horrified and directed the defeat of my proposal to the Democratic Congress to balance the budget by a manufacturers' sales tax of 2½ per cent. My proposal exempted food and cheaper clothing. We did that in order that we should not impose the burden upon the poor. Yet, as President Roosevelt, he places a manufacturers' sales tax of 25 per cent on pork, and 30 per cent on flour, both absolute essentials to the poor. That blow at the poor was no doubt softened by calling it a 'processing' tax. The implication was that some wicked middleman would pay it. The housewife rebelled at this more abundant life. One result of it was that the consumption of food in 1935 fell below the worst year, 1932, by the product of over 15,000,000 acres."

"We may explore what these New Deal principles did to our export and import market. You will remember that 1932 was the year when 'it could not be worse.' So we will take that worst year and compare it with the New Deal year of 1935. From that worst year exports of cotton have decreased 4,250,000 bales; our grain 93,000,000 bushels; our animal products by 500,000,000 pounds. This is estimated to be the product of about 20,000,000 acres. But, worse than that, this greatest food-producing country on earth has imported this year about 100,000,-000 bushels of grain, 700,000,000 pounds of animal products, and increased its imports of vegetable oils to be used as substitutes by another 700,000,000 pounds. It would take another probable 15,000,000 acres to produce these imports. The Secretary of Agriculture says America must choose one of three courses in foreign trade. The three are various degrees of the theory of more industrial imports in order that the American farmer may sell more to foreign countries. But what he produced was a fourth choice; that is, to give the foreign farmer the American farmer's market."

"From all this decrease in home consumption and shift in foreign trade the farmer has lost the market for more acres than the whole New Deal curtailment of 50,000,000 fertile acres. Is that not the principle of the Economic Dog chasing his tail?"

"On January 10 President Roosevelt declared himself in opposition to 'shipping our soil fertility to foreign nations.' The logical conclusion of all that is to stop exports altogether. There is a futility here somewhere.

The idea is that we encourage imports of industrial products and create unemployment at home. We are told we must do this in order that the farmer may export his products. Now we are told that it is not to our advantage to export farm products at all. He overlooks the fact that we can manufacture synthetic fertilizers to any amount necessary to cover export of 'soil fertility.' "

"In May, 1932, when I vetoed a bill for reciprocal tariff treaties, I stated that most of such treaties would sacrifice the American farmer. The New Deal method of testing poison is apparently to make the Nation swallow it. By just these reciprocal treaties the American market is today being opened to farmers of Cuba, Canada, Spain, and Italy. Yet under these principles farmers are told they must allow fertile acres to be idle because there is no market for their products. It is very confusing. The Economic Dog whirls even faster under this stimulus."

"We must explore as to where we get to when we start controlling crops. This principle of scarcity gets scarcer and scarcer. The moment one farm product was regimented, another had to be mobilized to prevent the farmers' energy from going into that. So we marched from seven controlled commodities in May, 1933, to five more in April, 1934, another in May, 1934, and finally we come to potatoes in 1935. Moreover, these measures are moving steadily to more and more coercion and less rain of checks—as witness the Cotton and the Potato Acts. As I read further and further into the 6250 verboten words of the potato law, I realized that one of the impulses to cheerfulness was about to be mashed out of American life. The potato had yielded not only food, but it had radiated humor to our daily conversation. It was once the happiest of all the vegetables. Its life would have been saddened by the bootlegger, the passive resister, and the Federal inspectors. Confined to a package by law, its eyes would have been dimmed by the alphabetical revenue stamps it must bear."

"One of the assured principles of New Deal farming is politics. One would think in the thunders of idealism that have accompanied Planned Agriculture it would be clean of politics. I have but one comment. That is to read two lines from a letter I hold written by a high officer in the AAA to a gentleman who spent his life in scientific work for the farmer and who was accepted for appointment in that service. It says, '. . . it will be necessary [for you] to secure political clearance, which means a letter of approval from the Democratic National Committee in California.' The Department of Agriculture was wholly under merit service before this sort of idealists got it. The execution of these principles required 120,000 part- or full-time Federal officials. Their pay was assessed against the farmers. This new breed of middlemen every day tried hard to bring agriculture into balance with politics."

"We may explore the effect of this economy of scarcity and crop control upon employment. For instance, the reduction of cotton by 10,000,-000 acres is producing a hideous poverty in the share croppers of the South. It is creating unemployment all over the Nation of some hundreds of thousands of agricultural laborers, railway men, and others who formerly lived by producing and handling the 20,000,000 tons of agricultural products that could come from the acres forced to idleness."

"And above all other consequences, the whole notion of regimenting the farmer under bureaucracy was the negation of the free American spirit. The system of scarcity was being applied to human freedom."

"Does all this corroborate President Roosevelt's indication on December 9 at Chicago that agriculture is 'making great strides' toward a 'balance either within itself or with industry and business?' If so, it was a juggler's balance."

"Finally—Does anybody believe that this flimsy structure under agriculture, of regimenting men, of putting fertile acres out of action, of giving American markets to foreigners, and levying its cost on the poor would not have fallen of its own weight, even without the Supreme Court?"

"We may now explore some of the roads to relief."

"And every country, including ourselves, has adopted measure after measure to protect the farmer and to speed a return to stability. Other nations tried most of the New Deal measures before the New Deal was born. From all this experience we should by now have learned some lessons in what is harmful, what is futile, and what will help."

"We shall be less than intelligent, and we shall be heartless of the farmers' problems if we do not distill from this wreckage of these experiments some lessons in truth. And there have been aids to recovery extended to the farmer both at home and abroad which have been successful. The first group of these aids is: Increase consumption of food by restoration of employment. That can come only with a balanced budget, stable currency and credit. Give the farmer our own home market. Adopt such sane national policies as will again restore reasonable export markets. Out of this group of policies we can restore demand to may millions of fertile acres."

"The second group of policies is: To retire submarginal lands where people cannot make a living. Do it in the more effective and humane way proposed by Secretary Hyde in 1932. Retard new reclamation projects until the land can be used."

"A third group of policies is: Encourage co-operative marketing and those marketing agreements which contribute to prevent gluts in the flow to markets. The farm credit machinery established by Republican administrations and improved by the New Deal should be still further improved."

"But beyond these measures this farm situation is now one where still further emergency measures pending general economic recovery are necessary. They are doubly necessary as a new road must be built by which agriculture can get back on to solid ground from the quicksand of the New Deal. We shall need to open our minds to further experiment."

"I suggest as one contribution to new methods that instead of trying to find a balance to agriculture by paying the farmer to curtail a crop, we should endeavor to expand another crop which can be marketed or which would improve the fertility of the soil. We import vast quantities of vegetable oils, sugar, and other commodities. There are industrial products that could be introduced by the American farmer. We need to replenish our soils with legumes and restore coverages. If we include this suggestion with the policies I have already mentioned, which would recover our lost acres from foreigners, we would be able to employ more than all the acres put out of action by the New Deal. We would reverse this economy of scarcity to an economy of plenty."

"This question of sustained fertility and better land use was brought to the forefront by former Governor Lowden in 1930. Nation-wide conferences under Secretary Hyde in 1932 further developed parts of this subject. The matter was still further advanced by the Republican side in the campaign of that year. These ideas have been further contributed to by many thinking men since that time. In order to secure these objectives I believe we must be prepared to subsidize directly such special crops until agriculture has again been brought into balance. At the end of such a road we could hope for a balanced agriculture in full production and increased fertility in our soils."

"I am advised that it can be done within the spirit as well as the letter of the Constitution."

"Since this paragraph was written these ideas have been discussed in Washington as a method of overcoming the debacle brought about by the New Deal. But if they are adopted it should be under certain fundamental safeguards. There should be no attempt to again impose New Deal ideas of controlling and regimenting the farmer or restricting production. He must be free of any restriction and control contracts. The farmer must be an entirely free man to use his own skill and judgment.

The administration of these methods should be handled by the Land Grant Colleges in order to free agriculture of politics and the vast bureaucracy now loaded upon the farmer. This work should be co-ordinated by a non-political national board. The cost should be borne by the general taxpayer and not loaded upon the poorest of the country through some tax like the processing tax. Otherwise this method will again be a subterfuge of pinkish National Planning under another alphabet."

"Somebody will shy at the blunt word 'subsidy.' And, in fact, the American people have been going all around Robin Hood's barn, rather than use it. Over a century ago we began it in canals and turnpikes; since then we have kept it up. Railroads, highways, ships and aviation, and silver mines and land reclamation—agriculture—we usually do it under some other name than subsidy. We had better begin to use straight words and we will act straight. A subsidy is a burden on the taxpayer, but it does not regiment or destroy the initiative or freedom of the receiver—it is to stimulate that."

"In conclusion may I offer a word of personal emotion. It lies far beyond the land of economics. I have spent years in public service in many countries during this most fateful period of human history. I saw as few men the backwash of war upon the common man of these countries. I saw at first hand revolution creeping in under promises of relief from the agonies of war destruction. I have seen the insidious destruction of liberty by propaganda. I have seen suffering humanity sacrifice that liberty, the greatest of all human achievements, for an illusion of security. The farmers of Russia supported the Bolsheviki against the new-born Democracy on the promise of the land. Today they have the choice of Siberia or the collectivist farms. I have seen freedom, the most priceless heritage, torn from children that this generation might escape its responsibilities. I wish to say to you unhesitatingly that our country has been following step by step the road through which these millions of people in foreign countries lost their liberties. Our farmers have had that blessing of individual liberty in greater fulness in their lives than any other part of even our own people. It was the farmers who fired the first shot at Lexington. It must be the farmers of America who defend that heritage. I ask you to stop, look, and listen."

TARIFF POLICIES

Hoover's tariff policies were ardently for protection of our workers and farmers from competition of the lower standards of living in foreign countries. He had seen their state of living. The Republican Party in its platform of 1928 was committed to increase of agricultural tariffs and a moderate revision of industrial tariffs. The public attitude was greatly influenced by the depression fall in prices and anxious for more protection.

Hoover was not an extremist. His basic tariff policy was to maintain duties that would represent "the difference in the cost of production at home and abroad." That basis maintained competition after American standards of living were taken into account. Hoover was probably the originator of this basis of tariff action.

Displeasure at this moderate position led to opposition to the President, by the Republican tariff extremists as well as the free traders. He did not believe in the tariff as an embargo or that it would cure chilblains, nor that free trade would do otherwise than demoralize the United States where cities, homes, schools and churches had been built around protection-industries and could not be moved elsewhere. Even if new industries could be built under the theory of free trade, it meant these people must be dispossessed of their living and skills with all the consequent misery and loss. He was keenly alive to the fact that the Democratic South, while professing free trade as a vote-catching device, was as keen for tariffs as any other part of the country.

Hoover's second policy in tariffs was that they should be placed in the hands of a bi-partisan Tariff Commission which should determine the rates based upon the cost of production and the difference at home and abroad. He had taken part in introducing a start toward such powers in the tariff of 1922. They were watered down till they were largely ineffective. As President he proposed to make them work and that the tariff should be made effectively flexible to changing time and circumstances; that it should be done in judicial form by open proceedings openly arrived at. He held that the greatest tariff reform was thus to get tariff-making out of politics and free the country from the orgy of greed which was witnessed at every legislative adjustment.

THE TARIFF LEGISLATION OF 1930

The misrepresentation of the Smoot-Hawley Tariff requires that its course and character should be shortly traced. In a Message to Congress on April 10, 1929, the President said:

"I have called this special session of Congress to redeem two pledges given in the last election—farm relief and limited changes in the tariff. . . ."

"An effective tariff upon agricultural products, that will compensate the farmer's higher costs and higher standards of living, has a dual purpose. Such a tariff not only protects the farmer in our domestic market, but it also stimulates him to diversify his crops and to grow products that he could not otherwise produce, and thus lessens his dependence upon exports to foreign markets. The great expansion of production abroad under the conditions I have mentioned renders foreign competition in our export markets increasingly serious. It seems but natural, therefore, that the American farmer, having been greatly handicapped in his foreign market by such competition from the younger expanding countries, should ask that foreign access to our domestic market should be regulated by taking into account the differences in our costs of production."

[*State Papers, Vol. I, pp. 35-6*]

". . . In considering the tariff for other industries than agriculture, we find that there have been economic shifts necessitating a readjustment of some of the tariff schedules. . . . What we need to remedy now is whatever substantial loss of employment may have resulted from shifts since that time."

"No discrimination against any foreign industry is involved in equalizing the difference in costs of production at home and abroad and thus taking from foreign producers the advantages they derive from paying lower wages to labor. Indeed, such equalization is not only a measure of social justice at home, but by the lift it gives to our standards of living we increase the demand for those goods from abroad that we do not ourselves produce. In a large sense we have learned that the cheapening of the toiler decreases rather than promotes permanent prosperity because it reduces the consuming power of the people . . . we also need important revision in some of the administrative phases of the tariff. The

Tariff Commission should be reorganized . . . administrative changes in the rates of duty should be made more automatic. . . . I believe a formula can be found that will insure rapid and accurate determination of needed changes in rates. . . ." *[State Papers, Vol. I, pp. 31–6]*

A struggle of months ensued over the revision with constant warning by the President that the revision must be "limited" and "the erection of the Tariff Commission with powers to revise the tariff to the differences in cost of producion at home and abroad" was a *sine-qua-non* of his approval, and that unduly high rates if enacted would be revised downward by the Commission.

After a hodgepodge bill had been passed by the House, the Senate Committee appreciably reduced the House rates. But once the bill was on the Senate floor there began a general game of hoist, fully participated in by the Democratic members accompanied always with demagogic misrepresentation by the same senators. The combined action of Republican Old Guards, the Progressives and Democrats in the Senate destroyed the flexible tariff provisions.

THE FLEXIBLE TARIFF

In a public warning on September 24, 1929, President Hoover said:

"In my Messages to Congress of April 16 at the opening of the Special Session I . . . presented the importance of . . . the flexible tariff. . . ."

"The reasons for the continued incorporation of such provisions are even more cogent today than ever before. No tariff bill ever enacted has been or ever will be perfect. It will contain injustices. . . . It could not be otherwise. Furthermore, if a perfect tariff bill were enacted the rapidity of our changing economic conditions and the constant shifting of our relations with economic life abroad would render some items in such an act imperfect in some particular within a year."

". . . The flexible provision is one of the most progressive steps taken in tariff making in all our history. It is entirely wrong that there shall be no remedy to isolated cases of injustice . . . through the failure to adequately protect certain industries, or to destroy the opportunity to revise duties which may prove higher than necessary to protect some industries and, therefore, become onerous upon the public. . . ."

". . . I regard it as o fthe utmost importance in justice to the public; as a protection for the sound progress in our economic system, and for

the future protection of our farmers and our industries and consumers. . . ."   [*State Papers, Vol. I, pp. 102–4*]

The tariff debate wore on over the winter of 1930. On
February 21, 1930, the differences between the President and
Senator Grundy were discussed in the Senate by Senator Pat
Harrison, of Mississippi. Senator Harrison frequently mentioned Senator Grundy's appeal to his Old Guard colleagues
to fight the President because of Hoover's moderate protection views and his efforts for a limited revision. Senator
Grundy likewise objected to the flexible tariff. He allied himself with Democrats and Progressives in his fight against a
Tariff Commission clothed with adequate flexible revision powers. All this did not prevent the Democrats from character-
izing this bill as the "Grundy tariff" in the succeeding campaign.

The bill having finally been passed by both Houses, it went
into conference.

The President demanded the flexible provisions in accordance with his principles. He stated to the Republican leaders that
without this provision there would be no bill. Through the
efforts of Senator Smoot and Representative Hawley, the President's formula was incorporated. In its final form the result
was a complete victory for the President in the flexible
provisions.

To cut short this debate, the President (on May 28, 1930)
authorized Senator Watson to state his position upon the flexible
tariff. The Senator said:

"I never quote the President of the United States, but I want
to say that in every talk I have had with the President about the
situation, he stated that he wanted a tariff commission to have all
the authority except that he should sign or veto the report of the
commission just as he signs or vetoes bills passed by Congress.
The President said, 'I want a straight non-partisan commission
to go into the whole question.' I think that so far as it is per-
missible to make rates and let those rates be submitted to the
President of the United States, I want a non-partisan commission. If the tariff can be taken out of politics, I want it taken out
of politics."

The debate still wore on and on June 5, 1930, Senate leaders
informed the President that Senator Grundy had concluded
not to vote for the Tariff Bill, as he did not consider the industrial rates high enough, and he was opposed to the flexible
provisions. There was some doubt whether the final bill with the
flexible provision would pass the Senate but several members on

the Democratic side who were making an appearance of opposition, but who had obtained sufficient local or regional advantages, would vote for the bill if necessary.

The bill finally passed and in a public statement on June 15, 1930, the President said:

"I shall approve the Tariff Bill. . . . It was undertaken as the result of pledges given by the Republican Party at Kansas City. . . ."

"Platform promises must not be empty gestures."

"A statistical estimate of the bill by the Tariff Commission shows that the average duties collected under the 1922 law were about 13.8 per cent of the value of all imports, both free and dutiable, while if the new law had been applied it would have increased this percentage to about 16.0 per cent."

"This compares with the average level of the tariff under

The McKinley Law of......................	23.0%
The Wilson Law of........................	20.9%
The Dingley Law of.......................	25.8%
The Payne-Aldrich Law of.................	19.3%
The Fordney-McCumber Law of.............	13.83%

"Under the Underwood Law of 1913 the amounts were disturbed by war conditions varying 6 per cent to 14.8 per cent."

"The proportion of imports which will be free of duty under the new law is estimated at from 61 to 63 per cent. This compares with averages under

The McKinley Law of......................	52.4%
The Wilson Law of........................	49.4%
The Dingley Law of.......................	45.2%
The Payne-Aldrich Law of.................	52.5%
The Fordney-McCumber Law of.............	63.8%

"Under the Underwood Law of 1913 disturbed conditions varied the free list from 60 per cent to 73 per cent averaging 66.3 per cent."

"The increases in tariff are largely directed to the interest of the farmer. Of the increases, it is stated by the Tariff Commission that 93.73 per cent are upon products of agricultural origin measured in value, as distinguished from 6.25 per cent upon commodities of strictly non-agricultural origin. The average rate upon agricultural raw materials shows an increase from 38.10 per cent to 48.92 per cent in contrast to dutiable articles of strictly other than agricultural origin which show an average increase of from 31.02 per cent to 34.31 per cent. Compensatory duties have necessarily been given on products manufactured from agricultural raw materials and protective rates added to these in some instances."

"The extent of rate revision as indicated by the Tariff Commission is that in value of the total imports the duties upon approximately 22.5 per cent have been increased, and 77.5 per cent were untouched or decreased. By number of the dutiable items mentioned in the bill, out of the total of about 3300 there were about 890 increased, 235 decreased, and 2170 untouched. The number of items increased was, therefore, 27 per cent of all dutiable items, and compares with 83 per cent of the number of items which were increased in the 1922 revision. . . ."

". . . No tariff bill has ever been enacted or ever will be enatced under the present system that will be perfect. . . . There are items upon which duties will prove too high and others upon which duties will prove to be too low. . . . I have insisted, however, that there should be created a new basis for the flexible tariff and it has been incorporated in this law. Thereby the means are established for objective and judicial review of these rates free from pressures inherent in legislative action. . . ."

[*State Papers, Vol. I, p. 314*]

The subsequent history of the flexible tariff in the Hoover Administration was that 250 industrial items were reviewed upon request by the Commission, and the rates changed in about seventy-five of these items.

There was never more misrepresentation than that of this tariff law.

As a campaign gesture, on May 11, 1932, the Democratic Congress passed a tariff bill which was vetoed by the President. It would have destroyed the flexible tariff. It also proposed reciprocal tariffs upon which the President's comment was:

"It has been the policy of our Government for many years to advance 'most favored nation' treaties with view to extinguishing these very processes, preferences, and trade frictions, and to secure equal treatment to us by the other nations in all their tariff and economic agreements. We have such treaties or executive agreements with thirty-one nations. If we adopted this complete reversal of policies and now negotiated reciprocal tariff agreements we should either under our 'most favored nation' obligations need extend these rights to all nations having such treaties with us, or to denounce such treaties."

"The struggle for special privileges by reciprocal agreements abroad has produced not only trade wars but has become the basis of political concessions and alliances which lead to international entanglements of the first order. These very processes are adding instability to the world today, and I am unwilling to enter upon any course which would result in the United States being involved in such complexities and such entanglements."

"Of high importance to us . . . is that the principal interest of a majority of the sixty or seventy other nations . . . would be to reduce the American agricultural tariffs. No concessions otherwise than those related to agricultural products would be of any importance to those particular nations . . . demoralize our agricultural industry and render us more and more dependent upon foreign countries for food supply; to drive our farmers into the towns and factories, and thus demoralize our whole national, economic, and social stability."

[*State Papers, Vol. II, p. 181*]

The President advised the Democratic Congress that if the rates were too high or should be abolished then to stand up and pass the legislation to do it. Far from doing so, they voted to increase the tariffs by taking oil and other Southern commodities off the free list and making them dutiable.

THE TARIFF DEBATE IN 1932

The tariff loomed up largely in the 1932 campaign and was debated to and fro. The Democrats insisted upon calling it the Grundy Tariff, and stated they would repeal the Tariff Commission as their first act. Hoover's comments were:

"All tariff acts contain injustices and inequities. That is the case with the last tariff bill. Some people get too much and some too little. But those of you who have followed the accomplishments of this administration will recollect that I secured in the last tariff act, twenty-five years after it had originally been advocated by President Theodore Roosevelt, the adoption of effective flexible tariff provisions to be administered by a bipartisan body. . . ."

"By maintaining that reform the country need no longer be faced with heartbreaking, logrolling selfishness and greed, which comes to the surface on every occasion when Congress revises the tariff."

"This bipartisan Tariff Commission has now been engaged for over eighteen months in an effective revision of the tariff. It has heard every complaint. It has found that many rates were just, some were too high, and some too low. But if there are tariffs which are too high and result in some damages to the United States, those tariffs can be readjusted by mere application to the Commission. That tribunal is open to all the people."

"Our opponents opposed this reform in tariff legislation. They passed a bill last session to destroy the independence of the Commission. They promise in their platform to destroy it. . . ."

[*State Papers, Vol. II, p. 311*]

Hoover's position on the tariff in general was stated in definite terms during the campaign. At Washington, D. C., on August 11, 1932, he said:

"I am squarely for a protective tariff. I am against the 'competitive tariff for revenue' advocated by our opponents. That would place our farmers and workers in competition with peasant and sweated labor products."

[*State Papers, Vol. II, p. 256*]

Speaking at Des Moines, Iowa, on October 4, 1932, the President said:

"The very basis of safety to American agriculture is the protective tariff on farm products."

"The Republican Party originated and proposes to maintain the protective tariff on agricultural products. We will even widen that tariff further where necessary to protect agriculture. Ninety per cent of your market is at home, and I propose to reserve this market to the American farmer."

"Has the Democratic Party ever proposed or supported a protective tariff on farm products? Has it ever given one single evidence of protection of the home market to the American farmer from the products raised by peasant labor on cheap land abroad?"

"The Democratic Party took the tariff off a large part of farm products in 1913, and placed them on the free list. A Republican Congress passed the emergency farm tariff in 1921 and a Democratic President vetoed it. The Democratic minority in the next Congress in 1921 voted against the revived emergency farm tariff. The Republican majority passed it and the Republican President signed it."

"The Democratic minority voted against the increase of agricultural tariffs in the Republican tariff of 1922. Most of the Democratic members of Congress voted against the increases in the tariff bill of 1930. Their platform enunciates the principle of 'a competitive tariff for revenue.' The competition that means is peasant labor and cheap lands. Their candidate states: 'We sit on a high wall of a Hawley-Smoot tariff'; 'sealed by the highest tariffs in the history of the world'; 'a wicked and exorbitant tariff'; 'a ghastly jest'; 'our policy declares for lowered tariffs.' This is a promise of reduction of farm tariffs. They will reduce agricultural tariffs if they come into power. Since when have our opponents become the friends of the farmer?"

"When you return to your homes you can compare prices with foreign countries and count up this proposed destruction at your own firesides. There are this minute 2,000,000 cattle in the northern states of Mexico seeking market. The price is about $2.50 per 100 pounds on the south bank of the Rio Grande. It is $4.50 on the north bank—and only the tariff wall between."

"Bad as our prices are, if we take comparable prices of farm products today in the United States and abroad, I am informed by the Department of Agriculture that you will find that except for the guardianship of the tariff, butter coulld be imported for 25 per cent below your prices, pork products for 30 per cent below your prices, lamb and beef products from 30 to 50 per cent below your prices, flaxseed for 35 per cent below your prices, beans for 40 per cent below your prices, and wool 30 per cent below your prices. Both corn and wheat could be sold in New York from the Argentine at prices below yours at this moment were it not for the tariff. I suppose these are ghastly jests."

"The removal of or reduction of the tariff on farm products means a flood of them into the United States from every direction, and either you would be forced to still further reduce your prices or your products would rot on your farms." [*State Papers, Vol. II, p. 309*]

Speaking at Cleveland, on October 15, 1932, the President said:

". . . In order to show you what the rates of wages are in the United States compared with other countries, I have this week secured through the Department of Commerce a calculation on a basis which I have used before for purposes of illustration. The actual wages in terms of the currencies of other countries are difficult to compare. We must find a common denominator."

"If we say that 5 per cent of butter and 95 per cent of flour form the basis of that useful mixture called "bread and butter," then the weekly

earnings in each country would buy, at retail in those countries, the
following totals of this useful compound:"

WEEKLY WAGES IF APPLIED TO THE PURCHASE OF "COMPOSITE POUNDS OF BREAD AND BUTTER" AS OF OCTOBER, 1932.

	Railway Engineers	Carpenters	Elec- tricians	Coal Miners	Weavers	Day Labor
U.S.	1069	1064	1300	734	565	393
U. K.[1]	342	253	276	223	161	184
Germany	271	176	169	162	120	106
France	246	183	164	123	86	86
Belgium	288	228	240	180	199	160
Italy	275	118	149	70	67	85
Japan	131	86	90	57	31	55

[1]United Kingdom.

"Do you want to compete with laborers whose wages in their own
money are only sufficient to buy from one-eighth to one-third of the
amount of bread and butter which you can buy at the present rates of
wages? That is a plain question. It does not require a great deal of
ingenious argument to support its correct answer. It is true we have the
most gigantic market in the world today, surrounded by nations clamoring to get in. But it has been my belief—and it is still my belief—that we
should protect this market for our own labor; not surrender it to the labor
of foreign countries, as the Democratic Party proposes to do. . . ."

[State Papers, Vol. II, p. 350]

Speaking at Indianapolis on October 28, the President said:

"In all this discussion about reducing tariffs, it should be remembered
that if any one of the rates or schedules of our tariff is too high, it has
been open to our opponents during the whole of the last session of the
House of Representatives to pass a simple resolution, and thereby secure
its review from the Tariff Commission. Did they do that? They did
not."   [State Papers, Vol. II, p. 398]

And in New York City, on October 31, 1932:

"Another proposal of our opponents which would wholly alter our
American system of life is to reduce the protective tariff to a competitive

tariff for revenue. The protective tariff and its results upon our economic structure has become gradually embedded into our economic life since the first protective tariff act passed by the American Congress under the administration of George Washington. There have been gaps at times of Democratic control when this protection has been taken away. But it has been so embedded that its removal has never failed to bring disaster. Whole towns, communities, and forms of agriculture with their homes, schools, and churches have been built up under this system of protection. The grass will grow in streets of a hundred cities, a thousand towns; the weeds will overrun the fields of millions of farms if that protection be taken away. Their churches and schoolhouses will decay."

"Incidentally, another one of the proposals of our opponents . . . [is] to repeal . . . the bipartisan Tariff Commission and thereby return the determination of import duties to the old log-rolling greed of group or sectional interest of Congressional action in review of the tariff."

[*State Papers, Vol. II, p. 418*]

Much distortion was given to this expression in later years. Speaking at Fort Wayne, Indiana, on April 4, 1936, Hoover said:

"You will remember Mr. Roosevelt's promises of 'immediate' 'drastic' reductions of the tariff. When Mr. Roosevelt made those promises I said that if protection to American industry and agriculture was taken away 'Grass will grow in the streets of a hundred cities, a thousand towns; the weeds will overrun the fields of a million farms.' At that time I believed in promises so I was wrong about that grass. They have not dared to carry out those promises. On the other hand, they have in fact increased the tariffs by devaluation of the dollar. They continue to nibble them through secretly made treaties."

"Tariff making by Congress has always been a sorry spectacle. Many duties are always made too high. Democrats as well as Republicans alike, log roll into that position. But the last Republican Administration established a new and vital reform in tariff making. We gave the first effective powers to the bipartisan tariff commission to lower or raise the tariffs on a proper basis. All proceedings were to be open to public hearings and in judicial form. The orgy of greed and privilege which surrounded constant change by Congress was at last done away with. This policy gave reality to the aspiration of progressive men over half a century."

"But the New Deal has sidetracked this Commission. It has been replaced by the secret determination of tariffs in back rooms without public hearings, through so-called reciprocal tariff negotiations. Men are deprived of their livelihood by secret covenants secretly arrived at."

"There is no greater exhibit of personal government in the whole New Deal. That is not democracy."[1]

[1]The history of the tariff subsequent to the Smoot-Hawley Act is of interest. Aside from the effective increase in the next administration of 59 per cent in the tariff by devaluation of the dollar, the tariffs have been widely extended by the Democratic Congress, removing from the free list such great imports as crude oil, gasoline, lubricating oils, coal, coke, lumber, copper, whale oil. Further duties have been increased on all items upon which processing taxes are levied and their manufactured products. One curious result is that the percentage of the free list—the duty-free goods coming in—has fallen from 66.5 per cent which it proved to be under the Smoot-Hawley Act (as shown by the actual imports for 1931 and 1932) down to 57 per cent in 1936 under a Democratic regime. This is the highest ratio of dutiable goods since the Payne-Aldrich Tariff of twenty-five years ago.

POLICIES IN RESPECT TO VETERANS

Hoover, having devoted years of his life to the War and having seen with his own eyes the actual service at the front, was naturally sympathetic with the veterans.

His policies were explicit—he wanted the nation to act generously, but he would not stand for political exploitation.

Each session of Congress sees the introduction of legislation increasing the services and payments to veterans. At times this legislation comes from politicians itching for veterans' votes and does not represent the sentiment of the veterans themselves. Indeed political opponents constantly drove such legislation in order to create ill will toward the President in the veterans. Nevertheless Hoover held to the generous and sympathetic view through his whole administration.

In an Armistice Day address on November 11, 1929, President Hoover said:

"Eleven years have gone by since the . . . guns ceased firing. It was a day of thanksgiving that marked the ending of the shambles of the trenches. For us it will be remembered always as a day of pride; pride in the memory of those who suffered and of those who made the last sacrifice of life in that great cause; pride in the proven valour of our Army and Navy; pride in the greatness of our National strength; pride in the high purpose for which we entered the war, and pride that we neither wanted nor got from it anything of profit for ourselves. Those stirring memories will always remain, and on each Armistice Day will glow again.

"From the war we have two paramount obligations. We owe to those who suffered and yet lived an obligation of national assistance, each according to his need. We owe it to the dead that we redeem our promise that their sacrifice would help bring peace to the world. The Nation will discharge its obligations."   [*State Papers, Vol. I, p. 125*]

CONSOLIDATION OF VETERANS' BUREAU

In his Annual Message to the Congress on December 3, 1929, President Hoover said:

"The administration of all laws concerning the veterans and their dependents has been upon the basis of dealing generously, humanely, and justly. While some inequalities have arisen, substantial and adequate care has been given and justice administered."

"I am convinced that we will gain in efficiency, economy, and more uniform administration and better definition of national policies if the Pension Bureau, the National Home for Volunteer Soldiers, and the Veterans' Bureau are brought together under a single agency."

[*State Papers, Vol. I, pp. 161–2*]

The President had appointed a committee on consolidation of veterans' services consisting of Secretary Wilbur, chairman, and General Hines, Colonel C. B. Hodges, and George H. Wood, with Presidential Secretary Newton as liaison. It brought in a workmanlike and comprehensive report, recommending consolidation of responsibility of the three divisions under a unified Veterans' Bureau. It further recommended that veterans' legislation be based in the future on need and on the facts gathered by such a study. The resulting consolidation of the veterans' services resulted in greatly increased economy and efficiency under the Veterans' Administrator General Hines.

In an address to the Annual Meeting of the American Legion on October 6, 1930, at Boston, the President said:

"I hope I may venture to claim from some years of service during the Great War, a measure of comradeship with the men who fought in that war. I understand your variety of French perfectly. I know from intimate experience, and I intend to hold in confidence, the first reaction you had from a passing shell, and the homelike appearance of shell holes under certain circumstances. I shall maintain secret your opinion of those who profess indifference to or the glory in passing bullets, or insects, or the mud and filth of the trenches, or days and weeks in the wet and cold."

"The glories of war are not in the heartbreaks of passing buddies and the thousand tragedies of the battle line. Its glories do not lie in its surroundings—they lie rather in the spirit, the sacrifices, the devotion of those who go cheerfully and courageously into the trenches, and the ultimate triumph of those lofty ideals for which they gave their all."

"It was inevitable that men who had lived through that great common experience, who had engaged in supreme adventure with death, should combine into associations of lifelong comradeship."

"The millions who shared in that experience came home from it rededicated to the further service of their country. . . . It was, therefore, with deep sympathy that I witnessed the birth of the American Legion in France in 1919."   [*State Papers, Vol. I, p. 384*]

EXTENSION OF HOSPITALIZATION

One of the Hoover policies was to extend hospitalization facilities to veterans suffering from both war and peace disabilities. He supported legislation repeatedly for that purpose. In a public statement approving an enactment on December 29, 1929, he indicated the need of even more facilities:

"I have been very glad to sign the bill authorizing the construction over a term of years of further hospitals for war veterans."

"The load seems likely to still further increase. . . . With view to an exhaustive examination of the subject I have asked General Hines to place the whole question before the Medical Council of the Veterans' Bureau for early study and report."   [*State Papers, Vol. I, p. 195*]

During the Hoover Administration twenty-five new hospitals were built and more contracted for—an increase from an original number of fifty. The accommodations for veterans in hospitals increased from about 26,000 at the beginning of his administration to 45,000 at the end, and with those in construction it was an increase of over 100 per cent.

INCREASE OF SPANISH WAR PENSIONS

The President was soon to meet in conflict with veterans' legislation. On May 28, 1930, the Congress passed an act greatly increasing pensions to Spanish-American War veterans, which included some most objectionable provisions. In vetoing it, the President said:

". . . I am in favor of proper discharge of the national obligation to men who have served in war who have become disabled and are in need. But certain principles in this legislation are opposed to the interest both of war veterans and of the public."

"In the whole of our pension legislation over past years we have excluded from such national award persons whose disabilities arise from 'vicious habits.' This bill breaks down that exclusion. . . . Certainly such claims for public help cannot be fairly based upon sacrifice to the Nation in war and must be opposed to national policy."

"Men who served only one day and during that suffered injury or impaired health became eligible for pensions. This law provides that if a man should incur any disability at any time in his life he may claim pension with only 70 days of service. The ninety day minimum service has been maintained against the Civil War veterans all these years because less service than this was not considered to imply personal danger or risk which warranted pension. . . ."

"There should be a requirement of 'need' as well as disability as a basis for these pensions. It is to me the height of injustice that citizens who are less well placed should be called upon to support from taxes those whose station in life enables them to support themselves or to live in independent security. The whole spirit of the pension system is that of a grateful nation rising to the support of those who have served in war, were injured or who have met with legitimate difficulties in after life which impose privation upon them." [State Papers, Vol. I, pp. 302–3]

In a press conference a few days later (June 3, 1930) the President said:

"I favored a liberalizing of the Spanish War Veteran pensions . . . but I have not changed my opinion that . . . rich men, or men having substantial incomes, should not draw pensions from the Government. . . ."

"I do not believe we should alter the principles which have been held for Civil War Veterans all these 70 years, requiring that men claiming pensions should have at least 90 days' service."

". . . I do not believe it is right to . . . call upon the Nation to pay disability allowances to men who have or who may tomorrow destroy their health by vicious habits."

"I have received numerous communications from veterans supporting these views." [State Papers, Vol. I, p. 307]

The legislation was passed over his veto but was amended some years afterwards to accord with Hoover's views.

INCREASE IN WORLD WAR VETERAN ALLOWANCES

A more serious conflict arose that same May, 1930, when the Congress passed a bill extending the period of "World War incurred disability" through which compensation or pensions would be greatly extended.

The Director of the Veterans' Bureau had advised the President that the bill would involve an immediate additional annual expenditure of $181,000,000, with a maximum annual outlay which would reach $400,000,000. The Senate amended the bill reducing the cost somewhat. The President made an earnest effort further to modify the bill but without success, and on May 26, the President vetoed the bill saying:

"One of the most repugnant tasks which can fall to this office is to disapprove of measures intended to benefit our sick or disabled men who have served our country in war. Perhaps as much as any other person, I have full realization of the task, the hardships, and the dangers to which the nation ordered its sons. In sentiment and in sympathy I should desire no greater satisfaction than to support just measures which are proposed for their benefit. But I want a square deal between veterans; not unjust discriminations between special groups, and I do not want wasteful or unnecessary expenditures. . . ."

"This measure except for a small part adds nothing to aid of veterans wounded or disabled in the war."

"I am informed by the Director of the Veterans' Bureau that the medical council of the bureau, consisting of most eminent physicians and surgeons, supported by the whole experience of the bureau, agree conclusively that this legal 'presumption,' that affliction from diseases mentioned in the bill between 1925 and 1930, is not a physical possibility and that the presumption constitutes a wholly false and fictitious basis for legislation in veterans' aid. This is confirmed by a recent resolution of so eminent a body as the American Medical Association."

"The spectacle of the government practicing subterfuge, in order to say that what did not happen in the war did happen in the war, impairs the integrity of government, reduces the respect for government, and undermines the morale of all the people. . . ."

"The further injustice of this bill may become more apparent when it is realized that men who were enrolled in the army who remained but comparatively a few days or weeks in service, without ever leaving their home States, will receive aid upon the same basis as those men who passed through the battle of the Argonne. . . ."

"There is no provision in this bill against men of independent means claiming benefits from the government for these disabilities arising in civil life. Surely it is of vital importance to the taxpayers, who, directly or indirectly, include all veterans themselves, that they shall not be called upon to contribute to such men of independent means. . . ."

". . . This bill contemplates compensation for some misconduct disabilities, the whole conception of which must be repugnant to decent family life."

"No government can proceed with intelligence that does not take into account the fiscal effects of its actions. The bill in a wasteful and extravagant manner goes far beyond the financial necessities of the situation. General Hines, after renewed examination, reports that this bill as finally passed will cost $110,000,000 the first year; that this will increase to an annual burden of $235,000,000, and continue during the life of these veterans. . . ."

"These costs are beyond the capacity of the government at the present time without increased taxation. They are larger than the veterans have themselves proposed. . . ."

". . . This Veterans' Bill is just bad legislation."

[*State Papers, Vol. I, p. 322*]

Hoover, however, felt that there was an undischarged obligation which the nation owed to veterans. To cover it, he proposed an entire revolution in veterans' legislation so as to meet a real need generously. He proposed that every veteran in need should be entitled to disability allowances and hospitalization for disability incurred in civil life for the whole of his life. He took the broad attitude that sick and destitute veterans would be a charge upon the community somewhere—or alternatively, they would suffer great privations. He insisted that it was the duty of the national government to care for them. At the same time, he felt it would cover the few injustices that the vetoed legislation would have cured. He further felt aside from justice and duty there was here a large element of relief to destitute unemployed which was also important. The President's proposal was accepted by the Republican caucus and carried through the Congress. Hoover had, however, to bear the attacks of the various economy leagues for years.

These agencies endeavored to destroy this legislation. To stop these attacks, the President stated in a Message to the Congress in December, 1932:

"The Nation should not ask for a reduction in allowances to men and dependents whose disabilities rise out of war service nor to those veterans with substantial service who have become totally disabled from non-war-connected causes and who are at the same time without other support. These latter veterans are a charge on the community at some point, and I feel that in view of their service to the Nation as a whole the responsibility should fall upon the Federal Government."

[*State Papers, Vol. II, p. 499*]

As the result of President Hoover's measure, there were in March, 1933, about 420,000 of these sick and destitute, non-service-connected disability veterans added to the rolls at a cost of about $75,000,000 per annum. The subject is further discussed on page 377.

WORLD WAR VETERANS' BONUS LEGISLATION

In 1931, Democratic leaders proposed to loan 50 per cent to veterans upon their bonus certificates under the guise of relief. The President favored the loans if they were limited to the men who needed relief—estimated at less than 20 per cent of the whole number. Congress, however, insisted on the whole, which implied a drain on the Treasury of $1,700,000. Hoover addressed a public protest to the Senate on February 18, 1931. He said:

". . . I have supported and the nation should maintain the important principle that when men have been called into jeopardy of their very lives in protection of the nation, then the nation as a whole incurs a special obligation beyond that to any other group of its citizens. . . . Over 700,-000 World War veterans or their dependents are today receiving . . . allowances. . . . The country should not be called upon, however, to support or make loans to those men who can by their own efforts support themselves . . . the largest part of this huge sum . . . is to be available to those who are not in distress. . . . Such action may . . . result in prolongation of this period of unemployment and suffering. . . . These burdens . . . cannot but have a damaging effect. . . . The one appealing argument for this legislation is for veterans in distress. . . . Placing a strain upon [the nation] . . . by a measure . . . for a vast sum beyond the call of distress . . . will not only nullify the benefits to the veterans but inflict injury to the country as a whole."

[*State Papers, Vol. I, p. 507*]

The bill was nevertheless passed, and on February 26, 1931, the President vetoed it, stating:

"It is now proposed . . . to impose . . . cash outlay on the government of about $1,700,000,000. . . ."

"There is not a penny in the Treasury to meet such a demand. The government must borrow this sum through the sale of reserve fund securities . . . or impose further taxation. . . . This proposal . . . is a requirement . . . to provide an enormous sum . . . to a vast majority who are able to care for themselves. . . . Among them are 387,000 veterans and 400,000 dependents . . . already receiving . . . support from the Federal Government. . . . These services now total an annual expenditure of . . . $800,000,000. . . . It is argued that . . . it would stimulate business. . . . We cannot further the restoration of prosperity by borrowing from some of our people, pledging the credit of all the people, to loan to some of our people who are not in need of the money. . . . It can be of no assistance to the return of real prosperity . . . if this argument is correct, we should make government loans to the whole people. . . . The need of the country today is to decrease the burden of taxes. . . . We must not forget the millions of hard-working families. . . . It is not the rich who suffer when we take taxes from our people, it is the poor who suffer. . . . I have no desire to present monetary aspects . . . except so far as they affect the human aspects. Surely it is a human aspect to transfer to the backs of those who toil, including veterans, a burden of those who by position and property can care for themselves. It is a human aspect to incur the danger of . . . continued unemployment. . . . Of much graver importance is the whole tendency to open the Federal Treasury to a thousand purposes, many admirable in their intentions . . . many . . . insidiously consume more and more of the savings . . . of our people . . . each of them breaks the barriers of self-reliance and self-support in our people."

[*State Papers, Vol. I, p. 512*]

But the Congress passed the bill over the President's veto. It was one of the things which contributed to deepen the depression. However, the President was a good sport and said:

"Although I have been greatly opposed to the passage of . . . loans . . . to people not in need, now that it is a law we propose to facilitate the working of it in every way possible."

"Inasmuch as the physical task of making loans to 3,500,000 veterans . . . will require many months, even with the most intensive organization, I have requested General Hines to give complete priority to applications from veterans who are in need. . . . The recent survey of the larger cities shows, in the opinion of the Administrator of Veterans' Affairs, that about 6½ of the total number of veterans in industrial centers are now receiving support from the local unemployment and other relief committees . . . as the amount possible for many veterans to borrow under the bill is so small, it is urgently necessary that the local committees shall continue their service to many veterans."

[*State Papers, Vol. I, pp. 517–8*]

In the fall of 1931, in the midst of the worst phase of the world panic, Democratic members proposed to pay the entire veterans' bonus in full, $3,400,000,000. The President went straight to the American Legion meeting at Detroit and addressed the veterans themselves on September 21, 1931. By that moving appeal, the Convention refused to support the Democratic leaders. The President said, in part:

". . . The world is passing through a great depression fraught with gruelling daily emergencies alike to men and to governments. This depression today flows largely from Europe through fundamental dislocations of economic and political forces caused by the Great War. . . . We would have recovered long since but for these forces from abroad. . . . Some individuals may have lost their nerve and faith. . . . You of the Legion have a peculiarly sacred stake in the future of the country which you fought to preserve. . . . During the past year our expenses have exceeded our income. . . . Today we face . . . large deficit . . . decrease . . . of yield of income taxes alone by . . . $1,200,000,000 . . . simultaneously we are carrying a huge and necessary extra burden of the unemployed . . . agriculture . . . and the veterans themselves. . . . Drastic economy [is needed] in every non-vital branch of government . . . the imperative moment has come when increased expenditure of the government must be avoided. . . . Your National Commander . . . came to me and offered your strength . . . to help in relief over [the] winter . . . and even greater service [is needed] today . . . [a] determined opposition by you to additional demands upon the nation. . . . I am speaking not alone of veterans' legislation . . . [but] equally of demands . . . which would require increased . . . expenditures. . . . The first stone in the foundation of recovery and stability . . . in the world is the stability of the Government of the United States. It is my purpose to maintain that stability and I invite you to enlist in that service. . . ."

"You would not have the President of the United States plead with . . . any group of citizens. . . . I make no plea to you. . . . But you would have your President point out the path of service in this nation. . . . My mind goes back to the days of the war . . . at the end of those years of heartsickness over the misery of it all, when peace came you and I knew that the wounds of the world were unhealed and that there would be further emergencies still before our country when self-denial and couragous service must be given. This is an emergency and these are the times for service. . . ."

[State Papers, Vol. I, p. 618]

Politicians still persisted and on March 29, 1932, the President issued a further warning:

"Informal polls of the House of Representatives have created apprehension in the country that a further bonus bill of $2,000,000,000 or thereabouts for World War veterans will be passed."

"I wish to state again that I am absolutely opposed to any such legislation. I made this position clear at the meeting of the American Legion in Detroit last September 21st, and the Legion has consistently supported that position. I do not believe any such legislation can become law."

"Such action would undo every effort that is being made to reduce government expenditures and balance the budget. The first duty of every citizen of the United States is to build up and sustain the credit of the United States Government. Such an action would irretrievably undermine it."   [*State Papers, Vol. I, p. 151*]

PRIVATE PENSION BILLS

President Hoover had a great antipathy to private pension bills, *i.e.*, bills granting individual pensions to specific persons. He shared this antipathy with President Cleveland and repeatedly vetoed such bills. In a veto message of April 27, 1932, he exposed the character of such bills by himself reporting on the cases.

"A proposed pension for a man who was courtmartialed for drunkenness and conduct prejudicial to good order, sentenced to six months' confinement, and whose conduct during confinement was so bad that he was finally discharged without honor for the good of the service."

"A proposed pension to a man who was discharged without honor because of chronic alcoholism."

"A proposed pension to a widow whose claim was filed five years after the death of the veteran, and upon call having been made for evidence of legal widowhood, claimant abandoned her claim for a period of 25 years. A recent investigation indicates claimant was never the legal wife of the soldier."

"A proposed pension to a man guilty of desertion and dishonorably discharged."

"A proposed pension to a man shown to have been a deserter, to have been punished by confinement and discharged without honor."

"A proposed pension to a man for self-inflicted injuries incurred in attempted suicide."

"A proposed pension to a man who was tried for desertion, convicted of absence without leave, and honorably discharged, having been found to have been mentally deficient, a condition that antedated his enlistment. There was no disability relating to service on which Federal pension should be granted."

"A proposed pension to a would-be suicide, no disability relating to service on which Federal pension should be granted being indicated."

"A proposed pension for a widow whose husband gave eight days' service, with no disability relating to the service."

"A proposed pension to a man who still suffers from a wound in the throat self-inflicted with a razor; with no disability relating to the service."

"A proposed pension for loss of a leg as the result of being struck by the fender of a street car while claimant was lying on the track in a completely intoxicated condition."

"A proposed pension to a widow whose husband had only nine days' service in a state militia, for which reimbursement was made by the United States; no disability relating to service being found."

"A proposed pension to a man who spent most of his service in the hospital, and was discharged without honor because of diseases not contracted in line of duty; was shown to have been guilty of malingering by taking soap pills to aid him in appearing anemic, and was recorded to have remarked that he knew 'how to play it and proposed doing it as long as he could.' His physical condition was not the result of service."

"A proposed pension to a man discharged without honor because of diseases not contracted in the service in line of duty. His condition not being one upon which Federal benefits should be based."

"I could add other instances, but it seems to me that even this number which appear neither to have law nor equity to justify them, warrants a revision of the bill, and that a larger dependence should be placed upon reports which are easily obtainable from the Pension Service."

[*State Papers, Vol. II, p. 188*]

PURGING THE PENSION ROLLS

By April, 1932, the President asked the Veterans' Bureau for a searching examination of wasteful and undue payments arising under technical interpretations of the older veterans' acts.

The Bureau reported a growth of something over $120,000,-000 a year of payments to able-bodied, self-supporting and even rich men as a result of such interpretations, or mistaken legislation. Mr. Hoover, in an endeavor to balance the budget, cou-

rageously proposed that these wrongful expenditures be suppressed; he said no honest veteran supported such expenditures;
that their continuation only gave fuel to the enemies of the
veterans and would result some day in much more drastic action
than was justified—and it did. The action was, of course, distorted by the political opposition.

THE "BONUS MARCHERS" OF 1932

In May to July, 1932, a large number of veteran "Bonus
Marchers" assembled in Washington to press for the bonus
legislation which the American Legion refused to support. Their
ranks were joined by a large number of hoodlums and some
Communists. They were frequently addressed by Democratic
members of Congress seeking to inflame them against the President for his opposition to this legislation and they were given
financial support by some of the publishers of the sensational
press. At the adjournment of Congress on July 16, 1932, when it
was evident that no legislation would be passed, the President requested a fund from Congress to pay the fares of the legitimate
veterans home again. Some six thousand availed themselves of
this, leaving about five thousand mixed veterans, hoodlums and
Communist agitators in Washington whose leaders were bent on
creating public disturbance. After the adjournment of Congress
the President through government agencies obtained the names
of upwards of two thousand of those remaining and found that
less than one-third of them had ever served in the armies.

Some old buildings on Pennsylvania Avenue had been occupied by some of the marchers. These buildings stood in the way
of construction work being carried out to give employment. On
July 28, the police requested some fifty veterans therein to move
to other quarters. Over one thousand of these men marched
from their camps outside of the city and made an organized
attack upon the police. In the melee Police Commissioner
Glassford became confused and the men were fired upon
by the police. Two were killed by the police and many policemen were injured. The District Commissioners, upon Glassford's urging, appealed to the President stating that they could
not preserve order in the Capital, that the police were greatly
outnumbered, and were being overwhelmed. With the same
right of call as the governor of any State they demanded military assistance to restore order. General McArthur took charge
and, without firing a shot or injuring a single person, restored
order. The President's orders to the Secretary of War, how-

ever, were not carried out for they were specific to confine the
action to restoring order in the city and to allow the men to return to their camps outside the business district. He proposed
that the next day they would be examined to eliminate the
Communist and hoodlum element. The army authorities, however, pressed all campers outside the District of Columbia, even
those not participating in the riots.

The misrepresentation of the bonus incident for political
purposes during the campaign by the opposition press and Democratic orators surpassed any similar action in American history.
Hoover was portrayed as a murderer and an enemy of the
veterans. A large part of the veterans probably believe to this
day that men who served their country in war were shot down
in the streets of Washington by the Regular Army at the President's orders—yet not a shot was fired or a person injured after
the Federal Government took charge.

And it was Hoover who gave more to veterans in need than
any President in history.

BONUS DEBATE IN THE CAMPAIGN OF 1932

The veterans' bonus questions again came up in the campaign of 1932. Roosevelt not having defined his stand on the
question, Hoover prophetically remarked on October 28, 1932:

"I have stated that I do not favor the prepayment of the soldiers' bonus.
It was passed by the last Democratic House of Representatives. With
the aid of the public it was stopped. It will be attempted again. The
Democratic candidate has not yet stated to the American people fairly
and squarely what his attitude is upon this subject."

"The reasons why I object to it can be illustrated by the father who
in a generous moment promised his young son a bonus of $100 when he
was 21 years old. The boy asked his father for the $100 thirteen years
in advance. His father said: 'Times are bad. I am hard pressed. I have
to bring up and educate all of the children, and I haven't the money. I
am placing $5 per annum in the savings bank and as it is compounded
it will amount to $100 when you are 21 years old.' "

"The moral of that story is you can not eat your loaf of compound
interest before the dough has had time to rise. And the further political
moral of this story is that it was said by the father's political opponents
that this son would never vote for his father for public office."

"Of one thing I will assure the veterans and that is when they are paid
they will be paid in real money."   [*State Papers, Vol. II, p. 402*]

Later (on November 4, 1932), Hoover said:

"The people have yet to learn what he [Roosevelt] proposes to do in respect to the soldiers' bonus. He seems to think that a cash sum to be paid 13 years hence is no different from cash but he says he intends it should be paid when there is a surplus in the Treasury with which to pay it. That means a surplus of $2,300,000,000. I assure the veterans that so long as there is a Democratic Congress there will never be a surplus of $2,300,000,000."[1]

[State Papers, Vol. II, p. 439]

[1] The new Administration as a matter of economy made a straight cut of some $300,-000,000 in veterans' allowances. As time has gone on this cut was found to be unjust and allowances have been restored until the veterans' expenditures have come back to the figure recommended by Hoover as shown on page 47. But the non-war-service disability men were only in a minor degree ever restored. By devaluing the currency the purchasing power of their allowances will possibly be diminished by another 41 per cent.

The following are the figures of total World War veterans or dead veterans' dependents receiving regularly either pensions or disability allowances from the Federal Government, which speak for themselves:

Hoover Administration

1930	376,500
1931	628,600
1932	840,300
1933	853,800

Roosevelt Administration

1934	462,900
1935	473,500
1936	479,000

Had the Hoover policies been preserved the 400,000 sick and needy would not have been forced off the veterans' roll onto relief and the total cost would have been no greater. This action also was one of the forces which led to the vast demands for relief and to the passage of the veterans' bonus payments of over $2,500,000,000 in 1935.

POLICIES IN RADIO, AVIATION, AND MERCHANT MARINE

RADIO

THE INITIATION OF GOVERNMENT CONTROL

The Hoover radio policies were (a) the channels through the air were public property; (b) broadcasters and others were tenants at the will of the Government; (c) they had to be regulated both for public interest and to prevent their destroying each other by interference. He was the father of these policies and chiefly instrumental in their adoption.

When Hoover became Secretary of Commerce in 1921 the radio was in use for telegraphic purposes—mostly ship to shore communication. Broadcasting was being done experimentally from two stations. In twelve months 320 broadcasting stations had sprung up and they were involved in a mess of interference with little authority in the Government to regulate them. The only authority for regulation was a minor law passed in 1912 regulating ship to shore use to secure freedom from interference. Moreover there at once loomed up a question of great public magnitude. Who owned the air channels? Many private interests assumed that the channels became theirs by right of occupation. With these problems in mind Secretary Hoover on February 27, 1922, called a conference of experts and broadcasters.

His address to this conference shows an uncanny grasp of the future. At the time the Department was without real authority but his intervention in mobilizing the broadcasters to voluntary action and acknowledgment of public ownership of the channels of communication was a great and enduring public service. In the light of development this address is a historic document. In part he said:

"We have witnessed in the last four or five months one of the most astounding things that has come under my observation of American life. This Department estimates that today over 600,000 (one estimate being 1,000,000) persons possess wireless telephone receiving sets, whereas there were less than fifty thousand such sets a year ago. We are indeed today upon a threshold of a new means of widespread communication of intelligence that has the most profound importance from the point of view of public education and public welfare. The comparative cheapness with which receiving stations can be installed, and the fact that the genius of the American boy is equal to construction of such stations within the limits of his own savings, bid fair to make the possession of receiving sets almost universal in the American home."

"I think that it will be agreed at the outset that the use of the radio telephone for communication between single individuals as in the case of the ordinary telephone is a perfectly hopeless notion. Obviously if ten million telephone subscribers are crying through the air for their mates they will never make a junction; the ether will be filled with frantic chaos, with no communication of any kind possible. In other words, the wireless telephone has one definite field, and that is for spread of certain predetermined material of public interest from central stations. This material must be limited to news, to education, and to entertainment, and the communication of such commercial matters as are of importance to large groups of the community at the same time."

"It is therefore primarily a question of broadcasting, and it becomes of primary public interest to say who is to do the broadcasting, under what circumstances, and with what type of material. It is inconceivable that we should allow so great a possibility for service, for news, for entertainment, for education, and for vital commercial purposes, to be drowned in advertising chatter, or for commercial purposes that can be quite well served by our other means of communication."

"The extraordinary development of the radio telephone, however, has brought us face to face with an entirely new condition. . . . It raises questions as to what extension in the powers of the Department should be requested of Congress in order that the maximum public good shall be secured from the development of this great invention."

"The problem is one of most intensely technical character, but is not one without hope of fairly complete solution. Fortunately, the sending of radio telephone messages can be arranged in wave lengths sufficiently far apart so as not to interfere with each other, and receivers can at their option tune their receiving instruments to the different wave bands. With the improvement in the art and in the delicacy of instruments, the distance between wave lengths may eventually decrease and thus the number of layers of messages increase. Furthermore, it is possible to increase the number of sending stations and thus the variety of material, if· the power applied to certain wave lengths is limited so as to circumscribe the area of distribution from a given station. . . ."

"One of the problems that enter into this whole question is that of who is to support the sending stations. In certain countries, the Government has prohibited the use of receiving instruments except upon payment of a fee, out of which are supported Government sending stations. I believe that such a plan would most seriously limit the development of the art and its social possibilities . . . I believe that we ought to allow any one to put in receiving stations who wishes to do so. But the immediate problem arises of who will do the broadcasting, and what will be his purpose. . . ."

"There is involved, however, in all of this regulation the necessity to so establish public right over the ether roads that there may be no national regret that we have parted with a great national asset into uncontrolled hands. I believe this conference with the high skill that it represents will be able to determine upon a method which should give satisfaction in all directions, and should stimulate the creation of a new addition to our national life."

One of the incidental results of the conference came from Secretary Hoover's insistence that the amateurs, mostly small boys, should have a definite wave band all of their own—which has held until this day.

Pending action by Congress to re-enforce the thread of authority and with the voluntary approval of broadcasters the Department put in a system of three months licenses. A second conference in March, 1923, expanded and perfected this mostly voluntary regulation. Hoover recommended to Congress that legislation be passed at once. Again on October 6, 1924, he called the Third Annual Conference of Broadcasters and again sought to hold the fort of semi-voluntary regulation in the face of 563 broadcasting stations all clamoring for free channels. At the same time he was incessantly urging Congress to legislate a real authority to some body.

In the meantime actions had been brought in the courts to break down the weak legal and largely voluntary control. The Secretary, in a public statement on March 10, 1924, said:

"I am in receipt of many requests for my views as to issues now before the courts bearing on the control of radio broadcasting . . . I can state emphatically that it would be most unfortunate for the people of this country, to whom broadcasting has become an important incident of life, if its control should come into the hands of any single corporation, individual, or combination."

"It would be in principle the same as though the entire press of the country were so controlled. The effect would be identical whether this control arose under a patent monopoly or under any form of combination, and from the standpoint of the people's interest the question of whether or not the broadcasting is for profit is immaterial. In the licensing system put in force by this Department the life of broadcasting licenses is limited to three months, so that no vested right can be obtained either in a wave length or a license. . . ."

In a statement to *The New York World* of March 16, 1924, he said:

"The regulation of radio is the most complex and difficult problem in regulation that has ever confronted the Government. Two conflicting principles assert themselves. One is the right of inventors to earn a profit on their patents, and the other is the broad principle that nobody must be permitted to monopolize or control the means of public communication. . . ."

"I believe, however, that everybody should be permitted to send out anything they like. The very moment that the Government begins to determine what can be sent, it establishes a censorship through the whole field of clashing ideas. . . ."

"You will recognize that if anybody should be able to have the exclusive use of a certain wave length he would have a monopoly on that part of the ether. That cannot be permitted. . . ."

In urging legislation he stated on March 26, 1924:

". . . there should become no vested right to a wave length on the part of a broadcasting station. This would be creating a monopoly of a certain road through the ether . . . we must limit the use of the ether to a definite period of years or months so that we can under any reasonable conditions return the use of this particular wave length to the Government. At the same time, we must be careful to give a reasonable continuity of service to a broadcasting station so as to warrant its erection and support."

Talking to the amateurs on March 26, 1924, he said:

"The amateurs as you all know have a certain wave band assigned to them, but within this band they do much of their own policing. In discussing with one of their leaders—a youngster of about sixteen—the method of preventing interference between them, he stated with some assurance that there would be no difficulties about enforcement if left to them. I pressed him as to the method they would employ in order to secure good results. He showed a good deal of diffidence but finally came through with the statement—'If you leave it to us and if anybody amongst the amateurs does not stick to the rules, we will see that somebody beats him up.' So far I have heard of no cases of assault and battery."

In addressing the Third Annual Radio Conference, October 6, 1924, he said:

"Radio has passed from the field of an adventure to that of a public utility. . . ."

"At the first radio conference I hazarded some modest anticipations as to its development and use. Some thought them visionary—yet we passed every point of these anticipations within eighteen months. We have, in fact, established an entirely new communication system."

December 4, 1924, Hoover again urged Congress, pending more exhaustive legislation, at once to enact a short bill to "preserve public interest . . . reserving Federal ownership" over the radio channels or as the expression was then "the ether," but opposing any censorship. He asked Congress to delay some parts of their proposed legislation until some problems were more clear.

In November, 1925, Congress having failed to act, the Fourth Annual Conference for voluntary regulation was called by Hoover. A bill was partially passed through Congress but had died on adjournment. There were now 563 stations being held under largely voluntary authority given from the industry to the Secretary. In addressing this conference he said:

"We have great reason to be proud of the results of these conferences. From them have been established principles upon which our country has led the world in the development of this service. We have accomplished this by a large measure of self-government in an art and industry of unheard of complexity, not only in its technical phases, but in its relations both to the Government and the public. Four years ago we were dealing with a scientific toy; today we are dealing with a vital force in American life. We are, I believe, bringing this lusty child out of its swaddling clothes without any infant diseases."

"Some of our major decisions of policy have been of far-reaching importance and have justified themselves a thousandfold. The decision that the public, through the Government, must retain the ownership of the channels through the air with just as zealous a care for open competition as we retain public ownership of our navigation channels has given freedom and development in service that would have otherwise been lost in private monopolies."

"We hear a great deal about the freedom of the air; but there are two parties to freedom of the air, and to freedom of speech, for that matter. There is the speechmaker and the listener. Certainly in radio I believe in freedom for the listener. He has much less option upon what he can reject, for the other fellow is occupying his receiving set. The listener's only option is to abandon his right to use his receiver. Freedom cannot mean a license to every person or corporation who wishes to broadcast his name or his wares, and thus monopolize the listener's set."

"We do not get much freedom of speech if fifty people speak at the same place at the same time, nor is there any freedom in a right to come into my sitting-room to make a speech whether I like it or not. So far as opportunity goes to explain one's views upon questions of controversy, political, religious, or social, it would seem that 578 independent stations, many competing in each locality, might give ample opportunity for great latitude in remarks; and in any event, without trying out all this question, we can surely agree that no one can raise a cry of deprivation of free speech if he is compelled to prove that there is something more than naked commercial selfishness in his purpose."

"The ether is a public medium, and its use must be for public benefit. The use of a radio channel is justified only if there is public benefit. The dominant element for consideration in the radio field is, and always will be, the great body of the listening public."

". . . we have in this development of governmental relations two distinct problems. First is a question of traffic control. This must be a Federal responsibility. . . . This is an administrative job, and for good administration must lie in a single responsibility."

"The second question is the determination of who shall use the traffic channels and under what conditions. This is a very large discretionary or semi-judicial function which should not devolve entirely upon any single official. . . ."

"We must bear in mind that radio broadcasting is the birth of the last five years and that our previous conferences have been largely concerned with trying to get the service established; to create an effective service that could reach every home. The agency is now established. When I called the first conference only thirty people were present. There were only two or three broadcasting stations and only a few hundred thousand listeners. Today there are nearly six hundred stations and about twenty-five million listeners."

By way of reporting progress Hoover said, on October 21, 1925, in a broadcast from Washington:

"Four million of our families have radio receiving sets, which have brought to them added education and cleanly entertainment. With the development of the radio one-half of the Nation can now receive the inspiration of a speech from our President and a score of million throbbed with the joys and sorrows of the dramatic presentation of minute-to-minute events in the last World Series. They even had knowledge of the progress of the games more quickly than some of the people in the grandstands. The radio is binding our Nation in great mutual understandings. And millions of us stay more by our own firesides while mother knits, father smokes, and son or daughter monkey with the dials instead of gadding about."

"Incidentally, I wish our engineers and inventors would invent another knob on our receiving sets by which we could express our feelings to the fellow who is broadcasting. Tuning out in disgust is an uncompleted mental reaction."

THE RADIO COMMISSION

Hoover did not believe in one-man-control of regulatory functions and in a public statement on December 26, 1925, took occasion to say so:

"A statement in one of this morning's newspapers seems to indicate a lack of information as to the basis I have proposed for radio control. The implication is that I have sought to have that job placed in my hands. Far to the contrary. I have both before Congressional committees and in at least a half dozen public addresses stated that no one official should dictate who is to use the radio wave lengths, and I have for years advocated that this being a semi-judicial function it should be placed in the hands of an independent commission."

"Moreover, for five years I have reiterated that these wave lengths are public property to be used by assignment of public authority. This view has been enforced by the Department of Commerce for the past five years. It was again reaffirmed by the last Radio Conference. This principle, together with a provision for a commission to control assignments, was incorporated into a bill introduced to Congress some weeks ago by Congressman Wallace White and approved by me. Somebody needs to find out what has already taken place before he starts something."

Finally the White Radio Law was passed by Congress on February 27, 1927, and the Radio Commission set up in accord with the Secretary's recommendations.

The law affirmed his view of public ownership of the channels; that operators had temporary license to use these channels subject to their performance in public interest. The first commissioners were selected by Hoover on behalf of President Coolidge.

The net results to the American people of these Hoover policies are of immeasurable public interest.

INTERNATIONAL REGULATION

On October 4, 1927, he presided as chairman at an international Radio Conference in Washington called for the purpose of establishing some order in air between nations. The Conference included delegates from seventy-six nations. The Conference lasted some months but finally agreed upon a division and regulation of wave lengths, control of interferences and a variety of other needed reforms which were so well worked out that they were generally accepted and have lasted to this day.

REORGANIZATION OF RADIO COMMISSION

The Radio Commission had been set up on a temporary basis and further legislation was needed. Hoover, now President, in his Message of December 3, 1929, recommended:

"I recommend the reorganization of the Radio Commission into a permanent body from its present temporary status. The requirement of the present law that the commissioners shall be appointed from specified zones should be abolished and a general provision made for their equitable selection from different parts of the country. Despite the effort of the commissioners, the present method develops a public insistence that the commissioners are specially charged with supervision of radio affairs in the zone from which each is appointed. As a result there is danger that the system will degenerate from a national system into five regional agencies with varying practices, varying policies, competitive tendencies, and consequent failure to attain its utmost capacity for service to the people as a whole."

[State Papers, Vol. I, p. 156]

In a public address to the Association of Broadcasters on October 26, 1931, Hoover said:

"As Secretary of Commerce I had the pleasure of wide acquaintance with the purposes of your Association in the Annual National Radio Conferences which were called at that time for the development of the national policies in relation to radio."

"The decisions reached at that early date have been of unending importance. The determination that radio channels were public property and should be controlled by the government; the determination that we should not have governmental broadcasting supported by a tax upon the listener, but that we should give license to use of these channels under private enterprise where there would be no restraint upon programs, has secured for us far greater variety of programs and excellence of service without cost to the listener. This decision has avoided the pitfalls of political and social conflicts in the use of speech over the radio which would have been involved in government broadcasting. It has preserved free speech to the country."

"These principles are now strongly imbedded in our law and in our entire public system. The industry has constantly faced new and complex problems. It is needless to mention the many-sided importance of radio in modern life . . . has become an essential element in the intellectual development of our country. It has brought most of the supposed values which were formerly available exclusively to life in the cities to every home throughout the land, for the treasures of music, of entertainment, and of information have been brought to the loneliest farm and the most remote hamlet. It is an incalculable extension of happiness and contentment."

As always in quasi-judicial commissions during the Hoover Administration the Radio Commission was free from any executive interference.

AVIATION

As Secretary of Commerce, Hoover pioneered the policy of government support and regulation of commercial aviation. His policies and objectives were sevenfold:

(*a*) Creation of a system of national airways with service from the Government similar to national waterways;

(*b*) Mail subsidy to develop the new system of transportation;

(*c*) Creation of an auxiliary to defense by large personnel and manufacturing capacity available to war:

(*d*) Regulation of pilots and machines to increase safety;

(*e*) Getting the government out of its expensive and unproductive attempt to carry the mails by government planes;

(*f*) Securing scientific research into aviation problems;

(*g*) Creation of a governmental agency to conduct these services.

In 1922, he called the first national conference on commercial aviation and here formulated safety legislation.

His report as the Secretary of Commerce for 1922 says:

". . . a conference upon commercial aviation was called comprising representatives of the manufacturers, of engineering societies, and public officials to consider the great loss of life due to faulty machines, faulty construction, and inadequate experience in aviators. The conference urgently recommended regulation and inspection similar in character to that applied to shipping, and the technical form of such legislation was drafted for recommendation to Congress."

In his reports as Secretary of Commerce for 1923 and 1924, the passage of this legislation was again urged.

THE MORROW COMMISSION

In order to get the whole subject, together with the problems of the Army and Navy, before the country and Congress, Secretary Hoover in 1925 joined in recommending to President Coolidge the appointment of an impressive national Commission to explore the situation. Mr. Dwight Morrow was appointed by the President as Chairman.

Hoover's memorandum of recommendations to the Commission were in part as follows:

". . . The essential . . . is the creation of a Bureau of Civil Aviation through which the Government should undertake to give services to commercial aviation comparable with those which the Government has over a century given to commercial navigation."

". . . we cannot have a successful commercial aviation until these

Government services are first provided. The Federal Government today provides for lighting and marking the channels of water of navigation; it provides for the accurate study of these channels and publication of charts of them; it maintains constant advice to navigators as to the shifting of channels and the changing of weather. It provides a service for safety inspection of craft for protection of travellers and seaworthiness to carry goods. It provides for the examination of officers of all such craft in order to maintain standards of skill and experience. It gives aid in the development and improvement of ports and waterways. We also have provided a body of law covering the many phases of the special relations in this industry. Were all these services and their vast accumulation of data and precedent to be wiped out tomorrow, our entire water-borne traffic would stop instantly. Nor would it be possible to re-establish water navigation except in the most primitive fashion unless these services were restored and maintained."

"We have to this, I believe, a complete analogy in aviation. Before we can expect to develop commercial aviation we must determine the air routes from the point of view of the best channels through the air in their relation to atmospheric conditions. We must develop a service for warnings of weather disturbance such as we have in navigation. We must prepare charts of these airways. We must secure the provision of landing fields and airports and for marking the routes."

"If we are to secure real economy of time, which is the basis of successful commercial aviation, we must provide for night movement and this necessitates the lighting of our airways."

"We must develop a system of inspection of both planes and personnel, not only from the point of view of protecting human life but also of establishing confidence in aviation as a method of safe and reliable transport. We must ultimately provide a body of law comparable with our merchant marine law and we must provide for the application of customs, emigration, and other regulation such as we have in water-borne commerce."

"Without such services my belief is that aviation can only develop in a primitive way. We can no more expect the individual aviator or the individual aviation company to provide these services on land than we could expect the individual navigator or the individual shipping company to provide them on the sea. If the airways service were provided by individuals or corporations they would either be free to competitors, which would be unfair, or we would have to concede monopoly to some one. Such a course would be the negation of equal opportunity and of stimulative competitive development. It would be as fatal to the long-view development of aviation to give exclusive monopoly over certain routes as it would be to give such monopolies over our water routes."

". . . In May I created a technical Commission for a study of the question. . . . This Commission is composed of . . . men who have an understanding of the problems involved. The Commission has raised considerable money from amongst its members and otherwise to defray expenses. . . ."

"These studies . . . will be supplied to your Commission."

"I need not emphasize the importance of commercial aviation as an arm of defense. While it is not probable that the actual commercial plane will be much used in actual battle, yet the building up of the manufacturing industry behind such aviation is of the most vital importance, and we must develop the airways across our own country, so that they may be used for purposes of defense. Beyond this, of course, a commercial development of the industry will give impulse in the development of the art. All these factors will contribute to the defense arm of the Government."

"And I wish to emphasize these additional propositions to your Committee:

"First. The establishment of an Aviation Bureau, so as to provide the services I have mentioned."

"Second. We should contract out the carriage of the mail. It is my belief that such contracts can now be let for an amount not to exceed 80 per cent of the postal receipts of the air mail. This income, together with the promise of additional revenue that could be obtained from express and passengers, appears to be sufficient to induce substantial concerns to undertake these ventures."

"Third. The establishment of airports at the important municipalities . . . the time has arrived when the airport will be a necessary adjunct to each important town. It has been our national policy in the past that the docks and terminal facilities for water-borne traffic should be supplied either by the municipalities or citizens of our cities and not by the Federal Government. I believe that many of our municipalities are prepared to find such facilities today if they could be assured of commercial service."

"To sum up, I believe that with this minimum extension of governmental activity we can secure a commercial aviation in the United States without subsidy."

THE DIVISION OF AERONAUTICS IN THE DEPARTMENT OF COMMERCE

Hoover's recommendations as to commercial aviation were adopted by the Commission. The Air Commerce Act of May, 1926, was the result. A division of Aeronautics was created in the Department of Commerce under an Assistant Secretary for Aeronautics with regulatory and development authority. The mail contracting was assigned to the Post Office. In the Secretary of Commerce's report for 1926 the beginnings of the new era in aviation are shown.

"On January 1, 1926, there were 369 miles of air transport services in operation by private enterprises, and there were 2665 miles operated by the Post Office Department. Assurance of congressional action and the official passage of the act have resulted in considerable preparatory activities by private enterprise. Little commercial aviation could be organized until the fundamental services above mentioned were assured, as no commercial concern could undertake to provide these aids to navigation at its individual expense, not only because of the large preliminary outlay but because such facilities would be equally available to competitors."

[*14th Annual Report, Secretary of Commerce*]

The work was rapidly organized under Assistant Secretary William MacCracken and Hoover was able the next year to report the establishment of 8390 miles of regular commercial transport routes, the establishment of 100 airports, etc. The following year the Department reported regular services over 11,191 miles of routes.

Colonel Clarence Young succeeded as Assistant Secretary of Aeronautics in 1928. In the President's first Annual Message of December 3, 1929, he informed Congress:

"During the past year progress in civil aeronautics has been remarkable. This is to a considerable degree due to the wise assistance of the Federal Government through the establishment and maintenance of airways by the Department of Commerce and the mail contracts from the Post Office Department. The Government-improved airways now exceed 25,000 miles—more than 14,000 miles of which will be lighted and equipped for night-flying operations by the close of the current year.

Airport construction through all the states is extremely active. There are now 1000 commercial and municipal airports in operation with an additional 1200 proposed for early development."

"Through this assistance the Nation is building a sound aviation system, operated by private enterprise. Over 6400 planes are in commercial use, and 9400 pilots are licensed by the Government. Our manufacturing capacity has risen to 7500 planes per annum. The aviation companies have increased regular air transportation until it now totals 90,000 miles per day—one-fourth of which is flown by night. Mail and express services now connect our principal cities, and extensive services for passenger transportation have been inaugurated, and others of importance are imminent. American air lines now reach into Canada and Mexico, to Cuba, Porto Rico, Central America, and most of the important countries of South America."   [State Papers, Vol. I, p. 152]

POST OFFICE MAIL CONTRACTS

The air mail contracts of the Post Office urgently required reorganization. The Postmaster-General, Walter F. Brown, in co-operation with Congress, revised these laws and the President on April 29, 1930, signed the resulting "Watres Act." Messsrs. Myers and Newton's statement of the President's policies follows:

"The intricate problems involved had been under examination by Postmaster-General Brown. The commercial air mail contracts had been established as the result of the report of the Morrow Commission in 1925. The commercial air transport industry was then young and experimental. There was but little experience upon which to fix the rates in the contracts, the routes which should be developed, or the conditions which should be required in order to stimulate traffic or serve best in national defense. Of even greater importance was the tremendous progress that had been made in aviation during the intervening years.

"Experience had proved the early rates to be too high. Exorbitant profits had been made, some contracts as high as $3 per mile. Great speculation in the securities of aviation companies had taken place in expectation of continuance of such rates. Some thirty companies had engaged in the traffic and in consequence many routes were not served by continuous lines. The conditions of the contracts had not developed equally the collateral services of passengers and express which it was hoped would bear an ever-increasing part of the costs. The planes were confined largely to purely mail-carrying types of no great speed. As many of the contracts for carrying the mail had in 1930 some years yet to run and could not honestly be cancelled, methods had to be devised to secure their voluntary surrender."

"As a result of the amended law and the able administration of Postmaster-General Brown, through negotiation the rates were greatly reduced, the routes were consolidated into a carefully planned national system of commercial airways, the type of plane was entirely changed to passenger and express service, which promised to reduce greatly the volume of subsidy required. The speed, safety and reliability of planes were greatly enhanced. The Nation was saved from a hodge-podge of airways similar to the tangle that had grown up in rail transportation, and above all, a great arm of national defense was created."

"In the fiscal year ending June 30, 1929, before the act went into effect, commercial aviation companies had flown 10,200,000 miles with the mail and the contractors had been paid $14,600,000 or $1.43 per mile. The air mail receipts were estimated at about $1,700,000, bringing the net cost to the Government down to about $1.26 per mile."

"In the fiscal year ending June 30, 1933, under the revised legislation, the contractors flew 35,900,000 miles with the mail and were paid $19,400,000, or about 54 cents per mile. Due to the greatly improved service, however, airmail receipts increased to about $10,000,000, which resulted in a net cost to the Government of about 26 cents per mile. The reduction in costs of transportation by the reform had been over 60 per cent on the gross cost per mile and about 80 per cent on the net cost per mile. Of equal importance, the subsidies had been so directed that the whole service was transformed into large passenger- and express-carrying planes, from which the revenues outside the Government were growing steadily and with the growth of the air mail traffic bade fair soon to reduce the subsidies to the amount of the mail receipts. Passengers had increased from 165,200 in 1929 to 550,000 in 1933. The manufacturing capacity for planes had increased enormously, and furnished the largest capacity in case of war of any country in the world. The planes had so much improved in character and quality that the mail time between the two seaboards had been reduced from forty-eight hours to twenty-one hours. The number of people directly employed had increased from 15,000 to 35,000, every one of whom in some capacity was a highly trained reserve of personnel in time of war. In military values alone the Government would have needed to expend five times the annual sum involved to build up the same organization if it had done so through the military department."[1]

[*Hoover Administration, p. 430*]

PAN–AMERICAN AIR POLICIES

After the election in 1928, Hoover undertook a journey to the South American states, where he laid the foundations with the different governments for the all-American air service. He made this a reality when on March 15, 1930, the Postmaster-General announced contracts for a new service of air mail to South America, to include Cuba, Honduras, Nicaragua, Costa Rica, Panama, Colombia, Ecuador, and Peru, three times a week. This service saved from six to nine days in transit to Peru.

On October 11, the first air mail to Argentina carried the President's congratulations to that government that the pre-inauguration visit had so direct a result. By October 9 of this year Uruguay had been added to the service.

MERCHANT MARINE

Hoover was a most ardent supporter of an American Merchant Marine. But he insisted that the only policy which would secure it was private ownership with subsidy.

At the end of the War, the Government owned a huge merchant fleet mostly poorly built and most expensive to operate. Hoover insisted from the first that merchant ships could never be successfully operated by the Government. Congress under radical and Southern leadership (the Southern states had many unprofitable lines operating at Government expense out of their ports) insisted on Government operation. Hoover, as Secretary of Commerce, fought it at every step, recommending, however,

---

[1] By savage partisan attacks the Roosevelt Administration in 1934 attempted to discolor this magnificent accomplishment in development of American aviation. False charges of collusion of operators in fixing routes and rates were used to cancel the contracts. The Army was substituted. A number of its aviators, inexperienced in the routes, were killed. Finally the contracts were restored to the same operators at presumably decreased rates. Later the Interstate Commerce Commission restored practically all the rates. The Government paid damages in concessions or directly for their action. The whole incident is one of the ugliest in American history. But it resulted in the complete vindication of Hoover's policy and the capacity and integrity of Postmaster-General Brown's administration.

that while in transition to private operation, the Government should maintain lines on the more important trade routes, the lines should be disposed of quickly. As time went on his views were well verified. Finally after eight years of futile action, enormous losses and a decadent marine, in 1928 Congress passed an act giving mail subsidies to private operation with the dual hope of inducing the sale of the Government lines and, by loans for ship construction, of securing the construction of new ships. Hoover did not like the Act because it was disguised subsidy, and mail as a basis of ship subsidy was bound to be wasteful and to lead to evasion.

He had for years advocated the abolition of the Shipping Board, but Congress insisted on retaining it as an executive body independent of the President. The members of Congress enjoyed its huge patronage and favors by playing politics with the Board's useless lines which were maintained particularly from the Southern and Pacific Coast ports.

Hoover first expressed his views in a public address in New York on February 17, 1920:

"If the Government continues in the shipping business, we shall be disappointed from the point of view of profits. For we shall be faced with the ability of private enterprise the world over to make profits from the margins of higher cost of Government operation alone. . . . The largest successfully managed cargo fleet in the world comprises about 120 ships, and yet we are attempting to manage 1900 ships at the hands of a Government bureau. . . . The . . . profit or loss in a ship is measured by a few hundred tons of coal wasted, . . . a little extravagance in repairs, or by the four or five days on a round trip. . . . Lest fault be found, our Government officials are unable to enter upon the detailed higgling in . . . rates required by every cargo. . . . They must take refuge . . . in fixed rates. In result, their competitors underbid by the smallest margins necessary to get the cargoes. . . . Our large fleet in the world's markets is thus to hold up rates. . . . Increasing number of our ships will be idle."

Speaking in November, 1923, he said:

"It is simply a truism to say that we must have an American Merchant Overseas Marine. . . . We must have our own ships for the protection of our foreign trade; we must have ships if we would expand our exports on sound lines and we must have them as an auxiliary to our national defense."

Secretary Hoover was appointed by President Harding chairman of a Cabinet Commission to inquire into the Merchant Marine and joined in their recommendation on December 29, 1924: "The Government can never operate commercial shipping as economically as private capital." The Commission recommended Government operations be continued on certain trade routes only until private enterprise could be established. They recommended the reorganization of the Shipping Board.

On November 4, 1925, at the request of the members of the House Committee on the Merchant Marine, Hoover gave them a report which says in part:

"I beg to acknowledge your request for my views upon the basis of policy that should be followed in the reorganization of the Government merchant marine."

"There are about twenty overseas trade routes which are the connecting links between our inland trade routes and foreign countries upon which our foreign trade is dependent."

"For the protection of our commerce from discrimination and from combinations which would impose onerous freight rates we must maintain upon each of these routes the operation of very substantial shipping under the American flag."

"Commerce cannot operate upon uncertainty of transportation; it requires regular ferrylike sailings over essential routes."

"The type of ship which is best adapted to such regular service and at the same time is the most profitable to operate is the cargo liner of from 10,000 to 18,000 gross tons, speed 12 to 18 knots, preferably Diesel-propelled, and having up to say, 20 per cent of passenger space. Replacements and extensions should be driven to this ideal."

"The national defense requires an American merchant marine and it also largely requires the cargo-liner type."

"We will never have a real or satisfactory merchant marine until it is owned and maintained by private enterprise. The Government cannot operate cheaply. It cannot secure a revenue as large as private enterprise. It cannot avoid the interminable difficulties and wastes of bureaucracy and above all, the direct and indirect political pressures. Furthermore, Government operation and competition with private enterprise, with the U. S. Treasury as a reserve fund, totally dulls private initiative. We must get out of Government operation as quickly as we can establish private operation. It is useless to renew proposals to subsidize shipping."

"Some of the lines on those trade routes are today successfully operated by American flag private enterprise. Some of the Government lines which are losing money today would pay private enterprise, and they could be disposed of under proper guarantee of continuance if private firms could be sure of future Government policies."

"We need some criteria for determining when successful operation is impossible on a particular route. We do not believe this could be done legislatively. Administratively it could be determined by experience. . . . No section of the country has a right to call upon the Government perpetually to operate ships at a loss."

"To our view it is vital, if we are to go on, that we provide a form of administration of the Government fleet that will reduce losses on those routes which the Government must operate pending trade growth."

"The Shipping Board was . . . established upon a bipartisan and later a regional basis. . . . The necessarily divided minds of the best Board on earth has always resulted in failure in executive work. . . . Each member has a four-way independent responsibility. He is responsible for every act of the Board to the country as a whole, to his particular constituency, to his political party, and, finally, to Congress. Responsibility to the President, the one responsibility which every administrative officer of the Government should acknowledge under the spirit of the Constitution, is denied by the Board."

"Therefore . . . the whole fleet and other property should be transferred to the Emergency Fleet Corporation and the president thereof should be appointed by the President of the United States."

". . . for certain major questions . . . an advisory board . . . is desirable."

Finally the Congress passed the White-Jones Merchant Marine Act of 1928.

At the beginning of his Presidential administration in 1929, Hoover found the Board and the Post Office were basing their mail contracts solely as inducement to purchasers to take over the old ships. This did not build new ships nor the types needed either to expand our trade or to support the navy as an auxiliary. He therefore appointed a Cabinet Committee to look into it and to direct any contracts let by the

Post Office as there was no control of the Shipping Board
by the administration.

In his first Annual Message President Hoover on December 3, 1929, made all this clear:

"Under the impulse of the Merchant Marine Act of 1928 the transfer to private enterprise of the Government-owned steamship lines is going forward with increasing success. The Shipping Board now operates about eighteen lines, which is less than half the number originally established, and the estimate of expenditures for the coming fiscal year is based upon reduction in losses on Government lines by approximately one-half. Construction loans have been made to the amount of approximately $75,000,000 out of the revolving fund authorized by Congress and have furnished an additional aid to American shipping and further stimulated the building of vessels in American yards."

"Desirous of securing the full values to the Nation of the great effort to develop our merchant marine by the Merchant Marine Act, soon after the inauguration of the present administration, I appointed an interdepartmental committee, consisting of the Secretary of Commerce, as chairman, the Secretary of the Navy, the Postmaster General, and the chairman of the Shipping Board, to make a survey of the policies being pursued under the Act of 1928 in respect of mail contracts; to inquire into its workings and to advise the Postmaster General in the administration of the act."

"In particular it seemed to me necessary to determine if the result of the contracts already let would assure the purpose expressed in the act, 'to further develop an American merchant marine, to assure its permanence in the transportation of the foreign trade of the United States, and for other purposes,' and to develop a co-ordinated policy by which these purposes may be translated into actualities."

"In review of the mail contracts already awarded it was found that they aggregated twenty-five separate awards imposing a governmental obligation of a little over $12,000,000 per annum. Provision had been imposed in five of the contracts for construction of new vessels with which to replace and expand services. These requirements come to a total of twelve vessels in the ten-year period, aggregating 122,000 tons. Some other conditions in the contracts had not worked out satisfactorily."

". . . The committee has advised the necessity of securing much larger undertakings as to service and new construction in future contracts. The committee at this time is recommending the advertising of fourteen additional routes, making substantial requirements for the construction of new vessels during the life of each contract recommended. A total of forty new vessels will be required under the contracts proposed, about half of which will be required to be built during the next three years. The capital cost of this new construction will be approximately $250,-000,000, involving approximately 460,000 gross tons. Should bidders be found who will make these undertakings, it will be necessary to recommend to Congress an increase in the authorized expenditure by the Post Office of about $5,500,000 annually. It will be most advantageous to grant such an authority."

"A conflict as to the administration of the act has arisen in the contention of persons who have purchased Shipping Board vessels that they are entitled to mail contracts irrespective of whether they are the lowest bidder, the Post Office, on the other hand, being required by law to let contracts in that manner. It is urgent that Congress should clarify this situation."

[State Papers, Vol. I, p. 153]

On several occasions actions by the Shipping Board raised great public criticism and the President without authority could do little but investigate them. As an instance, on June 6, 1930, in a letter to the Board, he wrote:

"The Board has had under consideration the bids for disposal of the Black Diamond and Cosmopolitan Lines. I understand it has also before it proposals which would lead to the lending of some $50,000,000 of Federal funds to the United States Line for new ship construction."

"While Congress has provided no authority to the President over the policies of the Shipping Board, yet these matters are of great importance to the future of the Merchant Marine, in which I am deeply interested. I propose, therefore, to appoint a committee of outstanding men who would review these questions and advise upon them, and on the broader policies in merchant marine organization." [State Papers, Vol. I, p. 308]

On July 9, 1930, the President appointed Ira A. Campbell, New York; H. G. Dalton, Cleveland; Edward N. Hurley, Chicago; George B. Jackson, Baltimore; and Clarence M. Woolley, New York, on this committee. As a result of the committee's report, certain contracts were very much changed.

Time and again the President urged upon Congress the abolition of the Shipping Board and recommended that its administrative functions should be placed under the control of the Executive, urging that great wastes were in progress. Such recommendations were made on December 3, 1929, December 8,

1931, February 17, 1932, April 1, 1932, December 1932, January 1933, and all times between. But the Democratic Congress would not release its grip.

Finally when the scandals and futilities of the Board's actions became a stench in the public nostrils, it was in 1933 finally abolished.

The action of President Hoover in directing the change in policy of the Post Office not to accept proposals of the Shipping Board for mail contracts unless it meant new ships did bring results. Whereas 128,000 tons of merchant ships were built in 1929, yearly numbers increased over 1929 despite the growing depression to 254,000 tons in 1930; 386,000 tons in 1931 and 213,000 tons in 1932. Some 30,000 men were given jobs in the shipyards. That the new tonnage of American shipping fell to 66,000 tons in 1934 and 63,000 tons in 1935 requires no comment.

POLICIES IN CONSERVATION

GENERAL POLICIES

Having spent a large part of his life in the West, and by training an engineer, Hoover was more familiar with the problems of conservation than any of our Presidents—and thereby the more genuinely zealous. He had in his youth served upon the geological and other government surveys in the West. He was well alive to the fact that our policies had been haphazard without co-ordinated plans of action, and had been subject to repeated raids by Congress and private interests. He was well aware of the problems of natural resource conservation. As Secretary of Commerce he had led in the conservation of the fisheries and of oil resources. He had long been an advocate of the systematic conservation of our water resources through integrated public works.

For convenience in arrangement, we will divide discussion of these policies into

    a. Conservation of the Public Lands.
    b. Conservation of the Forest.
    c. Conservation of the Parks.
    d. Conservation of Oil Resources.
    e. Conservation of Water Resources (see Public Works, p. 245).
    f. Conservation of the Fisheries.

PUBLIC LANDS

The President with Secretary Wilbur early took up better conservation of the remaining public lands—about 250,000,000 acres. Here his policies were:

(*a*) Creation of a nation-wide commission to study and recommend the best management;

(*b*) A set-up of reservations to the Federal Government of all possible oil and fuel lands;

(*c*) Establishment of governmental control to stop overgrazing and the impairment of water-supply upon public lands and reservations.

(*d*) Transfer of strictly grazing lands to the states for joint administration with the school lands of the state.

In a message to a meeting of Western governors at Salt Lake City sent through Assistant Secretary Dixon on August 26, 1929, the President said:

"I have for some years given thought to the necessity and desirability for a further step in development of the relations between the Federal and state governments in respect to the Public Lands. . . ."

"It may be stated at once that our Western states have long since passed from their swaddling clothes and are today more competent to manage much of these affairs than is the Federal Government. Moreover, we must seek every opportunity to retard the expansion of Federal bureaucracy and to place our communities in control of their own destinies."

"It seems to me that the time has come when we should determine the facts in the present situation, should consider the policies now being pursued and the changes which I might recommend to Congress."

"That these matters may be gone into exhaustively and that I may be advised intelligently, I propose to appoint a commission of nine or ten members, at least five of whom should be chosen from leading citizens of the public land states, and I should like to secure the co-operation of the governors by submission from them of names for such a commission. This commission would naturally co-operate with the Department of the Interior."

The President made the following tentative suggestion for consideration by the governors:

"The most vital question in respect to the remaining free public lands for both the individual states and the Nation is the preservation of their most important value—that is grazing. The remaining free lands of the public domain (that is, not including lands reserved for parks, forests, Indians, minerals, power sites, and other minor reserves) are valuable in the main only for that purpose."

"The first of the tentative suggestions, therefore, is that the surface rights of the remaining unappropriated, unreserved public lands should, subject to certain details for protection of homesteaders and the smaller stockmen, be transferred to the state governments for public school purposes and thus be placed under state administration."

"At the present time these unappropriated lands aggregate in the neighborhood of 190,000,000 acres and in addition some 10,000,000 acres have been withdrawn for purposes of stock watering places and stock drives which might be transferred as a part of the program of range preservation. In addition, some 35,000,000 acres have been withdrawn for coal and shale reserves, the surface rights of which with proper reservations might be added to this program of range development in the hands of the states."

"Reports which I have received indicate that due to lack of constructive regulation the grazing value of these lands is steadily decreasing due to overgrazing and their deterioration, aside from their decreased value in the production of herds, is likely to have a marked effect upon the destruction of the soil and ultimately upon the water supply. They bring no revenue to the Federal Government. The Federal Government is incapable of the adequate administration of matters which require so large a matter of local understanding. Practically none of these lands can be commercially afforested but in any event the forest reserves could be rounded out from them where this is desirable. Therefore, for the best interest of the people as a whole, and people of the Western states and the small farmers and stockmen by whom they are primarily used, they should be managed and the policies for their use determined by the state governments."

"The capacity which the individual states have shown in handling school lands already ceded out of every township, which are of the same character, is in itself proof of this and most of the individual states already maintain administrative organization for this purpose so that but little added burden would thus be imposed. They could to the advantage of the animal industry be made to ultimately yield some proper return to the states for school purposes and the fundamental values could be safeguarded in a fashion not possible by the Federal Government. They would also increase the tax base of the state governments."

[*State Papers, Vol. I, p. 91*]

On October 18, the President announced this commission.

"In co-operation with Secretary Wilbur, I have now made a start at the selection of this commission."

"In order that each of the all-important public land states may be represented and that there may be representatives from other sections of the country, I have decided to make the commission approximately twenty in number, of whom two will be women. The following have accepted the invitations so far sent out":

"Mr. James R. Garfield, Secretary of the Interior during Mr. Roosevelt's Administration, who is to be the chairman."

"Of the general representatives Mr. George Horace Lorimer of Philadelphia, Mary Roberts Rinehart, ex-Governor James P. Goodrich of Indiana, Colonel W. B. Greely, former head of the Forestry Service, and Mr. Gardner Cowles of Des Moines, Iowa, have so far accepted invitations to serve."

"As to representatives from the public land states the following have so far accepted: California, Elwood Mead; Montana, I. M. Brandjord; Washington, R. K. Tiffany; Arizona, Rudolph Koechler; Colorado, Chas. J. Moynihan; Nevada, George W. Malone; Utah, William Peterson; Idaho, I. H. Nash."

"The purpose of the commission is to study the whole question of the public domain particularly the unreserved lands. We have within it three outstanding problems:"

"First, there has been overgrazing throughout these lands, the value of the ranges having diminished as much as 80 to 90 per cent in some localities. The major disaster, however, is that destruction of the natural cover of the land imperils the water supply. The problem therefore in this sense is really a problem of water conservation."

"Second, the question as to what is the best method of applying a reclamation service to the West in order to gain real and enlarged conservation of water resources."

"Third, the commission is free to consider the questions of conservation of oil, coal, and other problems that arise in connection with the domain."

"I have recently had opportunity to confer with the Chairmen of the Senate and House Committees covering Public Land and Irrigation, and they have expressed their warm approval of the creation of this commission and have undertaken to introduce the necessary legislation to provide funds for its work."   [*State Papers, Vol. I, pp. 109, 110, 111*]

In his Annual Message to Congress on December 3, 1929, the President said:

"We are also confronted with a major problem in conservation due to the overgrazing on public lands. The effect of overgrazing (which has now become general) is not only to destroy the ranges but by impairing the ground coverage seriously to menace the water supply in many parts of the West through quick run-off, spring floods, and autumn drought."

[*State Papers, Vol. I, p. 157*]

On September 29, 1931, this Garfield Commission made its report. The report recommended:

1. That additional reserves to the Federal Government should be set up, including all possible oil and coal reclamation areas, forests, parks, bird refuges and national defense areas.

2. That the remaining areas (*i.e.*, grazing lands) should be granted to the states. The areas in those states which do not accept should be put under definite Federal administration.

The Commission pointed out the urgency of these recommendations—that the grazing lands were being ruined and should be regulated by the people who knew how—the states themselves. Most of the states expressed their desire to undertake the task.

While the grazing law passed by the New Deal did not give the job of control to the states as it should have, yet it was the outgrowth of this work.

In a special Message to the Congress on February 17, 1932, the President said:

"There should be a change in policy in dealing with public lands if we are to preserve their value for grazing and other purposes. The Committee on Conservation and Administration of the Public Domain, authorized by act of the Congress approved April 10, 1930, completed the task assigned to it a year ago. Its report has been transmitted to members of the Congress. Legislation carrying into effect the recommendations of the committee also is before the Congress. These proposals are the result of painstaking study and earnest deliberation. They offer a solution of the problems, connected with this remnant of our public domain, which have persisted for the past twenty-five years. I commend the report to the attention of the Congress, deeming the legislation of sufficient importance to justify early action."

[*State Papers, Vol. II, pp. 117–18*]

NATIONAL FORESTS

The forest policies of the Hoover Administration were direct and simple: to transfer any remaining forest lands from the public lands and to purchase additional lands.

The conservation and development of the forests was pushed vigorously by Secretary of Agriculture Hyde during the Hoover Administration. The total acreage of the forests was increased by 2,000,000 acres.

In order further to conserve the forests, the President, on May 14, 1931, directed all leasing of the forests for new lumbering operations should cease.

NATIONAL PARKS

The policies for the Parks were also very direct: to create new parks and enlarge the existing ones by transfer from public lands and by purchase or gift.

The area of National Parks and Monuments was extended by 40 per cent during the Hoover Administration under the direction of Secretary Wilbur with over 3,000,000 acres being added including ten new places. The principal sites developed were Death Valley, the Great Smokies, Shenandoah, the Great Dunes of Colorado, George Washington's Birthplace, and the Carlsbad Caverns.

The park service had now a high position in the public mind by its effective and non-political administration under Hoover's predecessors. For many years Stephen Mather had given extraordinary service in building up the parks for public use. Upon Mr. Mather's death his principal assistant, Mr. Horace Albright, was placed in charge. That high ideal was maintained and improved.

CONSERVATION OF OIL

The policies of the Hoover Administration were to conserve the oil resources (a) by withdrawal of all public lands from entry for oil and the establishment of permanent Federal oil reserves; (b) by securing co-operation among the states, through interstate compacts, to so regulate oil exploitation as to prevent the huge wastes in progress.

WITHDRAWAL OF PUBLIC LANDS

President Coolidge, in 1924, appointed four Cabinet members, including Secretary Hoover, upon an Oil Conservation

Board. The purpose was primarily to assure naval and military oil and gasoline supply, but further to study and report the entire question of oil conservation. Experts were employed, hearings were held, and the whole of the factual material then known as to America's oil reserves was determined and the waste in oil production was for the first time pointed out in a vigorous and scientific manner.

The Board, in a preliminary report in 1926, said as to the public domain:

"The Federal Government is still the owner of vast areas embracing several hundred millions of acres of land the title to which is held really in trust for the public generally. Within these areas are proven oil fields and also much unexploited territory holding promise of oil in commercial quantities. All these areas (except some special reserves) may fairly be said to be wide open to private appropriation through lease or otherwise. There seems to be no discretionary power anywhere to resist the exploitation of these lands and the dissipation of the Government's resources."

The Board urged action.

In 1928 and 1929, the Board made systematic recommendation of methods for reducing waste in private oil production, including the flush flow of new pools. It recommended that states should enact rigid laws to prevent waste of gas and oil and to regulate drilling and production so as to prevent such waste.

By one stroke in the first eight days of his administration Hoover did more for oil conservation than all of his predecessors or successors together. On March 8, 1929, he announced:

"There will be no leases or disposal of Government oil lands, no matter what emergency they may lie in, of Government holdings or Government controls, except those which may be mandatory by Congress. In other words, there will be complete conservation of Government oil in this administration."
[State Papers, Vol. I, p. 15]

On March 15, 1929, the President amplified this statement:

"Not only do we propose to stop the issue of development permits over public domain and other lands in control of the Government, which permits constitute the first step in the leasing of oil resources, but Secretary Wilbur proposes to review all outstanding permits to determine their status. Where holders are complying with the law, they need have no anxiety as to retrospective action, but some 34,000 permits for oil exploration by drilling have been issued since the leasing law was passed in President Wilson's Administration. Of these some 20,000 are outstanding at the present time. Under these permits drilling must proceed in definite stages under time limits. It is obvious that no large proportion of 20,000 oil wells are being drilled on lands under these permits. Thus, many persons have not complied with the requirements of the law and in effect have abandoned their rights."

"I have approved the recommendation of Secretary Wilbur to appoint a Departmental Board representing the different Bureaus interested, which will review the whole situation. Being fairly familiar with the sentiment of our Western states, I can at once refute the statement that the people of the West object to conservation of oil resources. They know that there is a limit to oil supplies and that the time will come when they and the nation will need this oil much more than it is needed now. There are no half measures in conservation of oil. The Government must cease to alienate its oil lands if we are to have conservation."

[*State Papers, Vol. I, pp. 16, 17*]

Under this order, hundreds of thousands of acres of oil leases which had not complied with the law were cancelled and returned to the Government.

Later on, a meeting of the governors of the public domain states having been called at Salt Lake City to protest the President's action, on August 21, 1929, he sent them a message:

"I know that the Western as well as the Eastern states agree that abuse of permits for mineral development or unnecessary production and waste in our national resources of minerals is a matter of deepest concern and must be vigorously prevented."

"Because of such abuse and waste I recently instituted measures to suspend further issue of oil prospecting permits on public lands and to clean up the misuse of outstanding permits, and thereby to clear the way for constructive conservation. It may interest the governors to know that when this decision was taken on the 12th of March there were prospecting permits in force covering over 40,000,000 acres of the public domain. We have now determined that over 40 per cent of these holders had not complied with the requirements of the law, that the large portion of these licenses were being used for the purpose of preventing others from engaging in honest development and some even as a basis of 'blue sky' promotions. After yielding to the claimants the widest latitude to show any genuine effort at development under the outstanding prospecting permits, the total will probably be reduced to about 10,000,000 acres, upon which genuine development is now in progress. The public domain is, therefore, being rapidly cleared of this abuse. The position is already restored to a point where measures can be discussed which will further effectually conserve the national resources, and at the same time take account of any necessity for local supplies."

[*State Papers, Vol. I, pp. 95, 96*]

In his Annual Message to the Congress on December 3, 1929, the President said:

"Conservation of our oil and gas resources against future need is a national necessity. The working of the oil permit system in development of oil and gas resources on the public domain has been subject to great abuse. I considered it necessary to suspend the issuance of such permits and to direct the review of all outstanding permits as to compliance of the holders with the law. The purpose was not only to end such abuse but to place the Government in position to review the entire subject."

[*State Papers, Vol. I, p. 157*]

POLICIES OF CONSERVATION OF NATIONAL OIL PRODUCTION

In April, 1929, the oil industry applied to President Hoover to have the Oil Conservation Board in effect grant an immunity from the Anti-Trust laws that the industry might restrict production and fix prices. The President in conference with Attorney-General Mitchell and Secretary of the Interior Wilbur determined that the Federal Oil Conservation Board had no authority to sanction any agreement proposing such immunity. The President stated at a press meeting that what was urgently needed in the oil industry was to stop the waste of oil, and to give stability to the industry by regulating the wasteful methods of overproduction from newly discovered pools. He proposed for the emergency that agreements among the states, through their conservation officials, should control activities upon these questions. The President further proposed that authority for such action should be had by interstate compacts as provided in the Constitution. Such compacts would retain to the states full control and avoided centralization of government in Washington.

To carry out real conservation as opposed to price fixing, etc.,

Secretary Wilbur under the authority of the President on June 10, 1929, called a conference of the oil states and of the industry to meet at Colorada Springs. The Secretary laid before them the President's plan of regional interstate compacts. This called for a compact by which the oil states agreed to each set up regulation to repress excessive drilling and wasteful methods and to do it in collaboration with each other. The President insisted that there were only five oil-producing states of consequence; that it would be more mobile, more effective and more within the responsibilities of these states to do their own job. Secretary Wilbur urged the necessity of action and stated:

"The position of the Federal Government is not to interfere with the rights and duties of the states, but to lend such aid as it can. . . . This administration has no desire to concentrate the forces of Government in Washington. It has every desire to co-operate with the states."

Mark Requa of California was chosen chairman of the meeting. After several days of debate the President's plan for stabilizing the industry was practically rejected in favor of Federal control of prices and production. The real opposition to the President's proposal was that it was a conservation measure, not a production control and price-fixing measure.[1]

The President and Secretary Wilbur nevertheless proceeded in two directions: (a) securing state conservation legislation; (b) securing conservation agreements among owners of larger oil pools where the Government also had holdings. In a review of progress, the President on March 13, 1931, said:

"In order to prevent enormous waste of gas and oil and to prevent the ruin of the independent oil producers, the Federal Oil Conservation Board brought about over a year ago, under the leadership of Secretary Wilbur, an almost entire restriction of production from the newly discovered great oil pool at Kettleman Hills, California, a large part of which is the property of the Federal Government. The state authorities of Oklahoma have brought about similar restraint upon an enormous new pool discovered at Oklahoma City. Coincident with these efforts, the State Commissions working with other producers of California, Oklahoma and Texas, brought about proration agreements amongst themselves. A

---

[1] It is of interest to note that after Federal control was adopted in the next administration and tried out for eighteen months, the same men who led the opposition to the proposal of President Hoover and Secretary Wilbur, advanced the "interstate compact proposal" based on the Hoover principle, and it was almost unanimously supported by the industry.

The United States still owns 97 per cent of all its original oil shale lands. . . ."

"There stands out the fact that Kelley, when placed in charge of this oil shale matter in your Washington office, immediately got in touch with a newspaper, refrained from presenting any of his complaints to you, and sold his story to the press, and refused then to give to authorized public officials any statement of the matter. It is a just inference that his refusal to assist the Assistant Attorney-General in his inquiry was merely to protect the news value of his proposed newspaper articles. . . ."

Despite this, *The World* persisted in the publication of these articles until the Congressional election in November, after which, upon threats of legal proceedings for libel by Secretary Wilbur, the newspaper apologized and admitted there was no basis for the assertions.

This yellow lie was used effectively in the Democratic campaign.

FISHERIES CONSERVATION

ALASKAN FISHERIES

When he was appointed Secretary of Commerce, Hoover began a whole new era of fisheries conservation policies. At once upon appointment to that office in 1921, he discovered that the great Alaskan fisheries were being rapidly destroyed by ruthless exploitation. These fisheries furnish more than half (by value), of the whole national fish supply. He at once determined upon extension of public control.

After investigation by experts and public hearings, on June, 1921, he recommended to Congress strong legislation "if the Alaska fisheries were not to be destroyed by over-fishing." Owing to oppositions, Congress refused to act. Secretary Hoover, in February, 1922, prevailed upon President Harding to use the Executive authority (Alaska being a Territory) to create a temporary fishing reservation of all Alaska, pending legislation by Congress of more constructive measures. Persons were thereafter only allowed to fish under license. This action created much fury. Sub-chasers from the navy were required to root out fishing pirates. Altogether a stiff battle of two years ensued in which a bitter opposition was led by certain fishing companies and the Alaskan delegate in Congress, aided by certain sensational journals.

In a public statement on July 23, 1923, Hoover, in reviewing the situation after a journey to Alaska, said:

"I have now had an opportunity of consulting with scores of people in Alaska on the fisheries question—with fishermen, canners, public officials, business men and experts, in public hearings and otherwise. There has not been a single dissent from the conclusion that there must be strong and immediate restrictions on salmon fishing, if we are to preserve the industry from the same destruction that has ruined many of our national fisheries elsewhere. In fact, it should have been undertaken in Alaska years ago. . . ."

"Restriction on activities naturally causes sacrifice and trouble. I regret that the purpose of the reserves has been deliberately misrepresented. . . ."

"It is to be hoped that Congress will take immediate action to give more constructive authority. In the meantime this administration does not intend to sit idly by denying responsibility under the authority already available, but to use it to the fullest effect. This is the largest of Alaska's industries. More than half her population and more than half her territorial revenues are dependent upon it. It can in time be built up to much larger dimensions than at present. If nothing is done, it will be lost in a few years. It is of vital importance to the whole American people as a source of national food supply. . . ."

"Our primary purpose is to restore this industry. The responsibility rests on the officials who have the authority to translate it into action. Pious statements, scientific discussion, and political oratory will not spawn salmon. . . ."

The battle became very bitter, and a characteristic communication of Hoover's to the chairman of the Senate Committee dated March 16, 1923, reads:

". . . So far as the statements of Delegate Southerland are concerned, there is no polite answer to them. The real issue is that having fitted a lid on the further destruction of the Alaskan fisheries until Congress acts, I intend to sit on it whether Delegate Southerland, certain canners, and certain fishermen like it or not."

On June 24, 1924, Congress passed the law as requested. The Secretary commenting upon this success said:

"The passing of the Alaskan fisheries conservation bill . . . assures the most important step yet accomplished in the preservation of our sea fisheries. I am naturally very much pleased as I have urged this legislation in every session of Congress for the last three years."

"I can stand any amount of personal abuse with all the amiability of the winner. . . ."

"I trust that this is the start of a series of effective measures for the redemption of American sea fisheries. We can, by equally constructive work, yet restore the great lost fisheries of shad, sturgeon, and salmon to the Atlantic coast. This is a great beginning toward conservation and with the public understanding that has come out of this discussion I believe we can make even further headway."

Today the fish in Alaskan waters have become so plentiful as to attract fishing fleets from several nations.

CONSERVATION OF ATLANTIC, PACIFIC AND INLAND FISHERIES

Other problems in fisheries conservation became of great importance. In May, 1921, Hoover called a nation-wide conference on pollution of streams and the ocean, especially by oil dumped in harbors and along the coast. It had not only become a great fire hazard (the great Baltimore fire), but was killing fish by the millions and destroying beaches. He said:

"Pollution of the coastal waters by industrial wastes is yearly becoming a graver menace to the fisheries, shipping, and use of our pleasure beaches. Owing to the recent great increase in the use of fuel oil on shipping and in the utilization of the many petroleum derivatives in industries, the pollution of waters by oil, especially in the vicinity of the more important harbors, has become particularly flagrant and damaging. Legislation is before Congress in this matter, and unless it is enacted great and serious damage will ensue."

After much agitation, Congress acted in June, 1924, and that pollution has disappeared.

In 1924, the Commerce Report said:

"The conservation of our fisheries is a matter of the utmost national importance. Many of them are threatened with extinction. Our great runs of salmon on the Atlantic coast long ago disappeared as a food supply, and the salmon of the Pacific coast were doomed until we recently called a halt on their destruction. The sturgeon fisheries of the Great Lakes have declined 98 per cent in forty years and the sturgeon has been almost displaced on the Atlantic coast. Since 1835 the annual catch of shad in the Potomac has dropped from 22,000,000 to 600,000. In ten years the crab fisheries of the Chesapeake and Delaware have been cut in half.

Our lobster catch is less than one-third of what it was thirty years ago."

"In an address before the Sixth Annual Convention of the United States Fisheries Association at Atlantic City on September 5, 1924, I summarized the situation as follows:"

The Work Accomplished

"First. Congress enacted last winter Federal legislation controlling oil pollution of coastal waters by oil-burning and oil-carrying ships. This measure was vital to the existence of our fisheries and the protection of our shellfish. It is only a beginning at solution of the pollution problem."

"Second. We secured by negotiation with Canada the Pacific coast halibut treaty and the enactment of legislation under which the two nations are now able to halt the depletion and destruction of that great fishery and to start its recuperation."

"Third. Congress, after three years of controversy, enacted the Alaska salmon fisheries conservation bill, and we have today vigorously stopped destruction and started the rejuvenation of these fisheries."

"Fourth. Congress enacted the upper Mississippi fish and game refuge bill through which the streams of the upper Mississippi will be preserved for the breeding of fish and game."

"Fifth. We have had some success in bringing about co-operation between different states for the protection of fisheries."

"These steps have not been accomplished without bitter opposition, part of it venal, part of it innocent, but they have been supported by every true fisherman."

The Next Steps in Conservation

"The steps now before us are still more important. They are:

"1. To cultivate a sense of national responsibility toward the fisheries and their maintenance; to make conservation of those priceless resources a part of the national instinct; to let the whole country understand that we can no more overfish and expect to have seafood than we can outcut the growth of our forests and expect to have timber."

"2. To make a vigorous attempt to restore the sturgeon, salmon, shad, lobster, crab, oyster, and clam and other littoral fisheries on the Atlantic coast."

"3. To secure the prevention of pollution from sources other than ships both in coastal and inland waters."

"4. To undertake the reinforcement of stocks of game fish throughout the United States."

Hoover, being a fisherman himself, did not miss the opportunity to further the interests of the game fishermen. The introduction here of a light touch in Government illuminates also the
Hoover policies in respect to game fish, in an address to the
Izaak Walton League:

"As the head of the Department of Commerce and thus charged with
such responsibilities for our game fisheries as weigh upon the mind of
the Federal Government, I wish to state a fact, to observe a condition,
to relate an experiment, to lay before you a proposition, to offer a protest,
and to give the reasons for all. I shall not discuss the commercial fisheries on this occasion because I wish to be cheerful and philosophical."

"The fact I refer to is that our game fishing is decreasing steadily and
rapidly. The condition is that the present method of rehabilitation
through hatcheries and distribution of fry and fingerlings is a failure
because of high infant mortality. The experiment in the cast indicates
that artificial hatching can be made successful if the fingerlings are carried
through infancy to childhood. The proposition is further to extend these
nurseries in co-operation with this association and all fish clubs. The
protest is that even this is useless unless we can check pollution of our
streams. The reason for all is that fishing is good for the soul of man."

The Fact

"Man and boy, the American is a fisherman. That comprehensive list
of human rights, the Declaration of Independence, is firm that all men
(and boys) are endowed with certain inalienable rights, including life,
liberty, and the pursuit of happiness, which obviously includes the pursuit
of fish. America is a well-watered country, and the inhabitants know all
of the fishing holes."

"The Americans also produce millions of automobiles. These co-ordinate forces of inalienable right, the automobile and the call of the fishing-
hole, propel the man and boy to a search of all the water within a radius
of 150 miles at week-ends alone. He extends it to a radius of 500 miles
on his summer holidays. These radii of operations of all these men and
boys greatly overlap. All of which has overworked the fishing-holes, and
the time between bites has become longer and longer, and the fish have
become wiser and wiser."

"Some millions of fishermen have invented thousands of new lures of
seductive order and devised many new and fearful incantations, with a
host of new kinds of clothes and labor-saving devices to carry them
about."

"We have indeed made stupendous progress in physical equipment to overcome the mysteries of fish. We have moved upward from the rude but social conditions of the willow pole with a butcher-string line, fixed with hooks, ten for a dime, whose compelling lure is one segment of an angle-worm and whose incantation is spitting on the bait. We have arrived at the high state of a tackle, assembled from the steed of Damascus, the bamboos of Siam, the silk of Japan, the lacquer of China, the tin of Bangkok, the nickel of Canada, the feathers of Brazil, and the silver of Colorado—all compounded by mass production at Chicago, Illinois, and Akron, Ohio. And for magic and incantations we have progressed to application of cosmetics for artificial flies and to wonders in special clothing with pigeon-holes for varied lures and liniments and to calling a bite a 'strike.' Nor do I need to repeat that fishing is not the rich man's sport, though his incantations are more expensive. I have said elsewhere that all men are equal before fishes. But I ask you if, in the face of all this overwhelming efficiency and progress, there is less time between bites?"

"However, our fishermen can put in many joyous hours at home polishing up the rods, reels and lures, discussing new flies when the imponderable forces of spring begin to move their bones. They could not get such joy out of a collection of live angleworms, and that is all a part of what we are trying to get at anyway—recreation and soul satisfaction. But I am off the track, because the Department of Commerce deals not in the beatitudes but in statistics. Moreover, we must also maintain the economic rather than the biologic method in discussion or some other department of the Government will accuse Commerce of invading their authority. Nevertheless, I may say, as an aside, that the fishing beatitudes are much amplified since Izaak Walton, for he did not spend his major life answering a bell. He never got the jumps from traffic signals or the price of wheat. Its blessings include not only Edgar Guest's 'wash of the soul' with pure air, but they also now include discipline in the equality of men, meekness and inspiration before the works of nature, charity and patience toward tackle-makers and the fish, a mockery of profits and conceits, a quieting of hate and a hushing to ambition, a rejoicing and gladness that you do not have to decide a blanked thing until next week."

"But to return to the economics of this sport. Having done everything to improve the tackle, lures and incantations we must conclude that the distance between bites has been increased because of rising ratio of water to fish. In other words, there are less fish. And, to slip back to the beatific side of fishing a minute, I might mention that there will be no joy on long winter nights making reinventories of the tackle unless there be behind it the indelible recollection of having caught a few bigger ones last summer. But I will say more on the economic importance of the fishing beatitudes later on."

"Based upon the number of fishing licenses issued in licensing states, the Bureau of Fisheries estimates that 10,000,000 people went game fishing in the year 1926. Any calculation of twenty years ago will show that not 1,000,000 people went fishing during those years. But I have no sympathy with attempts at disarmament of the gigantic army which every year marches against the fish, nor any limitations on its equipment of automobiles, tackle, or incantations. I am for force, more force, and more fish."

"Despite the statistical efficiency of our department, I do not know how many each one of the army captured last year. Judging by my own experience it was not so good. I spent several days searching fishing holes at various points between Chesapeake Bay and the Pacific; I tried to find some spot where not more than six automobiles had already camped, or where the campers did not get up before daylight and thus get the two or three fish which were off guard at that time of day. The state of New Jersey secures an accounting from its licenses of the number of game fish they catch. It works out at about 4.5 fish per fisherman per annum. Fishermen are not liars, and therefore I conclude that even in that well-organized state it was heavy going."

"Now I want to propose to you an idea. I submit to you that each fisherman ought to catch at least fifty during the season. I would like more than that myself, but that ought to be demanded as a minimum under the 'rights' as implied in the Declaration, provided it included one big one for purpose of indelible memory, conversation, and historic record."

"And at once I come to a powerful statistic—that is, 50 fish times 10,-000,000 men and boys—the purpose of which I will establish presently. This minimum ideal of a national catch of 500,000,000 game fish is of the most fundamental importance if we as a nation are to approach a beatific state for even two weeks in the year."

"And as we are thinking nationally, 500,000,000 fish divided amongst 120,000,000 people is not so much as you might think at first, for it is only about 4.1 fish per person, and it includes the little ones as well, and each of us eats 1095 times a year, less whatever meals we miss while fishing."

"At this point some one will deny that we have ever taken any 500,-000,000 fish in a year. I agree with him that we have not attained any such ideal per fisherman in long years. If it had been true, the moral state of the Nation would have been better maintained during the last calendar year. There were lots of people who committed crimes during the year who would not have done so if they had been fishing, and I assure you that the increase in crime is due to a lack of those qualities of mind and character which impregnate the soul of every fisherman except those who get no bites. Unless we can promise at least fifty fish per annum, including that occasional big one for recounting and memory purposes, we may despair of keeping the population from further moral turpitude."

The Condition

"Nearly fifty years ago the game fishermen in certain localities began to complain bitterly to their Congressmen about all this expanding distance between bites, which in economic terms is called the lag. As an equal opportunity for fishing must be properly considered by any great government as a necessity to public tranquility, measures were at once taken. The great Government said: 'we will now apply artificial means to the natural birth and distribution of fish.'"

"Thereafter the Federal Government built 40 game-fish hatcheries. The state governments built 191 hatcheries for game fish, and private enterprise has constructed 60 more. In these mass-production works the maternal carelessness of laying eggs out loose in the water to be eaten by cannibalistic relatives and friends was to be halted and they were thereafter carefully safeguarded in glass jars and troughs and temperatures. The baby fry and fingerlings thus born in security and reared in comfort to half an inch long or so were then placed in private railway cars and distributed back to the streams, being thereupon started on their happy way to be eaten by the same relatives and friends as fresh meat instead of fresh eggs."

"We have steadily increased in zeal in all these endeavors to beat the lag between bites until during the last few years these 291 hatcheries working on fifteen species of game fish turn out an average of 1,100,000,000 infant game fish to be duly launched into life amongst the cannibals."

"In addition to these paternalistic and maternal endeavors on the part of the Government, I am aware that mother nature has herself been busy also. Private enterprise in the shape of responsible mother fish is working upon the same problem; they are probably doing more than the paternal Government, for all I know. Private enterprise usually does. One thing we do know, and that is that it takes a host of fingerlings to provide for the survival of a fish of blessed memory. At a particular control over Alaskan salmon it is estimated that 1,668,750,000 eggs and fry were launched into life and 3,740,000 adult fish came back—and it is thought all who escaped infant mortality did come back—so that the loss was 99.77 per cent. Or, in other words, it took 450 fry to make a fish. And at this rate the annual 1,100,000,000 fry and fingerlings from the whole battery of hatcheries would produce one-third of a fish per fisherman per annum."

"I may say parenthetically that I introduce these statistics of birth registration and infant mortality among fish because it will relieve your minds of anxiety as to accuracy. But if any one feels these figures may be wrong, he has my permission to divide or multiply them by any factor based upon his own experience with the time element in bites, the size of fish, or the special incantations."

"In any event, 1,100,000,000 bureaucratic-mothered fry from all our combined Government hatcheries was only 2.2 fry for each fish in the modest minimum national ideal which I have insisted upon. And if anybody thinks that it only takes 2.2 fry to make a fish he is mightily mistaken. I conclude statistically from my own experience of the time between bites that the Alaskan figure of mortality should be corrected from 99.77 to 99.99 per cent."

"What I am coming to is that it is the solemn fact that only some microscopic per cent of these fry or fingerlings, whether synthetic or natural, ever live to that state of grandeur which will serve as inspiration to polish the tackle or insure the approach to the battle in renewed hope with each oncoming season. And we lose ground every year, sector by sector, as the highways include more fishing holes in the route. We must either multiply the output of our hatcheries by some fearful number or find some other way out."

The Experiment

"Some four years ago I expressed to Commissioner O'Malley, when inducting him into the headship of the Bureau of Fisheries, my complete scepticism over the effectiveness of our synthetic incubation and its statistical relations to the realistic life of a fish. My general thesis was that those infants did not have a dog's chance to gain that maturity which was required either by public policy or to produce the fishing beatitudes. He and his able assistant, Mr. Leach, thereupon started experiments to see if we could not apply mass production in nursing infant trout, bass, and other game fish to an age when they could survive traffic accidents or do battle with cannibals or enter the cannibal ranks themselves—and, in any event, hope to survive. It was my aspiration that if these adolescent youths could not win in open combat, at least some of them reared to

three inches long might make a full meal for a cannibal, instead of his requiring 200 fry fresh out of the eggs and then we would save 199 or so.
These experiments were seriously successful. And the same authorities,
Messrs. O'Malley and Leach, are convinced that by this same means we
have improved the fighting chances of these children of fish up to about a
50-50 go, and thereby our 1,100,000,000 governmental fingerlings might
serve as a base to produce the national ideal of 500,000,000 big ones.
I again refer you to my previous statement on the safety factor in the
magic of statistics."

Nor was it so expensive. One hundred bass couples in specially prepared pools produced 200,000 offsprings and raised them to three inches
long for a total outlay of $500, omitting rent and experts, or four fish for
a cent. Likewise, trout were carried along in life under the shelter of
hated bureaucracy until they could do battle."

"After this preliminary experience I, two years ago, appealed to your
chapters and to fish-and-game clubs throughout the country to co-operate
with us in establishing more experimental nurseries—the Department of
Commerce to furnish free fingerlings, free breeding stock, and free technical supervision. It was as one of the conditions that all streams in each
neighborhood should be stocked with the product so as to give the boy
a chance also. Fifteen chapters of the league, sixteen clubs and private
individuals, five states and municipalities have co-operated and established nurseries in nine states. Pennsylvania leads with fourteen stations.
Minnesota is next with thirteen stations, every one of the latter being
league chapters whose officers should be taken to the heart of every man
and boy who has hopes for the fishing beatitudes. The state of New
Jersey, working independently from the same conclusions, has done wonders on their own."

"Last year was our first year; 4,667,000 fish were raised up to battling
age in these co-operative nurseries and delivered into the streams. The
annual capacity of these nurseries when going full blast is probably near
20,000,000 fish. I believe those who have overcome their initial troubles
are enthusiastic of success."

The Proposition

"Now, the purpose of this speech and these statistics is to demonstrate
that we need more nurseries. We ought to have several hundred. They
are inexpensive compared to the annual outlay on tackle and the automobile journey to the fishing-holes. When you get through at that fish-
ing-hole you would have been glad to have paid for several hundred fish
at the rate of four to a cent. And by stocking all streams in the neigh-

borhood, they offer a large opportunity for establishing fealty from the small boy to the ideals of the sportsman. He may, for sound reasons of his own, continue to use his worn fly or even a worm, but be assured he will grow up to refined tackle all right later on."

"Our Government, national and state, is today spending nearly $2,000,-000 a year on game-fish hatcheries. We are convinced of their futility unless we can carry their work this one stage further. That stage should be accomplished through local effort and co-operation, and the Federal Government is prepared to furnish instruction, advice, breeding-stock, and fingerlings free to any chapter or club which will undertake it. If every state in the Union would respond as Minnesota, Pennsylvania, and New Jersey have responded, the job is done."

"The hatcheries are the necessary works for mass production of infant fish. That is a technical job requiring large expense, high skill, and training. Clubs cannot well undertake to run them, and we have long since accepted that as a proper function of the Federal and state governments."

"But the nurseries require only a few thousand dollars for plant and but a few hundred dollars annually for operation. It is our view that the nurseries are the only agency that will make the hatcheries worth while. If our nurseries could turn out 500,000,000 three-inch fish, we could trust the natural mothers to supply the balance."

"And I appeal to the fishermen of America to take up and further exhaust this great hope of permanent game-fishing in our country. It is your problem, and the remedy for a departing sport is with you. Not by demanding that an already maternally and paternally responsible Government do everything on earth, but in the pride of sportsmen to do their own job. Unless something like this be done, our sons will not be catching the limit. It is the real hope of triumph over the discouragement between bites."

The Protest

"And there is another phase of all this. Aside from the cannibalistic enemies of infant, adolescent and adult fish, acting in lively alliance with the organized army of 10,000,000 fishermen, we have still another fish enemy to deal with. That is pollution. Herein is the poison cup which we give to eggs, fry, fingerlings, adolescence, and adult fish alike."

"Now, if we want fish we have to reserve some place for them to live. They all occur in the water, but it happens that nature adapted them to clean water. I suppose that was because nature foresaw no fishing beatitudes along a sewer."

"And this question of pollution has a multitude of complications and lack of understanding."

"There are as many opinions about pollution as there are minds concerning it. Those who oppose it are not under the spell of the fishing lure. Pollution exists in different waters in different degrees—from ships, factories, coal mines, chemical works in cities and towns—only to mention a few of them. Many of these things damage public health, destroy the outdoor appeal of the streams, and all of them damage the fish."

"But after all we are an industrial people. We have to work at least eight hours a day and all but two or three weeks in the year, and we cannot abolish our industries and still pay for fishing tackle. So I have long since come to the conclusion that what we really need in every state, through our state authorities, is that there should be a survey of all the streams and a division of them into three categories."

"First, to determine the streams that have not yet been polluted, then give immediate protection to these streams, or parts of them, that they never shall be polluted; that no industry shall be allowed to settle upon them unless there is adequate guaranty that there will be no pollution. The second category includes the streams that are polluted to the finish. There are many of these that could never be recovered, as a matter of practical fact, without the displacement of hundreds of thousands of people from their homes through the crushing of their industries. The numbers who would benefit by clearing them would be infinitesimal compared to the suffering and loss implied in such an operation."

"Then we should have a third category of streams—those that are perhaps partially polluted, where we could get correction by systematic and sound action and gradually restore them to the first category."

"There are also problems of pollution of our coastal waters. I have discussed that before and will not enter upon it now. The same handling of our stream pollution is the first conservation measure in our country. For various reasons of states' rights it is but little a Federal problem. But states' rights are state responsibility and the mental complex of some states that their rights extend to passing the buck to the Federal Government needs psychopathic treatment by indignant chapters of the Izaak Walton League."

The Reason for It

"Now, the reasons for all this are some of them economic in their nature, some moral, and some spiritual. Our standards of material progress include the notion and the hope that we shall lessen the daily hours of labor on the farm, at the bench, and in the office—except for public servants. We also dream of longer annual holidays and more of them, as scientific routine and mass production do our production job faster and faster. And when they do the job at all they dull the souls of men unless their leisure hours become the period of life's objective—stimulation and fishing."

"We are decreasing hours. These same infallible clocks of progress, the humble statistics, tell us that the gainfully employed have steadily decreased in hours of work during the whole of thirty years. The great majority of us (except public officials) really work no more than eight hours a day except during the stress of planting or harvest or elections. Anyway, if we sleep eight hours we have eight hours in which to ruminate and make merry or stir the caldron of evil. This civilization is not going to depend upon what we do when we work so much as what we do in our time off. The moral and spiritual forces of our country do not lose ground in the hours we are busy on our jobs; their battle is the leisure time. We are organizing the production of leisure. We need better organization of its consumption. We devote vast departments of Government, the great agencies of commerce and industry, science and invention, to decreasing the hours of work, but we devote comparatively little to improving the hours of recreation. We associate joy with leisure. We have great machinery of joy, some of it destructive, some of it synthetic, some of it mass production. We go to chain theatres and movies; we watch somebody else knock a ball over the fence or kick it over the goal post. I do that and I believe in it. I do, however, insist that no other organized joy has values comparable to the outdoor experience. We gain less from the other forms in moral stature, in renewed purpose in life, in kindness, and in all the fishing beatitudes. We gain none of the constructive, rejuvenating joy that comes from return to the solemnity, the calm and inspiration of primitive nature. The joyous rush of the brook, the contemplation of the eternal flow of the stream, the stretch of forest and mountain all reduce our egotism, soothe our troubles, and shame our wickedness."

"And in it we make a physical effort that no sitting on cushions, benches, or side lines provides. To induce people to take its joy they need some stimulant from the hunt, the fish, or the climb. I am for fish. Fishing is not so much getting fish as it is a state of mind and a lure to the human soul into refreshment."

"But it is too long between bites; we must have more fish in proportion to the water."

[Hoover After Dinner, p. 91]

PUBLIC WORKS POLICIES

NATIONAL PLANNING

Hoover was the pioneer in advocating the policy of national planning of public works—(national planning in its true sense—not a cover-up for economic coercion). He was by instinct and profession a builder. During his four years as President, more peace-time public construction was started and consummated than under all the preceding administrations for thirty-six years including the Panama Canal. His policies called for useful works. He strongly opposed Federal "made" work, both from a moral and from an economic point of view.

Immediately after the War, Hoover began a crusade for this practical brand of national planning, calling for the establishment of a national Department of Public Works as the first step. (See also *Reorganization of the Federal Government,* page 561.) Speaking at Minneapolis, on August 26, 1920, he said:

"The time has arrived in our national development when we must have a definite national program in the development of our great engineering problems. Our rail and water transport, our water supply for irrigation, our reclamation, the provision of future fuel resources, the development of distribution of electrical power, all cry out for some broad-visioned national guidance. We must create a national engineering sense of provision for the Nation as a whole. . . . Just as our medical associations voice the necessity of safeguards to national health; as the bar associations of safeguards to our judiciary, so the engineers should exert themselves in our national engineering policies. We have none; but we need some, or the next generation will face a lower instead of a higher standard of living than ours."

"The development of our transportation, fuel, power, and water under private initiative has been one of the stimuli that has created the greatness of our people . . . this haphazard development must be co-ordinated . . . involves problems beyond individual initiative alone . . . the problems involve political, financial, interstate matters. . . ."

". . . All of these problems are much akin, and the time has come when they need some illumination, guidance, co-operation in their solution from the Federal Government. Nor do I mean a vast extension of Federal bureaucracy in Federal ownership. If . . . through an agency of the central government, we could have an adequate study and preparation of plan and method made of these problems, for engineering development over the next fifty years . . . we would have taken the first step toward . . . an increasing standard of living . . . for our descendants. . . ."

". . . In order that we shall have some central point in the Federal Government where these problems may be adequately considered, from which they can be ventilated for the verdict of public opinion, where the business brains of the country can be called into conference and co-operation with the Government, and therefore with the people, the engineers of the United States have proposed time and time again that a Cabinet department should be established in Washington, either new or to replace the Interior Department, to which should be assigned the whole question of public works . . . such a department has become an essential . . . proper consideration and presentation to the American people of these broader national engineering problems, upon which the next generation must depend if our country is to march forward."

He developed this concept on many occasions. In a notable address in Seattle, on August 21, 1926, he said:

"The time has come when we must take an enlarged vision of the future. . . . We have need that we formulate a new and broad national program for the full utilization of our streams, our rivers, and our lakes."

"Water is today our greatest undeveloped resource. Our streams and rivers offer us a possible total of 55,000,000 horespower and of this less than 11,000,000 has been developed. Of our 25,000 miles of possible inland waterways, probably less than 7000 are really modernized, and the utility of much of these 7000 miles is minimized by their isolation into segments of what should be connected transportation systems. We still have 20,000,000 acres of possible reclaimable and irrigable lands."

"These water resources lie in every part of the Union. The great basins of the Columbia, the Colorado, the Sacramento, the San Joaquin, the Mississippi, the Arkansas, the Platte, the Missouri, the Ohio, the Cumberland, the Tennessee, the Warrior, the Hudson, the Great Lakes, the St. Lawrence, and many others.

"True conservation of water is not the prevention of use. Every drop of water that runs to the sea without yielding its full commercial returns to the Nation is an economic loss."

"We have for a century and a half concentrated ourselves upon development of our land and our mineral resources; we have conserved our forests and developed our rail and highway transportation. Our Government has done some effective work with water but we have wasted vast sums of public money under political pressures; and we have now skimmed off the easy jobs. Today it is the major engineering jobs and the opportunity of great national design which lie before us."

"We must broaden our sights and determine great policies and programs. The great policy we need adopt is a resolution of vigorous development. The program is a problem of each great drainage. We must no longer think in terms of single power sites or single storage dams or single land projects, or single navigation improvements; we must think (and thanks to science and engineering we can think) in terms of the co-ordinated long-view development of each river system to its maximum utilization."

"If we study each of our great systems, we shall find that their possibilities lie each in its own case either in navigation, flood control, reclamation, irrigation, or electrical power. On some drainages all these uses are available, in others but part of them. But, in any event, each system must be considered as a whole and organized to the maximum results."

He then outlined the different great river drainages and their possibilities and continued as to finance and administration:

"The question at once arises as to who is to finance and own these great developments. . . . The development of these rivers and lake systems involve either the development of navigation, flood control, reclamation, irrigation, or electrical power. Some of these systems involve only one kind of development—some several."

"Navigation should be improved at the direct cost of the Federal Government, but with contributions from local governments. . . . The Federal Government has long since contributed directly to flood control in support of local and state action. The Federal Government has given assistance . . . irrigation and reclamation works, but with the presumed provision that the cost should be recovered from the land."

"Other forms of finance lie in the undertakings of irrigation or reclamation districts; the undertakings of municipalities in the procurement of their domestic water supplies; the undertakings of states and local parties in flood control and navigation works and in the great undertakings of our hydro-electric companies. . . . We have here also a problem of determining the limits of private and public development. It appears to me obvious that where the major purpose of a given development is navigation or irrigation, reclamation or flood control, then either the Federal Government or the states or some particular local district must assume the burden and ownership of the permament works."

"Our problems become more complex when electrical power is involved. It is my own view that the Federal Government should not go into the busines of either generation or distributing electrical power. There may be some special cases, but our general policy should be against it. Where power is a by-product of dams for other major public purposes such as navigation, etc., then the Federal Government should lease the power rights so as to recover as much or the whole of its total investment as can be. . . . It should be leased under provisions of the Federal Water Power Acts which amply provide for control by the Government."

Hoover was the first to set up the idea of national planning of these public works through commissions assigned to different drainages. Reviewing this question, he said, on August 21, 1926:

". . . primary requirement to national advance in these questions is better organization, both for determination of plans and for their execution. I hesitate to discuss the subject because it presents such an appalling picture of what is otherwise a very efficient Nation. Our first need is complete engineering studies of every drainage that we may have the basic fact upon which to determine engineering plans. We already have such information but in no case complete. Our second need is organization to determine a procedure and to co-ordinate interests."

". . . in most of these projects there is involved . . . the Federal Government, often several state governments, municipalities, irrigation, reclamation and flood-control districts and power companies. I might add that some of these projects involve international relationships with Mexico and Canada. I have mentioned the quarrels, litigation, and political obstructions in progress with respect to many of these projects. . . . There are four independent Federal administrative departments concerned; there are two or three different administrative departments in each state and there is conflict of opinion between representatives of counties, municipalities, and districts. Congress and committees thereof, the governments and legislatures of several states are also concerned, not to mention town councils and district boards. There are also involved the hydro-electric companies."

". . . there are no agencies which can pull these policies into some definite form."

". . . finance . . . must be created by securing the co-operation of Federal, state, municipal and district governments, and often the power companies. There is nobody to formulate financial plans. . . ."

"Nor am I about to propose any extension of Federal bureaucracy. I want to see more local responsibility. Moreover, we are a democracy and we must proceed by persuasion."

". . . the Lower Mississippi River Commission . . . through whose skill over a term of years we have at last evolved peace, finance, construction, navigation, and flood control on the lower river. I should like to see a commission set up separately on each of these great drainages, on which not only the Federal Government but also state governments concerned could be represented and which would also include independent technical members. I would not give to these commissions the power and task of spending money, of construction or administration. We have efficient engineering corps in our Federal and local governments for technical determinations and the execution of construction can be administered through existing agencies of the Government or by way of Federal contributions to the states or districts."

"The job of these commissions should be to consider the engineering data, to think, to plan, to devise, advise, co-ordinate, negotiate, persuade, and set upon the obstreperous. They should determine major lines of policy to be undertaken; they should organize the financial support and recommend what administrative bodies—national, state, or local—should undertake execution (if they are governmental works) and they should make recommendations to Congress or state legislatures for action. . . ."

". . . better organizations of our agencies for construction and administration, with view to reducing conflicting agencies in the Federal Government and with a view to building up a center point for real and constructive national policies and for administration in engineering and construction and great economy in expenditure. . . . I have many times recommended that all of our different Federal activities in public works be concentrated into a Public Works Division of the Interior Department, . . . our able army engineers assigned to that section in peace time. . . ."

Hoover elaborated upon these proposals in addresses delivered from 1920 to 1932 before public bodies in some thirty

cities. In order to build up regional understanding of co-ordina-
tion and planning, he designated "The Mississippi System,"
"The Great Lakes-St. Lawrence System," "The Colorado River
System," "The Columbia River System," the "Great Valleys of
California," "The Intercoastal Waterways" and others. (Report
of Secretary of Commerce, 1926, pp. 9, 10, 11.)

At one time or another, he was instrumental in securing, in
addition to the existing Mississippi River Commission, the
erection of preliminary commissions for study and co-ordination
of the St. Lawrence, the Colorado, and the Great Valleys of
California, and in securing preliminary studies and surveys by
the Government engineers in practically every other drainage
of the country. Here was the birth of real national planning.

A typical address developing these questions is one before the
National Rivers and Harbors Conference in Washington, D. C.,
on December 9, 1925, where Secretary Hoover outlined a new
national policy:

"If we were to make a survey of the many great problems of progress
that lie before us, the development of the whole of our internal waterways
would stand at the forefront. And we have reached an entirely new era
in this development. We need to take a re-inventory of these resources
in the light of new economic necessities, new facts, and the older forces
that have been slowly crystallizing over recent years. From them we
have need to adopt an entirely new and enlarged conception of these
questions. . . ."

"But their planning and construction will test our vision and our
statesmanship. For we must consider their development not alone in the
light of the needs of today, but of those beyond our time and our
generation."

"The new setting, the new departure, in which we find ourselves develops from many causes. Of these the most vital are the competitive
difficulties in which our Middle West agriculture has been thrown by the
shifting economic currents resulting from the War. . . . But there are
involved in this question also other great national problems. There is high
need of better distribution of our population in relief of the increasing
congestion of our seaboard states."

"We must plan and provide greatly increased transportation facilities
for the 40,000,000 of added population that we must serve within the
next quarter of a century. . . ."

"Such solutions are now made possible by the development in the art
of engineering. . . ."

"But first and foremost, we must envisage our inland waterways as great unified transportation systems, not as isolated units. We must conceive and attack their construction as a connected whole, not as a collection of disconnected lake and river projects which has been our habit in the past. The success and usefulness of any transportation system whether rail or water or highway will depend upon a broad inter-connection of numbers of great cities and their agricultural and industrial hinterlands not only between themselves, but with the seaboard. Nor are the economic problems of the Middle West, such as our agricultural problems, limited to the valley of one river or tributary. They are vivid in every state and we must march to their relief as a whole with a broad vision of their needs and the full utilization of our resources."

"The topography of our country, the present and future necessities of our population, the development we have already accomplished, and above all, the goodness of Providence in our natural water channels clearly define for us two such major inland waterways systems, the Mississippi system and the Great Lakes system. Beyond these and connecting with them is our overseas merchant marine. . . . We could project a system of main trunk lines and laterals of a total of 9000 miles in a consolidated barge system."

The Mississippi System

"This would comprise an east-west trunk line from Pittsburgh through Cairo to St. Louis and to Kansas City, a distance of 1600 miles, and it would comprise a north-south trunk waterway of 1500 miles from New Orleans to Chicago, connecting at that point with the Great Lakes . . . by improvement of the upper Mississippi . . . by improvement of the upper Missouri . . . by improvement of the Tennessee and the Cumberland . . . by improvement of the Arkansas, we could bring in Little Rock, and by improvement of the coastal canal, we could bring in Galveston and Houston; and so on with the other possible laterals. We could create this one consolidated system of transportation. . . ."

The Great Lakes System

"The Great Lakes system is a co-ordinating part of this whole problem. The Lakes today are the greatest inland transportation system in the world. . . . This system for ocean-going ships would comprise over 3000 miles of routes. These two great systems of inland transportation together will have a combined length of nearly 12,000 miles."

"The people of our Middle West need and insist that the seagoing ships on the Great Lakes shall have access to the ocean. . . . There are three major reasons . . . the agricultural situation . . . the industrial situation . . . the distribution of population in the country. . . ."

". . . Industry . . . is greatly congested in our Atlantic seaboard states. One of our great social problems today is this overgrowth of cities. Through the improvement of our interior waterways it will be possible to better distribute industry and population because these waterways will make it advantageous to move much production nearer to the area of consumption. . . ."

In an address at St. Louis, on November 22, 1926, Secretary Hoover said:

". . . The public necessity of a broader national policy, larger vision, and better organization in the treatment of these, our greatest undeveloped national resources. Every important river, stream, and lake presents some opportunity to increase our natural assets through the development of either navigation, power, reclamation, land protection, or flood control—or all of them. That we shall develop this heritage in public interest with economy and efficiency is of first national importance."

"There are some things which we must keep ever before us in connection with the whole problem of the utilization of our water resources."

"1. We must have a larger, broader, more definite national policy and better organization in the development of all of our water resources—for transportation, power, flood control, reclamation—in order that we may bring them in as rapidly as national need requires."

"2. The Midwest is primarily interested in the development of the Mississippi system, in navigation problems on the Great Lakes themselves, and in the shipway from the Lakes to the sea—a transportation system of 12,000 miles in length. Better distribution of population, relief from burdensome freight rates imposed by the War, aid to agriculture and to industry will result from the development of these resources in the heart of the country."

"3. The whole interior waterways system is a problem of greater depth—a six or nine-foot channel in all of our rivers, stabilization of the depths of the Great Lakes, deepening their channels and the construction of the great shipway."

"4. A unified connected system, with interconnection of the great Mississippi system and the Lakes, is essential. Disconnected though improved segments are of no avail. The whole chain is only as useful as the weakest link."

"5. The opening of the Great Lakes to the sea is feasible and must come. Determination of the route will be made speedily."

"6. Controversies between states and municipalities over the lowering of lake levels will not bring relief as speedily as will the pouring of cement and can be solved by engineering, not by law, for the largest part of it is climatic."

"7. A unified program for completing the whole Mississippi system is necessary. The capital cost will not exceed $120,000,000 beyond present appropriations and not more than five years in time."

"On this occasion I propose to review briefly these questions as they concern your immediate interest—the waterways of the Midwest, and to attempt a summary of the reasons why we advocate the vigorous prosecution of this development."

"It warrants oft repeating that in the Mississippi River and its tributaries—the Mississippi system—in the Great Lakes and their possible outlet to the sea, we possess 12,000 miles of inland waterways; that these waterways penetrate more than twenty states; that scores of cities are on their banks, that they cover the agricultural heart of America; that they cannot only be interconnected among themselves, but they lead from the Great Lakes to the sea, both at the Gulf and the North Atlantic."

"These are not new channels that we have suddenly discovered. All these miles of waterways were at one time or another the scene of water-borne commerce for more than a hundred years—some of them were the trade routes of North America three centuries ago."

"On our rivers the romantic three-foot packet boats with their few tons of burden were the pioneers of Western transportation. Their teeming life faded before the more economical transportation of the railways. In the meantime, engineering has given to us the prosaic trains of tugs pushing 500 to 2000-ton steel barges, the box-cars of inland waterways—if we but deepen our rivers by a six or nine feet. . . ."

"Our Government has worked at deepening these channels in spots and isolated projects for many years, but in our national policies what we have missed is the idea that to make a really successful transportation system requires large interconnected systems of trunk lines from seaboard with great feeders from our lateral rivers and its consequent widespread and diversified traffic. We have begun important works at the outer ends and worked back. We would not build a great railway system begun at the outer ends and building back toward the terminals and expect traffic to develop in the meantime."

"Moreover, we have wasted vast sums of money in interrupted execution and sporadic and irresolute policies, until today we find ourselves with a mass of disconnected segments of a transportation system, the peacefulness of some of which from the noise of commerce furnished constant munitions of criticism to our opponents. . . ."

"If we are to substitute trains of steel barges on our rivers for box-cars, we must not only have depth but we must have interconnection so that we may find employment for these box-cars with diversified traffic meshing into the different seasons of the year. Without such a completed and interconnected transportation system we cannot expect the most economic transportation of any one section; we cannot expect that our waterways will perform their real function either as to cost of transportation or as to supply of sufficient craft, or the building up of sound transportation companies to take advantage of their opportunities. Nor without interconnection of our great Mississippi system with the Lakes will we realize the full values of either. . . ."

"I should like to avail myself of this occasion to carry your thought to even wider aspects of national development of our water resources. Speaking recently in the Northwest, I commented upon the necessity of a larger, broader, and more definite national policy in development of all of our water resources."

"The development of science, in construction work, in transportation craft, in electrical power, in intensive agriculture, together with the new economic pressures resulting from the War and increasing population, have created possibilities of great wealth in practically every important river, stream, and lake in our country. In each of our great drainages some one or all of these different possible assets in navigation, power, reclamation, land protection, or flood control are to be found. . . ."

"I have spoken here today on the three great possible developments—that is, the Mississippi system, improvement of the Great Lakes, and their connection with the sea. Beyond this again there are great projects in our intercoastal canals and other great hydrographic basins such as the Columbia, Colorado, and other important streams. There are intricate problems of relationship of different forms of development, intricate questions of organization and finance which can only find solution if we shall develop some organization for broad consideration of the program for the development of each of these great drainages."

"First, we must have the engineering facts with regard to the potentialities of each drainage. We do not adequately possess it today. Second, we must have some center point from which broad policies can be evolved and directed. Third, we must have better organization in the administration of construction of the great works which they involve."

THE MISSISSIPPI FLOOD OF 1927 AND THE DEVELOPMENT
OF NEW FLOOD CONTROL

In 1927, there occurred an unprecedented flood of the Mississippi. Secretary Hoover was drafted by the President and the governors of those states to take charge of the situation. Over one million people had to be moved out and the destruction of property was enormous. He took a large part with the army engineers in the formulation of the new plan for flood control; helped to pass it through the Congress and to secure President Coolidge's support to it.

In his report to President Coolidge released to the press, on July 20, 1927, he said:

"The flood relief embraces four stages with four district organizations required—*i.e.,* rescue, care of exiles, rehabilitation, and flood control. . . ."

"The rescue organization has been mobilized, several hundred thousand people were brought out of the water . . . loss of only three lives. The . . . organization has been largely demobilized."

"The county reconstruction committees are making substantial progress with rehabilitation in 101 counties considerably flooded; 2,000,000 acres of crops that were lost have been replanted with staple crops mostly from seed furnished by the relief."

"In all . . . the destitute sufferers were furnished with a supply of food and feed on leaving camps; and, if their homes were destroyed, they were given their tents; they are being given household furniture, implements, and animals. The repairs of damaged homes and building of new homes, for those who cannot provide for themselves, are now in progress. . . . Sanitary measures are being set up in every county to put down malaria and other communicable diseases. . . . We shall have spent on the whole relief operation $13,400,000 from the Red Cross fund, $7,000,000 equipment and supplies from the Federal Government, $3,-000,000 free railway transportation, and provided $1,100,000 for county health clean-up units from other sources."

"The greatest of all measures needed is prompt and effective flood control and quick legislation, for that will restore confidence and from confidence will come a recovery in values and in business. It seems clear that flood control must embrace the following principles:

"(a) Higher and consequently wider levees and the extension of Federal responsibility for levees on some of the tributaries."

"(b) A safety valve upon the levees system by the provision of a 'spillway,' or more properly called a 'by-pass,' to the Gulf to protect New Orleans and Southern Louisiana—most probably using the Atchafalaya River for this purpose."

"(c) Of further safety measures the engineers are examining the possible extension of the by-pass in the northward from the Atchafalaya towards the Arkansas, the possible erection of emergency flood basins and the possibilities of storage in the tributaries."

"There is no question that the Mississippi River can be controlled if a bold and proper engineering plan is developed. It is not possible for the country to contemplate the constant jeopardy which now exists to 1,500,-000 of its citizens or the stupendous losses which the lack of adequate control periodically brings about. Furthermore, flood control means the secure development of some 20,000,000 acres of land capable of supporting five to ten millions of Americans. The cost of such work if spread over ten years would be an inconsiderable burden upon the country. It is not incompatible with national economy to prevent $10 of economic loss by the expenditure of $1 Federal outlay."

During the 1928 Presidential campaign, Hoover put forward these policies of planned public works vigorously.

Speaking at Palo Alto, on August 11, 1928, he said:

"Nearly all of our greater drainages contain within themselves possibilities of cheapened transportation, irrigation, reclamation, domestic water supply, hydro-electric power, and frequently the necessities of flood control. But this development of our waters requires more definite national policies in the systematic co-ordination of those different works upon each drainage area. We have wasted scores of millions by projects undertaken not as a part of a whole but as the consequence of purely local demands. We cannot develop modernized water transportation by isolated projects. We must develop it as a definite and positive interconnected system of transportation. We must adjust reclamation and irrigation to our needs for more land. Where they lie together we must co-ordinate transportation with flood control, the development of hydro-electric power and of irrigation, else we shall as in the past commit errors that will take years and millions to remedy."

"All these projects will probably require an expenditure of upward of one billion dollars within the next four years. It comprises the largest engineering construction ever undertaken by any government. It involves three times the expenditure laid out upon the Panama Canal. It is justified by the growth, need, and wealth of our country."

REVISION OF THE MISSISSIPPI–GREAT LAKES PROJECTS

Speaking at Louisville, Kentucky, on October 23, 1929, he discussed the policies to be applied to what he had five years before designated as the Mississippi System and to the other waterways.

". . . I suggested that all these tributaries of the Mississippi and the Great Lakes comprised a single great transportation system. That it must be developed in vision of the whole and not in parts. . . ."

"I may well summarize their present condition and enunciate the policies of my administration in respect to them :"

"1. As a general and broad policy I favor modernizing of every part of our waterways which will show economic justification in aid of our farmers and industries."

"2. The Mississippi system comprises over 9000 miles of navigable streams. I find that about 2200 miles have now been modernized to 9 feet in depth, and about 1400 miles have been modernized to at least 6 feet in depth. Therefore some 5000 miles are yet to be connected or completed so as to be of purpose to modern commerce. We should establish a 9-foot depth in the trunk system. While it is desirable that some of the tributaries be made accessible to traffic at 6 or 7 feet, yet we should in the long view look forward to increasing this latter depth as fast as traffic justifies it."

"This administration will insist upon building these waterways as we would build any other transportation system—that is, by extending its ramifications solidly outward from the main trunk lines. Substantial traffic or public service cannot be developed upon a patchwork of disconnected local improvement and intermediate segments. Such patchwork has in past years been the sink of hundreds of millions of public money."

"3. We must design our policies so as to establish private enterprise in substitution for Government operation of the barges and craft upon these waterways. We must continue Government barge lines through the pioneering stages, but we must look forward to private initiative not only as the cheapest method of operation but as the only way to assured and adequate public service."

"4. We should complete the entire Mississippi system within the next five years. We shall then have built a great north and south trunk waterway entirely across our country from the Gulf to the northern boundaries, and a great east and west route, halfway across the United States. Through the tributaries we shall have created a network of transportation. We shall then have brought a dozen great cities into direct communication by water; we shall have opened cheaper transportation of primary goods to the farmers and manufacturers of over a score of states."

"5. At the present time we have completed 746 miles of intracoastal canals. We still have approximately 1000 miles to build. We should complete this program over a period of less than ten years."

"6. We should continue improvement of the channels in the Great Lakes; we should determine and construct those works necessary for stabilizing the lake levels."

"7. One of the most vital improvements to transportation on the North American Continent is the removal of the obstacles in the St. Lawrence River to ocean-going vessels inward to the Great Lakes. Our Nation should undertake to do its part whenever our Canadian friends have overcome those difficulties which lie in the path of their making similar undertakings. . . ."

"8. We shall expedite the work of flood control on the lower Mississippi in every manner possible. In the working out of plans we find it necessary to reconsider one portion of the project, that is, the floodway below the Arkansas, but work in other directions will proceed in such fashion that there will be no delay of its completion under the ten-year program assigned to it."

"9. With the increasing size of ocean-going vessels and the constantly expanding volume of our commerce, we must maintain unceasing development of our harbors and the littoral waterways which extend inland from them."

"10. The total construction of these works which I have mentioned amounts to projects three and four times as great as the Panama Canal. In order that there may be no failure in administration, and as an indication of our determination to pursue these works with resolution, we have in the past month entirely recast the organization of this executive staff in the Government. With the approval of the Secretary of War, and under the newly appointed Chief of Engineers, we have assigned to each of these major projects a single responsible engineer. We thus secure a modern business organization, direct responsibility, and continuous administration."

"At the present time we are expending approximately $85,000,000 per annum on new construction and maintenance of these works. To complete these programs within the periods I have mentioned will require an increase in the Government outlay by about $10,000,000 per annum not including the St. Lawrence; at most, including that item, an increase in our expenditures of say $20,000,000 a year. A considerable proportion of this will end in five years' time. It is of the nature of a capital investment."

"This annual increase is equal to the cost of one-half of one battleship. If we are so fortunate as to save this annual outlay on naval construction as the result of the forthcoming naval conference in London, nothing could be a finer or more vivid conversion of swords to plowshares."

[*State Papers, Vol. I, pp. 119 ff.*]

As President, Hoover and the Secretary of War, Patrick Hurley, proceeded to carry out these policies with vigor. They had already reorganized the work of the Corps of Army Engineers into decentralized districts to make progress more effective. Congress responded and legislation was passed authorizing the engineers to study and report upon practically the entire program. It authorized the construction of a large part of it in an act signed July 4, 1930.

In a public statement in respect to this legislation, Hoover said:

"It was with particular satisfaction that I signed the Rivers and Harbors Bill as it represents the final authorization of the engineering work by which we construct and co-ordinate our great systems of waterways and harbors, which I have advocated for over five years; it was promised in the last campaign and in my recommendations to Congress."

"We can now build the many remaining segments of a definite canalization of our river systems through which modern barge trains of 10,000 to 15,000 tons of burden can operate systematically through the Midwest and to the Gulf of Mexico, and through the Lakes to the Atlantic The system, when completed, will have 12,000 miles of waterways and will give waterway connections between such great cities as New Orleans, Memphis, Knoxville, Chattanooga, St. Louis, Kansas City, Omaha, and Sioux City, Keokuk, Minneapolis, St. Paul, Chicago, Evansville, Cincinnati, Wheeling, and Pittsburgh. Through the Great Lakes and the Erie Canal many of those points will have access to central New York and the Atlantic. By its authorization for deepening of lake channels we shall support the present commerce of the Great Lakes and make preparation for ocean shipping by the ultimate deepening of the St. Lawrence. It authorizes numerous improvements in our harbors."

"It is a long view plan for the future. It will require many years to complete its construction. I do not propose that we should proceed in a haphazard manner, but that we should approach the problem on sound engineering lines, completing the main trunk systems and gradually extending the work outward along the lateral rivers. . . ."

"In aggregate this inland waterway undertaking represents a larger project than even the Panama Canal. It will provide employment for thousands of men. It should be fruitful of decreased transportation charges on bulk goods, should bring great benefits to our farms and to our industries. It should result in a better distribution of population away from the congested centers."   [*State Papers, Vol. I, p. 349*]

On August 24, 1930, the President directed the speeding up of governmental waterways and flood control projects to relieve unemployment. The War Department apportioned special funds for this construction and Congressional appropriations were steadily increased. (See *Relief: Public Works,* page 389.)

The deepening of the lower Mississippi for navigation was largely finished during the Hoover Administration. The canalization of the Ohio was completed. The deepening of the upper Mississippi, the canalization to Chicago and the lower Missouri were greatly advanced. The deep waterway to Stockton, the enlargement of the San Pedro Harbor, the deepening of the Hudson to Albany for ocean-going vessels were completed. The intercoastal canal system was greatly extended. Studies of coordinated development on the Columbia, Tennessee, Cumberland, upper Missouri and upper Mississippi Rivers were finished.

The flood control of the Mississippi and the Sacramento Rivers was largely completed.

During the Hoover Administration a total of over $700,000,-000 was expended in river, harbor, flood control, and reclamation projects, advancing them further in this four years than in the previous thirty years.

The great Flood Control plan for the thousand miles below Cairo on the Mississippi River with which Hoover had been so much identified proved so sound and so substantial that when the unprecedented Ohio flood of 1937 poured into it, there was not the loss of a life or consequential property.

ST. LAWRENCE WATERWAY

This great North American improvement which would make seaports of all the Great Lakes cities, would develop some 3,-000,000 electrical horsepower and decrease farmers' freight rates had been under desultory discussion for some years. As Secretary of Commerce, Hoover brought the subject to real life by securing in 1922 the opening of formal negotiations with Canada. As a result of these negotiations national engineering commissions were created by each government. New projects and estimated costs were reviewed. The engineering commissions divided sharply upon methods and the project seemed hopeless.

In 1924, President Coolidge appointed Secretary Hoover chairman of the American St. Lawrence Commission, to review the project, to undertake discussions with the Canadian Government and to find a common basis of engineering and public action. As Canada was not yet prepared for definite action, the negotiations lagged greatly. Furthermore, divisions grew up among the Lake cities as to the method and there was opposition from the power companies and seaboard cities fearful that it would divert their traffic. Hoover painstakingly planed out oppositions, conciliating conflicts and differences, engineering, economic and political.

The thirteenth Annual Report, 1925, of the Secretary of Commerce said:

"Some progress has been made toward the ultimate foundation of the project to open a route between the Great Lakes and the ocean, thus enabling deep-sea vessels to penetrate the interior of the country, with great advantages to our farmers, our manufacturers, and particularly the whole of the people in the eighteen states adjacent to the Lakes."

"Negotiations were initiated with Canada in 1922, at the request of Secretary Hoover, for a consideration of the improvement of the St. Lawrence River from Lake Ontario to Montreal, providing not only canalization for deep-sea navigation to the Lakes, but the development of large quantities of electrical power. National commissions were created in both Canada and this country.[1] . . . A joint engineering board . . . is actively at work on the engineering aspects and will report early next year. Concurrent with this, the Department of Commerce has in process a critical economic study of the effects and benefits of this great project."

[1]On the American St. Lawrence Commission were Charles L. Allen, William C. Breed, Charles P. Craig, James F. Davidson, Stephen B. Davis, James P. Goodrich, James R. Howard, and James P. Noonan.

"Irrespective of the route selected, there is urgent need of both Canada and ourselves for the regulation of the levels of the Lakes by works at the foot of Lake Erie, thereby providing greater depths for navigation, the lowered levels of which (in the main due to climatic conditions) have imposed great wastes upon Lake shipping."

The St. Lawrence Commission in reporting its recommendations to President Coolidge said:

"Dear Mr. President:

"This Commission appointed by you on March 14, 1924, to advise upon development of shipway from the Great Lakes to the sea has directed me to transmit to you their conclusions."

"In accordance with this recommendation, and upon the appointment of the present Commission, and also a like body by Canada known as the National Advisory Committee of Canada, it was agreed between the two governments that a Joint Board of six engineers should be created to further exhaustively examine the subject. This Joint Engineering Board has now completed an exhaustive investigation of all the engineering features involved in the Lake and River development. Its report is herewith submitted."

"1. The construction of a shipway of sufficient depth to admit ocean shipping from the Atlantic to the Great Lakes will lessen the economic handicaps of adverse transportation costs to a vast area in the interior of the continent. Within the United States, it embraces all or large portions of the states of Ohio, Indiana, Kentucky, Illinois, Iowa, Missouri, Kansas, Nebraska, North and South Dakota, Montana, Wisconsin, Minnesota, Michigan, Pennsylvania, and New York. It includes a large part of Canada. Within this area, there are more than 40,000,000 inhabitants who gain their livelihood from its basic industries."

"These sections have always been under natural transportation disadvantages in the exportation and importation of commodities. But the building of the Panama Canal artifically created a still further dislocation of its competitive relations and beyond this the necessary increase in railway rates following the War has shifted greatly the economic position of the mid-continent to the great detriment of that area."

"This becomes apparent if we cease to think of distance merely as a matter of miles and consider it in terms of cost. If we take as a unit of measurement the cost in cents of carrying a ton of staple goods at present rate, taking the cheapest route in each case, we find that before the War, New York was 1904 cents away from San Francisco, while now it is only 1680 cents away. Chicago, which was 2610 cents away from the Pacific coast before the War, is today 2946 cents away. In other words, Chicago has moved 336 cents away from the Pacific coast, while New York has moved 224 cents closer. A similar calculation will show that in the same period, since ocean rates have remained about the same, Chicago has moved 594 cents away from the markets of the Atlantic seaboard and South America. The same ratios apply to the other Midwest points. The increased transportation costs to world markets from the mid-continent have had serious results to agriculture."

"2. Three different routes for such a shipway have been put forward:"

"(a) By reconstruction of the present canal from Lake Ontario to the Hudson, making use of the new Welland Canal now being constructed by the Canadian Government to connect Lake Ontario and Lake Erie. The United States has treaty protection of equal treatment in the use of the Welland."

"(b) By developing an 'All-American' route, which would include the Lake Ontario-Hudson project plus a new ship canal on the south side of Niagara which would duplicate the new Welland Canal."

"(c) By utilizing the St. Lawrence River, as a joint undertaking with Canada."

"5. The reports of the United States engineers of December 6, 1926, estimate the cost of constructing the Lake-Ontario-Hudson route at $506,000,000; the All-American route at $631,000,000 (both estimates without interest during construction). No consequential relief by water-power can be developed upon these routes. The net cost to the joint governments of the improvement of the St. Lawrence route upon procedure indicated below would be upon the joint engineers' estimates of between $123,000,000 and $148,000,000 from which some further reductions should be made from further realization upon hydro-electric power."

"6. The development of the St. Lawrence Waterway is necessarily also a development of the huge hydro-electric power from the great rapids which now obstruct navigation on the river. The complete practicable power development of the river will provide a total of about 5,000,000 installed HP of which about 2,250,000 lies in the upper rapids along the international section between New York State and the Province of Ontario, the remainder lying in the lower rapids and wholly within the

Dominion of Canada. This is not only the largest possible hydro-electric power development upon the continent, but the reports of the engineers indicate that the capital outlay per horsepower is less than most of the hydro-electric installations now in progress in the United States."

"10. It is estimated that maintenance plus interest at 4½ per cent on the All-American route would be $36,000,000 per annum, upon the Ontario-Hudson route $28,770,000 upon this plan of development of the St. Lawrence route, say $10,000,000 after deduction of power returns from power actually developed as above. These charges applied to the estimated annual medial tonnages is as follows:"

	Per ton
All-American	$2.06
Lake Ontario-Hudson	1.64
St. Lawrence	.43

"11. There are other important considerations in comparison of routes. The amount of restricted and therefore retarded navigation through actual canals would be 137 miles on the All-American route, 128 miles on the Ontario-Hudson route, 21 to 25 miles on the St. Lawrence."

"12. It is estimated that the construction of the waterway upon the St. Lawrence will require eight years, but ten years may be assumed as a minimum period even if all international questions, legislation, administrative and financial problems were rapidly overcome."

"The conclusions of this Commission are therefore:"

"First: The construction of the shipway from the Great Lakes to the sea is imperative both for the relief and for the future development of a vast area in the interior of the continent."

"Second: The shipway should be constructed on the St. Lawrence route, provided suitable agreement can be made for its joint undertaking with the Dominion of Canada."

"Third: That the development of the power resources of the St. Lawrence should be undertaken by appropriate agencies."

"Fourth: That negotiations should be entered into with Canada in an endeavor to arrive at agreement upon all these subjects. In such negotiations the United States should recognize the proper relations of New York to the power development in the International Section."

Speaking of this project in his 1928 campaign, Hoover said:

". . . This means more than the mere saving upon the actual goods shipped over these routes. If part of our crops can move to market at a seven- to ten-cent saving per bushel, the buyers' competitive bidding for this portion of the crop will force upward the price of the whole crop."

"This development concerns not alone agriculture, but every industry and business in the Midwest. . . . This development should tend to increase manufacturing industry in the Midwest and thereby create a larger diversity of employment and a greater local market for agricultural products. . . . The policy of rapid consummation of this great project will be continued."

Soon after Hoover entered the White House, all the engineering differences were planed out. However, it was not until December 10, 1931, that the President was able to report to Congress that definite negotiations of a treaty were under way:

"Conversations were begun between the Secretary of State and the Canadian minister at Washington on November 14 looking to the framing of a treaty for the development of the St. Lawrence seaway. The negotiations are continuing. I am hopeful that an agreement may result within a reasonable time enabling us to begin work on this great project, which will be of much importance economically to Canada and to the United States." [*State Papers, Vol. II, p. 77*]

Incidentally arising out of the work of the St. Lawrence Commission under Hoover's chairmanship were the measures saving the scenic values of Niagara Falls. In the fall of 1928 at his instance negotiations were undertaken with Canada for remedial measures. A special Niagara Board was in consequence appointed in 1926. Finally a treaty with Canada was negotiated by the Hoover Administration and signed on April 9, 1930. The treaty provides for such joint conservation work as is necessary to preserve the beauties of the Falls.

In an address at Des Moines, Iowa, on October 4, 1932, Hoover reviewed the progress on this great project:

"Four years ago, in this state, I gave assurance to the farmers that one of the first policies of my administration would be the vigorous prosecution and completion of the inland waterway system and advancement of the Great Lakes-St. Lawrence seaway as a fundamental relief to agriculture by cheaper transportation. I am glad to report to you that more than twice the amount of work has been done on the waterways in the last three years than in any similar period in the history of the United States. I am also glad to report that after twenty years of discussion, examination, and intermittent negotiation a treaty has been signed with Canada which only awaits ratification by the United States Senate and the Dominion Parliament for us to undertake that great contribution to the strengthening of Midwest agriculture in reaching out to world markets." [State Papers, Vol. I, p. 293]

On July 14, 1932, President Hoover announced that the treaty with Canada had been completed, and four days later it was published with this Presidential comment:

"The signing of the Great Lakes-St. Lawrence Waterway Treaty marks another step forward in this the greatest internal improvement yet undertaken on the North American continent. The treaty must yet be ratified by the legislative bodies of the two governments and is not effective unless this is done."

"The treaty represents to me the redemption of a promise which I made to the people of the Midwest. It provides for the construction of a twenty-seven-foot waterway from the sea to all Canadian and American points, on the Great Lakes. Such a depth will admit practically 90 per cent of ocean shipping of the world to our lake cities in the states of New York, Ohio, Michigan, Indiana, Illinois, Wisconsin, and Minnesota. Its influence in cheapening transportation of oversea goods will stretch widely into the interior from these points. Its completion will have a profoundly favorable effect upon the development of agriculture and industry throughout the Midwest. The large by-product of power will benefit the Northeast. These benefits are mutual with the great Dominion to the north."

"The waterway will probably require ten years for completion, during which time normal growth of traffic in the Nation will far more than compensate for any diversions from American railways and other American port facilities. The economic gains from improved transportation have always benefited the whole people. . . ."

[State Papers, Vol. II, p. 237]

On December 6, 1932, the President submitted the treaty to the Senate.

RECLAMATION POLICIES

The reclamation policies of President Hoover and Secretary Wilbur were to confine Government activities to projects already begun and to take in hand only those new projects which required years of preparation and construction. These policies of delay were most advisable in the face of the great surplus of agricultural production which developed in 1930. Rapid development of new lands would be unfair to the farming community.

Surveys and estimates were prepared for practically all the known irrigation projects. They were scheduled for construction over future years as population requirements and need for their products should become evident. The aim was to make them economically sound.

Hoover had long held the view that Federal participation in reclamation should be confined to the construction of dams and other major engineering works, leaving it to the local communities and private citizens to do the other development. Under its original set-up the Reclamation Service did all the collateral development as well, and sold the land to settlers upon their undertaking to repay the entire cost of the project. Hoover often stated that the settlers could never bear such cost and that the history of such projects was often a series of painful bankruptcies to most of the original settlers. He believed the Government should bear the cost of the major engineering works itself out of public interest—and then keep out of the land business.

In his Message to the meeting of the Western governors, on on August 21, 1929, before referred to, the President said:

"It seems to me that the vital questions here are to reorient the direction of the Reclamation Service primarily to the storage of water and to simplify its administration."

"The Reclamation Fund and the Reclamation Service were created in 1902 and the situation has since changed materially. The present plan as you are aware is that receipts from sale of public lands, mineral royalties and repayments by the beneficiaries for expenditures upon projects all accrue to this fund. The Reclamation Service undertakes special projects upon the authorization of Congress, which are financed from the fund on the basis of return by the land owners or purchasers of the cost of the project but without interest for a term of years. A total of approximately $182,000,000 has been expended from the fund."

"The present Reclamation Act is based fundamentally on the reclamation of Government-owned lands. Possible areas available for reclamation have now passed almost wholly into private ownership and the use of the Reclamation Fund for further projects may be legally criticized owing to the fact that the land is no longer a part of the public domain and circumlocution by voluntary agreements may not always be possible."

"Moreover the application of the fund under the present organization results in very large Federal administrative activities within the states of a character which was never originally contemplated and which could be much better administered by the local state governments themselves. In many ways it duplicates the state water administrations."

"There are several tentative suggestions for more effective handling of the fund. For instance, the Reclamation Service for all new projects might well be confined to the construction of permanent works, that is, dams and such construction as results in water storage—and at the completion of such construction the entire works be handed over to the states with no obligation for repayment to the Reclamation Fund except such revenues as might arise from electrical power and possibly in some cases from the sale of water until the outlay has been repaid or in any event for not longer than, say fifty years."

"Under such arrangements the states would have the entire management of all new reclamation projects and would themselves deal with the irrigation land questions and land settlements. It is only through the powers of the states that reclamation districts can legally be organized which would incorporate the liability of privately-owned lands for irrigation expenditure and by such organization it ought to be possible to finance the subsidiary works."

"It is not suggested that the states should take over the administration of the established projects but that the system should be set up for future undertakings. If it were instituted it would, of course, be necessary to set up some safeguards to cover interstate projects. No doubt each new project as at present should be specifically authorized by Congress."

[*State Papers, Vol. I, p. 93*]

In his first Message to the Congress, on December 3, 1929, the President said:

"We have a third problem of major dimensions in the reconsideration of our reclamation policy. The inclusion of most of the available lands of the public domain in existing or planned reclamation projects largely completes the original purpose of the Reclamation Service. There still remains the necessity for extensive storage of water in the arid states which renders it desirable that we should give a wider vision and purpose to this service." [*State Papers, Vol. I, pp. 157–8*]

"Reclamation should have a broader import than that of bringing unproductive land under cultivation. We do not need further additions to our agricultural land at present. Additional agricultural production except such marginal expansion as present projects warrant is inadvisable."

"The conservation of water by storage is required, not alone in the West, but in all parts of the country."

"The effective development of water conservation through storage is largely an interstate question in the aid of domestic and industrial water supply, transportation, irrigation, and flood control. Where construction work for storage relates to these larger issues, it is properly the work of the Federal Government. Where water power is developed as a by-product, it should be disposed of in advance by contracts which will fairly reimburse the Government for its outlay. The Reclamation Service should be extended to cover these broad purposes of storage and conservation of water rather than the narrow purpose of irrigation. Such important projects as the dam at Boulder Canyon, the dam at Cove Creek, and the development of the Columbia, should ultimately be undertaken when there is need for such service and when contracts can be made for the sale of power to amortize the cost of construction to the Government."

[*State Papers, Vol. II, p. 117*]

The Congress was, however, too engaged in the depression to attend to the question.

COLORADO RIVER DEVELOPMENT

Some time before the World War it had been proposed to build a dam in the Colorado River Canyon. Hoover had visited the site and was much interested in seeing it undertaken for the primary purpose of protecting the Imperial Valley from floods and for the provision of a better water supply to Southern California. Incidentally, it would produce a sufficient electrical power to pay for its construction. After the War the project was revived but fierce contentions arose over the effect of this dam upon the water rights of the seven states in the Colorado River drainage.

At a meeting of the governors and other representatives of these states in 1921, it was proposed that an interstate compact should be undertaken. The governors afterward requested of President Harding that Secretary Hoover should be appointed chairman of a commission to be authorized by the Congress, to forward these purposes. The Annual Report of Secretary of Commerce Hoover for the year 1922 contains this mention:

"On December 17, 1921, at your request I undertook, as chairman, to represent the Federal Government upon a commission set up by the seven states in the Colorado River Basin, the purpose of which is to formulate a treaty between these states . . . to settle the conflict of water rights and a program of systematic development for that great national asset. Meetings of this commission were held in Washington in January, 1922; in Phoenix, March 15; in Los Angeles, March 20; in Salt Lake City, March 27; in Denver, March 31; and in Cheyenne, April 2, at which public hearings were held and necessary information recruited for the forthcoming final sessions of the commission."   [Pages 10–11]

The Annual Report of the Secretary of Commerce for 1923 (page 25), states:

"The Colorado River Commission, on which I . . . acted as chairman, held its final sessions at Santa Fé, New Mexico, from November 9 to November 24, 1922. On the latter date the Colorado River Compact was signed by the representatives of the seven states (Arizona, California, Colorado, Nevada, New Mexico, Utah, and Wyoming) and approved by me as the representative of the Federal Government."

"The major purposes of the Compact are to provide for the equitable division and apportionment of the use of the waters of the Colorado River; to establish the relative importance of different beneficial uses of water; to promote interstate comity; to remove causes of present and future controversies; and to secure the expeditious agricultural and industrial development of the Colorado River Basin, the storage of its waters, and the protection of life and property from floods. To these ends the Colorado River Basin is divided into two basins, and an apportionment of the use of part of the water of the river is made to each of them with the provision that further equitable apportionments may be made."

"The Compact provides a basis for the carrying out of one of the greatest of our national developments. The land under irrigation in 1920 from the river and its tributaries amounted to about 2,464,000 acres. . . .

It is estimated that the irrigated land can be increased to over 5,000,000 acres. Development of 5,000,000 horsepower is a possibility. With long distance transmission all of this can probably be brought into national use. . . ."

"The successful negotiation of an interstate compact in settlement of so important and complex a problem is significant in that it marks the first time that so large a number of states have been able to settle fundamental interstate rights by process of treaty. The Compact becomes effective when approved by the legislatures of each of the signatory states and by the Congress of the United States. The legislature of six of the seven states have now ratified it, only Arizona having failed to take final action. Congressional action will doubtless await the approval of all of the seven states."

The report does not mention that Hoover visited all the seven states to secure the ratification of the Compact by the legislatures and governors, and engaged himself incessantly in public addresses and press advocacy of the development. The Compact was first held up by Arizona. California initially ratified it against the opposition of certain Senators and Congressmen, but Hoover carried the day. But the opposition forces rallied, and California's legislature later withdrew its ratification and substituted "reservations," despite Hoover's vigorous protests that it would delay the construction of the dam—which it did.

However, in January, 1926, the Secretary announced a new plan for solving this difficulty, and secured the ratification of five states in such fashion as overcame the California difficulties. Arizona still opposed.

In the meantime, oppositions to the construction of the dam had grown in other quarters. Charges of infeasibility of a dam, the highest in all history, were met by the appointment of an eminent engineering commission nominated by Hoover. Together with Secretary Work, Secretary Hoover drafted changes in the proposed authorizing legislation which met other objections from the Eastern states. With these efforts of Hoover and with those of President Coolidge, Senator Johnson's and Congressman Swing's united action finally pushed the legislation over in 1928.

And on June 25, 1929, President Hoover announced the signing of a proclamation, making effective the Compact between six of the seven states in the Colorado River Basin.

". . . The Compact . . . is the final settlement of disputes that have extended over twenty-five years and which have stopped the development

of the river. . . . It opens the avenue for some hope of the settlement
of other regional questions as between the states rather than the imposition of these problems on the Federal Government."

[*State Papers, Vol. I, p. 71*]

There yet remained the job of making the contracts for sale
of electrical power which would pay for the dam and of securing
a contractor to build it. These contracts were consummated by
Secretary Wilbur in April, 1930. On July 7, 1930, orders were
given to start construction on this $325,000,000 public improve-
ment.

These contracts provided for the purchase of the falling
water by municipalities and private companies in such fashion
as to protect the public and the Government. They kept the
Federal Government out of the business of generating and distributing power.

Following the national custom of naming large Federal reservoirs for the Presidents, Secretary Wilbur on September 8,
1930, when starting work on the railway to the Colorado Dam
named it the Hoover Dam. There had previously been named
the Roosevelt Dam for Theodore Roosevelt, the Wilson Dam
for Woodrow Wilson, the Coolidge Dam for Calvin Coolidge.
None of those Presidents had taken more than casual interest
in securing the establishment of these great works. Hoover's
service in the creation of the Colorado River dam had been far
more than ministerial: it had been personal over years, and without him it would not be in existence today. The naming of the
dam was in usual course and Congress approved it through appropriations in the name of Hoover Dam.[1]

On President Hoover's trip back to Washington after the election (November 12, 1932), he stopped to make a short inspection by night of the progress on the dam. At this time he made a
short review of his policies in this matter:

"This is not the first time I have visited the site of this great dam.
And it does give me extraordinary pleasure to see the great dream I have
long held taking form in actual reality of stone and cement."

"It is now ten years since I became chairman of the Colorado River
Commission. That Commission solved in a unique way the legal conflicts
as to water rights amongst six of the states. It was the first time that a
provision in the Constitution of the United States for treaties amongst
the several states was utilized on so great a scale. And I again had the

[1]The attempt of Secretary Ickes to change the name was unprecedented and has met
with much criticism.

satisfaction of presenting, both as an engineer and as the head of the Commission, to President Coolidge and to the Congress, the great importance of these works. And I had a further part in the drafting of the final legislation which ultimately brought them into being."

"This legislation required the making of an extremely intricate arrangement by which the Federal Government should advance the money but the by-product of power arising from this dam should be sold in such fashion as to return to the Federal Government its entire cost with interest. That contract for the sale of power was successfully negotiated by the present Secretary of the Interior with my approval and contracts were let for actual construction which was begun during my administration. The work has been carried forward with such rapidity that it is already more than a year ahead of schedule in its progress toward the specified period for its completion. Within a few days the river will be diverted through massive tunnels in order that the foundations of the dam may be laid."

"This dam is the greatest engineering work of its character ever attempted by the hand of man. Its height alone is nearly 700 feet, making it more than 100 feet higher than the Washington Monument, and far higher than any other such construction ever undertaken."

"Its major purposes are four in number."

"Its first purpose was to stabilize the flow of the river from these gigantic annual floods, thus preventing destruction of the great Imperial Valley and the agriculture which has grown up in neighboring states and in Mexico. Most Americans will remember how President Theodore Roosevelt many years ago had to intervene to stop the break in the levees on the river through which the whole of this river was pouring in torrent into the arena of the Imperial Valley which, being below sea-level, would have been turned into an irredeemable sea. This danger is forever removed by the construction of this dam."

"Second, to provide a supply of domestic water accessible to Southern California and parts of Arizona. Southern California has a population grown almost to the point where its entire water supply is absorbed, as evidenced by the periodic necessity to ration water in that quarter. With these new supplies of water its growth can go on for generations. And in this connection I may mention that through loans from the Reconstruction Corporation, work starts at once on the great aqueduct to carry this water into Los Angeles and the surrounding towns."

"The third purpose was to provide an adequate supply of irrigation water to the large areas of Arizona, the Imperial Valley and other valleys of Southern California."

"The fourth purpose is to preserve American rights in the flow of the river."

"But the whole of this translates itself into something infinitely more important. It translates itself into millions of happy homes for Americans out under the blue sky of the West. It will in fact in its various ramifications assure livelihood to a new population nearly as great as that of the State of Maryland."

"I know that I express the appreciation of the people of the Southwest to all those now engaged in direction and work upon this magnificent construction. It will be a source of pride to every man and woman to have had association with so great a work. I hope to be present at its final completion as a bystander. Even so I shall feel a special personal satisfaction."

"The waters of this great river, instead of being wasted in the sea, will now be brought into use by man. Civilization advances with the practical application of knowledge in such structures as the one being built here in the pathway of one of the great rivers of the continent. The spread of its values in human happiness is beyond computation."

[*State Papers, Vol. II, p. 481*]

THE GREAT VALLEYS OF CALIFORNIA

The President naturally had a great interest in the development of the water resources of the Great Valleys of California, his own state, with whose problems he was familiar. At Sacramento on June 27, 1925, he reviewed the problem and policies that should be adopted, saying:

"If we were to scan the whole nation for the greatest opportunity of national development we would find that it lies right here in the Great Central Valley of California."

"In the Sacramento and San Joaquin valleys we have about 14,000,000 acres of arable land of which about 4,000,000 are under irrigation. Of the remainder perhaps 6,000,000 can be brought into intensive cultivation —some people claim all of it, but we do not need to be extremists to make a great case. We have from these river systems an average of some 37,000,000 acre feet of annual water supply—enough water for all the 14,000,000 acres, if its engineering application can be solved. But a large part of these new acres must be watered from the flood flow of the waters, which means storage. We have mountain and hill storage sites of at least 30,000,000 acre feet capacity strung around the Great Central Valley, as against our present constructed storage of 2,500,000 acre feet. There is at some price all the storage we need. Beyond storage we have the possibilities of pumping by the cheapest power supply in the world, which is itself the by-product of our storage."

"If we can accomplish the great thing of providing water for 6,000,000 acres more we shall have added fully a million people to the state, and a wealth of one or two billion dollars—an addition to America as great as the fine state of Maryland. This is no dry statistical statement. . . . There lie in its possibilities hundreds of thousands of the happiest homes in the world."

"I have said that today we are entering upon a new era in this development. The period of easy projects is over. No doubt the new era must be made up as the sum of hundreds of different projects of reclamation, irrigation, storage, power and flood control, just as it has in the past. But they will be more difficult projects than hitherto. They will be more expensive. Many of them will need be indirect in their effect. They may be hundreds of miles from the land which they serve. And above all they will materially affect each other. Thus their planning will require much greater vision than ever before. They must have co-ordination on some general plan or we will waste infinite effort; we shall waste much of both our water and our land; we shall be involved in bitter quarrels between communities; we shall be involved in costly litigation which permanently will stifle much development and above all we shall never be able to assemble the concentrated energy of the local communities, the state, and the national governments which alone can make them financially possible."

"Now some would think this to be a great dream. There are those who contend that the American farmer is already overproducing and that more irrigation development will be his ruin. We are also told that California already has more intensive cultivation than she can find market for. That is absolutely true in the short view. If a magic wand could bring this 6,000,000 acres into orchards and watered fields in the next twenty-four hours or the next ten years, I would be for suppressing the wand. But there is no magic wand. The only genuine wand is long, laborious construction. It takes time to build dams and canals and to plant orchards."

"If we were to start tomorrow upon this great work of dams in the hills and mountains, the improvement of the rivers, the pumping plants and distribution systems, it would be more than twenty-five years before we accomplished all this. The population of the United States will have increased by 40,000,000 people in that period and we would have accomplished an unparalleled task if we brought in this 6,000,000 acres by that time."

". . . There is conflicting interest between districts, between different private interests, between governmental bureaus, between engineers."

"If sixty years ago we could have had a sound plan of flood control and conformed every development to it we should have saved tens of millions in construction and more tens of millions in losses and quarrels. . . ."

"Another of the questions raised as to this great enterprise is that the cost of the huge works to accomplish this great development will be in excess of what the land can bear. There can be no doubt that, by and large, water will be more expensive in its development and application per acre in the fuutre than have been the easier projects of the past. And in this respect I should like to make a suggestion that seems to me must control our future hopes."

"That is, it is not alone the landowner who gains by these great permanent additions to the national wealth. The neighboring village, the great cities of the state, and the Nation at large will gain some part of their livelihood from these 6,000,000 acres through the services they sell, the merchandising they do, the transportation, the manufacture they carry on for these added farms. More people will make a living who actually live away from these acres than the number who live upon them."

"Therefore, in the large fundamental works which only indirectly improve specific land, not only the state but the Nation should bear some part of the burden as well as the land. And there is the power by-product."

"Hitherto we have considered it a Federal obligation to contribute to the improvement of our waterways and to flood control. This new era of development requires expenditure on both these accounts and the Federal Government should undertake a substantial part of the burden for both these purposes—and mountain reservoirs will yet be a part of our flood control and navigation maintenance."

"But again we require co-ordination in forming plans. Which brings me to my major proposition—that is, how to definitely organize effective action."

"It is the essence of self-government, that these problems must be solved under state leadership, not by absentee Federal control."

"Therefore, it seems to me the time has come when the state should move upon this problem by setting up the state engineer as the chairman of a committee. That the Railway Commission and the Division of Water Rights should be given a membership; that the reclamation and irrigation districts should nominate some engineer members; that the Federal departments, that is, the War Department, Interior Department, Federal Power Commission, should be asked to instruct their engineers in this region to become members. I am never particular over names or details; what we want is an organism that will function."

"All these works—the dams and reservoirs, the power plants, the irrigation canals, the pumps, the levees, and the orchards—are not an end in themselves. They are but the means with which we may create happy homes, and under God better men and women. It is a great thing to accomplish. It is a great heritage to hand down to our children."

"There are two problems confronting the state; they are water supply and the marketing of perishable products."

Larger Vision Needed

"If we are to bring under production the millions of acres of undeveloped land in the state, it must be done with a larger vision than any heretofore employed. Water is probably our greatest undeveloped resource. We have developed our lands and our industries, but we have not developed our water resources to their full extent. We have done some jobs with water, but they have been the easier jobs. In studying the problem, we found that what applied to California insofar as the development of water resources is concerned, also applied to the rest of the United States. Taxpayers in other sections do not care to dig down in their pockets for California, but if the resources of the Mississippi, the Great Lakes, the St. Lawrence, and the others, are also developed, California will share in the benefits."

Nothing was, however, done by the California authorities. But four months after coming to the White House, Hoover proposed to Governor Young the appointment of a joint commission to examine the subject.[1] In his statement to the press he said (August 17, 1929):

"Some years ago I advocated the co-ordination of the multitude of activities, governmental and otherwise, engaged in direct and indirect control and development of California water supply and the provision

[1]The commission members were Lt.-Colonel Thomas M. Robins, U. S. A., Frank E. Bonner, Federal Power Commission, and Doctor Elwood Mead of the Interior Department, for the Federal Government; and for the state, George Pardee, William Durbrow, B. A. Etcheverry, Alfred Harrell, W. B. Mathews, Judge Warren Olney, Jr., Frank E. Weymouth, B. B. Meek and W. J. Carr.

of some definite policies instead of the haphazard and often conflicting action of different agencies. Governor Young had forwarded this idea by enactment of certain state legislation which now enables us to bring about a larger measure of such co-ordination. The first step is the creation of a commission to supervise an exhaustive investigation of the engineering facts and to determine the policies which should be pursued in the long-view development of the state, as to irrigation, flood control, navigation, and power."

"In order that all of the commission should embrace all agencies, I have requested the War Department which controls the navigation channels and flood control, the Power Commission which controls water-power permits, and the Interior Department which is interested in irrigation, each to designate a member of the commission which the governor is now appointing. The governor's representatives will embrace the state agencies and leading citizens."

Fifteen months later on December 27, 1930, the California Joint Federal and State Water Commission, appointed by the President and Governor Young, submitted its report. The report proposed a comprehensive basis for the development and conservation of California water supplies and defined the relations of Federal, state, and private action. It exerted a large influence in the plans for the development of the state.

PUBLIC ROADS AND HIGHWAYS

Here the Hoover policies were simple—more and more road construction. Hoover advocated these policies in his 1928 campaign.

In his first Message to the Congress, on December 3, 1929, he said:

"There are over 3,000,000 miles of legally established highways in the United States, of which about 10 per cent are included in the state highway systems, the remainder being county and other local roads. About 626,000 miles have been improved with some type of surfacing, comprising some 63 per cent of the state highway systems and 16 per cent of the local roads. Of the improved roads about 102,000 miles are hard surfaced, comprising about 22 per cent of the state highway systems and about 8 per cent of the local roads."

"While proper planning should materially reduce the listed mileage of public roads, particularly in the agricultural districts, and turn these roads back to useful purposes, it is evident that road construction must be a long-continued program. Progress in improvement is about 50,000 miles of all types per annum, of which some 12,000 miles are of the more durable types. The total expenditures of Federal, state, and local governments last year for construction and maintenance assumed the huge total of $1,660,000,000."

"Federal aid in the construction of the highway systems in conjunction with the states has proved to be beneficial and stimulating. We must ultimately give consideration to the increase of our contribution to these systems, particularly with a view to stimulating the improvement of farm-to-market roads."

[*State Papers, Vol. I, pp. 150–1*]

With the depression he advanced highway construction over normal programs as an aid to unemployment.

In a press statement, on July 3, 1931, he pointed out:

"Federal aid for 1931 is $259,897,000, as compared with $105,648,-000 for 1930, an increased Federal program of $154,249,000."

[*State Papers, Vol. I, p. 594*]

During the Hoover Administration, under the direction of Secretary Hyde and Bureau Chief Thomas H. McDonald the completed Federal aid highways increased from 78,000 miles to 115,000 miles. The rate of construction was raised from 7400 miles in 1929 to 16,000 miles in 1932. The number of men employed on public and forest roads rose from 110,000 to 280,000.

PUBLIC BUILDINGS

The Federal Government had for years lagged behind its need in office buildings until it was occupying thousands of rented buildings both in Washington and throughout the country. During the thirty years from 1900 to 1930 it had expended a total of less than $250,000,000, or an average of less than $10,000,-000 per annum in providing itself with facilities and housing. A definite building program was undertaken in Coolidge's Administration to save exorbitant rents for the Government.

Secretary of the Treasury Mellon had taken a large part in formulating the original program and has especially interested himself in the opportunity architecturally to improve the national capital and this interest was continued under Secretary Mills. Hoover had also taken an active part in the formulation of this program and something like $250,000,000 had been authorized by the Congress for this purpose. Of this program, buildings costing a total of about $10,000,000 had been completed when Hoover came to the White House in 1929.

Partially to secure the economies for the Government and largely to aid employment, President Hoover enormously speeded up this program. During his administration the authorizations from Congress were increased to over $802,000,000. Ferry Heath, Assistant Secretary of the Treasury, was placed in charge of the work and for the first time architects outside of the Government bureaus were employed, not only for expedition, but more especially to secure a reform in the drab architecture so common in Federal construction.

Hoover was deeply interested in the beautification of the national capital. Under his leadership acts were passed giving authority to the Fine Arts Commission of Washington which had they been enacted twenty-five years earlier would have saved many an eyesore in that city. Speaking on April 25, 1929, he said:

"I am glad that the opportunity has come to me as President to contribute to impulse and leadership in the improvement of the national capital. This is more than merely the making of a beautiful city. Washington is not only the Nation's capital, it is the symbol of America. By its dignity and architectural inspiration we stimulate pride in our country, we encourage that elevation of thought and character which comes from great architecture."

"Our Government in Washington has grown greatly during the past fifteen years. We have a working force of nearly 70,000 employees as compared with 35,000 a score of years ago."

"War and economic recovery have delayed us in providing even our bare necessities of office space. Nearly 25,000 employees are today in rented buildings or temporary structures built during the War which were expected to last but a year or two. Many of the buildings are insanitary. Above all, the departments are divided among scores of unworkable and scattered buildings. For instance, agriculture is housed in forty-six different places in the city and the Treasury in twenty-seven places, commerce in twenty places. We are paying rents and losing efficiency in sums far greater than the interest upon adequate buildings. Many of the buildings we occupy are an eyesore to the city. We have an authorized building program for, say, 18,000 employees, yet if we would satisfy even our present need, we should have new buildings to accommodate more than 30,000 Government workers."

"Congress has authorized the beginning of a great program which must extend over many years. It is our primary duty to do more than erect offices. We must fit that program into the traditions and the symbolism of the capital. Our forefathers had a great vision of the capital for America, unique from its birth in its inspired conception, flexibility and wonderful beauty. No one in one hundred and fifty years has been able to improve upon it."

"The founders of the Republic also gave us a great tradition in architecture. In after years we have held to it in some periods and in others we have fallen sadly away from it. Although it is perhaps too early to envisage such a glorious future, I do hope to live to see the day when we shall remove from Washington the evidences of those falls from the high standards which would have been deplored by the founders of our Republic and have been deplored by the citizens of good taste ever since these transgressions." [*State Papers, Vol. I, p. 47*]

> As indication of the gigantic character of this work, we quote from the President's reports. He said on November 4, 1931:

"That portion of the Federal program of aid to unemployment comprised in the great expansion of public buildings under the Treasury Department shows the following progress since the report of September 1. There is a total of 817 projects which have so far been specifically authorized, and 222 firms of architects are engaged in plans and supervision. The attached tables show the progress of individual projects which may be summarized:"

"*First:* A total of 131 buildings have been completed at a total cost of $41,934,569. Sixteen buildings have been completed during the months of September and October."

"*Second:* There were 270 buildings in construction at the first of November by contract, at an estimated cost of $229,772,700. There have been 41 contracts let during the months of September and October with a total value in excess of $48,000,000."

"*Third:* There are 64 projects in which sites have been arranged, drawings are completed, for which construction contracts have been invited, of a total estimated cost of $19,970,500."

"*Fourth:* There are 240 projects in which sites have been selected and on which plans are now under way of a total estimated cost of $141,-947,923."

"*Fifth:* At the first of this month there were 100 projects in which the sites have been determined upon and are in process of being acquired. The estimated cost of the buildings thereon is $31,133,500."

"*Sixth:* There are 12 projects held for amended legislation or for other reasons with a total estimated cost of $3,145,000."

"It is estimated that the number of men now directly and indirectly employed on this program is 50,000. It is estimated by the Treasury Department that the number that will be directly and indirectly employed on January first is 100,000."   [*State Papers, Vol. II, p. 26*]

Again on December 8, 1932, he reported to the Congress:

". . . 817 projects have been specifically authorized. . . . On October 31, last, 254 of these projects had been completed, 400 projects were under contract either in whole or in part, and 110 projects were being processed toward the contract stage, the drawings therefore having been completed."   [*State Papers, Vol. II, pp. 514–15*]

By the end of the Hoover Administration 360 buildings of the national program had been completed and some 460 more were under contract, or at an advanced stage of preparation. The total expenditures and obligations amounted to about $700,000,000.

One of the President's running fights with the Congress was to hold this construction to justifiable projects and keep it from becoming a general pork barrel. (See p. 482.)[1]

SAN FRANCISCO BAY BRIDGE

The problem of a bridge across San Francisco Bay was familiar to Hoover. As Secretary of Commerce he had interested himself in it and had secured direction from President Harding to the army engineers that they should report upon the question. Their report was not favorable to the Goat Island route but to some less serviceable route. The navy opposed any bridge as a danger to fleet mobilization in time of war. The Secretary

-----

[1]In April, 1933, the uncommitted balances of about $95,000,000 on Hoover's building program were appropriated by Roosevelt for other purposes, much of it "made" work, and this great policy brought to an end.

attempted to conciliate the military departments but his authority without the backing of the President was insufficient.

The subject of the route was also one of long divided opinion and acrimony among the Bay communities. Beyond this there was apparently no way of financing it.

In the campaign of 1928, Hoover gave public assurances to the Bay cities that he would do his best to bring about a bridge. On August 13, 1929, soon after assuming the Presidency, he announced the appointment of a committee jointly with Governor Young to solve the problem of locating the bridge and its design. He said to the press:

"There can be no question as to the necessity for such a bridge for the economic development of these communities. In addition to the cities of San Francisco, Oakland, and Alameda, the governor of California through recent legislation has recently taken an interest in this problem. In order that we may have an exhaustive investigation with a view to final determination which I hope will be acceptable to all parties, I have consulted the Secretary of War and the Secretary of the Navy, as well as Mr. Meek, the representative of Governor Young, and I shall appoint a commission comprising two representatives from the Navy, two from the Army, and I shall ask the authorities of the east side of the Bay to appoint another member. I shall ask the governor to appoint one or two members and I shall appoint a leading citizen, Mr. Mark Requa, if he will undertake it, in the hope that we may arrive at a determination of the common interest."

[*State Papers, Vol. I, p. 90*]

The President issued instructions to the governmental agencies to come to an understanding. They did. The commission comprised: Mark L. Requa, chairman; George T. Cameron, vice-chairman; Rear-Admiral L. E. Gregory and W. H. Stanley, General G. B. Pillsbury, Colonel E. C. Daley, State Senator Arthur H. Breed, Professor Charles D. Marx, and C. H. Purcell.

The President on August 12, 1930, announced the successful completion of the work of the commission. This report was the result of the first real open-minded, comprehensive engineering survey made upon the subject. The commission recommended the Rincon Hill-Goat Island location.

This bridge constitutes the greatest engineering undertaking of its kind, and to the commission is due a great measure of gratitude from the communities served. The President issued a statement reviewing the matter:

"After several years of delay in settlement of a site for a much-needed bridge across San Francisco Bay, due to disagreements between the naval authorities, the army engineers, the municipal and state authorities, the commission, representing all of these agencies, under the chairmanship of Mr. Mark L. Requa, has now come to unanimous agreement, and appears to have found a solution which has commended itself in all directions, and a much-needed improvement may now be carried forward."

[State Papers, Vol. I, p. 367]

The next great problem was to finance the bridge. Certainly during the midst of the depression it was hopeless of local accomplishment. The President had it in mind.

In proposing the Reconstruction Finance Corporation in 1931, Hoover included the request for power to the Corporation to loan for reproductive public works, but Congress deleted this authority from the act. In the winter of 1932, the President again urged this authority be given to the R. F. C. and used the San Francisco Bridge Report as the type of public improvements which should be undertaken and emphasized its service to unemployment. When this authority was granted in June, 1932, he suggested to San Francisco that it should send its representatives to Washington to negotiate with the R. F. C. He advised with them and the R. F. C. and finally brought to successful conclusion the necessary loans of upward of $75,-000,000. Thus, great employment was created and the greatest bridge in the world was built. And it will obviously repay to the Federal Government every cent of loans with interest.

POLICIES IN REGULATION OF BUSINESS

The Hoover attitude on government regulation of business is summarized in an address delivered in Colorado Springs on March 7, 1936.

"And at once we come to the relation of government to economic life. I have discussed many of its phases elsewhere. On this occasion time permits me to refer only to the relations of government to business. For in this field lies a large part of the choice that youth must make."

"We have three alternatives."

"First: Unregulated business."

"Second: Government-regulated business, which I believe is the American System."

"Third: Government-dictated business, whether by dictation to business or by government in business. This is the New Deal choice. These ideas are dipped from cauldrons of European Fascism or Socialism."

Unregulated Business

"While some gentlemen may not agree, we may dismiss any system of unregulated business. We know from experience that the vast tools of technology and mechanical power can be seized for purposes of oppression. They have been used to limit production and to strangle competition and opportunity. We can no more have economic power without checks and balances than we can have political power without checks and balances. Either one leads to tyranny."

"And there must be regulation of the traffic even when it is honest. We have too many people and too many devices to allow them to riot all over the streets of commerce. But a traffic policeman must only enforce the rules. He will block the traffic if he stands on the corner demanding to know their business and telling them how to run it."

The American System of Regulation

"I am one who believes that the only system which will preserve liberty and hold open the doors of opportunity is government-regulated business.

And this is as far from government-dictated business as the two poles. Democracy can regulate its citizens through law and judicial bodies. No democracy can dictate and survive as a democracy. The only way to preserve individual initiative and enterprise is for the government to make the same rules for everybody and act as umpire."

"But if we are to preserve freedom we must face the fact that ours is a regulatory system."

"And let us be definite once and for all as to what we mean by a system of regulation. It looms up more clearly against the past three years."

"1. A great area of business will regulate its own prices and profits through competition. Competition is also the restless pillow of progress. But we must compel honest competition through prevention of monopolies and unfair practices. That is indirect regulation."

"2. The semi- yet natural monopolies, such as railways and utilities, must be directly regulated as to rates to prevent the misuse of their privilege."

"3. Banking, finance, public markets, and other functions of trust must be regulated to prevent abuse and misuse of trust."

"The failure of the states, particularly New York, to do their part during the boom years has necessitated an extension of Federal action. The New Deal regulations of stock and security promotion in various aspects have the right objectives. They were hastily and poorly formed without proper consideration by Congress. But they point right."

"4. Certain groups must be appropriately regulated to prevent waste of natural resources."

"5. Labor must have the right to free collective bargaining. But it must have responsibilities as well as rights."

"6. At one time we relied upon the theory of 'shirtsleeves to shirtsleeves in three generations' to regulate over-accumulations of wealth. This is now guaranteed by our income and inheritance taxes. Some people feel these taxes take the shirt also."

"But there are certain principles that must run through these methods."

"1. The first principle of regulation is the least regulation that will preserve equality of opportunity and liberty itself. We cannot afford to stifle a thousand honest men in order to smother one evil person."

"2. To preserve Liberty the major burden of regulation must fall upon the states and local government. But where the states hopelessly fail or when the problem grows beyond their powers we should call upon the Federal Government. Or we should invoke the machinery of interstate compacts."

"3. Regulation should be by specific law, that all who run may read.

That alone holds open the doors of the courts to the citizen. This must be 'a government of laws and not of men.' "

"4. And the American System of Liberty will not function solely through traffic policemen. The fundamental regulation of the nation is the Ten Commandments and the Sermon on the Mount."

"Incidentally, the government might regulate its own business by some of the standards it imposes on others."

"There are certain humanities which run through all business. As we become more experienced, more humane, as conditions change, we recognize things as abuses which we once passed over. There are the abuses of slums, child labor, sweated hours, and sweated wages. They have been diminishing for decades before the New Deal. They have not been solved yet. They must be solved. We must not be afraid to use the powers of government to eliminate them."

"There will be periodic unemployment in any system. It is even so in the self-declared economic heavens of Socialism and Fascism. With common sense we could provide insurance programs against it. We could go further and prevent many causes of depressions."

"Out of medical and public health discoveries we have in eighty years increased the number of people over sixty years of age from 4 per cent to 8 per cent. That imposes another problem upon us."

"This American System has sprung from the spirit of our people. It has been developing progressively over many generations. However grave its faults may be they are but marginal to a great area of human well-being. The test of a system is its comparative results with others and whether it has the impulses within to cure its faults. This system based on ordered liberty alone answers these tests."

"The doors of opportunity cannot be held open by inaction. That is an ideal that must be incessantly fought for."

"These doors are partly closed by every gentleman who hatches some special privilege. They are closed to somebody by every betrayal of trust. But because brickbats can be used for murder we do not need to stop building houses. These doors are partly shut by every needless bureaucrat. And there is the tax collector. He stands today right in the door."

"Every new invention, every new idea, every new war shifts and changes our economic life. That greatest instrument of American joy, the automobile, has in twenty years shifted regulation in a hundred directions."

"Many obstructions and abuses have been added by the New Deal. Many of them are older but no worse. While the inspiration to reform comes from the human heart, it is achieved only by the intellect. Enthusiastic hearts have flooded us with illusions. Ideals without illusions are good. Ideals with illusions are no good. You may remember that youth with a banner of strange device. Was it 'Excelsior' or was it 'Planned Economy?' He froze to death."

Hoover's general attitude to business was always that in the vast majority the business transactions of the American people were honest and they were efficient. There were margins of abuse and exploitation which must be controlled and corrected. In an address at Cleveland, Ohio, on May 7, 1924, he said:

"I am one of those who believe in the substratum of inherent honesty, the fine vein of service and kindliness in our citizenship. The vast volume of goods and services that daily flow through the land would cease instantly were it not for the instinctive dependence of our people upon the moral responsibility of the men who labor in the shops and farms and the men who direct our production and distribution."

"In these times of muddled thought it is sometimes worth repeating a truism. Industry and commerce are not based upon taking advantage of other persons. Their foundations lie in the division of labor and exchange of products. For through specialization we increase the total and variety of production and secure its diffusion into consumption. By some false analogy to the 'survival of the fittest' many have conceived the whole business world to be a sort of economic 'dog eat dog.' We often lay too much emphasis upon its competitive features, too little upon the fact that it is in essence a great co-operative effort. And our homemade Bolshevist-minded critics to the contrary, the whole economic structure of our nation and the survival of our high general levels of comfort are dependent upon the maintenance and development of leadership in the world of industry and commerce. Any contribution to larger production, to wider diffusion of things consumable and enjoyable, is a service to the community and the men who honestly accomplish it deserve high public esteem."

In an address on April 20, 1920, he said:

"The combination of capital for larger unit production and distribution is in itself economically sound up to some point of expansion. It is not, however, sufficiently recognized that overgrowth of such units leads them to bureaucratic administration and eventually renders them less efficient than smaller units. From a social point of view the moment they begin to dominate the community, either in wages or prices or production, or to prevent the growth of competition, they are in flagrant violation of the primary principle of equality of opportunity."

"There can be no equality of opportunity if the ownership of the tools of production and service is to become frozen to a narrow group of holders either through large combination of capital or unrestricted accumulation of wealth."

> *The Challenge to Liberty,* written in 1934, expands this subject further:

"The abuses of Liberty fall naturally into two separate groups. First is the betrayal of public and private trust by individuals, and second are the problems of economic exploitation and domination which arise in modern business organization."

"Such betrayals are not alone stealing of money. They injure the most precious faith that has ever come to a people—faith in Liberty. They cannot be atoned for by restitution or punishment. The men who have been guilty of these betrayals have, by breaking down confidence in our institutions and our economic system, by the prejudice, hate, and discouragement they brought to our people, by the furious impulse to insensate action they aroused, contributed more to the cause of Regimentation, Fascism, Socialism, and Communism in the United States than all the preachments of Mussolini, Hitler, Karl Marx, or Lenin. No one has a right to condone an atom of it; any one of even feeble instincts of righteousness will condemn every particle of it."

"Because for a time a gangster runs loose, we must not assume that crime prevails through the whole American people, nor that the law or national ideals of decency and honesty have ceased to function. It is equally untrue that the more cultivated gangsters in big business represent either the morals or the regard for law in the general conduct of the financial and industrial institutions of the country. Betrayals of trust are not a part of the American System. They are violations of it. It is individual men who violate laws and public rights."

"The effects of economic abuse, exploitation of labor and of the public, and other economic dominations are of vastly greater importance than the occasional betrayal of trust. They are largely correctable by economic organization and legal administration. Their greatest corrective however is devotion to the Sermon on the Mount."

"Competition is in a large measure the most effective and dependable check upon rapacity and a preventive of economic domination and tyranny. Yet competition is open to marginal abuses which must be regulated. Common honesty is not universal; some groups will conspire to avoid competition; some competitive processes, while not dishonest, yet result in destructive action which oppresses labor and the public; and some industries, by their nature, are semi-monopolies, where reliance upon competition is an insufficient safeguard of the public interest."

"Perverse initiative will not do. There is no Liberty if the initiative of men may be freely devoted to robbery and tyranny, no matter in what guise. . . . The opponents of the American System cite these misuses of Liberty as if they were its overwhelming characteristics. That they are marginal problems can be demonstrated in a few sentences. The billions of daily transactions among our people are carried on in justifiable confidence in integrity and fairness, or the economic clock would stop. The oft-repeated statement that 200 corporations control 90 per cent of the nation's wealth diminishes on examination to the fact that all corporations in the country, outside of banking and insurance companies, hold 30 per cent of the national wealth. Of this about one-third are small enterprises. Of the whole figure of 30 per cent, about one-third are railroads and utilities whose profits or rates are regulated, and the balance are of the competitive category."

"Economic abuses or tyrannies do not always spring from greed, though that is often enough their origin. They often arise from a desire for power. The man of feudal type of mind is often generous and honest with a tinge of benevolence in his tyrannies, convinced that his is the correct service to his fellowmen. His legal defense and his excuse is usually his false interpretation that the right of property or power over property exceeds the other rights, protections, and duties of Liberty. Liberty denies that the right of private property can be used to invade other rights and the establishment of this fact has been one of the struggles between true Liberalism and 'the public be damned' attitude. But to deny that property can be so used is not a denial of the right of property. It is a denial of the right to use it for oppression. This type of mind will become even more obnoxious and dangerous in the opportunities for grasp of power in other social systems."

"The movements in regulation have all been battlegrounds in the definition of the borders between Liberty and economic oppression. These borders are not always exact, but they are capable of discovery and reasonable determination."

"In regulation there must be the minimum necessary to attain true public ends. That is sound economics as well as Liberty. Otherwise industry is frozen and its development stunted. In our regulating devices there must be a sharp separation of judicial from executive powers through a definition of what is required by specific statutory laws. And enforcement of these laws must be by a politically free judicial system in which there is full access to higher courts. The individual must know precisely what his obligations and securities are, and must have the full protection of the courts in their inviolability. Thus we hold to the preservation of a 'government of laws and not of men'—the first bulwark of Liberty. Our increasing tendency over years has been to vest vital regulatory powers in executive officials or alternatively to subject some judicial commissions to effective executive control. That is a crack in the wall against political tyranny. It chills initiative and enterprise by uncertainty and subjects it to politics, which is worse. But still worse, where judicial authority is held by executive officials, the threat of their executive authority leads the citizen to acquiesce in injustice."

"There is another boundary between those necessary regulations defining and inhibiting wrongdoing with property and, on the other hand, the inevitable tyranny of the state when it directs and dictates to men how they shall use their property. That is the distinction between the state as a policing agency and bureaucracy as the manager of business. The essence of American Liberty is to assure men the secured right to every activity which does not trespass the rights of others. Regulation as to what men may not do must not be confused with regimentation of men into platoons under a governmental corporal. That is the whole distinction between men possessing rights which cannot be transgressed by the state, and men merely as pawns of the state."

"In all regulation we have another and very practical problem—that is, in building walls against oppression, that we do not, in seeking to save all the foolish and to prevent all the possible permutations of sin, damage the contributions to progress by thousands of honest mne."

UNFAIR COMPETITION AND BUSINESS ETHICS

As Secretary of Commerce Hoover undertook a voluntary campaign of co-operaion with business to remove unfair practices and to set up standards of business ethics. In this effort he established co-operation among the Department, the trade associations and the Federal Trade Commission to create voluntary codes of business ethics. He brought into these associations a new purpose—to use them not alone for economic advancement but for moral improvement.

Of many statements we choose an address at Cleveland, Ohio, on May 7, 1924, where he reviewed these efforts, and explained his policies:

"The advancement of science and our increasing population require constantly new standards of conduct and breed an increasing multitude of new rules and regulations. The basic principles laid down in the Ten Commandments and the Sermon on the Mount are as applicable today as when they were declared, but they require a host of subsidiary clauses. The ten ways to evil in the time of Moses have increased to ten thousand now."

"A whole host of rules and regulations are necessary to maintain human rights with this amazing transformation into an industrial era. Ten people in a whole country, with a plow apiece, did not elbow each other very much. But when we put 7,000,000 people in a county with the tools of electric, steam, thirty-floor buildings, telephones, miscellaneous noises, street-cars, railways, motors, stock exchanges, and what not, then we do jostle each other in a multitude of directions. Thereupon our law-makers supply the demand by the ceaseless piling up of statutes."

". . . Moreover, with increasing education our senses become more offended and our moral discriminations increase; for all of which we discover new things to remedy. In one of our states over 1000 laws and ordinances have been added in the last eight months. It is also true that a large part of them will sleep peacefully in the statute book."

"The question we need to consider is whether these rules and regulations are to be developed solely by government or whether they cannot be in some large part developed out of voluntary forces in the nation. In other words, can the abuses which give rise to government in business be eliminated by the systematic and voluntary action of commerce and industry itself? . . ."

"National character cannot be built by law. It is the sum of the moral fibre of its individuals. When abuses which rise from our growing system are cured by live individual conscience, by initiative in the creation of voluntary standards, then is the growth of moral perceptions fertilized in every individual character."

"No one disputes the necessity for constantly new standards of conduct in relation to all these tools and inventions. Even our latest great invention—radio—has brought a host of new questions. No one disputes that much of these subsidiary additions to the Ten Commandments must be made by legislation. Our public utilities are wasteful and costly unless we give them a privilege more or less monopolistic. At once when we have business affected with monopoly we must have regulation by law.

Much of even this phase might have been unnecessary had there been a higher degree of responsibility to the public, higher standards of business practice among those who dominated these agencies in years gone by. . . ."

"When legislation penetrates the business world it is because there is abuse somewhere. A great deal of this legislation is due rather to the inability of business hitherto to so organize as to correct abuses than to any lack of desire to have it done. Sometimes the abuses are more apparent than real, but anything is a handle for demagoguery. In the main, however, the public acts only when it has lost confidence in the ability or willingness of business to correct its own abuses."

"Legislative action is always clumsy—it is incapable of adjustment to shifting needs. It often enough produces new economic currents more abusive than those intended to be cured. Government too often becomes the persecutor instead of the regulator."

"The thing we all need to searchingly consider is the practical question of the method by which the business world can develop and enforce its own standards and thus stem the tide of governmental regulation. The cure does not lie in mere opposition. It lies in the correction of abuse. It lies in an adaptability to changing human outlook."

"The problem of business ethics as a prevention of abuse is of two categories: those where the standard must be one of individual moral perceptions, and those where we must have a determination of standards of conduct for a whole group in order that there may be a basis for ethics."

"The standards of honesty, of a sense of mutual obligation, and of service, were determined two thousand years ago. They may require at times to be recalled. And the responsibility for them increases infinitely in high places either in business or government, for there rests the high responsibility for leadership in fineness of moral perception. Their failure is a blow at the repute of business and at confidence in government itself."

"The second field and the one which I am primarily discussing is the great area of indirect economic wrong and unethical practices that spring up under the pressures of competition and habit. There is also the great field of economic waste through destructive competition, through strikes, booms, and slumps, unemployment, through failure of our different industries to synchronize, and a hundred other causes which directly lower our productivity and employment. Waste may be abstractly unethical, but in any event it can only be remedied by economic action."

"If we are to find solution to these collective issues outside of government regulation we must meet two practical problems:"

"First, there must be organization in such form as can establish the standards of conduct in this vast complex of shifting invention, production, and use. There is no existing basis to check the failure of service or the sacrifice of public interest. Some one must determine such standards. They must be determined and held flexibly in tune with the intense technology of trade."

"Second, there must be some sort of enforcement. There is the perpetual difficulty of a small minority who will not play the game. They too often bring disrepute upon the vast majority; they drive many others to adopt unfair competitive methods which all deplore; their abuses give rise to public indignation and clamor which breed legislative action."

"I believe we now for the first time have the method at hand for voluntarily organized determination of standards and their adoption. I would go further; I believe we are in the presence of a new era in the organization of industry and commerce in which, if properly directed, lies forces pregnant with infinite possibilities of moral progress. I believe that we are, almost unnoticed, in the midst of a great revolution—or perhaps a better word, a transformation in the whole super-organization of our economic life. We are passing from a period of extremely individualistic action into a period of associational activities."

"Practically our entire American working world is now organized into some form of economic association. We have trade associations and trade institutes embracing particular industries and occupations. We have chambers of commerce embracing representatives of different industries and commerce. We have the labor unions representing the different crafts. We have associations embracing all the different professions—law, engineering, medicine, banking, real estate, and what not. We have farmers' associations, and we have the enormous growth of farmers' co-operatives for actual dealing in commodities. Of indirect kin to this is the great increase in ownership of industries by their employees, and customers, and again we have a tremendous expansion of mutualized insurance and banking."

"Associational activities are, I believe, driving upon a new road where the objectives can be made wholly and vitally of public interest. . . ."

"Three years of study and intimate contact with associations of economic groups whether in production, distribution, labor, or finance, convince me that there lies within them a great moving impulse toward betterment."

"If these organizations accept as their primary purpose the lifting of standards, if they will co-operate together for voluntary enforcement of high standards, we shall have proceeded far along the road of the elimination of government from business. . . ."

"The test of our whole economic and social system is its capacity to cure its own abuses. New abuses and new relationships to the public interest will occur as long as we continue to progress. If we are to be wholly dependent upon government to cure these abuses we shall by this very method have created an enlarged and deadening abuse through the extension of bureaucracy and the clumsy and incapable handling of delicate economic forces. . . ."

"American business needs a lifting purpose greater than the struggle of materialism. Nor can it lie in some evanescent, emotional, dramatic crusade. It lies in the higher pitch of economic life, in a finer regard for the rights of others, a stronger devotion to obligations of citizenship that will assure an improved leadership in every community and the nation; it lies in the organization of the forces of our economic life so that they may produce happier individual lives, more secure in employment and comfort, wider in the possibilities of enjoyment of nature, larger in its opportunities of intellectual life."

In the implementation of these ideas Secretary Hoover set up an entire division in the Department of Commerce. "Codes of ethics" were worked out with trade associations to eliminate abuse and unfair competition in each trade and were defined and adopted as applicable to their special trade. Hoover enlisted the co-operation of the Federal Trade Commission to assure that these codes had no element of violation of the Anti-Trust laws. To assure confidence these codes were promulgated by the Trade Commission as standards of fair practice. There was no force attempted or implied. They were solely voluntary. They covered the largest part of American business. By degrees they were becoming part of the business custom of the country.[1]

Speaking upon these codes on November 7, 1924, at Del Monte, California, he said:

". . . The very publication of codes of ethics by many associations instilling service as the primary purpose, the condemnation of specific unfair practices, the insistence upon a higher plane of relationships between employer and employee—all of them are at least indications of improving thought and growing moral perceptions."

[1]The attempt of the NRA to make these codes of ethics compulsory at once lost the moral lift.

"All of this is the strong beginning of a new force in the business world. . . ."

"If these organizations accept as their primary purpose the lifting of standards, if they will co-operate together for voluntary enforcement of high standards, we shall have proceeded far along the road of the elimination of government from business. American business is never secure unless it has public confidence behind it. Otherwise it will always be a prey to demagoguery and filled with discouragement."

MONOPOLIES, AND MONOPOLISTIC PRACTICES

The Hoover policies were implacably against monopoly in every form. His whole concept was based upon maintaining competition. In certain directions where a semi-natural monopoly exists, such as railways and utilities, he held there must be regulation of rates and profits but with as much stimulation of competition even here as possible. However, against those who believed every co-operative action was monopoly, he insisted that there were great areas of proper co-operation in business which not only did not diminsh competition but in fact actually strengthened it. His discussion and actions in these matters form a whole economic literature in themselves. A few quotations only are necessary.

Hoover's fundamental approach to the question of monopoly was from the side of its destruction of human liberty. In discussing freedom in this aspect, he said:

"Our system has at all times had to contend with internal encroachments upon Liberty. Greed in economic agencies invades it from the Right, and greed for power in bureaucracy and government infringes it from the Left. Its battles against betrayal of trust, business exploitation, and all forms of economic tyranny have long demonstrated that it was no system of *laissez faire*. Its battles against the spoils system or the expansion of bureaucracy have long demonstrated its live sense of opposition to the subtle approach of political tyranny."

"It holds that the other freedoms cannot be maintained if economic freedom be impaired—not alone because the most insidious mastery of men's minds and lives is through economic domination, but because the maximum possible economic freedom is the most nearly universal field for release of the creative spirit of men. It has ever held that injury to others is an encroachment upon Liberty; and that restraints as well as freedoms are the very rights of men. Therefore, in fashioning its economic system, it does not hold that there is a license of business to exploit; on the contrary, it holds that economic oppression is servitude. The American System holds equally that monopoly, group or class advantage, economic domination, Regimentation, Fascism, Socialism, Communism, or any other form of tyranny, small or great, are violations of the basis of Liberty."

[Challenge to Liberty, p. 33]

One of Hoover's earliest actions in defining the line between co-operation and monopoly was in 1922. At that time there was an extremist interpretation by Attorney-General Daugherty of the Anti-Trust laws which included even co-operative action in public interest. As Secretary of Commerce he set out his views in a memorandum which became the subject of widespread discussion. Shortly afterwards the Supreme Court by two notable decisions greatly clarified the issue and in fact supported the Hoover philosophy. Legislation on the question therefore became less vital.

The statement, however, is an important contribution to economic policies:

"The country has now had many years' experience with these acts [Anti-Trust]; they have received constant interpretation by the courts, and the working results in our economic fabric in some directions are out of tune with our economic development. No one would contend that there be relaxation in the restraints against undue capital combinations, monopoly, price-fixing, domination, unfair practices, and the whole category of collective action damaging to public interest. There has been, however, a profound growth of understanding of the need and possibilities of co-operative action in business that is in the interest of public welfare. Some parts of these co-operative efforts are inhibited by law today, but, of much wider result, many are stifled out of fear or shackled from uncertainty of the law. The two latter factors are far more widespread than can be appreciated except through wide contact with economic activities, and they definitely impede our national progress upon right lines. Relaxation of the acts has already been given by legislation in favor of the farmer and trades-unions, but the farmer and laborer are being even more greatly injured by these destructive shackles upon business in many directions, which produce instability of employment and increase distribution costs, than they were by the direct influence of these acts upon their own affairs."

"At the time the Sherman Act was passed, the country was in the throes of growing consolidations of capital. These were consolidations of actual ownership, and the country was alive with deserved complaint of domination in business, in attempts to crush competitors with unfair practices and destructive competition. Collective action in its sense of benefit to public interest was much less known and, at any rate, was probably not contemplated as coming within the meaning of the act. In any event there is a wide difference between the whole social conception of capital combinations against public interest and co-operative action between individuals which may be profoundly in the public interest. The former extinguishes individualism through domination; the latter greatly advances it and protects it. Co-operative action has, however, struggled for development through the growth of chambers of commerce, trade associations, and conferences of one kind and another in an effort to meet various sorts of crises, to improve business standards, and to eliminate waste in production and distribution."

"It is true that some minority of such activities has been used as a cloak for action against public interest, but it is also true that a vast amount of action in public interest has been lost and even greater national calamities brought upon us by lack of co-operative action. A case in point is that the instability of the bituminous coal industry and the disintegration of its employers' associations by pressure under the restraint of trade acts contributed directly to the prolongation of the coal strike, as no adequate organization of operators existed which could meet and bargain with the workers who were free from all restraint. The whole movement toward co-operative action arises from a fundamental need to which we must give heed. Where the objectives of co-operation are to eliminate waste in production and distribution, to increase education as to better methods of business, to expand research in processes of production, to take collective action in policing business ethics, to maintain standards of quality, to secure adequate representation of problems before the government and other economic groups and to improve conditions of labor, to negotiate collectively with highly organized groups of labor, to prevent unemployment, to supply information equally to members and to the public, upon which better judgment may be formulated in the conduct of business; then these activities are working in public interest. There are some twenty-odd different functions of co-operative action which are at the same time in the interest of the different trades and the community at large. Any collective activity can be used as a cloak for conspiracy against public interest, as can any meeting of men engaged in business but it does not follow because bricks have been used for murder that we should prohibit bricks. There is, moreover, a very wide differentiation between co-operative action open to an entire trade or region of a trade and capital combinations, because the former may be dissolved instantly without any disturbance of capital or production and does not represent increasing domination of a group of individuals in a trade, but the democratic development of a whole industry."

"It has often been argued that the original intent of the restraint of trade acts was not to inhibit any sort of economic collective action which was in interest of public welfare, and that the time has come when the act should be limited so as to leave free all such action. Without entering upon debate as to the difficulties of such a course it is possible to consider a narrower field of liberalization of law; that is, for the law to be liberalized to the extent that co-operative organizations generally, as distinguished from capital consolidations, should be permitted to file with some appropriate governmental agency the plan of their operations, the functions they proposed to carry on, and the objectives they proposed to reach; that upon approval such of these functions as did not apparently contravene public interest might be proceeded with; that upon complaint, however, either of individuals or the law officers of the Government that these functions had reacted against public interest, then after a hearing before some suitable tribunal the right to continue these particular functions should, if the complaints are justified, be suspended. If thereafter these functions were continued, or if it should be proved that the activities had been extended beyond the functions in the original proposals, the organization should be likewise subject to prosecution under the present acts. Parties who did not wish to avail themselves of this privilege could continue in the present status."

"All who know the situation in such matters will realize that the problems of co-operative action are mainly the concern of the smaller businesses. Such a measure as that suggested above would serve actually to protect small business and thus to maintain competition. Big business takes care of itself. Legitimate trade associations and other forms of business co-operation would be greatly stimulated along lines of public welfare if such a plan were adopted."

"It appears to me that the time has come when we should take cognizance of these necessities if we are to have a progressive economic system. Its growing complexity, its shift of objective and service, require a determination based upon a proper sense of maintenance of long-view competition, initiative, business stability, and public interest."

[*Report of the Secretary of Commerce, 1922, pp. 29–31*]

Another phase of the Anti-Trust legislation arose in the waste of natural resources through destructive competition. President Hoover considered that we must in some manner have Federal regulation to prevent gigantic wastes in natural resources—oil, coal, etc. In his second Annual Message to the Congress, on December 2, 1930, he said:

"I recommend that the Congress institute an inquiry into some aspects of the economic working of these laws. I do not favor repeal of the Sherman Act. The prevention of monopolies is of most vital public importance. Competition is not only the basis of protection to the consumer but is the incentive to progress. However, the interpretation of these laws by the courts, the changes in business, especially in the economic effects upon those enterprises closely related to the use of the natural resources of the country, make such an inquiry advisable. The producers of these materials assert that certain unfortunate results of wasteful and destructive use of these natural resources together with a destructive competition which impoverishes both operator and worker cannot be remedied because of the prohibitive interpretation of the Anti-Trust laws. The well-known condition of the bituminous coal industry is an illustration. The people have a vital interest in the conservation of their natural resources; in the prevention of wasteful practices; in conditions of destructive competition which may impoverish the producer and the wage earner; and they have an equal interest in maintaining adequate competition. I therefore suggest that an inquiry be directed especially to the effect of the workings of the Anti-Trust laws in these particular fields to determine if these evils can be remedied without sacrifice of the fundamental purpose of these laws."

[*State Papers, Vol. I, pp. 437–8*]

He wished Congress to investigate all aspects of the question. His own view was that regulation should be accomplished through the interstate compacts provided in the Constitution; that this preserved the element of local government without expanding Federal power by a Constitutional amendment. He strongly urged it upon the states for application to the oil industry. (See page 237.)

The downward movement of the depression with its slackening demand, however, stopped wastes and shifted the question temporarily from exploitation to overproduction.

ENFORCEMENT OF ANTI-TRUST LAWS

Upon assuming the Presidency Hoover, with Attorney-General Mitchell, chose John Lord O'Brian as Assistant Attorney-General, to head the Anti-Trust division of the Department of Justice. Hoover's instructions were to enforce the law without flinching. A number of notable infractions were pursued and stopped.

Complaint was made in some business journals in the earlier period of his administration that the number of prosecutions exceeded the same period in any other administration. As a matter of fact the oncoming depression by the natural sharpening of competition effectively ended any considerable violation. With this sharpening of competition from the depression, however, certain groups of the business world swung over to the idea that the only salvation was to repeal the Anti-Trust laws. The President refused every such suggestion.

Certain groups developed another idea, that the Government should itself organize monopolies in business. On September 17, 1931, President Gerald Swope of the General Electric Company in a public address took the lead in a "plan" for the reorganization of American industry. The President's office memorandum written at the time was as follows:

"This plan provides for the consolidation of all industries into trade associations, which are legalized by the government and authorized to 'stabilize prices.' There is no stabilization of prices without price-fixing, and this feature at once becomes the organization of gigantic trusts such as have never been dreamed of in the history of the world. This is the creation of a series of complete monopolies over the American people. It means the repeal of the entire Sherman and Clayton Acts, and all other restrictions on combinations and monopoly. In fact, if such a thing were ever done, it means the decay of American industry from the day this scheme is born, because one cannot stabilize prices without protecting obsolete plants and inferior managements. It is the most gigantic proposal of monopoly ever made in history."

The President sought the opinion of the Attorney-General upon it, who reported it to be wholly unconstitutional.

This same idea reappeared on December 19, 1931, when the

Chamber of Commerce of the United States reported the results of a referendum of its members on the subject. Their more important points were that (a) the Anti-Trust laws should be modified to permit combinations to keep "production related to consumption"; (b) there should be governmental supervision and enforcement of these processes; (c) each representative trade association should perform the functions of an economic council to bring about these agreements, the whole to be governed by a superior economic council; (d) there should be curtailment of production in natural resource industries wherever there was overproduction.

The President expressed the opinion that if this plan were carried into practice, it would, through the creation of government monopolies, drive the country toward the Fascism of which it was a pattern, or toward Socialism as the result of public exasperation.

Later, on September 23, 1932, Henry I. Harriman, president of the United States Chamber of Commerce, called upon the President to urge that he pledge himself in the presidential campaign to support the Chamber's recommendations of December, 1931, that is, to set up what subsequently became the NRA. The President naturally refused, as to him it was a violation of the most primary elements of human liberty. In 1934, in commenting on the NRA Hoover said:

"The most effective part of code operations is devoted to limitation of real competition. It is true that the law provided that there should be no monopolies or monopolistic practices. The major aspiration of those seeking to avoid the Anti-Trust acts always has been precisely the fixing of minimum prices and restriction of output, and these objectives, so earnestly yearned for in some quarters, now have been imposed by law. The economic results, so far as the trades and consumers are concerned, are about the same as if the Anti-Trust acts had been abolished. Naturally, if these industrial regiments hold to discipline they are at once constituted as complete guild monopolies as any in the Elizabethan period, from which we derived much of our American antagonism to monopoly."

In a public statement on these acts (prior to the Supreme Court's unanimous decision on their unconstitutionality) Hoover said on May 15, 1935:

"Present NRA proposals are as bad, in many ways, as the original. With its continuation until the next Congress and with Federal agents putting pressure on state legislatures to get them to enact state laws in support of NRA, it is evident that there has been no real retreat."

"This whole idea of ruling business through code authorities with delegated powers of law is un-American in principle and a proved failure in practice. The codes are retarding recovery. They are a cloak for conspiracy against the public interest. They are and will continue to be a weapon of bureaucracy, a device for intimidation of decent citizens."

"To the customary answer of 'destructive criticism' or the other question 'what substitute is offered?' I suggest that the only substitute for an action that rests on definite and proved economic error is to abandon it. We do not construct new buildings on false foundations, and we cannot build a nation's economy on a fundamental error."

"The beneficent objectives of a great social justice and the prevention of sweating, child labor, and abuse in business practices should be and can be better attained by specific statutory law."

"There are already sufficient agencies of government for full enforcement of the laws of the land. Where necessary those laws should be strengthened, but not replaced with personal government."

"The prevention of waste in mineral resources should be carried out by the states operating under Federally encouraged interstate compacts. That is an American method of eradicating economic abuses and wastes, as distinguished from Fascist regimentation."

"The multitude of code administrators, agents, or committees has spread into every hamlet, and, whether authorized or not, they have engaged in the coercion and intimidation of presumably free citizens. People have been sent to jail, but far more have been threatened with jail. Direct and indirect boycotts have been organized by the bureaucracy itself. Many are being used today. Claiming to cure immoral business practices, the codes have increased them a thousandfold through 'chiseling.' They have not protected legitimate business from unfair competition, but they have deprived the public of the benefits of fair competition."

"This whole NRA scheme has saddled the American people with the worst era of monopolies we have ever experienced. However monopoly is defined, its objective is to fix prices or to limit production or to stifle competition. Any one of those evils produces the other two, and it is no remedy to take part of them out. These have been the very aim of certain business elements ever since Queen Elizabeth. Most of the 700 NRA codes effect those very purposes."

"Exactly such schemes to avoid competition in business were rejected by my administration because they were born from a desire to escape the Anti-Trust laws. If the Anti-Trust laws had not been effective in a major way, there would have been no such desire to escape them. If they do not meet modern conditions, they should be openly amended, not circumvented."

"My investigations over the country show that the codes have increased costs of production and distribution, and therefore prices. Thus they have driven toward decreased consumption and increased unemployment. They have increased the cost of living, and placed a heavier burden on the American farmer."

"NRA has been crushing the life out of small business, and they are crushing the life out of the very heart of the local community body. There are 1,500,000 small businesses in this country, and our purpose should be to protect them."

"The codes are preventing new enterprises. In this they deprive America's youth of the opportunity and the liberty to start and build their independence, and thus stop the men and women of tomorrow from building soundly toward a true social security."

"Publishers have had to resist arduously the encroachment of these NRA codes upon such fundamental, constitutionally guaranteed American liberties as free speech."

"The whole concept of NRA is rooted in a regimented 'economy of scarcity'—an idea that increased costs, restricted production and hampered enterprise will enrich a nation. That notion may enrich a few individuals and help a few businesses, but it will impoverish the nation and undermine the principles of real social justice upon which this nation was founded."

"If the NRA has increased employment, it is not apparent. If we subtract the persons temporarily employed by the coded industries as the direct result of the enormous Government expenditures, we find that the numbers being employed are not materially greater than when it was enacted. NRA's pretended promises to labor were intentionally vague and have never been clarified. They have only promoted conflict without establishing real rights."

"That original ballyhoo used to hypnotize and coerce the people into acquiescence is now gone. Most of the originally grandiose schemes now are conceded to be a violation of the spirit and the letter of the American Constitution."

"Some business interests already have established advantages out of the codes, and therefore seek the perpetuation of NRA. Even these interests should recognize that in the end they, themselves, will become either the pawns of a bureaucracy that they do not want or the instruments of a bureaucracy the American people do not want."

There could be no better evidence that the Anti-Trust laws

were active and effective in the Hoover Administration than the constant agitation from those they restrained to have them modified or repealed, and the triumph of effective repeal in the NRA. Any one who contemplates the activity of competition during Hoover's time and the total cessation of it under the NRA can grasp that evidence.

Speaking at Fort Wayne, Indiana, on April 4, 1936, Hoover said:

"You remember that promise so often repeated by Mr. Roosevelt in 1932—'Impartial enforcement of the Anti-Trust laws to prevent monopoly,' etc. You also remember that statement of the President—'History will record the NRA as the most important and far-reaching legislation ever enacted.' Everybody knows the NRA piled up the most gigantic monopolistic practices since Qeen Elizabeth. They restricted production, fixed prices, and brought destruction to small business men."

"Time and again the last Republican Administration refused to listen to the siren of these NRA ideas. But no better proof is needed that competition was maintained by the Republican Administration than the orgy of monopolistic practices which broke loose on its abandonment by the New Deal. Today we have before us the full import of the NRA: It was framed on the exact pattern of Mr. Mussolini. And now Mr. Mussolini discloses that it is but the first step to complete Socialism. He has taken over the monopolies for the government. And we are promised that the NRA will be born again in America."

REGULATION OF ELECTRIC POWER

In the early part of Hoover's service as Secretary of Commerce, water power was already under some Federal regulation. However at that time hardly 2 per cent of all the power supply of the country passed over state lines. Hoover for this reason did not at that early period favor Federal regulation except as to water power from streams under Federal jurisdiction. He believed that other power could be better handled by the states. But with the development of long transmissions and the consequent increasing volume of interstate power, together with the building up of huge holding companies, he decided that the time had come for Federal regulation.

In his first Message to Congress of December 3, 1929, he requested the creation of a full-time Federal Power Commission for general regulation of power to replace the Cabinet Committee which had theretofore administered the limited Federal water power acts. He said:

"It is also desirable that the authority of the commission should be extended to certain phases of power regulation. The nature of the electric utilities industry is such that about 90 per cent of all power generation and distribution is intrastate in character, and most of the states have developed their own regulatory systems as to certificates of convenience, rates, and profits of such utilities. To encroach upon their authorities and responsibilities would be an encroachment upon the rights of the states. There are cases, however, of interstate character beyond the jurisdiction of the states. To meet these cases it would be most desirable if a method could be worked out by which initial action may be taken between the commissions of the states whose joint action should be made effective by the Federal Power Commission with a reserve to act on its own motion in case of disagreement of non-action by the states."

[*State Papers, Vol. I, pp. 155–6*]

Draft bills for regulation of interstate power were furnished to the Chairmen of the Committees concerned. The recommendations were opposed by power interests and radical members of Congress as well.

Finally (June 3, 1930), however, Congress passed the portion of the act creating the Federal Power Commission but transferred to it only the authorities of the old Cabinet Committee over water powers on navigable rivers. They refused to follow the President's request for authority to the Commission to regulate interstate rates in co-operation with the state regulatory commissions and to regulate the accounting and financing of companies engaged in interstate power distribution. The President was very indignant at some of the so-called Progressives in Congress whose opposition was born of desire to force the Government operation of power. Their theory was apparently to oppose adequate control of private operation in the hope that public resentment over unrestrained greedy action would forward their cause. Here was the whole question of the American system of regulation as against Socialism.

In his second Annual Message to Congress on December 2, 1930, President Hoover urged again:

"I have in a previous Message recommended effective regulation of interstate electrical power. Such regulation should preserve the independence and responsibility of the states."

[*State Papers, Vol. I, p. 437*]

He took occasion to remind Congress again a month later on January 10, 1931:

"It will be recalled that on my recommendation the Federal Power Commission was reorganized from the old basis of three Cabinet members giving a small part of their time, to a full commission of five members, in order that adequate protection could be given to public interest in the water resources of the country, and that I further recommended that the Commission should be given authority to regulate all interstate power rates. The law establishing the new commission became effective last June, although legislation giving it authority to regulate rates has not yet been enacted."   [*State Papers, Vol. I, p. 485*]

SENATE ATTEMPT TO DIRECT THE COMMISSION

Hoover had appointed a most distinguished Commission under the new law and the Senate had confirmed their appointments. Upon taking office they discharged some employees of the previous Commission who turned out to have alliances with certain senators. These senators endeavored to recall the confirmations of the members of the Commission. The President stoutly defended the independence of the Executive and when the opposition senators took the matter into the courts they were beaten. In a public statement at the time the President said on March 10, 1931:

"I have today notified the Senate that I will not accede to their resolution. . . ."

". . . these appointments were constitutionally made, are not subject to recall . . . the objective of the Senate constitutes an attempt to dictate to an administrative agency upon the appointment of subordinates and an attempted invasion of the authority of the Executive. These as President, I am bound to resist."

"I cannot, however, allow a false issue to be placed before the country. There is no issue for or against power companies. . . ."

"The resolutions of the Senate may have the attractive political merit of giving rise to a legend that those who voted for it are 'enemies of the power interests,' and, inferentially, those who voted against it are 'friends of the power interests,' and it may contain a hope of symbolizing me as the defender of power interests if I refuse to sacrifice three outstanding public servants."   [*State Papers, Vol. I, p. 485*]

MUSCLE SHOALS

On March 3, 1931, Hoover vetoed a Congressional act to put the Government into the fertilizer and power business at Muscle Shoals. After analyzing and riddling it from a business point of view, he said:

"I am firmly opposed to the government entering into any business the major purpose of which is competition with our citizens. There are national emergencies which require that the government should temporarily enter the field of business, but they must be emergency actions and in matters where the cost of the project is secondary to much higher considerations. There are many localities where the Federal Government is justified in the construction of great dams and reservoirs, where navigation, flood control, reclamation, or stream regulation are of dominant importance, and where they are beyond the capacity or purpose of private or local government capital to construct. In these cases power is often a by-product and should be disposed of by contract or lease. But for the Federal Government deliberately to go out to build up and expand such an occasion to the major purpose of a power and manufacturing business is to break down the initiative and enterprise of the American people; it is destruction of equality of opportunity amongst our people; it is the negation of the ideals upon which our civilization has been based."

"This bill raises one of the important issues confronting our people. That is squarely the issue of Federal Government ownership and operation of power and manufacturing business not as a minor by-product but as a major purpose. Involved in this question is the agitation against the conduct of the power industry. The power problem is not to be solved by the Federal Government going into the power business, nor is it to be solved by the project in this bill. The remedy for abuses in the conduct of that industry lies in regulation and not by the Federal Government entering upon the business itself. I have recommended to the Congress on various occasions that action should be taken to establish Federal regulation of interstate power in co-operation with state authorities. This bill would launch the Federal Government upon a policy of ownership and operation of power utilities upon a basis of competition instead of by the proper government function of regulation for the protection of all the people. I hesitate to contemplate the future of our institutions, of our government, and of our country if the preoccupation of its officials is to be no longer the promotion of justice and equal opportunity but is to be devoted to barter in the markets. That is not liberalism, it is degeneration."

"The real development of the resources and the industries of the Tennessee Valley can only be accomplished by the people in that valley themselves. Muscle Shoals can only be administered by the people upon the ground, responsible to their own communities, directing them solely for the benefit of their communities and not for purposes of pursuit of social theories or national politics. Any other course deprives them of liberty."

"I would therefore suggest that the states of Alabama and Tennessee, who are the ones primarily concerned, should set up a commission of their own representatives together with a representative from the national farm organizations and the Corps of Army Engineers; that there be vested in that commission full authority to lease the plants at Muscle Shoals in the interest of the local community and agriculture generally."

"The Federal Government should, as in the case of Boulder Canyon, construct Cove Creek Dam as a regulatory measure for the flood protection of the Tennessee Valley and the development of its water resources, but on the same bases as those imposed at Boulder Canyon—that is, that construction should be undertaken at such time as the proposed commission is able to secure contracts for use of the increased water supply to power users or the lease of the power produced as a by-product from such a dam on terms that will return to the government interest upon its outlay with amortization."   [*State Papers, Vol. I, pp. 526–7–8*]

FURTHER REGULATION URGED

Again in his third Annual Message, President Hoover returned to this subject:

"I have recommended in previous Messages the effective regulation of interstate electrical power as the essential function of the reorganized Federal Power Commission. I renew the recommendation. It is urgently needed in public protection."   [*State Papers, Vol. II, p. 53*]

Speaking in the campaign of 1932 (Washington, August 11), he said:

"I have repeatedly recommended the Federal regulation of interstate power. I shall persist in that. I have opposed the Federal Government undertaking the operation of the power business. I shall continue that opposition."   [*State Papers, Vol. II, p. 257*]

During 1932, under the economic strains of the depression, several of the electric holding company castles began to collapse with great public losses and indignation. Had the Democratic radical Congress acted upon Hoover's recommendations, considerable part of these losses would have been prevented. For instance, the Insull "Empire" of fantastic holding companies which collapsed in Chicago with such dire results was mostly constructed after his recommendations.

Speaking in the 1932 campaign, on October 31, he said:

"Three years ago, in view of the extension of the use of transmission of power over state borders and the difficulties of state regulatory bodies in the face of this interstate action, I recommended to the Congress that such interstate power should be placed under regulation by the Federal Government in co-operation with the state authorities."

"That recommendation was in accord with the principles of the Republican Party over the past fifty years, to provide regulation where public interest had developed in tools of industry which was beyond control and regulation of the states."

"I succeeded in creating an independent Power Commission to handle such matters, but the Democratic House declined to approve the further powers to this commission necessary for such regulation."

[*State Papers, Vol. II, p. 419*]

In general comment upon the refusal of a Democratic Congress to act on Electric Power regulation, the President stated in a private letter on February 17, 1933, since published:

"There is a phase of all this that must cause anxiety to every American. Democracy cannot survive unless it is master in its own house. The economic system cannot survive unless there are real restraints upon unbridled greed or dishonest reach for power. Greed and dishonesty are not attributes solely of our system—they are human and will infect socialism or any ism. But if our production and distribution systems are to function we must have effective restraints on manipulation, greed and dishonesty. Our Democracy has proved its ability to put its unruly occupants under control but never until their conduct has been a public scandal and a stench. For instance, you will recollect my own opposition to government operation of electric power, for that is a violation of the very fundamentals of our system; but parallel with it I asked and preached for regulation of it to protect the public from its financial manipulation. We gained the Power Commission but Congress refused it the regulatory authority we asked. I have time and again warned, asked and urged the reorganization of the banking system. The inertia of the Democracy is never more marked than in promotion of what seems abstract or indirect ideas. The recent scandals are the result. Democracy, always lagging, will no doubt now act and may act destructively to the system, for it is mad. It is this lag, the failure to act in time for prevention which I fear most in the sane advancement of economic life. For an outraged people may destroy the whole economic system rather than reconstruct and control the segment which has failed in its function. I trust the new administration will recognize the difference between crime and economic functioning; between constructive prevention and organization as contrasted with destruction."

[*Hoover Administration, p. 319–20*]

REGULATION OF RAILWAYS

The President's policies toward the railways were first, private ownership and operation; second, consummation of the Congressional Railroad Acts calling for consolidation into larger systems; third, reform in the methods of regulation to create more financial stability.

As Secretary of Commerce it was his duty to take part in the formulation of these policies and in advising the President thereon.

The reports of that Department are replete with the formulation of these policies.

CONSOLIDATION INTO LARGER SYSTEMS

In a contribution to *The Saturday Evening Post* of February 9, 1924, the Secretary summed up the policies to that date. He said:

"The development of policies that will provide adequate, economical and nondiscriminatory transportation for a population which requires doubling the amount of goods to be moved about every fifteen years, is task enough for the independent thought of the nation. But these policies are also a good component for political and financial medicines, and it is a job in itself to secure their consideration solely on the basis of long-view public interest."

"We have three possible courses open to us: to adopt Government ownership; to abandon regulation and control in expectation that free exploitation will secure results; or to make effective the policies already indicated in legislation. The nation must have settled policies of some sort in these matters or we shall yet have the country strangled for lack of transportation."

"The case against Government ownership or nationalization or whatever you wish to call it goes to the very mainsprings of our whole national life. The stifling of individual initiative, of equality of individual opportunity through the blight of bureaucracy would be a lasting blow to the development of the intelligence and character of our people. It is a definite step to socialism. It is a certainty that our political system has not developed—and will not develop in our generation—to a point where we could stand the political implications of another 2,000,000 Government employees and their method of selection. Moreover, the pressures exerted by special localities upon two joint boards of directors, consisting of 435 Congressmen and 96 Senators, for special service at Government expense would become as noteworthy as they have become in the administration of the Shipping Board and the River and Harbor appropriations, and any coherent growth would become impossible. And as to practical results in business efficiency we need no better exhibit to refresh our souls in resolution than the spectacle of the United States Government engaged in the operation of overseas shipping."

"There is nothing that would be a greater disaster to our railway employees than to be placed under a wage control where the hand of every other citizen would be against them with the implied prohibition of the right to strike which comes with Government service."

"Those who believe in the other alternative of retreat from tight regulation in public interest to the good old days of free competition and uncontrolled consolidation have little understanding of the public mind, or a short memory as to the practical workings of these freedoms. The pernicious political activities of the railways of a generation ago in practically every state—their resistance to every attempt to secure public rights, their debauchery of everything that is wholesome in democracy, the scandalous operation of many roads with alternate ruin and inflation, the vast increase in capitalization at many consolidations, the discrimination in rates—are a category of evils which required years to overcome. They lie in the annals of every state in the Union. It is possible that there would never have been regulation of rates or prohibition of the plain economic need of consolidation into larger systems had the public been protected against discrimination and the evils that crept into the consolidation finance of that period. If the advantages from the great consolidations of that time had been passed on to the public in decreased rates and to the stockholders in more stable earnings, the process would doubtless have been permitted to continue to full completion. The outrages on the public in all these directions created a foundation of resentment which extends to the present day, supplies gas for every demagogue, and makes a just and objective handling of the problem next to impossible. Had the railway managers of the last generation been guiltless of these practices we probably should have no more of a railway problem today than of a telephone problem."

"We have a new generation of railway operators. I have no hesitation in saying that with very few exceptions they have a high sense of public responsibility. They have given us a record of efficiency in management and consideration of public need during the past year which has never been equaled in railway history. Nevertheless, public memory of past wrongs will stifle at birth any attempt at abrogation of regulatory control, and it is a waste of time to talk about it. It is a certainty that so long as we have private ownership we shall have regulation of rates, service and capitalization in public utilities not only nationally but in each of the forty-eight states. It has come to stay. It ought to stay on its own merits; for we cannot intrust the conduct of a monopoly or a semi-monopoly solely to goodwill."

"If we are going to think along lines of private ownership we must start with this primary acceptance—that future rates and capitalization will be publicly controlled. The very moment we arrive at this point we have eliminated the whole justification for maintaining a multitude of independent utilities for the purpose of securing reasonable rates by competition, and if we would prepare for our national needs and effect obvious economies we should at once promote the creation of larger units. A big element of the whole problem is that certain roads are now unable under any reasonable maximum of rates to earn enough to perform their share of public service and to finance themselves to this end. Yet we have not a single mile of railway more than the country will yet need. We have about 1600 companies in the business, of which 186 have an operating revenue of $1,000,000 a year or more. Some of these roads are strong, prosperous and efficient. Others are semi-bankrupt and unable to perform the public service which constitutes their only warrant for existence. Between these two extremes are roads unable in varying degrees to supply the transportation service necessary to the present life of the communities dependent upon them or to expend for the needs of future years."

"Nor are these deficits in service wholly local to each particular railroad. In their inability to provide their share of common rolling stock the weak roads thrust an excessive burden of finance and support upon the strong railways. Our car shortages should be blamed on the weak and not the strong roads."

"Rate regulation is not responsible for all the weakness of the weak roads. Many of them could not earn enough to finance themselves even under free competition, yet they are necessary to the communities they serve. Any maximum of rates no doubt renders their position more difficult. Rates sufficient merely to support the weak, even if they could be collected, would be extortionate if collected by the strong. Yet great communities have grown up on railway rates below the needed earnings of weak roads. Congress, in struggling with this dilemma, included in the present Transportation Act a requirement of a fair return, which is declared by the Interstate Commerce Commission to be an average of 5¾ per cent net on the physical valuation of the whole railway property with a recapture to Government control of one-half the earnings of individual railways in excess of 6 per cent. The establishment of this figure of an average implies that some railways will earn in excess of this amount and that others will earn less. During these recent times of the highest traffics on record, about 70,000 miles earned less than 4 per cent net on the Interstate Commerce Commission valuation, many did not earn their fixed charges, while 70,000 miles earned more than 5¾ per cent. Every railway that earns less has been put in a position where it cannot adequately enter the financial markets to secure capital for future development or adequately maintain service. Yet no one is likely to advocate any increase in the present national average of earnings. Whether this provision were in the Transportation Act or not, constitutionally the Government could not fix rates which would yield other than a fair return on the value of the property devoted to transportation uses. But whatever the background of this provision may be, from the point of view of the development of our railway system it must be obvious that the fixing of any fair average or maximum will imply that many railways are unable to earn enough to maintain their service, and yet we must have their expansion if the country is to go forward. The only solution lies in their incorporation with such other railways as will give the combined whole a sound financial foundation."

"It may be complained that the poorer railways should not be foisted upon the richer ones. This, however, is a question partly of the prices at which they are absorbed and of their prospective value rather than of their present earning power, for the latter will increase through the growth of the country. Moreover, there is a large question that has not yet been fully investigated in that many weak roads are feeder lines and the division of joint rates between them and the trunk lines perhaps ought to be on a basis more favorable to the feeders. If we are not to have consolidation this question must be examined, and I believe it would result in the earnings of many strong roads being diminished by diversion to feeders. With consolidation such questions will not arise. The problem of stable finance is even broader than the problem of the weak roads. We have seen long periods in the last decade when we were stifled for transportation because of the inability of even average good railways to compete in the markets for capital. . . ."

"A railway in the hands of a receiver never gives full service. This is exactly what happens to scores of weaker railways in bad times, and it will be an evergrowing menace unless all of them are placed upon a sounder footing of finance."

"The second reason for consolidation lies in the necessity for a more equitable distribution of rates as between different commodities. Our rate structure is a most amazing complex of local and commodity compromises with the theory of charging all that the traffic will bear. The inequalities and injustices arising out of the structure have been greatly exaggerated by the horizontal increases due to the war. A silk dress worth $200 pays less freight from Chicago to New York than does a bushel of wheat worth one dollar. . . ."

"The third major reason for consolidation—and one that is perhaps sometimes unduly emphasized—is the economy in operation that may be obtained. There would be undoubted economies, not so much in overhead as in the better handling of traffic, the better utilization of common terminals and other facilities, wider home use of cars, more direct routing, and more universal standards and cheaper maintenance of equipment. . . ."

"Voluntary consolidations of our railways were frequent until 1904, when the Supreme Court in the Northern Securities Case construed the antitrust laws to forbid them, the dominant theory at that stage in our national development being that equitable rates should be maintained through competition. . . ."

"The present Transportation Act provides for consolidations only to the extent they are approved by the Interstate Commerce Commission and are in accordance with its general plan. . . . Obviously consolidations cannot be allowed to proceed merely at the wish of the companies concerned. The purpose to be accomplished is public."

"If we accept consolidation as a fundamental policy, then we should

have its consummation in the most rapid manner after the system out-
lines are determined. Under the present purely voluntary provisions,
with no stimulation to accomplishment, it is likely to be long delayed.
The weakness of the present law lies precisely at this point."

"The urgent importance of the early consummation of consolidation
warrants consideration of methods to expedite it. Early in 1923 President Harding instructed the Department of Commerce to give consideration to such methods. As a result I put forward the following outline
of a plan last April. This plan provides for:

"1. Groups for consolidation to be formulated by the Interstate Commerce Commission as provided in the present Act."

"2. Consolidated systems to be permitted incorporation under Federal law, the issue of the securities of such corporations to be subject
to the approval of the Interstate Commerce Commission."

"3. The total par value of securities in no event to exceed the total
value of the component roads as established by the Interstate Commerce
Commission as of June 30, 1914, plus the value of actual capital expenditures and deducting depreciation and abandonments since that date."

"4. Voluntary consolidations, with the consent of the Interstate Commerce Commission, to be made within two years after promulgation of
the commission groups."

"5. At the end of the two-year period the Interstate Commerce Commission to appoint an organization committee for each group not then
consolidated; this committee to consist of representatives of each of
the component roads and three representatives of the public."

"6. Each organization committee to determine the value of the outstanding securities of the component roads, valuing each class or issue
separately; the total value so fixed for the securities of any road in no
event to exceed the value of that road as established by the Interstate
Commerce Commission under the terms of the Transportation Act. . . ."

"7. Each organization committee to use all proper means to bring
about consolidation; to have the right to proceed to create a Federal
corporation for the consolidation of its group, and to offer its securities
in exchange to the then holders of securities of the component roads
upon the basis of the relative values established; securities constituting
prior liens to be either exchanged or left in effect as may be most advantageous under the particular circumstances."

"8. The securities of the consolidated companies to be issued as soon
as a majority of the holders of the stock of the component roads have
agreed to the exchange; having acquired a majority, the consolidated
corporation to have the right by law to acquire the nonconsenting minor-

ity, and to take the necessary legal steps for that purpose, compensating them for their stock at its fair value."

"9. If a majority of the stockholders in a component road shall fail to exchange, then the organization committee may, if the approving roads agree to finance the operation, acquire the dissenting road or the stock in it under powers of eminent domain."

"10. If any organization committee is unable to agree as to values or terms of exchange to be offered they may be fixed by the Interstate Commerce Commission."

"In effect the plan makes available all the usual methods by which railroads have been reorganized or consolidated in the past."

"Historically, as I have indicated, consolidation enabled the railroads to serve the transportation needs of the country; but the privilege was abused to such a point that it was finally denied. A strict regulatory policy has now developed to the stage where it can with entire safety to the public be trusted to encourage railroad consolidations anew without danger of a recurrence of their former abuses. Consolidation is economically sound and, when subjected to intelligent supervision and control, cannot be other than directly beneficial to the public."

In his first Annual Message to Congress, on December 3, 1929, he said:

"We have, however, not yet assured for the future that adequate system of transportation through consolidations which was the objective of the Congress in the Transportation Act. The chief purpose of consolidation is to secure well-balanced systems with more uniform and satisfactory rate structure, a more stable financial structure, more equitable distribution of traffic, greater efficiency, and single-line instead of multiple-line hauls. In this way the country will have the assurance of better service and ultimately at lower and more even rates than would otherwise be attained. Legislation to simplify and expedite consolidation methods and better to protect public interest should be enacted."

[State Papers, Vol. I, pp. 152–3]

In his second Message, on December 2, 1930, he said:

"We have determined upon a national policy of consolidation of the railways as a necessity of more stable and more economically operated transportation. Further legislation is necessary to facilitate such consolidation. In the public interest we should strengthen the railways that they may meet our future needs."

". . . The provisions dealing with corporate reorganizations should be applicable to railroads, and in such cases the plan of reorganization should not become effective until it has been approved by the Interstate Commerce Commission."

[*State Papers, Vol. I, p. 437*]

THE CONSOLIDATION AGREEMENT OF 1930

In an endeavor to make practical the provisions of the Transportation Act of 1920 for consolidation of the railways into larger systems the President initiated direct negotiations between the railways to that end in the Eastern Trunkline territory. His further purpose was to give greater financial strength to the railways which were rapidly falling into difficulties due to the depression.

On December 31, 1930, he announced the success of these negotiations, saying:

"As a result of meetings . . . a plan for consolidation of the different railways in official classification territory (except New England) into four independent systems was agreed upon for presentation to the Interstate Commerce Commission."

"The four new systems embrace the territory east of the Mississippi River, including the Virginian Railway on the south, the New York Central on the north."

"These negotiations have been in progress for some weeks, and were undertaken at my suggestion in the hope of effecting the consolidation policies declared by Congress in 1920 and especially at this time as a contribution to the recovery of business by enlarging opportunity for employment and by increasing the financial stability of all the railways, and particularly some of the weaker roads."

"The Transportation Act passed by Congress in 1920 provides for a consolidation of railways into a limited number of strong systems in order to maintain broader competition, more adequate service, simplification of rate structure, lower operating costs and in the long run lower rates to the public."

"During the past ten years a possible grouping of the roads so as to carry out the law has been under constant discussion. The Interstate Commerce Commission has no power to compel such consolidations. They can only be effected upon initiation of the carriers. During this period a number of negotiations have been undertaken in respect to these railways, with view to carrying out the wishes of Congress, but they have proved abortive. A year ago the Interstate Commerce Commission issued a suggested plan for consolidating these roads into five systems. This plan, like others, has met with objections which apparently made it an unsolvable basis."

"These uncertainties and delays over nearly ten years have seriously retarded development of the railways and have prevented a desirable growth in many directions, and have diminished their ability to compete with other forms of transportation. Such questions as electrification, linking up of different railroads, development of terminals and many other major improvements have been retarded because of uncertainty with respect to the position which particular roads are to occupy in the permanent grouping."

"It is my understanding that the plan provided for the protection of the interests of the employees and full consideration of the interest of the various communities and carries out the requirements of the law in protection of public interest generally. The presidents of the major systems have agreed upon the many details of the plan with the exception of a minor point, which is left to arbitration."

"The plan, of course, must be submitted to the Interstate Commerce Commission, who have the independent duty to determine if it meets with every requirement of public interest."

[*State Papers, Vol. I, p. 474*]

In a single-handed obstruction by Senator Couzens with some Democratic encouragement, this was held up until the agreement was no longer possible. Thereby a great constructive action was destroyed and the Government later on compelled to find huge loans to these railways which would not have been necessary.

REVISION OF RAILWAY REGULATION

At the urging of the President the Interstate Commerce Commission developed an entire revision of the railway regulation acts which would have given a great deal more stability to the railways and greater protecion to the public. The President was anxious for its enactment. In his third Message to Congress, on December 8, 1931, he urged it upon Congress as an emergency necessity.

"The railways present one of our immediate and pressing problems. They are and must remain the backbone of our transportation system. Their prosperity is interrelated with the prosperity of all industries. Their fundamental service in transportation, the volume of their employment, their buying power for supplies from other industries, the enormous investment in their securities, particularly their bonds, by insurance companies, savings banks, benevolent and other trusts, all reflect their partnership in the whole economic fabric. Through these institutions the railway bonds are in a large sense the investment of every family. The well-maintained and successful operation and the stability of railway finances are of primary importance to economic recovery. They should have more effective opportunity to reduce operating costs by proper consolidation. As their rates must be regulated in public interest, so also approximate regulation should be applied to competing services by some authority. The methods of their regulation should be revised. The Interstate Commerce Commission has made important and far-reaching recommendations upon the whole subject, which I commend to the early consideration of the Congress."   [*State Papers, Vol. II, p. 51*]

> The reforms proposed by the Commission covered the repeal of Section 15A which gave the Government an uncollectable 50 per cent of profits over certain earnings and required the reexpenditure of these profits on other railroads. They included regulation of bus and truck traffic, the regulation of port to port rates, and regulation of car companies. They provided that the Commission have authority over stock purchases of one railroad by another. The recommendations included provisions to strengthen the Commission's authority to bring about consolidations.
>
> On October 28, 1932, in an address at Indianapolis, Hoover said:

"I have repeatedly recommended to the Congress a revision of our railway transportation laws in order that we might create greater stability and greater assurance of this vital service in our transportation. . . . I have set this matter out in numerous Messages to Congress. I have supported the recommendations of the Interstate Commerce Commission, which are specific and not generalities. Our opponents have adopted my program in this matter during this campaign except certain glittering generalizations, as to which they do not inform us how they are to be accomplished, and upon which I enter a reservation."

[*State Papers, Vol. II, pp. 399-400*]

AIDS TO RAILWAYS

The railways had shown signs of recovery from the depression in early 1931. But with the European financial collapse and its impact upon us in the summer and fall of 1931 they developed great distress. Renewal of loans was impossible and receiverships were imminent over three-quarters of the systems. The shock to insurance companies, banks and public institutions generally who held railroad bonds and securities would have brought disaster of immeasurable dimensions. The inevitable curtailment of railway operations in receivership would have increased unemployment. The situation was one of the most serious with which the President was confronted.

This crisis was one of those solved in the formation of the Reconstruction Finance Corporation in 1931–32. The total loans to railroads at no one time have been greater than $300,000,000 and the very existence of this reserve power enabled much private financing otherwise impossible. The Government will lose nothing.

Conflict having grown up among the various Government agencies dealing with the railways which threatened to delay financial support to them, the President undertook the co-ordination of these agencies. On March 19, 1932, he made the following public statement which hardly indicated the battle he had been through:

"I have held a number of conferences for survey of the railway situation and of the Reconstruction Finance Corporation, members of the Interstate Commerce Commission, and representatives of the Railway Credit Corporation."

"It is estimated that the financial necessities of the important railways of the country which are likely to require aid in meeting the interest and renewal of their maturing securities, during 1932, will be from $300,-000,000 to $400,000,000."

"The problem is to handle the situation as a whole so as to lay the foundations for restored employment on the railways and through their purchases of supplies, and at the same time to establish confidence in the security of the bonds which are the reliance of great trustee institutions of the United States which are in fact the property of the entire people."

"The co-ordination of programs and policies has been arrived at."

[*State Papers, Vol. II, p. 143*]

RAILWAY REORGANIZATION

The financial organization of many of the railways was top-heavy. Aside from depression troubles they had permanently lost traffic by the highways, by the pipe lines for oil and by the electrification of industry. Many railroads needed reorganization to reduce their fixed charges. To go through the customary receiverships and bankruptcy was disastrous both to public confidence and to their security holders. To remedy this was the President's proposed change in the bankruptcy laws, to permit orderly reorganization. (See Adjustment of Private Debt, pages 486 ff.)

This act was passed in February, 1933, and is today the vehicle of great re-arrangement of railroad capital under conditions much more just and constructive to the public and the holders of securities than ever before.

BANKING REFORM

President Hoover inherited 24,000 independent banks all involved in a gigantic credit inflation originating in the Federal Reserve System—and a speculative madness over the entire country. In numbers, 7600 of these banks were national and 15,000 were state banks under 48 different state laws. The weakness of the whole system was indicated by the fact that in three previous "prosperous" years there were net failures of 199 national banks with deposits of $177,000,000 and 1387 state banks with deposits of $362,000,000. The four subsequent years showed vividly enough the weakness of the whole system.

A great forward step in banking reform had taken place in the Wilson Administration when the Federal Reserve System was established, and the banking laws revised. The Democratic leaders held it was the final and ultimate solution of all banking dangers to the country. In the speeches of President Wilson, Secretary McAdoo, Senator Glass and other leaders, they assured the American people:

"We shall have no more financial panics."

"Panics are impossible."

"Business men can now proceed in perfect confidence that they will no longer put their property in peril."

"Now the business man may work out his destiny without living in terror of panic and hard times."

"Panics in the future are unthinkable."

"Never again can panic come to the American people."

As Secretary of Commerce, Hoover had no part in banking control but had protested vigorously at the policies of artificial expansion of credit by the Reserve Board which contributed so much to the mad boom of 1929.

Hoover had been nominated and elected with the opposition of many of the New York banks. Their opposition combined with the partisan attitude of the Senate made any program of reform difficult. And on top of all this came the crash before his administration had time to turn around, and the problem became one of saving the ship in a desperate storm rather than putting new machinery in it. Nevertheless President Hoover went at the job.

In his first Annual Message to the Congress on December 3, 1929 (this was before the real crisis), he urged that a special joint commission embracing members of Congress and the leading administration officials be created for the purpose of investigation of the whole banking system with recommendations for legislation. The idea of such an important commission was squelched and it was not until April 19, 1930, that the Senate Banking and Currency Committee passed a resolution to make an investigation themselves.

These promises not having been realized, Hoover advocated drastic reforms upon the following lines:

"(a) To compel every commercial bank to join the Federal Reserve System;

"(b) to establish inspection of all commercial banks by the Federal Reserve System;

"(c) to attain gradual separation of promotion affiliates;

"(d) to exclude long-term credits from demand deposit banks;

"(e) to separate savings and long-term loan institutions from demand deposit institutions;

"(f) to establish state-wide branch banking by national banks under suitable regulations with provision that no new branches be established where there were adequate facilities, except by purchase of an existing bank."

[*Hoover Administration, p. 166*]

The Hoover methods included reorganization of Mortgage Banking and of Agricultural Credit Institutions (a) to create a national system of Mortgage Discount Banks of which the Home Loan Banks were the first step; (b) to expand Federal Land Banks; (c) to create the national system of Agricultural Credit Banks for purposes of production and livestock credit (to absorb the Intermediate Credit Banks); (d) to extend credit facilities to farm co-operatives through the Farm Board.

The Democratic-radical combination in the Senate made the majority of that body opposed to President Hoover from the day his Administration opened. Senator Glass with this backing became at once the dictator of all banking legislation.

On May 5, 1930, Senator Glass introduced a banking bill himself and on May 30 the Committee announced it hoped to have a bill ready for the next session.

On October 2, 1930, in an address to the American Bankers' Convention he vigorously attacked the effect of banking credit inflation on the creation of booms and of mad speculation with subsequent depressions and misery. He appealed to the bankers to study the whole problem and to take part in reform and cure abuses. . . . "A great human problem."

In the session of the Congress of December, 1930, to March, 1931, it was expected that the Senate Banking and Currency Committee under the leadership of Senator Glass would bring forward its banking reform bill. They were, however, not able to agree upon it and wished for more time for investigation.

In a public address at Indianapolis on June 15, 1931, the President again returned to the need for reform in banking.

"The Federal Reserve System was inadequate to prevent a large diversion of capital and bank deposits from commercial and industrial business into wasteful speculation and stock promotion. It is obvious our banking system must be organized to give greater protection to depositors against failures. It is equally obvious that we must determine whether the facilities of our security and commodity exchanges are not being used to create illegitimate speculation and intensify depressions."

[State Papers, Vol. I, p. 581]

The second stage of the great depression emerged immediately after the adjournment of the Congress in 1931. The European financial collapse began in May of that year and culminated in the default of the Bank of England at the end of September. The terrific impacts upon us threw our weak banking system completely out of gear. The emergency policies injected by Hoover to save the collapse of our banking system are dealt with elsewhere. They comprised the creation of the National Credit Association with a capital of $500,000,000; the German Standstill Agreement; the expansion of the credit authority of the Federal Land Banks by a billion; the Reconstruction Finance Corporation with $3,000,000,000; the expansion of eligibility in the Federal Reserve System so as to save the gold standard; the expansion of Federal Reserve credit by several billion through open market operations; the creation of the Home Loan Banks; and the creation if the Agricultural Credit Banks. All these supports were thrown behind the banking and business situation, a large part of which would never have been necessary if we had possessed a sound banking system.

Gradually even the banking leaders were beginning to realize that the President was right and that there must be reform.

One of the obvious weaknesses of our banking system was the investing of demand deposits in long-term mortgage real estate loans which could not be realized in time of stress. With view to building a more flexible structure, on October 7, 1931, the President summoned a committee representing insurance, banking, building and loan, real estate and construction interests and proposed to them the creation of a national system of Mortgage Discount Banks somewhat comparable in function with the Federal Reserve Banks in discount of commercial loans. His idea was that the Government should furnish the initial capital as was done in the Federal Reserve Banks; that this capital should ultimately be absorbed by the members of the new mortgage banks. The members were to be building and loan associations, insurance and mortgage companies, the banks and other institutions making real estate mortgage loans. The new mortgage system was to discount "live" mortgages up to 80 per cent if they did not exceed a reasonable proportion of property valuation and in turn to secure its funds (outside the initial capital) from the issue of debentures to the public in the manner of the Federal Land Banks.

The President urged that this would save home owners and farmers from foreclosure, would thaw out billions of frozen assets, would save many banks from collapse, and would be a long step toward the needed separation of long-term and short-term credit systems in national economy.

The insurance companies and certain mortgage companies immediately began opposition, as it would undoubtedly lower mortgage interest rates. The building and loan associations, real estate and construction interests favored it. Other financial interests opposed it. Because Hoover favored it was enough to stir up those who, for purely partisan reasons, wished to stop any accomplishment.

The President soon found that the oppositions were too strong for a broad reform and proceeded to narrow the plan down to include discount of home and farm mortgages and to restrict the discount percentages, in the hope that at least this foundation could be laid. The Home Loan Banks were the result. (See page 436.)

The President's Message to the Congress on December 8, 1931, dealt largely with emergency matters, but in the longer view of banking reform, he said:

". . . The paralysis has been further augmented by the steady increase in recent years of the proportion of bank assets invested in long-term securities, such as mortgages and bonds. These securities tend to lose their liquidity in depression or temporarily to fall in value so that the ability of the banks to meet the shock of sudden withdrawal is greatly lessened and the restriction of all kinds of credit is thereby increased. The continuing credit paralysis has operated to accentuate the deflation and liquidation of commodities, real estate, and securities below any reasonable basis of values."

"A method should be devised to make available quickly to depositors some portion of their deposits in closed banks as the assets of such banks may warrant. Such provision would go far to relieve distress in a multitude of families, would stabilize values in many communities, and would liberate working capital to thousands of concerns. I recommend that measures be enacted promptly to accomplish these results and I suggest that the Congress should consider the development of such a plan through the Federal Reserve Banks."

"I recommend the establishment of a system of home-loan discount banks as the necessary companion in our financial structure of the Federal Reserve Banks and our Federal Land Banks. Such action will relieve present distressing pressures against home and farm property owners. It will relieve pressures upon and give added strength to building and loan associations, savings banks, and deposit banks, engaged in extending such credits. Such action would further decentralize our credit structure. It would revive residential construction and employment. It would enable such loaning institutions more effectually to promote home ownership. I discussed this plan at some length in a statement made public November 14, last. This plan has been warmly indorsed by the recent National Conference upon Home Ownership and Housing, whose members were designated by the governors of the states and the groups interested."

"Our people have a right to a banking system in which their deposits shall be safeguarded and the flow of credit less subject to storms. The need of a sounder system is plainly shown by the extent of bank failures. I recommend the prompt improvement of the banking laws. Changed financial conditions and commercial practices must be met. The Congress should investigate the need for separation between different kinds of banking; an enlargement of branch banking under proper restrictions; and the methods by which enlarged membership in the Federal Reserve system may be brought about."   [*State Papers, Vol. II, pp. 46–7*]

On December 11, the President requested of Congress as one of the most important requirements of the day:

"The revision of our banking laws so as to safeguard the depositors."
[*State Papers, Vol. II, p. 84*]

He urged again at the next Congress on January 4, 1932:

"Revision of banking laws in order to better safeguard deposits."
[*State Papers, Vol. II, p. 103*]

The Senate Banking and Finance Committee now belatedly began in real earnest the formulation of broad banking reform. The President consulted with their members frequently, urging expedition.

On January 22, 1932, Senator Glass introduced his Banking Reform Bill which partially covered the field. On January 27, it was returned to the subcommittee for revision. The President conferred with the senator, assuring his support. The bill was reported to the Senate on March 16, 1932. It provided for revision of laws on group banking and promotion affiliates, for encouragement to branch banking, insistence upon membership in the Reserve System, limits on loans for speculation. It also created a corporation for loans to expedite liquidation of closed banks. Public hearings were held with a deluge of banking opposition. The bill again was sent back to a subcommittee for revision, and again introduced to the Senate on April 9, 1932, and on April 27 was put on the calendar of Privileged Business. The banking world again was in opposition over the elimination of their promotion affiliates; opposed compulsory membership in the Federal Reserve System and branch banking, and other leading features. The battle raged furiously through May and on June 16, the Senate displaced it on the calendar.

During the winter of 1932, the President took up the question of a new institution of banking for farmers, and in result the Agricultural Credit Banks were created through the R. F. C. (See page 442.)

During the campaign of 1932, Hoover frequently urged the need of thorough-going banking reform. At Washington on on August 11, 1932:

"In soil poisoned by speculation grew those ugly weeds of waste, of exploitation, of abuse, of financial power."

"This depression has exposed many weaknesses in our economic system. There have been exploitation and abuse of financial power. We will fearlessly and unremittingly reform such abuses. I have recommended

to the Congress the reform of our banking laws. Unfortunately this
legislation has not yet been enacted. The American people must have
protection from insecure banking through a stronger system. They must
be relieved from conditions which permit the credit machinery of the
country to be made available without adequate check for wholesale speculation in securities with ruinous consequences to millions of our citizens
and to national economy."   [*State Papers, Vol. II, p. 247*]

Again at Indianapolis on October 28, 1932, President Hoover
repeated:

". . . this depression has exposed many weaknesses in our economic
system. It has shown much wrongdoing. There has been exploitation
and abuse of financial power. These weaknesses must be corrected and
that wrongdoing must be punished. We will continue to reform such
abuses and correct such wrongdoing as falls within the powers of the
Federal Government."

"The American people must have protection from insecure banking
through a stronger system. They must be relieved from conditions which
permit the credit machinery of the country to be made available without
adequate check for wholesale speculation in securities, with its ruinous
consequences to millions of our citizens and to national economy. . . ."

"I recommended to the Congress the sane reform of our banking laws.
The Democratic House of Representatives did not see fit to pass that
legislation in the last session. I shall persist in securing its accomplishment."   [*State Papers, Vol. II, p. 389*]

Even though defeated in the election, President Hoover returned to the charge in his fourth Annual and final Message to
the Congress on December 6, 1932:

"The second direction for action is the complete reorganization at once
of our banking system. The shocks to our economic life have undoubtedly been multiplied by the weakness of this system, and until they are
remedied recovery will be greatly hampered."

"The basis of every other and every further effort toward recovery
is to reorganize at once our banking system. The shocks to our economic
system have undoubtedly multiplied by the weakness of our financial system. I first called attention of the Congress in 1929 to this condition,
and I have unceasingly recommended remedy since that time. The subject has been exhaustively investigated both by the committees of the
Congress and the officers of the Federal Reserve System."

"The banking and financial system is presumed to serve in furnishing the essential lubricant to the wheels of industry, agriculture, and commerce, that is, credit. Its diversion from proper use, its improper use, or its insufficiency instantly brings hardship and dislocation in economic life. As a system our banking has failed to meet this great emergency. It can be said without question of doubt that our losses and distress have been greatly augmented by its wholly inadequate organization. Its inability as a system to respond to our needs is today a constant drain upon progress toward recovery. In this statement I am not referring to individual banks or bankers. Thousands of them have shown distinguished courage and ability. On the contrary, I am referring to the system itself, which is so organized, or so lacking in organization, that in an emergency its very mechanism jeopardizes or paralyzes the action of sound banks and its instability is responsible for periodic dangers to our whole economic system."

"Bank failures rose in 1931 to 10½ per cent of all the banks as compared to 1½ per cent of the failures of all other types of enterprise. Since January 1, 1930, we have had 4665 banks suspend, with $3,300,000,000 in deposits. Partly from fears and drains from abroad, partly from these failures themselves (which indeed often caused closing of sound banks), we have witnessed hoarding of currency to an enormous sum, rising during the height of the crisis to over $1,600,000,000. The results from interreaction of cause and effect have expressed themselves in strangulation of credit which at times has almost stifled the Nation's business and agriculture. The losses, suffering, and tragedies of our people are incalculable. Not alone do they lie in the losses of savings to millions of homes, injury by deprival of working capital to thousands of small businesses, but also, in the frantic pressure to recall loans to meet pressures of hoarding and in liquidation of failed banks, millions of other people have suffered in the loss of their homes and farms, businesses have been ruined, unemployment increased, and farmers' prices diminished."

"That this failure to function is unnecessary and is the fault of our particular system is plainly indicated by the fact that in Great Britain, where the economic mechanism has suffered far greater shocks than our own, there has not been a single bank failure during the depression. Again in Canada, where the situation has been in large degree identical with our own, there have not been substantial bank failures."

"The creation of the Reconstruction Finance Corporation and the amendments to the Federal Reserve Act served to defend the Nation in a great crisis. They are not remedies; they are relief. It is inconceivable that the Reconstruction Corporation, which has extended aid to nearly 6000 institutions and is manifestly but a temporary device, can go on indefinitely."

"It is today a matter of satisfaction that the rate of bank failures, of hoarding, and the demands upon the Reconstruction Corporation have greatly lessened. The acute phases of the crisis have obviously passed and the time has now come when this national danger and this failure to respond to national necessities must be ended and the measures to end them can be safely undertaken. Methods of reform have been exhaustively examined. There is no reason now why solution should not be found at the present session of the Congress. Inflation of currency or governmental conduct of banking can have no part in these reforms. The Government must abide within the field of constructive organization, regulation, and the enforcement of safe practices only."

"Parallel with reform in the banking laws must be changes in the Federal Farm Loan Banking system and in the Joint Stock Land Banks. Some of these changes should be directed to permanent improvement and some to emergency aid to our people where they wish to fight to save their farms and homes."

"I wish again to emphasize this view—that these widespread banking reforms are a national necessity and are the first requisites for further recovery in agriculture and business. They should have immediate consideration as steps greatly needed to further recovery."

[*State Papers, Vol. II, p. 500*]

On December 8, 1932, the Glass Banking Reform Bill was given privileged position on the calendar. The fight, however, revived even though Senator Glass offered to compromise certain features. A filibuster against the bill was undertaken by Senators Huey Long and Thomas. The bill was passed by the Senate on January 26, 1933, but was greatly attenuated. The Democratic leaders of the House refused to take action. The President made a final push to get even this bill through in a special Message to the Congress on February 20, 1933.

"There are certain measures looking to the promotion of economic recovery which have been under consideration by the Congress and are so advanced toward completion or understanding as to seem possible of enactment during the present session."

"The enactment by the House of the general principles embodied in the Glass Banking Bill which has already passed the Senate will greatly contribute to re-establish confidence. It is the first constructive step to remedy the prime weakness of our whole economic life—that is the organization of our credit system."[1]   [*State Papers, Vol. II, p. 597*]

In a published letter to Mr. Arch W. Shaw of February 17, 1933, Hoover made an over-all review of the problem.

"The last four years have shown unquestionably that it is mainly the third element of our system—that is, finance—which has failed and produced by far the largest part of the demoralization of our systems of production and distribution with its thousand tragedies which wring the heart of the Nation. I am not insensible to the disturbing war inheritances, of our expansion of production in certain branches, nor to the effect of increased labor-saving devices on employment, but these are minor notes of discord compared to that arising from failure of the financial system. This failure has been evidenced in two directions: That is, the lack of organization for domestic purposes and the weakness presented by a disintegrated front to the world through which we have been infinitely more demoralized by repeated shocks from abroad."

"The credit system in all its phases should be merely a lubricant to the systems of production and distribution. It is not its function to control these systems. That it should be so badly organized, that the volume of currency and credit, whether long or short term, should expand and shrink irrespective of the needs of production and distribution; that its stability should be the particular creature of emotional fear or optimism; that it should be insecure; that it should dominate and not be subordinate to production and distribution—all this is intolerable if we are to maintain our civilization. Yet these things have happened on a gigantic scale. We could have weathered through these failures with some losses and could have secured reorganization as we went along, planing out failures in the fundamental organization of the financial system. The rain of blows from abroad, however, on the system of such weakness has wholly prostrated us by a second phase of this depression which came from a collapse of the financial systems in Europe."

"I am referring to the system itself, which is so organized, or so lacking in organization, that it fails in its primary function of stable and steady service to the production and distribution system. In an emergency its very mechanism increases the jeopardy and paralyzes action of the community."

"Clearly we must secure sound organization of our financial system as

[1]The banking reforms of the Roosevelt Administration have not embraced the vital Hoover policies.

a prerequisite of the functioning of the whole economic system. The first steps in that system are sound currency, economy in Government, balanced governmental budgets, whether national or local. The second step is an adequate separation of commercial banking from investment banking, whether in mortgages, bonds or other forms of long-term securities. The next step is to secure effective co-ordination between national and state systems. We cannot endure forty-nine separate regulatory systems which are both conflicting and weakening. We must accept the large view that the mismanagement, instability, and bad functioning of any single institution affects the stability of some part of production and distribution and a multitude of other financial institutions. Therefore there must be co-operation within the financial system enforced by control and regulation by the Government, that will assure that this segment of our economic system does not, through faulty organization and action, bring our people again to these tragedies of unemployment and loss of homes which are today a stigma upon national life. We cannot endure that enormous sums of the people's savings shall be poured out either at home or abroad without making the promoter responsible for his every statement. We cannot endure that men will either manipulate the savings of the people so abundantly evidenced in recent exposures."

"That it has been necessary for the Government, through emergency action, to protect us while holding a wealth of gold from being taken off the gold standard, to erect gigantic credit institutions with the full pledge of Government credit to save the Nation from chaos through this failure of the financial system, that it is necessary for us to devise schemes of clearing-house protections and to install such temporary devices throughout the Nation, is full proof of all I have said. That is the big question. If we can solve this, then we must take in hand the faults of the production and distribution systems—and many problems in the social and political system. But this financial system simply must be made to function first."

"There is a phase of all this that must cause anxiety to every American. Democracy cannot survive unless it is master in its own house. The economic system cannot survive unless there are real restraints upon unbridled greed or dishonest reach for power."

"I have time and again warned, asked and urged the reorganization of the banking system. The inertia of the Democracy is never more marked than in promotion of what seems abstract or indirect ideas. The recent scandals are the result. Democracy, always lagging, will no doubt now act and may act destructively to the system, for it is mad. It is this lag, the failure to act in time for prevention which I fear most in the sane advancement of economic life."

"During these four years I have been fighting to preserve this fundamental system of production and distribution from destruction through collapse and bad functioning of the financial system."

"If we succeed in the job of preservation, certainly the next effort before the country is to reorganize the financial system so that all this will not happen again."   [*Hoover Administration, pp. 317–20*]

REFORM OF THE STOCK EXCHANGE AND OF SECURITY ISSUES

The mad boom of 1927–29 brought into being every evil of speculation. It was not until long afterwards that its underground character became evident. During the years 1925–27 Secretary Hoover had repeatedly protested the Federal Reserve Board's policies of inflation of credit. It nevertheless persisted and thereby contributed greatly to the creation of the boom.

After coming to the White House in 1929, Hoover in cooperation with the Federal Reserve Board applied various restraints on the boom. But it had gone too far for any restraint except its own collapse.

The President made an attack upon one phase of it quickly after taking office. He instructed the Department of Justice to make a drive to prevent the bucketshops and market tipsters from using the mails to stimulate speculation. This was the only Federal jurisdiction. These bucketshops were violating the laws of the State of New York, but the officials of that state had failed entirely to do anything about it. Hoover hoped this exposure would open the eyes of the public. Some fifty establishments were closed, and the press noted that telephone calls in New York City decreased by 150,000 per day after the drive was started, accounting for it as the drying up of bucketshops and tipsters. The Better Business Bureau stated that this was the most significant clean-up in the history of the Exchange. As time went on it became evident that wrong-doing was much more important than bucketshops.

President Hoover, on October 13, 1930, sent for the officials of the Stock Exchange. He informed them that, despite the fact that primarily the Exchange, for purposes of regulation, was under the jurisdiction of the State of New York, and not under the Federal Government, unless the Exchange reformed its rules and conduct so as to eliminate the manipulation then generally going on, and enforced those rules, then Federal regulation would be inevitable. He informed them further that he would make no public statement at that time in order that they might first have the opportunity to correct the situation themselves.

Some evil practices were corrected. But others remained and were defended strongly by the officials of the Exchange, particularly the "making of markets" and large short operations.

On June 15, 1931, in a public address at Indianapolis the President said:

". . . It is equally obvious that we must determine whether the facilities of our security and commodity exchanges are not being used to create illegitimate speculation and intensify depressions."

[*State Papers, Vol. I, p. 581*]

During the fall of 1931 and early winter of 1932 it became evident that, despite constant assurances, there was little real accomplishment in cleaning house by the Exchange itself.

On February 19, 1932, the President said at a press conference:

"There have been discussions, as is reported, between myself and other officials of the administration with officials of the New York Stock Exchange. Stock Exchange officials have, during the past eight months, from time to time taken steps to restrain bear raiding with a degree of success, but during the latter part of January, despite these steps, there was a large increase in the short account which unquestionably affected the price of securities and brought discouragement to the country as a whole. I, and other administration officials, again expressed our views to the managers of the Exchange that they should take adequate measures to protect investors from artificial depression of the price of securities for speculative profit. Individuals who use the facilities of the Exchange for such purposes are not contributing to recovery of the United States."

[*State Papers, Vol. I, p. 118*]

SENATE INVESTIGATION OF 1932–33

During the winter of 1932 the evidence of high financial misdoings which had centered chiefly in New York were gradually coming to light.

After the European financial crash, and when the Reconstruction Finance Corporation was formed and some semblance of financial order was re-established, President Hoover determined that Federal action would be necessary. Nothing could definitely get at the facts but the powers of a Congressional inquiry. Therefore on February 26, 1932, he requested Senators Norbeck and Walcott of the Senate Banking and Currency Committee to urge a Senatorial investigation into manipulative practices against the public interest, and to bring them into the daylight.

Messrs. Myers and Newton continue the story:

"It was evident that certain speculators were at work endeavoring to stifle the Senate investigation of the New York Stock Exchange. The President was determined that the methods used by certain members of this institution should be thoroughly reviewed, first with the view to determining if the authorities of the Exchange were doing their part to bring certain immediate practices to an end; and second, to determine if the New York State authorities could any longer be entrusted with protection of the public interest under their power to regulate it. The bear raids and pools formed in anticipation of the German collapse, in anticipation of the British crisis, and in anticipation of the gold crisis, all of them greatly had increased public apprehension at the time and had caused hoarding, flights of capital, and bank failures. Every occasion was to be 'the last.' Since the New York State authorities, who had primary responsibility, would not intervene, the President had determined that the information must be secured upon which action could be founded that would protect the public interest."

"Senator Walcott, who was familiar with the Exchange, was equally earnest in the belief that self-government of the Exchange had failed and that the New York State authorities would do nothing."

"The truth could be brought out only under the compulsion that a Senate committee could exert. His hope was that such important institutions could govern themselves, or at least the states would recognize their fundamental responsibility. In any event, he was tired of having reform promises broken."   [*Hoover Administration, p. 192*]

Some statements having been made later in respect to the origin of this inquiry, Senator F. C. Walcott wrote to Hoover in answer to it as follows:

"I recall vividly the events which led up to our meetings at the White House, when you urged me, toward the end of February, 1932, to persuade the Banking and Currency Committee of the

Senate to use every effort to determine the facts connected with
. . . the New York Stock Exchange."

"You explained very definitely to Senator Norbeck and me
your reasons. . . . I then talked the matter over fully with
several of the more active members of the Banking and Currency Committee, who were eager to get at the facts."

"The situation was critical. You, as President, were urging
haste and definite action. . . ."

"Previous to these events, you had talked with me several
times at the White House about the danger. . . . You gave me
definite instructions to proceed without delay. . . ."

"Those were critical days, and you were determined to get
at some evil practices. . . ."

". . . the complete study was made by the Banking and
Currency Committee of the affairs of the bank affiliates. That
subcommittee was composed of Senators Glass, Townsend,
Bulkley, and myself. It made a thorough study, by public hearings and expert investigations, of the operations and ramifications of certain investment companies that were affiliates of some
of the large national banks. . . ."

"It was this investigation into certain pool operations and
manipulations involving some of the bank officials that led to
the uncovering. . . ."

"You were backing courageously and without fear or favor
all of these endeavors to get at the facts and correct the evils,
and you, more than any one else, were responsible for the constructive reforms that were eventually adopted in connection with
the correction of the abuses among the banks and bankers."

The action of the President brought him a hail of abuse from
the financial world. Many honest bankers thought it ill-advised
and many protestors were scared on their own account.

In reply to one of these sincere protestors the President wrote
on April 2, 1932:

"Men are not justified in deliberately making profits from the losses
of other people."

In its results this investigation has proved one of the most
far-reaching in the history of inquires made by the Senate.

Speaking at Indianapolis on October 28, 1932, he said:

"There have been exploitation and abuse of financial power. That
wrongdoing must be punished. We will continue to reform such abuses

and correct such wrongdoing as falls within the powers of the Federal Government."

> In reply to Governor Roosevelt's criticism in the 1932 campaign that banking reforms had not been brought about, Hoover said:

"The governor does not inform the American people that there is no Federal law of regulation of the sale of securities and that there is doubtful constitutional authority for such law; that most of these bonds are issued from New York State, which has such authority; and that the governor has done nothing to reform that evil, if it be one. I recollect a Republican governor of New York who, believing wrong was being done to citizens of his own and other states on their life insurance, found a man in Charles Evans Hughes who cleaned it up once and for all."

"The governor has the advantage of me in experience in that particular. As late as 1928 the governor was engaged in that business for profit and actively occupied in promoting such loans. At that time he was chairman of the organization committee of the Federal International Banking Company, a corporation organized for the selling of foreign securities and bonds to the American people. I have in my hand a prospectus of that corporation in which the foreword was written by Mr. Roosevelt."

"The governor as a private promoter for profit during the boom of 1928 believed and practiced what the governor, as presidential candidate, now denounces as immoral and a cause of our calamities."

[*State Papers, Vol. II, p. 389*]

At New York on October 31, 1932, the President said:

". . . I have already stated that democracy must remain master in its own house. I have stated that abuse and wrongdoing must be punished and controlled."

". . . Our American system demands economic justice as well as political and social justice; it is not a system of *laissez faire.*"

"In the ebb and flow of economic life our people in times of prosperity and ease naturally tend to neglect the vigilance over their rights. Moreover, wrongdoing is obscured by apparent success in enterprise. Then insidious diseases and wrongdoings grow apace. But we have in the past seen in times of distress and difficulty that wrongdoing and weakness come to the surface, and our people, in their endeavors to correct these wrongs, are tempted to extremes which may destroy rather than build."

"It is men who do wrong, not our institutions. It is men who violate the laws and public rights. It is men, not institutions, who must be punished."   [*State Papers, Vol. II, p. 408*]

Hoover supported the New Deal efforts to regulate security issues and the Stock Exchange practices. In 1934 he said:

"For this immediate discussion I may state that reform and revision of our older regulatory laws in banking, commodity and stock markets, transportation, utilities and natural resource industries are absolutely necessary. So long as these revisions conform to the conditions of Liberty there can be no difference of opinion except as to method. All reform entails some degree of experiment. I have no fear of experiments which take account of experience, do not remake the errors of history, and do not set out to experiment with the principles of Liberty. We may feel that some reform measures do not reach to the heart of the problems they undertake to solve; that they are in part punitive rather than constructive; that they are in part impractical of producing the desired result; that in attempting to suppress a dozen scoundrels they are retarding the normal and active flow of economic life among a thousand honest men, and are thus retarding recovery from the depression. But we must remember that reform is a hard horse to ride in the blinding storm of world war liquidation."   [*The Challenge to Liberty, pp. 107–8*]

Speaking at Colorado Springs on March 7, 1936, he said:

"The failure of the states, particularly New York, to do their part during the boom years has necessitated an extension of Federal action. The New Deal regulations of stock and security promotion in various aspects have the right objectives. They were hastily and poorly formed without proper consideration by Congress. But they point right."

AMERICAN PRIVATE LOANS TO FOREIGNERS

The subject of American investments in foreign countries was not acute during the Hoover Administration. The general crash which came in October, 1929, practically brought the pub-

lic flotation of foreign bond issues in the United States to an
end. The subject has some interest both because of the Hoover
policies when Secretary of Commerce and President, and because of the Democratic propaganda upon the subject in the
elections of 1932 and 1936.

PRIVATE LOANS AS A RELIEF MEASURE IN 1920

Hoover became Secretary of Commerce in March, 1921,
in the midst of the immediate post-war depression. At that
time, the United States had an enormous surplus of commodities. We had some four or five million unemployed. Farm
prices were falling rapidly. Foreign countries just out of the
war were in need of both food and raw materials—but they had
no method of immediate payment. The flotation of foreign loans
for private subscription in the United States which in effect
enabled them to buy American commodities had reached considerable dimensions in the after-war period of the Wilson Administration but had slacked off during the post-war depression.

A movement was started in Congress and elsewhere for the
Federal Government to make loans to foreigners to enable them
to buy. Secretary Hoover denounced any further lending by the
Federal Government. He contended that the Government should
stop lending and that the business world should undertake to
extend properly secured credits.

This latter proposal was organized into a definite campaign.
In the course of this campaign, Hoover made an address
in Chicago, on December 10, 1920, at a public meeting called to
consider ways and means:

"Our farmers are suffering great losses and workmen great unemployment. It is due to a considerable degree to the stagnation in orders for
our export surplus. From this stagnation the consuming power of our
home market is reduced and the effects cumulate upon us. . . . With
these forces thundering at every door we can now heed the oft-repeated
warning that our welfare is no longer isolated from the welfare of the
world."

". . . The vicious economic cycle can be broken . . . by the establishment of credits abroad . . . the long-time investment in reproductive
enterprise abroad. . . . If we would give full time of the employment
of our farmers, our laborers and our business men, we must be prepared to invest some part of the value of these surplus products abroad."

"The social and economic demoralization of Europe . . . renders her unable to buy largely today unless she receives certain credits of material and food. . . ."

". . . The resort to direct loans by our Government to foreign governments to promote commerce can lead only to a dozen vicious ends . . . our great nation could not exact a higher rate than our Government is paid. . . . Foreign merchants and manufacturers would obtain such loans . . . at lower rates than our own merchants and manufacturers. . . . Our Government would be subject to every political pressure that desperate foreign statesmen can invent . . . their nationals in our borders would clamor at the hall of Congress for special favors to their mother countries. . . . Our governments cannot higgle in the market to exact the securities and returns appropriate to risk. . . . The collection of a debt to our Treasury from a foreign government sets afoot propaganda against our officials, against our Government. There is no court to which a government can appeal for collection of debt except a battleship." . . . .

". . . Every argument comes back . . . to the . . . conclusion that we must organize for private long-term foreign investment. . . ."

". . . I hope this meeting . . . will be a milestone in the development of organized co-operation between our banks, our business, our farmers, and our working communities."

This co-operation to extend credits was organized and built up rapidly during the next eighteen months. It served the great purpose of the least expensive relief of unemployment and agriculture ever devised. It contributed greatly to recovery from that depression.

HARDING–COOLIDGE ADMINISTRATION CONTROL OF LOANS

As time went on, however, these loans began to multiply greatly and to raise some disturbing questions. President Harding at the suggestion of Secretaries Hughes, Mellon and Hoover, called a conference of representatives of the bond-issuing houses at Washington, to discuss the question. The bankers agreed to be guided by the administration. As a result, the administration requested that all issues should first be submitted to the State Department for their opinion, on certain phases, and a public notice to that effect was issued on March 3, 1922. The New York banks became disturbed at the extent to which these opinions might go, and in April a memorandum on the subject was filed with the administration by Governor Strong of New York Federal Reserve Bank.

In reply on April 29, 1922, Hoover addressed a recommendation to the Secretary of State, urging that certain standards should be set up in respect to these loans beyond those proposed by the banks; and that the bankers be requested to hold to these standards. His letter was as follows:

"My dear Mr. Secretary:

"I am in receipt of the very able memorandum prepared by Governor Strong upon the subject of foreign loans. I do not think any one disputes Governor Strong's economic premise that foreign loans made in the American market will be represented by the ultimate export of goods or gold to some destination—either to the borrowing country or otherwise. It can at once be agreed that in principle foreign loans are vital in the present situation of the world and of our commerce."

"I am not, however, prepared to accept Governor Strong's implied conclusion that no standards should be set up in the placing of foreign loans in the American market. I believe these standards can be developed in the banking community itself. I am convinced that unless they are so developed Congress will, sooner or later, impose control on the placing of such obligations, as there are other and larger considerations than those enumerated by Governor Strong. It appears to me that the Federal Government has certain unavoidable political and moral responsibilities toward these operations and that our bankers have certain internal responsibilities to our commerce."

Political Responsibilities

"In the political category it may be stated that credits from our citizens to foreign governments or municipalities have a different complexion from either internal credit operations or even of credits to private persons abroad, in that there is no method by which failure in payment of such loans can be prosecuted, except by the diplomatic intervention of our Government. There rests upon the Federal Government, whether desired or not, an implication that it will assist our citizens in relation to such transactions. To impose such lines of conduct on defaulting governmental creditors as will recover to our citizens their due is a path which has led to infinite complexities in international relations. It is perfectly possible to carry an argument against foreign loans to an extreme, but even a moderate view should certainly go to the extent of creating some concern in the Federal Government that the security and form of these loans should, at the outset, involve a fair hope that the Federal Government will not be required to enter upon intervention."

"A further political interest lies in finance which lends itself directly or indirectly to war or to the maintenance of political and economic instability. We are morally and selfishly interested in the economic and political recovery of all the world. America is practically the final reservoir of international capital. Unless this capital is to be employed for reproductive purposes there is little hope of economic recovery. The expenditure of American capital, whether represented by goods or gold in the maintenance of unbalanced budgets or the support of armies, is destructive use of capital. It is piling up dangers for the future of the world and while it may bring temporary values to the lender of the money, or the exporter of goods, it makes no contribution to the increase of economic stability and in fact contributes directly toward the continuation of instability, and thus indirectly robs both the lender and the exporter of goods of the real benefit that would otherwise accrue."

"Broadly, the reproductive use of export gold or goods means an increased standard of living, increased demand for further goods and increased social stability, whereas the unproductive use is the negation of these ends."

"The most pertinent fact with regard to Europe today is that the whole political and economic life is enveloped in an atmosphere of war and not of peace. Restrictions on loans made from the United States to reproductive purposes will at least give the tendency to render impossible that form of statesmanship which would maintain such an atmosphere."

Moral Responsibilities

"In the second category, that of moral responsibilities, the problem is also much involved and argument can be carried to extremes, but again some middle ground does exist. Our citizens have had but little experience in international investment. They are not possessed of the information with regard to the security of many of these offerings which is possessed by the Government or such offerings would not be entertained. A serious question arises in my mind as to whether the Federal Government has the moral right to withhold this information from its citizens."

"For instance, a vast amount of foreign currencies, and securities in foreign currencies, have been sold to the American investor, which have resulted in a national loss of probably upwards of five hundred millions of dollars in the last three years. It may be contended that it is the duty of the different state governments to protect their citizens from such frauds, but in the international field it seems to me improbable that any action of the state governments would be practical, and if once undertaken under the various investment control laws of the different states, might lead to a large amount of international complication."

"Even in the field of more respectable finance, the loan history of some of the nations who are borrowing freely in these markets for the first time could not be familiar to the American investor or there would be less facility in placing these loans with other than speculative investors."

"Another instance of these moral responsibilities lies in loans to countries already indebted to the United States Government in large sums and who from every apparent prospect will not be able to meet these obligations to the American people. Our Federal authorities must have some responsibility in not informing our citizens (or the promoters to them) that these nations will probably have to confess inability to meet their creditors. Unless some such action is taken the citizens from whom such information has been withheld would seem to me to have the moral right to insist that the Federal Government should not press its governmental claims to the prejudice of their investment."

"The only justification for allowing loans to proceed to countries already unable to meet their liabilities, would be that the resources obtained from such loans would be applied to reproductive purposes which would increase the assets of such a borrowing nation in such manner as to strengthen its ability to meet its obligations to the United States Treasury. Therefore, the Federal Government must from this reason alone be at once interested in the purpose to which such loans are to be applied."

"The whole of these problems or moral responsibilities are perfectly capable of dialectics in ethics to their total obliteration, but the test of action of the Federal Government in these particulars should at least be the standard that would be expected of a reputable business man dealing with his own customers. . . ."

Hoover's policies were strongly opposed and neither the administration of Harding nor of Coolidge was willing to attempt to establish standards of the character he advocated. A committee was set up of the three Cabinet members whose duty it was to pass upon the effect which any particular loan might have on our Government.

Nevertheless, the Secretary sought to educate the public and in an address at Washington on May 16, 1922, said, in respect to loans to foreigners:

"There are some matters in the lending of private capital that are of concern to the nation as a whole. For instance, it is essential that these loans should be confined to reproductive purposes. All loans to foreign nations which are not employed for reproductive work are a destruction of the capital. The furnishing of raw materials, the construction of transportation facilities, public utilities, factories and production throughout the world, are uses for American capital that bless both the borrower and the lender. The upbuilding of the rest of the world and its consuming power adds primarily to world well-being, but it also adds to the future demands for our own labor, the products of our own farmers, and the services of our own merchants."

"But loans that are dissipated either directly or indirectly in military expenditure or in unbalanced budgets, in the bolstering up of inflated currencies, are a double loss to the world. They are not only a loss in that they add nothing to increased productivity, but they are a loss in that they entail the postponement of those measures which are vital for the economic rehabilitation of the world."

Again, speaking to a Bankers' Convention on October 30, 1923, he said:

"There are responsibilities which come to you—responsibilities for the Nation as a whole—not alone in the development of a better understanding of the difference between speculation and investments at home, but of even more importance, in the safeguarding of our country in the matter of investments abroad. In the case of loans, either private or governmental, made to foreign countries our people are even less able to judge of the security than they are in the case of domestic issues, and thus where foreign loans are involved even more depends upon the character of the bankers concerned."

"The loaning of some of our surplus capital abroad is a necessary part of our foreign trade relations. Surplus capital is really surplus goods, and of these we have many. Such loans of surplus capital in rightful proportion promote our exports, increase the productivity of foreign lands, increase their standard of living, and increase their buying power. Trade grown through the increase of prosperity in foreign countries, and capital is often necessary to develop their resources. But it is essential in the interest of stability, that these loans should be used for reproductive purposes. All loans to foreign nations which are not used for reproductive work are a destruction of the capital. The furnishing of raw materials, the construction of transportation facilities, public utilities, factories, and other productive enterprises throughout the world are uses for American capital that bless both the borrower and the lender. The upbuilding of the rest of the world and its consuming power adds primarily to world well-being; and it also adds to future demand for our own labor, for the products of our own farmers, for the services of our own merchants. But loans that are dissipated either directly or indirectly in military expenditures, or in expenditures upon political adventure, or in the financing of deficient budgets due to military costs, are a destruction of capital."

Again, in addressing the Pan-American Commercial Conference in 1927, the Secretary returned to this subject:
He said of such loans that they were helpful in world development

"provided always one essential principle dominates the character of these transactions. That is, that no nation as a government should borrow or no government lend and nations should discourage their citizens from borrowing or lending unless this money is to be devoted to productive enterprise."

"Out of the wealth and the higher standards of living created from enterprise itself must come the ability to repay the capital to the borrowing country. Any other course of action creates obligations impossible of repayment except by a direct subtraction from the standards of living of the borrowing country and the impoverishment of its people."

"In fact, if this principle could be adopted between nations of the world—that is, if nations would do away with the lending of money for the balancing of budgets for purposes of military equipment or war purposes, or even that type of public works which does not bring some direct or indirect productive return—a great number of blessings would follow to the entire world."

"There could be no question as to the ability to repay; with this increasing security capital would become steadily cheaper, the dangers to national and individual independence in attempts of the lender to collect his defaulted debts would be avoided; there would be definite increase in the standard of living and the comfort and prosperity of the borrower."

"There could be no greater step taken in the prevention of war itself. This is perhaps a little further toward the millennium than our practical world has reached, and I do not propose that these are matters that can be regulated by law or treaty. They are matters that can be regulated solely by the commercial and financial sentiment of each of our countries; and if this body may be able to develop the firm conviction, develop the understanding that the financial transactions between nations must be built upon the primary foundation that money transferred is for reproductive purposes, it will have contributed to the future of the Western Hemisphere in a degree seldom open to a conference of this character."

The Cabinet Committee during the Harding and Coolidge Administrations did exert pressures in two particulars. The first was in advising the bankers that the Government did not wish private loans made to countries who had not made settlement and payments upon the war debts. This inhibition was voluntarily maintained by the banks and had some importance on the war debt settlements. It may be noted that this policy was renewed by the Roosevelt Administration with a trumpet-flourish of legislation.

On another occasion official warnings were given that German municipal and other bond issues ranked after reparations—a warning that was not heeded.

In the latter part of 1925, Secretary Hoover protested publicly at certain loans to the Brazilian Coffee Valorization and European Potash cartel. The real purpose of this financing was to extend the monopolies so as to advance prices against the American consumer. The following press statement by Hoover (January 4, 1926) explains itself.

"I note that The Wall Street Journal scolds me for the suggestion of the administration to American bankers that they should not make loans to the foreign monopolies which control the price of import products to American consumers."

"The particular loans which The Wall Street Journal seems to favor are those to the potash combination and the coffee combination. I also note that they realize that 'potash is used principally by our cotton and truck farmers and scarcely at all by the great wheat and corn farmers.' No mention is made of the numerical importance of the coffee consumer."

Early in the Hoover Administration the President requested the Departments of Justice and Commerce to formulate legislation giving the Government authority to assure certain standards in such loans. The subject was prepared for the Congress of December, 1929, but the general crash having occurred two months previously, the subject became wholly academic and was displaced for more important issues. No consequential loans were made during the depression period of sequential loans were made during the depression period of the Hoover Administration.[1]

Roosevelt raised the question again in the 1936 campaign in a speech at Pittsburgh, to which Hoover replied in an address on October 17, 1936:

"In this speech President Roosevelt made the statement that between 1920 and 1930 eight billions of money out of American pockets had been sent to foreign countries and used by them to give employment to their citizens. He says that most of that money is gone for good. He implies that it was taken away from American workmen and given to foreign workmen. That reflects mostly upon my predecessors in office, including President Wilson. But I shall not let that smear rest upon them. President Roosevelt did not mention that this money was borrowed by foreigners on interest and was not gifts. He does not mention that it was borrowed from private Americans and not from our Government."

"I have had each of these foreign borrowings which were offered to the American public carefully traced. I am informed their total was seven billions, not eight billions. That is, however, an error of only 12½ per cent and we can let that pass. Of these seven billions that are supposed to be lost, two billions have become due and have been paid in full. Three billions are not yet due but interest and amortization are being met regularly. The remaining two billions are partly in default but are being salvaged as the world recovers. The net result is that this is an error of about 87½ per cent."

"But even that is not the whole story. It is an economic fact that loans to foreigners must ultimately be transmitted in goods, services, or gold. Gold was provably not shipped. Therefore these private loans made employment of American workmen and American farmers in producing this amount of goods. In fact, those private loans contributed greatly to full employment in the United States during the whole decade of the twenties when unemployment existed in practically every other country in the world. President Roosevelt's statement is the more astonishing as he has himself advocated the loaning of money to foreigners, including Russia, thus to create markets for products of American shops and farms. He created the so-called Export Banks for this exact purpose. But in his case he has placed the risk on the taxpayer and not upon the private banker."

[1] The Roosevelt Administration revived the Hoover policy of 1922 of inducing exports by again lending money to foreigners to buy such commodities. As set up by the Roosevelt Administration, however, our Government was to loan the money, instead of Hoover's policy of 1922, that loans should be made by private agencies. Governments seldom get their money back, private agencies usually do.

"But still more interesting in this connection is the fact that Mr. Roosevelt has automatically and without consent of these private American citizens cancelled 41 per cent of these debts from foreigners. He did that when he devalued the dollar. He made the foreigners a gift of about three billions of dollars from American pockets. Before the dollar was devalued these people had to send 41 per cent more gold or its equivalent in goods to the United States to meet their obligations than they have to send today. And I may add that this cancellation of foreign debts applies also to the eleven billions of war debts owed the American people. Here the President made a present to foreigners of another four billions of American dollars."

DEPRESSION RELIEF, CREDIT AND FISCAL POLICIES

THE CAUSES AND COURSE OF THE DEPRESSION

The origins and the progress of the depression largely determined the policies required to combat it.

Its origins lay in the World War and it was world wide. The destruction of 20,000,000 lives, of hundreds of billions of property, the creation of 200 billion dollar governmental debts, the inflated expansion of certain industries, including agriculture, the uneconomic boundaries of the Peace Treaties, the unbalanced budgets, the fugitive flight of capital from one country to another seeking safety, and the constant inflations of credit and currency over the world in attempts to stand off the evil day of liquidation—all piled up a flood that had to burst.

There were immediate causes in the United States which contributed to precipitate and to intensify the crash. After the war Presidents Harding and Coolidge had prudently balanced the budget, reduced the debt and we were slowly liquidating our war losses and rebuilding a great prosperity on the sole basis of increasing national efficiency. But the United States also, in 1927, started credit inflation on the mistaken notion of our Federal Reserve leaders that we could help to tide over a threatening European slackening of business. Out of this inflation and other causes, including too much optimism and failure to pass on decreasing costs to the consumer, the United States was enveloped in a period of mad speculation which crashed in October, 1929.

Hoover as Secretary of Commerce had made repeated protests against these Federal Reserve Board policies and repeated warnings against the wild speculation. At the first proposal of these policies[1] he had protested, "The Reserve policies . . . mean inflation with inevitable collapse which will bring calamities upon our farmers, our workers and legitimate business."

[1]See Myers and Newton, p. 10.

We may quote his statements on the rise of speculation at various times, "The . . . safety of continued prosperity will depend on . . . caution and resistance to . . . speculation . . . our bankers can check the dangers of speculative credits. . . ." "The real test . . . will be whether we can hold this . . . prosperity without . . . an era of speculation and extravagance with its inevitable debacle. . . ." "Unless our financial policies are guided with courage and wisdom this speculation . . . can only land us on the shores of depression. . . . Not since 1920 have we required . . . a more capable administration of credit facilities than now. . . ."

When Hoover became President he inherited three things: first, a crazy speculative boom in the United States; second, a hidden impending European financial collapse; and third, a weak and badly organized banking system.

It is necessary to remember that depressions are the retribution of previous economic follies and wrong-doings and not the cause of them. It is obvious that, when they break, the inflationary and speculative values must be liquidated down to realities. Time is required for such readjustments, both in values of stocks, real estate, fictitiously high commodities and in the fictitious debts founded upon them. Further, the waste, bad management and extravagance in industry incident to booms and speculation must be eliminated. But of equal importance, the minds of individual citizens and of the nation must be adjusted to better moral standards and the change to a less extravagant form of life than those which existed in the boom. Again boom periods are always the scene of extra wrong-doing and villainy. And the depression brings about the exposure of accumulated weaknesses in the economic system which must be met by great economic and social reforms.

The movements of the depression and recovery during the Hoover Administration divide themselves into four definite periods, each requiring adaptations of policies and methods.

The first period of eighteen months extended from the market crash in October, 1929, while the United States and the rest of the world were liquidating their inflated stock and business boom. Had that been all there was to it, our beginnings of recovery in early 1931 would have lifted us out of it and it would have been but an episode, not dangerous to our civilization.

The second period of about fourteen months began in the spring of 1931, when the war-born but hidden weaknesses and follies of Europe broke into the greatest business and financial debacle of history. We were already weakened by our boom-depression; these hurricanes swept over our borders and drew us deep into the maëlstrom. Our banking system instead of serving as a shock absorber became a liability to the Nation itself. This period reached its bottom in July, 1932.

The third period was the four months extending from July to October, 1932, of definite world-wide recovery in which the United State participated. This was stifled by the oncoming election in November.

The fourth period extended from the election in November, 1932, to the inauguration in March, 1933. At this point the United States alone departed from the upward course of the general world recovery and took a swift nose dive into bank panic. This divergence of the United States arose from the fear of the change in national policies which began even before the actual election and was fanned into panic by fears of the evident intent of devaluing the dollar and hugely increasing Government expenditures.

A number of points of acute crises developed during this period. Had they not been handled with courage, any one of them would have brought about a general panic.

The first of these crises was the result of the stock market crash of October-November, 1929.

The second crisis was the result of the Central European financial collapse of June, 1931.

The third crisis was the result of the abandonment of the gold standard by England which caused the departure of thirty countries from the gold standard in October, 1931.

The fourth crisis was in February, 1932, when European pressures upon the United States, and our inflexible currency laws brought about a threatened forcing of the United States from the gold standard.

The fifth crisis in June, 1932, was caused by the breakdown of public confidence due to obstruction in Congress.

The sixth crisis came in February, 1933, when Hoover, himself denuded of power, was refused co-operation by Roosevelt.

On each of these occasions, save the last, the tide of general panic was turned by the policies of the Hoover Administration.

GENERAL POLICIES

Hoover's first, and in fact revolutionary, policy in handling the depression was to hold that the Federal Government had an obligation to perform in mitigating the effects of the depression and expediting recovery. Never before in a score of depressions, some almost as severe, had any President taken any part or used any of the strength of the Federal Government in such a battle in behalf of the people.

The dominant Hoover policies were:

1. To stimulate and organize the people to themselves take co-operative action in every direction to meet the problems of the depression.

2. To insist on the full action of local and state governments.

3. When such action was insufficient then to bring the full strength of the Federal Government behind the people's organizations and their local and state governments.

Under these dominant policies, the President set up these principal lines of Federal action.

a. To provide against suffering from hunger and cold among the dislocated and unemployed, by staggering employment, by increased construction work and by relief.

b. To cushion the inevitable downward readjustments of wages and farm prices which inevitably must recede from boom levels.

c. To secure co-operation between employers and employees which would preserve the country from industrial conflicts and the social disorder which had usually arisen in depression.

d. To preserve sound currency, to secure, if possible, from Congress a balanced budget as the very bulwark of National credit.

e. To buttress the credit institutions of the country so as to prevent panic and business bankruptcy and the widespread dispossession of homes and farms.

f. To co-operate with other nations in remedying the world-wide forces of the depression.

g. To build fundamental reforms in business and banking but, where these reforms would dislocate recovery, then to suspend reform for the greater purpose of returning people to work.

h. To sustain the courage of the people.

i. To hold rigidly to the Constitution and the liberties of the people under any stress that might arise.

President Hoover gave his own explanation of the spirit behind these aims in an address at Indianapolis on June 15, 1931:

"For the first time in history the Federal Government has taken an extensive and positive part in mitigating the effects of depression and expediting recovery. I have conceived that if we would preserve our democracy this leadership must take the part not of attempted dictatorship, but of organizing co-operation in the constructive forces of the community and of stimulating every element of initiative and self-reliance in the country. There is no sudden stroke of either governmental or private action which can dissolve these world difficulties; patient constructive action in a multitude of directions is the strategy of success. This battle is upon a thousand fronts. . . . Some . . . people . . . demand abrupt change . . . in our American system. . . . Others have indomitable confidence that by some legerdemain we can legislate ourselves out of a world-wide depression. Such views are as accurate as the belief we can exorcise a Caribbean hurricane by statutory law."

[*State Papers, Vol. I, p. 574*]

Through the crisis the President refused to be an alarmist. Nothing is more subject to hysteria than fear of banking and credit. For the President ever to have stated his fears or to have disclosed in public statement the dangers around him would have precipitated a bank panic itself. He said on October 2, 1930:

"I wish to say that no one can occupy the high office of President and conceivably be other than completely confident of the future of the United States. Perhaps as to no other place does the cheerful courage and power of a confident people reflect as to his office. There are a few folks in business and several folks in the political world who resent the notion that things will ever get better and who wish to enjoy our temporary misery. To recount to these persons the progress of co-operation between the people and the Government in amelioration of this situation, or to mention that we are suffering far less than other countries, only inspires the unkind retort that we should fix our gaze solely upon the unhappy features of the decline. And, above all, to chide the pessimism of persons who have assumed the end of those mighty forces which for one hundred and fifty years have driven this land further and further toward that great human goal—the abolition of intellectual and economic poverty—is perhaps not a sympathetic approach. This is no time to talk of any surrender. We have known a thousand temporary setbacks, but the spirit of this people will never brook defeat."

[*State Papers, Vol. I, p. 377*]

And again on June 15, 1931:

"These fears and apprehensions are unnecessarily increased by that minority of people who would make political capital out of the depression through magnifying our unemployment and losses. Other small groups make their contribution to distress by raids on our markets with purpose to profit from depreciation of securities and commodities. Both groups are within the law; they are equally condemned by our public and business opinion; they are by no means helpful to the Nation."

"Fear and apprehension, whether their origins are domestic or foreign, are very real, tangible, economic forces. Fear of loss of a job or uncertainty as to the future has caused millions of our people unnecessarily to reduce their purchases of goods, thereby decreasing our production and employment. These uncertainties lead our bankers and business men to extreme caution, and in consequence a mania for liquidation has reduced our stocks of goods and our credits far below any necessity. All these apprehensions and actions check enterprise and lessen our national activities. We are suffering today more from frozen confidence than we are from frozen securities."   [*State Papers, Vol. I, p. 575*]

At two periods in the depression the President became optimistic that the tide had turned. One was in the first part of 1931 before the financial collapse in Europe had struck us and the other in the spring of 1932 when the tide had finally turned. Both occasions were justified. We may mention here that the President never used the expression that "prosperity was around the corner" or any equivalent of it. That was the coinage of the opposition.

President Hoover himself illuminated his policies and actions in an address at Washington on August 11, 1932, when he said:

"I wish to say something of my conception of the relation of our Government to the people and of the responsibilities of both, particularly as applied to these times. The spirit and devising of this Government by the people was to sustain a dual purpose—on the one hand to protect our people amongst nations and in domestic emergencies by great national power, and on the other to preserve individual liberty and freedom through local government."

"The function of the Federal Government in these times is to use its reserve powers and its strength for the protection of citizens and local governments by support to our institutions against forces beyond their control. It is not the function of the Government to relieve individuals of their responsibilities to their neighbors, or to relieve private institutions of their responsibilities to the public, or of local government to the states, or of state governments to the Federal Government. In giving that protection and that aid the Federal Government must insist that all of them exert their responsibilities in full. It is vital that the programs of the Government shall not compete with or replace any of them but shall add to their initiative and their strength. It is vital that by the use of public revenues and public credit in emergency the Nation shall be strengthened and not weakened."

". . . It is only by this release of initiative, this insistence upon individual responsibility, that there accrue the great sums of individual accomplishment which carry this Nation forward. . . ."

"The solution of our many problems is not to be found in haphazard experimentation or by revolution. It must be through organic development of our national life under these ideals. It must secure that cooperative action which builds initiative and strength outside of government. It does not follow, because our difficulties are stupendous, because there are some souls timorous enough to doubt the validity and effectiveness of our ideals and our system, that we must turn to a state controlled or state directed social or economic system in order to cure our troubles. That is not liberalism; it is tyranny. It is the regimentation of men under autocratic bureaucracy with all its extinction of liberty, of hope, and of opportunity. Of course, no man of understanding says that our system works perfectly. It does not. The human race is not perfect. Nevertheless, the movement of a true civilization is toward freedom rather than regimentation. This is our ideal."

"Ofttimes the tendency of democracy in presence of national danger is to strike blindly, to listen to demagogues and slogans, all of which would destroy and would not save. We have refused to be stampeded into such courses. . . ."

"Our emergency measures of the past three years form a definite strategy dominated in the background by these American principles and ideals, forming a continuous campaign waged against the forces of destruction on an ever-widening or constantly shifting front."

". . . where it becomes necessary to meet emergencies beyond the power of these agencies by the creation of new Government instrumentalities, they should be of such character as not to supplant or weaken, but rather to supplement and strengthen, the initiative and enterprise of the people. . . ."

"We have not feared boldly to adopt unprecedented measures to meet the unprecedented violence of the storm. But, because we have kept ever before us these eternal principles of our Nation, the American Government in its ideals is the same as it was when the people gave the Presidency into my trust. We shall keep it so. . . ."

"It was in accordance with these principles that in the first stage of the depression I called the leaders of business and of labor and agriculture to meet with me and induced them, by their own initiative, to organize against panic with all its devastating destruction; to uphold wages until the cost of living was adjusted; to spread existing employment through shortened hours; and to advance construction work, public and private, against future need."

"In pursuance of that same policy, I each winter thereafter assumed the leadership in mobilizing all the voluntary and official organizations throughout the country to prevent suffering from hunger and cold, and to protect the million families stricken by drought. When it became advisable to strengthen the states who could not longer carry the full burden of relief to distress, I held that the Federal Government should do so. . . ."

"It is in accordance with these principles that, in aid to unemployment, we are expending some six hundred millions [a year] in Federal construction of such public works as can be justified as bringing early and definite returns."

"It is in accord with these principles and purposes that we have made provision for one billion five hundred millions of loans to self-supporting works so that we may increase employment in productive labor."

"It was in accordance with these principles that we have strengthened the capital of the Federal Land Banks—that farmers indebted to them should not be unduly deprived of their homes. The Farm Board by emergency loans to the farmers' co-operatives served to stem panics in agricultural prices and saved hundreds of thousands of farmers and their creditors from bankruptcy. We have created agencies to prevent bankruptcy and failure of their co-operative organizations, and we are erecting new instrumentalities to give credit facilities for livestock growers and the orderly marketing of farm products."

"It was in accordance with these principles that in the face of the looming European crises we sought to change the trend of European economic degeneration by my proposal of the German moratorium and the standstill agreements as to German private debts."

"It was in accordance with these principles that I first secured the creation by private initiative of the National Credit Association, whose efforts prevented the failure of hundreds of banks, and loss to countless thousands of depositors who had loaned all their savings to them."

"As the storm grew in intensity we created the Reconstruction Finance Corporation with a capital of $2,000,000,000 to uphold the credit structure of the Nation, and by thus raising the shield of Government credit we prevented the wholesale failure of banks, of insurance companies, of building and loan associations, of farm-mortgage associations, of live-stock-loan associations, and of railroads in all of which the public interest is paramount. This disaster has been averted through the saving of more than 5000 institutions and the knowledge that adequate assistance was available to tide others over the stress. This was done not to save a few stockholders, but to save 25,000,000 of American families, every one of whose very savings and employment might have been wiped out and whose whole future would have been blighted had those institutions gone down."

"It was in accordance with these principles that we expanded the functions and powers of the Federal Reserve Banks that they might counteract the stupendous shrinkage of credit due to fear, to hoarding, and to foreign withdrawals."

"It is in accordance with these principles that we are now in process of establishing a new system of home-loan banks so that through added strength by co-operation in the building and loan associations, the savings banks, and the insurance companies we may relax the pressure of forfeiture upon home owners, and procure the release of new resources for the construction of more homes and the employment of more men."

"It was in accordance with these principles that we have insisted upon a reduction of governmental expense, for no country can squander itself to prosperity on the ruins of its taxpayers, and it was in accordance with these purposes that we have sought new revenues to equalize the diminishing income of the Government in order that the power of the Federal Government to meet the emergency should be impregnable."

"It is in accordance with these principles that we have joined in the development of a world economic conference to bulwark the whole international fabric of finance, monetary values, and the expansion of world commerce."

"It is in accordance with these principles that I am today organizing the private industrial and financial resources of the country to co-operate effectively with the vast Governmental instrumentalities which we have in motion, so that through their united and co-ordinated efforts we may move from defense to powerful attack upon the depression along the whole national front."

"These programs, unparalleled in the history of depressions in any country and in any time, to care for distress, to provide employment, to aid agriculture, to maintain the financial stability of the country, to safeguard the savings of the people, to protect their homes, are not in the past tense—they are in action. I shall propose such other measures, public and private, as may be necessary from time to time to meet the changing situations and to further speed economic recovery. That recovery may be slow, but we will succeed."

"And come what may, I shall maintain through all these measures the sanctity of the great principles under which the Republic over a period of one hundred and fifty years has grown to be the greatest Nation on earth."

"I should like to digress for one instant for an observation on the past three years which should exhilarate the faith of all Americans—that is the profound growth of the sense of social responsibility which this depression has demonstrated."

"No government in Washington has hitherto considered that it held so broad a responsibility for leadership in such times. Despite hardships, the devotion of our men and women to those in distress is demonstrated by the national averages of infant mortality, general mortality, and sickness, which are less today than in times of prosperity. For the first time in the history of depressions, dividends, profits, and cost of living have been reduced before wages have suffered. We have been more free from industrial conflict through strikes and lockouts and all forms of social disorder than even in normal times. The Nation is building the initiative of men toward new fields of social co-operation and endeavor."

We shall discuss the President's detailed policies and actions during the depression under the following headings:

RELIEF

EMERGENCY STRENGTHENING OF CREDIT, BANKING AND CURRENCY IN THE FIRST PERIOD OF THE DEPRESSION

> The Crash of the Boom in 1929
> The Start of Recovery in 1930–31

EMERGENCY POLICIES OF THE SECOND PERIOD
FROM APRIL, 1931

> The Moratorium
> The German Standstill Agreement
> The British Crash in September, 1931
> The National Credit Association
> Long-term Credit Stringency
> The Reconstruction Finance Corporation

Home Loan Banks
Expansion of Agricultural Credit
Expansion of Federal Reserve Credit
Hoarding
National Business and Industrial Committees
Balancing the Budget
Protecting the Gold Standard
Congressional Obstruction Crisis of 1932
Adjustment of Private Debt
World Stabilization of Currency
World War Debt
The Beginning of Recovery in 1932
The Panic of March, 1933

RELIEF

Herbert Hoover had had the largest experience in relief of any human being. He had given five years to that service abroad and at home without a cent of remuneration. During those years he had organized relief one time or another to over 150,000,000 people in some thirty countries and under a variety of calamities. His ideas of the public obligation had been long fixed. His long experience pointed the policies of organization for the depression of 1930.

In 1887 President Cleveland refused to approve a bill for Federal Government action in relief of a drought and announced his famous doctrine "though the people support the Government, the Government should not support the people." This had held as the policy of the Federal Government steadily through both Republican and Democratic administrations and no President had ever considered that there was a governmental obligation to take part in mitigating business depressions or in the restoration of recovery.

President Hoover, humanitarian, was the first to announce, on October 17, 1930, a new national policy in the responsibilities of Government to relief.

"As a nation we must prevent hunger and cold to those of our people who are in honest difficulties."   [*State Papers, Vol. I, p. 402*]

Indeed, he had urged the governmental obligation in time of national calamity often as a private citizen. Nine years before as Secretary of Commerce, and chairman, he addressed the Unemployment Conference of September, 1921:

". . . Obviously our unemployment arises from the aftermath of the great World War. We have been plunged into a period of violent readjustment and one of the bitter fruits of this readjustment is large unemployment. . . . There is no economic failure so terrible in its import as that of a country possessing a surplus of every necessity of life in which numbers, willing and anxious to work, are deprived of these necessities. It simply cannot be if our moral and economic system is to survive. It is the duty of this conference to find definite and organized remedy for this emergency and I hope also that you may be able to outline for public consideration such plans as will in the long view tend to mitigate its recurrences. . . ."

". . . The administration has felt that a large degree of solution could be expected through the mobilization of the fine co-operative action of our manufacturers and employers, of our public bodies and local authorities, and that if solution could be found in these directions we could have accomplished even more than the care of our unemployed, that we will have again demonstrated that independence and ability of action amongst our own people that saves our Government from that ultimate paternalism that will undermine our whole political system. . . ."

"What our people wish is the opportunity to earn their daily bread, and surely in a country with its warehouses bursting with surpluses of food, of clothing, with its mines capable of indefinite production of fuel, with sufficient housing for comfort and health, we possess the intelligence to find solution. Without it our whole system is open to serious charges of failure. . . ."

That conference organized the Nation to a co-operative and successful handling of the first post-war unemployment crisis under the Hoover leadership.

But President Hoover was in agreement with President Cleveland that the Federal Government should not itself directly extend aid to individuals. His principles, policies and methods in dealing with relief as shown later were:

1. That the Federal Government must give leadership and see that the job was done in every part of the country.

2. That the voluntary forces of the country should be completely mobilized into nation-wide co-operation.

   a. That railway, utility and industrial construction work should be expanded.

   b. That wages should be maintained until decreased cost of living made reductions just.

   c. That employment should be staggered so as to give some income to as many as possible.

   d. That committees of leading citizens in every state and local community, free from politics, must be organized to undertake and administer direct relief—or made work as they saw fit— thus completely decentralizing the problems into the hands of the communities themselves under their own administration and leadership.

e. That municipal, state and Federal Public Works should be expanded.

In the use of Federal Public Works, he insisted that they must be real and purposeful and not "made work." As the problem deepened, he determined that non-productive Public Works were a danger to public finance and substituted Federal loans to reproductive works.

In direct relief, as the depression deepened beyond private resources, he insisted:

a. That municipal, county and state governments should assume the first obligation to support local committees from public funds.

b. That if and when state resources weakened then the Federal Government should give supplementary support, but only through money or commodities supplied to state and local committees for their administration.

c. That the Federal Government should never engage in direct relief to individuals; that its service should never be centralized into Federal bureaucracy.

To the end, he fought every attempt to centralize relief in the Federal Government either directly to individuals or through the fiction of "made work." He rightly insisted (as has been abundantly proved) that such action would waste hundreds of millions upon inefficient bureaucracy, would undermine local responsibility, would lead only to chronic relief, to corruption, and politics which would undermine the whole American structure.

That is, his policies were decentralized local administration and local responsibility; supplemental support of taxpayers' money to these organizations from local government; and further support from the Federal Government to the extent that their needs could not be met otherwise.

The first stage of relief began immediately after the crash when the President summoned conferences at the White House of separate groups of leaders in industry, labor, agriculture, and banking for the purpose of establishing co-operative action. It was at the first of these conferences, on November 21, 1929, that President Hoover first proposed relief measures. Mr. Newton's report of this conference is given in full on page 129. We may repeat part in this aspect:

"The President further proceeded to point out that our immediate duty was to consider the human problem of unemployment and distress; that our second problem was to maintain social order and industrial peace; the third was orderly liquidation and the prevention of panic, and the final readjustment of new concepts of living. He explained that immediate 'liquidation' of labor had been the industrial policy of previous depressions; that his every instinct was opposed to both the term and the policy, for labor was not a commodity. It represented human homes. Moreover, from an economic viewpoint such action would deepen the depression by suddenly reducing purchasing power and, as a still worse consequence, it would bring about industrial strife, bitterness, disorder, and fear. He put forward his own view that, in our modern economy and on account of the intensified competition from shrinkage in demand and the inevitable loss of profits due to a depression, the cost of living would fall even if wages were temporarily maintained. Hence if wages were reduced subsequently, and then no more and no faster than the cost of living had previously fallen, the burden would not fall primarily on labor, and values could be 'stepped down.' Thereby great hardships and economic and social difficulties would be avoided. In any event the first shock must fall on profits and not on wages."

"President Hoover held the fundamental view that wages should be maintained for the present; that planned construction work should be maintained by industry, and governmental agencies even should increase construction to give as much employment as possible; that the available work should be spread among all employees by temporarily shortening the work-week of individuals; and that each industry should look after distress among its own employees. By these means industry would help to 'cushion down' the situation."

"The same afternoon (November 21) the President held conferences with the outstanding labor leaders and secured their adherence to the program. This co-operation required the patriotic withdrawal of some wage demands which already had been made. The labor leaders loyally carried out their part in these withdrawals."

". . . The purpose of these declarations is to give assurance that conflicts should not occur during the present situation which will affect the continuity of work, and thus to maintain stability of employment."   [*State Papers, Vol. I, p. 136*]

To follow the Hoover relief policies and actions from this point onward we must divide them into:

> Direct Relief.
> Relief through Public Works.
> Private Construction.

Relief of the Drought of 1930.
Agricultural Relief (see Agricultural Policies page 146).
Veterans' Relief (see Veterans' Policies, page 193).
Employment Through Shortened Hours (see p. 129 ff).

DIRECT RELIEF

CENSUS OF UNEMPLOYED

On April 30, 1930, the first (and only) accurate census of unemployment was carried out under Secretary Lamont on Hoover's instruction. It showed that 45,600,000 persons were at work gainfully employed; that 2,429,000 persons were out of work and looking for work; and in addition there were 758,-000 temporarily laid off, making a total of about 3,187,000. As there are always about 1,000,000 to 2,000,000 unemployables and persons out of work between jobs and as there is an average of more than one breadwinner per family, the number of families under strain appeared to be between 1,000,000 and 1,500,000. At this time the local authorities everywhere reported that their actual wants were being looked after by local effort where necessary.

PRESIDENT'S RELIEF ORGANIZATION

By October the unemployment had increased by at least 1,000,000 and to provide for the coming winter, the President set national organization in motion to see that no one suffered.

He announced on October 21, 1930, the creation of the "President's Emergency Relief Organization" and the appointment of Colonel Arthur Woods as its administrator. Colonel Woods had directed the Federal unemployment activities under Secretary Hoover in 1922. Colonel Woods secured through the governors the creation of State Unemployment Relief Committees in those states where relief was needed. This organization was further decentralized until over 3000 such committees of leading citizens, state and local, were functioning over the country. Colonel Woods served from that date to August 19, 1931, and was succeeded by Walter Gifford, who served from then until August 5, 1932. Mr. Gifford was succeeded in turn by Fred C. Croxton, who served until March, 1933. The Washington staff was comprised mostly of volunteers and its field staff was comprised of inspectors and organizers to see that there were no failures.

Following a Senate attempt to create direct Federal relief, President Hoover made a clear statement of his policies to the press in a statement of February 3, 1931:

"Certain senators have issued a public statement to the effect that unless the President and the House of Representatives agree to appropriations from the Federal Treasury for charitable purposes they will force an extra session of Congress."

"I do not wish to add acrimony to a discussion, but would rather state this case as I see its fundamentals."

"This is not an issue as to whether people shall go hungry or cold in the United States. It is solely a question of the best method by which hunger and cold shall be prevented. It is a question as to whether the American people on one hand will maintain the spirit of charity and mutual self help through voluntary giving and the responsibility of local government as distinguished on the other hand from appropriations out of the Federal Treasury for such purposes. My own conviction is strongly that if we break down this sense of responsibility of individual generosity to individual and mutual self help in the country in times of national difficulty and if we start appropriations of this character we have not only impaired something infinitely valuable in the life of the American people but have struck at the roots of self-government. Once this has happened it is not the cost of a few more millions but we are faced with the abyss of reliance in future upon Government charity in some form or other. The money involved is indeed the least of the costs to American ideals and American institutions."

"The basis of successful relief in national distress is to mobilize and organize the infinite number of agencies of self help in the community. That has been the American way of relieving distress among our own people and the country is successfully meeting its problem in the American way today."

"But after and coincidently with voluntary relief, our American system requires that municipal, county, and state governments shall use their own resources and credit before seeking such assistance from the Federal Treasury."

"I have indeed spent much of my life in fighting hardship and starvation both abroad and in the Southern states. I do not feel that I should be charged with lack of human sympathy for those who suffer but I recall that in all the organizations with which I have been connected over these many years, the foundation has been to summon the maximum of self help. I am proud to have sought the help of Congress in the past for nations who were so disorganized by war and anarchy that self help was impossible. But even these appropriations were but a tithe of that which was coincidently mobilized from the public charity of the United States and foreign countries. There is no such paralysis in the United States and I am confident that our people have the resources, the initiative, the courage, the stamina and kindliness of spirit to meet this situation in the way they have met their problems over generations."

"I will accredit to those who advocate Federal charity a natural anxiety for the people of their states. I am willing to pledge myself that if the time should ever come that the voluntary agencies of the country together with the local and state governments are unable to find resources with which to prevent hunger and suffering in my country, I will ask the aid of every resource of the Federal Government because I would no more see starvation amongst our countrymen than would any senator or congressman. I have the faith in the American people that such a day will not come."

"The American people are doing their job today. They should be given a chance to show whether they wish to preserve the principles of individual and local responsibility and mutual self help before they embark on what I believe is a disastrous system. I feel sure they will succeed if given the opportunity." [State Papers, Vol. I, p. 496]

The next year, in July, 1931, the President undertook an entire resurvey of the relief situation. The governors reported that the relief organizations set up in co-operation with Colonel Woods were functioning in every state—227 large cities, some 2000 smaller cities, and over 1000 counties each had special committees. The governors and the committees reported that they believed they could carry over the winter of 1931–32 with the measures then in force. Only one governor considered Federal aid, aside from the measures in force, was necessary. A survey by the Federal Public Health Service showed that there had been no failure for the public health was generally better than in prosperous times. Infant mortality especially was less owing to the unusual solicitude of women's committee organizations for the children.

A month later the President induced Walter Gifford to take over the direction of relief, Colonel Woods having been compelled to return to his own personal work. The employment situation was degenerating badly because of the European financial collapse. The number of unemployed had increased to an estimated number of over 7,000,000. Hoover in his letter of appointment to Gifford (August 19, 1931) said:

"It is clear . . . that the United States will be faced . . . with a heavy relief load. . . . I am asking you to set up such further organization as may be desirable . . . this care of misfortunes our first duty to the Nation . . . the whole forces of the administration are at your disposal."

[*State Papers, Vol. I, p. 609*]

Gifford stiffened the organization to meet the coming winter. The various Federal departments reported they would be giving employment to over 750,000 men on public works through the winter. Through the inclusion of non-service connected sick and destitute veterans in regular allowances of the Federal Government in June of the previous year, nearly 400,-000 men who would otherwise have been on the local communities were being carried by the Federal Government. (See Veterans, page 193.)

In this autumn of 1931, Hoover engaged the Friends' Service Committee to initiate and carry on the special feeding of the children in the coal regions. He raised several hundred thousand dollars privately for their support.

During the winter of 1931–32 a constant check upon the situation was kept through periodic surveys made through the governors and other agencies, and an even closer independent check was maintained through public health officers. Gifford kept daily in touch with the state officials and state committees. Repeated surveys were made by Public Health officials. Any consequential undernourishment or exposure in the people shows instantly in the mortality statistics—and they were lower than even in prosperous times. Their report of January 2, 1932, is typical:

". . . Mortality in the United States during the year . . . [was] definitely lower than in the two previous years. . . ."

"Records for this last quarter . . . indicate that the mortality at the beginning of the winter of 1931–32 has continued on a very favorable level, the rate being only 10.7 per 1000 as compared to 11.4, 12.0 and 13.2 in the last quarters of 1930, 1929, and 1928, respectively. . . ."

"Infant mortality during the past year . . . was definitely lower than in any preceding year on record, the rate being 55.8 against 58.1 for 1930. . . . This . . . showing has persisted during the last weeks of the year, the rate for the final quarter being 46.6 against an average of 56.9

for the corresponding period in the three preceding years and against 51.9 for the same period of 1929, the lowest previous rate."

[*State Papers, Vol. II, p. 101*]

DISTRIBUTION OF FARM BOARD COMMODITIES

At this time [February, 1932] Hoover determined to use for relief the surplus commodities in the hands of the Farm Board. On March 7, 1932, Congress authorized the first lot of 40,000,-000 bushels of wheat, and on July 5 a further 45,000,000 bushels of wheat and 250,000,000 pounds of cotton. This amount of wheat would yield over 20,000,000 barrels of flour—sufficient for over 6,000,000 families for nine months or until the next session of Congress. The cotton was sufficient, after deducting the cost of spinning, to make garments for over 4,000,000 families. The President secured the voluntary management of the Red Cross for its distribution from the Farm Board to the state and local committees. There was much addition in supplies and service in making garments from the Red Cross' devoted membership—mostly the women.

FEDERAL AID TO THE STATES

By February, the unemployment had increased to 10,000,000. It had become evident that certain states would require more help from the Federal Government than the public works in progress and the commodities from the Farm Board. This was particularly true of Illinois, Ohio, and Michigan.

The President felt that further aid must be given before the Congressional session was over. At once the problem of the method arose. The disposition of Congress was to set up direct Federal aid to the individuals under a Federal organization. Hoover was convinced that this could lead only to politics and petty corruption and still worse to the undermining of local responsibility and the magnificent work of voluntary committees in action all over the country. He finally determined that the aid should be given as loans to the states from the Federal Government, that it should be based upon the need of the states and not upon any quota basis, that it should be administered through the state and local committees. He had much difficulty in convincing Congress of this basis of action.

On May 31, 1932, in personally addressing the Senate, the President said:

"I hold that the maintenance of the sense of individual and personal responsibility of men to their neighbors and the proper separation of functions of the Federal and local governments requires the maintenance of the fundamental principle that the obligation of distress rests upon the individuals, upon the communities and upon the states. In order, however, that there may be no failure on the part of any state to meet its obligation in this direction I have, after consultation with some of the party leaders on both sides, favored authorization to the Reconstruction Finance Corporation to loan up to $300,000,000 to state governments where they are unable to finance themselves in provision of relief to distress."

[*State Papers, Vol. II, p. 201*]

After a great deal of battling in which the Congress attempted to make the Federal allotments on a population basis (pork barrel) instead of based on need and local effort, the President got his way and on July 17, 1932, he signed the bill with the statement that:

"Through provision of $300,000,000 of temporary loans by the Reconstruction Corporation to such states as are absolutely unable to finance the relief of distress, we have a solid back-log of assurance that there need be no hunger and cold in the United States. These loans are to be based upon absolute need and evidence of financial exhaustion. I do not expect any state to resort to it except as a last extremity."

[*State Papers, Vol. I, p. 236*]

CONGRESSIONAL REFUSAL TO SUPPORT THE PRESIDENT'S ORGANIZATION

The President's Washington organization was voluntary except for clerical hire. To cover this, the President addressed the Congress on July 5, 1932, saying:

"The second Deficiency Bill just passed omitted an appropriation for continuance of the activities of the President's Organization on Unemployment Relief. I urgently request that Congress make a special appropriation of $120,000 to continue this work over the next fiscal year."

"This organization, of which Mr. Walter S. Gifford is director, is comprised of leading men and women throughout every state in the Union and has served to establish and co-ordinate state and local volunteer effort in relief of distress throughout the Nation. The organization has secured in a large way the co-operation of industry and labor, of the national social welfare organizations, and has assisted in mobilizing a large amount of voluntary funds and administering local recources to the best advantage. This organization is the only agency for national co-ordination and stimulation. . . ."

". . . The organization is made up primarily of volunteers serving without pay or expense. It is non-partisan. . . . To function success-fully it must have funds to employ a relatively small number of trained personnel together with necessary office help. . . ."

[*State Papers, Vol. II, pp. 220–1*]

The pettiness of Democratic leaders who resented his resist-ance to per capita appropriations led them to refuse his request. The President, however, arranged for the Reconstruction Finance Corporation to conduct the relief organization as a part of the administration of the $300,000,000 appropriation.

Because Gifford had completed his year and was compelled to return to the presidency of the American Telephone and Telegraph Company, Fred C. Croxton was placed in charge of the President's organization and directed the allocation of the R. F. C. funds.

Gifford in relinquishing his office and with his experience of a year in administration made comment upon the many pro-posals to centralize relief in the Federal Government:

"To centralize the responsibility . . . would demoralize the greatest voluntary decentralized organization ever assembled in peace times in this country."

HOOVER'S REVIEW OF RELIEF ACTIVITIES

In an address of September 15, 1932, reviewing the relief work, the President said:

"Our tasks are definite. The first is to see that no man, woman, or child shall go hungry or unsheltered through the approaching winter."

"The second is to see that our great benevolent agencies for character building, for hospitalization, for care of children and all their vast num-ber of agencies of voluntary solicitude for the less fortunate are main-tained in full strength."

"The third is to maintain the bedrock principle of our liberties by the full mobilization of individual and local resources and responsibilities."

"The fourth is that we may maintain the spiritual impulses in our people for generous giving and generous service—in the spirit that each is his brother's keeper. Personal feeling and personal responsibility of men to their neighbors is the soul of genuine good will; it is the essential foundation of modern society. A cold and distant charity which puts out its sympathy only through the tax collector yields a very meager dole of unloving and perfunctory relief."

"With each succeeding winter in this period of great distress our problem has become larger and more difficult. Yet the American people have responded to meet it."

"The time has gone by when a depression could be regarded only as a depression of business. It must be regarded now as something deeper, involving a social responsibility not merely for measures helpful to the restoration of business, for fundamentally they are actions on behalf of those whom business has ceased to be able to employ. They are not the authors of the misery which is upon the land. They are its victims."

"That the American people have made a broad and courageous attack upon the consequences of our present unparalleled calamity is amply suggested by the state of public health in the Nation. I recognize that there are exceptions both local and individual to any general statement, yet no one can deny the scientific determination of our public health officials throughout the land. Their reports to the Surgeon General of the United States represent the final word upon the efficient and devoted sense of responsibility of our people in this obligation to our fellow citizens. Overwhelmingly they confirm the fact that general mortality rate, infant mortality rate, epidemics, the disease rate—are less than in normal times. There is but one explanation. That is, that through an aroused sense of public responsibility, those in destitution and their children are receiving actually more regular and more adequate care than even in normal times."

"With the possibility of still larger tasks and lessened individual local resources for the next winter, before the close of the last Congress I secured to the Red Cross 85,000,000 bushels of wheat, 500,000 bales of cotton and an authorization to the Reconstruction Finance Corporation to advance $300,000,000 to such states as could not finance themselves to care for distress."

"Nor are we seeking relief only by direct provision for distress, which is your problem. In the Federal Government we are providing employment during this year through the speeding up of necessary Federal construction work to a huge total of over $750,000,000. In addition we have provided for loans of $1,500,000,000 for construction of public enterprises of self-sustaining character. Wherever possible we are concentrating that effort for the winter months. In addition, our employers and our labor groups have been organized anew in a systematic nation-wide campaign to further spread the available work and to shorten working hours."[1]   [*State Papers, Vol. II, p. 281*]

Under Croxton's direction the disposition of the Federal relief fund supplemental to state and local needs was based upon Federal investigation of actual need and upon a showing that the states and local divisions themselves were providing a proper share of the burden. The funds were administered through the committees which had been established in 1930 and there has never been a breath of corruption, waste, or politics found by the earnest searchers therefor.

The amounts allocated to the states through the R. F. C. during President Hoover's Administration were as follows:

July, 1932..............................$ 3,000,000
August, 1932.......................... 13,931,669
September, 1932...................... 18,523,502
October, 1932......................... 22,594,762
November, 1932....................... 18,484,823
December, 1932........................ 35,958,117
January, 1933.......................... 49,435,416
February, 1933......................... 48,187,271

This of course was only part of the relief measures. The action of states and local communities, the large amounts of food and clothing distributed from the Farm Board supplies [see page 378], the large extension of Federal aid to needy veterans, the large extension of public and private works [see page 389] —all were part of the national effort.

On December 6, 1932, in his last Annual Message to the Congress—three months before the end of his term, Hoover said:

"In the face of widespread hardship our people have demonstrated daily a magnificent sense of humanity, of individual and community responsibility for the welfare of the less fortunate. They have grown in their conceptions and organization for co-operative action for the common welfare."

"In the provision against distress during this winter, the great private

[1] In view of the assertions of the Roosevelt Administration of inadequacy in relief under Hoover, it is curious that no such charge was made in the campaign of 1932 when every conceivable charge was made. It could not be made with honesty and every community would have sensed its dishonesty if it had been made.

agencies of the country have been mobilized again; the local authorities and the states are engaged everywhere in relief. The provisions made for loans from the Reconstruction Finance Corporation to states that have exhausted their own resources, guarantee that there should be no hunger or suffering from cold in the country. The large majority of states are showing a sturdy co-operation in the spirit of the Federal aid."

"The Surgeon General, in charge of the Public Health Service, furnishes me with the following information upon the state of public health:

MORTALITY RATE PER 1000 OF POPULATION ON AN ANNUAL BASIS
FROM REPRESENTATIVE STATES

First 9 months of—	General	Infant
1928	11.9	67.8
1929	12.0	65.8
1930	11.4	62.0
1931	11.2	60.0
1932	10.6	55.0

"The sickness rates from data available show the same trends. These facts indicate the fine endeavor of the agencies which have been mobilized for care of those in distress."   [*State Papers, Vol. II, p. 495*]

COMPARISON OF HOOVER AND NEW DEAL RELIEF METHODS

After three years of the Roosevelt Federal control and centralization of relief, Hoover, in an address at St. Louis on December 16, 1935, reviewed the comparative methods.

"Let me say one thing right at the outset. There is no disagreement upon the public obligation to relieve distress which flows from national calamity. The support of that comes from the conscience of a people. It comes from their fidelity to the Sermon on the Mount. They know the weary days of tramping the streets in search for a chance to work. They know the discouragement and despair which have stalked those homes."

"Some five years ago I stated that, 'as a Nation we must prevent hunger and cold to those of our people who are in honest difficulties.' I have never heard a disagreement with that."

"I believe I can without egotism claim to have had some special experience in relief. At one time or another it became my task to organize and administer relief to over 150,000,000 people who had been reduced to destitution by war or by famine or by flood, both at home and abroad. I gave some years to that service in the aspiration to save life, to allay suffering, to restore courage and faith in humanity."

"It also became my duty in 1930 to see that relief was organized for our unemployed. Organization of relief upon a nation-wide basis was practically unknown in the world before those experiences. It therefore fell to me and my colleagues to pioneer in methods. I spent long, weary days listening to arguments whether to have direct money relief, or relief in kind, or public works or made-work or 'boondoggling,' or centralized administration, or decentralized responsibility. We tried out these alternatives. Out of those poignant experiences we learned certain fundamentals. We quickly learned that there were four types of persons who rush into relief. There were the starry-eyed who periodically discover that relief is needed and that everything up to date is wrong. There were those whose major passion was sociological experiment upon a mass of distress. There were those who would make profit from misery. There were always those present who do not neglect the political possibilities of relief. But there were the sterling, solid men and women in every city and hamlet who willingly served and sacrificed."

"We learned that relief was an emergency operation, not a social experiment; that the object was to serve the people in genuine distress and nobody else. We learned that the dreamers cannot effectually conduct the grinding tasks of relief; that politics must be shunned as a plague. We learned that centralized bureaucracy gives the sufferers more red tape than relief. We learned that we must mobilize on a voluntary basis the best hearts and brains in every community to serve their neighbors. We learned that there must be complete decentralization to them of both authority and administration. We did not have to learn that local self-government and local responsibility was the basis of American life."

"In 1930 by co-operation with the states, we secured the creation of state committees of leading citizens. With them we secured the creation of similar committees in every city, town, and county where relief was needed. These committees had no politics. They were men and women experienced in large affairs, sympathetic, understanding of the needs of their neighbors in distress. And they served without pay. In those days one did not enter into relief of his countrymen through the portals of a payroll. American men and women of such stature cannot be had as a paid bureaucracy, yet they will serve voluntarily all hours of the day and defer their own affairs to night."

"These committees used the existing officials; they engaged their own tested organizations; they employed their own trusted citizens. They had the complete authority to determine the methods best adapted to their neighborhoods. They knew the problem of the man next door better than anybody in Washington. They themselves determined for their locality what method was to be used. They adapted these needs to the individual families. Their stewardship was under the limelight of their own community. They gave spiritual aid and encouragement."

"At the start the relief in 1930 depended upon private giving. As times became more difficult, the committees co-operated in the use of county and municipal funds; and as it became still more difficult many of the state governments provided them with funds. Finally, as state resources weakened, we provided Federal Government funds to be distributed to the state governments and by them redistributed to the local organizations. That we built up no bureaucracy is evident from the fact that although the Government had many new emergency tasks, yet during the Hoover administration the total number of all Government officials decreased by 10,000. That form of organization expressed in its noblest form the whole American ideal of local self-government, local responsibility, national co-operation, and the voluntary spirit of human service."

"There was no important failure to provide for those in real need. There was no substantial complaint or suggestion of waste, politics, or corruption. Neither the Republican Party nor any of its agencies ever asked for votes or claimed that its administration deserved votes for it. That idea was repugnant to every decent sense of Americanism."

"However, all this was forgotten on March 3, 1933. We may accept that the date of Creation was moved to March 4, and we may examine what sort of a world has been made."

"At that moment good men appeared who were certain that before their advent everything was done wrong. Also came the visionaries, the profit-maker, and above all, the politician. They all yearned to serve their fellowmen."

"The whole relief work was promptly centralized from Washington. State and local organizations were dismissed or reduced to mere window dressing. A paid bureaucracy was spread over the land. The history of the last two and one-half years shows the floundering of this administration. That needs no more proof than the buffeting of those in distress from FERA or PWA or its subsidiaries to EPW, then to SERA, then to CWA, partly to FRSC, then back to FERA, and over to WPA. As each of these alphabetical organizations flares up in folly and waste its victims and its accounts have been buried by juggling of the alphabet. When they are all buried their spirit will live on as IOU.''

"We may compare the cost of these two forms of administration—the one founded on local self-government under the glare of its local public opinion; the other being run by a political bureaucracy from Washington.''

"Statistics are dry subjects, but just now figures are the most important thing in our national life. The entire cost of relief to unemployment during the last year of the Republican administration was about $1,100,000,000. That includes Federal, state, municipal, county, and private giving. It includes Federal public works above normal and does not include relief to agriculture. The Federal overhead was not over $250,000 a year. The total number of paid Federal employees was less than 200.''

"Now let us examine the respective needs in these two periods. The average of the monthly figures of the American Federation of Labor shows 11,600,000 unemployed during the last year of the Hoover administration. During the year of the New Deal ending this October the unemployed have averaged about 11,100,000. That was a decrease of the unemployment load by about 5 per cent.''

"Now let us note the increase in relief cost. However, the marvellous migratory habits of these relief funds from one place in the alphabet to another make them difficult hunting. But judging from Treasury and other statements the expenditures on all relief alphabets in the year ending last October for Federal, state, and local were over $3,500,000,-000. This also includes Federal Public Works over normal, but does not include relief to agriculture. There were over 140,000 officials on the Federal payroll, not including the people on relief. The salaries of these officials alone must come to about $300,000,000 a year. It is easy to detect another $200,000,000 in pencils, typewriters, offices, automobiles, Pullman fares, etc., not to mention press releases. That is an overhead of four or five hundred million per annum. Some increase in relief was necessary, but an increase of 300 per cent in costs in the face of a 5 per cent decrease in unemployment load is significant. And the overhead amounts to nearly one-half the whole cost of relief three years ago.''

"In confirmation of this, I have inquired as to the figures of several cities and counties. To cite one of them, the number on relief increased 5 per cent, the cost 250 per cent. The others confirm these increases.''

"Every community has been forced to conspire to get its share from the Federal grab bag. And saddest of all, the responsibility of local self-government has been dulled; we are becoming a nation of prayer wheels directed to Washington."

"We may well wonder why local organization of relief, consonant with the whole spirit of democracy, has been shifted to a Federal Bureaucracy at Washington. Some part of it has to do with politics and yearning for sociological experiments. Jobs have been thereby found for over 140,000 new Federal officials. If it was decided to bureaucratize relief from Washington, then every call of good government demanded that the staff be selected by nonpartisan merit tests through the Civil Service Commission. But that service which has been built up over many years by every President was ignored and repudiated, and the spoils system substituted. You know and I know and the people know that this horde of officials has been appointed by the advice and consent of Democratic politicians."

"The inevitable and driving purpose of any political bureaucracy is to use its powers to secure its jobs. The sudden appropriations to cities, counties, and states were singularly timed to elections. And this is not the only method of making politics out of human misery. Governor Smith has said that nobody shoots Santa Claus. But the people may learn that there are other things moving around in the dark besides Santa Claus."

"A mass of propaganda spreads over the country to the effect that relief to the unemployed originates with the New Deal and would end with the New Deal. Those in distress will not be misled. Whatever aid they receive comes not from any official or party. It comes out of the pockets of their fellow-citizens. It will not end as long as there is need or any resources left."

"Do you want more proofs of waste, folly, chiselers, and petty corruption? You know it in your own town, city, or village. Read your own newspapers, whose columns periodically reek with accounts of disorganization and waste. Their editorials cry to heaven against the use being made of relief for politics. If only the money taken from the taxpayers could go to those in distress there would be less cause for public indignation."

"The administration of relief needs reform right now. It needs it in the interest of good government. It needs it in the interest of the 85 per cent of our citizens who have to pay for it. They include everybody who works. The cost of these wastes and follies is collected by hidden taxes in every package that comes from the store. Or worse, we are laying it onto our children by debt. Reform is needed in the interest of the 15 per cent who are on relief, that they get better and more secure service. To the self-respecting Americans on relief these wastes and follies are a tragedy. They know it dissipates money they need. It delays their deliverance to a real job. The inspiration of relief comes from the heart, but its effectiveness must come from the head."

"As the New Deal always demands alternative plans, I offer four:

"1. Stop these wasteful Federal public works projects; confine them to projects which meet the needs of the Nation."

"2. Decentralize the administration of all other forms of relief. Turn them back to the states and local communities. Do it in joint co-opera-tion with the governors, mayors, and county authorities. Enlist again the voluntary services of American men and women on a nonpartisan basis. Give such responsible committees as they create the entire de-termination of how it should be done. Allot to the states less than one-half the present funds being spent in relief. Require the local authorities to find from their local funds at least 5 per cent as a check on waste. Require the state to do its share. Discharge most of the Federal officials connected with these relief agencies. Those in real need will be better cared for than they are today."

"3. Do it now. That would go far to assure a clean election. But it is more than that. It would relieve human distress which suffers enough without the poison of politics in its bread."

Speaking in New York on September 23, 1936, Hoover con-tinued his analysis of the relief problem:

"The dominant question of all questions is not costs but results. Did this sort of administration of relief by sympathetic highly qualified groups of citizens that prevailed from 1930 to 1932 care for the de-serving people who were in need? No human system of organization is perfect. But read the press of those years. It discloses that, aside from the sporadic accidents of any system, there were no criticisms for relief failure. No one starved. There were no daily headlines of fraud. There was much appeal for funds and painting of the need, but no painting of failure to provide. In the presidential campaign of 1932, every charge that human ingenuity could invent was brought. And yet relief was scarcely discussed. Not a single charge against relief was made of politics, of waste, of corruption, or of failure to prevent hunger or cold."

"Public health records are also a useful test. Undernourishment and cold are at once expressed in terms of increased disease and mortality. A study of the insurance, public health, and other statistics will show the surprising result that the population was in better physical health in 1932 than even during the boom year of 1928. The most illuminating figures are those of infant mortality which show that 1932 was the lowest in all American history. And remember, this was the third full year of depression. That the infant mortality has been rising since the relief was taken from local administration and centralized under political Washington is shown in the Public Health indexes:

1928	6880 deaths per 100,000
1929	6730 deaths per 100,000
1930	6460 deaths per 100,000
1931	6170 deaths per 100,000
1932	5760 deaths per 100,000
1933	5810 deaths per 100,000
1934	5990 deaths per 100,000

"Today instead of sympathy for the unemployed and the destitute there is a growing resentment. The real sympathy from the national heart flows far more truly through personal leadership in the community than through Federal agents."

"There is a spiritual loss in all this which cannot be estimated. Instead of building up the solicitude of neighbor for neighbor, instead of building the responsibility of good neighbors among men and women, we are cultivating hardness for the destitute, we are undermining self-respect of men and women. We are creating contempt for government."

"One need of the Nation today is a recall of a spirit of individual service. That spirit springs from the human heart not from politics. Upon that spirit alone can this democracy survive. No greater call to service could be made than to remobilize local administration of relief."

PUBLIC WORKS RELIEF

Hoover was probably the original exponent of enlarging government programs of public works and private programs of construction as relief to unemployment in time of business depression.

As stated, he had served as chairman of the Unemployment Conference in September, 1921. The methods by which that comparatively minor depression was met have considerable

importance. Out of this Conference came the first tangible
definite proposal of the use of speeded-up public and private
construction to mitigate slumps and relieve unemployment. Co-
operation of Federal, state, local and industrial agencies was
then effectively organized by Hoover and served a fine purpose.

EXPANSION OF PRIVATE CONSTRUCTION AND
LOCAL PUBLIC WORKS

As mentioned, immediately upon the crash in 1929, the
President undertook again to organize co-operative action of industry. On November 19, 20, and 22, 1929, he summoned a
series of conferences of industrial leaders (see page 129) and
through them organized co-operation in continuance and expansion of private works. Secretary Lamont organized a division
in the Department of Commerce and administered the plan. On
November 23, President Hoover issued an appeal to governors
and mayors as follows:

"With view to giving strength to the present economic situation and
providing for the absorption of any unemployment which might result
from present disturbed conditions, I have asked for collective action of
industry in the expansion of construction activities and in stabilization
of wages. As I have publicly stated, one of the largest factors that can
be brought to bear is that of the energetic yet prudent pursuit of public
works by the Federal Government and state, municipal, and country authorities."

"The Federal Government will exert itself to the utmost within its
own province and I should like to feel that I have the co-operation of
yourself and the municipal county and other local officials in the same
direction. It would be helpful if road, street, public building and other
construction of this type could be speeded up and adjusted in such fashion
as to further employment."

"I would also appreciate it if your officials would canvass the state,
municipal, and county programs and give me such information as you
can as to the volume of expenditure that can be prudently arranged for
the next twelve months and for the next six months and inform me
thereof."

"I am asking Secretary Lamont of the Department of Commerce to
take in hand the detailed measures of co-operation with you which may
arise in this matter."

[State Papers, Vol. I, p. 137]

On December 3, 1929, in his Message to Congress he urged
immediate expansion of Federal public building, waterways,
flood control, and Hoover Dam construction. In an address to
the United States Chamber of Commerce on December 5,
1929, he stated:

"The third line of action has been to undertake through voluntary
organization of industry the continuity and expansion of the construction and maintenance work of the country, so as to take up any slack
in employment which arises in other directions. The extension and organization of this work are the purpose of this meeting . . . this great
field of expenditure could by its acceleration in time of need, be made
into a great balance wheel of stability. . . . No one would advocate the
production of consumable goods beyond the daily demand; that in itself
only stirs up future difficulty."

"I am glad to report that such a program has met with universal
approval of all those in responsible positions. Our railways and utilities
and many of our larger manufacturers have shown a most distinguished
spirit in undertaking to maintain and even to expand their construction
and betterment programs. The state, county, and municipal governments
are responding in the most gratifying way to the requests to co-operate
with the Federal Government in every prudent expansion of public
works."   [*State Papers, Vol. I, p. 182*]

On January 3, 1930, he reported to the press:

"Our drive for increase in construction and improvement work to
take up unemployment is showing most encouraging results, and it looks
as if the work undertaken will be larger for 1930 than for 1929."
"The Department of Commerce now has complete returns from the
governors of sixteen states covering public works to be undertaken in
1930 by the state, municipal, and county authorities. They have partial
returns from thirteen more states. The total so far reported, and including the Federal Government, is about $1,550,000,000, and in nearly
all cases larger than for 1929. The surveys are coming in daily, and
should be completed by mid-January."
"The preliminary estimate of the railways for construction and betterments for 1930 was $1,050,000,000, and for the public utilities
$2,100,000,000, including the telephones. The total of these items so
far is $4,700,000,000. This does not include the balance of the state,

municipal, and county work, nor the building construction, nor the industrial and factory improvements, which latter are now under survey by the Special Business Committee." [State Papers, Vol. I, p. 201]

On October 6, 1930, in an address to the American Federation of Labor, President Hoover, referring to this co-operation in expansion of private construction, said:

"The fine co-operation in the providing of organized emergency employment through Federal, state, and municipal public works and utility construction has been an important contribution in taking up the slack of unemployment. The measure of success is easily demonstrated. The Department of Commerce reports to me that public works and the construction work by the railways and utilities in the last eight months amount to about $4,500,000,000 as compared with about $4,000,000,000 in the same period of the boom year of 1929, or an increase of about $500,000,000. In all previous depressions these works decreased, so that the gain is more than even the apparent figures." [State Papers, Vol. I, p. 391]

In reporting to Congress upon this subject on December 2, 1930, the President said:

"The third direction of co-operation has been to maintain and even extend construction work and betterments in anticipation of the future. It has been the universal experience in previous depressions that public works and private construction have fallen off rapidly with the general tide of depression. On this occasion, however, the increased authorization and generous appropriations by the Congress and the action of states and municipalities have resulted in the expansion of public construction to an amount even above that in the most prosperous years. In addition the co-operation of public utilities, railways, and other large organizations has been generously given in construction and betterment work in anticipation of future need. The Department of Commerce advises me that as a result, the volume of this type of construction work, which amounted to roughly $6,300,000,000 in 1929, instead of decreasing will show a total of about $7,000,000,000 for 1930. There has, of course, been a substantial decrease in the types of construction which could not be undertaken in advance of need." [State Papers, Vol. I, p. 430]

FURTHER EXPANSION OF FEDERAL PUBLIC WORKS

On November 8, 1930, the President announced he would recommend to Congress still further expansion of Federal public works:

"It will be remembered that the appropriations for Federal construction were greatly increased upon the President's recommendation by the last Congress as aid to employment during the current year. The departments were also authorized to undertake necessary technical preparation for future construction work which was authorized but not appropriated for. As a result of appropriations available during the present fiscal year, the construction work of all kinds in the Federal Government will be increased to a total exceeding $500,000,000. The Emergency appropriations that will be requested will be in the nature of an addition to this already enlarged program and will be in anticipation of such construction work as would normally have taken place a year or two hence."

[*State Papers, Vol. I, p. 411*]

Promptly a Democratic-radical political phenomenon developed when the members of the Congress scented the political possibilities of the pork-barrel in public works. By forcing the President to oppose their proposals of several billions they hoped at least for a display of public feeling against him. Hoover issued this crisp warning (December 9, 1930):

"I observe that measures have been already introduced in Congress and are having advocacy, which, if passed, would impose an increased expenditure beyond the sums which I have recommended for the present and next fiscal year by a total of nearly $4,500,000,000, and mostly under the guise of giving relief of some kind or another."

"Some of these schemes are ill-considered; some represent enthusiasts, and some represent the desire of individuals to show that they are more generous than the administration or that they are more generous than even the leaders of their own parties. They are playing politics at the expense of human misery. . . . The American people will not be misled by such tactics."

[*State Papers, Vol. I, p. 459*]

As the depression went on the Federal expenditures were steadily increased for construction work of all kinds including naval vessels, military construction, etc. The normal expenditures for public works, buildings, highways, etc., during Mr.

Coolidge's Administration were at the rate of about $150,000,-000 per annum with an additional amount for naval and military construction. During the depression years all construction as shown in the President's Message to Congress of December 6, 1932, was:

Fiscal Year	Amount
1930	$410,420,000
1931	574,870,000
1932	655,880,000
1933	717,260,000 (in progress)

About 700,000 men, and therefore families, were being provided for.

During this time demagogic agitation for expansion of public works grew louder and finally called for $5,000,000,000 per annum. These agitations were chiefly fathered by the sensational press (which later bitterly criticized the Roosevelt Administration for just such action).

SHIFT FROM FEDERAL PUBLIC WORKS TO FEDERAL LOANS FOR REPRODUCTIVE WORKS

A certan amount of expansion of Federal public works was advisable. A fire in the grate is useful but to burn the house down does not serve the same purpose. As experience was gained with large programs certain limits became evident. As a method of relief it was costing the Government $1200 to $1500 a year to give relief to a single family and no government could solve the size of the problem in that direction. It was two or three times as expensive as direct aid through local committees. The works must be really sound in their benefits, whether social or economic. Such works were mostly away from the centers of unemployment and only people skilled in such work could be employed, which often resulted in employing people not in need.

In search for economically sound undertakings that could be near the centers of unemployment, the President developed the idea of "income-producing" works which would subsequently earn their cost and repay loans, as distinguished from non-productive public works. This program was developed with Senate leaders and in a press statement on May 12, 1932, the President said:

"There are a large number of economically sound and self-supporting projects that would unquestionably be carried forward were it not for the present situation existing in the capital markets and the inadequate functioning of the credit machinery of the country. They exist, both in the field of public bodies and of industry."

"It is proposed to use the instrumentality of the Reconstruction Finance Corporation which has a nation-wide organization by authorizing the Corporation either to underwrite or make loans for income producing and self sustaining enterprises which will increase employment whether undertaken by public bodies or by private enterprises."

"It is proposed to provide the necessary funds as they are required by the sale of securities of the Reconstruction Corporation and its total borrowing powers to be increased up to $3,000,000,000."

"It is necessary to sharply distinguish between the use of capital for the above purposes and its use for unproductive public works. This proposal represents a flow of funds into productive enterprises, which is not taking place today because of abnormal conditions. These being loans on security and being self-liquidating in character, do not constitute a charge against the taxpayer or the public credit."

"An examination shows that to increase Federal Government construction work during the next year beyond the amounts already provided for would be to undertake works of largely artificial character far in advance of public return and would represent a wasteful use of capital and public credit."

[State Papers, Vol. II, p. 187]

On May 21 in amplification of his plan as opposed to expansion of nonproductive public-works projects, he stated in a letter to one of the nonproductive works proponents:

"These proposals of huge expansion of public works' have a vital relation to balancing the Federal Budget and to the stabilizing of national credit. The financing of 'income-producing works' by the Reconstruction Corporation is an investment operation. . . . does not involve added burdens upon the taxpayer either now or in the future. It will liquidate itself with the return of the investor to the money markets."

"The proposal to build non-productive 'public works' . . . necessitates making increased appropriations by the Congress. . . . Whatever the method employed, they are inescapably a burden upon the taxpayer."

"I have for many years advocated the speeding up of public works in times of depression. That has been done upon a huge scale and is proceeding at as great a pace as fiscal stability will warrant. All branches of Government—Federal, state, and municipal—have greatly expanded their 'public works' and have now reached a stage where they have anticipated the need for many such works for a long time to come. Therefore, the new projects which might be undertaken are of even more remote usefulness. . . . We have largely anticipated the future and have rendered further expansion beyond our present program of very remote usefulness. . . . We cannot thus squander ourselves into prosperity."

"A still further and overriding reason for not undertaking such programs of further expansions of Federal 'public works' is evident if we examine the individual projects which might be undertaken from an engineering and economic point of view. . . . Construction . . . physically requires years for completion such as naval vessels, buildings, canalization of rivers, etc. . . . could only be expended over four or five years; . . . projects not already started will require legal and technical preparation and therefore could not be brought to the point of employment of labor during the next year . . . a portion are in localities where there is little unemployment. . . . A portion are of remote utility and are not justified, such as extension of agricultural acerage at the present time. . . . That means the employment of say less than 40,000 men. Thus the whole of these grandiose contentions of possible expansion of Federal 'public works' fall absolutely to the ground for these reasons if there were no other."

". . . the program I have proposed gives people employment in all parts of the country in their normal jobs under normal conditions at the normal place of abode, tends to re-establish normal processes in business and industry and will do so on a much larger scale than the projects proposed in the so-called 'public works' program."

". . . It is generally agreed that the balancing of the Federal Budget and unimpaired national credit are indispensable to the restoration of confidence and to the very start of economic recovery. The administration and Congress have pledged themselves to this end. A 'public works' program such as is suggested by your committee . . . creates at once an enormous further deficit."

"It will serve no good purpose and will fool no one to try to cover appearances by restoring to a so-called 'extraordinary budget.' That device is well known. It brought the governments of certain foreign countries to the brink of financial disaster."

[*State Papers, Vol. II, p. 189*]

On May 31, 1932, the President urged the plan in person to the Senate.

"In order to aid unemployment and to avoid wasteful expansion of public works I have favored an authority to the Reconstruction Corporation to increase its issues of its securities to the maximum of $3,000,-000,000 in order that it may extend its services both in aid to employment and agriculture on a wide scale. Under the methods proposed the Corporation is to be (a) authorized to buy bonds from political subdivisions or public bodies to aid in construction of income-producing or self-liquidating projects; (b) to make loans to established enterprise upon adequate security, for advancement of sound projects that will increase employment but safeguarded by requirement that some portion of outside capital is also provided."

"I have not been able to favor the expansion of public works beyond the program already proposed in the Budget. I have for many years advocated speeding up of public works as relief to unemployment in times of depression. Since the beginning of this depression, in consonance with this view, the Federal Government will have expended in excess of $1,500,000,000 in construction and maintenance of one kind or another as against a normal program of perhaps $650,000,000 for a similar period. The Budget for next year calls for over $550,000,000 or double our usual outlay. If we shall now increase these programs we shall need instantly to increase taxes still further. We have already forced every project for which we have justification with any regard to the taxpayer and the avoidance of sheer waste."   [*State Papers, Vol. II, p. 202*]

The President had a long struggle to get his program through in shape. To make an example of the pork barrel and political injection into the program he denounced (on May 27, 1932) a measure introduced into the House of Representatives as follows:

"There should be an understanding of the character of the draft bill made public yesterday in the House of Representatives. That draft bill supports some proposals we have already made in aid to unemployment through the use of the Reconstruction Finance Corporation to make loans for projects which have been in abeyance and which proposal makes no drain on the taxpayer. But in addition it proposes to expend about $900,000,000 for Federal public works."

". . . thus creating a deficit in the Budget that could only be met with more taxes and more Federal bond issues."

"An examination of only one group of these proposals—that is, proposed authorizations for new post offices—shows a list of about 2300 such buildings, at a total cost of about $150,000,000. The Post Office Department informs me that the interest and upkeep of these buildings would amount to $14,000,000 per annum, whereas the upkeep and rent of buildings at present in use amounts to less than $3,000,000. Many of the other groups in this bill will no more stand the light of day than this example."

"A total of over 3500 projects of various kinds are proposed in this bill, scattered into every quarter of the United States. Many of these projects have heretofore been discredited by Congress because of useless extravagance involved. Many were originally authorizd as justified only in the long distant future. I do not believe that 20 per cent could be brought to the stage of employment for a year. I am advised by he engineers that the amount of labor required to complete a group of $400,000,000 of these works would amount to only 100,000 men for one year, because they are in large degree mechanical jobs."

"This is not unemployment relief. It is the most gigantic pork barrel ever proposed to the American Congress."

"Detailed lists of all these projects have been broadcast to every part of the country during the past twenty-four hours, to the cities, towns, villages, and sections who would receive a portion of this pork barrel. It is apparently expected that the cupidity of these towns and sections will demand that their congressmen and senators vote for this bill or threaten to penalize them if they fail to join in this squandering of money."

"I just do not believe that such lack of intelligence or cupidity exists amongst the people of our United States. . . . Our Nation was not founded on the pork barrel, and it has not become great by political log-rolling. I hope that those many members of Congress of both parties who I know will oppose this bill will receive the definite support of the people in their districts in resisting it." [State Papers, Vol. II, p. 195]

In his Message on the state of the Nation of December 6, 1932, the President said in review:

"Speeding up of Federal public works during the past four years as an aid to employment has advanced many types of such improvements to the point where further expansion cannot be justified in their usefulness to the Government or the people. As an aid to unemployment we should beyond the normal constructive programs substitute reproductive or so-called self-liquidating works. Loans for such purposes have been provided for through the Reconstruction Finance Corporation. This change in character of projects directly relieves the taxpayer and is capable of expansion into a larger field than the direct Federal works. The reproductive works constitute an addition to national wealth and to future employment, whereas further undue expansion of Federal public works is but a burden upon the future."

[*State Papers, Vol. II, p. 498*]

In the nine months between the passage of the act and the end of the Hoover Administration about $175,000,000 of reproductive projects had been authorized and some $500,000,000 more were in advanced stage of preparation.

RELIEF OF THE 1930 DROUGHT

A farm drought in twenty states occurred in 1930 approaching the severity of any of those in subsequent years. It is of interest to observe Hoover's consistency of policies in avoiding to the utmost degree centralization and the use of Federal bureaucracy but yet getting the job done handsomely by co-operation.

The first move of the President was to secure (August 5, 1930) a voluntary reduction of 50 per cent in railway rates for feed to drought areas.

On August 8 he summoned a meeting of drought state governors to Washington. At this meeting of the governors and Federal officials on August 19, State and County Relief Committees were set up to co-ordinate Federal services, the Red Cross, and private credit agencies. The President instituted an immediate additional Federal road and other public works program in those areas. He directed the Federal Land Bank and the Farm Board to expand their credit facilities. He secured an initial appropriation of $5,000,000 from the National Red Cross. All of these were co-ordinated under the committee organization headed by Secretary of Agriculture Arthur Hyde.

In his Annual Message to Congress on December 2, 1930, he recommended $30,000,000 for loans to farmers for seed and feed. Democratic leaders wanting to show their superior generosity raised the amount to $85,000,000 and included taking over to the Federal Government the direct relief to families then being efficiently carried on by the Red Cross. The Red Cross had underway a drive for an additional $10,000,000 from voluntary sources which this Congressional action greatly injured. President Hoover refused to discard his program and himself led the Red Cross drive for $10,000,000 to successful conclusion. In a public appeal on January 22, 1931, he said:

". . . It is unthinkable that any of our people should be allowed to suffer from hunger or want. The heart of the Nation will not permit it. It is to the heart of the Nation that I am appealing tonight. I urge all of my fellow countrymen to contribute promptly and in accordance with their means. It is a call to citizenship and to generosity in time of trial, but it is a call for protection to our greatest American institution of charity and above all a call on behalf of those in need."

"I want to take this occasion to thank the thousands of devoted members of the Red Cross throughout the land who in the drought-stricken areas are devoting their time and effort to the relief of suffering and in the other parts of the country to providing the means of doing so. In the face of calamity let us unite in a common effort to drive suffering and want from our country. There can be no higher duty. To the call of that duty the Nation will respond." [*State Papers, Vol. I, p. 494*]

The debate over Congressional appropriations stretched over two months. It was charged in Congress that there was attempt to get loans into the hands of southern planters for distribution to their tenants instead of directly from the Department of Agriculture. This the President would not agree to. There was also a desire of the Progressives and Democratic members to make the President appear as heartless to the distressed. In the meantime the President's organization was doing the job until Congress finally gave way to the President's insistence.

In reporting to the Congress in his Annual Message on December 8, 1931, the President said:

". . . The loans authorized by Congress for rehabilitation in the drought areas have enabled farmers to produce abundant crops in those districts. The Red Cross undertook and magnificently administered relief for over 2,500,000 drought sufferers last winter. . . . The action of the Federal Farm Board in granting credits to farm co-operatives saved many of them from bankruptcy and increased their purpose and strength." [*State Paper, Vol. II, p. 45*]

The total Government loans to drought relief sufferers for seed and feed were $47,000,000 administered by the local relief committees in co-operation with the Department of Agriculture. Ultimately 75 per cent were repaid. There was no loss of animals and no yield to the demands for rash slaughter of animals by Government agents. The Red Cross expenditures were under $10,000,000 and no one was allowed to suffer.

EMERGENCY STRENGTHENING OF CREDIT, BANKING, AND CURRENCY

In a major sense the depression was dominated by credit and banking disturbances. We deal with the President's policies in long-view banking reform elsewhere. Here we are concerned with the emergency actions.

It is not our purpose here to enter upon a long account of incidents that have been well described elsewhere. Our purpose is to describe the policies of the President in meeting these terrific economic shocks not by the traditional inaction of all previous American Presidents, but by a series of the most courageous actions in our history.

THE FIRST PERIOD OF THE DEPRESSION

The first credit and banking problem was to get over the crash in the stock markets without a banking panic. The total loans against speculative stocks in the crash month of October exceeded $11,000,000,000 and they had to be liquidated. They were liquidated to under $2,000,000,000 with the help of the Federal Reserve System. The cushioning of farm prices had been done with the help of the Farm Board. By mid-February, 1930, the acute crisis was past and any danger of panic at this time was averted.

The balance of the year 1930 was a period of moderate economic readjustment and by the opening of 1931, the whole situation showed a turn for the better. The general spirit by the end of March, 1931, was confident of recovery. Current press and economic opinions everywhere were voicing evidences of improvement. The Federal Reserve Board reported an improvement in the banking situation and a decrease in commercial failures and in increase in industrial output. Economic indices of the Federal Reserve Board showed that for the first three months of 1931, there were either increases or steadiness in payrolls, employment, wholesale prices, security prices, construction contracts, freight-car loadings, etc. *The New York Times* concluded that the depression had reached bottom and that recovery signs were showing. As the result of a survey of the country, the American Telephone and Telegraph Company announced that the economic tide had turned. The cost of living had decreased by 12 per cent, the rate of wages generally had been upheld. Unemployment, which reached its deep point in January, 1931, began to improve by March. A realignment of the public mind against extravagance had taken place and serious reforms had been achieved in business management.

Thus the economic picture of the United States at the end of March, 1931, showed not only an ending of the decline but a tendency to upturn. The United States was steadying up and it was clear that, if no external influences intervened, the country was making for general recovery.

But the collapse of Europe was yet to come.

The measures taken by the President had been effective in cushioning the shocks. The destitute had been cared for. There had been no industrial friction. The depression up to this time was not serious as depressions go. It is true that the stock crash was dramatic, and had brought great hardships upon individuals, but the productivity of the country still was running strongly. Unemployment had not exceeded that of the short post-war depression of 1921, or, in proportion, that of the depression of 1907–1908, from both of which recuperation had been easy and rapid.

The President commenting upon this period said, on June 15, 1931:

"As we look beyond the horizons of our own troubles and consider the events in other lands, we know that the main causes of the extreme violence and the long continuance of this depression came not from within but from outside the United States. Had our wild speculation, our stock promotion with its infinite losses and hardship to innocent people, our loose and extravagant business methods, and our unprecedented drought, been our only disasters we should have recovered months ago."

[State Papers, Vol. I, p. 574]

THE CRISIS FROM THE CENTRAL EUROPEAN COLLAPSE

Every morning from March, 1931, to July 1932, Hoover rose to find some new calamity from abroad. He was forced constantly to devise new methods to meet a repeated series of crises which swept from the whole world. He was forced to do it in the face of the Democratic opposition in Congress intent upon delaying recovery until the election, even though it would bring infinite misery upon the people. And despite them, the President forced measure after measure until, as the world recognizes, the tide was turned in 1932 and only retreated in the United States because of the reversal of the Hoover policies prior to the Inauguration.

The events of the fourteen months from the spring of 1931 to the summer of 1932 have never been more accurately nor more graphically summarized than by the President himself when he spoke eighteen months later on October 4, 1932, at Des Moines, Iowa. Although it somewhat anticipates the record of policies it is desirable to have a general picture of what he had to meet:

"I wish to describe one of the battles we have fought to save this Nation from a defeat that would have dragged farmers and city dwellers alike down to a common ruin. This battle was fought parallel with other battles on other fronts. Much of what I will tell you has been hitherto undisclosed. It had to be fought in silence, for it will be evident to you that had the whole of the forces in motion been made public at the time there would have been no hope of victory because of the panic through fear and destruction of confidence that very disclosure would have brought. . . ."

"Our own speculative boom had weakened our own economic structure, but the critical assaults and dangers swept upon us from foreign countries. We were therefore plunged into a battle against invading forces of destruction from abroad to preserve the financial integrity of our Government; to counteract the terrific forces of deflation aligned against us; to protect the debtor class who were being strangled by . . . the demands for payment of debt; to prevent our being pushed off the gold standard . . . to preserve the savings of the American people."

"We were fighting to hold the Gibraltar of world stability because only by holding this last fortress could we be saved from a crashing world, with a decade of misery and the very destruction of our form of government and our ideals of national life."

"When eighteen months ago the financial systems of Europe were no longer able to stand the strain of their war inheritances and of their after-war economic and political policies, an earthquake ran through forty nations. Financial panics; governments unable to meet their obligations; banks unable to pay their depositors; citizens, fearing inflation of currency, seeking to export their savings to foreign countries for safety; citizens of other nations demanding payment of their loans; financial and monetary systems either in collapse or remaining only in appearance. The shocks of this earthquake ran from Vienna to Berlin, from Berlin to

London, from London to Asia and South America. From all those countries they came to this country, to every city and farm in the United States."

"First one and then another of these forty nations either abandoned payment in gold of their obligations to other countries, or restricted payments by their citizens to foreign countries, so as practically to amount to at least temporary or partial repudiation of public and private debts. Every one of them in a frantic endeavor to reduce the expenditures of their citizens, imposed drastic restrictions upon their imports of goods. These events were not as children playing with blocks. They brought revolutions, mutinies, riots, downfalls of governments, and a seething of despair which threatened civilization."

"The first effect of these shocks on us was from foreign dumping of American securities on our markets which demoralized prices upon our exchanges, foreign buying power stagnated because .of their internal paralysis and this in turn stifled the markets for our farm and factory products, increased our unemployment and by piling up our surpluses demoralized our commodity prices."

"The frantic restrictive measures on exchanges and the abandonment of gold standards made it impossible for American citizens to collect billions of the moneys due to us for goods which our ciitzens had sold abroad, or short-term loans they had made to facilitate commerce. At the same time citizens of those countries demanded payment from our citizens of the moneys due for goods they had sold to our merchants and for securities they had sold in our country."

"Before the end foreign countries drained us of nearly a billion dollars of gold and a vast amount of other exchange."

"Then we had also to meet an attack upon our own flank by some of our own people, who, becoming infected with world fear and panic, withdrew vast sums from our own banks and hoarded it from the use of our own people, to the amount of $1,500,000,000. This brought its own train of failures and bankruptcies. Even worse, many of our less patriotic citizens started to export their money to foreign countries for fear we should be forced onto a paper money basis. . . ."

"Three of the great perils were invisible except to those who had the responsibility of dealing with the situation."

"The first of these perils was the steady strangulation of credit through the removal of $3,000,000,000 of gold and currency by foreign drains and by hoarding from the channels of our commerce and business. And let me remind you that credit is the lifeblood of business, or prices, and of jobs."

"Had the full consequences of this action been allowed to run their full extent, it would have resulted, under our system of currency and banking, in the deflation of credit anywhere from twenty to twenty-five billions, or the destruction of nearly half the immediate working capital of the country. There would have been almost a universal call for payment of debt which would have brought about universal bankruptcy, because property could not be converted into cash, no matter what its value."

"And there were other forces equally dangerous. The tax income of the Federal Government is largely based upon profits and income. As these profits and income disappeared, the Federal revenues fell by nearly one-half, and thus the very stability of the Federal Treasury was imperiled. The Government was compelled to borrow enormous sums to pay current expenses."

"The third peril, which we escaped only by the most drastic action, was that of being forced off the gold standard. . . ."

"I believe I can make clear why we were in danger of being forced off even with our theoretically large stocks of gold. I have told you of the enormous sums of gold and exchange drained from us by foreigners. You will realize also that our citizens who hoard Federal Reserve and some other forms of currency are in effect hoarding gold, because under the law we must maintain 40 per cent gold reserve behind such currency. Owing to the lack in the Federal Reserve System of the kind of securities required by the law for the additional 60 per cent of coverage of the currency, the Reserve System was forced to increase their gold reserve up to 75 per cent. Thus with $1,500,000,000 of hoarded currency there was in effect over $1,000,000,000 of gold hoarded by our own citizens."

"These drains had at one moment reduced the amount of gold we could spare for current payments to a point where the Secretary of the Treasury informed me that unless we could put into effect a remedy, we could not hold to the gold standard but two weeks longer because of inability to meet the demands of foreigners and our own citizens for gold."

"Being forced off the gold standard in the United States meant utter chaos. Never was our Nation in greater peril, not alone in banks and financial systems, money and currency, but that forebode dangers, moral and social chaos, with years of conflict and derangement."

"In the midst of this hurricane the Republican Administration kept a cool head and rejected every counsel of weakness and cowardice. Some of the reactionary economists urged that we should allow the liquidation to take its course until we had found bottom. Some people talked of vast issues of paper money. Some talked of suspending payments of Government issues. Some talked of setting up a council of national defense. Some talked foolishly of dictatorship—any of which would have produced panic itself. Some assured me that no man could propose increased taxes in the United States to balance the Budget in the midst of a depression and survive an election."

"We determined that we should not enter the morass of using the printing press for currency or bonds. All human experience has demonstrated that that path once taken cannot be stopped, and that the moral integrity of the Government would be sacrificed, because ultimately both currency and bonds would become valueless."

"We determined that we would not follow the advice of the bitter-end liquidationists and see the whole body of debtors of the United States brought to bankruptcy and the savings of our people brought to destruction."

"We determined we would stand up like men and render the credit of the United States Government impregnable through the drastic reduction of Government expenditures and increased revenues until we balanced our Budget. We determined that if necessary we should lend the full credit of the Government thus made impregnable, to aid private institutions to protect the debtor and the savings of our people."

"We decided upon changes in the Federal Reserve System which would make our gold active in commercial use and that we would keep the American dollar ringing true in every city in America and in the world; that we would expand credit to offset the contraction brought about by hoarding and foreign withdrawals; that we would strengthen the Federal Land Banks and all other mortgage institutions; that we would lend to the farmers for production; that we would protect the insurance companies, the building and loan associations, the savings banks, the country banks, and every other point of weakness."

"We determined to place the shield of the Federal Government in front of the local communities in protection of those in distress and that we would increase employment through profitable construction work with the aid of Government credit." [*State Papers, Vol. II, p. 298*]

Important as was this Des Moines speech to his own political fortunes, he could not tell the entire story, for fear of damaging the situation. He did not tell of that discouraging day in July, 1931, when he discovered the imminent collapse of a hundred American banks, from the Atlantic to the Pacific, because of the greedy purchase of European short-term bills.

(See page 411.) The breath of suspicion might again have set panic afloat. The President knew what bank panic would mean to the American home. The people were not to know until after his authority and leadership, which had so often saved them, had been destroyed by the election.

THE MORATORIUM ON INTERGOVERNMENTAL DEBTS

The financial panic which began in Austria in April, 1931, had spread over Germany and Central Europe.

The first major policy of the President to meet the shock of the European collapse was a moratorium upon intergovernmental debts over the whole world. These intergovernmental payments between all war nations exceeded $800,000,000 or $900,-000,000 annually and obviously were a crushing impediment to any recovery in Central Europe. The effect of their collapse was daily spreading over the world and had reached the United States through shrinkage of our export markets, falling prices of securities, of farm products and of raw materials, and increased unemployment. This country was daily becoming more apprehensive. Fear to extend credit, hoarding of currency and runs on banks were steadily pulling down our already weak banking structure.

The President's announcement of the moratorium proposal, on June 20, 1931, was in part:

"The American Government proposes the postponement during one year of all payments on intergovernmental debts, reparations, and relief debts, both principal and interest, of course not including obligations of governments held by private parties. Subject to confirmation by Congress, the American Government will postpone all payments upon the debts of foreign governments to the American Government payable during the fiscal year beginning July 1 next, conditional on a like postponement for one year of all payments on intergovernmental debts owing the important creditor powers."

"Wise and timely action should contribute to relieve the pressure of these adverse forces in foreign countries and should assist in the re-establishment of confidence, thus forwarding political peace and economic stability in the world."　　　　　　　　　　　　　　　[*State Papers, Vol. I, p. 591*]

The moratorium was finally accepted by all the fifteen governments involved on July 6, 1931, at which time the President issued the following statement:[1]

"I am glad to announce that the American proposal for one year's postponement of all intergovernmental debts and reparations has now been accepted in principle by all of the important creditor governments. . . ."

"The technical difficulties arising from many complicated international agreements, which involve the aggregate payment between governments of over $800,000,000 per annum, are now in the course of solution by the good will and earnest co-operation of governmental leaders everywhere."

"The American part of the plan is, of course, subject to the approval by Congress, but I have received the individual assurances of support from a very large majority of the members of both Senate and House, irrespective of political affiliations."

"The acceptance of this proposal has meant sacrifices by the American people and by the former Allied Governments, who are with all others suffering from world-wide depression and deficits in governmental budgets. The economic load most seriously oppressing the peoples of Germany and Central Europe will be immensely lightened."

"While the plan is particularly aimed to economic relief, yet economic relief means the swinging of men's minds from fear to confidence, the swinging of nations from the apprehension of disorder and governmental collapse to hope and confidence of the future. It means tangible aid to unemployment and agriculture. . . ." [*State Papers, Vol. I, pp. 595–6*]

Hoover described the entire negotiation at St. Louis on November 4, 1932, from which we can take but a few extracts:

"In the latter part of May a year ago Ambassador Sackett made an emergency journey from Berlin to see me to present to me the desperate situation of the German people. His evidence showed that under the burden of unbearable debts and the cost of war, that great nation was rapidly disintegrating. . . . They had lost all heart for the future and were steadily coming to the conclusion that nothing short of a revolution such as that which had taken place in Russia offered them any hope of deliverance."

". . . I took up that problem, not alone from the interest of this great

[1]For a fuller account of these negotiations see Myers and Newton, *The Hoover Administration,* pp. 90 ff.

mass of humanity but knowing that if that nation should fall, the reactions upon the rest of the world and the United States would be irreparable. President Von Hindenburg, knowing of Mr. Sackett's visit, sent me an appeal of a character between heads of nations without precedent in diplomatic history. That appeal was for preservation of a great people that I should use the good offices and prestige of the United States for their rescue."

"In order to give a year in which the world, particularly European nations, could come to a comprehension of what this disintegration was doing to civilization itself, I proposed the postponement of all international debts for one year."

"This was not easy to accomplish. Day after day, night after night, I was in communication first with one ambassador and then another, proposing methods to meet difficulties which arose, building up adjustments amongst different nations, until finally that year of postponement was secured."

"And it was not merely a postponement of a year in the payments on debts for which I was seeking. I was seeking for a year in which Europe could solemnly consider the situation into which she was drifting. I was seeking to remove from the mind of the world the fears of débâcle in civilization which were breaking down all security of credit and to bring to their attention the healing powers of international co-operation."

"You yourselves are familiar with the history of the year which followed. I know that the proposal of the moratorium diverted the entire current of thought and changed the history of what otherwise would have been a tragedy to the whole of civilization. It brought to new understanding the realization of the burdens under which Germany had been laboring."

"Under the impulses of these agreements and the recognition of the peril in which they stood, there came a great measure of redemption to the German people, a sense of greater security to the world from Lausanne."

"That agreement and the human sympathies which were evoked by that new understanding of the postwar difficulties in the world has served greatly in the healing of the wounds of the Great War."

[*State Papers, Vol. II, pp. 447–49*]

THE GERMAN STANDSTILL AGREEMENT

The result of the moratorium and its release of a great strain was an immediate wave of confidence, stiffening of prices, and a great sense of relief all over the world. Soon it became evident, however, that there was some other gigantic strain pressing on the world from which degeneration again began. It quickly developed that there was a huge undisclosed international indebtedness hanging over the world in the shape of short-term banking bills issued by banks to banks at high interest rates which could not be met.

The total of these bills according to the subsequent report of the Bank of International Settlements aggregated over $10,-000,000,000. Of them, huge amounts had been issued by Germany and the other Central European countries to the American, British, French, and Scandinavian and other banks of creditor countries. Over a hundred American banks held an aggregate of over $1,600,000,000 of Central European bills in amounts, in some cases, equal to their capital and surplus. Unless the problem was promptly dealt with, it meant that American banks holding over $15,000,000,000 of deposits might collapse.

The President had secured a conference in London to consider the situation, where he was represented by Secretaries Stimson and Mellon. But Europe simply stood paralyzed but talking. As the conference was getting nowhere, Hoover, on July 17, 1931, proposed the Standstill Agreement by which the banks of the world should agree to hold these bills for a stipulated time; and that a committee should be appointed to administer them. The President's proposal was accepted on July 23, 1931, after a good deal of growling and opposition by the banks. The banks of America, England, and France, in the meantime, had been busy trying to get their governments to loan money to Central Europe. In fact, this was at one stage recommended by Messrs. Mellon and Stimson. Hoover was, however, adamant that neither our Government nor our banks should loan any more money to Central Europe—that he could allow no more American money either private or public to be poured into this bucket without a bottom.

The Hoover plan as dispatched to this conference was as follows:

"1. On the political side, the United States hopes that, through mutual good will and understanding, the European nations may eliminate all friction, so that the world may rely upon the political stability of Europe."

"2. On the economic side, the present emergency is strictly a short-term credit crisis. . . . Germany has financed her economic activities to a very great extent through the medium of short-term foreign credits. . . . There is no reason why the present emergency cannot be immediately and definitely surmounted."

"(*a*) . . . The internal flight from the mark can be . . . successfully combated by the vigorous action of the German Government. . . ."

"(*b*) As to the external credits, we believe that the first approach to this problem is the development of a program that will permit the maintenance for an adequate period of time of the present outstanding lines of credit. . . ."

"In the development of such a program the governments of the countries haviing principal banking centers, including the United States, Belgium, France, Great Britain, Holland, Italy, Japan, and Switzerland, and other important banking centers, might well undertake to encourage their bankers so to organize as to permit the maintenance for an adequate period of time of present-day outstanding lines of credit to Germany. . . ."

"3. It is our belief that if such a program could be made promptly effective it would result in an immediate restoration of confidence. . . ."

"4. A committee should be selected by the Bank for International Settlements or created by some other appropriate method to secure co-operation on the following question."

"(*a*) In consultation with the banking interests in the different countries to provide for the renewal of the present volume of outstanding short-term credits from those countries."

"(*b*) In making an inquiry into the immediate further needs in credit of Germany."

"(*c*) In the development during the course of the next six or eight months of plans for a conversion of some proportion of the short-term credits to long-term credits."

Upon acceptance of these proposals, the President, on July 23, 1931, said:

"The London Conference has laid sound foundations for the establishment of stability in Germany."

"The major problem is one affecting primarily the banking and credit conditions and can best be solved by the voluntary co-operation of the bankers of the world rather than by governments with their conflicting interests. Such a basis of co-operation is assured."

"The program supplements the suspension of inter-governmental debts already in effect. . . ."

"The world is indebted to Premiers MacDonald, Laval, and Bruening, to Messrs. Stimson, Mellon, Grandi, Francqui, and other governmental representatives in this conference. The conference has demonstrated a fine spirit of conciliation and consideration amongst nations that will have lasting benefits in establishment of stability."

[*State Papers, Vol. I, p. 600*]

Upon the completion of these arrangements the whole world again breathed easier. The American situation improved visibly. The American people had again been saved from a bank panic.

THE CRISIS FOLLOWING THE BRITISH COLLAPSE

The British financial system proved too weak to withstand the shocks from failure of Central Europe, South America, etc., to meet their obligations to British banks. Their difficulties were accentuated by the continuing withdrawal of gold by France. Although the American bankers with the approval of Hoover loaned $200,000,000 to uphold the Bank of England, that institution defaulted on gold payments on September 21, 1931. The fears of the world were still further accentuated by the reports of a mutiny in the British Navy. The commodity and security markets over the most of Europe closed.

A new situation confronted the President. Heavy withdrawals of American gold and exchange began to foreign countries, thus shrinking our credit structure. Foreign countries began increasing tariffs and embargoing imports to protect their currencies. In the general world alarm our people began hoarding currency and gold and took out of circulation a total of over a billion dollars. Smaller and weaker banks again began to fail daily. Our prices were again falling and our unemployment increasing.

President Hoover now was confronted with a third great crisis. The first was the stock crash of 1929. The second was the Central European collapse of June and July, 1931. The new situation extended from September, 1931, to May, 1932. It arose not alone from the British collapse but from the default in gold payments in some twenty nations all followed by embargoes or restrictions on imports to protect their exchange. Revolutions occurred in many of them. During this period Hoover had the collaboration of Secretary of the Treasury Mellon, shortly to be succeeded by Ogden Mills, Secretary of Commerce Lamont, Under Secretary Ballantine and Mr. Henry M. Robinson. This new situation has been summarized by Messrs. Myers and Newton:

"(a) He was faced with renewed financial collapse abroad, following the British crisis, which again was breaking down our export markets and causing a domestic fall of prices and increased unemployment. It was placing decided strains on our security markets and our financial system. It was radiating fear and panic in the country.

(b) He was faced with the inadequacy of a badly organized banking system which already was weakened by the collapse of our own boom and that of Central Europe. As stated before, our system consisted of thousands of separate banks operating under different and uncorrelated state systems of supervision, with a superimposed Federal system. Our Federal Reserve System was not sufficiently flexible to meet the situation.

(c) He was faced with a fall of over $2,000,000,000 in Government revenues from the pre-depression normal, which forecast a budget deficit of over $1,500,000,000 at a time when expenditures on relief must be increased.

(d) He was faced with a Democratic-controlled House and an opposition Senate.

(e) Finally, a general calling of loans by the banks, under the pressure of the foreign situation and domestic hoarding, would mean the collapse of the banking and business system with the possibility of our being forced off the gold standard.

He now had two alternatives: first, the one advocated by many orthodox economists and bankers, of allowing unrestrained liquidation; second, that of adopting unprecedented measures. Many counselled the former course. The President realized that would mean infinite hardship through a general foreclosure of mortgages on homes and farms, through widespread receiverships for railways and industries, through the collapse of securities which would draw in its train the insurance companies and saving banks with a possibility of general repudiation, and finally through enormously extended unemployment, with all the social consequences of these great dangers to the entire nation. His view was that if America failed, the whole of modern civilization might be paralyzed.

Together with his Cabinet members and other advisers, he determined upon a broad program both of defense and offense to meet the new situation. His first move was to summon the heads of the Clearing House banks in New York and the heads of the leading insurance companies within reach, to meet with him on Sunday evening, the 4th of October.

At the same time, the President requested the ranking members of the banking, finance, and other committees in both Houses of Congress, including members of both political parties, to meet him at the White House the evening of the 6th."

MEETING OF THE NEW YORK BANK AND
INSURANCE HEADS

At the meeting with the New York bankers, the President stated:

". . . the situation since the British collapse ten days ago is approaching disaster at an accelerated speed until it has reached a panic condition. . . . That while a similar situation due to the economic breakdown in Central Europe in the spring . . . had been overcome by the action of the Government . . . the rise of recovery therefrom had been again stifled by the . . . fears over the British situation, those fears had been realized . . . we are again faced with a new and even worse emergency. . . . A survey shows . . . at least twenty other countries will be forced off the gold standard with Great Britain . . . inevitably they would increase tariffs, quotas and other restrictions on their imports . . . their depreciated currencies make further barriers to our exports . . . our prices of agricultural commodities are again further demoralized . . . current European attitude is that we will collapse next . . . a drain of at least one billion of the gold, hitherto here for refuge, by export and earmarking is in progress. . . . [causing] the greatest withdrawal of all time. . . . The Federal Reserve system is expanding credit by every device to meet the sapping of our credit foundations . . . the fears of the people were, since the British failed ten days ago, expressed in unprecedented hoarding of currency . . . the volume of hoarding has reached $150,000,000 a week . . . it totalled over $500,000,000 since the middle of August and $900,000,000 over May 1. . . . Security prices were demoralized by European selling and forced liquidations. . . . This with hoarding is breaking down an already weak banking system by compelling a sacrifice of their assets to meet withdrawals. . . . Bank failures in the twelve days since the British collapse already exceeded $500,000,-

ooo. . . . But beyond this, the banks in the large centers are calling interior loans to fortify themselves against foreign drains . . . the secondary banking centers being drained are fortifying themselves against it by calling loans from country banks and customers . . . the imminent collapse of banks threatens in many interior centers particularly in the the South and Midwest . . . [and] the inability of farmers and home owners to meet mortgage requirements. . . . In all, a senseless 'bankers' panic' and public fears are contributing to dragging the country down."

The President then stated his plan:

The bankers were to create a national credit association with $500,000,000 capital to support the financial structure, to be subscribed by all the banks in a ratio of 2 per cent of their deposits.

The insurance companies, with the Federal Farm Loan Banks, were to announce to the farmers and homeowners that no mortgages would be foreclosed so long as the borrowers made an honest effort to repay. He proposed that the institutions join in forming a national mortgage discount system to relieve permanently the "frozen" mortgage capital and the assets of financial institutions.

MEETING WITH CONGRESSIONAL LEADERS

On October 6, 1931, the President together with Secretary of the Treasury and the Chairman of the Federal Reserve Board met with the thirty Congressional leaders, members of the committees involved, whom he had summoned to his study at the White House. Mr. Newton's account of the meeting follows:

"President Hoover reviewed the whole economic situation very fully. He stated that we were faced with another crisis as great as that of the previous June, with the world much weaker to withstand the shock and with a banking system defective in organization. He announced that the time had come when national unity and the abandonment of political opposition were imperative. He recounted the agreement with the bankers and added that he had invited the Premier of France to visit the United States to discuss the world situation. He assured those present that he had a program for the immediate moment; that he would have further proposals when Congress met; that whether the Congress would be called earlier than its regular session on December 2 would depend upon the development of the crisis. He had prepared a memorandum of his proposals in the form of a joint public statement to be issued on the part of all present if they felt they could agree with it or with modifications of it."

"A frank discussion followed, in which practically all present took part. Generally speaking, both Republicans and Democrats alike expressed apprehension about the proposal to set up another governmental financial agency similar to the old War Finance Corporation, and hoped it would not be necessary and only a last resort. The desire not to project the Government into the business of lending money was quite generally expressed. . . ."

"The discussion lasted until one o'clock in the morning. Congressman Garner was outspoken in his lack of sympathy with the program, but the others present were helpful and cooperative. Senator Borah questioned the reference in the proposed statement to the Laval visit. To obviate any possible objection the Laval paragraph was phrased so that the President took the entire responsibility for its implications. The statement was finally agreed upon."

[*Hoover Administration, p. 125*]

This agreement in peacetime between the President and Congressional leaders representing both parties gave great hopes. Later on we shall see the extent of the performance by the Democratic members by their partisanship in the face of a great crisis. The memorandum of the President's policies appeared in the press the same morning and was as follows:

"The prolongation of the depression by the succession of events in Europe, affecting as they have both commodity and security prices, has produced in some localities in the United States an apprehension wholly unjustified in view of the thousand-fold resources we have for meeting any demand. Foolish alarm in these sections has been accompanied by wholly unjustifiable withdrawal of currency from the banks. Such action results in limiting the ability of the banks in these localities to extend credit to business men and farmers for the normal conduct of business, but beyond this to be prepared to meet the possibility of unreasoning demands of depositors the banks are compelled to place their assets in liquid form by sales of securities and restriction of credits, so as to enable them to meet unnecessary and unjustified drains. This affects the conduct of banking further afield. It is unnecessary to specify the unfortunate consequences of such a situation in the districts affected both in its further effect on national prices of agricultural products, upon securities and upon the normal conduct of business and employment of labor. It is a deflationary factor and a definite impediment to agricultural and business recovery."

"In order to deal with this wholly abnormal situation and to bring about an early restoration of confidence, unity of action on the part of our bankers and co-operative action on the part of the Government is essential. Therefore, I propose the following definite program of action, to which I ask our citizens to give their full co-operation."

"1. To mobilize the banking resources of the country to meet these conditions, I request the bankers of the Nation to form a national institution of at least $500,000,000. The purpose of this institution to be the rediscount of banking assets not now eligible for rediscount at the Federal Reserve Banks in order to assure our banks, being sound, that they may attain liquidity in case of necessity, and thereby enable them to continue their business without the restriction of credits or the sacrifice of their assets."

"It is a movement of national assurance and of unity of action in an American way to assist business, employment, and agriculture."

"2. On September 8, I requested the governors of the Federal Reserve Banks to endeavor to secure the co-operation of the bankers of their territory to make some advances on the security of the assets of closed banks or to take over some of these assets in order that the receivers of those banks may pay some dividends to their depositors in advance of what would otherwise be the case pending liquidation."

"3. In order that the above program may be carried out, I request the governors of the Federal Reserve Banks in each district to secure the appointment of working committees of bankers for each Reserve district to co-operate.

"4. I shall propose to the Congress that the eligibility provisions of the Federal Reserve Act should be broadened in order to give greater liquidity to the assets of the banks. . . ."

"5. Furthermore, if necessity requires, I will recommend the creation of a finance corporation similar in character and purpose to the War Finance Corporation, with available funds sufficient for any legitimate call in support of credit."

"6. I shall recommend to Congress the subscription of further capital stock by the government to the Federal Land Banks (as was done at their founding) to strengthen their resources so that the farmer may be assured of such accommodation as he may require. . . ."

"7. I have submitted the above-mentioned proposals which require legislation to the members of Congress, whose attendance I was able to secure on short notice at the evening's meeting—being largely the members of committees particularly concerned—and they approve of them in principle."

"8. Premier Laval of France is visiting the United States. It is my purpose to discuss with him the question of such further arrangements as are imperative during the period of the depression in respect of intergovernmental debts. . . ."

"9. The times call for unity of action on the part of our people. We have met with great difficulties not of our own making. It requires determination to overcome these difficulties and above all to restore and maintain confidence. Our people owe it not only to themselves and in their own interest, but they can by such an example of stability and purpose give hope and confidence in our own country and to the rest of the world."

THE NATIONAL CREDIT ASSOCIATION

As stated the President's move to meet the further weakening bank situation was to secure support by voluntary action outside of the Government.

In amplification of his statement at the meeting of bankers and insurance heads on October 4th he addressed the following letter to Mr. George Harrison, the governor of the Federal Reserve Bank of New York:

"DEAR MR. HARRISON:

"The request which I laid before the leading New York bankers last night for co-operation in unity of national action to assure credit security can, in the light of our discussions, be simplified to the following concrete measures:

"1. They are to take the lead in immediate formulation of a national institution with a capital of $500,000,000. The function of this institution to be:

"(a) The rediscount of bank assets not now eligible in the Federal Reserve System in order to assure the stability of banks throughout the country from attack by unreasoning depositors. That is to prevent bank failures."

"(b) Loans against the assets of closed banks to enable them to pay some early dividend to depositors and thus revive many business activities and relieve families from destitution."

"2. It is proposed that the capital be underwritten by the banks of the United States as a national effort, possibly with the support of the industrials. New York being the financial center of the Nation must of necessity assume both the initiative and the major burden. The effort should be participated in by the country at large by appropriate organization."

"3. As I said last night, we are in a degenerating vicious cycle. Economic events of Europe have demoralized our farm produce and security prices. This has given rise to an unsettlement of public mind. There have been in some localities foolish alarm over the stability of our credit structure and considerable withdrawals of currency. In consequence, bankers in many other parts of the country in fear of the possibility of such unreasoning demands of depositors have deemed it necessary to place their assets in such liquid form as to enable them to meet drains and runs. To do this they sell securities and restrict credit. The sale of securities demoralizes their price and jeopardizes other banks. The restriction on credit has grown greatly in the past few weeks. There are a multitude of complaints that farmers cannot secure loans for their livestock feeding or to carry their commodities until the markets improve. There are a multitude of complaints of business men that they cannot secure the usual credit to carry their operations on a normal basis and must discharge labor. There are complaints of manufacturers who use agricultural and other raw materials that they cannot secure credits beyond day to day needs with which to lay in their customary seasonal supplies. The effect of this is to thrust on the back of the farmer the load of carrying the Nation's stocks. The whole cumulative effect is today to decrease prices of commodities and securities and to spread the relations of the debtor and creditor."

"4. The only way to break this cycle is to restore confidence in the people at large. To do this requires major unified action that will give confidence to the country. It is this that I have asked of the New York bankers."

"5. I stated that if the New York banks will undertake to comply with this request, I will seek to secure assurance from the leaders of appropriate committees in Congress of both political parties to support my recommendation at the next session for

"(a) The extension of rediscount eligibility in the Federal Reserve System."

"(b) If necessity requires to recreate the War Finance Corporation with available funds sufficient for any emergency in our credit system."

"(c) To strengthen the Federal Farm Loan Bank System."

"Yours faithfully,

"HERBERT HOOVER."

The following day, the banks undertook this task. A corporation of $500,000,000 in capital was formed with George M. Reynolds, Chicago, chairman; Mortimer Buckner, New York, president; Daniel Wing, Boston; Livingston Jones, Philadelphia; Arthur Braun, Pittsburgh; John M. Miller, Jr., Richmond; John K. Ottley, Atlanta; Walter W. Smith, St. Louis; Edward W. Decker, Minneapolis; W. S. McLucas, Kansas City; Nathan Adams, Dallas; and Frank Anderson, San Francisco.

Acute banking situations in Louisiana, South Carolina, Tennessee, and California were given relief and closing prevented. In other centers the Association also met great pressures. In all the Association made loans to over 750 banks involving over $400,000,000, and unquestionably contributed to stiffen the situation temporarily. Under this impulse the country again showed distinct improvement during the last half of October and early November, but the situation then began to weaken and the much larger measures already indicated by the President became necessary.

MORTGAGE CREDIT ACTION

In addition to the problems of commercial banking (short-term credit), a further great credit strain lay in the real-estate mortgage field. Many of these mortgages had been placed at inflationary levels and owners could never pay out. Our inadequate banking system had permitted demand or short-term deposits to be invested in them and the banks were confronted with vast investments, most of them sound, out of which they could not meet depositors' demands or runs. The building and loan associations were in the same fix. These institutions could not give renewals and altogether pressures upon home-owners, farmers and others developed and widespread foreclosure threatened. The whole situation was driving the country to panic.

The President had, on October 4, asked the representatives of the larger life-insurance companies and savings banks to help by giving time and relief. They had objected to any publicity but promised to give extensions and relief from interest.

The President, on October 7, 1931, called to the White House a committee which he had appointed from important insurance, mortgage, building and loan, and construction interests. As stated elsewhere, he laid before them a proposal to

establish a national system of mortgage discount banks, somewhat comparable with the Federal Reserve System. As in that
system, the Government was to provide for the initial capital,
but in this case the capital should be absorbed by the members,
who were to embrace all kinds of institutions making real-estate
mortgages. He proposed that the mortgage banks thus created
should issue debentures for funds which would be available at
all times to discount up to 90 per cent any "live" mortgage, so
long as the 90 per cent did not exceed 60 per cent of the reasonable value of the property in normal times. He urged that
this was of the greatest emergency importance, that it would
thaw out billions of frozen assets. It would relieve the pressure
of foreclosure upon millions of farmers and home-owners.

Inquiry in Congress and elsewhere developed that it would
be impossible to secure enough support to so broad-visioned
and so clean-cut a proposal and the President, therefore, determined to attack it piecemeal with the hope that later on he
could develop it further. He therefore divided his attack on the
question into several segments, as will be seen later. (See
Agricultural Credit, page 442, Home Loan Banks, page 436,
R. F. C., page 427.)

In addition, grave situations arose over the inability of railways and others to refund bond issues and to meet interest
obligations which threatened the stability of all such investing
public institutions such as the life-insurance companies, etc.

HOOVER'S PROGRAM TO MEET THE CRISIS

By the convening of the Congress (December 7, 1931) the
situation required the full action forecast in the October
meeting, and still more.

The President then brought forward the most stupendous
program of Government action. His policies and program of
action were as follows:

1. Creation of the Reconstruction Finance Corporation with
authority to loan:

(a) to building and loan associations, savings banks, insurance companies, banks, and trust and mortgage companies to
enable them to meet the needs of their depositors;

(b) to railroads to prevent default on bonds and receiverships which would jeopardize the insurance companies, savings banks and small investors;

(c) to railroads and industry for improvements that would give employment;

(d) to public bodies for slum clearance, bridges, water-works, and other improvements of a reproductive character which would give employment;

2. Creation of the Home Loan Banks as the first step in banking reform and the amelioration of farm and home mortgage foreclosure.

3. Creation of a system of Agricultural Credit Banks to make livestock and production loans; further, to authorize the R. F. C. to make agricultural loans and to loan for export purposes.

4. Expansion of the capital of the Federal Land Banks by $125,000,000 which would expand their lending capacity by a billion; and entirely to revise their procedure.

5. The Federal Reserve Banks to loan to the closed banks on their assets so that they could at once pay their depositors without forced liquidation of their assets.

6. Expansion of the character of eligible paper for discount at the Federal Reserve Banks so as to protect the gold standard and at the same time spread out credit.

7. Expansion of credit to meet the shrinkage caused by European action and local withdrawals with open market operations and easy money policies through the Federal Reserve Banks.

8. Reform of the banking laws at once.

9. Reform of the railway regulation laws at once.

10. Immediate reform of the bankruptcy laws so as to promote orderly adjustment of inflated debt.

11. At a little later stage, he proposed Federal loans to needy states for direct relief and further appropriations of Farm Board surpluses of wheat and cotton for relief.

12. Further expansion of public works.

13. Appointment of a World War Debt Commission to consider that question.

14. Finding new taxes.

15. Reducing the ordinary Government expenses.

16. Balancing the Federal Budget.

The President proposed this program to a hostile Congress bent upon destruction of his every policy and proposal, in the hopes that by the plunge of the country into the depths they would win an election. The Message containing the proposal ap-

pealed for national unity and put in definite form his proposed
financial measures.

"Our first step toward recovery is to re-establish confidence and thus
restore the flow of credit which is the very basis of our economic life.
We must put some steel beams in the foundations of our credit structure."

"The recommendations which I here lay before the Congress are designed to meet these needs by strengthening financial, industrial, and
agricultural life through the medium of our existing institutions, and
thus to avoid the entry of the Government into competition with private
business."

Federal Government Finance

"The first requirement of confidence and of economic recovery is financial stability of the United States Government. I must at this time
call attention to the magnitude of the deficits which have developed and
the resulting necessity for determined and courageous policies. These
deficits arise in the main from the heavy decrease in tax receipts due to
the depression and to the increase in expenditure on construction in aid
to unemployment, aids to agriculture, and upon services to veterans."

[*State Papers, Vol. II, p. 47*]

"The Budget for the fiscal year beginning July 1 next, after allowing
for some increase of taxes under the present laws and after allowing for
drastic reduction in expenditures, still indicates a deficit of $1,417,-
000,000. After offsetting the statutory debt retirements this would
indicate an increase in the national debt for the fiscal year 1933 of about
$921,000,000."

"Several conclusions are inevitable. We must have insistent and determined reduction in Government expenses. We must face a temporary
increase in taxes. Such increase should not cover the whole of these
deficits or it will retard recovery. We must partially finance the deficit by
borrowing."

Federal Land Banks

"I recommend that the Congress authorize the subscription by the
Treasury of further capital to the Federal Land Banks. It is urgent that
the banks be supported so as to stabilize the market values of their bonds
and thus secure capital for the farmers at low rates."

Deposits in Closed Banks

"A method should be devised to make available quickly to depositors
some portion of their deposits in closed banks as the assets of such banks

may warrant. Such provision would go far to relieve distress in a multitude of families, would stabilize values in many communities, and would liberate working capital to thousands of concerns. I recommend that measures be enacted promptly to accomplish these results."

Home-Loan Discount Banks

"I recommend the establishment of a system of home-loan discount banks as the necessary companion in our financial structure of the Federal Reserve Banks and our Federal Land Banks. Such action will relieve present distressing pressures against home and farm property owners. It will relieve pressures upon and give added strength to building and loan associations, savings banks, and deposit banks, engaged in extending such credits. Such action would further decentralize our credit structure. It would revive residential construction and employment. It would enable such loaning institutions more effectually to promote home ownership."

Reconstruction Finance Corporation

"In order that the public may be absolutely assured and that the Government may be in position to meet any public necessity, I recommend that an emergency Reconstruction Corporation of the nature of the former War Finance Corporation should be established. It may not be necessary to use such an instrumentality very extensively. The very existence of such a bulwark will strengthen confidence. The Treasury should be authorized to subscribe a reasonable capital to it, and it should be given authority to issue its own debentures. It should be placed in liquidation at the end of two years. Its purpose is by strengthening the weak spots to thus liberate the full strength of the Nation's resources. It should be in position to facilitate exports by American agencies; make advances to agricultural credit agencies where necessary to protect and aid the agricultural industry; to make temporary advances upon proper securities to established industries, railways, and financial institutions which cannot otherwise secure credit, and where such advances will protect the credit structure and stimulate employment."

Federal Reserve Eligibility

"On October 6 I issued a statement that I should recommend to the Congress an extension during emergencies of the eligibility provisions in the Federal Reserve Act. This statement was approved by a representative gathering of the members of both Houses of the Congress, including members of the appropriate committees. It was approved by the officials of the Treasury Department, and I understand such an extension has been approved by a majority of the governors of the Federal Reserve banks."

Banking Laws

"Our people have a right to a banking system in which their deposits shall be safeguarded and the flow of credit less subject to storms. The need of a sounder system is plainly shown by the extent of bank failures. I recommend the prompt improvement of the banking laws. Changed financial conditions and commercial practices must be met. The Congress should investigate the need for separation between different kinds of banking; an enlargement of branch banking under proper restrictions; and the methods by which enlarged membership in the Federal Reserve system may be brought about. . . ."

Railways

"The railways present one of our immediate and pressing problems. They are and must remain the backbone of our transportation system. Their prosperity is interrelated with the prosperity of all industries. . . ."

"The well-maintained and successful operation and the stability of railway finances are of primary importance to economic recovery. . . ."

"The Interstate Commerce Commission has made important and far-reaching recommendations upon the whole subject."

HOOVER'S FURTHER PROGRAM TO MEET THE CRISIS

Later, as the session progressed and as the economic situation developed, the President added further recommendations, which can be summarized as follows:

1. He proposed to make Government bonds eligible for coverage of the currency in the Federal Reserve System to prevent our being forced off the gold standard.

2. In consequence of Congressional refusal of parts of the original program, he subsequently returned to the charge, asking Congress to authorize the Reconstruction Finance Corporation to lend up to $1,800,000,000 for reproductive public and semi-public and industrial works, slum clearance, etc., to states, municipalities, etc.

3. He asked authority for the Reconstruction Finance Corporation to establish a system of Agricultural Credit Banks.

4. He urged reform of the bankruptcy laws to facilitate readjustment of debt.

5. He proposed to lend $300,000,000 to the states for direct relief of distress.

THE RECONSTRUCTION FINANCE CORPORATION

The President's proposal was that $500,000,000 of capital should be provided to a temporary corporation by the Government with authority to issue up to $3,000,000,000 of tax exempt bonds; that the corporation should have the widest powers to extend credit against security to building and loan associations, savings banks, real estate and mortgage concerns; to banks, trust and insurance companies; to railways and industries; to states and municipalities and public bodies for new construction work, these proposals were whittled down in committee and in Congress, both the capital and scope being reduced.

The Congress greatly delayed action, even taking a two weeks' Christmas holiday. On January 4, the President sent an urgent Message:

"The need is manifestly even more urgent than at the date of my Message a month ago. I should be derelict in my duty if I did not at this time emphasize the paramount importance to the Nation of constructive action. . . . We can and must replace the unjustifiable fear in the country with confidence. Our hope and confidence for the future rest upon unity of our people and of the Government in prompt and courageous action."

[State Papers, Vol. II, p. 102]

The bill having finally passed, the President signed it on January 22, 1932, although he was disappointed at the failure to grant all the credit power he had requested. In a press statement, he said:

"It brings into being a powerful organization with adequate resources, able to strengthen weaknesses that may develop in our credit, banking and railway structure, in order to permit business and industry to carry on normal activities free from the fear of unexpected shocks and retarding influences."

"Its purpose is to stop deflation in agriculture and industry and thus to increase employment by the restoration of men to their normal jobs. It is not created for the aid of big industries or big banks. Such institutions are amply able to take care of themselves. It is created for the support of the smaller banks and financial institutions, and through rendering their resources liquid to give renewed support to business, industry, and agriculture. It should give opportunity to mobilize the gigantic strength of our country for recovery." [State Papers, Vol. II, p. 106]

He at once appointed the head of the Federal Reserve, Eugene Meyer, chairman, General Charles G. Dawes, president, with Secretary Ogden Mills and Messrs. Harvey C. Couch, Jesse H. Jones, Gardner Cowles, and Wilson McCarthy as directors. On January 24, the Board met with the President and stated they were already functioning and making loans. The President expressed the hope that they would use every power to stop bank failures at once.

The effect of the Corporation upon confidence was positive. The following table shows monthly bank failures and the loans made by the R. F. C. in corresponding months:

[In millions of dollars]

Bank Failures (net closings in deposits)		R. F. C. Loans to Credit Institutions
1931		
September	—229.2	
October	—466.3	
(National Credit Association formed)		
November	— 54.9	
December	—258.5	
1932		
January	—207.9	
(R. F. C. formed)		
February	— 42.5	45.0
March	+ 4.1	127.0
April	— 20.6	188.0
May	— 1.1	236.0
June	—121.2	331.0
(Congressional crisis)		
July	+ 21.2	123.0
August	+ 4.0	105.0
September	+ 0.6	41.0
October	+ 18.4	31.0
(Roosevelt elected)		
November	— 30.8	32.0
December	— 63.6	65.0
1933		
January	—120.5	64.0

EXPANSION OF THE POWERS OF THE R. F. C.

Early in May, the President began a series of conferences with members of Congress to secure the full grant of powers to the R. F. C. originally asked, and to extend its work in still other directions. Through those powers he proposed that four major things could be accomplished. First, the Corporation should make loans to public and semi-public institutions for construction of reproductive works such as toll bridges, water-works, clearance of slums; second, to industry for modernization of plant and housing; third, to agriculture to create a real system of "production credits"; fourth, to the creation of emergency export credits.

The proposals for loans from the Reconstruction Finance Corporation for "income-producing works" having met some criticism which might delay action, the President stated at the press conference on May 13, 1932:

"When our people recover from frozen confidence then our credit machinery will begin to function once more on a normal basis and there will be no need to exercise the emergency powers already vested in any of our governmental agencies or the further extensions we are proposing for the Reconstruction Corporation. If by unity of action these extensions of powers are kept within the limits I have proposed they do not affect the Budget. They do not constitute a drain on the taxpayer. They constitute temporary mobilization of timid capital for positive and definite purpose of speeding the recovery of business, agriculture, and employment."

"I have, however, no taste for any such emergency powers in the Government. But we are fighting the economic consequences of over-liquidation and unjustified fear as to the future of the United States. The battle to set our economic machine in motion in this emergency takes new forms and requires new tactics from time to time. We used such emergency powers to win the war; we can use them to fight the depression, the misery and suffering from which are equally great."

[State Papers, Vol. II, p. 188]

In the meantime, another panic situation had arisen owing to the actions of Congress. (See page 478.) On that occasion, May 31, 1932, President Hoover addressed the Senate in person, mostly upon other measures but including restoration of the original powers and expansion of the Reconstruction Finance Corporation.

". . . that there may be no failure . . . authorization to the Reconstruction Finance Corporation to loan up to $300,000,000 to state governments . . . relief to distress. . . ."

". . . to aid unemployment and to avoid wasteful expansion of public works . . . an authority to the Reconstruction Corporation to increase its issues of its securities to the maximum of $3,000,000,000 in order that it may extend its services both in aid to employment and agriculture on a wide scale. Under the methods proposed the Corporation is to be (a) authorized to buy bonds from political subdivisions or public bodies to aid in construction of income-producing or self-liquidating projects; (b) to make loans to established enterprise upon adequate security, for advancement of sound projects that will increase employment but safeguarded by requirement that some portion of outside capital is also provided; (c) to divert a portion of the unexpended authorizations of agricultural loans through the Secretary of Agriculture to finance the exports of agricultural products; (d) to make loans to institutions upon security of agricultural commodities to assure the carrying of normal stocks of these commodities and thus by stabilizing their loan value to steady their price levels; (e) to make loans to the Federal Farm Board to enable extension of finance of farm co-operatives."

[*State Papers, Vol. II, p. 201*]

On June 5, 1932, the President published a review of the R. F. C.'s work up to that time:

". . . in the fourteen weeks of its life loans of about $500,000,000 were authorized to something like 4000 banks, agricultural credit corporations, life insurance companies and other financial institutions, and in addition thereto about $170,000,000 to railroads."

"Of nearly 3000 borrowing banks, more than 70 per cent are located in towns of 5000 in population or less; while 84 per cent are located in towns of 25,000 in population or less; and that only 4.5 per cent of money loaned to banks has gone to institutions in cities of over 1,000,000 in population."

"In all these communities, these banks have been able to meet the demands of their depositors and to minimize the necessity of forced collections, foreclosures and sales of securities and have thus contributed to protect community values. One hundred and twenty-five closed banks have either been reopened or their depositors paid out. And bank failures which amounted to nearly 100 a week when the Corporation began are now down to about the casualties of normal times. It is estimated that altogether over 10,000,000 individual depositors borrowers have been benefited by the margins provided by the Reconstruction Finance Corporation to these banks."

"Over 250 building and loan associations have borrowed from the Corporation in order to enable them on the one hand to make their routine payments to their depositors and participants, and on the other to avoid the foreclosures of mortgages. The result again has been benefits to hundreds of thousands of individuals."

"In the agricultural field, the Corporation has underwritten or subscribed for issues placing $68,000,000 of the Federal Intermediate Credit Bank debentures, the whole of which sums are loaned directly to farmers for production and marketing purposes. Loans have been made to a number of agricultural, market and live stock finance corporations, which in turn has enabled them to extend and continue loans particularly upon livestock and loans to a great number of farmers. Beyond this, loans to the extent of $75,000,000 have been made directly to about 450,000 farmers for seed purposes through the Department of Agriculture. Altogether probably 1,000,000 individual farmers have been directly or indirectly helped."

"The net result of approximately $170,000,000 authorized loans to railroads has been on one hand to increase employment by continuing necessary construction work, and on the other hand by preventing receiverships, and thus safeguarding the great investments of the trustee institutions such as insurance companies, savings banks, etc. The deterioration of service and other standards which accompany receiverships have also been avoided."

"Generally about $670,000,000 of loans authorized to date have filtered through to the use and protection of a very large segment of the whole country. An encouraging feature is that the repayment of loans has begun, some $30,000,000 having been repaid."

[*State Papers, Vol. II, pp. 203–5*]

By June 24, the Senate and House had each passed bills extending the powers of the R. F. C. but carrying provisions of political purpose, which were intolerable in good government. The President made an effort with their conferees to secure revision so as to avoid veto and delay.

On July 11, 1932, the Democratic leaders insisted on passing their vote-catching bill for universal loans from the R. F. C. The President vetoed the bill, saying:

"On the 31st of May last I addressed the Senate recommending further definite and large-scale measures to aid in relief of distress and unemployment imposed upon us by the continued degeneration in the world economic situation."

"The creation of the Reconstruction Finance Corporation itself was warranted only as a temporary measure to safely pass a grave national emergency which would otherwise have plunged us into destructive panic in consequence of the financial collapse in Europe. Its purpose was to preserve the credit structure of the Nation and thereby protect every individual in his employment, his farm, his bank deposits, his insurance policy, and his other savings."

"So far as those portions of the proposed extension of authority to the Corporation provide authorization temporarily to finance self-liquidating works up to the sum of $1,500,000,000, it is in accord with my recommendations. The section dealing with agricultural relief does not provide for loans to sound institutions upon the security of agricultural products so sorely needed at the present time."

". . . my major objection to the measure, as now formulated, lies in the inclusion of an extraordinary extension of authority to the Reconstruction Corporation to make loans to 'individuals, to trusts, estates, partnerships, corporations (public or quasi-public or private), to associations, joint-stock companies, states, political subdivisions of states, municipalities, or political subdivisions thereof.' The following objections are directed to this particular provision:"

"This expansion of authority of the Reconstruction Corporation would mean loans against security for any conceivable purpose on any conceivable security for anybody who wants money."

"The purpose of the expansion is no longer in the spirit of solving a great major emergency but to establish a privilege whether it serves a great national end or not."

"This proposal violates every sound principle of public finance and of Government. Never before has so dangerous a suggestion been seriously made to our country. Never before has so much power for evil been placed at the unlimited discretion of seven individuals."

"In view of the short time left to the Congress for consideration of this legislation and of the urgent need for sound relief measures, the necessity of which I have on several occasions urged upon the Congress, I recommend that a compromise should be reached upon terms suggested by members of both Houses and both parties, and that the Congress should not adjourn until this is accomplished. Such compromise proposal should embrace:"

". . . provisions for loans to states in amount of $300,000,000 for the care of distress in states where needed."

". . . loans for construction work of projects of self-liquidating character but also essential aids to agriculture."

"That the Corporation be authorized to increase its issues of capital by $1,800,000,000 for these purposes."

"With the utmost seriousness I urge the Congress to enact a relief measure, but I cannot approve the measure before me, fraught as it is with possibilities of misfeasance and special privileges, so impracticable of administration, so dangerous to public credit and so damaging to our whole conception of governmental relations to the people as to bring far more distress than it will cure." [*State Papers, Vol. II, p. 228*]

"I expect to sign the Relief Bill on Tuesday. . . ."

"Its three major features are:"

"First—Through provision of $300,000,000 of temporary loans by the Reconstruction Corporation to such states as are absolutely unable to finance the relief of distress."

"Second—Through the provision of $1,500,000,000 of loans by the Reconstruction Corporation for reproductive construction work of public character, on terms which will be repaid, we should ultimately be able to find employment for hundreds of thousands of people without drain on the taxpayer."

"Third—Through the broadening of the powers of the Corporation in the character of loans it can make to assist agriculture, we should materially improve the position of the farmer."

"While there are some secondary features of the measure to which I have objection, they are not so great as to warrant refusal to approve the measure in the face of the great service that the major provisions will be to the Nation. It is a strong step toward recovery." [*State Papers, Vol. II, p. 235*]

This measure provided the powers, originally asked for eight months before, to make loans for construction work to public and private agencies and to establish wider credit for agriculture.

On July 17, 1932, the extension of powers to the Reconstruction Finance Corporation was passed, mainly in the form insisted upon by the President. The House bill had contained Speaker Garner's provisions for publication of the Reconstruction Finance Corporation loans. The President appealed to the Senate to eliminate this as it would cause runs upon banks, and affect adversely insurance companies, and building and loan associations. The Senate modified the provision slightly and both Democratic and Republican senators made a public statement that as amended it would necessitate only a confidential communication to the House and Senate.

CHANGE IN R. F. C. ADMINISTRATION

On June 6, General Dawes resigned as president of the R. F. C. The Central Republic Bank of Chicago, of which he had been one of the founders, had fallen into difficulty and although he had not been an official of the bank for many years, he felt he must resign from the R. F. C. The President appointed Charles A. Miller of Utica, New York, to succeed him.

On July 26, Eugene Meyer, who was also governor of the Federal Reserve Board, retired from the R. F. C. Former Senator Atlee Pomerene was appointed his successor. The President was determined that the R. F. C. should never be charged with partisan action. He therefore selected an outstanding Democrat so that there could be no such charge.

DAWES LOAN

The Democratic Party did, however, charge the President with having used the R. F. C. to favor General Dawes's bank. To this, Hoover made vigorous reply at St. Louis, on November 4, 1932. As a matter of fact, General Dawes never asked for help. He preferred to close the bank. It was the other banks of Chicago who demanded help and they were led by Melvin A. Traylor, president of the First National Bank, who was a leading Democrat and at that time discussed as a Democratic candidate for the Presidency. The loan was insisted upon by Messrs. Jones, McCarthy, and Couch, the Democratic members of the R. F. C. Board, as absolutely necessary to stop a financial panic in Chicago.

PUBLICATION OF R. F. C. LOANS

The reversal of a minor Hoover policy by Democratic leaders had some importance in creating the bank panic on March 4, 1933. It was his policy not to publish the names of borrowers from the R. F. C. as that would, with the nervous temper of the times, create suspicions as to the financial standing of any particular bank, insurance company or building and loan association, if it were known that they were borrowing from the

Government. The full details were, however, sent confidentially to the clerks of the House and Senate.

The Garner Amendment, mentioned on page 433, was publicly proclaimed by Democratic senators as not calling for publication. But in January, 1933, Mr. Garner insisted upon publication of this information which was in the hands of the clerk of the House. Appeals to the President-elect by some of his friends to use his influence received no response.[1]

On March 5, 1933, *The New York Herald Tribune* said that Congress "virtually sealed the fate of the Corporation and of the banks by insisting on including in the relief bill of last July the indefensibly vicious provision of detailed publicity of all loans."

We may quote also from two Democratic leaders:

Chairman Pomerene, of the Reconstruction Finance Corporation, later made a statement to the press saying:

"The banks which got R. F. C. loans were good banks. The loans were amply secured as the law required. Request for loans did not mean that applicant banks were unsound, but some silly persons construed them that way. It was the most damnable and vicious thing that was ever done. It almost counteracted all the good that we had been able to do."

and

"Hon. W. Warren Barbour,
United States Senate,
Washington, D. C.

Jersey City
Apr. 5, 1933

The last publication of Reconstruction Finance loans to banks did incalculable harm. To continue these publications will mean further runs on banks and ruin to many. Again I vehemently repeat my protest as governor of New Jersey to the publication of the names of banks. Such publication can serve no purpose and only serves to undo the good work which the President has accomplished in restoring confidence. Senator Robinson deserves support and co-operation in his effort to remedy this situation.

A. HARRY MOORE,
Governor of New Jersey"

RECORD OF THE R. F. C.

The record of work of the R. F. C. under President Hoover's Administration (to the end of February, 1933) is only partly indicated by figures. Much of its efficacy was in prevention.

[1] It is interesting to note that after the panic Hoover's policy of non-publication was resumed by Roosevelt.

During this time

Loans authorized were.............$2,297,434,592
Actually disbursed were............ 1,842,151,761
Repaid were...................... 363,391,326
Outstanding were.................. 1,473,850,437

Of these loans those drawn and outstanding were:

Building and loan associations and
    mortgage loan companies........... $197,177,382
Insurance companies................ 63,060,480
Federal Land Banks and other agricul-
    tural loans...................... 73,016,670
Railroads 296,229,010
Banks and trust companies........... 669,218,661

Further loans authorized to borrowers but not yet drawn included $38,000,000 to building and loan and mortgage companies and $81,000,000 to Federal Land Banks and other agricultural credits. In addition to direct loans for agricultural purposes a further sum of $130,000,000 was loaned to farmers through the Secretary of Agriculture. A total of $210,115,000 had been authorized for direct relief and a total of $159,500,000 disbursed. A total of $179,500,000 of self-liquidating public works, slum clearance, etc., had been settled but only $18,600,-000 actually drawn due to time required for engineering plans, etc.; and a further $500,000,000 was in advanced stage of preparation. These sums were loaned to over 6000 different institutions and public bodies of which 92 per cent by numbers were in towns of less than 100,000 population—and loans were authorized to over 10,000 different institutions. The largest part of all these loans have now been repaid or will be soon liquidated. The real service of the R. F. C. was that literally millions of people were preserved from loss of their savings and bankruptcy.

HOME LOAN BANKS

We have referred elsewhere to the Hoover proposal to create a permanent National Mortgage Discount System which would parallel the Federal Reserve System. (See Banking Reform, page 332, and Emergency Credit, page 422.) As this seemed impossible of immediate accomplishment he determined to establish such a discount system over the more limited field of home and farm mortgages. To advance this he secured the support of the committees of the National Housing Conference then about to assemble. On November 13, 1931, he publicly and in detail stated his plan. After discussing its importance both to the emergency and as a measure of vast permanent importance he gave the following details:

"I shall propose to Congress the establishment of a system of Home Loan Discount Banks for four purposes:"

"1. For the present emergency purpose of relieving the financial strains upon sound building and loan associations, savings banks, deposit banks, and farm loan banks that have been giving credit through the medium of small mortgage loans upon urban and farm properties used for homes. Thereby to relieve pressures upon home and farm owners."

"2. To put the various types of institutions loaning on mortgage in a position to assist in the revival of home construction in many parts of the country and with its resultant increase in employment."

"3. To safeguard against the repetition of such experiences in the future."

"4. For the long-view purpose of strengthening such institutions in the promotion of home ownership particularly through the financial strength thus made available to building and loan associations."

"The immediate credit situation has for the time being in many parts of the country restricted severely the activities of building and loan associations, deposit banks including country banks, and savings departments, savings banks, and farm loan companies in such a fashion that they are not only not able to extend credit through new mortgages to home and farm owners, but are only too often unable to renew mortgages or give consideration to those in difficulty with resultant great hardships to borrowers and a definite depreciation of real estate values in the areas where such pressures exist."

"A considerable part of our unemployment is due to stagnation in residential construction."

"The high importance of residential construction as a matter of employment is indicated by the fact that more than 200,000 individual homes are erected annually in normal times, which with initial furnishings contribute more than $2,000,000,000 to our construction and other industries. This construction has greatly diminished. Its revival would provide for employment in the most vital way. As a people we need at all times the encouragement of home ownership, and a large part of such action is only possible through an opportunity to obtain long-term loans payable in installments. It is urgently important, therefore, that we provide some method for bringing into continuing and steady action the great facilities of such of these great national and local loaning concerns as have been under pressure and should provide against such difficulties in the future."

"The farm mortgage situation presents many difficulties to which this plan would give aid."

"(a) That there be established twelve Home Loan Discount Banks . . . under the direction of a Federal Home Loan Board."

"(b) The capital of these discount banks shall be initially a minimum of five to thirty million as may be determined by the Federal Board. . . ."

"(c) The proposed discount banks to make no initial or direct mortgages but to loan only upon the obligations of the loaning institutions secured by the mortgage loans as collateral so as to assure and expand the functioning of such institutions."

"(d) Building and loan associations, saving banks, deposit banks, farm loan banks, etc., may become members of the System. . . ."

"(e) The mortgage loans eligible for collateral shall not exceed $15,000 each and shall be limited to urban and farm property used for home purposes."

"(f) The maximum amount to be advanced against the mortgage collateral not to exceed more than 50 per cent of the unpaid balance on unamortized or short-term mortgage loans and not more than 60 per cent of the unpaid balance of amortized long-term mortgages. . . ."

"(g) The discount banks as their needs require from time to time to issue bonds or short-term notes to investors to an amount not to exceed in the aggregate twelve times the capital of the issuing bank. . . ."

"(h) If the aggregate initial capital of the discount banks should in the beginning be fixed at $150,000,000, it would be possible for the twelve banks to finance approximately something over $1,800,000,000 of advance to the borrowing institutions which could be further expanded by increase in their capital."

"(i) It is proposed to find the initial capital stock for the discount banks in much the same way, in so far as is applicable, as the capital was found for the Federal Reserve Banks . . . first offer the capital to the institutions which would participate in the service. . . . And as was provided in respect to the Federal Reserve Banks, if the initial capital is not wholly thus provided, it should be subscribed by the Federal Government; and, further, somewhat as was provided in the case of the Federal Land Banks, other institutions using the facilities of the discount banks should be required to purchase from time to time from the Government some proportionate amount of its holdings of stock if there be any. In this manner any Government capital will gradually pass over to private owner-ship as was the case in the Federal Land Bank. . . ."

"There is no element of inflation in the plan but simply a better organization of credit for these purposes. . . ."

[*State Papers, Vol. II, p. 33*]

On December 2, 1931, the plan received the vigorous approval of the Housing Conference comprised of a thousand members under Secretary Wilbur and through them received active support from every state. (See page 385.)

The President recommended the creation of the system to Congress in his Message of December 8, 1931.

Representative Luce introduced the Home Loan Bank Bill in the House on December 10, and Senator Watson introduced it to the Senate. The bill was sabotaged and delayed for nearly nine months. Senator Couzens led the opposition. Finally it was passed but considerably attenuated in its functions and restricted as to its action.[1]

On July 22, 1932, the bill was finally signed by the President. It made available $1,250,000,000 of credits to home owners.

In signing the bill the President said:

"This institution has been created on the general lines advocated by me in a statement to the press on November 13 last. . . . Its purpose is to establish a series of discount banks for home mortgages, performing a function for home owners somewhat similar to that performed in the commercial field by the Federal Reserve Banks through their discount facilities."

"There are to be eight to twelve such banks established in different parts of the country with a total capital of $125,000,000 to be initially subscribed by the Reconstruction Finance Corporation. Building and loan associations, savings banks, insurance companies, etc., are to be eligible for membership in the system. Member institutions are required to subscribe for stock of the Home Loan Banks and to absorb gradually the capital and they may borrow from the banks upon their notes to be secured by the collateral of sound home mortgages."

"The Home Loan Banks are in turn to obtain the resources required by them through the issue of debentures and notes. These notes have back of them the obligation of the members, the mortgages pledged as securities of such obligations and the capital of the Home Loan Banks themselves. The debentures and notes thus have a triple security."

[1]The Roosevelt Administration has reinstated some part of Hoover's ideas.

"The creation of these institutions does not involve the Government in business except in the initial work of the Reconstruction Corporation, and the setting up of the Board in Washington to determine standards of practice. The cost of this Board in Washington is to be paid by the Home Loan Banks and the banks are to be owned and run by their members. In effect it is using the good offices of the Government and the Reconstruction Finance Corporation to set up co-operative action amongst these member institutions to mobilize their credit and resources. There are several thousand institutions eligible for membership."

"The purpose of the system is both to meet the present emergency and to build up home ownership on more favorable terms than exist to-day . . . in thousands of instances they have been unable to renew existing mortgages with resultant foreclosures and great hardships."

"A considerable part of our unemployment is due to stagnation in residential construction."

"In the long view we need at all times to encourage home ownership and for such encouragement it must be possible for home owners to obtain long-term loans payable in installments. These institutions should provide the method for bringing into continuous and steady action the great home loaning associations which are so greatly restricted due to present pressures."   [*State Papers, Vol. II, pp. 238–9*]

On August 6, the President announced the appointment of the members of the Home Loan Bank Board. They were Franklin W. Fort, chairman, Nathan Miller, William E. Best, H. Morton Bodfish and John M. Gries. All were men experienced in mortgage banking and building loan association work. They had to be drafted to the work by the President. Shortly after the Board was formed, Chairman Fort issued a moving appeal to the country to stay foreclosures upon homes until the bank could be brought into action. It met a fine response.

Referring to the Home Loan Banks, President Hoover said at Cleveland, on October 15, 1932:

"The literally thousands of heart-breaking instances of inability of working people to attain renewal of expiring mortgages on favorable terms, and the consequent loss of their homes, have been one of the tragedies of this depression. Had the Democratic House of Representatives acted upon this measure at the time of its recommendation, we would have saved hundreds of thousands of these tragedies."

"I finally secured the passage of that bill through the Congress. Those

banks will be operating by the end of this month. The system is not as perfect as I would wish, yet it has already had one immensely beneficial effect, and there will be others."
[State Papers, Vol. II, p. 337]

Speaking at Indianapolis on October 28, 1932, he said:

"The bill was drafted and presented to Congress on December 8 last. The refusal of the Democratic House of Representatives to act prevented its passage until the last hour of the session eight months later, when the pressures from women and men devoted to the upbuilding of the American home had become so great that they did not dare defeat it in the face of this campaign."

"Had that bill been passed when it was introduced, nearly a year ago, the suffering and losses of thousands of small-home owners in the United States would have been prevented. I consider that act was the greatest act yet undertaken by any government at any time on behalf of the thousands of owners of small homes. It provides the machinery, through the mobilization of building and loan associations and savings banks, by which we may assure to men and women the opportunity to bring up their children in the surroundings which make for true unity and true purpose in American life."
[State Papers, Vol. II, p. 389]

Senator Borah on December 8, 1932, introduced a bill to repeal the Home Loan Banks. It was not passed.

Had the legislation been passed promptly, thousands of families would have been able to save their homes from foreclosure and had its terms been made as designed, the creation of the Home Owner's Loan Corporation would probably never have been necessary. But these Home Loan banks have proved of inestimable value. Today (1937) over 4000 building and loan associations or other eligible institutions are members. They are rapidly returning the Government's advances of original capital and bid fair to be free of Government ownership in a very few years. The members of the system have over a billion dollars of loans out to home owners.

It was Hoover's intention to build a real national mortgage rediscount system upon these banks had he continued in office.

EXPANSION OF AGRICULTURAL CREDIT

The President's policy was to reorganize the whole foundations of agricultural credits so that farmers would never again be threatened with deprival of credit by a depression, and to lay these foundations in the emergency actions.

During previous years the Government had established the Federal Land Banks which had placed over 499,577 farm mortgages aggregating over $1,605,796,644. The capital had originally been set up by the Government but gradually all of it had been transferred to farmers who, in fact, conducted the banks under the supervision of the Federal Farm Loan Board. There had also been set up the Intermediate Credit Banks to provide farmers with production loans, a system which was operated under the supervision of the same Board.

The Federal Farm Board had been set up by President Hoover primarily for the purpose of creating and financing farm co-operatives. It had by 1932 made loans of upward of $200,000,000 to such organizations. The Farm Board also had authority to make loans on farm products stored in public warehouses. (See Agricultural Policies, page 146.)

In his conference with representatives of the leading insurance companies on October 5, 1931, the President had proposed that they co-operate in the emergency by not foreclosing mortgages except where absolutely unavoidable. In his conference with Congressional committees on October 6, 1931, he announced he would recommend to Congress the subscription of a further $125,000,000 capital to the Federal Land Banks which would enable them to place another $1,000,000,000 of their bonds. By including an authority to the R. F. C. to buy these bonds he made sure they would have a market.

On October 7, 1931, the President settled with Secretary of Agriculture Hyde and Chairman Bestor of the Federal Farm Loan Board immediate policies of mortgage relief to be followed and legislation to be asked for. He emphasized that "every man who in fact was doing his best to meet his obligations should be aided in every possible way." A letter of suggestions from the Board to the officers of the Land Banks was agreed upon, under which foreclosures would be limited to those who wished to or had already abandoned their farms; the banks should function in a thoroughly humane way in respect to their own loans; and they would make every effort where feasible to assume the loans of others in danger of foreclosure, so as to prevent such dispossession.

A few days later the President completed the longer-view revision with Chairman Bestor. These legislative proposals were:

Permission to the Federal Land Banks to make direct loans to farmers, where the Farm Loan Association was not functioning.

Enlarging the purposes for which loans might be made by the Federal Land Banks.

Granting authority to Federal Land Banks to carry real estate for five years at its normal value. This was to relieve the situation as regards the collateral which banks place back of their bonds.

Permission to Federal Land Banks to postpone payment of delinquent installments for a period of ten years.

Change in the act so that farmers would not be compelled to pay penalty interest.

Permission to the Banks to amortize delinquent items over a period of forty years.

Liberalization of the collection policy of the Banks and permission to substitute purchase money mortgages as collateral in place of amortized mortgages provided under the original act.

Providing a basis of rates to clear up the faulty provision of the act of 1923 permitting Land Banks to issue consolidated bonds.

Those proposals were drafted into amendments to the existing law and were introduced into the Senate. They passed the Senate but consideration and passage were delayed in the Democratic House for many months and much of their contribution to stemming the tide of farm losses was dissipated.

The increase of capital to the Federal Land Banks was recommended in the President's Message of December 8, 1931, and was passed by the Congress on January 23, 1932. The amount of $125,000,000 permitted the expansion of bonds for land loans by about one billion. Under its powers the R. F. C. was able to buy these bonds. It was also able to buy Intermediate Credit bank paper.

These provisions did not, however, prove full enough to meet the stringency in agricultural credit. The President on May 7, 1932, recommended further authority to the R. F. C. to erect a definite organism to furnish livestock and production loans to farmers and to set up export credits for agricultural produce. On May 31 in personal address to the Senate the President urged that the R. F. C. be given the authority to extend the whole basis of agricultural credits.

In a public statement on June 5 reviewing the agencies already in action, he showed that through various channels over 1,000,000 farmers had already been aided during the emergency with credit. He urged the further expansion of such credit.

In order to cover the field effectively, the President proposed the creation of the Agricultural Credit Banks. The plan was enacted in the Emergency Relief Bill of July 21, 1932. It provided for the establishment of twelve regional banks of $3,-000,000 capital each, the capital being provided by the Reconstruction Finance Corporation. The banks were to make loans on livestock and for production, or to discount such loans. The Agricultural Credit Banks in turn were given a rediscount privilege with the Federal Reserve System and the Reconstruction Finance Corporation. The total credit thus made available would exceed $1,360,000,000. The President urged that a small overcharge in interest rates should be made by these banks, the borrower to receive capital stock in the banks to that amount. The purpose of this was to dispose of the Government capital to the farmers themselves who would then own and could conduct the banks. This provision was lost in the shuffle. Had Hoover been elected it was his intention to have introduced this principle and to have consolidated these institutions with the Intermediate Credit Banks, thus giving the farmers a complete production and livestock credit system of their own ownership and management.

In reviewing this expansion of Agricultural Credits, Hoover, speaking on October 4, 1932, said:

"The very first necessity to prevent collapse and secure recovery in agriculture has been to keep open to the farmer the banking and other sources from which to make short-term loans for planting, harvesting, feeding livestock, and other production necessities. That has been accomplished indirectly in a large measure through the increased authority to the Federal Reserve System and its expansion of credits, and indirectly through the Reconstruction Corporation loans to your banks. It has been aided directly through the Intermediate Credit Banks and through the ten new Agricultural Credit institutions which alone can command over $300,000,000 credit and which are now being erected in all parts of the country."

"We are thus rapidly everywhere restoring normal short-term credits to agriculture."

"In another direction upon my recommendation the Reconstruction Corporation has been authorized to make credit available to processors to purchase and carry their usual stocks of agricultural products and thus relieve a burden which was resting upon farm prices because the farmer was forced to carry these stocks. But even more important than this, at my recommendation the Reconstruction Corporation has been authorized to make credits available for sales of farm products in new markets aroad. This is today and will, with increasing activity, extend immediate markets in relief of farmers and the prices of products."

"The mortgage situation—that is, long-term credits—is one of our most difficult problems. On October 6 a year ago, I secured and published an undertaking . . . that we should extend aid to this situation. In December we appropriated $125,000,000 directly to increase the capital of the Federal Land Banks and we provided further capital through authority that the Reconstruction Corporation should purchase the bonds of these banks."

"A little over 1 per cent of the farms held under mortgage by the Federal Land Bank System today are under foreclosure, and these mostly cases where men wished to give up."

"The character of the organization of the Joint Stock Land Banks whose business methods are not controlled by the Federal Farm Loan Board has resulted in disastrous and unjust pressure for payments in some of these banks. The basis of that organization should be remedied. We have sought to further aid the whole mortgage situation by loans from the Reconstruction Corporation to banks, mortgage companies, and insurance companies to enable them to show consideration to their farmer borrowers. As a result of these actions hundreds of thousands of foreclosures have been prevented. . . ."

"But despite the relief afforded by these measures, the mortgage situation has become more acute. There must be more effective relief. In it lies a primary social problem."

"I conceive that in this civilization of ours, and more particularly under our distinctive American system, there is one primary necessity to its permanent success. That is, we must build up men and women in their own homes, on their own farms, where they may have their own security and express their own individuality."

"A nation on such foundations is a nation where the real satisfactions of life and happiness thrive, and where real freedom of mind and aspiration secure that individual progress in morals, in spirit and accomplishment, the sum of which makes up the greatness of America. Some will say this is a mere ideal. I am not ashamed of ideals. America was founded upon them, but they must be the premise for practical action."

"And for prompt and practical action I have, during the past month, secured definite and positive steps in co-ordination of the policies not only of the Federal agencies but the important private mortgage agencies as well. These agencies have undertaken to give their help."

"But further and more definitely than this I shall propose to Congress at the next session that we further reorganize the Federal Land Banks and give to them the resources and liberty of action necessary to enable them definitely and positively to expand in the refinancing of the farm-mortgage situation where it is necessary to give men who want to fight for it a chance to hold their homes."　　[*State Papers, Vol. II, p. 315*]

The President through the Bankruptcy Reform Bill provided another and major aid to farmers in difficulty. The passage of this act was delayed for over a year but finally passed on June 10, 1933. Under it hundreds of thousands of farmers have equitably compounded with their creditors and saved their homes. Further particulars are given in the section on Adjustment of Debt, p. 486.

EXPANDING FEDERAL RESERVE CREDIT

Under the Federal Reserve law the securities "eligible" for discount at the Federal Reserve Banks had been very tightly limited to commercial bills and a few minor securities. The Federal Reserve currency issues had to be covered with a minimum of 40 per cent gold and the balance by "eligible" securities. The foreign drain on gold after the European collapse, the shrinkage in commercial activities and consequently of bills, and the hoarding of gold and currency all contributed to make the Reserve System itself strangle credit. The President considered it imperative not only to remove this strangulation but to enable the System to expand credit.

At the conference with Congressional Committees on October 6, 1931, the President proposed that other types of bank loans should be made "eligible." This was agreed to at the time, and recommended to Congress by the President on December 8, 1931. He urged it in a further Message on January 4. The Senate Committee, however, refused to act.

Quickly this strangulation of credit appeared from another

direction which made action imperative. The foreign drains of gold and our own hoarding had so exhausted our "free" gold that we were in danger of being unable to meet foreign demands and we should practically be forced off the gold standard.

After a series of conferences, the President finally secured action (see *Protecting the Gold Standard,* page 470), and the so-called Glass-Steagall Bill was passed on February 27, 1932.

The President on signing it said:

"The bill should accomplish two major purposes."

"First.   In a sense this bill is a national defense measure.   By freeing the vast amounts of gold in our Federal Reserve System (in excess of the gold reserve required by law), it so increases the already large available resources of the Federal Reserve Banks as to enable them beyond question to meet any conceivable demands that might be made on them at home or from abroad."

"Second.   It liberalizes existing provisions with regard to eligibility of collateral, and thereby enables the Federal Reserve Banks to furnish accommodations to many banks on sound assets heretofore unavailable for rediscount purposes."

"The gradual credit contraction during the past eight months, arising indirectly from causes originating in foreign countries and continued domestic deflation, but more directly from hoarding, has been unquestionably the major factor in depressing prices and delaying business recovery."

"This measure . . . will so strengthen our whole credit structure and open the channels of credit as now to permit our banks more adequately to serve the needs of agriculture, industry, and commerce."

"I trust that our banks, with the assurance and facilities now provided, will reach out to aid business and industry in such fashion as to increase employment and aid agriculture."   [*State Papers, Vol. II, p. 128*]

The Glass-Steagall Act served even a wider purpose in the President's policies than freeing the gold standard from danger. By freeing the Federal Reserve banks from this danger, it enabled a definitely large scale of credit expansion through open market operations.

This was one of President Hoover's most important policies for militant action against the depression. The "governments" held previous to this action had ranged around $700,000,000. Acting promptly, the Federal Reserve banks increased their holdings of "governments" through open market purchase by over $1,100,000,000 before August, 1932. At the usual ratios, these "governments" so bought theoretically expanded credit to the ultimate borrower by $10,000,000,000. Without this expansion to meet the contraction of credit due to foreign and other withdrawals, we should have been plunged into widespread bankruptcy.

HOARDING

Many people, terrorized by the constant shocks from abroad and the bank failures, periodically during the depression engaged in large-scale hoarding of currency and gold. The effect was of course to strangle credit and to cause still more bank failures. Such a wave had been checked by the restoration of confidence through the Moratorium in June, 1931. Another sprang up with the British collapse in October, but was checked by the creation of the National Credit Association. In December, 1931, increased hoarding began to be very serious.

Early in February, the President instituted a public campaign of education upon its effects under the leadership of Colonel Frank Knox. The President's appeal issued on February 3, 1932, said:

". . . now a patriotic . . . service is to secure the return of hoarded money into the channels of industry. During the past year and with an accelerated rate during the last few months a total of over a billion three hundred millions of money has been hoarded. That sum is still outstanding. I am convinced that citizens hoarding currency or money do not realize its serious effect on our country. It diminishes the credit facilities by many billions. Every dollar hoarded means a destruction of from five to ten dollars of credit. Credit is the bloodstream of our economic life. Restriction or destruction of credit cripples the revival and expansion of agriculture, industry, commerce and employment. Every dollar returned from hoarding to circulation means putting men to work. It means help to agriculture and to business. Every one hoarding currency injures not only his own prospects and those of his family, but is acting contrary to the common good. The credit institutions are greatly crippled in furnishing these needed credits, unless the hoarded money is returned. Therefore, I urge all those persons to put their dollars to work—either by conservative investment, or by deposit in sound institutions in order that it may thus return into the channels of economic life."

[State Papers, Vol. II, p. 108]

This campaign, together with the work of the R. F. C., served to stop the movement for the moment and on February 6, the President stated to the press:

"I am glad to report that since February 4 when I took action on hoarding, there has been an entire turn in the tide. . . . It is estimated that $34,000,000 has been returned to circulation from hoarding."

The volume of currency out remained fairly stable until the panic of March, 1933. There was one flurry during which about $300,000,000 was drawn at the time of the Congressional Crisis referred to on page 478.

NATIONAL BUSINESS AND INDUSTRIAL COMMITTEES

Secretary Mills undertook the organization of a committee of business men and bankers in each Federal Reserve District to secure that the ample credit now available through the R. F. C. and the Federal Reserve System was put to work in the country. The first committee was organized in the New York Reserve District on May 19, 1932. On the 20th, the President issued a statement requesting the governors of the other Reserve Districts to organize similar committees.

On August 14, 1932, the President announced:

"I have called a national conference for August 26 of the Business and Industrial Committees of the twelve Federal Reserve Districts for the purpose of organizing a concerted program of action along the whole economic front. The conference will deal with specific projects. . . ."

"A canvass of the means, methods, agencies, and powers available in the country for general advancement; wider expansion of credit facilities to business and industry where consumption of goods is assued; co-ordination and expansion of livestock and agricultural credit facilities; co-ordination and expansion of financial facilities for the movement of commodities into consumption; expansion of programs for repairs and maintenance of the railways; and creation of organization for further spread of existing employment and expansion of employment."

". . . It is expected to outline a basis for public, commercial and trade group co-operation in the execution of the purposes of the con-ference. . . ."

[State Papers, Vol. II, p. 266]

The Conference convened on August 26 under the chairmanship of Henry M. Robinson. The President opened its session:

"We have asked you . . . to confer together and with the officials of the Government agencies which are engaged in the problems of the depression. The purpose of the Conference is to better organize private initiative and to co-ordinate it with governmental activities, so as to further aid in the progress of recovery. . . . This is a meeting not to pass resolutions on economic questions but to give you the opportunity to organize for action."

". . . we are convinced that we have overcome the major financial crisis—a crisis in severity unparalleled in the history of the world—and that with its relaxation confidence and hope have reappeared in the world. We are now able to take further steps."

"It is not proposed to engage in artificialities. Nor is it proposed that you attempt to settle here in a day great economic problems of the future. It is simply proposed that you organize for action in the problems immediately before us. Great future problems will occur to you as they are in the minds of all of us. . . ."

"We have a powerful governmental program in action for aid to recovery. . . ."

"We need a better distribution of credit."

". . . It is clearly necessary that there be co-ordination of effort in hastening the return of unemployed to employment in their natural industries. . . ."

". . . the distressing problems of agriculture are not alone the problems of the farmer and the Government. Its relief is one of the primary foundations of all progress in our country, and upon it does the progress of your business depend. It is as much your problem as it is the problem of the farmer."   [*State Papers, Vol. II, p. 268*]

The committees started most effective service, but, of course, dissolved with the election in November.

BALANCING THE BUDGET

President Hoover's major and insistent fiscal policy was to balance the Federal Budget as a primary necessity to public confidence and economic recovery.

REDUCTION OF EXPENDITURES

It may come a surprise yet it is none the less true that President Hoover conducted the routine expenditures of the Government more economically than Calvin Coolidge. The total expenditures of the Hoover Administration were $17,576,767,206 of which $4,656,368,095 were emergency expenditures due to the depression. These deducted, the ordinary expenditures of his administration were $12,920,389,111 net. (Myers and Newton, p. 533.) The last four years of Mr. Coolidge's Administration cost $14,570,600,000, when there was no emergency.

Had the Democratic Congress accepted the President's proposals, the expenditures would have been substantially further reduced. As it was, President Hoover had to meet five forces: (a) a collapse of 50 per cent in tax receipts, (b) increased emergency expenditures for relief of unemployment and agriculture, (c) the opposition to reduction of ordinary expenses so as to accommodate this increase, (d) a multitude of grab-bag raids on the Treasury, which must be withstood, (e) an opposition Congress.

As an indication of Mr. Hoover's resolute determination to hold down expenditures and to balance the Budget against all opposition, we may barely outline a long catalogue of incidents.

On February 25, 1930, President Hoover in a vigorous public protest called for a stop to demands upon the Federal Government for money. He called attention to the fact that bills for increased expenditures then in Congress exceeded four billions and that he would have none of them.

On April 16, 1930, the President addressed the Chairman of the Senate Appropriations Committee calling his attention to the fact that partially matured appropriations exceeded the Budget and must be reduced: "We cannot contemplate any such deficit."

On May 28, 1930, President Hoover vetoed a huge pension bill.

On June 26, 1930, the President vetoed another huge pension bill.

On July 18, 1930, at a special Cabinet meeting on the reduction of the expenditures of the Government the President directed that the situation had so developed that non-essential appropriations already made by the Congress should not be spent. He stated publicly, "In view of falling revenue, without interfering in the program in aid of unemployment . . . we will find . . . reductions."

On October 10, 1930, the President announced a reduction of $67,000,000 in certain departments and indicated more coming.

On December 2, 1930, the President's Annual Message forecast a deficit due to falling income and corporation taxes:

"While it will be necessary in public interest to further increase expenditures . . . in aid of unemployment . . . and farmers . . . absolute necessity to defer any . . . unnecessary increase of Government expenses . . . most rigid economy . . . a necessity. . . ."

[State Papers, Vol. I, p. 436]

On December 3, 1930, the President in his Budget Message said:

"This is not the time to embark upon any new or enlarged ventures of Government. It will tax our every resource to . . . provide for employment and relief."

[State Papers, Vol. I, p. 457]

On December 9, 1930, in a public warning to Congress, Mr. Hoover said:

"Prosperity cannot be restored by raids on the public treasury . . . They (proposers of wild schemes) are playing politics at the expense of human misery."

[State Papers, Vol. I, p. 460]

On February 7, 1931, President Hoover publicly warned the Congress he would veto the Veterans' Bonus Bill providing for loans to veterans of 50 per cent of their bonus unless it was limited to those who were unemployed. (See Veterans, page 197.)

On February 18, 1931, the President vetoed a series of Indian claims bills.

On February 18, 1931, the President vigorously and publicly protested his opposition to the Soldiers' Bonus Bill again.

On February 18, 1931, the President sought to end the postal deficit by increasing postage rates. The Democratic Congress refused.

On February 23, 1931, the President vetoed a bill to give soldiers' benefits to civilians employed in war.

On February 23, 1931, the President vetoed a long list of private pension bills.

On February 26, 1931, the President vetoed the Bonus Bill.

"There is not a penny in the Treasury to meet such a demand . . ." Congress passed it over his veto.

On March 3, 1931, the President vetoed a bill to spend hundreds of millions on fertilizer factories, etc., at Muscle Shoals.

On June 2, 1931, the President started another drive to reduce ordinary departmental expenditures. Various departments reported reductions. Tax receipts further decreased.

On September 21, 1931, the President undertook a special journey to the Detroit Convention of the American Legion, where after a moving address, he secured a promise to abandon pressures for further bonus appropriations. The President said:

"The imperative moment has come when increase in Government expenditures must be avoided. . . . The first stone in the foundation of stability and recovery . . . is the stability of the Government. . . . It is my purpose to maintain that stability. I invite you to enlist in that fight."

[*State Papers, Vol. I, p. 619*]

On September 25, 1931, the President stated to the press that the action of the Legion should be a model for other groups pressing on Congress.

On October 16, 1931, in refusing a program for Naval expansion, the President said:

"The essential services of the Government must and will be maintained but these are times when with a large deficit facing the country . . . projects . . . must be deferred . . . but must make contributions to relief."

[*State Papers, Vol. II, p. 11*]

On November 6, 1931, the President announced that direct cuts of $350,000,000 in ordinary expenses of the Government would be provided in the budget recommendation to the Congress.

On November 12, 1931, the President announced a cut in Naval Budget of $51,000,000 to $343,000,000.

On December 8, 1931, the President in his Annual Message said:

"First requirement . . . of economic recovery is financial stability of the Government . . . deficits . . . from heavy decrease in tax receipts . . . aid to unemployment and agriculture . . . the magnitude of deficit . . . necessitate determined and courageous policies. We must have insistent and determined reduction in Government expenses. We must face temporary increase in taxes."

[*State Papers, Vol. II, p. 72*]

HOOVER PROPOSES INCREASED TAXES

The Message proposed further cuts in ordinary expenditures of $360,000,000 and increase in taxes by $1,300,000,000.

On December 11, 1931, the President made a public appeal that only by drastic economy in ordinary expenditures, resolute opposition to increased expenditure except for relief and temporary increase in taxation, could the budget be balanced. The original tax proposal was to increase income and estate taxes together with a restoration of other taxes to the 1924 tax base. Later the latter was changed to a proposal of a manufacturers' sales tax excluding food and cheaper clothing.

On December 29, 1931, he issued a public statement urging upon Congress the reorganization and consolidation of routine Government bureaus to bring about economy.

On January 4, 1931, in a public review of recovery legislation, the President again emphasized the necessity of drastic economy and temporary increase in taxation to provide a balanced budget.

"I have made proposals designed to check further degeneration in prices and values to fortify us against continued shocks . . . and to unshackle the forces of recovery. . . . The country must have confidence that the credit and stability of the Federal Government will be maintained by adequate increase in taxes. . . ." [*State Papers, Vol. II, p. 102*]

On January 8, 1932, the President issued a public appeal for support in resisting the profligate proposals of Congress. He said:

"We cannot squander ourselves into prosperity. . . . Drastic economy requires sacrifice. . . . We must balance our budget . . . provide against distress. . . ." [*State Papers, Vol. II, p. 104*]

On February 17, 1932, the President again urged upon Congress the reorganization of Government departments, abolishing many agencies and bureaus.

On February 26, 1932, the President vetoed private pension bills again.

On March 7, 1932, the House Ways and Means Committee reported a revenue bill to raise $1,246,000,000 in revenue including a manufacturers' sales tax.

On March 8, 1932, a press statement of the President showed that so far the House had failed to carry out budget recommendations and instead had already increased expenditure by $200,000,000 instead of reducing them.

On March 11, 1932, certain of the President's economy proposals were defeated by the Democratic Senate.

On March 25, 1932, the new Revenue Bill including the manufacturers' sales tax was defeated in the Democratic House. The President in a statement to the country said:

"To balance the budget is the keynote of real recovery. . . . It must be done. We must eliminate this deficit." [*State Papers, Vol. II, p. 147*]

He stated the deficit would exceed $2,000,000,000.

On March 29, 1932, another Soldiers' Bonus Bill was proposed in the House. The President denounced it.

On April 1, 1932, the House passed a patch-work tax bill providing for about $1,000,000,000 revenue.

On April 4, 1932, the President sent a most vigorous Message to the Congress stating that revenue and economy actions were inadequate. He urged a joint bi-partisan Committee with Congress to re-examine his economy program in the ordinary expenditures of the Government.

On April 5, 1932, Democrats attacked this proposal and asked for his specific recommendations of cuts.

On April 9, 1932, the President appointed a committee of the Cabinet comprising Secretaries Mills and Wilbur and Postmaster General Brown to meet with the Economy Commitee appointed by the House of Representatives. The Cabinet members proposed additional $250,000,000 specific cuts in expenses by legislative action in addition to the $360,000,000 already recommended in the Executive Budget.

On April 16, 1932, at the Committee's request, the President sent in an "Omnibus" legislative economy bill of $250,000,000 specific cuts in addition to $360,000,000 already proposed in the Budget Message.

On April 25, 1932, the House Committee reported out the Economy Bill omitting $135,000,000 of the President's proposals.

On April 25, 1932, the President vetoed more bills for Indian claims.

On April 27, 1932, the President vetoed 327 private pension bills—now totalling more than those celebrated by Grover Cleveland's vetoes.

On April 27, 1932, the President in an address to state governors at Richmond, Virginia, said:

"The economic safety of the Republic depends upon the joint financial stability of all our governments . . . the foundations of recovery of business, of employment, and of agriculture depend upon the success of our efforts (to balance our budgets). . . ."

"Today we are clearly absorbing too great a portion of the national income for the conduct of our various branches of Government . . . before the War the total cost of . . . governments represented only about 8 per cent of our national income. In boom times . . . the cost of Government actually increased to . . . 15 per cent of the national income, of which less than 3 per cent was directly due to the War. Today, with the falling off of business, the aggregate expenditures (are) . . . more than 20 per cent of the national income."

"Before the War theoretically every man worked twenty-five days a year for the national, state and local governments combined. In 1924 he worked forty-six days a year. Today he works for the support of all forms of government sixty-one days out of a year. Continued progress on this road is the way to national impoverishment. . . ."

". . . We cannot restore economic stability in the Nation by continuing to siphon so large a part of private effort into the coffers of the Government—it . . . stifles productivity, . . . consumption, . . . employment. Nor can we hide our heads in the sand by borrowing to cover current Government expenses, for thus we drain the capital of the country into public securities and draft it away from industry and commerce . . . dominant national necessity is to reduce the expenditures. . . ."

". . . every dollar of decrease in expense, every plan of consolidation in Government acticities . . . causes pain and resentment. . . ."

". . . upon the success (of our task) depends a momentous contribution to our united security . . . the common welfare of every man, woman, and child in our Nation." [State Papers, Vol. II, pp. 169–175]

On May 2, 1932, the Democratic House passed another bonus bill. It was stopped by the President's warning to the Senate.

On May 3, 1932, the House finally passed the Omnibus Economy Bill with only $30,000,000 cuts left in it.

On May 5, 1932, the whole country was discouraged by the actions of the Congress. The President sent a drastic Message to the House of Representatives:

"The most essential factor to economic recovery today is the restoration of confidence. In spite of the unquestioned beneficial effect of the

remedial measures already taken and the gradual improvement in fundamental conditions, fear and alarm prevail in the country because of events
in Washington which have greatly disturbed the public mind."

"The manner in which the House of Representatives rejected both the
revenue program proposed by the Treasury and the program unanimously
reported by the Committee on Ways and Means; the character of the tax
measures passed; the action of the House which would increase governmental expenditure by $132,000,000 for road building; the action further
to enlarge expenditures in non-service-connected benefits from the Veterans' Bureau at the very time when the House was refusing to remedy
abuse in these same services; the virtual destruction of both the national
economy program proposed by the Executive officials and the program
of the Special House Committee on Economy; the failure of the House
to give adequate authority for early reduction of Government bureaus
and commissions; the passage of legislation by the House placing burdens
of impossible execution upon the Federal Reserve System over the protest
of the Federal Reserve Board; the threat of further legislation looking
to uncontrolled inflation—have all resulted in diminishing public confidence and offsetting the constructive, unified efforts of the Executive and
the Congress undertaken earlier in the year for recovery of employment
and agriculture."

"I need not recount that the revenues of the Government as estimated
for the next fiscal year show a decrease of about $1,700,000,000 below
the fiscal year 1929 and inexorably require a broader basis of taxation
and a drastic reduction of expenditures in order to balance the budget.
Nothing is more necessary at this time than balancing the budget. Nothing will put more heart into the country than prompt and courageous
and united action in enacting the legislation which this situation impera-
tively demands, and an equally determined stand in defeating unwise and
unnecessary legislation."

"Most expeditious action is necessary if the revenues, appropriations,
economy legislation and a balanced budget are to be attained before the
beginning of the new fiscal year on July 1 next."

"The details and requirements of the situation are now well known to
the Congress and plainly require:"

"1. The prompt enactment of a revenue bill adequate to produce the
necessary revenue and so designed as to distribute the burdens equitably
and not to impede economic recovery."

"2. A drastic program of economy which, including the savings already made in the Executive budget of $369,000,000, can be increased to
exceed $700,000,000 per annum. Considering that the whole Federal

expenditure, except about $1,700,000,000, is for uncontrollable obligations this would represent an unprecedented reduction. Such a program, to accomplish its purpose, must embrace the rejection of all measures that increase expenditures unless they be for undoubted emergency; the reduction in appropriations now pending below the figures submitted in the Executive budget on December 9 last; a reconsideration of the legislation covering those economy projects which require repeal or amendment to the laws; and an effective grant of authority to the Executive to reorganize and consolidate and eliminate unnecessary Government bureaus and establishments." [*State Papers, Vol. II, pp. 175–6*]

"The imperative need of the Nation today is a definite and conclusive program for balancing the budget. Uncertainty is disastrous. It must be in every sense a national program. Sectional, partisan, group, or class considerations can have no place in it. Ours is a government of all the people, created to protect and promote the common good, and when the claims of any group or class are inconsistent with the welfare of all, they must give way. Various groups and sections of the country have brought insistent and delaying pressures to bear for the adoption or rejection of various projects which would yield great economy and revenue. They have not realized that sacrifice by all groups is essential to the salvation of the Nation. They have not recognized the gravity of the problems with which we are confronted. They apparently do not know that by their actions they are imposing losses on members of their own groups and sections through stagnation, unemployment, decreased commodity prices, far greater than the sacrifices called for under these suggestions. The Government cannot be dictated to by organized minorities. Such action will undermine all popular government. I know that these actions do not reflect the will of the country, and I refuse to believe that the country is unable to reflect its will in legislation."

"In conclusion, let me urge the national necessity for prompt and resolute and unified action, keeping constantly in mind the larger aspects of the problem and that the necessity for these measures is born of a great national emergency. If such a program should be agreed to by the leaders and members of both Houses it would go far to restore business, employment, and agriculture alike. It would have a most reassuring effect on the country." [*State Papers, Vol. II, pp. 175–76*]

On May 6, 1932, the President stated to the country:

"The issue before the country is the re-establishment of confidence and speed toward recovery by ending these delays in balancing the budget through immediate passage of revenue measures and reduction of Government expenditures. It is not a partisan issue. This was one of the most important steps of the non-partisan program for restoring stability proposed by me and patriotically accepted by the leaders of both political parties last December. Effective programs, projects, estimates and possibilities for both economy and revenue have been presented and are known in every detail."

"This is not a controversy between the President and Congress or its members. It is an issue of the people against delays and destructive legislation which impair the credit of the United States. It is also an issue between the people and the locust swarm of lobbyists who haunt the halls of Congress seeking selfish privilege for special groups and sections of the country, misleading members as to the real views of the people by showers of propaganda."

"What is urgently required is immediate action upon and conclusion of these questions. This is a serious hour which demands that all elements of the Government and the people rise with stern courage above partisanship to meet the needs of our national life."

[State Papers, Vol. II, p. 180]

On May 9, 1932, the President vetoed the soldiers' benefits
for civilians who served in the Spanish-American War.
On May 13, 1932, the President stated:

"Our job in the Government is unity of action to do our part in an unceasing campaign to re-establish public confidence. That is fundamental to recovery. The imperative and immediate step is to balance the budget and I am sure the Government will stay at this job until it is accomplished."   [<i>State Papers, Vol. II, pp. 188–89</i>]

On May 27, 1932, the President, commenting upon a bill introduced into the House at the instance of Speaker Garner, said:

"The urgent question today is to balance the budget. . . ."

"This is not unemployment relief. It is the most gigantic pork barrel ever proposed to the American Congress. It is an unexampled raid on the public treasury."   [<i>State Papers, Vol. II, p. 195</i>]

On May 31, 1932, the House having passed some futile economy and tax bills up to the Senate, the President addressed that body in person:

"An emergency has developed in the last few days which it is my duty to lay before the Senate."

"The continued downward movement in the economic life of the country has been particularly accelerated during the past few days and it relates in part definitely to the financial program of the Government. There can be no doubt that superimposed upon other causes the long continued delays in the passage of legislation providing for such reduction in expenses and such addition to revenues as would balance the budget, together with proposals of projects which would greatly increase governmental expenditures, have given rise to doubt and anxiety as to the ability of our Government to meet its responsibilities. These fears and doubts have been foolishly exaggerated in foreign countries. They know from bitter experience that the course of unbalanced budgets is the road of ruin. They do not realize that slow as our processes may be we are determined and have the resources to place the finances of the United States on an unassailable basis."

"The immediate result has been to create an entirely unjustified run upon the American dollar from foreign countries and within the past few days despite our national wealth and resources and our unparalleled gold reserves our dollar stands at a serious discount in the markets of the world for the first time in half a century. This can be and must be immediately corrected or the reaction upon our economic situation will be such as to cause great losses to our people and will still further retard recovery. Nor is the confusion in public mind and the rising feeling of doubt and fear confined to foreign countries. It reflects itself directly in diminished economic activity and increased unemployment within our own borders and among our own citizens. There is thus further stress upon already diminished and strained economic life of the country."

"No one has a more sympathetic realization than I of the difficulties and complexities of the problem with which the Congress is confronted. The decrease in revenues due to the depression by upwards of $1,700,-000,000 and the consequent necessity to reduce Government expenditures, the sacrifice such reduction calls for from many groups and sections, the further sacrifice called for in the distribution of the remaining burden by the imposition of new taxes all constitute a problem which naturally arouses wide divergence of sectional interest and individual views. Yet if we are to secure a just distribution of these sacrifices in such fashion as to establish confidence in the integrity of the Government we must secure an adjustment of these views to quick and prompt national action, directed at one sole purpose, that is to unfetter the rehabilitation of industry, agriculture, and employment. The time has come when we must all make sacrifices of some parts of our particular views and bring these dangers and degenerations to a halt by expeditious action."

"In the stress of this emergency I have conferred with members of both parties of the Senate as to methods by which the strains and stresses could be overcome and the gigantic resources and energies of our people released from the fetters in which they are held. I have felt in the stress of this emergency a grave responsibility rests upon me not only to present the situation to the Senate but to make suggestions as to the basis of adjustment between these views which I hope will lead to early action. And I am addressing myself to the Senate on this occasion as the major questions under consideration are now before this body."

"We have three major duties in legislation in order to accomplish our fundamental purposes."

"1. Drastic reduction of expenditures."

"2. Passage of adequate revenue legislation, the combination of which with reductions will unquestionably beyond all manner of doubt declare to the world the balancing of the Federal budget and the stabilizing of the American dollar."

"3. Passage of adequate relief legislation to assure the country against distress and to aid in employment pending the next session of Congress."

"It is essential that when we ask our citizens to undertake the burdens of increased taxation we must give to them evidence of reduction of every expenditure not absolutely vital to the immediate conduct of the Government. The Executive budget of last December provided for a reduction of expenditures in the next fiscal year over the then estimated expenditures of the current year by about $370,000,000. I have recommended to the Congress from time to time the necessity for passage of legislation which would give authority for further important reductions in expenditures not possible for consideration by either the Executive or the Committees of Congress without such legislation."

"The natural wealth of this country is unimpaired and the inherent abilities of our people to meet their problems are being restrained by failure of the Government to act. Time is of the essence. Every day's delay makes new wounds and extends them. I come before you in sympathy with the difficulties which the problem presents and in a sincere spirit of helpfulness. I ask of you to accept such a basis of practical adjustment essential to the welfare of our people. In your hands at this moment is the answer to the question whether democracy has the capacity to act speedily enough to save itself in emergency. The Nation urgently needs unity. It needs solidarity before the world in demonstrating that America has the courage to look its difficulties in the face and the capacity and resolution to meet them." [*State Papers, Vol. II, pp. 197–99, 203*]

That there could be no feeling that the President was not justly imposing burdens on all, he urged the Senate to increase income taxes to 55 per cent in the upper brackets. For both emergency and social reasons, he urged also that the upper brackets of the estate taxes also be increased to 55 per cent. (See Distribution of Property, page 93.)

On June 1, 1932, the Senate passed a tax bill but it yielded much less than the President hoped.

On June 8, 1932, the Senate passed the Omnibus Economy Bill, but trimmed it down to $134,000,000.

On June 11, 1932, the President urged the House and Senate Conferees to restore full $250,000,000 in the legislative Economy Bill.

On June 19, 1932, the President held a conference of House and Senate leaders in an endeavor to eliminate pork-barrel appropriations attached to the Relief Bill.

On June 30, 1932, the Legislative Economy Bill was finally passed but reduced from $250,000,000 to $130,000,000. The President's observation in signing was "with limited satisfaction."

On July 11, 1932, the President vetoed a Relief Bill because there had been attached to it by the Democratic leaders pork-barrel and certain provisions for Government loans to individuals.

". . . (the Government) subjected to conspiracies and of predatory interest, individuals and private corporations. . . ."

"Huge losses and scandals must inevitably result . . . threatening the credit of the United States. . . . Never before has so dangerous a suggestion been made seriously to our country."

[*State Papers, Vol. II, p. 228*]

INCREASE IN REVENUES

On July 18, 1932, one of the worst Congresses in history adjourned. (See Congressional Obstruction, page 478.) The President had secured reduction of $300,000,000 out of $700,-000,000 he had proposed; he had secured an increase of taxes by $1,000,000,000 instead of $1,300,000,000.

On August 11, 1932, the President in a public address at Washington said:

"I have insisted upon a balanced budget as the foundation of all public and private financial stability and of all public confidence. I shall insist on the maintenance of that policy. Recent increases in revenues, while temporary, should be again examined, and if they tend to sap the vitality of industry, and thus retard employment, they must be revised."

"The first necessity of the Nation, the wealth and income of whose citizens have been reduced, is to reduce expenditures on government, national, state, and local. It is the relief of taxes from the backs of men which liberates their powers. It is through lower expenditures that we get lower taxes. This must be done. Considerable reduction in Federal expenditures has been attained. If we except those extraordinary expenditures imposed upon us by the depression, it will be found that the Federal Government is operating for $200,000,000 less annually today than four years ago. The Congress rejected recommendations which would have saved . . ."

"I shall repeat my proposals for economy. . . . I shall continue to oppose raids on the Federal Treasury."   [*State Papers, Vol. II, p. 250*]

At the final session of Congress in his administration in the fall of 1932, the President again returned to the balancing of the budget. On December 6, 1932, in his Message to the Congress, the President said:

"I shall in due course present the Executive budget to the Congress. It will show proposed reductions in appropriations below those enacted by the last session of the Congress by over $830,000,000. In addition, I shall present the necessary Executive Orders under the recent act authorizing the reorganization of the Federal Government which, if permitted to go into force, will produce still further substantial economies. . . ."

"Many of the economies recommended in the budget were presented at the last session of the Congress, but failed of adoption. . . ."

"Some of the older revenues and some of the revenues provided under the act passed during the last session of the Congress, particularly those generally referred to as the nuisance taxes, have not been as prolific of income as had been hoped. Further revenue is necessary in addition to the amount of reductions in expenditures recommended. Many of the manufacturers' excise taxes upon selected industries not only failed to produce satisfactory revenue but they are in many ways unjust and discriminatory. The time has come when, if the Government is to have an adequate basis of revenue to assure a balanced budget, this system of special manufacturers' excise taxes should be extended to cover practically all manufactures at a uniform rate, except necessary food and possibly some grades of clothing. . . ."   [*State Papers, Vol. II, p. 532*]

The budget estimates immediately showed the effect of these recommendations. A threatened deficit of nearly two billions would be reduced to only $300,000,000. That is, the first fiscal year of the Roosevelt Administration—between July 1, 1933 and June 30, 1934—would see the Nation back on a practically balanced budget, which also could have been the case the year be-before if the Democratic Congress had been willing to co-operate.

As an additional step in the same direction, the President sent to Congress on December 9 a complete series of executive orders reorganizing the entire administrative structure of the Government.

On December 23, 1932, the Republican leaders reported to the President that in discussions with Democratic leaders of the House, the latter had agreed to support a general revenue bill this session which, with reductions of expenditures, would practically balance the budget; also that they would again support a manufacturers' sales tax. This major item alone was estimated to raise $500,000,000. Other items of increased revenues also were to be included.

According to *The New York Times* dispatch, Speaker Garner, now Vice-President-elect, taking the 1932 platform of his party seriously, "reiterated his desire to balance the budget in the present session of Congress and his willingness to use his influence for the adoption of the sales tax if that should be necessary to accomplish his purpose. . . ." Mr. Garner stated:

"We must balance the budget and carry out what appeared to be the mandate of the people in November. . . . I feel we must carry out our promises."

According to the same journal, Senator Pat Harrison gave similar assurances.

President-elect Roosevelt the next day announced in Albany, through the press, that he was "amazed" and "horrified" at the action of the Democratic leaders in agreeing to a manufacturers' sales tax. It is to be noted that the manufacturers' sales tax of 2 per cent, as proposed by President Hoover, excluded food and the cheaper forms of clothing. There could have been no principle here involved, for President Roosevelt, within ninety days thereafter, advocated and imposed a form of manufacturers' sales tax—under the term "processing tax"—exclusively upon foods and cheaper clothing, which amounted to from 20 to 40 per cent.

On December 28, 1932, *The New York Times* dispatch from Washington stated:

"The Democratic framers of revenue measures were in a state of confusion today over the tax situation. Speaker Garner re-iterated his desire to balance the budget, but indicated unmis-takably a feeling of perplexity since the revelation of Governor Roosevelt's opposition. . . . The quick rebound from Albany occasioned by the support of Speaker Garner and Chairman Collier of the sales tax as a last resort was declared by a member of the committee to have 'taken the heart out of the boys!' . . . House leaders declared it extremely doubtful that any general revenue bill would be reported in the short session."

The country again shook on the verge of a panic. The President's answer to President-elect Roosevelt was an exhaustive analysis of his proposals and the need of a balanced budget in a Message to the Congress on January 17, 1932, in which he said in part:

"In my Budget Message of December 5 I laid before the Congress the financial situation of the Government together with proposals for the next fiscal year. . . . I urged upon the Congress the necessity for further drastic reduction in expenditures and increase in revenues."

"I now approach the Congress again upon this subject, knowing that the members are fully possessed of the complete necessity of a balanced budget as the foundation of economic recovery and to urge that action should be taken during the present session to bring this about."

"The great problem before the world today is a restoration and main-tenance of confidence. I need scarcely repeat that the maintenance of con-fidence in the financial stability of the United States Government is the first contribution to all financial stability within our borders, and in fact in the world as a whole. Upon that confidence rests the credit of the states, the municipalities, all our financial institutions and industry—it is the basis of recovered employment and agriculture."

"The increases in revenues enacted at the last session have not had the results hoped for because of continued economic stagnation. The income of the Government for the next fiscal year nominally estimated at $2,950,-000,000 is likely to fall short under present world conditions by any-where from $100,000,000 to $300,000,000."

"Expenditures (and I speak in terms of expenditures rather than ap-propriations because of the confusion caused by carry-over of appropria-tions for the present fiscal year) including post-office deficit but excluding debt redemption, are estimated at about $3,771,000,000. If expenditures are continued during the next fiscal year at the present rate there would thus be a deficit of from $920,000,000 to $1,120,000,000 in the next fiscal year exclusive of sinking fund charges."

"Obviously the first necessity of a nation of decreasing income is reduction in expenditures. . . ."

"In canvassing the three major fields of possible income, that is income taxes, customs and excise taxes, I believe that inquiry by the Congress will develop that income taxes under the Act of 1932 have been developed to the point of maximum productivity unless we are prepared to abandon our American system of fairly high exemption and reasonably low rates applicable to the smaller incomes and in any event by keeping to these principles no further burdens in this direction would substantially increase revenues and solve the questions. One of the first economic effects of the increases already made is the retreat of capital into tax-exempt securities and the denudation of industry and commerce of that much available capital."

"The customs revenues and other miscellaneous revenues are not likely to be increased except through recovery in trade. In my view, therefore, the field for substantial increase in Federal Government revenues resolves itself to the exploration of the possibilities of so-called excise or sales taxes. In the estimated revenues for the next fiscal year nearly $700,-000,000 is comprised of so-called excise taxes which are levied on a few score different manufactured commodities. These taxes are in fact manufacturers' sales taxes. Any attempted distinction between 'excise' taxes on manufactured commodities, or 'sales' taxes on manufactured commodities is mere juggling with words. Of the taxes now levied nearly $200,000,000 are upon essentials as distinguished from so-called nonessentials. The Congress has thus already established a 'sales' tax as the basis for one quarter of the whole public revenues, and has already adopted 'sales' taxes upon essentials as distinguished from non-essentials. To extend this form of taxation is neither new nor revolutionary. Instead of spreading it over a few scores of commodities and services at irregular rates which cause discrimination and hardship between industries, it would seem the essence of good statesmanship to apply such a tax generally at a low rate upon all manufactures except upon food and cheaper grades of clothing, and thereby give to the Federal Government a stable basis of income during the period of depression."

"One of the most helpful contributions which the Congress and this administration could give to the next administration would be to enable them to start with the Federal budget in balance and the Federal finances in order." [State Papers, Vol. I, pp. 580–81]

The following statement was issued by the President on January 30, 1933:

"The appropriation bills for the next fiscal year for the State, Justice, Commerce, and Labor Departments—together with the Independent Offices Bill—have now been reported out from the House Appropriations Committee. The President recommended total appropriations for these services of $977,637,002, excluding permanent appropriations. The House Committee recommended $1,106,172,812 . . . or $128,535,810 increase over the President's recommendations. To this should be added $1,268,480 for deferments which will be required in the fiscal year, making a total increase for these services of $129,804,290.

"The totals of the increases over the President's recommendations to date are . . . $163,319,642 and, if finally adopted by the Congress, will make an increase in the estimated deficit by that amount."

[State Papers, Vol. II, p. 584]

The same day, the President vetoed another Indian claims bill.

Fighting to the last to keep down appropriations, at 11:45 A.M., on March 4, 1933, the President issued this statement with his pocket veto of the Independent Offices Appropriation Bill:

"The appropriation bills passed by the Congress when taking into account mere postponements to later deficiency bills show that the total appropriations for the next fiscal year were approximately $161,000,000 above the President's recommendations. Of this increase, $130,900,000 is in the Independent Offices Bill. The President is not signing this bill in order that it may be reviewed in the next session."

[State Papers, Vol. II, p. 602]

[1]President Roosevelt's Message to the Democratic Congress a few days later, on March 10, 1933, drastically blamed the Hoover Administration for not balancing the budget, by saying:

"Thus we shall have piled up an accumulated deficit of $5,000,000,000.

"With the utmost seriousness I point out to the Congress the profound effect of this fact upon our national economy. It has contributed to the recent collapse of our banking structure. It has accentuated the stagnation of the economic life of our people. It has added to the ranks of the unemployed. Our Government's house is not in order and for many reasons no effective action has been taken to restore it to order."

"Upon the unimpaired credit of the United States Government rest the safety of deposits, the security of insurance policies, the activity of industrial enterprises, the value of our agricultural products and the availability of employment. The credit of the United States Government definitely affects those fundamental human values. It, therefore, becomes our first concern to make secure the foundation. National recovery depends upon it."

"Too often in recent history liberal governments have been wrecked on rocks of loose fiscal policy. We must avoid this danger."

It is unfortunate that Roosevelt did not think of this months earlier. In that case his budget would have been balanced by Hoover.

NATIONAL DEBT UNDER HOOVER ADMINISTRATION

As it finally washed out, the national debt at the beginning of the Hoover Administration was $17,378,514,363. It was $20,858,055,366 four years later at the end of March, 1933. The increase was $3,479,541,003. Of this, however, $2,397,-267,363 were recoverable loans which had been made by the Government in emergency aids, leaving a net increase of the burden upon the taxpayer of $1,082,273,640.

Commenting at Philadelphia, on October 16, 1936, on the subsequent events, Hoover said:

"I propose to discuss the New Deal morals in arithmetic. Another title might be 'Government by Deception.' A subtitle might be 'Intellectual Honesty in Political Campaigns.' And I may say at once that the loss to this Nation by the corruption of public thinking is far greater than the waste of public money."

"To illustrate this subject I shall examine two speeches of President Roosevelt which relate to Government expenditures. And I shall explore some of the published accounts of the Government. I choose these samples because figures are given, and there is something to get hold of besides Utopia. There is something we can test for old-fashioned integrity. The first of these speeches was at Pittsburgh in October, four years ago, when he was running for President. The second was at Pittsburgh two weeks ago, when he was defending what he had done in the meantime. And I shall at the end of this examination give you a constructive suggestion."

"In that Pittsburgh speech of four years ago Mr. Roosevelt said that the Republican spending was 'the most reckless and extravagant pace I have ever been able to discover in the statistical record of any peacetime government anywhere, anytime.' That speech showed high artistry in denunciation. It showed high imagination in figures. He exhausted the hard words of the political vocabulary—'desperate,' 'futile,' 'false,' 'pretty picture,' 'shocking,' 'unreliable,' 'spendthrift,' 'gamble,' 'bankruptcy,' 'prodigality,' 'extravagance,' 'muddle,' 'appalling.' All that in one single speech. And all this was applied to an increase of the national debt during the last Republican Administration of something over three billions without deducting recoverable loans. Mr. Roosevelt having exhausted these words on three billions what is there left to us to use on his ultimate fourteen billions?"

"He denied Republicans any mercy from the fact that Federal revenues had precipitously dropped off by two billions through a world-wide calamity. He denied us any quarter because we had placed humanity first in the American budget and spent and loaned public funds to a people in distress. Now he claims a patent on that idea. He gave us no credit marks for fighting a pork barrel Democratic Congress to get a balanced budget. He has patented many improvements on that barrel. With solemnity he promised to save 25 per cent a year from expenditures of the Government and to at once balance the budget. And he tearfully appealed to the woman in her home struggling to balance her budget. And he vigorously asserted he would never conceal anything."

"In reply at that time I corrected these mis-statements. But misrepresentation can only be washed up in the laundry of time. That laundry is working."

"Mr. Roosevelt in the 1936 model Pittsburgh speech naturally omitted correction of his inexactitudes of four years before. He now dismisses his own immensely greater deficits and all the evidences of his wastes and follies by the pious remark that for him and his supine Congress to have balanced his budget would 'have been a crime against the American people.' Thus he changes the rules between these two innings."

"In the Pittsburgh speech two weeks ago the President develops the idea of a baseball scoreboard and sets certain figures upon it for the fans to look at. For instance, he said that the last Republican Administration had increased the national debt by over three billions. He admitted that he had already increased it by thirteen billions. But he claims a deduction of six and one-half billions from his increase because of the bonus and for recoverable loans. Any umpire would call that statement out on three strikes of which one was a foul."

"Strike one: He deducts the present recoverable loans from his debt. But he misses the opportunity to be intellectually honest and likewise deduct from the last Republican Administration over two billions of recoverable loans. They were handed to him, largely collected by him and spent by him. Second, no publication of the United States Government warrants Mr. Roosevelt's valuation of five billions on recoverable assets, especially when we consider the enormous hidden losses in the New Deal guaranteed loans. The third strike is that the debt for veterans was not paid off. It was merely borrowed from the banks and has yet to be paid off. Incidentally he did not include the further increase of debt he is piling up. Thus the score of Republican increase in taxpayers' debt is one billion not three billions. His own score on the same basis will be about ten billions not six and one-half billions. If such an unmoral scoreboard had been put before any baseball game in the country the manager would be driven off the field."

PROTECTING THE GOLD STANDARD

President Hoover's currency policy was the straight Republican gospel of a convertible gold currency of the "present weight and fineness."

The abandonment of the gold standard by some forty countries during the European crisis from April, 1931 to January, 1932, created great pressures against the remaining gold standard countries. The President's policies in the international monetary field are discussed elsewhere. (See World Stabilization of Currencies, page 494.)

No occasion arose publicly to define or defend the gold standard in the United States until the winter of 1932. Then drain of gold from the United States because of the bank panics abroad and hoarding at home reduced the free gold available to meet the demands of foreign depositors in the United States to a point where according to figures furnished by the Federal Reserve Board a further two or three weeks' drain would have exhausted it. We had about $430,000,000 of "free" gold and foreigners still had $1,300,000,000 of deposits in the United States subject to call. Hoover acted promptly, stated the peril to the gold standard and proposed in conference with the Senate and House leaders those constructive measures that later became the Glass-Steagall Bill.

This act, by making "governments" eligible for currency reserves at the Federal Reserve Banks, freed enough gold to save the country from being forced off the gold standard through inability to meet foreign demands. (A more extensive account may be found in Myers and Newton, page 169.)

In describing these events at Des Moines on October 4, 1932, Hoover said:

"We were fighting to hold the Gibraltar of world stability, because only by holding this last fortress could we be saved from a crashing world, with a decade of misery and the very destruction of our form of Government and our ideals of national life."

"When eighteen months ago the financial systems of Europe were no longer able to stand the strain of their war inheritances and of their after-war economic and political policies, an earthquake ran through forty nations. Financial panics; governments unable to meet their obligations; banks unable to pay their depositors; citizens, fearing inflation of currency, seeking to export their savings to foreign countries for safety; citizens of other nations demanding payment of their loans; financial and monetary systems either in collapse or remaining only in appearance. The shocks of this earthquake ran from Vienna to Berlin, from Berlin to London, from London to Asia and South America. From all those countries they came to this country, to every city and farm in the United States."

"First one and then another of these forty nations either abandoned payment in gold or their obligations to other countries, or restricted payments by their citizens to foreign countries, so as practically to amount to at least temporary or partial repudiation of public and private debts. Every one of them, in a frantic endeavor to reduce the expenditures of their citizens, imposed drastic restrictions upon their imports of goods. These events were not as children playing with blocks. They brought revolutions, mutinies, riots, downfalls of governments, and a seething of despair which threatened civilization."

"I believe I can make clear why we were in danger of being forced off even with our theoretically large stocks of gold. I have told you of the enormous sums of gold and exchange drained from us by foreigners (in excess of $1,000,000,000). You will realize also that our citizens who hoard Federal Reserve and some other forms of currency are in effect hoarding gold, because under the law we must maintain 40 per cent gold reserve behind such currency. Owing to the lack in the Federal Reserve System of the kind of securities required by the law for the additional 60 per cent of coverage of the currency, the Reserve System was forced to increase their gold reserve up to 75 per cent. Thus with $1,500,000,000 of hoarded currency, there was in effect over $1,000,-000,000 of gold hoarded by our own citizens."

"These drains had at one moment reduced the amount of gold we could spare for current payments to a point where the Secretary of the Treasury informed me that unless we could put into effect a remedy, we could not hold to the gold standard but two weeks longer because of inability to meet the demands of foreigners and our own citizens for gold."

"Being forced off the gold standard in the United States meant utter chaos. Never was our Nation in greater peril, not alone in banks and financial systems, money and currency, but that forebode dangers, moral and social chaos, with years of conflict and derangement."

"We decided upon changes in the Federal Reserve System which would make our gold active in commercial use and that we would keep the American dollar ringing true in every city in America and in the world; that we would expand credit to offset the contraction brought about by hoarding and foreign withdrawals; that we would strengthen the Federal Land Banks and all other mortgage institutions; that we would lend to the farmers for production; that we would protect the insurance companies, the building and loan associations, the savings banks, the country banks, and every other point of weakness."

[*State Papers, Vol. II, pp. 298–303*]

In view of the currency inflation proposals passed by the Democratic House, Hoover pressed the currency policies during the campaign of 1932. Speaking at Des Moines on October 4, he said as to the Patman $2,300,000,000 fiat money bill:

". . . the bill they passed . . . would have made our currency a football of every speculator and every vicious element in the financial world at the very time when we were fighting for the honesty of the American dollar. I can do no better than to quote Daniel Webster, who, one hundred years ago, made one of the most prophetic statements ever made when he said:

" 'He who tampers with the currency robs labor of its bread. He panders, indeed, to greedy capital, which is keen-sighted and may shift for itself, but he beggars labor, which is unsuspecting and too busy with the present to calculate for the future. The prosperity of the workpeople lives, moves and has its being in established credit and steady medium of payment.' "

"The experience of scores of governments in the world since that day has confirmed Webster's statement, and yet the dominant leadership of the Democratic Party passed that measure to issue paper money through the House of Representatives."

". . . These ideas and measures represented the true sentiments and doctrines of the majority of the control of the Democratic Party. A small minority of Democratic members disapproved these measures, but these men obviously have no voice today. This program was passed through the Democratic House of Representatives under the leadership of the gentleman who has been nominated the Democratic candidate for Vice-President and thus these measures and policies were approved by their party.

"At no time in public discussion of the vital issues of this campaign has any Democratic candidate, high or low, disavowed these destructive acts, which must emerge again if they come to power."

[*State Papers, Vol. II, p. 306*]

Speaking at Cleveland on October 15, Hoover said:

"There is nothing in which the American workman is more concerned than in preserving the integrity of the American dollar. The Democratic Party has at various times, and specifically by the passage of the Patman Bill by the Democratic House of Representatives on June 15 last, endeavored to undermine the integrity of the American currency through the issue of $2,300,000,000 of greenbacks—harking back to the disastrous experience of sixty years ago. If any of you will study what happened in Germany, or France, or Austria, or any other European country when they resorted to these measures in order to meet their immediate difficulties, you will find that the major hardship fell upon the working people. There was a time when the value of the German mark was five to the dollar. They tried this plan of relief. I have in my desk a five-million mark note which before the entrance into these processes would have been worth one million dollars, and yet which I bought for actually one dollar. The effect of their experiment was a subtle and steady reduction of real wages, right and left."

"We have fought a great battle to maintain the stability of the American dollar, the stability of its exchange, in order that we might protect the working people of the United States."

[*State Papers, Vol. II, p. 352*]

Speaking at Indianapolis on October 28, he said:

"One of the most important issues of this campaign arises from the fact that the Democratic candidate has not yet disavowed the bill passed by the Democratic House of Representatives under the leadership of the Democratic candidate for Vice-President to issue $2,300,000,000 of greenback currency—that is, unconvertible paper money. That is money purporting to come from the horn of plenty but with the death's-head engraved upon it. Tampering with the currency has been a perennial policy of the Democratic Party. The Republican Party has had to repel that before now. In the absence of any declaration by the Democratic candidate on this subject for seven weeks of this campaign, no delayed promise now can effectually disavow that policy. The taint of it is firmly embedded in the Democratic Party. The dangers of it are embedded in this election. If you want to know what this 'new deal' and this sort of money does to the people, ask any of your neighbors who have relatives in Europe, especially as to German marks."

[*State Papers, Vol. II, p. 401*]

And at New York, October 31, he said:

"Another proposal of our opponents is that of inflation of the currency. The bill which passed the last session of the Democratic House called upon the Treasury of the United States to issue $2,300,000,000 in paper currency that would be unconvertible into solid values. Call it what you will, greenbacks or fiat money. It was that nightmare which overhung our own country for years after the Civil War."

"In our special situation today the issuance of greenbacks means the immediate departure of this country from the gold standard, as there could be no provision for the redemption of such currency in gold. The new currency must obviously go to immediate and constantly fluctuating discount when associated with currency convertible in gold. . . ."

"No candidate and no speaker in this campaign has disavowed this action of the Democratic House. In spite of this visible experience within recollection of this generation, with all its pitiable results, fiat money is proposed by the Democratic Party as a potent measure for relief from this depression." [*State Papers, Vol. II, p. 416*]

Finally Senator Glass was requested by Roosevelt to make reply to Hoover.

The speech of Senator Glass was of bitter denunciation of Hoover's statements, including a denial of the whole incident the President had mentioned in connection with the gold crisis of the previous February. Senator Watson at once made reply:

"Senator Glass has made the statement that he had no record of having been presented with the facts as to the gold crisis in the United States. . . . The Senator will perhaps remember the two-hour confidential conference of Senate leaders, including Senator Glass, called in February of last winter by the President, together with officials of the Treasury, the Federal Reserve System and the Reconstruction Finance Corporation. In that conference the President and these gentlemen urged the great gravity of the situation and the necessity for the immediate enactment of the legislation recommended by the President for extension of authority to the Federal Reserve System to enable them to prevent imminent jeopardy to the gold standard in the United States."

"I well recall that it was pointed out by these officials that under the foreign drains of gold and the hoarding then current, together with the inflexibility of the Federal Reserve laws, and despite our nominal gold holdings, we had at that time only about $350,000,000 of free gold and that losses to foreigners and hoarders were going on at a rate of $150,000,000 a week."

"Although Senator Glass had been opposed to these proposed measures, in the face of the evidence presented he patriotically agreed to proceed wtih the increased authority asked for, and to introduce them in the Congress, where they were enacted and the dangers from this quarter were finally and completely averted."

At last, on November 4, Mr. Roosevelt asserted his devotion to "the promise, yes, the covenant" embodied in Government securities. The covenant on Government bonds is "The principal and interest hereof are payable in United States gold coin of the present standard of value."

This debate would be of little consequence but for subsequent events. Senator Glass was to see the day in April, 1933, when he divulged to the Senate how he had been misled, and continued:

"To me the suggestion that we may devalue the currency gold dollar by 50 per cent means national repudiation. To me it means dishonor; in my conception of it, it is immoral. . . . It means not only the contravention of my party's platform in that respect but of the promises of the party's spokesmen during that campaign. . . . There has been no need for it."

As shown elsewhere the news, soon after the election of November, of President-elect Roosevelt's intentions to devalue or tinker with the currency was a major cause in producing the bank panic on March 4, 1933. (See page 527.)

President Hoover, on February 14, 1933, delivered an important address upon the whole question of maintaining the gold standard (see page 501). The international stabilization of currencies is also a part of this subject and is dealt with on page 494.

Hoover, in *The Challenge to Liberty,* discusses at length the New Deal managed currencies (page 92). (See also Adjustment of Debt, page 486.)

He again discussed this theory of currency in New York on November 16, 1935. He said:

"The new 'Economic Planning' has included repudiation of Government covenants, which raises somber questions of Government morals and honor. In any event it devalued the dollar by 41 per cent. It gave us the gift of 'Managed Currency.' As potent devices for destroying confidence these have merit. Through politically managed credit it has brought us to the threshold of devastating inflation. The stock market is already peeking into that Bluebeard's cave."

"In the few moments of this address I shall explore a little further into the price and consequences of these monetary and credit policies."

"There is the folly of buying foreign silver. I could at least see some reason for spending ten to fifteen million a year to subsidize employment in our Western silver mines by buying their product at a profitable price. But what earthly reason we have for buying vast amounts of foreign silver will take generations of politicians to explain. If we are to have managed currency, we do not require any metallic base. There is in fact no metallic base today. If there were, you could exchange currency for gold. If we want a metallic base, the Government already has $9,700,-000,000 of gold and only $5,600,000,000 of currency in circulation. Thus it would seem that we have plenty of metallic base for the currency when we have nearly one dollar and eighty cents in gold metal for every dollar of currency. That leaves plenty over to pay international balances. Yet we deliberately bid up the price of foreign silver by 50 per cent. Then we proceed to buy vast quantities of that commodity, for which we have no earthly use, at enormous profits to foreigners. Upon that folly we have already spent about $250,000,000 and under the new 'Economic Planning' we are to spend about $1,000,000,000 more. The siphon runs either through the taxpayer's pocket or inflation. You can be sure no foreigner would buy this silver back from us at what we pay for it."

"It is no doubt a part of our good-neighbor policies that we have joyfully subsidized every foreign speculator in silver. We have also subsidized every silver mine in Australia, India, Mexico, and Peru. But we have pursued these good-neighbor policies further. We have stirred up currency troubles in China and other silver currency countries. We have stimulated their good feelings by flooding them with bankruptcies, labor troubles, and jiggling their cost of living."

"Another result of 'Economic Planning' has been the attraction of billions in gold—over two billions in two years—that we do not need for any conceivable purpose. We ought to have had goods instead. Apparently 'Planned Economy' aims to become a bi-metallic Midas."

"Although we cannot recall 100 per cent dollars we can well consider the results of devaluation. We devalued the dollar 41 per cent under the hypnosis that if we reduced the length of a yard to 21.2 inches we would have more cloth in the bolt. One result is that the foreigner is shipping us more gold every day to buy our good domestic assets for the price of 21.2 inches to the yard. That is a complicated problem of New Deal economics, but if you will search around in it you will find much of interest. It is likely to represent more loss to the American people than a whole year's treasury deficit."

"While on this romantic subject of currencies I may mention that when we entered new 'National Planning' in currency we were promised a 'managed currency' that would be adjusted to American life and conditions. Of course if it worked it would increase the cost of living by 41 per cent. Thus it would reduce the living to be obtained from all life insurance policies, college endowments, pensions, wages and salaries, and would increase the housewife's cost of living. By it we forgave 41 per cent of most of our foreign debts. That is, they can pay them today with 41 per cent less gold than they expected to pay. You will remember those private foreign loans. They were denounced as the cause of all evil, so we now reduce the evil by reducing them 41 per cent. But offsetting all these pains, it was supposed to reduce the burden of mortgages. And equally if it works it lessens the burdens of all bonds, Government and otherwise. Here we again enter higher economics, but if you explore it thoroughly you will find that the 10,000,000 stockholders of corporations, including the wicked power companies, profit at the expense of the 65,-000,000 insurance policy holders. The sum of all these shifts do not make the poor any richer."

"But above all, this managed currency was to be thoroughly American and would make us independent of world influences. Two billions of dollars were appropriated to stabilize secretly foreign exchange and no accounting of the losses appears in the national deficit—that is, not yet. But behold! Our mystery fund has been most successful in stabilizing our currency to within a few per cent of the pound sterling for over a year. We have attained that stability which comes from leaning up against the British. We are the thirty-first member of the 'Sterling Bloc' of nations. Let us remember that the British also have a managed currency, and in the 'Sterling Bloc' we are only one of the thirty-one planets which revolve around the British sun. We have thus trustingly reposed in London a large influence in American values and freedom of American trade. I do not pretend to know where all this will take us, but I do know that I prefer a currency that no 'National Planning' can manage for us. not even the British."

"In any event so long as 'managed currency' lasts the purchasing value of the dollar lies at the whim of political government. Politics are bound be in every government-managed currency. You can never make the

American dollar ring true on the counters of the world nor on the counters of our savings banks so long as there is the alloy of politics in it. So long as it has that alloy in it people cannot invest $100 today with full confidence as to what it will be worth in old age. One result has been delayed recovery in the construction industries and continued unemployment in millions of unhappy homes. That goes into the realm of higher economics, but I assure you it is a huge burden in money and misery on the country not included in the Budget."

CONGRESSIONAL OBSTRUCTION CRISIS, MAY, 1932

No clear exposition of the policies of the Hoover Administration is possible without realization of the character of the Congress of 1931–33. The House of 1929 was Republican and co-operative. The Congressional elections of 1930 had produced a House that was in majority Democratic. The Senate was in majority Democratic and Radical Republican. In the face of the great crises which culminated with the British collapse in October, 1931, President Hoover called movingly for national unity and co-operation outside of politics. He took council with Democratic leaders equally with Republicans. Some Democratic members did co-operate and genuine tributes were paid to their patriotism by the President. But aside from those exceptions and some lip service, it was obvious that the Democratic control was resolved to sabotage the President's program and to delay recovery itself with the hope of winning the election a year later. This can be made evident if we review the fate of the President's urgent emergency program during the session of 1931–32.

1. On December 8, 1931, the President proposed the creation of the R. F. C. with widespread powers to support the financial and industrial fabric. The act was passed forty-six days later with reduced resources and more limited scope. The balance of the powers vital to employment and agriculture asked for were not enacted for 221 days. (See R. F. C., page 427.)

2. The President, on December 8, proposed an increase in the Land Bank capital and an entire revision of the Land Banks to enable them to handle farm mortgage emergencies. The increase of capital was given forty-four days later and the revision was not passed until a year later. In the R. F. C. proposals were provisions which would have allowed the establishment of a system of agricultural production and livestock loan banks. This provision was enacted 221 days after its proposal. (See Agricultural Credit, p. 442.)

3. The President, on December 8, proposed the creation of a system of Home Loan Banks to relieve pressure on home owners and to stimulate home building. The act in attenuated form was passed 220 days later. Foreclosures on thousands of homes would have been saved by reasonable promptness. (See Home Loan Banks, page 436.)

4. On December 8 the President proposed an extension of "eligibility" paper in the Federal Reserve System. The purpose was to allow immediate expansion of credit to meet the contraction due to foreign withdrawals of gold. It was not until the situation became so acute as to threaten the gold standard and to force the country to the edge of panic that this action was taken by Congress eighty days late. (See Protecting the Gold Standard, page 470, and Expansion of Federal Reserve Credit, page 449.)

5. On February 29, 1932, the President proposed his great reform of the bankruptcy laws to bring about an adjustment of overwhelming debt to farmers, home owners, railways and business. This law was not passed until a year later, just prior to the Roosevelt inauguration. (See Adjustment of Debt, page 486.)

6. On December 3, 1929 (and often before), the President proposed a drastic reform of the whole banking system so as to make deposits safe. Nothing was done but talk till 1933 and then only an attenuated bill passed by the Senate in 1933. (See Banking Reform, page 332.)

7. On December 8, 1931, the President proposed that loans should be made on the assets of closed banks to enable distributions to depositors and to conserve the assets for their benefit. It was not passed until the Roosevelt Administration.

8. On December 8, 1931 (and before), the President urged a revision of railway regulation so as to strengthen railway service and finance. It has never been adequately done. (See Reform of Railway Regulation, page 320.)

9. Beginning in December, 1929, repeatedly, the President urged the regulation of electrical power companies. The Federal Power Commission was created but the full authorities recommended by Hoover were not accepted. (See Electrical Power Regulation, page 314.)

10. On December 8, 1931, the President urged the absolute necessity of balancing the Federal Budget. On December 9, he presented an Executive Budget with a cut of over $350,000,000 in the ordinary Federal expenditures. The Congress refused all but about $150,000,000. In February the President proposed

additional reductions of ordinary Federal expenditures of $300,-000,000 which required legislative action. It finally passed on June 30 as $130,000,000 savings. (See Balancing the Budget, page 450.)

11. On February 17, 1932, the President presented a plan of reorganization of Federal bureaus that would make great savings. In June a make-believe authority was passed that meant nothing. (See Reorganization of Federal Departments, page 561.)

12. On December 9, 1931, the President proposed an increase of over a billion in taxes in order to balance the budget. It was not until ninety days later that a revenue bill was reported out of committee. With its large membership, for years it had been the practice of the House to consider its revenue legislation under a special rule, limiting the number of hours that the bill could be considered under general debate. The Democratic House leaders refused such a rule in considering this particular bill. The bill was debated for fifteen days. In the face of a national emergency it was talked to death. The President was angry but held his tongue to soft words and conciliation, for it was the Democrats who had to legislate if the country was to be saved from panic, and a few decent Democrats had supported the President.

From February to May no progress had been made on the President's program. By the month of May it became clear to the country that this sabotage of recovery was in progress and alarm became general. The hopefulness and confidence inspired by the R. F. C., the Glass-Steagall Bill, the Agricultural Land Bank Bill and other measures were dissipated.

In the meantime the Democratic leadership in Congress had been busy in proposing measures intensely discouraging to the country. On January 8 the President issued an appeal to the Congress, "We cannot squander ourselves into prosperity." On January 28 the President had to notify Senate leaders that he would not approve a Democratic proposal to issue $1,000,-000,000 fiat money. On March 9 the President had to notify the House that he would not approve their Soldier's Bonus Bill and the $2,400,000,000 fiat money bill. Constantly bills were being promoted to increase hugely Federal expenditures. On April 27 the President had to veto a great omnibus private pension bill. On May 2 the House passed the "Rubber Dollar" bill—a forerunner of "managed currency."

By this program of sabotage and delay they not only destroyed confidence and hope at home but confidence abroad in the stability of the United States Government. As a result, a new flight of capital from America was in full swing. The drain of gold, which had slackened from $300,000,000 in October to $25,000,000 in March, rose again rapidly and reached $200,000,-000 in June. The hoarding of currency again grew apace. The prices of wheat dropped 25 per cent from March and cotton dropped 16 per cent. The prices of industrial stocks had dropped over 50 per cent from March. Unemployment increased. The dollar went to a 7½ per cent discount in Paris. The foreign press again considered it was but a matter of days until we should be compelled to abandon the gold standard. The dollar reached a 7½ per cent descent by June. We were in the presence of another bank panic—this time the creation of Congress—"the Congressional Crisis of 1932."

On May 5 the President addressed an extraordinarily sharp Message to Congress:

"I should not be discharging my Constitutional responsibility to give to the Congress information on the state of the Union and to recommend for its consideration such measures as may be necessary and expedient, if I did not report to the Congress the situation which has arisen in the country in large degrees as the result of incidents of legislation during the past six weeks."

"The most essential factor to economic recovery today is the restoration of confidence. In spite of the unquestioned beneficial effect of the remedial measures already taken and the gradual improvement in fundamental conditions, fear and alarm prevail in the country because of events in Washington which have greatly disturbed the public mind."

"The manner in which the House of Representatives rejected both the revenue program proposed by the Treasury and the program unanimously reported by the Committee on Ways and Means; the character of the tax measures passed; the action of the House which would increase governmental expenditure . . .; the virtual destruction of both the national economy program proposed by the executive officials and the program of the Special House Committee on Economy; the failure of the House to give adequate authority for early reduction of Government bureaus and commissions; the passage of legislation by the House placing burdens of impossible execution upon the Federal Reserve System over the protest of the Federal Reserve Board; the threat of further legislation looking to uncontrolled inflation—have all resulted in diminishing public confidence and offsetting the constructive, unified efforts of the Executive and the Congress undertaken earlier in the year for recovery of employment and agriculture."

". . . the imperative need of the Nation today is a definite and conclusive program . . . uncertainty is disastrous . . . prompt, resolute, and unified action . . . the necessity for these measures is born of a great national emergency . . . such a program . . . would have a most reassuring effect. . . ." [*State Papers, Vol. II, p. 178*]

The reaction of the press was impressive.

The Baltimore Sun (Democratic): "Congress deserves what it has been given. It asked for all it has been given. Mr. Hoover's Message is an unanswerable indictment. Bitter and savage as it is, in substance it is no more than a summary of the proceedings of Congress in the last two months. Any bare recital of those proceedings would inevitably give forth the bitter and savage tone of this Presidential Message. Congress has flagrantly and disgracefully deserted its own standards. . . . Congress has missed no opportunity to disembowel the policy of orthodox finance."

The New York Times: "A Democratic senator, Mr. Harrison, calls upon the President to bring order out of chaos. The budget is not balanced. Tax plans have gone astray. 'If ever there was a time,' he says, 'when the President ought to speak out to his leaders in Congress, it is now.' But the President has been speaking out to his leaders and appealing to his adversaries, vigorously and consistently since Congress convened five months ago. On the importance of Federal retrenchment and the necessity of balancing the budget he has spoken in no less than twenty-one Messages, statements and addresses. . . . Responsibility for the chaos which now exists in Washington rests upon those members of Congress who have blocked the President at every turn and bolted their own party leadership."

Despite all this the Democratic leaders introduced into the House an enormous pork-barrel bill. The President at once attacked it (May 27):

"The urgent question today is the prompt balancing of the budget . . . it is essential that there should be an understanding of the character of the draft bill made public yesterday in the House of Representatives. . . . That draft bill supports some proposals we have already made in aid of unemployment. . . . But in addition it proposes to expend about $900,000,000."

"An examination of only one group of these proposals—that is, proposed authorizations for new post offices—shows a list of about 2300 such buildings, at a total cost of about $150,000,000. The Post Office Department informs me that the interest and upkeep of these buildings would amount to $14,000,000 per annum, whereas the upkeep and rent of buildings at present in use amounts to less than $3,000,000. Many of the other groups in this bill will no more stand the light of day than this example."

"A total of over 3500 projects of various kinds are proposed in this bill, scattered into every quarter of the United States. I do not believe that 20 per cent could be brought to the stage of employment for a year. I am advised by the engineers that the amount of labor required to complete a group of $400,000,000 of these works would amount to only 100,000 men for one year, because they are in large degree mechanical jobs."

"This is not unemployment relief. It is the most gigantic pork barrel ever proposed to the American Congress. It is an unexampled raid on the public treasury."

"Detailed lists of all these projects have been broadcast to every part of the country during the past twenty-four hours, to the cities, towns, villages, and sections who would receive a portion of this pork barrel. It is apparently expected that the cupidity of these towns and sections will demand that their congressmen and senators vote for this bill or threaten to penalize them if they fail to join in this squandering of money."

"I just do not believe that such lack of intelligence or cupidity exists amongst the people of our United States. . . . Our Nation was not founded on the pork barrel, and it has not become great by political logrolling."

[*State Papers, Vol. II, p. 195*]

On May 31 the President addressed the Senate in person:

"The continued downward movement in the economic life of the country has been particularly accelerated during the past few days and it relates in part definitely to the financial program of the Government. There can be no doubt that superimposed upon other causes the long-continued delays in the passage of legislation providing for such reduction in expenses and such addition to revenues as would balance the budget, together with proposals of projects which would greatly increase governmental expenditures, have given rise to doubt and anxiety as to the ability of our Government to meet its responsibilities. These fears and doubts have been foolishly exaggerated in foreign countries. They know from bitter experience that the course of unbalanced budgets is the road of ruin. They do not realize that slow as our processes may be we are determined and have the resources to place the finances of the United States on an unassailable basis."

"The immediate result has been to create an entirely unjustified run upon the American dollar from foreign countries and within the past few days, despite our national wealth and resources and our unparalleled gold reserves, our dollar stands at a serious discount in the markets of the world for the first time in half a century. This can and must be immediately corrected or the reaction upon our economic situation will be such as to cause great losses to our people and will still further retard recovery. Nor is the confusion in public mind and the rising feeling of doubt and fear confined to foreign countries. It reflects itself directly in diminished economic activity and increased unemployment within our own borders and among our own citizens. There is thus further stress upon already diminished and strained economic life of the country."

". . . The time has come when we must all make sacrifice of some parts of our particular views and bring these dangers and degenerations to halt by expeditious action. . . ."

"We have three major duties in legislation in order to accomplish our fundamental purposes."

"1. Drastic reduction of expenditures."

"2. Passage of adequate revenue legislation, the combination of which with reductions will unquestionably beyond all manner of doubt declare to the world the balancing of the Federal budget and the stabilizing of the American dollar."

"3. Passage of adequate relief legislation to assure the country against distress and to aid in employment pending the next session of Congress."

". . . authorization to the Reconstruction Finance Corporation to loan up to $300,000,000 to state governments where they are unable to finance themselves in provision of relief to distress."

". . . an authority to the Reconstruction Corporation to increase its issues of its securities to the maximum of $3,000,000,000 in order that it may extend its services both in aid to employment and agriculture on a wide scale. . . ."

". . . the inherent abilities of our people to meet their problems are being restrained by failure of the Government to act. Time is of the essence. Every day's delay makes new wounds and extends them. In your hands at this moment is the answer to the question whether democracy has the capacity to act speedily enough to save itself in emergency."

[*State Papers, Vol. II, p. 197*]

The President again got partial results.

But continuing its obstruction, the Democratic House of Representatives passed the Garner pork-barrel bill of $2,300,-000,000. On June 8, 1932, the Senate passed the "legislative" Economy Bill, having trimmed it from the $300,000,000 originally proposed by the President down to $134,000,000.

On June 15, 1932, the House passed the Patman Bonus Bill of $2,400,000,000 to be paid with fiat money. This inflation measure backed largely by Democratic votes gave a greater shock to the country than the proposed payment of the bonus, and even more stimulated the flight of capital. The President stopped it by threat of veto to the Senate.

By the end of June it was evident that the President would defeat this destructive legislation at every point. It was evident that though delayed, he would secure the major parts of this constructive program. The country began to breathe easier and the panic which seemed certain early in June was again defeated.

On July 18, 1932, the Congress adjourned. The President, delayed and sabotaged, had secured the R. F. C. with the authorities to save building and loan associations, banks, insurance companies, and railways; extension of Agricultural Credits; the Home Loan Banks; the expansion of Federal Reserve Credits; an increase in Federal revenues by $1,000,000,000 out of $1,-300,000,000; a decrease in Federal expenditures by $300,000,000 out of $700,000,000; further relief to employment through expanded public works, through loans for reproductive work by the R. F. C., through loans for direct relief and appropriation of Farm Board commodities. He had got the moratorium confirmed and the world started to an international stablization of currency.

Aside from emergency measures, useful legislation was enacted limiting the use of injunctions in labor disputes and prison and criminal law reform, including the kidnapping law.

He had saved the fidelity of the Government to its obligations. He had protected the people by relief and by saving the financial structure. He had laid the foundation for great permanent reforms. He had brought about these measures within the Constitution and he had preserved freedom itself.

GENERAL MEASURES OF DEPRESSION ADJUSTMENT

ADJUSTMENT OF PRIVATE DEBT

One of the outstanding phenomena of any depression is the adjustment of private debts. The inflation which precedes all depression creates debt upon a basis that cannot be supported. Readjustment downward of such debt is inexorable. Unsupportable debt arises often enough in ordinary times but in depression it is widespread. The social importance of the subject was recognized in the formulation of the Constitution itself. The social objective is to keep every producing unit operating whether individual or corporate. Often enough in ordinary times bankruptcy is the result of bad management, and dispossession is a necessity if the unit is to be kept producing. But in widespread depression those best able and most interested in keeping the business alive are also caught. In 1930 the operation of the bankruptcy laws gave very little opportunity to save those who were efficient or interested in making a fight for recovery. And it also resulted in the dissolution of many units the preservation of which was needed. Dispossession did not apply alone to farmers or home-owners, but likewise to the operators and managers of enterprise.

Beyond this larger problem, the old form of bankruptcy proceedings had become the scene of much malpractice and fraud.

President Hoover proposed new national policies and an entire reform not only for the emergency but permanently. On July 29, 1930, he directed the Departments of Justice and Commerce to undertake an exhaustive investigation of bankruptcy law and practice with view to the elimination of malpractice and to development of a more constructive method of readjustment of debts, so as to avoid many bankruptcies and foreclosures. This inquiry resulted in the proposal by himself with the support of Attorney General Mitchell of definite reforms.

Broadly they provided for

(*a*) elimination of fraud in bankruptcy practice;

(*b*) conciliation and adjustment of debt with the aid of the courts;

(*c*) protection during the period of negotiation;

486

(*d*) creation of a system of conciliators under the courts for farmers, home-owners and small debtors;

(*e*) provision against speculators buying up debt in order to seize property;

(*f*) provision for a two-thirds rule to bind security holders in corporations under protection of the courts—the latter safe-guarded against the current hold-ups of minorities and the necessity of property sale, usually to speculators.

In December, 1931, the exhaustive report of the Departments was transmitted to the Congress with the President's recom-mendation and with draft legislation for the committees of Congress. In the accompanying Message the President said:

"The Federal Government is charged under the Constitution with the responsibility of providing the country with an adequate system for the administration of bankrupt estates. The importance of such a system to the business life of the community is apparent. The number of cases in bankruptcy has steadily increased from 23,000 in the fiscal year 1921 to 53,000 in 1928 and to 65,000 in 1931. The liabilities involved have increased from $171,000,000 in 1921 to $830,000,000 in 1928 and to $1,008,000,000 in 1931, and the losses to creditors have increased from $144,000,000 in 1921 to $740,000,000 in 1928 and to $911,000,000 in 1931. The increases are therefore obviously not due to the economic sit-uation, but to deeper causes."

"A sound bankruptcy system should operate—

"First, to relieve honest but unfortunate debtors of an overwhelming burden of debt;

"Second, to effect a prompt and economical liquidation and distribu-tion of insolvent estates; and

"Third, to discourage fraud and needless waste of assets by withhold-ing relief from debtors in proper cases."

"For some time the prevailing opinion has been that our present bank-ruptcy act has failed in its purpose and needs thorough revision. During the past year the Department of Justice, with my approval, has conducted an investigation into the administration of bankrupt estates in the Federal courts. Nation-wide in its scope, the inquiry has involved intensive study of the practical operation of the bankruptcy act under varying local con-ditions throughout the United States. Court records and special reports of referees have been analyzed. Organizations of business men and law-yers have assisted in gathering information not available through official channels. Judges, prosecuting officers, referees, merchants, bankers, and others have made available their experience. Data gathered by the Department of Commerce relating to causes of failure and the effect of bad debts upon business have been studied. The history of bankruptcy legislation and administration in this country, and in Great Britain, Canada, and other countries, has been reviewed."

"The inquiry has now been completed. Its result is embodied in a report which is transmitted herewith for the consideration of the Congress. Thorough and exhaustive in detail, it presents the information necessary to enable the Congress to determine the faults in the present law and to devise their cure."

"The present bankruptcy act is defective in that it holds out every inducement for waste of assets long after business failure has become inevitable. It permits exploitation of its own process and wasteful administration by those who are neither truly representative of the creditor nor the bankrupt."

"Except in rare cases it results in the grant of a full discharge of all debts without sufficient inquiry as to the conduct of the bankrupt or of the causes of failure. It discharges from their debts large numbers of persons who might have paid without hardship had the law discriminated between those overwhelmed by misfortune and those needing only temporary relief and the opportunity to deal fairly with their creditors."

"The bankruptcy act should be amended to provide remedial processes in voluntary proceedings under which debtors, unable to pay their debts in due course, may have the protection of the court without being adjudged bankrupt, for the purpose of composing or extending the maturity of their debts, of amortizing the payment of their debts out of future earnings, of procuring the liquidation of their property under voluntary assignment to a trustee; or, in the case of corporations, for the purpose of reorganization."

"The act should be amended to require the examination of every bankrupt by a responsible official and a full disclosure of the cause of his failure and of his conduct in connection therewith for the consideration of the court in determining whether he should have his discharge."

"The discretion of the courts in granting or refusing discharges should be broadened, and they should be authorized to postpone discharges for a time and require bankrupts, during the period of suspension, to make some satisfaction out of after-acquired property as a condition to the granting of a full discharge." [*State Papers, Vol. II, pp. 134–5*]

The President did not sit idly waiting for Congress to act. In conferences with senators and representatives he urged its importance, stating, as recorded by Myers and Newton:

". . . One of the essentials to recovery from the depression was the readjustment of inflated and unbearable debt. While it is certain that the processes of war and of booms build up inflated debts, the processes of depression, in turn, correct this ill balance between the debtor and the creditor."

"He urged that 'debtors should not be sacrificed for causes beyond their control and to an advantage of the creditor.' 'Sacrifices must be mutual.' But he likewise insisted that 'debts are individual, not collective.' It must be a process of 'individual adjustment.' He held that these adjustments could be greatly facilitated by taking advantage of the constitutional control of bankruptcy vested in the Federal Government to provide a more workable method of mutual readjustment between debtors and creditors."

"He urged it as one of the most important policies of the administration. . . . That it would make a valuable contribution to the necessary readjustments . . . the mutual interests of both creditors and debtors. Moreover, there was a vast amount of graft and plunder current in old bankruptcy practices, in certain localities, which required immediate reform."

[Hoover Administration, p. 321]

He did not succeed, due to Democratic opposition, in getting the bill further than committees in the winter session of 1931–32.

He returned to the charge, however, after the election and on January 11, 1933, he addressed a special Message to Congress:

"On February 29 last I addressed the Congress on the urgent necessity for revision of the bankruptcy laws, and presented detailed proposals to that end. These proposals were based upon most searching inquiry into the whole subject which had been undertaken by the Attorney-General at my direction. . . . I urge that the matter be given attention in this session, for effective legislation would have most helpful economic and social results in the welfare and recovery of the Nation."

"The process of forced liquidation through foreclosure and bankruptcy sale of the assets of individual and corporate debtors, who through no fault of their own are unable in the present emergency to provide for the payment of their debts in ordinary course as they mature, is utterly destructive of the interests of debtor and creditor alike, and if this process is allowed to take its usual course misery will be suffered by thousands without substantial gain to their creditors, who insist upon liquidation and foreclosure in the vain hope of collecting their claims. In the great majority of cases such liquidation under present conditions is so futile and destructive that voluntary readjustments through the extension or composition of individual debts and the reorganization of corporations must be desirable to a large majority of the creditors."

"I wish again to emphasize that the passage of legislation for this relief of individual and corporate debtors at this session of Congress is a matter of the most vital importance. It has a major bearing upon the whole economic situation in the adjustment of the relation of debtors and creditors. I therefore recommend its immediate consideration as an emergency action." [*State Papers, Vol. II, p. 567*]

The House passed a bill, but it was held up in the Senate. President Hoover addressed yet another Message to Congress on February 20, 1933, in which he said:

"It is most necessary that the principles of the Bankruptcy Bill which has already been acted upon by the House should be passed by the Senate. The whole object of the bill is to secure orderly co-operation between creditors and debtors, whether farmers, individuals, general corporations or railroads, for mutual adjustment which will preserve the integrity and continuous operation of business, save the values of good will and the continuation of people in their occupations and thus avoid destruction of the interest of both parties. This legislation is of the most critical importance in this period of readjustment. Incidentally such a workable system is highly necessary in order to permit a certain minority of railroads to be so reorganized as to reduce fixed charges and thus relieve the Reconstruction Finance Corporation of drains in prevention of destructive receiverships." [*State Papers, Vol. II, p. 597*]

Congress ultimately passed a bill, but the Senate had excluded the provisions for corporation reorganization, retaining the provision for individual adjustment and railway reorganization. In the previous October the President had canvassed many leading insurance and mortgage companies and received assurance that if such a bill were passed, they would immediately undertake co-operation with their debtors for wide-scale and rapid readjustments. Had the bill been passed promptly and completely the year before, it would greatly have alleviated hu-

man hardship by the readjustment of the oppressive debts of
the farm and home owners. It would have offered a method
for the readjustment of impossible corporation and railway
debts. It would have saved much fraud and waste current
under the old bankruptcy processes, kept thousands of concerns
from bankruptcy, and also have prevented much of that spread
of fear which is so destructive to public confidence when large
and continuous closures of business and dispossession of home
owners are in process. Even had it been promptly passed after
the election, it would have contributed greatly to stability. The
deletion of the corporation feature and this delay in passage
have prevented the use of it to the extent possible had it been made
a feature of the original legislation as recommended.

The destructive attitude of the Democratic majority toward
this legislation, and the delays in its passage, only added to the
general discouragement of the country.[1]

The Hoover policy in this legislation was a new approach to
the whole question of debt readjustments from inflated values.
The Democratic method of readjustment of inflated debt was to
devalue the currency.

In discussing the comparative methods Hoover later on stated:

"One of the major objectives stated [for devaluation] was to reduce
unbearable debt. It was asserted that the value of the dollar as represented in its purchasing power for goods or services had changed from
its value when the original bargains of debt were made. Under this operation the citizens were regimented into two groups, debtors and creditors. An empirical and universal amount of 40 to 50 per cent was set
as the degree of shift in the value of all property to the debtor regiment
from the creditor regiment."

"This act involved the widest responsibility which the Government
bears to its citizens, and that individuals bear toward each other. For
fidelity to contract, unless determined unconscionable by an independent
tribunal, is the very integrity of Liberty and of any economic society."

"These monetary acts extend the assumption of unbearable debt over
the whole of the private and public debts of the Nation. That this attempt at universal shift of 40 to 50 per cent of the value of all debts was
neither necessary nor just can be demonstrated in a few sentences. The
theory mistakenly assumed that the distorted prices and values at the
depth of a banking panic were permanent. It assumed that the recovery

[1]It is interesting to note that the incoming administration caused Congress to pass the
clauses which had been deleted from Hoover's bill.

from depression in progress through the world would not extend to the United States. Of even more importance, this theory also assumed that every single debt had become oppressive; that every single creditor had benefited by about one-half since the initial bargain; that every single debtor had lost by this amount; that no debtor could carry out his initial bargain; and that the respective rights of every debtor and every creditor in every kind of property should be shifted from debtor to creditor without any inquiry or process of justice. Debt is an individual thing, not a mass transaction. The circumstances of every debt vary."

"Certainly the Government cannot contend that its debt was oppressive. No man has yet stated that the Government could not have paid its obligations in full. It was not insolvent. It was not bankrupt."

"In large areas of private debt the borrower was amply able to meet his obligations. In other great areas he had already profited by large dividends or earnings, or otherwise by the use of the savings of lenders which he had deliberately solicited. A huge part of the bond issues of railways, of power companies, of industrial companies, of foreign governments, current commercial debt, the bank deposits, urban mortgages and what not belong to these categories."

"The evidence of the volume of debts which require governmental relief as a social necessity does not by any conceivable calculation indicate more than a very minor percentage of the total public and private debt. Extensive provisions for the adjustment between individuals of their debts were made by new facilities under the bankruptcy acts and the further relief measures provided through the use of Government credit."

"But let us examine the injustice under this managed currency more particularly. In a great category where debt required adjustment there had already been many compromises between debtors and investors, as witness the many reorganizations of urban building loans, and corporate and other obligations, which were the products of inflation. The people's savings invested in these cases are required, by depreciation of the dollar, to submit to a still further loss."

"Most lending is ultimately from savings which mean somebody's self-denial of the joy of spending today in order to provide for the future. But the borrower is often enough a person who secured these joys and is now to be relieved of part payment, although a large part of these borrowers are able to pay. The man who borrowed from an insurance company to build himself a more expensive and enjoyable house has secured these joys at the cost of the policyholder, who had hoped by self-denial to escape dependency. This applies equally to the huge debt of industrial and commercial businesses which profited by their borrowings from the policyholder and the depositor in a savings bank."

"Those self-denying investors—the thrifty of the Nation—who were willing to accept a low rate of interest in order to obtain the maximum security are under this theory to have the purchasing value of their savings now shrunken in exactly the same ratio as the avaricious who received extortionate rates, or the reckless who took high risks. The holders of hard-won savings—the widow's mite—invested in 3¼ per cent first mortgage industrial bonds are called upon to sacrifice the same proportion as the holders of 7 per cent third mortgages. By the transfer of values from the first mortgage bondholder to the common stockholder the security of these speculative bonds is even increased. At once we see the evidence of this in the marked advance in the prices of these speculative debts. This disregard of prudence and this benefit to recklessness particularly penalizes a very large part of insurance and the great public endowment assets."

"Ten billions of endowments in educational, hospitalization, and welfare activities—creditors whose debtors are mostly corporations and governments—are to be depleted in purchasing power. These endowed institutions give the leadership necessary to all our vast complex of public institutions. Yet if this theory eventuate, their activities must diminish by 40 per cent."

"Furthermore, if this theory shall succeed, in the great bulk of industrial debt, the empirical reduction of purchasing power of the regiments of bondholders transfers this purchasing power to the regiments of common stockholders. Any inspection of who are the rank and file in these regiments will at once demonstrate the double injustice. The holders of bonds are largely the insurance company, the savings bank depositor, the small investor, and the endowed institution."

"If this intent of devaluation shall eventuate, the transfer of property by Government fiat from 60,000,000 insurance policyholders to 10,000,000 stockholders is not even diffusion of wealth. It is further concentration of wealth. As a matter of fact, any survey of the total results would show (if the theory of these acts works out) that it will benefit the richest members of the community, because their property is, in the main, in equities. The hardship will fall upon the great mass of the people who are indirect holders of obligations through their savings in insurance, in savings bank deposits, as well as those who directly hold bonds and mortgages. That is, in our modern American economy the rich are more largely the holders of equities and those of moderate means more largely the holders of obligations. Thus the rich hereby become richer, the poor poorer."[1]   [*The Challenge to Liberty, pp. 92–98*]

WORLD STABILIZATION OF CURRENCIES

The abandonment of the gold standard by some forty countries, beginning with the Central European financial collapse in April, 1931, continuing after the British collapse in September, threw the whole world trade into confusion. There began a direct and indirect gigantic trade war using currencies as the major weapon. Nations were seeking advantages in exports and at the same time raising tariffs, placing embargoes and quotas on imports.

One of the objects of the French Premier Laval's visit to the United States in October, 1931, was mutual discussion of this subject. President Hoover, accompanied by Secretaries Stimson and Mills, and Premier Laval both agreed that the first essential of stability in a rocking world was that these two countries hold fast. It was concluded that it was too early to call a world conference for currency stabilization but that it must be undertaken later in an effort to stop the disintegration then in progress. The joint statement issued by President Hoover and Premier Laval on October 25, 1931, said:

"We canvassed the economic situation in the world, the trends in international relations bearing upon it; the problems of the forthcoming conference for limitation and reduction of armaments; the effect of the depression on payments under inter-governmental debts; the stabilization of international exchanges and other financial and economic subjects."

"Our especial emphasis has been upon the more important means

---

[1]Debt readjustment by devaluation, undertaken by the Roosevelt Administration, proved a futility because of the slowness in the inflationary effect upon prices. The difficulties of debtors and creditors still continued. In consequence the Hoover policies have proved invaluable to the country. Literally hundreds of thousands of farm mortgages have been readjusted under these laws and the farms saved to the owners. Over 6000 corporation reorganizations are under progress of adjustment by these provisions without destructive bankruptcy.

Had Hoover's plan been allowed to work out it would have served every purpose of righteous debt readjustment without devaluating the currency.

through which the efforts of our government could be exerted toward restoration of economic stability and confidence. Particularly we are convinced of the importance of monetary stability as an essential factor in the restoration of normal economic life in the world in which the maintenance of the gold standard in France and the United States will serve as a major influence." [*State Papers, Vol. II, pp. 20–1*]

After some preliminary inquiries, the President, on May 24, 1932, requested Secretary Stimson to open conversations with Prime Minister MacDonald of Great Britain upon an international conference to bring about stabilization of currencies, exchanges, and removal of trade barriers that had sprung from these instabilities. The President not only considered action imperative but that the time had come for action. He further felt that the announcements and organization of such a conference would in itself give some increase in confidence and hope. He felt it desirable that the British should lead in calling the conference rather than we who had held to stable currency and had imposed no trade barriers during the crisis. The Prime Minister accepted these proposals and on May 21 the calling of the conference was announced. It was understood that the conference would meet after the Presidential elections in the fall, probably in January or February, 1933.

In the meantime, a body of experts was chosen by each of the nations who met at Geneva on November 1, 1932, and formulated the program of the conference. The American delegates were Ambassador Sackett, Norman Davis, E. E. Day, and J. H. Williams. This preliminary conference did more than arrange a program; they reported upon the urgent necessity for prompt agreement to end these destructive competitions and made some progress in preparing methods. The unanimity in this preliminary conference again added confidence to the world.

In reporting to the Congress upon the purposes of the conference, President Hoover said, on December 19, 1932:

"While it is difficult in any analysis of world economic forces to separate the cause from the effect or the symptom from the disease, or to separate one segment of a vicious cycle from another, we must begin somewhere by determination of our objectives."

". . . the most urgent economic effort still before the world is the restoration of price levels. The undue and continued fall in prices and trade obviously has many origins. One dangerous consequence however is visible enough in the increased difficulties which are arising between many debtors and creditors. The values behind a multitude of securities are lessened, the income of debtors is insufficient to meet their obligations, creditors are unable to undertake new commitments for fear of the safety of present undertakings."

"It is not enough to say that the fall in prices is due to decreased consumption and thus the sole remedy is the adjustment by reduced production. That is in part true but decreased consumption is brought about by certain economic forces which, if overcome, would result in a great measure of recovery of consumption and thus recovery from the depression. Any competent study of the causes of continued abnormal levels of prices would at once establish the fact that the general price movement is world-wide in character and international influences therefore have a part in them. Further exploration in this field brings us at once to the fact that price levels have been seriously affected by abandonment of the gold standard by many countries and the consequent instability and depreciation of foreign currencies. These fluctuations in themselves, through the uncertainties they create, stifle trade, cause invasions of unnatural marketing territory, result in arbitrary trade restrictions and ultimate diminished consumption of goods, followed by a further fall in prices."

". . . Restrictions have not alone been put upon the movement of gold and exchange but they have been imposed upon imports of goods in endeavor to prevent the spending of undue sums abroad by their nationals as a further precaution to prevent the outflow of gold reserves and thus undermining of currency. These steps have again reduced consumption and diminished prices and are but parts of the vicious cycles which must be broken at some point if we are to assure economic recovery."

"We have abundant proof of the effect of these forces within our own borders. The depreciation of foreign currencies lowers the cost of production abroad compared to our costs of production, thus undermining the effect of our protective tariffs. Prices of agricultural and other commodities in the United States are being seriously affected and thousands of our workers are today being thrown out of employment through the invasion of such goods."

". . . one of the first and most fundamental points of attack is to re-establish stability of currencies and foreign exchange, and thereby release an infinite number of barriers against the movement of commodities, the general effect of which would be to raise the prices of commodities throughout the world."

". . . While the gold standard has worked badly since the War due to the huge economic dislocations of the War, yet it is still the only practicable basis of international settlements and monetary stability so far as the more advanced industrial nations are concerned. The larger use of silver as a supplementary currency would aid to stability in many quarters of the world. In any event it is a certainty that trade and prices must be disorganized until some method of monetary and exchange stability is attained."

"It is for the purpose of discussing these and other matters most vital to us and the rest of the world that we have joined in the World Economic Conference, where . . . measures for the turning of the tide of business and price levels . . . can be fully and effectively considered, and if possible undertaken simultaneously between nations. . . ."

[*State Papers, Vol. II, pp. 548–9*]

Prior to the election President Hoover had determined upon the men whom he would send as American delegates to the Economic Conference, representatives and leaders of both political parties.[1] He had deferred communicating with them on the subject until the results of the approaching election might be known. With Roosevelt's election, Hoover recognized that Roosevelt might wish to appoint a different delegation. He assumed that the new President would wish to proceed at the earliest possible moment, since a successful and early consummation of the Conference would give further impulse to the world recovery already in progress. The conferees would, of course, come to no conclusion before Roosevelt was in office. On November 12, 1932, President Hoover telegraphed President-elect Roosevelt suggesting a personal conference upon pressing questions, after discussing the World War Debt.

". . . The building up of world economic stability is of the greatest importance to the building up of our recovery . . . as you know a world economic conference will be held during the course of the coming winter. . . . While this conference may be begun during my administration it is certain it will not complete its labors until after you have assumed office.

[1]These were Secretary of the Treasury Mills, Senators David Reed and Carter Glass, Congressmen Luce and Crisp, with Silas Strawn, Henry Robinson, Colonel Edward House, William Green of the A. F. of L., Louis Taber of the National Grange, and one unselected.

. . . Time is of the greatest importance in all these questions. . . . I hope you will find it convenient . . . for me to advise with you. . . ."

The President and the President-elect conferred on November 22. The President proposed that a delegation should be selected at once in order that they might have the ensuing months to prepare for their task. He proposed they should simultaneously deal with War Debt questions (see War Debts, page 516) and the stabilization conference and co-ordinate with the World Disarmament Conference then in session. He considered all these problems must be interrelated if we were to secure real results. Roosevelt rejected the idea of any delegation and suggested that Hoover negotiate through his ambassadors. This was manifestly impractical since no round-table action can be taken in forty capitals, and, of more importance, no agreement would be binding upon Roosevelt. Moreover, no nation would negotiate with an administration which had but three months to live.

All these efforts by their very promise had contributed to world recovery and President Hoover was most anxious to give continued support to the gradually improving situation. All the world, including our our own business men, looked anxiously for the attitude of Roosevelt on forwarding these policies. The objectives were wholly non-political and every one was hopeful of co-operative action.

The press expressed great disappointment at Roosevelt's attitude both toward stablization progress and the delay in the War Debt question.

Said the *Detroit Free Press:* "It is highly unfortunate that Governor Roosevelt was unable to bring himself to meet the President half way. The refusal of the governor to co-operate actively with Mr. Hoover and his subsequent statement that the matter at issue was 'not his baby,' are indicative of the lack of largeness and vision most disquieting in a person about to become the Chief Executive of the Nation. . . . Mr. Roosevelt had an opportunity unique in the history of the American Presidency, and he failed to grasp it."

The New York Herald Tribune stated (November 24, 1932): "Americans are so accustomed to having Mr. Hoover do the right and courageous thing that his admirable statement on the debts will hardly occasion surprise. It covers a complex issue, endlessly bedeviled by national prejudices and selfishness, clearly, fairly, and with a minimum of words. . . ."

"It may be recalled that during the campaign there was heat

and resentment in Democratic quarters when it was argued that a change of administration inevitably meant marking time for a number of months. Mr. Hoover has now done his utmost to prevent such a delay in respect to the debt issue. Mr. Roosevelt has felt unable to aid him. The delay must ensue."

The Baltimore Sun said (November 24) that "the debts may not be legally his baby until the fourth of March, but it seems to us that Mr. Roosevelt might wisely have given thought to the possibility that this baby, which is not now his, may soon develop into an unruly stepchild, permanently lodged under his roof, and disposed to play with matches."

Within a month the effects of this attitude had begun to affect adversely the economic situation and on December 17, President Hoover returned to the subject in a telegram to Governor Roosevelt, again urging the selection of representatives to discuss some phases of the War Debts and the stablization:

"These problems cannot be disassociated from the problems which will come before the World Economic Conference. As the economic situation in foreign countries is one of the dominant depressants of prices and employment in the United States it is urgent that the World Economic Conference should assemble at as early a date as possible. The United States should be represented by a strong and effective delegation. This delegation should be chosen at an early moment in order that it may give necessary consideration and familiarize itself with the problems, and secure that such investigation and study are made as will be necessary for its use at the Conference. . . ."

". . . it seems clear that the successful outcome of the World Economic Conference will be greatly furthered if the debt problems can be satisfactorily advanced before that Conference although final agreement in some cases may be contingent upon the satisfactory solution of certain economic questions in which our country has a direct interest and the final determination of which may well form a part of the matters coming before the Economic Conference."

"It is desirable that such delegation should include members of the Congress in order that such intricate facts and circumstances can be effectively presented to the Congress. . . ."

"If it were not for the urgency of the situation both at home and abroad and the possible great helpfulness to employment and agricultural prices and general restoration of confidence which could be brought about by successful issue of all these questions and the corresponding great dangers of inaction, it would be normal to allow the whole matter to rest until after the change of administration, but in the emergency such as exists at the moment I would be neglectful of my duty if I did not facilitate in every way the earliest possible dealing with these questions. It is obvious that no conclusions would be reached from such discussions prior to March 4, but a great deal of time could be saved if the machinery could be created at once by the appointment of the delegates as I have mentioned. . . ."

"I should be glad to know if you could join with me in the selection of such delegation at the present time or if you feel that the whole matter should be deferred until after March 4. I believe that there would be no difficulty in agreeing upon an adequate representation for the purpose."

[*State Papers, Vol. II, p. 554 et seq.*]

As President-elect Roosevelt stated he was unwilling to proceed on the line suggested by President Hoover, the latter, on December 20, replied:

"I have your telegram expressing the difficulties which you find in co-operation at the present time. In the face of foreign conditions which are continually degenerating agricultural prices, increasing unemployment and creating economic difficulties for our people, I am unwilling to admit that co-operation cannot be established between the outgoing and incoming administrations which will give earlier solution and recovery from these difficulties."

". . . my proposals to you have been directed to the setting up not of solutions but of the machinery through which by preparedness the ultimate solution of these questions can be expedited . . . that many months of delay and increasing losses to our people may be avoided."

". . . conclusions obviously cannot be attained in my administration and will lie entirely within your administration. . . . What I deem of the utmost importance is that . . . on March 4 machinery of your approval will be here, fully informed and ready to function according to the policies you may determine. . . ."

"With view to again making an effort to secure co-operation and that solidarity of national action which the situation needs, I would be glad if you could designate Mr. Owen D. Young, Colonel House, or any other men of your party possessed of your views and your confidence and at the same time familiar with these problems, to sit with the principal officers of this administration, in endeavor to see what steps can be taken to avoid delays of precious time and inevitable losses that will ensue from such delays."

Again Roosevelt declined and Hoover reluctantly dropped the matter with the statement on December 22:

"Governor Roosevelt considers it undesirable for him to accede to my suggestions for co-operative action. . . . I will respect his wishes. . . ."

When it became evident in the winter of 1933 that President-elect Roosevelt intended to tinker with the currency and thus to delay world stabilization, President Hoover made a powerful address in support of the gold standard and his stabilization policies in New York on February 14, 1933. He said in part:

"Economic degeneration is always a series of vicious cycles of cause and effect. Whatever the causes may be, we must grasp these cycles at some segment and deal with them. Perhaps it would add clarity to the position I wish to make later if I should shortly follow through the cycle of financial failure which has at least in part taken place in countries abroad. Many countries . . . were overburdened with debt . . . unbalanced budgets . . . finally reaching the point where collapse in governmental credit was inevitable. Foreigners in fear withdrew their deposits in such countries. Citizens in fright exported their capital. The result was a large movement of gold from such a country followed by the immediate undermining of confidence in its currency and its credit system. Runs on its banks ensued. Restrictions were imposed upon exchange to stop the flight of capital. Barriers were erected against the imports of commodities in endeavor to reduce the spending of their citizens for foreign goods and in an effort to establish equilibrium in exchange and retention of their gold reserves. Failure in such efforts resulted in abandonment of the gold standard. Currency depreciation, stagnation of their industries, increase in their unemployment and further shrinkage in consumption of world goods, again and again affecting all other nations. Depreciated currencies gave some nations the hope to manufacture goods more cheaply than their neighbors and thus to rehabilitate their financial position by invasion of the markets of other nations. Those nations in turn have sought to protect themselves by erecting barriers, until today as a result of such financial breakdown we are in the presence of an incipient outbreak of economic war in the world with the weapons of depreciated currencies, artificial barriers to trade by quotas, reciprocal trade agreements, discriminations, nationalistic campaigns to consume home-made goods, and a score of tactics each of which can be justified for the moment, but each of which adds to world confusion and dangers."

"Out of the storm center of Europe this devastation has spread until, if we survey the world situation at the present moment, we find some forty-four countries which have placed restrictions upon the movement of gold and exchange or are otherwise definitely off the gold standard. In practically all of them these actions have within the past twelve months been accompanied by new restrictions upon imports in an endeavor to hold or attract gold or to give some stability to currencies."

"These depreciations of currency and regulations of exchange and restrictions of imports originated as defense measures by nations to meet their domestic financial difficulties. But a new phase is now developing among these nations, that is the rapid degeneration into economic war which threatens to engulf the world. The imperative call to the world today is to prevent this war."

"Ever since the storm began in Europe the United States has held stanchly to the gold standard. In the present setting of depreciated currencies and in the light of differences in costs of production our tariffs are below those of most countries; we have held free from quotas, preferences, discriminations among nations. We have thereby maintained one Gibraltar of stability in the world and contributed to check the movement to chaos."

"We are ourselves now confronted with an unnatural movement of goods from the lowered costs and standards of countries of depreciated currencies, which daily increase our unemployment and our difficulties. We are confronted with discriminatory actions and barriers stifling our agricultural and other markets. We will be ourselves forced to defensive action to protect ourselves unless this mad race is stopped. We must not be the major victim of it all."

"In all this competition of degeneration, these beginnings of economic war between scores of nations, we see a gradual shrinkage in demand for international commodities throughout the world, and continuing fall of prices in terms of gold. From falling prices and unemployment we have at once the inability of debtors to meet obligations to their creditors, the dispossession of people from their farms and homes and businesses."

"If the world is to secure economic peace, if it is to turn in the tide of degeneration, if it is to restore the functioning of the production and distribution systems of the world, it must start somewhere to break these vicious fiscal and financial circles. I am convinced that the first point of attack is to secure assured greater stability in the currencies of the important commercial nations. Without such stability the continued results of uncertainty, the destruction of confidence by currency fluctuations, exchange controls, and artificial import restrictions cannot be overcome but will continue to increase. With effective stability of currencies these dangers can be at once relaxed. I am not unaware that currency instability is both a cause and an effect in the vicious cycle—but we must start somewhere."

"In all the welter of discussion over these problems we find some who are maintaining that the world has outgrown the use of gold as a basis of currency and exchange. We can all agree that gold as a commodity of universal exchange has not worked perfectly in the face of this great economic eruption. But we have to remember that it is a commodity the value of which is enshrined in human instincts for over 10,000 years. The time may come when the world can safely abandon its use altogether for these purposes, but it has not yet reached that point. It may be that by theoretically managed currencies some form of stability may be found a score or two years hence, but we have no time to wait. They are subject to great human fallibilities. Sooner or later political pressure of special groups and interests will direct their use. But in any event it would take many years' demonstration to convince men that a non-gold currency would certainly a year hence be worth what he paid for it today."

"To add to the confusion, another phenomenon of the gold situation has increased disturbance and wrought havoc. That is the effect of waves of fear and apprehension. We have a parallel in nations to an unreasoning panic run on a bank. The fears and apprehensions directed in turn to the stability of first one nation and then another have caused the withdrawal of foreign balances from a particular nation, followed by flights of capital, through purchases of exchange by its own citizens seeking refuge and security for their property. These movements are followed by large flows of gold to meet exchange demands, thus undermining the domestic currency and credit system of the victim nation and leading to an unnatural piling up of gold in some nation temporarily considered safe. These movements, themselves in large degree unwarranted, have forced some nations off the gold standard that could otherwise have maintaind their position. We ourselves a year ago suffered from the effects of such a movement. Thus a mass of the gold dashing hither and yon from one nation to another, seeking maximum safety, has acted like a cannon loose on the deck of the world in a storm."

"Broadly, the solution lies in the re-establishment of confidence. That confidence cannot be re-established by the abandonment of gold as a standard in the world. So far as the human race has yet developed and established its methods and systems of stable exchange, that solution can only be found now and found quickly through the re-establishment of gold standards among important nations. The huge gold reserves of the world can be made to function in relation to currencies, standards of value, and exchange. And I say with emphasis that I am not proposing this as a favor to the United States. It is the need of the whole world. The United States is so situated that it can protect itself better than almost any country on earth."

"Nor is it necessary from an international point of view that those nations who have been forced off the gold standard shall be again restored to former gold values. It will suffice if it only is fixed. From this source are the principal hopes for restoring world confidence and reversing the growing barriers to the movement of goods, and making possible the security in trade which will again revive a demand for such goods. To do this it is necessary to have strong and courageous action on the part of the leading commercial nations. If some sort of international financial action is necessary to enable central banks to co-operate for the purpose of stabilizing currencies, nations should have no hesitation in joining in such an operation under proper safeguards. If some part of the debt payments to us could be set aside for temporary use for this purpose, we should not hesitate to do so. At the same time the world should endeavor to find a place for silver, at least in enlarged subsidiary coinage."

"If the major nations will enter the road leading to the early re-establishment of the gold standard, then and then only can the abnormal barriers to trade, the quotas, preferences, discriminatory agreements, and tariffs which exceed the differences in costs of production between nations be removed, uniform trade privileges among all nations be re-established and the threat of economic war averted. A reasonable period of comparative stability in the world's currencies would repay the cost of such effort a hundred times over in the increase of consumption, the increase of employment, the lessening of the difficulties of debtors throughout the land, with the avoidance of millions of tragedies. The world would quickly see a renewed movement of goods and would have an immediate rise in prices everywhere thereby bringing immediate relief to the whole economic system."

"I do not underestimate the difficulties nor the vast fiscal and financial problems which lie behind the restoration of stability and economic peace. Bold action alone can succeed. The alternative to such constructive action is a condition too grave to be contemplated in passive acceptance."

"The American people will soon be at the fork of three roads. The first is the highway of co-operation among nations, thereby to remove the obstructions to world consumption and rising prices. This road leads to real stability, to expanding standards of living, to a resumption of the march of progress by all peoples. It is today the immediate road to relief of agriculture and unemployment, not alone for us but the entire world."

"The second road is to rely upon our high degree of national self-containment, to increase our tariffs, to create quotas and discriminations, and to engage in definite methods of curtailment of production of agricultural and other products and thus to secure a larger measure of economic isolation from world influences. It would be a long road of readjustments into unknown and uncertain fields. But it may be necessary if the first way out is closed to us. Some measures may be necessary pending co-operative conclusions with other nations."

"The third road is that we inflate our currency, consequently abandon the gold standard, and with our depreciated currency attempt to enter a world economic war, with the certainty that it leads to complete destruction, both at home and abroad."

"In its broad light the problem before the world today is to work together to prevent the dangers of developing economic conflict—to secure economic peace. That is a field in which the world can co-operate even more easily than in the field of prevention of war, because there is involved in it no background of century-old controversies, injustices, or hates. The problems in that economic field contain less of the imponderables and more of the concrete. There is involved in it the most important and appealing self-interest of every nation. Through such co-operation the world can mitigate the forces which are destroying the systems of production and distribution upon the maintenance of which its gigantic population is dependent. There is a driving force before the eyes of every statesman in the misery and suffering which have infected every nation. Throughout the world the people are distraught with unemployment; the decline of prices which has plunged farmers into despair; the loss of homes, of savings and provisions for old age. Therefore, just as there is an obligation amongst nations to engage in every possible step for the prevention of war itself, there is before us today the necessity for world co-operation to prevent economic warfare. And who can say but the greatest act in prevention of war is to allay economic friction."

"On our side this problem is not to be solved by partisan action but by national unity. Whatever our differences of view may be on domestic policies, the welfare of the American people rests upon solidarity before the world, not merely in resisting proposals which would weaken the United States and the world but solidarity in co-operation with other nations in strengthening the whole economic fabric of the world. These problems are not insoluble. There is a latent, earnest, and underlying purpose on the part of all nations to find their solution. Of our own determination there should be no question."

"The problem before the world is to restore confidence and hope by the release of the strong, natural forces of recovery which are inherent in this civilization. Civilization is the history of surmounted difficulties. We of this world today are of the same strain as our fathers who builded this civilization. They passed through most terrible conflicts. They met many great depressions. They created a state of human well-being in normal times such as the world has never seen. The next forward step is as great as any in history. It is that we perpetuate the welfare of mankind through the immense objectives of world recovery and world peace."

[*State Papers, Vol. II, p. 588*]

The Stabilization Conference (the London Economic Conference) was not convened until July, 1933. Its results are well known. The failure to carry on President Hoover's policies in this field have been a disaster not alone to the United States but to the world as a whole. And the end of these disasters is not yet. Certainly the hand that successfully guided the Naval Limitations Conference, the Moratorium, and the Standstill Agreement, was no longer at the helm.

WORLD WAR DEBTS

The Hoover policies on the War Debts were clear and emphatic. He wholly opposed cancellation. The War Debt borrowers should pay up to their capacity to pay. He was prepared to favor readjustment to capacity to pay at any time revision could be proved necessary. And he considered that the integrity and ultimate payment of the debt required fore-handed co-operation with the debtors during the depression.

On October 16, 1922, he delivered an address at Toledo, Ohio, which had much to do with formulating public opinion on the subject:

"Proposals have been repeatedly made over the last three years that the loans from our Government to foreign countries during the War should in part or in whole be cancelled, either for moral reasons or in the interest of economic stability. . . . Full understanding can be advanced only by full and frank discussion. . . ."

"There are certain phases . . . that . . . require emphasis."

"First. These loans are often spoken of as debts to our Government. They are, in fact, debts owing to our taxpayers. These loans were made at the urgent request of the borrowers and under their solemn assurance of repayment. The loans were individual to each nation. They have no relation to other nations or other debts. The American taxpayer did not participate in reparations and acquired no territory or any other benefits under the Treaty, as did our debtors. There is no question as to the moral or contractual obligation. The repudiation of these loans would undermine the whole fabric of international good faith. I do not believe any public official, either of the United States or any other country, could or should approve their cancellation. Certainly *I* do not."

"Second. . . . I am convinced that the *capital sum* of these debts can be paid some time with the exception of say 5 per cent. I am also convinced that this can be done without realization of the oft-expressed undue strain on the debtor countries or the threat of a flood of goods from debtor countries in such quantity as would endanger employment of the factories and workmen of the United States. . . ."

"Third. . . . The burden of payments falls with different weight upon each of the nineteen different debtors . . . it will be found that respective annual payments due to us from different countries vary in their burden upon them from 2 to 12 per cent of their governmental income."

"Fourth. If there be some of these countries who should be relieved . . . in order to promote economic stability, then there needs be a demonstration . . . that would be convincing to the American public and to Congress. The taxpayer will . . . naturally consider that . . . there must be such political and economic readjustment . . . of Europe as will bring about an atmosphere of peace in replacement of an atmosphere of war. . . . There must be a reduction of armament . . . as a guarantee of peace. . . . There must be a general intent to create good will and peaceful working together . . . instead of constant recurrence of political crises which so narrowly escape war and so sadly disturb commerce. . . ."

"Fifth. America has dealt with Europe during the past few years in terms of idealism. . . . What the American people would do in the circumstances that the forces of real world peace and prosperity were put in motion, could be looked forward to with confidence. . . ."

"In arguments . . . that the loans must be cancelled, the claim is seldom made that the payment cannot be provided out of taxation or reduction of expenditures in the debtor country, and payments made in the local currency of that country. The economic contention is that such currency must be transformed into goods or gold in order to be shipped to the American people. . . ."

". . . that these shipments would necessarily be direct from the debtor country to us; that such shipments might embarrass our industries and employment; . . . that present trade balances should be taken as an indication of future paying power . . . the whole of these assumptions need to be seriously modified. . . ."

". . . For instance, the annual expenditure of American tourists abroad, the remittances of emigrants in the United States to their relatives abroad, the growing volume of investment made by our people in foreign countries, interest upon investments in the United States . . . and other items of so-called invisible exchange . . . with which they in turn can make payments . . . amounted to about $1,500,000,000 in the last fiscal year. . . ."

". . . it does not follow that these debts are either to be paid in goods or that competitive goods necessarily come into our market. . . ."

"Large international debt is not a new phenomenon. It is precisely the same thing in its effect upon exchange and trade whether the debt is intergovernmental or private. Before the War, the rest of the world owed to Europe generally probably $30,000,000,000 and this burden was carried without disturbance to the world's commerce. . . ."

Speaking upon this subject in New York on March 16, 1926, Secretary Hoover said:

". . . Alarm has been repeatedly raised that repayment of the war debts must necessitate the increase of imports of competitive goods in order to provide for these payments—to the damage of our industry and workmen. These ideas are out of perspective. Our war debt when settled upon our own views of the capacity to pay will yield about $300,000,000 per annum, although as yet the actual payments are much less than this. The private foreign loans and investments today require repayments in principal and interest of about $600,000,000 annually, or nearly twice the war debt. I have heard of no suggestion that interest and repayment of these private debts will bring the disaster attributed to the war debt. The question is of importance, however, as to how this $800,000,000 or $900,-000,000 of annual payments may affect our merchandise movement. There is a compensating factor in American trade relations unique to our country which has a large bearing upon this question—that is, the vast dimension of our invisible exports in the form of tourist expenditure, emigrants' remittances, and other forms of American expenditure abroad. These items in 1925 amounted to about $900,000,000 or about $100,-000,000 more than our incoming payments on debts of all kinds. In other words, at this stage of calculation the balance of trade should be in our favour by about $100,000,000. But beyond this we are making, and shall long continue to make, loans abroad. For the last four years these loans have averaged nearly $700,000,000 a year, and in fact the merchandise balance in our favor has been running just about this same amount."

"Now the summation and purpose of all these words is the conclusion that there is no disastrous shift in our imports and exports of merchandise in prospect from debt causes."

Hoover was in 1922 appointed a member of the World War Debt Commission which in the following years made the settlements with the debtors. For one case he had argued for more lenient treatment than that accorded by the Commission—for Belgium, to whom he felt terms at least as lenient as those to Italy should have been given.

Constant agitation and pressures were maintained chiefly by New York bankers for cancellation of these debts. Hoover at all times refused, and was therefore a "reactionary." The financial collapse of war finance and inflation in Europe in the spring of 1931, however, placed temporarily a new phase on the whole question. An interim readjustment toward capacity to pay became necessary—and should extend to all other debts between governments in the world as well.

On June 5, 1931, the President proposed to the Cabinet members that if the situation continued to degenerate it would be necessary to suspend the payments to the United States of about $250,000,000 per annum, but at the same time it should be made a condition that all other payments from one government to another arising out of the War, including reparations, should also be suspended. The total of such payments was about $900,000,-000 per annum.

On June 18, the President received an appeal from President von Hindenburg that Germany was sinking under pressures and asking President Hoover's aid. On July 20 the President proposed the moratorium which was to be effective for eighteen months. The subject is discussed in detail under Emergency Actions on page 408.

He emphasized however the general policies of the United States:

"I wish to take this occasion also to frankly state my views upon our relations to German reparations and the debts owed to us by the Allied governments of Europe. Our Government has not been a party to, or exerted any voice in determination of reparation obligations. We purposely did not participate in either general reparations or the division of colonies or property. The repayment of debts due to us from the Allies for the advance for war and reconstruction was settled upon a basis not contingent upon German reparations or related thereto. Therefore, reparations is necessarily wholly a European problem with which we have no relation."

"I do not approve in any remote sense of the cancellation of the debts to us. World confidence would not be enhanced by such action. None of our debtor nations has ever suggested it. But as the basis of the settlement of these debts was the capacity under normal conditions of the debtor to pay, we should be consistent with our own policies and principles if we take into account the abnormal situation now existing in the world. I am sure the American people have no desire to attempt to extract any sum beyond the capacity of any debtor to pay and it is our view that broad vision requires that our Government should recognize the situation as it exists."

"This course of action is entirely consistent with the policy which we have hitherto pursued. We are not involved in the discussion of strictly European problems, of which the payment of German reparations is one. It represents our willingness to make a contribution to the early restoration of world prosperity in which our own people have so deep an interest."

[*State Papers, Vol. I, p. 591*]

The benefits from the proposal were considerably damaged by the delays due to the French but the action was consummated in July, 1931, and definitely contributed to stemming the economic tide.

With the further collapse of European finance and currencies it became evident by October, 1931, that some of the European countries would need longer temporary relief from their debt-payments to us if we were not to force them to repudiate. Moreover, in the acute panicky situation all over the world some word of encouragement was badly needed. In an important statement of October 6, 1931, the President said:

"Premier Laval of France is visiting the United States. It is my purpose to discuss with him the question of such further arrangements as are imperative during the period of the depression with respect to intergovernmental debts. The policy of the American Government in this matter is well known and was set out by me in public statement on June 20 in announcing the American proposal for a year's postponement of debt payments. Our problem in this respect is one of such adjustment during the period of depression as will at the same time aid our own and world recovery. . . ."

". . . Our people owe it not only to themselves and in their own interest but they can by such an example of stability and purpose give hope and confidence in our own country and to the rest of the world."

[*State Papers, Vol. II, p. 6*]

In the discussions with Premier Laval, Hoover insisted upon the consistent American policy of war debt payments within the capacity of each individual debtor to pay and that any further extensions must be the result of inquiry which would satisfy Congress and the people on this point. He expressed the hope that although they had no direct relation to the United States, the German, Austrian, Hungarian, and other reparation payments during depression should be looked upon in the same spirit by their creditors. And he suggested that it would give hope to those people and to the world if machinery should be set up in Europe at once to really determine their capacity to pay.

The joint statement by President Hoover and Premier Laval, issued on October 25, 1931, said:

"In so far as intergovernmental obligations are concerned we recognize that prior to the expiration of the Hoover year of postponement, some agreement regarding them may be necessary covering the period of business depression, as to the terms and conditions of which the two governments make all reservations. The initiative in this matter should be taken at an early date by the European powers principally concerned within the framework of agreements existing prior to July 1, 1931. . . ."

[*State Papers, Vol. II, p. 20*]

The President presented the Moratorium to Congress for ratification on December 10, 1931, with the attached recommendation:

"As we approach the new year it is clear that a number of the governments indebted to us will be unable to meet further payments to us in full pending recovery in their economic life. It is useless to blind ourselves to an obvious fact. Therefore it will be necessary in some cases to make still further temporary adjustments."

"I recommend the re-creation of the World War Foreign Debt Commission, with authority to examine such problems as may arise in connection with these debts during the present economic emergency, and to report to the Congress its conclusions and recommendations."

[*State Papers, Vol. II, p. 75*]

The former Debt Commission had been a joint body representing the President, the Senate and the House. The Congress refused, and instead passed a resolution denouncing any such action. The effect was, of course, discouraging to recovery.

The President gave an account of the Moratorium at some length in an address at St. Louis, Missouri, on November 4, 1932, for further account of which see page 409.

From it, however, the following significant paragraph may be repeated in this place:

"In order to give a year in which the world, particularly European nations, could come to a comprehension of what this disintegration was doing to civilization itself, I proposed the postponement of all international debts for one year."

"And it was not merely a postponement of a year in the payments on debts for which I was seeking. I was seeking for a year in which Europe could solemnly consider the situation into which she was drifting. I was seeking to remove from the mind of the world the fears of débâcle in civilization which were breaking down all security of credit and to bring to their attention the healing powers of international co-operation."

"You yourselves are familiar with the history of the year which followed. I know that the proposal of the moratorium diverted the entire current of thought and changed the history of what otherwise would have been a tragedy to the whole of civilization. It brought to new understanding the realization of the burdens under which Germany had been laboring."

"Under the impulses of these agreements and the recognition at least of the peril in which they stood, there came out of this agreement a great measure of redemption to the German people, a sense of greater security to the world from the agreements at Lausanne."

"That agreement and the new understanding of the postwar difficulties in the world has served greatly in the healing of the wounds of the Great War."

". . . overriding all these incidents, the world has witnessed the courage of men and the willingness to place their fate and their political future at stake for the world's progress . . . for the guidance of this world back toward stability and common interest in the development of human welfare."

[*State Papers, Vol. II, p. 431*]

EUROPEAN DRIVE TO REDUCE THE WAR DEBTS
IRRESPECTIVE OF CAPACITY TO PAY

In the European Conference at Lausanne, on July 8, 1932, the German and other reparation payments to European creditors were not simply postponed for a further period during the depression but were completely abandoned, except for about one billion, by their creditors.

Soon, however, it developed that the Lausanne settlement was conditional upon the consummation of a secret "gentleman's agreement." The bargain was to be conditional upon the United States cancelling her War debts. Not having any direct interest in German reparations, we had not been represented at Lausanne in any way, directly or indirectly. To bring the matter into the open and to avoid any misunderstanding, the President directed Under-Secretary Castle, in Secretary Stimson's absence, to issue the following statement:

"The American Government is pleased that, in reaching an agreement on the question of reparations, the nations assembled at Lausanne have made a great step forward in stabilization of the economic situation in Europe."

"On the question of War debts to the United States by European governments there is no change in the attitude of the American Government which was clearly expressed in the President's statement concerning the proposed moratorium on intergovernmental debts on June 20 of last year."

That it was the intention of European debtors to unite against us was clear when on July 11, 1932, Mr. Neville Chamberlain, British Chancellor of the Exchequer, stated in the House of Commons that we had taken part in the conclusions of the Lausanne Conference and implied an obligation rested on us. The President immediately directed the State Department to issue a denial of this misrepresentation. The only activity of Hoover had been to urge through Premier Laval that the nations get together and settle with Germany on the basis of real capacity to pay.

On July 12, 1932, Prime Minister MacDonald of Great Britain acknowledged that we had taken no part at Lausanne, directly or indirectly. Persistence in trying to force the United States continued, however.

On July 14, 1932, the British announced an agreement with France as to a "solid front" on our war debts due to us. In answer to an inquiry by Senator Borah, the President wrote him the following letter:

"MY DEAR MR. SENATOR:

"I have your inquiry this morning, through Secretary Stimson, as to the effect on the United States of recent agreements in Europe."

"Our people are, of course, gratified at the settlement of the strictly European problem of reparations or any of the other political or economic questions that have impeded European recovery. Such action, together with the real progress in disarmament, will contribute greatly to world stability."

"I wish to make it absolutely clear, however, that the United States has not been consulted regarding any of the agreements reported by the press to have been concluded recently at Lausanne and that of course it is not a party to, nor in any way committed to, any such agreements."

"While I do not assume it to be the purpose of any of these agreements to effect combined action of our debtors, if it shall be so interpreted then I do not propose that the American people shall be pressed into any line of action or that our policies shall be in any way influenced by such a combination either open or implied."

"Yours faithfully,
[*State Papers, Vol. II, p. 235*]

The publication of this letter resulted in an immediate statement from Europe that the pact was not directed against us and did not affect debts to us.

It was nevertheless obvious that if repudiation was to be avoided, some temporary extension to those debtors unable to pay at once or some form of payment other than cash would need to be set up for still a longer period other than the year's moratorium. In a statement on August 11, 1932, Hoover threw out a hint to them to come forward:

"My views in opposition to cancellation of war debts are a matter of detailed record in many public statements and a recent Message to the Congress. They mark a continuity of that policy maintained by my predecessors. I am hopeful of such drastic reduction of world armament as will save the taxpayers in debtor countries a large part of the cost of their payments to us. If for any particular annual payment we were offered some other tangible form of compensation such as the expansion of markets for American agriculture and labor, and the restoration and maintenance of our prosperity, then I am sure our citizens would consider such a proposal. But it is a certainty that these debts must not be cancelled or the burdens transferred to our people."

[*State Papers, Vol. II, p. 257*]

Speaking at Des Moines, on October 4, 1932, the President said:

"And in connection with agriculture, I may mention the question of War debts. I do not approve cancellation of these debts. I certainly do not approve the proposal of our opponents to lower our tariffs in order that by profits gained from a flood of goods into the United States this debt should be transferred to our workers by putting them out of employment and to our farmers by forcing their produce to rot in their barns."

"In my acceptance address I stated the exact reverse of this proposal. I said: 'If for some particular annual payment we are offered some other tangible form of compensation, such as the expansion of markets for American agriculture and labor and the restoration and maintenance of our prosperity, then I am sure our citizens would consider a proposal.'"

"I am prepared to go farther. I am prepared to recommend that any annual payment on the foreign debt be used for the specific purpose of securing an expansion of the foreign markets for American agricultural products. There is justice in that, for the difficulties inherited from the War are part of your difficulties today. That is a proposal of more importance to the farmer than any panacea."

[*State Papers, Vol. II, p. 316*]

At Cleveland, on October 15, 1932, Hoover further stated:

"In this connection with all these problems, the European War debts to the United States constantly arise. I have consistently opposed cancellation of these debts. The Democratic candidate, to use his own words, proposes to reduce our tariffs so that out of Europe's profits through the increased trade they would obtain from us Europe would pay us these debt annuities. That is vastly worse than cancellation. This would take money out of the pockets of the farmer, laborer, and business man to pay Europe's debts."

"In the constructive handling of this question I have said that I would favor the utilization of War debts to advantage agriculture and labor. Such action has received support of many leaders of labor and agriculture."

[*State Papers, Vol. II, p. 355*]

THE DEBT CRISIS OF DECEMBER 1932

The Moratorium being about to expire, immediately after the election of November 4, 1932, all of the debtor governments, each in almost identical terms, asked the United States for suspension of all payment pending a complete review of the entire debt question. Hoover had just been defeated and Roosevelt would not take office for three months. Hoover at once stated that any creditor should be willing to discuss with his debtor but that as there was no time for discussion before December 15, it was a *sine qua non* of any discussion that the December 15 payments be made.

Hoover believed that some of the governments needed temporary extensions of the Moratorium. That certainly did not apply to France, who held large gold deposits in the United States. Above all, he held it was a matter between the United States and each country individually based upon that country's capacity to pay.

Hoover requested Roosevelt's co-operation in dealing with the problem but met with scant response (see page 497 ff. and Myers and Newton, *Hoover Administration,* page 279).

The President, however, set out his views in a press statement on November 23, 1932:

"To avoid misunderstanding it seems desirable to summarize briefly the complex questions and the policies consistently followed by the United States in respect to these debts and my views as to the course which should be pursued."

"1. These debts were created, and were undoubtedly based, on the proposal of the borrowers, no doubt in good faith, and the assumption of the Government of the United States, that they were actual loans which would be repaid. Had it not been for this assumption, it is hardly to be supposed that this Government would have been so largely involved. . . ."

"2. The United States Government from the beginning has taken the position that it would deal with each of the debtor governments separately, as separate and distinct circumstances surrounded each case. . . ."

"3. Debt settlements made in each case took into consideration the economic conditions and the capacity to pay of the individual debtor nation . . . show concessions ranging from 30 per cent to 80 per cent of the total amounts that were due."

"4. From the time of the creation of these debts to the United States, this Government has uniformly insisted that they must be treated as entirely separate from reparation claims arising out of the War. The reasons for adherence to this position are plain. After the War we refused to accept general reparations or any compensation in territory, economic privileges, or Government indemnity."

"Moreover, in the matter of reparations and other intergovernmental debts arising from the War, our position is entirely different from that of governments that are both creditors and debtors."

[*State Papers, Vol. II, pp. 487–8*]

> He referred to a previous statement by Treasury Secretary Houston of March 1, 1920, in response to a note from the British Government suggesting a general cancellation of war debts:

". . . Of course I recognize that a general cancellation of such debts would be of advantage to Great Britain and that it probably would not involve any losses on her part. As there are no obligations of the United States Government which would be cancelled under such a plan, the effect would be that, in consideration of a cancellation by the United States Government of obligations which it holds for advances made to the British Government and other allied governments, the British Government would cancel its debts against France, Italy, Russia, and her other allies. Such a proposal does not involve mutual sacrifices on the part of the nations concerned. It simply involves a contribution mainly by the United States. . . ."

"The debt agreements are, through force of law, unalterable save by Congressional action. Without entering into legalistic consideration of the respective powers of the Executive and the Congress, it may be said at once that, based upon the relation of these debts to revenue, the Congress has insisted upon participation in initiation of negotiations and in any ultimate decisions in respect to the war debts."

[*State Papers, Vol. II, p. 489*]

". . . from a practical point of view, that no progress is possible without active co-operation of the Congress."

"The necessity of this authority does not, however, relieve me of the responsibilities of this office, and I therefore shall state my own views."

"The world-wide crisis has at least temporarily increased the weight of all debts throughout the world. Tremendous disparity in price levels, contraction in markets, depreciation in currency, stagnation of trade and industry—are all part of this world-wide depression which is not only increasing the weight of these debts and has made their payment more difficult to some nations, but have thrust them as well into the problem of world recovery and its effect upon our own farmers, workers, and business. These are realities. We cannot blind ourselves to their existence. They are vital factors in the problem now before us for consideration."

"At the same time, it must be emphatically recalled that the aftermath of the Great War and these incidents of the depression have also fallen with great weight on the American people, and the effect upon them directly as taxpayers, of any modification with respect to the debts due this country, must not be disregarded. Other nations have their budgetary problems. So have we. Other people are heavily burdened with taxes. So are our people."

"I do not feel that the American people should be called upon to make further sacrifices. I have held, however, that advantages to us could be found by other forms of tangible compensation than cash, such as expansion of markets for products of American agriculture and labor. There are other possible compensations in economic relations which might be developed on study which would contribute to recovery of prices and trade. Such compensations could be made mutually advantageous."

"The World Economic Conference will convene in a few months. A world disarmament conference is now in progress. And I must reiterate that the problem of foreign debts has in the American mind very definite relationship. There are, therefore, important avenues of mutual advantage which should be genuinely explored."

"It is unthinkable that, within the comity of nations and the maintenance of international good-will, our people should refuse to consider the request of a friendly people to discuss an important question in which they and we both have a vital interest, irrespective of what conclusions might arise from such a discussion. This is particularly true in a world greatly afflicted, where co-operation and good-will are essential to the welfare of all."

"I believe, therefore, that Congress in view of the requests made by these governments should authorize the creation of an agency to exchange views with those governments, enlarging the field of discussion as above indicated and to report to Congress such recommendations as they deem desirable." [*State Papers, Vol. II, pp. 490–1*]

". . . We may thus take . . . co-ordinated steps towards the solution of the many underlying causes of the present calamity."

"As to the suspension of installments due on December 15, no facts have been presented by the debtor governments which would justify such postponement under the principles heretofore laid down by this country. At the Lausanne Conference, which has been referred to as a precedent, that postponement was the natural result of the facts which had been elaborately presented during many months of previous inquiry."

"The suggestion that the suspension of the December 15 payments would permit the governments to enter undisturbed into discussions now proposed does not appear to me to carry weight. Contrary to this view, it seems to me that discussion would proceed under more favorable circumstances if the terms of these obligations are carried out rather than suspended prior to discussion. By that I do not mean to say that if extraordinary circumstances . . . exist and are called to the attention of this Government, I shall transmit them to Congress for prompt consideration, but I must insist that existing agreements be respected until they have been mutually modified by duly authorized representatives of the governments affected."

"There is a larger aspect to this question of responding to an invitation from a friendly nation to discuss, . . . Discussion does not involve abandonment on our part of what we believe to be sound and right. On the other hand, a refusal to afford others the opportunity to present in conference their views and to hear ours upon a question in which we are both concerned, and an insistence upon dealing with our neighbors at arms' length, would be the negation of the very principles upon which rests the hope of rebuilding a new and better world from the shattered remnants of the old."

"If our civilization is to be perpetuated, the great causes of world peace, world disarmament, and world recovery must prevail. They cannot prevail until a path to their attainment is built upon honest friendship, mutual confidence, and proper co-operation among the nations."

"These immense objectives upon which the future and welfare of all mankind depend must be ever in our thought in dealing with immediate and difficult problems. The solution of each one of these, upon the basis of an understanding reached after frank and fair discussion, in and of itself strengthens the foundation of the edifice of world progress we seek to erect; whereas our failure to approach difficulties and differences among nations in such a spirit serves but to undermine constructive effort."

"Peace and honest friendship with all nations have been the cardinal principles by which we have ever guided our foreign relations. They are the stars by which the world must today guide its course—a world in which our country must assume its share of leadership and responsibility."

[*State Papers, Vol. II, pp. 492-3*]

Most of the important debtors made the December 15 payments except the French who publicly claimed there was an assurance from President-elect Roosevelt that payment was not a *sine-qua non* of negotiations.

President Hoover set out the subject again in a full Message to Congress on December 19, 1932. After discussing the proposed Economic Conference and Disarmament Conference, he said:

"The problem of the war debts to the United States has entered into this world situation. It is my belief that their importance, relative to the other world economic forces in action, is exaggerated. Nevertheless in times of deep depression some nations are unable to pay and in some cases payments do weigh heavily upon foreign exchange and currency stability. In dealing with an economically sick world many factors become distorted in their relative importance and the emotions of peoples must be taken into account."

"As Congress is aware the principal debtor nations recently requested that the December payments on these debts should be postponed and that we should undertake an exchange of views upon possible revision in the light of altered world conditions."

"We have declined to postpone this payment as we considered that such action (*a*) would amount to practical breakdown of the integrity of these agreements, (*b*) would impose an abandonment of the national policies of dealing with these obligations separately with each nation, (*c*) would create a situation where debts would have been regarded as being a counterpart of German reparations and indemnities and thus not only destroy their individual character and obligation but become an effective transfer of German reparations to the American taxpayer, (*d*) would be no real relief to the world situation without consideration of the destructive forces militating against economic recovery, (*e*) would not be a proper call upon the American people to further sacrifices unless there were definite compensations. It is essential in our national interest that we accept none of these implications and undertake no commitments before these economic and other problems are canvassed and so far as possible are solved."

"Of the total of about $125,500,000 due, Czechoslovakia, Finland,

Great Britain, Italy, Latvia, and Lithuania have met payments amounting to $98,685,910, despite the difficulties inherent in the times. Austria, Belgium, Esthonia, France, Greece, Hungary, and Poland have not made their payments. In the case of some of these countries such failure was unquestionably due to inability in the present situation to make the payments contemplated by the agreements."

"Certain nations have specifically stated that they do not see their way clear to make payments under these agreements for the future. Thus our Government and our people are confronted with the realities of a situation in connection with the debts not heretofore contemplated."

"It is not necessary for me at this time to enter upon the subject of the origins of these debts, the sacrifices already made by the American people, the respective capacities of other governments to pay, or to answer the arguments put forward which look toward cancellation of these obligations. I may, however, point out that except in one country the taxation required for the payments upon the debts owing to our Government does not exceed one-quarter of the amounts now being imposed to support their military establishments. As their maintained armaments call for a large increase in expenditures on our defensive forces beyond those before the war, the American people naturally feel that cancellation of these debts, would give us no relief from arms but only free large sums for further military preparations abroad. Further, it is not amiss to note that the contention that payment of these debts is confined to direct shipment of goods or payment in gold is not a proper representation since in normal times triangular trade is a very large factor in world exchanges, nor is any presentation of the trade balance situation complete without taking into account services as for instance American tourist expenditures and emigrant remittances alone to most of the debtor countries exceed the amount of payments. I may also mention that our country made double the total sacrifice of any other nation in bringing about the moratorium which served to prevent the collapse of many nations of Europe with its reactions upon the world. This act of good-will on our part must not now be made either the excuse or opportuny for demanding still larger sacrifices."

"My views are well known; I will not entertain the thought of cancellation. I believe that whatever further sacrifices the American people might make by way of adjustment of cash payments must be compensated by definite benefits in markets and otherwise."

"In any event in protection to our own vital interests, as good neighbors and in accord with our traditional duty as wise and fair creditors whether to individuals or nations, we must honor the request for discussion of these questions by nations who have sought to maintain their obligations to us."

". . . It seems clear that the successful outcome of the Economic Conference would be greatly furthered if the debt problem were explored in advance, even though final agreement might well be contingent on the satisfactory solution of economic and armament questions in which our country has direct interest."

"Thus from this present complex situation certain definite conclusions are unavoidable :"

"1. A number of the most serious problems have now arisen and we are bound to recognize and deal with them."

"2. It is of great importance that preparatory action should be taken at once otherwise time will be lost while destructive forces are continuing against our agriculture, employment, and business."

"3. Adequate and proper machinery for dealing with them must be created. It is clear that ordinary diplomatic agencies and facilities are not suitable for the conduct of negotiations which can best be carried on across the table by specially qualified representatives."

"4. As I have pointed out, the discussion of debts is necessarily connected with the solution of major problems at the World Economic Conference and the Arms Conference."

"5. Discussions in respect to both debt questions and the World Economic Conference cannot be concluded during my administration, yet the economic situation in the world necessitates the preliminary work essential to its success. The undertaking of these preliminary questions should not be delayed until after March 4."

"I propose, therefore, to seek the co-operation of President-elect Roosevelt in the organization of machinery for advancement of consideration of these problems."

"A year ago I requested that the Congress should authorize the creation of a Debt Commission to deal with situations which were bound to arise. The Congress did not consider this wise. In the situation as it has developed it appears necessary for the Executive to proceed. Obviously any conclusions would be subject to approval by the Congress."

"On the other hand should the Congress prefer to authorize by legislative enactment a commission set up along the lines above indicated it would meet my hearty approval." [*State Papers, Vol. II, pp. 550–4*]

President Hoover again proposed that the President-elect should join in the selection of the Commission to work out these questions.

The Democratic leaders after consultation with President-elect Roosevelt, however, refused to join in the creation of such a Commission or to approve its purpose. It is useless to conjecture what Hoover could have obtained by his policies by way of a *quid pro quo* in currency stability, agricultural privilege, continued limitation of arms and some payments, had he been re-elected.

All of the debtors except Finland defaulted. Once defaulted, they justify it at home by arguments that make it difficult for them to think of an immediate resumption of payments—or ever. Also, since that time each of them has increased their military expenditures for more than the amount of the debt payments.

A more detailed account of these negotiations may be found in Myers and Newton, *The Hoover Administration,* page 280.

THE BEGINNING OF RECOVERY

As quickly as it became evident at the end of June, 1932, that the President would secure a large part of his financial program; that he would defeat destructive legislation; that credit would flow free, that the American dollar would ring true on every counter of the world, at once new hope sprang up in the country. The forces of liquidation abroad had also in large part exhausted themselves. The Lausanne Conference, practically abolishing reparations, had stiffened the European economic situation. The prospect of balanced budgets and stabilized currencies all began to have their effect.

History now records that the Great Depression turned in late June or early July of 1932. Recovery began in all the great commercial countries and continued upward for the next two years. President Hoover was the world leader who had contributed most to this victory over chaos. The battle against the depression had been won.

Hoover's assurance in 1932 that world recovery including the United States had begun in June-July, 1932, is now recognized the world over. To quote only a few authorities:

The Annalist, February 21, 1936, by D. W. Ellsworth: ". . . the bottom of depression was reached in 1932."

Leonard P. Ayres (*Economics of Recovery,* page 137): ". . . the corner was turned in the country in the summer of 1932 . . . the most important factor in preventing our incipient recovery in 1932 . . . from . . . recovering . . . as did that begun abroad was political in nature."

Irving Fisher (*American Economic Association Speech,* December 28, 1933) : "We should have been further on the road toward recovery today had there been no election last year. Recovery started under Mr. Hoover but . . . a recession because of fear over political uncertainties."

The Department of Commerce under President Roosevelt, in its *World Economic Review,* for 1933, said: ". . . Then (1932) business in the more important commercial nations of the world was showing a tendency toward recovery. The decline generally had been long and steep, and forces of recovery were at work.

In the United States business improved substantially, from July until September, and held firm without much definite tendency either way in October and November. . . . The relatively long interval between the election and the inauguration of the new President proved unsettling to business and was a factor militating against further immediate improvement.

Kansas City Star, January 26, 1936: ". . . the depression here, according the League (of Nations) charts, reached its low point in June, 1932. Then there was an abrupt and important revival during the summer. In November began a deterioration."

Frank Kent (March 9, 1936): ". . . there is general agreement that the low point was reached in June, 1932, and all over the world recovery began about that time."

Walter Lippmann (November, 1933): "There is very good statistical evidence which goes to prove . . . the world depression reached its low point in midsummer of 1932." (June 18, 1936): "The historians will . . . see that President Hoover, Secretary Mills, and Governor Meyer had hold of the essence of the matter in the spring of 1932 when . . . they arrested the depression."

National City Bank, January, 1936: ". . . signs of recovery (in 1935) more widespread than at any time since the turn in the depression was reached in 1932."

National Industrial Conference Board (November 10, 1934): ". . . the facts presented in the chart bring out clearly that the first steps toward recovery were taken in the year 1932."

Edmund Platt, former vice-chairman of the Federal Reserve Board (*New York Times,* July 4, 1933): "If 1932 had not happened to be a Presidentiail year, the recovery begun then might might have continued without any serious interruption."

New York Times (June 16, 1934): "The change for the better in the last half of 1932 is beyond dispute. That this evident revival of confidence was suddenly reversed in February, 1933, is equally true." (November 24, 1935): ". . . the beginning of the turn must be assigned to 1932." (November 26, 1935) "We have already travelled far since the depression turned in 1932." (January 2, 1936): "Recovery . . . really began in 1932."

The Brookings Institute in 1937 reaches much the same conclusions.

The question is not, however, when the statistical low was reached. The sole question is, did the forces of recovery take possession in the world including the United States in July,

1932? It is true they were reversed by the election and the disturbing policies of Roosevelt which became known prior to his inauguration. That the country was plunged into deeper statistical troughs in some directions by his actions does not negative the fact that had Hoover been re-elected we should have gone straight to recovery.

All this is attested by the actual facts.

In the months of August, September, and October, 1932, bank failures had almost ceased while banks re-opened were more than suspensions. The great flow of gold the months previous to July reversed itself into an enormous inflow. The whole banking structure greatly strengthened. Wholesale commodity prices and farm prices advanced steadily through July and August and September. Cotton and wheat advanced over 20 per cent. United States cotton manufacturing advanced from 51.5 per cent of mill capacity in July to 97 per cent in October. Domestic wool consumption advanced from 16,500,000 pounds in May to 46,100,000 pounds in September.

The Federal Reserve Board's index of industrial production swept upward from 56 in July to 68 for both September and October.

The American Federation of Labor reported 12,300,000 unemployed on July 1, and 11,586,000 on October 1. The construction industries, as reflected in the Federal Reserve Board's index of contracts awarded, improved over 30 per cent.

The Federal Reserve Board's seasonally adjusted index of department-store sales moved upward 8 per cent from July to October, a level not recorded again until August, 1933. Electric power production hit the 1932 low in July, at 6,112,000,000 kilowatt hours and then registered consistent monthly advances until the end of October.

Freight car loadings advanced from an average of 80,000 cars daily early in July, 1932, to 96,000 cars daily during the first two weeks of October. Moody reported net earnings of sixty-three principal railroads in the third quarter of 1932 as 95 per cent above the second quarter.

Dun and Bradstreet's index of business failures fell off precipitously through August and September. In the stock market, which is the barometer of national psychology as well as of economic values, the Standard Statistics index of 351 industrial stocks swept from a low of 34 in early July to a high of 56 in September. Leading industrial issues doubled in price, while rail shares nearly trebled.

The Standard Bond index bounded up from 72.2 for June to 85.8 for September. The weighted average of seventeen New York bank stocks advanced from a depression low of $31 to $70.76 on September 7.

There is no doubt recovery was under way—until the election.

THE PANIC OF MARCH, 1933

Roosevelt carried the election on November 8, 1932, by a vote of 57 per cent of the people.

The election obviously meant a reversal in many national policies. Until these new policies developed hesitation was a certainty. The business community never waits for an event that is coming. In fact, hundreds of millions of orders for goods were cancelled instantly. Business men following the assertions in the campaign expected a reduction in tariff and great increases in government expense with further increases in taxes. Although Roosevelt had denied that there would be tampering with the currency, the actions of the last Democratic Congress, and the expressed intent of Roosevelt's principal supporters, left an immediate feeling of uneasiness in this respect also.

The constructive influence and the program of the Hoover Administration was over on November 9. From that moment the people naturally looked to Roosevelt. His policies, in fact, controlled any action of the Congress, for the Democratic House of Representatives and the opposition Senate would take no action without Roosevelt's approval.

Hoover at once announced a policy of co-operation with the incoming administration. On November 12, in a short speech at Glendale, California, while en route to Washington, he said:

"The majority of the people have decided to entrust the Government to a new administration. The political campaign is over. . . . If we are to continue the recovery so evidently in progress during the last few months by overcoming the many difficulties which still confront us, we must have continued unity in constructive action all along the economic front. I shall work for that unity during the remaining four months of this administration. . . ."

"The first consideration today of every American citizen is the continued recovery of the country—a consideration far above partisanship."

[*State Papers, Vol. II, p. 480*]

The history of this period has already been written at length
by Myers and Newton (*Hoover Administration*), and Lawrence Sullivan (*Prelude to Panic*).[1] It is not our purpose to
enter into the incidents except so far as they indicate the policies of the Hoover Administration.

Hoover's first action was to invite Roosevelt's co-operation upon
the problems which could not rightly be deferred without great
injury to the country, but which must extend over into the
Roosevelt Administration.

In the main these problems proved to be: (*a*) policies in respect to the War Debts; (*b*) the World Economic Conference;
(*c*) The World Disarmament Conference; (*d*) Balancing of
the Budget; (*e*) Reforms of the Banking Laws; (*f*) Reform of
Bankruptcy Acts; (*g*) the banking and currency crisis of February, 1933.

Hoover's detailed policies in these matters after the election
are dealt with in the pages devoted to these subjects.

Unfortunately, Roosevelt either evaded or declined the co-
operation which Hoover offered. But of more importance, for
the first time in American history, an incoming President either
by positive or negative action began the making of his policies
before his inauguration. History will amply record that co-
operation by Roosevelt and his withdrawal from a discussion of
public questions and from interferences with Congress would
have saved a bank panic and would have assured steady progress
toward recovery.

We may note here some results. The World Conference to
stabilize currency was postponed from February to July. By
postponement of war debt questions the debtors defaulted their
payments. For lack of co-ordinating the American strength, the
world stabilization of currencies, the limitation of arms, concessions on war debts for quid pro quo all weakened and failed.
President-elect Roosevelt's instructions to the Democratic Congress defeated President Hoover's balancing of the budget. He
refused to instruct his obedient leaders not to publicize R. F. C.
loans. But more important than all were his intimations of
tinkering with the currency and his refusal to confirm to Hoover
and others his campaign assurances of holding to the existing
gold standard. All culminated to create a banking panic. On

[1]*Statesman Press,* 1936.

this episode the historical statement that will stand for all time is the graphic and accurate account of Hoover himself—and it has never been denied. Speaking at St. Louis on December 16, 1935, he said:

"In speaking at Atlanta two weeks ago the President's first basis of defense for his gigantic spending, deficits, and debts was the assertion that 'The mechanics of civilization came to a dead stop on March 3, 1933.'"

"What happened on March 3, 1933, was an induced hysteria of bank depositors. The banking structure at large subsequently proved to be sound. That is scarcely a dead stop to civilization."

"I have always believed that the newspapers are one of the mechanisms of civilization. They did not quit. At that time I saw no headlines that the farmers had ceased to till the fields. Most of you did not detect that the delivery of food to your doors had stopped. Railway managers apparently did not know that their trains had stalled. Somebody failed to inform us that the hum of our factories was silent. We still had to jump out of the way of the 23,000,000 automobiles. Our churches, schools, and courts are a part of the mechanics of civilization. They did not close. And the Supreme Court seems to be functioning yet. If civilization came to a dead stop the press missed a great piece of news that day."

"If this notion is to be the excuse for this spending and other vagaries of the New Deal, we had better examine into it further."

"The truth is that the world-wide depression was turned in June-July, 1932, all over the world. That was before the election of the New Deal. That is supported by scores of leading American economists, business men, and public leaders. It is supported by the economic publications throughout the world."

"That turning was aided by the measures of our Republican Government. These measures were within the Constitution of the United States. They were not that futile financial juggling which has violated economic law, morals, the Constitution, and the structure of American liberty. The turnings was aided by the efforts of foreign governments. Every commercial country, including the United States, surged forward. Prices rose, employment increased, the whole agricultural, financial, and business structure grew in strength. After the election of the New Deal we began a retreat. Only in the United States was there an interruption. We were the strongest and should have led the van. And we lagged behind for two years. The other countries of the world went forward without interruption. They adopted no New Deal. Apparently those nations did not hear that the mechanics of civilization came to a dead stop on March 3, 1933."

"It did not come to a stop even in the United States. It was meddled with. We have not got over it yet. But why did we have a panic of bank depositors in 1933? Because they were scared. We had no bank panic from the crash of the boom in 1929. We had no panic at the financial collapse in Europe in 1931. We had no panic at the most dangerous point in the depression when our banks were weakest in the spring of 1932. There was no panic before the election of November, 1932. When did they become frightened? They became scared a few weeks before the inauguration of the New Deal on March 4, 1933."

"What were they frightened of? They could not have been scared by the out-going administration which had only a few days to run. They were frightened at the incoming New Deal. Why were they scared at the New Deal? Because soon after the election large numbers of people awoke to the fact that promises given in the campaign would be violated. Among other things it gradually spread that the gold standard would be abandoned or that the currency would be tinkered with. It was evident that a wholesale orgy of spending of public money would be undertaken. Business slackened its energies. Shrewd speculators shipped their money abroad at fabulous profits. Bankers tried to protect themselves. The public in blind fear demanded gold and the 'covenants' of the United States which called for gold. Some of them were scared at the banks by the destructive publication of R. F. C. loans. The banking structure was not insolvent. After the banks were closed it was found that the solvent banks, measured by deposits, comprised 92 per cent of the banking strength of the country. The President himself stated they were sound. Subsequently more banks were found sound and reopened. And beyond this, important banks wrongfully closed by the New Deal, such as in the Detroit area, are now paying out 100 per cent to the depositors. It was the most political and the most unnecessary bank panic in all our history. It would have been prevented by simple co-operation."

Speaking at Fort Wayne, on April 4, 1936, he said:

"There is an elaborate phantasmagoria to which the New Deal spokesmen seek to give life with their pulmotor of propaganda. That relates to the situation in the country when they came into power on March 4, 1933."

"Mr. Roosevelt is anxious that the American people shall believe that the Nation was 'in ruins' when he took office. From the panic of bank depositors which greeted his inauguration he concludes that the Republicans did it."

"That incident is still used to justify his abandoned promises. It is still used as the excuse for the attempt to transform the fate of a nation. We may, therefore, explore a little further into this particular question."

"I hardly need restate the fact, now well established by disinterested economists the world over, that America was shaking itself clear of the depression, under its Republican Administration, in June-July, 1932. The whole world started forward. Prosperity had actually swung around the corner and was on its way up the street of our national life when it encountered the change in national policies. After Mr. Roosevelt's election in 1932 we alone of all great nations were set back. Most other nations continued forward."

"The causes which produced that skid in national progress are now a matter of documented public record available to everybody."

"I may mention just one incident. On February 17, 1933, fifteen days before Mr. Roosevelt's inauguration it had become apparent that a panic was inevitable unless Mr. Roosevelt would co-operate to allay fear. I, as President of all the people, addressed to Mr. Roosevelt as President-elect of all the people a personal appeal in my own handwriting which was delivered personally to him by a trusted messenger. It contained these words:"

" 'A most critical situation has arisen. The major difficulty is the state of public mind . . . a statement by you upon two or three policies of your administration would restore public confidence . . . by the removal of fear.' "

" 'With the election there came the natural and inevitable hesitation. . . . A number of discouraging things have happened on top of this. . . . The breakdown in balancing the budget. . . . The proposals for inflation . . . the publication of R. F. C. loans [by the Democratic Congress] . . . a state of alarm . . . rapidly reaching a crisis . . . flight of capital . . . foreign withdrawals of gold . . . hoarding. It is obvious that you . . . are the only one who can give prompt assurance that there will be no tampering or inflation of the currency, that the budget will be unquestionably balanced.' "

"But no such assurance was forthcoming. In a word I asked that the whispers of speculators and others that Mr. Roosevelt did not intend to keep his campaign promises should be stopped by an emphatic public confirmation of those promises. That those speculators and insiders were right was plain enough later on. This first contact of the 'money changers' with the New Deal netted those who removed their money from the country a profit of up to 60 per cent when the dollar was debased."

"The urgent necessity for the President-elect to make such a statement to stop the panic was urged by others including the Advisory Council of the Federal Reserve Board and by responsible newspapers. The usual reply is that the President-elect had no responsibilities until March 4. There are a dozen answers to that. One is that every American citizen has a responsibility. Another is that as President-elect he had not hesitated on December 29, 1932, to take the unprecedented responsibility of ordering the Democratic Congress to oppose the steps I had taken to balance the budget."

"Having got the Nation into that hole, the administration showed great determination and speed in getting us out. For this latter they deserve credit."

"That unnecessary bank panic created a temporary slump in the upward movement of farm and other prices and employment. And we listen every day to the New Dealers chant like a Greek chorus of the doleful bottom from which they started."

"Some of their spokesmen are so tragic as to announce that the 'tramp of revolution' was in the air. Those young men have yet to learn that bank depositors even in a panic have not been known to lead revolutions. A sane people with a heritage of orderly democracy do not revolt by violence. America had no thought of revolution. But revolution was in the minds of the Brain Trust. They had nothing else on their minds. However they did deeply touch the national funny-bone."

"These men did use the occasion to grasp for power. They did try to impose a new system on the American people. For months they called it the Roosevelt Revolution. They liked that word revolution for quite a while! The implication of that thrilling heroic word has now been softened to the soothing idea of a more abundant life."

Speaking at Philadelphia on October 17, 1936, Hoover said:

"The President in this last Pittsburgh speech implies delicately that he brought about recovery from the depression. His minions of course shout it."

"We can examine this also for a moment. The origins of this depression are agreed on by almost every economist, every scholar, every informed statesman in the world. It was the inexorable and inevitable world-wide aftermath of the World War. Its causes lay in the pit of destruction dug by the most titanic struggle in which humanity has yet engaged. Our own credit inflation contributed to our own difficulties. But this depression began in other countries before it touched the United States. No man or no government brought about that depression. Governments could do much to protect their citizens, their citizens' institutions and their savings from its blasts. But its sweep was as inexorable as a Caribbean hurricane."

"Likewise the recovery from this depression was not the work of any one official or government or all of them. Recovery was the invincible result of a billiion of human beings on the seven continents struggling to repair the breaches in their daily lives. Governments could aid their citizens in recovery; by foolish action they could retard it."

"That the beginnings of recovery were world-wide, including the United States in the spring of 1932, is recognized by almost every economist, every scholar, every informed statesman. That was nine months before Mr. Roosevelt ever came to the Presidency. And in many of these countries without the interferences of New Deals recovery has marched further and faster than in the United States."

"Mr. Roosevelt naturally does not emphasize the fact that at his election the United States alone faltered in the world-wide march of recovery. He does not recall that the American bank panic was a panic of fear that he would not keep his campaign promises, particularly as to the currency. He does not mention that in the dark days of European panics Republican policies had twice or thrice prevented the spread of these panics to the United States. He does not mention all his delays on recovery that were removed by the Supreme Court."

"He paints a poignant picture of the difficulties of the country resulting from the bank panic which marked his inauguration day of 1933. He implies that the people were in danger of starving, that riot was in the air. Mr. Roosevelt does not mention that due to a Republican Administration which had first put humanity first there had not been starvation in the previous three years of the depression. He does not mention that there had not been hunger riots in that four years and there had been no industrial riots."

"And today he lays his claims to re-election upon the improvement in the country from the bottom of that ditch. He quotes a vast amount of figures to prove that. Those figures would look different if they were drawn before his election and were increased in accordance with his own devaluation of the dollar. He now claims political reward for that unnecessary forcing of the country into the ditch of panic. I am reminded of the boy who murdered his father and mother, then appealed to the judge not only for acquittal but for future support on the ground he was an orphan."

"The President illustrated his views of this period by recounting a story of a nice old gentleman who fell off the dock in 1933 and was rescued. The gentleman was effusive in thanks but three years later he complained that he had lost his hat."

"I have some inside information about that incident. The old gentleman was surreptitiously pushed off the dock in order that the hero could gain the plaudits of the crowd as a life saver."

"With apologies to Governor Smith may I not suggest that Santa Claus has turned into Chanticleer whose crow each morning claimed credit for the rising sun."

PROBLEMS OF GOVERNMENT
ADMINISTRATION

PROBITY IN GOVERNMENT

In a telegram to the Republican Convention of June 14, 1928, Hoover demanded: "Shall honesty and righteousness in government and business confirm the confidence of the people in their institutions and their laws?"

In the 1928 campaign, Hoover said in his Acceptance Address, on August 11, 1928:

"In the past years there has been corruption participated in by individual officials and members of both political parties in national, state, and municipal affairs. Too often this corruption has been viewed with indifference. . . . It would seem unnecessary to state the elemental requirement that government must inspire confidence not only in its ability but in its integrity. Dishonesty in government, whether national, state, or municipal, is a double wrong. It is treason to the state. It is destructive of self-government. Government in the United States rests not only upon the consent of the governed, but upon the conscience of the Nation. Government weakens the moment that its integrity is even doubted. Moral incompetency by those entrusted with government is a blighting wind upon private integrity."

These were not matters of oratory with Hoover, but of daily practice of which there are multitudes of incidents.

Four days after the Inauguration, President Hoover announced that there was to be no theory "to the victor belong the spoils" in his administration. In a public statement he said that every honest and zealous public servant would be retained irrespective of politics, and thereby created great antagonism among politicians. Four days later, Hoover announced there "will be no leases or disposal of Government oil lands no matter what the emergency they may be in except where mandatory by Congress or the Courts." It brought him a storm of protest from oil operators and governors and members of the Congress from oil-land states. Two days later the President announced that government transactions should be open to the light of day and ordered the publication in the press of tax refunds in excess of $20,000.

Twenty days after his Inauguration, the President took in hand the nettle of corrupt Federal patronage in the South in a public statement on the subject:

"Recent exposures of abuse in recommendations for Federal office, particularly in some parts of the states of South Carolina, Georgia, and Mississippi, under which some of the Federal departments, mainly the postoffice, were misled in appointments, obviously render it impossible for the old organizations in those states to command the confidence of the administration, although many members of these organizations are not subject to criticism. But such conditions are intolerable to public service, are repugnant to the ideals and purposes of the Republican Party, are unjust to the people of the South and must be ended. The duty of reorganization so as to correct these conditions rests with the people of those states, and all efforts to that end will receive the hearty co-operation of the administration. If these three states are unable to initiate such organization through the leadership of men who will command confidence and protect the public service, the different Federal departments will be compelled to adopt other methods to secure advice as to the selection of Federal employees." [*State Papers, Vol. I, p. 22*]

The President subsequently appointed committees of leading citizens, independent of the political organizations, in Georgia, Mississippi, and South Carolina, to advise him upon public appointments.

On December 22, 1929, as a part of the Democratic smearing campaign, Congressman Garner charged the President with corrupt relations with sugar lobbyists and a Senate investigation was launched in which every device of misrepresentation was employed. On January 14, 1930, the Senate Committee brought in a report: "There is no impropriety nor anything open to criticism upon the President's part."

Early in the administration, the President had the whole Federal service reviewed for fidelity in administration. He established the practice of having every suspicion of wrongdoing on the part of public servants at once referred to the Department of Justice for investigation. As a sample of action, the President announced on May 1, 1929, that following an investigation and report by the Department of Justice, he had that day summarily removed William A. DeGroot, the United

States District Attorney for the Eastern District of New York. Speaking at Marion, Ohio, on June 16, 1931, Mr. Hoover said:

"There are disloyalties and there are crimes which shock our sensibilities, which may bring suffering upon those who are touched by their immediate results. But there is no disloyalty and no crime in all the category of human weaknesses which compares with the failure of probity in the conduct of public trust. Monetary loss or even the shock to moral sensibilities is perhaps a passing thing, but the breaking down of the faith of a people in the honesty of their Government and in the integrity of their institutions, the lowering of respect for the standards of honor which prevail in high places, are crimes for which punishment can never atone."[1]   [*State Papers, Vol. I, p. 586*]

Hoover assembled a strong staff in the Federal Government. The principal officers were:

State Department
  Secretary, Henry L. Stimson.
    Under-Secretary, Joseph P. Cotton.
      (later) William R. Castle, Jr.
    Assistant Secretaries, Wilbur Carr, Francis White, James Grafton Rogers, Harvey Bundy.
Treasury Department
  Secretary, Andrew W. Mellon.
    (later) Ogden L. Mills.
    Under-Secretary, Ogden L. Mills.
      (later) Arthur A. Ballantine.
  Heads of Bureaus
    Bureau of Customs, F. X. A. Eble.
    Bureau of Internal Revenue, David Burnet.
    Bureau of the Mint, Robert J. Grant.
    Bureau of Industrial Alcohol, J. M. Doran.
    Bureau of Narcotics, H. J. Anslinger.
    Bureau of the Public Health Service, Hugh S. Cumming.
    Bureau of the Budget, J. Clawson Roop.

---

[1]With all the search of bitter partisanship and large expenditure into the highways and byways for some shred of dishonesty in the Hoover Administration not one particle of dishonesty could be found in the handling of over twenty-five billion of income and expenditures during that period or in the many public relations where honesty is at test. That was because of the Hoover policy in choosing men for probity and ability and not primarily for politics. Never has the public service been raised to as high a level as during the four Hoover years.

War Department
   Secretary, James W. Good.
     (later) Patrick J. Hurley.
     Assistant Secretaries, Patrick J. Hurley, Frederick H. Payne, F. Trubee Davison.
     Chief of Staff, Major-General Summerall.
     (later) Major-General Douglas MacArthur.
     Chief of Engineers, Major-General Lytle Brown.

Department of Justice
   Attorney-General, William D. Mitchell.
   Solicitor-General, Charles Evans Hughes, Jr.
     (later) Thomas D. Thacher.
   Assistant to the Attorney-General, John Lord O'Brien.
   Assistant Attorneys-General, Charles P. Sisson, Seth Richardson, Roy St. Lewis, G. Aaron Youngquist, Monte Appel, Charles Rugg, Nugent Dodds, Charles Lawrence.
   Heads of Bureaus
     Bureau of Investigation, J. Edgar Hoover.
     Bureau of Prisons, Sanford Bates.
     Bureau of Prohibition, Amos Woodcock.

Post-Office Department
   Postmaster-General, Walter F. Brown.
     Assistant Postmasters-General, Arch Coleman, W. Irving Glover, Frederick Tilton, John W. Philp.
     Director of Postal Savings, William T. S. Rollins.

Navy Department
   Secretary, Charles Francis Adams.
     Assistant Secretaries, Ernest Lee Jahncke and David Ingalls.
     Chief of Naval Operations, Admiral C. F. Hughes.
     (later) Admiral William V. Pratt.

Department of the Interior
   Secretary, Ray Lyman Wilbur.
     Assistant Secretaries, Josph H. Dixon and John H. Edwards.
   Solicitor, Edward Finney.
   Heads of Bureaus
     National Park Service, Horace M. Albright.
     Land Office, Charles Moore.
     Indian Bureau, Charles J. Rhoads, Assistant, J. Henry Scattergood.
     Reclamation, Elwood Mead.
     Education, William J. Cooper.

Geological Survey, George Otis Smith.
(later) William Mendenhall.

Department of Agriculture

Secretary, Arthur M. Hyde.

Assistant Secretary, R. W. Dunlap.

Heads of Bureaus

Extension Service, C. W. Warburton.
Weather Bureau, Charles F. Marvin.
Animal Industry, John R. Mohler.
Dairy Industry, O. E. Reed.
Plant Industry, William A. Taylor.
Forest Service, R. Y. Stuart.
Chemistry and Soils, Henry C. Knight.
Entomology, C. L. Marlatt.
Biological Survey, Paul G. Redington.
Public Roads, Thomas MacDonald.
Agricultural Economics, Nils A. Olsen.
Plant Quarantine and Control Administration, Lee A. Strong.
Grain Futures Administration, J. W. T. Duval.
Food and Drug Administration, W. G. Campbell.

Department of Commerce

Secretary, Robert P. Lamont.
(later) Roy D. Chapin.

Assistant Secretaries, Julius Klein and Clarence M. Young.

Heads of Bureaus

Census, William M. Steuart.
Foreign and Domestic Commerce, William L. Cooper.
Fisheries, Henry O'Malley.
Lighthouses, George Putnam.
Coast and Geodetic Survey, R. S. Patton.
Navigation, Arthur Tyrer.
Patent Office, Thomas Robertson.
Mines, Scott Turner.

Department of Labor

Secretary, James J. Davis.
(later) William N. Doak.

Assistant Secretaries, Robe Carl White and W. W. Husband.

Heads of Bureaus

Immigration, Harry E. Hull.
Children's Bureau, Grace Abbott.
Naturalization, Raymond F. Crist.

Women's Bureau, Mary Anderson.
United States Employment Service, Francis I. Jones.
(later)   John R. Alpine.

The Presidential Secretaries were Walter H. Newton, Lawrence Richey, George Akerson and later Theodore Joslin, and French Strother.

Among President Hoover's appointments to positions to the Independent Offices and Establishments were the following:

Civil Service Commission, Thomas E. Campbell, Commissioner.

Interstate Commerce Commission, William E. Lee, Hugh M. Tate, and Charles D. Mahaffie.

Tariff Commission, Robert Lord O'Brien, Thomas Walker Page, John Lee Coulter, Ira M. Ornburn, and Charles R. Crisp.

Federal Radio Commission, Commissioner Charles McK. Saltzman, Harold Lafount, William Starbuck, and Thad H. Brown.

Federal Power Commission, George Otis Smith, Chairman, Frank R. McNinch, and Claude L. Draper.

District of Columbia Commissioners, Doctor Luther Reichelderfer, Major-General Herbert Crosby, and Major John C. Gotwals.

POLICIES OF REFORM IN THE ADMINISTRATION AND ENFORCEMENT OF LAW

President Hoover was as stern as Lincoln in his policies on law enforcement and obedience to law. In his Inaugural Address, he said:

"The most malign of all these dangers today is disregard and disobedience of law. Crime is increasing. Confidence in rigid and speedy justice is decreasing. I am not prepared to believe that this indicates any decay in the moral fiber of the American people. I am not prepared to believe that it indicates an impotence of the Federal Government to enforce its laws."

"It is only in part due to the additional burdens imposed upon our judicial system by the eighteenth amendment. The problem is much wider than that. Many influences had increasingly complicated and weakened our law enforcement organization long before the adoption of the eighteenth amendment."

"To re-establish the vigor and effectiveness of law enforcement we must critically consider the entire Federal machinery of justice."

"Its intricate and involved rules of procedure have become the refuge of both big and little criminals. There is a belief abroad that by invoking technicalities, subterfuge, and delay, the ends of justice may be thwarted by those who can pay the cost."

"Reform, reorganization and strengthening of our whole judicial and enforcement system both in civil and criminal sides have been advocated for years by statesmen, judges, and bar associations. First steps toward that end should not longer be delayed. Rigid and expeditious justice is the first safeguard of freedom, the basis of all ordered liberty."

"I have been selected by you to execute and enforce the laws of the country. I propose to do so to the extent of my own abilities, but the measure of success that the Government shall attain will depend upon the moral support which you, as citizens, extend. The duty of citizens to support the laws of the land is co-equal with the duty of their Government to enforce the laws which exist."

"Our whole system of self-government will crumble either if officials elect what laws they will enforce or citizens elect what laws they will support. The worst evil of disregard for some law is that it destroys respect for all law. If citizens do not like a law, their duty as honest men and women is to discourage its violation; their right is openly to work for its repeal."   [*State Papers, Vol. I, pp. 4–6*]

Hoover delivered a notable address upon this subject before the Associated Press in New York on April 22, 1929:

"I ask only that you weigh this for yourselves, and if my position is right, that you support it—not to support me but to support something infinitely more precious—the one force that holds our civilization together —law. And I wish to discuss it as law, not as to the merits or demerits of a particular law but all law, Federal and state, for ours is a Government of laws made by the people themselves."

"A surprising number of our people, otherwise of responsibility in the community, have drifted into the extraordinary notion that laws are made for those who choose to obey them. And, in addition, our law enforcement machinery is suffering from many infirmities arising out of its technicalities, its circumlocutions, its involved procedures, and too often, I regret, from inefficient and delinquent officials."

"We are reaping the harvest of these defects. More than 9000 human beings are lawlessly killed every year in the United States. Little more than half as many arrests follow. Less than one-sixth of these slayers are convicted, and but a scandalously small percentage are adequately punished. Twenty times as many people in proportion to population are lawlessly killed in the United States as in Great Britain. In many of our great cities murder can apparently be committed with impunity. At least fifty times as many robberies in proportion to population are committed in the United States as in Great Britain, and three times as many burglaries."

"Even in such premeditated crimes as embezzlement and forgery our record stands no comparison with stable nations. No part of the country, rural or urban, is immune. Life and property are relatively more unsafe than in any other civilized country in the world. In spite of all this we have reason to pride ourselves on our institutions and the high moral instincts of the great majority of our people. No one will assert that such crimes would be committed if we had even a normal respect for law and if the laws of our country were properly enforced."

"In order to dispel certain illusions in the public mind on this subject, let me say at once that while violations of law have been increased by inclusion of crimes under the eighteenth amendment and by the vast sums that are poured into the hands of the criminal classes by the patronage of illicit liquor by otherwise responsible citizens, yet this is but one segment of our problem. I have purposely cited the extent of murder, burglary, robbery, forgery, and embezzlement, for but a small percentage of these can be attributed to the eighteenth amendment. In fact, of the total number of convictions for felony last year, less than 8 per cent came from that source. It is therefore but a sector of the invasion of lawlessness."

"What we are facing today is something far larger and more fundamental: the possibility that respect for law is fading from the sensibilities of our people. . . . Law should be observed and must be enforced until it is repealed by the proper processes of our democracy. The duty to enforce the law rests upon every public official and the duty to obey it rests upon every citizen."

"No individual has the right to determine what law shall be obeyed and what law shall not be enforced. If a law is wrong, its rigid enforcement is the surest guaranty of its repeal. . . . "

"In my position, with my obligations, there can be no argument on these points. There is no citizen who would approve of the President of the United States assuming any other attitude. . . . Respect for law and obedience to law does not distinguish between Federal and stae laws—it is a common conscience."

"We have two immediate problems before us in Government. To investigate our existing agencies of enforcement and to reorganize our system of enforcement in such manner as to eliminate its weaknesses. It is the purpose of the Federal Administration systematically to strengthen its law enforcement agencies week by week, month by month, year by year, not by dramatic displays and violent attacks in order to make headlines, not by violating the law itself through misuse of the law in its enforcement, but by steady pressure, steady weeding out of all incapable and negligent officials, no matter what their status; by encourgement, promotion, and recognition for those who do their duty; and by the most rigid scrutiny of the records and attitudes of all persons suggested for appointment to official posts in our entire law enforcement machinery. That is administration for which my colleagues and I are fully responsible so far as the human material which can be assembled for the task will permit. . . ."

"There is another and vastly wider field than the nature of laws and the methods of their enforcement. This is the basic question of the understanding, the ideals, the relationship of the individual citizen to the law itself. It is in this field that the press plays a dominant part. It is almost final in its potency to arouse the interest and consciousness of our people. It can destroy their finer sensibilities or it can invigorate them."

". . . I wonder, sometimes, however, if perhaps a little more support to our laws could not be given in one direction. If, instead of the glamour of romance and heroism, which our American imaginative minds too frequently throw around those who break the laws, we would invest with a little romance and heroism those thousands of our officers who are endeavoring to enforce the law, it would itself decrease crime. Praise and respect for those who properly enforce the laws and daily condemnation of those who defy the laws would help. Perhaps a little better proportioned balance of news concerning those criminals who are convicted and punished would serve to instill the fear of the law."

"Finally, I wish to again reiterate that the problem of law enforcement is not alone a function or business of Government. If law can be upheld only by enforcement officers, then our scheme of goverment is at an end. Every citizen has a personal duty in it—the duty to order his own actions, to so weigh the effect of his example, that his conduct shall be a positive force in his community with respect to the law."

"It is unnecessary for me to argue the fact that the very essence of freedom is obedience to law; that liberty itself has but one foundation, and that is in the law."   [*State Papers Vol. I, pp. 42–7*]

His addresses and statements to the end of his administration were constant in insistence on these basic policies of government but he carried these policies far further than preachments. His first act was to choose an Attorney-General (William D. Mitchell) free from all political associations, and set the Department of Justice absolutely outside of politics. Attorney-General Mitchell recruited the strongest law enforcement staff ever assembled in any administration. Messrs. Myers and Newton, commenting upon this, stated:

"A drastic reform of the whole Federal law enforcement machinery was carried out. The most careful scrutiny was given to the appointment of Feedral judges and district attorneys. A score of weak district attorneys were removed or failed of reappointment. But, of even more importance, the whole machinery of enforcement was tightened up all along the line. As stated elsewhere, the criminal procedure in Federal courts was simplified and greatly improved. The Criminal Investigation Division under J. Edgar Hoover was built up into a real Scotland Yard, with a personnel of legally trained men instead of the old-fashioned detectives. These men created the spirit of the 'G' men who now are the terror of the criminals."   [*Hoover Administration, p. 535*]

In result, 11,000 more civil cases were terminated in 1932 than in 1929. And in criminal law the inhabitants of Federal prisons were increased from less than 30,000 to over 53,000. Of this increase only about 3000 were due to a more strict enforcement of prohibition.

As an instance of bringing policy into action, we may give an example from Myers and Newton:

"On March 19, 1929, Walter Strong, publisher of *The Chicago Daily News,* called upon the President and stated that Chicago had so fallen into the hands of the gangsters that the courts and police were impotent to act, and that some outside force must intervene if the city's ability to protect itself was to be restored. The President directed that the various Government law enforcement agencies at once and without publicity should combine and, regardless of expense, send these gangsters to jail if they had violated Federal laws."

"The only Federal criminal statutes to invoke were the Prohibition Act and the Income Tax laws. The grip of the gangs was broken up with the conviction of Al Capone and others in the Federal courts during the succeeding two years."   [*The Hoover Administration, p. 376*]

As an example of the refusal to allow politics to enter into law enforcement questions, the President addressed a Republican State Chairman as follows:

"DEAR SIR:

"I have your letter of September 21st."

"I cannot believe that you and the many . . . who have protested the appointment of Mr. Hughes [United States Attorney], overlook the primary responsibility which rests upon the President of the United States. That responsibility is one of the most sacred which he assumes upon his oath of office. It is that he shall, to his utmost capacity, appoint men to public office who will execute the laws of the United States with integriy and without fear, favor, or political collusion. The appointive responsibility rests in the President, not in any organization. . . ."

"The success of the Republican Party rests upon good government, not on patronage, and Florida will have good government so far as it is within my powers to give it. . . . I note your demands that the organization shall dictate appointments . . . and that you appeal to the opponents of the administration to attack me. I enclose a statement which I issued last March. That statement was no idle gesture."

[*State Papers, Vol. I, p. 105*]

Another such instance arose in February, 1931. A vacancy existed in the United States District Court for Minnesota. Senator Schall had been asked for suggestions. He responded, urging the appointment of a certain lawyer. Appropriate inquiry was made by the Department of Justice. The Attorney-General advised the President that he could not recommend the appointment. The Senator was advised that the nomination could not be made. Further suggestions were requested. There was a deadlock for several months. Finally, under local pressure, the entire Congressional delegation from Minnesota joined the Senator in urging the President to send in the nomination. The latter was convinced that the appointment ought not to be made, and refused to do so. Ultimately, the delegation gave way and the President's choice was confirmed by the Senate.

On January 13, 1930, the President, with the support of the Attorney-General and the Wickersham Commission, sent a special Message to Congress urging immediate changes in law enforcement machinery, which read in part:

"In my previous Messages I have requested the attention of the Congress to the urgent situation which has grown up in the matter of enforcement of Federal criminal laws. . . ."

"The development of the facts shows the necessity for certain important and evident administrative reforms in the enforcement and judicial machinery, concrete proposals for which are available from Government departments. They are in the main :"

"1. Reorganization of the Federal court structure so as to give relief from congestion."

"2. Concentration of responsibility in detection and prosecution of prohibition violations."

"3. Consolidation of the various agencies engaged in prevention of smuggling of liquor, narcotics, other merchandise, and aliens over our frontiers."

"4. Provision of adequate court and prosecuting officials."

"5. Expansion of Federal prisons and reorganization of parole and other practices."

"6. Specific legislation for the District of Columbia."

"I believe the administrative changes mentioned above will contribute to cure many abuses. . . ." [*State Papers, Vol. I, p. 203*]

The President followed this up on April 28 asking for expedition because of the urgency of certain of the measures. By May, a considerable progress had been made in the enactment of this program. The number of Federal judges were increased. The Division of Identification and Information was established in the Bureau of Investigation of the Department of Justice. Its purpose was to exchange criminal records between state and municipal authorities. Under this authority the Federal Government was able for the first time to concentrate criminal records and fingerprints in one national unit.

In addition, large measures of prison reform were passed which are referred to elsewhere. (See page 89.)

The President's program—backed by the Attorney-General—was by no means complete. On February 29, 1932, he sent another special Message to the Congress on further reform of the Judicial system. It said in part:

"On previous occasions I have called the attention of the Congress to the necessity of strengthening and making certain changes in our judicial and law enforcement machinery. Since then substantial progress has been made both through improved methods of administration and additional legislation. However, there is room for further improvement. . . ."

Congestion in the Courts

"Improvement has been shown during the past three years through steps taken under direction of the Attorney-General in more efficient organization of enforcement agencies through Congressional action in concentration of the responsibilities in the Department of Justice and through the prison reform laws passed by the Congress. Yet despite every effort there is still undue congestion in the courts in a number of districts."

"The following statistics indicate this congestion as well as the progress made:"

"Criminal cases commenced have increased from 1928 to 1931, but the number pending shows a decrease from 30,400 at the end of 1928 to 27,900 at the end of 1931. In 1931 alone, 4000 more criminal cases were disposed of than commenced, showing a definite gain in this field. There has also been a steady improvement in the quality of the work of the prosecuting agencies. Despite an increase in the volume of criminal cases begun, there has been a steady reduction in the number left pending each year. The results attained show a greater percentage of convictions and a lower ratio of dismissals and acquittals. In 1928, 78.3 per cent of criminal cases terminated were by verdict and plea of guilty, while in 1931 this ratio has increased to 84.2 per cent. In 1928, 21.7 per cent of criminal cases were terminated by dismissal or acquittal, while in 1931 this figure had fallen to 15.8 per cent."

"Final results of the more effective work of the Federal agencies for enforcement of criminal laws are evidenced by increase of prisoners. The number of Federal convicts in prison institutions and on parole increased from 19,110 at the end of 1928 to 27,871 on June 30, 1931. During the same period the number on probation increased from 3500 to 12,000. The total number of Federal convicts under some form of restraint was 39,900 on June 30, 1931, as compared with 22,600 on June 30, 1928. The recent reorganization of the parole and probation systems not only has produced a humane result, but has relieved an otherwise impossible prison congestion. These gains in effectiveness have been the result mainly of improvement in personnel, of administrative effort and reorganization, and not of reforms in judicial procedure. . . ."

Reform in Criminal Procedure

"The extent of crime is and must be a subject of increasing concern to the Government and to every well-disposed citizen. This increase is by no means confined to the violation of new criminal laws.

"Some part of all crime is due to confidence of criminals in the delays of the law and to their ability to avoid conviction and to delay penalties by misuse of the procedure and provisions of the law intended to assure fair trial."

"The present procedure in criminal appeals to the United States circuit courts of appeal and the procedure in the United States district courts, in preparation for appeals after verdicts of guilty, lend themselves to delay and unnecessary expense. . . ."

". . . I suggest that the Supreme Court of the United States be authorized to prescribe uniform rules of practice and procedure in criminal cases for all proceedings after verdicts in the district courts, and for the circuit courts of appeal, including the courts of the District of Columbia. . . ."

"Legislation should be enacted to permit an accused person to waive the requirement of indictment by grand jury. Where the accused admits his guilt, preliminary hearings and grand jury proceedings are not necessary for his protection, they cause unnecessary expense and delay. . . ."

"There have been many instances, some recently in the Supreme Court of the District of Columbia, where indictments, returned after long and expensive hearings, have been invalidated by the discovery of the presence on the grand jury of a single ineligible juror. . . . Legislation should be enacted limiting the time for making motions to quash indictments because of disqualifications of grand jurors. . . ."

"Each year many juveniles charged with violation of law fall into the custody of the Federal authorities. In the interest of child welfare there should be legislation enabling the Attorney-General to forego prosecution of children in the Federal courts and to return them to state authorities to be dealt with by juvenile courts and other state agencies equipped to deal with juvenile delinquents."

"The Constitution provides that the judicial power of the Federal courts shall extend to cases between citizens of different states and the Judiciary Acts have provided for the exercise of this jurisdiction. . . ."

"I recommend the consideration by the Congress of a measure to modify this jurisdiction to a limited extent by providing that where a corporation, organized under the laws of one state, carries on business in another state it shall be treated as a citizen of the state wherein it carries on business as respects suits brought within that state between it and the residents thereof and arising out of the business carried on in such state. Such a change in the law would keep out of the Federal courts cases which do not really belong there and reduce the burdens of the Federal courts without impairing in any degree the diversity of citizenship jurisdiction which the framers of the Constitution had in mind."

"I have hitherto recommended legislation effectively to supplement the Prohibition law for the District of Columbia. . . ."

"Reform in judicial procedure is, for many reasons, a slow process. It is not to be brought about by any single measure. It can best be accomplished by dealing with the subject step by step, the sum of which, in the course of time, will result in definite improvement. . . ."

[State Papers, Vol. II, p. 129]

Proposals for reform in the bankruptcy laws will be found elsewhere.

June 29, 1932, the President signed the law carrying out his reforms as to reorganization of Federal procedure in criminal jury cases. On July 8, he signed another law following these recommendations in form of a model law against sale or carrying concealed weapons in the District of Columbia. On February 25, 1933, he signed another of his reform measures with the following public statement:

"I have signed with great satisfaction the bill, S. 4020, to transfer to the Supreme Court of the United States the authority to prescribe rules of practice and procedure to be followed by the lower Federal courts in criminal cases after verdict. It represents the recommendations of myself and the Attorney-General over the past four years. It realizes, in part, a quarter of a century of demands for reform in Federal criminal procedure. It should prevent well endowed criminals, who have been convicted by juries, from delaying punishment by years of resort to sharp technicalities of judicial procedure. It will increase the respect for law."

[State Papers, Vol. I, p. 600]

Upon the importance of this law enforcement measure, the Attorney-General commented to the President.

"This is the most important measure directed at the reform of criminal procedure in the Federal courts that has been enacted for many years. The necessity for such legislation has more than once been brought to the attention of the Congress in your Messages and repeatedly urged in my reports to the Congress."

". . . Convicted persons supplied with ample funds and resourceful lawyers have been able to delay final judgment and the commencement of their sentences from one to four years after juries have returned verdicts of guilty. There have been innumerable instances of this kind. . . .

While a convicted person should have the right to have his conviction reviewed by an Appellate Court, he has no right to interminable delay. . . . This bill, which allows the Supreme Court of the United States to regulate all these proceedings, opens the way to throwing overboard the entire system of proceedings in Federal criminal cases after verdicts of guilty and to substitute new rules which will compel speedy disposition of these cases. . . ."

"One class of cases in which these abuses have been greatest is that including prosecutions for use of the mails to defraud. We have had many instances where thousands of persons have been defrauded out of their savings and robbed of vast sums by unscrupulous operators in worthless securities and where the malefactors, finally convicted by juries in Federal courts of using the mails to defraud, have gone at large on bail for years before their cases were finally disposed of in the intermediate courts of appeals."

". . . we have here the means of putting an end to practices after verdicts of guilty which have tended to make people lose confidence in the administration of criminal law."   [*State Papers, Vol. II, pp. 600–1*]

No President has more vigorously enforced the laws or consummated so many policies in judicial reform as Hoover. No word as to the Hoover policies of law enforcement would be complete without mention of the care taken by both the Attorney-General and himself in judicial appointment. The whole Federal Bench was stronger at the end of his administration than at the beginning.

President Hoover's judicial appointments were as follows:

Justices of the Supreme Court: Chief Justice Charles Evans Hughes and Associate Justices Owen D. Roberts and Benjamin N. Cardozo.
United States Circuit Judges:
First Circuit, Scott Wilson and James M. Morton, Jr.
Third Circuit, J. Whitaker Thompson.
Fourth Circuit, Morris A. Soper.
Fifth Circuit, Samuel Sibley and Joseph Hutcheson.
Sixth Circuit, Charles C. Simons.
Seventh Circuit, William Sparks.
Eighth Circuit, John B. Sanborn and Archibald Gardner.
Ninth Circuit, Curtis D. Wilbur and William H. Sawtelle.
Tenth Circuit, George McDermott and Orie L. Phillips.

Judges of the Court of Customs and Patent Appeals: Irvine L. Lenroot.

United States District Courts:

First Circuit, Ira K. Wells and Hugh D. McLellan.

Second Circuit, John M. Woolsey, Francis G. Caffey, Alfred Coxe, Robert Patterson, Clarence G. Galston, Mortimer W. Byers, Carroll C. Hincks, John Knight.

Third Circuit, John P. Nields, Albert Watson, John Avis, Philip Forman, George Welch.

Fourth Circuit, J. Lyles Glenn, W. Calvin, Luther B. Way, John Paul.

Fifth Circuit, Charles B. Kennamer, Louis W. Strum, E. Marvin Underwood, Thomas Kennedy, Randolph Bryant, Robert McMillan.

Sixth Circuit, Ernest A. O'Brien, Robert Nevin.

Seventh Circuit, John H. Barnes, Charles G. Briggle.

Eighth Circuit, A. Lee Wyman.

Ninth Circuit, George Cosgrave, E. Coke Hill, Albert Sames, Henry Hollzer, James Alger Fee.

Tenth Circuit, Richard J. Hopkins.

Judges of the Court of Claims: Thomas S. Williams, Benjamin Littleton, and Richard Whaley.

United States Court of Appeals of the District of Columbia: William Hitz and D. Lawrence Croner.

Judges of the United States Customs Court: David Kincheloe, Slater H. Evans, William J. Tilson and Frederick Dallinger.

Territory of Hawaii: Supreme Court, Chief Justice, Antonio M. Perry; Associate Justices, James J. Banks and Charles F. Parsons; 1st Circuit, Albert Cristy; 2nd Circuit, Daniel Case.

THE WICKERSHAM COMMISSION

Hoover announced in his campaign of 1928 that he would appoint a commission to examine and recommend improvement in the whole of the law enforcement machinery. That commission was appointed in May, 1929, under the chairmanship of former Attorney-General George W. Wickersham.

The Commission in addition to George Wickersham, chairman, was former Secretary of War Newton D. Baker, U. S. Circuit Judge William S. Kenyon, U. S. District Judges Paul McCormick and William Grubb, former Chief Justice Kenneth MacKintosh of the Washington Supreme Court, Dean Roscoe Pound of Harvard, Doctor Ada Comstock and Messrs. Henry Anderson, Monte Leman and Frank Loesch.

The commission was usually known as the Wickersham Commission. The public came to regard it solely in the aspects of Prohibition, although its greatest contribution was in the much broader field.

At the initial meeting of the commission on May 28, 1929, at the White House, the President said:

"The American people are deeply concerned over the alarming disobedience of law, the abuses in law enforcement and the growth of organized crime, which has spread in every field of evil-doing and in every part of our country. A nation does not fail from its growth of wealth or power. But no nation can for long survive the failure of its citizens to respect and obey the laws which they themselves make. Nor can it survive a decadence of the moral and spiritual concepts that are the basis of respect for law, nor from neglect to organize itself to defeat crime and the corruption that flows from it. Nor is this a problem confined to the enforcement and obedience of one law or the laws of the Federal or state governments separately. The problem is partly the attitude toward all law."

"It is my hope that the commission shall secure an accurate determination of fact and cause, following them with constructive, courageous conclusions which will bring public understanding and command public support of its solutions. . . . I do pray for the success of your endeavors, for by such success you will have performed one of the greatest services to our generation."   [*State Papers, Vol. I, p. 63*]

The Wickersham Commission made exhaustive examination and report upon the many problems of law enforcement and crime. These reports had a profound effect in directing public and legislative attitudes on procedure of the courts, and upon police and preventive measures in respect to crime and its suppression. The Commission dealt with the prohibition question and while the initial report was against repeal the supplementary reports showed great division in the Commission as to the methods of handling the problem, reflecting in fact the greatly divided opinion in the country.

PROHIBITION

This was a most troublesome question throughout the Hoover Administration. Mr. Joslin correctly stated Mr. Hoover's policies in respect to it when he says:

"Mr. Hoover did not believe the Eighteenth Amendment

was anywhere near perfect. Far from it. To him it was what he described it—an experiment. The great body of the people believe he said prohibition was a 'noble experiment.' He never said anything of the kind. What he did say, not once but many times, was:

"'Our country has deliberately undertaken a great social and economic experiment, noble in motive and far-reaching in purpose. It must be worked out constructively.'"

"It was the motive that was 'noble.' The 'experiment' was 'social and economic.' There is a marked distinction."

"To the extent of my ability I shall now describe the President's position on Prohibition. It was his attitude throughout his administration. It is his attitude today to the best of my knowledge and belief."

"He was and is a stickler for law observance, whether of Prohibition or any other law. To his mind, the worst evil of disregard for some law is that it destroys respect for all law. He often observed that for citizens to patronize the violation of a particular law on the ground that they were opposed to it was destructive of the very basis of that protection of life, homes, and property which they rightly claimed under other laws. He firmly believed that if the citizens did not like a law, their duty as honest men and women was to discourage its violation. Equally, their right was openly to work for its repeal."

"He believed that the human race would be better off without alcoholic beverages. There is no use mincing words in this particular. He looked upon the problem presented by Prohibition as being a practical one. He was most implacably opposed to the return of the saloon with its enormous corruption of politics and the morals of the community. He believed the only way to prove the merits of the experiment in prohibition provided by the Eighteenth Amendment was to give it a fair and honest trial."

"It must be borne in mind that the enforcement of the Eighteenth Amendment was made 'concurrent' between the Federal Government and the states. The whole assumption was that the police powers of the states, counties, and municipalities would be applied to its enforcement. It was not originally expected that the Federal Government would do more than look after interstate commerce, imports, and major conspiracies extending over several states."

"In order that the Federal Government should not be delinquent, Mr. Hoover entirely reorganized and enlarged the Federal enforcement service to the very maximum that all could be used practically. He placed them under the Civil Service and eliminated every political employee with men chosen absolutely on merit. He eliminated to the extent he possibly could graft, collusion, and brutality which had been prevalent in the service."

"It became obvious, however, that enforcement would fail unless the state and municipal authorities would do their part. Otherwise, it would be necessary for the Federal Government to employ 250,000 agents and duplicate every local peace official with the consequent practical destruction of all state and local responsibility—not alone for Prohibition but in a much wider sense."

"He repeatedly sent for the governors of dry states to come to Washington and he urged upon them that, unless at least the dry states were willing to do their part and make an example of successful 'concurrent' enforcement, the whole experiment would break down."

"It requires no reiteration of the fact that even the dry states in the Union slacked more and more on enforcement and it became obvious that, regardless of the merits or demerits of the experiment, it was a form of prohibition which never could be enforced. These states were wetter than under their own laws."

To this we may add that Hoover energized the Government to give the law a fair trial. The prohibition experience at least proved the wisdom of effecting constitutional reforms by giving authority to Congress to act instead of placing inflexible powers in the Constitution.

At what time Hoover determined the law should be repealed is not known. He repeatedly stated to his colleagues: "I am under the most sacred oath to 'preserve, protect and defend' the Constitution. The Eighteenth Amendment is part of the Constitution. The Constitution gives the President no part in its amendment. Under the Constitution, legislation submitting the amendment is not subject to the President's veto. There is reason in that. If I, as President, were to go out and denounce the Eighteenth Amendment, there is not a judge or a jury in the United States that would give a conviction from that day on. I should have nullified the Constitution and violated my oath. On the other hand when I get to the campaign the country must know, but it would be wrong to do it a moment before."

On August 11, 1932, ninety days before the election, he stated that the amendment should be repealed but that the Federal Government should retain a veto on methods of distribution to prevent the return of the old saloon system. We give his statement in part:

"Across the path of the Nation's consideration of these vast problems of economic and social order there has arisen a bitter controversy over the control of the liquor traffic. I have always sympathized with the high purpose of the Eighteenth Amendment, and I have used every power at my command to make it effective over the entire country. I have hoped it was the final solution of the evils of the liquor traffic against which our people have striven for generations. It has succeeded in great measure in those many communities where the majority sentiment is favorable to it. But in other and increasing number of communities there is a majority sentiment unfavorable to it. Laws opposed by majority sentiment create resentment which undermines enforcement and in the end produces degenration and crime."

". . . the return of the saloon system with its corruption, its moral and social abuse which debauched the home, its deliberate interference with those states endeavoring to find honest solution, its permeation of political parties and its pervasion of legislatures, even touched at the capital of the Nation. . . . I cannot consent to the return of that system."

". . . we must recognize the difficulties which have developed in making the Eighteenth Amendment effective and that grave abuses have grown up. . . . An increasing number of states and municipalities are proving themselves unwilling to engage in such enforcement. Owing to this . . . in large sections an increasing illegal traffic in liquor. But worse than this there has been in those areas a spread of disrespect not only for this law but for all laws, grave dangers of practical nullification of the Constitution, a degeneration in municipal government, and an increase in subsidized crime and violence. I cannot consent to the continuation of this regime."

"I refuse to accept either of these destinies, on the one hand to return to the old saloon with its political and social corruption, or on the other to endure the bootlegger and the speakeasy with their abuses and crime. Either is intolerable. These are not the ways out. . . ."

"It is my conviction that the nature of this change, and one upon which all reasonable people can find common ground, is that each state shall be given the right to deal with the problem as it may determine, but subject to absolute guarantees in the Constitution to protect each state from interference and invasion by its neighbors, and that in no part of the United States shall there be a return of the saloon system with its inevitable political and social corruption and its organized interference with other states."

"American statesmanship is capable of working out such a solution and making it effective." [State Papers, Vol. II, p. 261]

THE LINDBERGH KIDNAPPING LAW

On March 1, 1932, word came that the son of Colonel and Mrs. Charles Lindbergh had been kidnapped. The President, shocked by this most inhumane of crimes, called upon the Attorney-General and instructed him to put his force on the job. Every aid possible was given but the lack of authority of the Federal Government was at once evident. The President said to the press:

"I have directed the law enforcement agencies and the several secret services of the Federal Government to make the kidnapping and murder of the Lindbergh baby a live and never-to-be-forgotten case, never to be relaxed until those criminals are implacably brought to justice. The Federal Government does not have police authority in such crimes but its agencies will be unceasingly alert to assist the New Jersey police in every possible way until this end has been accomplished."

In the meantime, the President urged to Congressional leaders the necessity for some real authority. A month later, on June 22, 1932, the President signed the anti-kidnapping bill. This act provided that transportation in interstate commerce of a kidnapped person should be a Federal penitentiary offense. The court was authorized to fix a maximum punishment of life imprisonment.

On July 10, 1932, the President signed an extension to the kidnapping law which made it a Federal crime to use the mails with intent to extort money from any person by threatening to kidnap or otherwise injure the person or property of any person. This concluded the authority he had requested to meet the kidnapping problem.

These laws, together with the reorganization of the Bureau of Investigation by the employment of a higher type of personnel and the installation of a system of national criminal records, formed the foundation for the Federal drive, then and later, against kidnapping and organized crime.

RESULTS OF REORGANIZED LAW ENFORCEMENT

Some indication of the increasing thoroughness of Hoover's policies in law enforcement under Attorney-General Mitchell is shown by the fact that 24,307 civil cases were commenced in 1929 while 34,189 civil cases were commenced in 1932. In 1929 a total of 21,733 civil cases were completed, while 29,591 were completed in 1932. In criminal cases 86,348 cases were commenced in 1929 as against 91,174 in 1932. Of these cases 85,324 were completed in 1929, while 96,946 were completed in 1932. The greater effectiveness is indicated by the fact that the Federal convicts in prisons, on parole or on probation increased from 32,868 in 1930 to 53,116 in 1932.

CIVIL SERVICE

One of the Hoover policies was the unflagging support of the merit service—the so-called Civil Service. In his Acceptance Address at Palo Alto, on August 11, 1928, he announced his policies:

"Our Civil Service has proved a great national boon. Appointive office, both North, South, East, and West, must be based solely on merit, character, and reputation in the community in which the appointee is to serve; as it is essential for the proper performance of their duties that officials shall enjoy the confidence and respect of the people with whom they serve."

Congress had for years failed to meet the recommendations of one President after another to place first-, second-, and third-class postmasters within the merit system of the Civil Service Commission. This was the only large group outside this requirement and it had been universally used as Congressional patronage. The President, however, had some power in that he could refuse to submit appointments to the Senate unless he was satisfied with their merits. A partial system of examination had been installed by President Harding. But in order to remove postmasters further from the spoils system into a more effective merit system, President Hoover revised upwards the previous methods of investigation. In effect all candidates had to pass an examination by the Civil Service Commission. While this gave assurance of efficiency, it did not build up

a permanent merit service in the Post Office. The President's
order on the subject (May 1, 1929) was in part:

"When a vacancy exists or occurs in the position of postmaster of an
office of the first, second, or third class, if such vacancy is not filled by
nomination of some qualified person within the competitive classified
Civil Service, the Postmaster-General shall certify the fact to the Commission, which shall forthwith hold an open competitive examination to
test the fitness of applicants to fill such vacancy, and when such examination has been held and the papers submitted therewith have been rated,
the Commission shall furnish a certificate of not less than three eligibles
for appointment to fill such vacancy . . . (certain requirements as to
residence, age, and character). . . . If pursuant to this order it is desired to submit to the President for nomination the name of a person
in the competitive classified service, such person must first be found by
the Civil Service Commission to possess the requisite qualifications."

[*State Papers, Vol. I, p. 49*]

He followed this in his first Message to the Congress on
December 3, 1929, by hoping that at least one more step could
be taken:

"Approximately four-fifths of all the employees in the executive Civil
Service now occupy positions subject to competitive examination under
the Civil Service law."

"There are, however, still commanding opportunities for extending the
system. These opportunities lie within the province of Congress and not
the President. I recommend that a further step be taken by authorization
that appointments of third-class postmasters be made under the Civil
Service law."   [*State Papers, Vol. I, p. 162*]

The President, by an executive order on November 18, 1930,
extended the civil service or merit system to the appointment of
employees of the District of Columbia. For the first time the
appointment of these municipal employees was taken out of
politics.

In the spring of 1930, the President through co-operation
with Congressman Lehlbach secured the revision of retirement
provisions and pensions to civil servants which placed them upon
a much improved basis. Through his co-operation with Congress the pensions of the Foreign Service of the State Department were revised.

On July 8, 1930, upon consolidating the various bureaus connected with Veterans' affairs, the President placed some 2000 officials who had hitherto been outside of the Civil Service requirements under that Commission.

On April 25, 1931, the President created the Council of Personnel Administration to improve the Civil Service. The undertaking was based on an able report by Chairman Thomas E. Campbell of the Civil Service Commission. The order stated:

"For the purpose of developing in the Federal Government a more effective and economical system of employment and personnel management . . . there is hereby established a Council of Personnel Administration, . . ."

". . . The president of the Civil Service Commission shall act as chairman of the Council. . . ."

"The Council of Personnel Administration shall:

"(a) Establish a liaison system between the Civil Service Commission and the several departments;

"(b) With the assistance of advisory committees . . . make available to the Government the best developments in personnel administration outside of Government service. . . ."

"(c) Prepare specific plans for improvement and co-ordination of personnel administration. . . ." [*State Papers, Vol. I, p. 552*]

At the close of the Hoover Administration over 81 per cent of the Federal employees were appointed under merit requirements of the Civil Service. With the Civil Service examinations required for postmasters, fully 95 per cent of all employees were under merit requirements. The remainder comprised mostly transient labor and policy-making officials. Furthermore, while the heads of some seventy bureaus in the Government were Presidential appointments and usually used for political supporters, at the end of the Hoover Administration all but a very small number were men promoted from the permanent employees of the bureaus themselves.

Speaking in Oakland, on October 5, 1935, Hoover commented on the change in these policies by Roosevelt:

"I would call your attention to the numbers and potency of the army of spenders which has been created. According to the reports of the Civil Service Commission, there were about 573,000 civilian employees in the Federal Government at the end of the Cooldige Administration. There were about 565,000 at the end of the Hoover Administration."

"There are 730,000 today. And this does not include some 100,000 part-time paid members of some 5000 committees and agencies of one sort or another who all spend money. Nor does it include the people on relief."

"The whole system of non-political appointments under the Civil Service which had been steadily built up by every administration for years has now been practically ignored. Almost this whole addition of 260,-000 new people on the Federal payroll constitutes the most gigantic spoils raid in our history. Even Andrew Jackson appointed less than 10,000."

"Whenever you increase the numbers of political bureaucracy you not only have to pay them but they are veritable research laboratories for new inventions in spending money. Bureaucracy rushes headlong into visions of the millennium and sends the bill to the Treasury. And there are three implacable spirits in bureaucracy—self-perpetuation, expansion, and demand for more power. Moreover, they also serve to help win elections."

"The Roosevelt Administration is now clutched in the meshes of the gigantic spending bureaucracy which it has created. Even with expenditures of some eight billions annually, with deficits of about $3,500,-000,000, there is to be no "breathing spell" in spending, as witness the ten billions of new appropriations just passed by Congress."

Speaking again at Portland, Oregon, on February 12, 1936, he referred to the subject:

"The New Deal is not confused in politics. National Planning has been a success in that field. But it is a moral confusion of every ideal of American Government. For fifty years it has been an aspiration of America that our Government officials should be removed from the political spoils system. The selection by merit through the Civil Service Commission was not alone to gain efficiency in Government. Its purpose was to raise the morals of public life. It was to make impossible the bribe-taker, the invisible government of the greedy, and the corruption of elections. Since 1880 every President has steadily builded that service."

"Let us examine the record. The Coolidge officials under the Civil Service were about 75 per cent. The Hoover increase was to over 81 per cent. The Roosevelt decrease has been to 57 per cent. This is exhibit A of New Deal idealism."

"All this sometimes reminds me of the small girl who said, 'Mother, you know that beautiful jug that you said had been handed down to us from generation to generation?' Mother replied, 'Yes, Ann, what of it?' And Ann answered solemnly, 'This generation dropped it.'"

"But we may explore that still further. During the Hoover Administration, despite the many emergency agencies needed to meet the depression, the total number of Federal officials was decreased by 10,000. But under the New Deal, part or full-time political officials have been increased by over 335,000."

POLICIES OF REORGANIZATION OF THE FEDERAL ADMINISTRATION

Hoover began agitation for reorganization of the Federal machinery in 1920. His views were later summed up in a public address on this subject at Washington, on May 21, 1925:

"Bad co-ordination among industries finally comes home to the people as a whole in the form of increased prices. And bad organization in Government comes home in many more directions than even the taxes it wastes."

". . . it is another of these laborious subjects in which stimulating oratory is about as serviceable as a sermon on high voltage and it contains about the same proportion of humor and good cheer as a reminder that we have to work when the trout are rising."

"As is said in the maiden speech of every constitutional orator, our Government is divided into the legislative, judicial, and executive branches. When our forefathers conceived this great plan they also conceived that legislation required the meeting of scores of minds of equal authority, and that judicial decision likewise required the meeting of many minds through appeals and final decision by a whole bench of judges; but they were no less emphatic that administration must be in single-headed responsibility. And in one hundred and fifty years of the highest development of skill in organization of big industry and commerce, we have right down to today proved the soundness of this principle of many minds for legislative, judicial, and advisory decisions, but a single mind for executive authority. Yet in Government we have been busy for the last century violating these primary principles of good organization."

"On the executive side of the Federal Government we have grown to have more than 200 different bureaus, boards, and commissions employing several hundred thousand people. For the most part they have been thrown hodge-podge into ten different executive departments, under Cabinet officers. But there are more than forty independent establishments either directly under the President or directly under Congress."

"As this immense number of bureaus and agencies is now grouped and organized there are six primary streams of confusion and waste.

There is a confusion of basic principles; there is a grouping of Federal bureaus which divides responsibility; there arises from this scattering a lack of definite national policies; direct wastes arise from overlap and conflict; indirectly large costs are imposed upon citizens by this scattering of functions and by the undue complexity of laws and regulations. There are too many floating islands in this dismal swamp of independent agencies only technically anchored to the President but really responsible to nobody—and with all this division of authority multiplies the urge for expansion of Federal activities in every direction."

"It is not my purpose to deal primarily with the legislative and judicial arms of the Government. With the growing complexity of problems it has been necessary for Congress to delegate . . . many secondary legislative functions in the making of regulations, and many secondary judicial functions in the enforcement of them. That is the so-called administrative law. And there has been the crudest mixing of these semi-legislative and semi-judicial and advisory functions with purely executive functions. Moreover, these semi-judicial and semi-legislative duties are frequently entrusted to single officers, while purely administrative functions are often carried on by boards. All of this is exactly the reverse of the basic principles of sound administration. Boards and commissions are soundly adapted to the deliberate processes necessary to semi-judicial and semi-legislative and advisory functions but they are absolutely hopeless where decisive administrative action is necessary. And likewise most of such functions should not be entrusted to a single mind. There is not a single successful business organization in the country that confuses such functions the way we do in Government."

"The Shipping Board has semi-judicial functions that quite properly were entrusted to a Board. Political jealousies and sectional jealousies, however, required a bipartisan body selected from different parts of the country although it was to perform an expert judicial function. Then this structure was suddenly loaded with the most difficult of administrative jobs—the actual construction of a great fleet. . . . The losses and waste . . . from assigning administrative functions to the joint and equal minds . . . a few hundred millions. . . . Not even two geniuses of equal authority could administer a competitive business—let alone seven."

"This same chaos of function is carried into other directions where administrative officials are given these semi-judicial and semi-legislative authorities. The Secretary of Agriculture has been loaded with powers of this character in the administration of the stockyards and commodity exchanges. The Secretary of Commerce has such powers . . . many bureau heads have such powers. The responsibilities in decisions . . . as important as those of Federal courts . . . and worst of all there are none of the safeguards to right in these determinations which surround our courts. Duties of this character should no longer be imposed upon administrative officials. . . . No individual should be at the same time legislator, policeman, prosecutor, judge, and jury. Yet we are. We do judgment the best we can in old Kadi fashion and the culprit usually knuckles down quietly because he feels we might look for him again if he protested. The dangers of oppression in these matters are not merely a theory—they are a fact."

"Every single department, bureau, and board in the entire Government should be placed upon the operating table and a cleancut separation established between semi-judicial and semi-legislative functions on the one hand, and administration on the other. The former rightly belongs to boards or commissions, the latter in individuals."

"Our other greatest weakness in organization is the division of authority over services directed to the same major purpose by scattering them through unrelated groups."

"To illustrate my point, I have made a partial collection of misfits and in so doing I have taken no account of either incidental functions or semi-legislative or semi-judicial agencies except so far as they have administrative functions."

	Number of Bureaus or Agencies	Number of Departments or Independent Agencies in which they are located
Public Works Construction	14	9
Conservation of Nation Resources	8	5
Direct Aids to Industry	5	2
Direct Aids to Merchant Marine	14	6
Direct Aids to Education	6	3
Direct Aids to Veterans	4	4
Government of Territories and Dependencies	4	3
Public Health	4	2
Purchase of $250,000,000 of supplies annually	In every bureau of the Government	

"It is not necessary that each of these groups should become a whole executive department, each under a Cabinet officer; but it is entirely feasible to place each of them under the supervision of a special assistant secretary, and if we were truly intelligent we would class him as an expert and outside selection on political grounds. It is entirely secondary what department these groups are in. The big thing is to bring these kindred agencies together under one authority so that their overlapping edges can be clipped and their fights stopped. . . . It all costs somebody money."

"The divided responsibility . . . consistent development of broad national policies. . . . Under the present system we have different bureau policies, department policies, board policies, and commission policies. We have a bundle of divergent ideas without focus; lumber piled together does not make a house. The treatment of our national resources furnishes a good instance. If anything is certain, it is that the Government should have a continuous, definite, and consistent policy directed to intelligent conservation and use of national resources. But it can have no such policy so long as responsibility is split up among half a dozen different departments. The recent occurrences in oil leases are a fair example of what may happen by the lack of single-headed responsibility in such matters. No policy of real guardianship of our reserve resources will exist until we put all conservation business in the hands of an Under Secretary for Conservation, with the spotlight of public opinion continuously focused upon him."

"The same is true of our deplorable lack of a definite and organized merchant marine policy."

"In our public works there has been no concept of the Nation's priority needs or its needs as a whole, and enormous sums have been sunk upon many fruitless works that got nowhere."

"The scattering of our purchasing agencies and the method of purchasing result in such obvious losses as to require no discussion."

"The multiplication and scattering of the agencies which are supposed to attend to different aspects of the same problem . . . impose a heavy burden upon those who have dealings with the Government. It costs somebody money."

"Under existing hodge-podge arrangement, the citizen is driven from pillar to post among the bureaus, seeking information he wants, settling the demands upon him or determining the regulations by which he is required to conduct his business. I have daily evidence. . . . Assistance to and regulation of navigation is not by any means one of the principal functions of our Government, but it must be a sore trial to the hardy mariner. The delay of ships, the time lost to masters and officers as they are shuttled from one office to another, or as one official after another operates on him from the fourteen agencies in six different departments which have to do with shipping must sorely try his temper. Perhaps hardships at sea make him immune to trouble ashore. But it is a great burden on the Merchant Marine."

"Again there are a great many bureaus at Washington which are given to important economic research. The boundary lines which separate these bureaus, one from another, are necessarily indeterminate. The business man who is accustomed to receive a bombardment of questionnaires from these establishments has good reason to dread the extension of Federal encroachment upon business. He would have much less cause for complaining if these Government activities were grouped in such fashion that these matters fell under the control of fewer superior officials."

"The forty governmental agencies which are now supposed to function directly under the President present another problem. . . . It is preposterous to expect that with his multitude of higher obligations the President can give them anything like adequate supervision."

"The largest of the independent establishments is, of course, the Veterans' Bureau. It is my belief that if this Bureau had been directly responsible to a Cabinet officer there would have been, as in the case of other departmental bureaus, so many more safeguards in management as to have prevented the frauds which have been exposed in the courts in the recent history of that Bureau."

"Every well-balanced citizen knows of something in this world that ought to be regulated that is not being regulated. Every agency of the Federal Government knows this also, but the difference is that every Government agency is under constant pressure, or sometimes is anxious, to expand its powers further than was originally contemplated. When any particular theme is large in the national mind, every bureau that has any relationship to the problem or thinks it can get some appropriation for it immediately rushes in that direction. They compete with each other, tread on each other's toes, fight each other, but the net effect is expansion. Much of it is originated from worthy zeal. And it costs somebody money. The very scattering of Government agencies gives impetus to this tendency. There would be far less of this if there were concentrated authority over related things."

"The natural tendency of most healthy things is to grow. There are of course Government bureaus which should grow, and as the country gets bigger and more complicated they must grow. But they should grow in directions approved by the whole people, and in line with fundamental Nation policies—not as scattered entities in a conglomerate bureaucracy."

"I wish to repeat that the faults of organization are not a matter of the taxpayers' small change. They form a total of waste which, considering the indirect results, runs into high figures. The waste from bad organization is not to be measured in loss of dollars of Congressional appropriations alone. That is bad enough, but still larger is the indirect loss in the unnecessary costs they impose on the citizen. All these weaknesses have been multiplied by the growth of the country, the enlargement of its problems and the burdens from the War."

"What we need is three primary reforms; first to group together all agencies having the same predominant major purpose under the same administrative supervision; second, to separate the semi-judicial and the semi-legislative and advisory functions from the administrative functions placing the former under joint minds, the latter under single responsibility, and third, we should relieve the President of a vast amount of direct administrative labor."

"Every President from Roosevelt to Coolidge has urged upon Congress a reorganization of the executive arm of the Government; commissions have been appointed, Congressional committees have investigated, reports have been made, confirming all this. Cabinet officers express their feelings in spirited annual reports with a circulation of a few hundred copies. More than once a complete program of reorganization has been formulated, and put forward as a basis for general consideration."

"But practically every single item in such a program has invariably met with opposition of some vested official, or it has disturbed some vested habit, and offended some organized minority. It has aroused paid propagandists. All these vested officials, vested habits, organized propaganda groups, are in favor of every item of reorganization except that which affects the bureau or the activity in which they are specially interested. No proposed change is so unimportant that it is not bitterly opposed by some one. In the aggregate, these directors of vested habits surround Congress with a confusing fog of opposition. Meantime the inchoate voice of the public gets nowhere but to swear at 'bureaucracy.'"

"Nor will we ever attain this until Congress will authorize the President or some board, if you will, or a committee of its own members to take the time to do it. Congress courageously removed the Civil Service from politics; it created the Budget, it established the Classification. The remaining great step is to authorize the reorganization of the administrative arm of the Government."

"I do not expect that the Federal Government will ever be a model of organization, but I have aspirations to see it improve. Some one has said that the first ten years in any needed reform are the hardest. The first ten years are up."

President Harding in an endeavor to solve the problem had secured a joint commission of the Administration and Congressional representatives under the chairmanship of Walter F. Brown to report on the whole subject. The commission made energetic recommendations to the Congress including new departments of Public Welfare, etc., but exactly the forces mentioned above by Hoover succeeded in stopping any effective action. President Coolidge time and again urged action upon Congress, and although he had a Republican Congress, the bureau forces and their allies again prevented action.

As Secretary of Commerce, Hoover proceeded to reorganize and consolidate within that department to the full extent permitted by law. The Bureau of Mines and the Bureau of Patents which were allied with functions of the Department of Commerce were transferred from the Interior to Commerce and their overlapping was wiped out.

In the campaign of 1928, Hoover pressed the subject:

"One of the greatest difficulties . . . is the multitude of . . . Government bureaus, . . . and the duplication of governmental activities."

"Our Republican Presidents have repeatedly recommended to Congress that it would not only greatly reduce expenses of business in its contacts with Government but that a great reduction could be made in governmental expenditure and more consistent and continued national policies could be developed if we could secure the grouping of these agencies devoted to one major purpose under single responsibility and authority. I have had the good fortune to be able to carry out such reorganization in respect to the Department of Commerce. The results have amply justified its expansion to other departments and I should consider it an obligation to enlist the support of Congress to effect it."

On coming to the White House in 1929, Hoover recommended reorganization to the Congress on December 3, 1929:

"This subject has been under consideration for over twenty years. It was promised by both political parties in the recent campaign. It has been repeatedly examined by committees and commissions—Congressional, executive, and voluntary. The conclusions of these investigations have been unanimous that reorganization is a necessity of sound administration; of economy; of more effective governmental policies and of relief to the citizen from unnecessary harassment in his relations with a multitude of scattered governmental agencies. But the presentation of any specific plan at once enlivens opposition from every official whose authority may be curtailed or who fears his position is imperiled by such a result; of bureaus and departments which wish to maintain their authority and activities; of citizens and their organizations who are selfishly interested, or who are inspired by fear that their favorite bureau may, in a new setting, be less subject to their influence or more subject to some other influence. . . ."

"The essential principles of reorganization are two in number. First, all administrative activities of the same major purpose should be placed in groups under single-headed responsibility; second, all executive and administrative functions should be separated from boards and commissions and placed under individual responsibility, while quasi-legislative and quasi-judicial and broadly advisory functions should be removed from individual authority and assigned to boards and commissions. . . ."

"With this background of all previous experience I can see no hope for the development of a sound reorganization of the Government unless Congress be willing to delegate its authority over the problem (subject to defined principles) to the Executive, who should act upon approval of a joint committee of Congress or with the reservation of power of revision by Congress within some limited period adequate for its consideration."

[*State Papers, Vol. I, pp. 162–3*]

During this year Hoover secured two successes in consolidation. On May 27, 1930, he signed a bill authorizing him to consolidate all the Prohibition enforcement agencies into the Department of Justice, which he did. On July 8, 1930, under authority of Congress, he issued an order creating the Veterans' Administration out of some four or five agencies previously scattered over the Government and bringing all veterans' business into one agency. General Hines who was appointed Administrator of Veterans' Affairs subsequently reported that the consolidation was saving $10,000,000 per annum. The Veterans' services were more efficient.

President Hoover returned to the charge again in his Message of December 8, 1931, hoping to get it done step at a time:

"I have referred in previous Messages to the profound need of further reorganization and consolidation of Federal administrative functions to eliminate overlap and waste, and to enable co-ordination and definition of Government policies now wholly impossible in scattered and conflicting agencies which deal with parts of the same major function. . . . There are two directions of such reorganization, however, which have an important bearing upon the emergency problems with which we are confronted."

"At present the Shipping Board exercises large administrative functions independent of the Executive. These administrative functions should be transferred to the Department of Commerce. . . ."

"The Shipping Board should be made a regulatory body acting also in advisory capacity on loans and policies, in keeping with its original conception. Its regulatory powers should be amended to include regulation of coastwise shipping so as to assure stability and better service. It is also worthy of consideration that the regulation of rates and services upon the inland waterways should be assigned to such a reorganized board."

"I recommend that all building and construction activities of the Government now carried on by many departments be consolidated into an independent establishment under the President to be known as the 'Public Works Administration' directed by a Public Works Administrator. This agency should undertake all construction work in service to the different departments of the Government (except naval and military work). The services of the Corps of Army Engineers should be delegated in rotation for military duty to this administration in continuation of their supervision of river and harbor work. Great economies, sounder policies, more effective co-ordination to employment, and expedition in all construction work would result from this consolidation."

[State Papers, Vol. II, pp. 53–4]

Hoover reinforced it in a public statement on December 29, 1931:

"The most constructive direction for economy in Federal expenditure beyond a rigid reduction of appropriations and the resolute opposition to new appropriations lies in the consolidation of Government bureaus and general reorganization of the Federal Government. I have recommended this reorganization in public addresses, reports and Messages to Congress throughout the past ten years."

"Outstanding amongst these reorganizations would be consolidation of all construction activities of the Government under an Administrator of Public Works to serve all the departments. Other cases are the consolidation of all Merchant Marine activities into the Department of Commerce; the consolidation of the conservation activities of the Government; of the public health services, of educational activities and numerous other groups on the same major purpose under single-headed responsibility. Such action would result in the elimination of many expensive agencies and overlap resulting in very great economies. These economies would run into many millions."

[*State Papers, Vol. II, pp. 97–8*]

The President continuously pressed the matter on the Congress without result until 1932, when he undertook a new drive upon the subject. In a special Message to the Congress on February 16, 1932, he said:

"Because of its direct relation to the cost of Government, I desire again to bring to the attention of the Congress the necessity of more effective organization of the Executive branch of the Government, the importance of which I have referred to in previous Messages. . . ."

"The need for reorganization is obvious. Today the Government embraces from 150 to 200 separate units. Governmental units when once set up have a tendency to grow independently of other units. This leads to overlapping and waste. The overlap and the number of agencies can be reduced."

"In the present crisis the absolute necessity for the most drastic economy makes the problem of governmental reorganization one of paramount importance."

"We may frankly admit the practical difficulties of such reorganization. Not only do different fractions of the Government fear such reorganization, but many associations and agencies throughout the country will be alarmed that the particular function to which they are devoted may in some fashion be curtailed. Proposals to the Congress of detailed plans for the reorganization of the many different bureaus and independent agencies have always proved in the past to be a signal for the mobilization of opposition from all quarters which has destroyed the possibility of constructive action."

"There is little hope for success in this task unless it is placed in the hands of some one responsible for it, with authority and direction to act. . . ."

"I recommend, therefore, that the Congress provide for"

"(*a*) Consolidation and grouping of the various executive and administrative activities according to their major purposes under single-headed responsibility, the Congress designating the title of the officer to be placed in immediate charge of such groups as are not now possible under existing organization."

"(*b*) Adoption of the general principle that executive and administrative functions should have single-headed responsibility and that advisory, regulatory, and quasi-judicial functions should be performed by boards and commissions, thus permitting the transfer of certain regulatory functions from executive officials to existing boards or commissions and executive functions from boards and commissions to executive officials."

"(*c*) Authority under proper safeguards to be lodged in the President to effect these transfers and consolidations and authority. . . ."

"The ten major executive departments and the major regulatory and financial boards and commissions should of course be maintained. Some of these existing agencies are already organized upon the basis of their major purpose, but functions of the same major·purpose now outside of these groups should be transferred to them. . . ."

"The most important of the posts of this character are the following:"

"Public Works Administrator (new office)."

"Personnel Administrator (change from chairman of Civil Service Commission)."

"Assistant Secretary for Public Health (new)."

"Assistant Secretary for Education (change from Commissioner)."

"Assistant Secretary for Merchant Marine (new office)."

"Assistant Secretary for Conservation (new office)."

"Assistant Secretary for Agricultural Research (change from present Assistant Secretary)."

"Assistant Secretary for Agricultural Economics (change from Director)."   [*State Papers, Vol. II, pp. 164 ff.*]

Hoover sent the Committees a draft bill. It made some progress in the House, but in a Message on May 5, he said:

"In the category of economies that can be made by consolidation, reorganization, and elimination of the less necessary bureaus, commissions, etc., the authority given in the measure passed by the House of Representatives is so restricted that it cannot be made effective until late in the next fiscal year. In order to expedite this economy, I earnestly recommend that the Executive be authorized to proceed immediately in the consolidation of Public Works, and Personnel, partly provided in the House Economy Bill, Public Health, Merchant Marine, Conservation, Education, Munitions manufacture, Army and Navy hospitals, aviation fields, and other specific Army and Navy activities which may advantageously be consolidated for the purpose of economy and more effective administration. The savings to be made are indeterminate but very considerable. If made by Executive action within the above direction from the Congress they can be made promptly."

[State Papers, Vol. II, pp. 178–9]

June 30, 1932, a partial authorization was given to the President to reorganize the Government by Executive orders, subject to the approval of Congress of such orders.

On December 9, 1932, he issued the Executive orders and sent the following Message to the Congress:

"A total of fifty-eight Executive agencies and parts of agencies have been grouped or consolidated. One effect is to reduce by about fifteen the number of independent agencies and commissions."

"These orders constitute the necessary initial action required in carrying out the policy which the Congress has proclaimed in connection with reorganization of the Executive branch of the Federal Government."

"I have established a Division of Public Works in the Department of the Interior and designated that the title of one of the present Assistant Secretaries shall be changed to 'Assistant Secretary of Interior for Public Works,' under whose direction I have grouped the following organizations and functions:"

"Bureau of Reclamation . . ."

"The Geological Survey . . ."

"The Office of the Supervising Architect . . ."

"The non-military activities (except the Survey of Northern and Northwestern Lakes and the Supervision of New York Harbor) administered under the direction or supervision of the Chief of Engineers, United States Army (seven bureaus and boards), harbors and flood control work, and the duties, powers . . ."

"The Bureau of Public Roads . . ."

"The Office of Public Buildings and Public Parks . . ."

"The National Capital Park and Planning Commission . . ."

"The Rock Creek and Potomac Parkway Commission . . ."

"The Arlington Memorial Bridge Commission . . ."

"The Commission of Fine Arts, which is transferred to the Department of the Interior . . ."

"The George Rogers Clark Sesquicentennial Commission . . ."

"Mount Rushmore National Memorial Commission . . . shall serve in an advisory capacity to the Secretary of the Interior."

"General Supply Committee . . ."

"The Government Fuel Yards. . . ."

"I have established a Division of Education, Health, and Recreation in the Department of the Interior and have designated that one of the Assistant Secretaries shall be called 'Assistant Secretary of Interior for Education, Health, and Recreation,' and have transferred to that division the following organizations and functions:"

"The Office of Education . . ."

"Howard University . . ."

"The Columbia Institution for the Deaf . . ."

"The American Printing House for the Blind . . ."

"The Federal Board for Vocational Education . . ."

"The Bureau of Indian Affairs . . ."

"The Public Health Service . . ."

"The Division of Vital Statistics . . ."

"St. Elizabeth's Hospital . . ."

"Freedmen's Hospital . . ."

"The National Park Service . . ."

"The National Parks, Monuments, and Cemeteries . . ."

"I have established a Division of Land Utilization in the Department of Agriculture . . . under an 'Assistant Secretary of Agriculture for Land Utilization,'"

"The Forest Service . . ."

"The General Land Office . . ."

"The Committee on the Conservation and Administration of the Public Domain . . ."

"The Advisory Council of the National Arboretum . . ."

"The Bureau of Biological Survey . . ."

"The Bureau of Chemistry and Soils . . ."

"Various fractions of bureaus already in the Department of Agriculture dealing with this major purpose. . . ."

"I have established a Merchant Marine Division in the Department of

Commerce, and an 'Assistant Secretary of Commerce for Merchant Marine,' and have transferred to that division the following organizations and functions:"

"The Coast and Geodetic Survey . . ."
"The Hydrographic Office . . ."
"The Survey of Northern and Northwestern Lakes . . ."
"The Bureau of Navigation and Steamboat Inspection . . ."
"The Supervisor of New York Harbor . . ."
"The Naval Observatory . . ."
"The United States Shipping Board Merchant Fleet Corporation . . ."
"The Inland Waterways Corporation . . ."
"The Bureau of Lighthouses. . . ."

"I have transferred to the Department of Commerce or the bureaus thereof, as indicated, the following organizations and functions which involve services in the interest of commerce and industry:"

". . . The Federal Oil Conservation Board . . ."
"The . . . National Screw Thread Commission . . ."
"The . . . National Advisory Committee for Aeronautics . . ."
"The Weather Bureau. . . ."

"I have transferred to and consolidated with the Department of Justice the . . . Alien Property Custodian. . . ."

"I have transferred to . . . the Department of Labor the powers and duties now exercised by the Employees' Compensation Commission the administration act of March 4, 1927 and the Act of May 17, 1928. . . ."

"I have transferred to and consolidated with the Civil Service Commission the . . . Employees' Compensation Commission. . . ."

"I have transferred to and consolidated with the Coast Guard in the Treasury Department the following services:"
"The Border Patrol from the Immigration Service . . ."
"The Border Patrol from the Customs Service. . . ."

"I have transferred and consolidated the following activities in the Bureau of the Budget:"
"The powers and duties now exercised by the General Accounting Office . . . except that the Comptroller General shall retain the power and duty to prescribe the form and manner in which accounts shall be submitted to his office for audit. . . ." [State Papers, Vol. II, p. 532]

Congress defeated the proposals. The press stated that the President-elect did not approve. Mr. Hoover stated on January 3:

"The proposals of Democratic leaders in Congress to stop the reorganization of Government functions which I have made is a backward step. The same opposition has now arisen which has defeated every effort at reorganization for twenty-five years. . . . The proposal to transfer the job of reorganization to my successor is simply a device by which it is hoped that these proposals can be defeated. Statements that I have made over ten years as to the opposition which has always thwarted reorganization have come true. Five years ago I said:"

" '. . . Practically every single item in such a program has invariably met with opposition of some vested official, or it has disturbed some vested habit, and offended some organized minority. It has aroused the paid propagandists. All these vested officials, vested habits, organized propaganda groups, are in favor of every item of reorganization except that which affects the bureau or the activity in which they are specially interested. No proposed change is so unimportant that it is not bitterly opposed by some one. In the aggregate, these directors of vested habits surround Congress with a confusing fog of opposition. Meantime, the inchoate voice of the public gets nowhere but to swear at "bureaucracy.' "

"Any real reorganization sensibly carried out will sooner or later embrace the very orders I have issued."

"Either Congress must keep its hands off now or they must give to my successor much larger powers of independent action than given to any President if there is ever to be reorganization. And that authority to be effective should be free of the limitations in the law passed last year which gives Congress the veto power, which prevents the abolition of functions, which prevents the rearrangement of major Departments. Otherwise it will, as is now being demonstrated in the present law, again be merely make believe." [State Papers, Vol. II, pp. 561–3]

In a press Statement on January 20, 1933, the President said:

"There is no question that the consolidations would have brought about great economies. No one wishes to estimate these economies until it is possible to determine accurately how many offices can be abolished, how much can be saved by the more advantageous purchase of supplies and the greater co-ordination of work. But it is a certainty that great economies would have been made if the program had been carried out. It would have been a contribution to lessening taxation in the forthcoming fiscal year."[1]

[State Papers, Vol. II, p. 582]

[1]Four years later Roosevelt presented to Congress similar action. His proposals set up new Cabinet officers for some groups instead of Under-Secretaries. Roosevelt's proposals, however, contain an invasion of the independence of the quasi-judicial bodies, a transformation of Civil Service and the Controller of the Currency's Office into positions subjective to the Executive, which Hoover never approved.

FOREIGN POLICIES

PRESERVING PEACE

By his personal familiarity with the war and with almost every country in the world, Herbert Hoover, more than any other President, was in position to take prompt and decisive stands on major policies of foreign relations.

There has never been in the White House a President more devoted to peace. Nor has there been any one more constructive in the practical paths of peace.

Long before he was President he made many an address on peace. On September 2, 1924, he summarized:

". . . Militarism is the direct or indirect fostering of the belief that war is ennobling to a nation, that war is the moment of a nation's greatness, that a martial spirit is a beneficent catalizer of the blood and spirit of the nation, that nations even in peace gain in power and add to their prestige and prosperity by dominating armament. In the persuasion of peoples to carry the burdens of great armament these arguments and beliefs are stimulated by painting some neighbor nation as the enemy, by fanning the flames of hate, of fear and of arrogance in their peoples, and thereby is created that spirit of aggression which in 1914 broke the peace of the world."

"Militarism feeds itself most successfully upon populations militarized through peace-time conscription of the whole manhood. It is only in such a nation-wide school that it can be well sustained. There can be little stimulation of these malign ideas in a nation where 10,000,000 men could be massed in arms, yet the whole of its standing army is but 140,000 men. Indeed, we are the only important nation today whose standing army is less than the policemen on its street corners. Our voluntary forces are but 180,000 men and the essence of voluntary forces is that of sacrifice which must be made by men whose callings and aspirations lie in peace—whose belief is that civilization progresses only in the path of peace."

"But to say that Americans are not militarists does not imply that they are pacifists. I, like almost a universality of Americans, am opposed to war. It has been . . . my fate, to see the incantations which raised the violence of the mob; to see the militant armies of many nations on many occasions. I have been present at great parades, tremendous spectacles of military prowess. I have seen soldiers going to battle, their faces set in grim determination and lit with belief in victory for a sacred cause. I have seen them returning from the struggle, their hopes sustained by success or shattered by defeat. I have seen the thousands of dead, the millions of starving women and children . . . the grief of millions of homes, the miseries of famine and anarchy, the revolutions that have swept many nations and threatened others, the lowered standards of living, the indelible impress of hate, the more terrible possibilities of future war, through ever advancing science . . . not alone the moral degeneration and the loss of life . . . but the delicate machinery of social organization . . . of commerce upon which civilization is founded cannot stand such a shock again. Our people know the narrow margins by which civilization and all that we hold dear barely escaped destruction six years ago."

"So it is that we in America have come to loathe war and to yearn for universal peace. We harbor neither fear nor hate, neither aggression nor desire for power or prestige other than that which lies in the arts of peace. Our country has led in the limitation of armament."

"Nevertheless, however we might fervently hope and pray that wars are over, we cannot found our national policies upon such a basis. Strive as we may for the ideal, we must look out upon the world through the clear glass of realism. We know how the seeds of war are planted and that human nature and understanding change but slowly; that man is proceeding only little by little toward the goal of perfection, and that nations are but aggregations of men. If we survey the world we find that it is as greatly armed as in the tinder-box days of 1914, though not in the same places. Preparedness for defense is a necessity so long as great armaments, and the spirits of fear, hate, militant nationalism, arrogance, or aggression linger in the world. And the world is not free from these uncomfortable bed-fellows though some of them be stunned by the exhaustion of the last ten years. We must needs maintain such forces as assure us in defense, whose equipment and morale keep ever ready, and whose public support is one of appreciation of a national service well given to the security of us all."

Declaring his policies in his Acceptance Speech of August 11, 1928, on the Stanford campus, he said:

"I think I may say that I have witnessed as much of the horror and suffering of war as any other American. From it I have deep passion for peace. Our foreign policy has one primary object, and that is peace. We have no hates; we wish no further possessions; we harbor no military threats. The unspeakable experiences of the Great War, the narrow margin by which civilization survived its exhaustion, is still vivid in men's minds. There is no nation in the world today that does not earnestly wish for peace—that is not striving for peace."

"There are two co-operating factors in the maintenance of peace—the building of good will by wise and sympathetic handling of international relations, and the adequate preparedness for defense. We must not only be just; we must be respected. The experiences of the war afforded final proof that we cannot isolate ourselves from the world, that the safeguarding of peace cannot be attained by negative action."

"We believe that the foundations of peace can be strengthened by the creation of methods and agencies by which a multitude of incidents may be transferred from the realm of prejudice and force to arbitration and the determination of right and wrong based upon international law."

"We have been and we are particularly desirous of furthering the limitation of armaments. But in the meantime we know that in an armed world there is only one certain guarantee of freedom—and that is preparedness for defense. . . . We earnestly wish that the burdens and dangers of armament upon every home in the world might be lessened."

In his Inaugural Address on March 4, 1929, Hoover said:

"The United States fully accepts the profound truth that our own progress, prosperity and peace are interlocked with the progress, prosperity and peace of all humanity. The whole world is at peace. The dangers to a continuation of this peace today are largely the fear and suspicion which still haunt the world. No suspicion or fear can be rightly directed toward our country."

"We not only desire peace with the world, but to see peace maintained throughout the world. We wish to advance the reign of justice and reason toward the extinction of force."

"The recent treaty for the renunciation of war as an instrument of national policy sets an advanced standard in our conception of the relations of nations. Its acceptance should pave the way to greater limitation of armament, the offer of which we sincerely extend to the world. But its full realization also implies a greater and greater perfection in the instrumentalities for pacific settlement of controversies between nations. In the creation and use of these instrumentalities we should support every sound method of conciliation, arbitration, and judicial settlement. American statesmen were among the first to propose and they have constantly urged upon the world, the establishment of a tribunal for the settlement of controversies of a justiciable character. The Permanent Court of International Justice in its major purpose is thus peculiarly identified with American ideals and with American statesmanship."

"Our people have determined that we should make no political engagements such as membership in the League of Nations, which may commit us in advance as a nation to become involved in the settlements of controversies between other countries."

"It is impossible, my countrymen, to speak of peace without profound emotion. In thousands of homes in America, in millions of homes around the world, there are vacant chairs. It would be a shameful confession of our unworthiness if it should develop that we have abandoned the hope for which all these men died. Surely civilization is old enough, surely mankind is mature enough so that we ought in our own lifetime to find a way to permanent peace. Abroad, to west and east, are nations whose sons mingled their blood with the blood of our sons on the battlefields. Most of these nations have contributed to our race, to our culture, our knowledge, and our progress. From one of them we derive our very language and from many of them much of the genius of our institutions. Their desire for peace is as deep and sincere as our own."

[*State Papers, Vol. I, p. 3*]

In the Armistice Day address on November 11, 1929, he amplified his policies on the requirements of peace:

"But peace is not a static thing. To maintain peace is as dynamic in its requirements as is the conduct of war. We cannot say 'Let there be peace' and go about other business. Nor are the methods by which peace is to be maintained and war prevented to be established by slogans or by abstract phrases or by academic theory. Progress toward peace can be attained only as a result of realistic practical daily conduct amongst nations. It can be the result only of a frank recognition of forces which may disturb peace. For instance, we must realize that our industrial life, our employment, our comfort, and our culture depend greatly upon our interchange of goods and ideas with other nations. We must realize that this interchange cannot be carried on unless our citizens are flung into every quarter of the globe and the citizens of every other nation are represented in our country."

"We must realize that some of them will get into trouble somewhere.

Certainly their troubles will multiply if other nations are at war. We have an obligation and every other nation has an obligation to see to the protection of their lives, and that justice is done to them so long as they comply with the laws of the countries in which they reside. From all these relationships frictions and controversies will arise daily."

"But there are other more deep-seated and more dangerous forces which produce friction and controversy than these eruptions over the rights of citizens. We must realize that there are many unsolved problems of boundaries between nations. There are peoples aspiring to a greater measure of self-government. There are the fears of invasion and domination bequeathed to all humanity from its former wars. There are a host of age-old controversies whose specters haunt the world, which at any time may touch the springs of fear and ill will."

"We must frankly accept the fact, therefore, that we and all the nations of the world will be involved, for all future time, in small or great controversies and frictions arising out of all of these multiple causes. In these controversies lurks the subtle danger that national temper at any moment may become a heat and that emotion may rise to the flaming point. Therefore, peace must be the result of unceasing endeavor."

"I have said that recently we have covenanted with other civilized nations not only to renounce war as an instrument of national policy but also we have agreed that we shall settle all controversies by pacific means. But the machinery for pacific settlement of disputes among nations is, as yet, inadequate. We need to strengthen our own provisions for it."

"Our State Department is the first of these means. It must be strengthened and supported as the great arm of our government, dedicated to the organization of peace."

"We need further to extend our treaties with other countries providing methods for reference of controversies to conference, to inquiry as to fact, or to arbitration, or to judicial determination."

"We have need to define the rules of conduct of nations and to formulate an authoritative system of international law. We have need under proper reservations to support the World Court in order that we may secure judicial determination of certain types of controversies and build up precedents which add to the body of international law. By these agencies we relegate a thousand frictions to orderly processes of settlement and by deliberation in action we prevent their development into national inflammation."

"We are also interested that other nations shall settle by pacific means the controversies arising between them. From every selfish point of view the preservation of peace among other nations is of interest to the

United States. In such wars we are in constant danger of entanglement because of interference with the widespread activities of our citizens. But of far more importance than this, our ideals and our hopes are for the progress of justice through the entire world."

"We desire to see all humanity relieved of the hideous blight of war and of the cruelties and injustices that lead to war. We are interested in all methods that can be devised to assure the settlement of all controversies between nations."

"There are today two roads to that end. The European nations have, by the covenant of the League of Nations, agreed that if nations fail to settle their differences peaceably then force should be applied by other nations to compel them to be reasonable. We have refused to travel this road. We are confident that at least in the Western Hemisphere public opinion will suffice to check violence. This is the road we propose to travel. What we urgently need in this direction is a further development of methods for reference of unsettled controversies to joint inquiry by the parties assisted by friendly nations, in order that action may be stayed and that the aggressor may be subjected to the searchlight of public opinion."

"And we have another task equally great as the settlement of incidental controversies. We must, where opportunity offers, work steadfastly to remove the deeper causes and frictions which lead to disputes and ill will. One of these causes is competition in armament. In order to stir a nation to the expenditures and burdens of increased armament, some danger and some enemy must be envisaged. Fears and distrust must be used as a goad to stir the Nation forward to competitive effort. No one denies that the maintenance of great armament is a burden upon the backs of all who toil. The expenditure for it curtails vast projects of human betterment which governments might undertake. Every man under arms means that some other man must bear an extra burden somewhere. But a greater cost is the ill will resulting from rivalry between nations in construction of armaments."

"It is first and foremost to rid ourselves of this danger that I have again initiated naval negotiations. I have full confidence in the success of the conference which will assemble next January. In setting up this conference we have already agreed with Great Britain that there shall be a parity in naval strength between us. I am in hopes that there will be a serious reduction in navies as a relief to the economic burdens of all peoples. And I believe that men and women throughout the world demand such reduction. We must reduce and limit warships by agreement only. I have no faith in the reduction of armaments by example alone."

"Until such time as nations can build the agencies of pacific settlement on stronger foundations; until fear, the most dangerous of all national emotions, has been proved groundless by long proof of international honesty, until the power of world public opinion as a restraint of aggression has had many years of test, there will not have been established that confidence which warrants the abandonment of preparedness for defense among nations. To do so may invite war."

"I am for adequate preparedness as a guaranty that no foreign soldier shall ever step upon the soil of our country."

"Men of good will throughout the world are working earnestly and honestly to perfect the equipment and preparedness for peace. But there is something high above and infinitely more powerful than the work of all ambassadors and ministers, something far more powerful than treaties and the machinery of arbitration and conciliation and judicial decision, something more vital than even our covenants to abolish war, something more mighty than armies and navies in defense."

"That is to build the spirit of good will and friendliness, to create respect and confidence, to stimulate esteem between peoples—this is the far greatest guaranty of peace. In that atmosphere, all controversies become but passing incidents of the day. Nor does this friendliness, respect, and esteem come to nations who behave weakly or supinely. It comes to those who are strong but who use their strength not in arrogance or injustice. It is through these means that we establish the sincerity, the justice, and the dignity of a great people. That is a new vision of diplomacy that is dawning in the world."

Speaking in Boston on October 6, 1930, the President said:

"Real peace in the world requires something more than the documents which we sign to terminate wars. Peace requires unremitting, courageous campaigns, laid with strategy and carried on successfully on a hundred fronts and sustained in the spirit and from the hearts of every individual in every town and village of our country."

"In the great intangibles of human emotion, respect is inseparable from good will. The maintenance of respect requires that we sustain a preparedness for defense that is impregnable yet that contains no threat of aggression." [State Papers, Vol. I, p. 384]

The first two years of the Hoover Administration saw the steady rise of peace in the world. The Kellogg Pact, the Locarno

Pact, the London Naval Limitation Treaty, the success of the League of Nations in minor European quarrels, all marked definite progress of world sentiment.

With the financial collapse of Europe in mid-1931, a wholly new spirit was born. Economic difficulties brought revolutions; the rise of military dictatorships and an evil spirit of exploitation and vicious nationalism; the Japanese repudiation of the Kellogg Pact; all were but signs of the times.

These changing times are echoed in the President's policies. In a statement of November 11, 1931, he said in the Armistice Day address at Washington:

"However great our desire for peace, we must not assume that the peace for which these men died has become assured to the world or that the obligations which they left to us, the living, have been discharged."

"The backwash of forces loosened by the Great War has grown until during the past two years the stability of many nations has been greatly shaken. This, with their fears and discouragement for the future, weakened confidence throughout the whole financial and economic world. From it all we have been passing through an emergency second only to the Great War."

[*State Papers, Vol. II, p. 28*]

And again in his Annual Message to Congress, on December 8, 1931, he said:

"Within two years there have been revolutions or acute social disorders in nineteen countries, embracing more than half the population of the world. . . ."

[*State Papers, Vol. II, p. 42*]

Reporting on his foreign policies in his second Acceptance address, Hoover said on August 11, 1932:

"My foreign policies have been devoted to strengthening the foundations of world peace. We inaugurated the London naval treaty which reduced arms and limited the ratios between the fleets of the three powers. We have made concrete proposals at Geneva to reduce armaments of the world by one-third. It would save the taxpayers of the world a billion a year. It would save us over $200,000,000 a year. It would reduce fear and danger of war. We have expanded the arbitration of disputes. I have recommended joining the World Court under proper reservations preserving our freedom of action. We have given leadership in transforming the Kellogg-Briand Pact from an inspiring outlawry of war to an organized instrument for peaceful settlements backed by definite mobilization of world public opinion against aggression. We shall, under the spirit of that pact, consult with other nations in times of emergency to promote world peace. We shall enter no agreements committing us to any future course of action or which call for use of force to preserve peace."

"Above all, I have projected a new doctrine into international affairs, the doctrine that we do not and never will recognize title to possession of territory gained in violation of the peace pacts. That doctrine has been accepted by all the nations of the world on a recent critical occasion, and within the last few days has been accepted again by all the nations of the Western Hemisphere. That is public opinion made tangible and effective."

"This world needs peace. It must have peace with justice. I shall continue to strive unceasingly, with every power of mind and spirit, to explore every possible path that leads toward a world in which right triumphs over force, in which reason rules over passion, in which men and women may rear their children not to be devoured by war but to pursue in safety the nobler arts of peace."

"I shall continue to build on that design."

[State Papers, Vol. II, pp. 260–1]

The practical steps of the Hoover Administration in foreign relations can be reviewed shortly under the following heads:
   Building up the instrumentalities of peace.
   Re-establishment of Latin-American good will.
   The limitation and reduction of naval arms.
   The Hoover proposal to immunize food ships in war.
   Far Eastern policies.
   The control of trade in arms.
   Reduction of world land arms.
   Moratorium on Intergovernmental Debts (see page 408).
   German Standstill agreement (see page 411).
   World War debts (see page 506).
   World Stabilization of Currency and Economic Stability (see page 494).

BUILDING UP THE INSTRUMENTALITIES
OF PEACE

During his Administration President Hoover with Secretary Stimson's aid greatly strengthened the whole diplomatic service. Through Congressional increase in the allowances to ambassadors and ministers they made it possible for "Career men" without private income to hold these posts. Too many such posts had been filled with men for political gratitude. Over four-fifths of all these posts in the Hoover Administration were filled by promotion of trained men.

These appointments included: Ambassadors, Cuba, Harry F. Guggenheim; France, Walter F. Edge; Germany, Frederick M. Sackett; Great Britain, Charles Gates Dawes and later Andrew W. Mellon; Italy, John W. Garrett; Japan, William R. Castle, Jr.* and then W. Cameron Forbes and Joseph C. Grew*; Peru, Fred Morris Dearing*; Poland, Alexander P. Moore, John N. Willys and F. Lammot Belin*; Spain, Irwin B. Laughlin*; Turkey, Charles H. Sherrill.

Among the Ministers were: Albania, Herman Bernstein; Austria, Gilchrist Stockton; Bolivia, Evan Young* and Edward F. Feely; Bulgaria, Henry Wharton Shoemaker*; Canada, Hanford MacNider; China, Nelson Johnson*; Costa Rica, H. F. Arthur Schoenfeld* and Charles C. Eberhardt*; Czechoslovakia, Abraham Ratshesky; Denmark, Ralph W. Booth and Frederick W. B. Coleman; Dominican Republic, H. F. Arthur Schoenfeld* and later Charles B. Curtis; Ecuador, William Dawson* and Franklin Gunther*; Egypt, William Jardine; El Salvador, Charles B. Curtis*; Finland, Edward Brodie; Guatemala, Sheldon Whitehouse*; Haiti, Dana Munro*; and Norman Armour*; Iraq, Paul Knabenshue*; Honduras, Julius Lay*; Latvia, Robert P. Skinner*; Liberia, Charles E. Mitchell; Netherlands, Gerritt John Diekema; Nicaragua, Matthew Hanna*; Norway, Hoffman Philip*; Panama, Roy T. Davis*; Paraguay, Post Wheeler*; Persia, Charles C. Hart; Portugal, John Glover South; Siam, Arthur Geissler* and David E. Kaufman*; Sweden, John Motley Morehead; Uruguay, Leland Harrison*; Venezuela, George T. Sumerlin*; Union of South Africa, Ralph T. Totten.

Territorial and other appointed Governors during the Hoover Administration were:

Alaska, George A. Parks.

Hawaii, Lawrence M. Judd.

Philippine Islands, Dwight Davis and later Theodore Roosevelt.

Puerto Rico, Theodore Roosevelt and later James R. Beverley.

Of far greater importance was the vigorous promotion of treaties for the promotion of peace. The great accomplishment of the Coolidge Administration, the Kellogg Pact, was supported and extended by Hoover. To make that Pact effective, the

*Career-men.

treaties providing methods for peaceful settlement of disputes require organization. During the Hoover Administration twenty-five new treaties of arbitration and seventeen new treaties of conciliation were entered into. Several score other treaties covering narcotics, slavery, commerce, aviation, and merchant marine were negotiated, all of which contribute to peaceful development.

THE WORLD COURT

Hoover had long been a staunch supporter of the settlement of international disputes by judicial processes. Early in his Administration he consulted with Elihu Root on the possibility of securing such changes in the constitution of the World Court as would meet the objections which had been previously raised in the Senate. Root secured these changes and the President submitted the protocols to the Senate with this message, on December 10, 1930:

"I have the honor to transmit to the Senate for its consideration and action, three documents concerning adherence of the United States to the Court of International Justice. I enclose also a report of November 18, 1929, by the Secretary of State. I trust the protocols may have consideration as soon as possible after the emergency relief and appropriation legislation has been disposed of."

"It will be recalled that on January 27, 1926, following extended consideration, the Senate advised and gave consent to adherence to the Court with five reservations; and it gave authorization to effect their acceptance by an exchange of notes. Consent to four of these reservations was promptly expressed at a meeting of the nations, members of the Court, and after negotiations undertaken with the approval of President Coolidge, two protocols were drawn to revise the statutes of the Court in order to embody this consent and also to meet the fifth reservation. The Protocol of Accession of the United States and the Protocol of Revision have now been signed by practically all the nations which are members of the Court and have also already been ratified by a large majority of those nations."

"The provisions of the protocols free us from any entanglement in the diplomacy of other nations. We cannot be summoned before this Court, we can from time to time seek its services by agreement with other nations. These protocols permit our withdrawal from the Court at any time without reproach or ill-will."

"The movement for the establishment of such a court originated with our country. It has been supported by Presidents Wilson, Harding, and Coolidge; by Secretaries of State Hughes, Kellogg, and Stimson; it springs from the earnest seeking of our people for justice in international relations and to strengthen the foundations of peace."

"Through the Kellogg-Briand Pact we have pledged ourselves to the use of pacific means in settlement of all controversies. Our great nation, so devoted to peace and justice, should lend its co-operation in this effort of the nations to establish a great agency for such pacific settlements."

"The White House,
"December 10, 1930." [*State Papers, Vol. I, p. 460*]

In his message of December 10, 1931, he again pressed the subject:

"In the past session of the Congress I transmitted to the Senate protocols providing for adherence by the United States to the Permanent Court of International Justice. Upon that occasion I expressed my views fully not only of the wisdom of such action, but that the safeguards against European entanglements stipulated for by the Senate had been in effect secured and the interest of the United States protected. I need not repeat that for over twelve years every President and every Secretary of State has urged this action as a material contribution to the pacific settlement of controversies among nations and a further assurance against war."

[*State Papers, Vol. II, pp. 80–1*]

The opposition, however, prevented its coming to a vote in the Senate.[1]

LATIN–AMERICAN RELATIONS

Hoover as President-elect made a good-will visit to the principal South American countries that he might personally exchange views with their officials. Four tangible results flowed from this visit: first, the reorganization of our Latin-American Diplomatic Service; second, the creation of an All-American air service; third, the settlement of the Tacna-Arica dispute; fourth, an advanced and courageous declaration by Hoover of our future Latin-American governmental policies which together with the abandonment of the Wilson-Coolidge policies of intervention entirely transformed our relations with these States.

[1]President Roosevelt has warmly urged the ratification of the Court upon the Senate.

Hoover removed the political appointees among our ministers and ambassadors in every Latin-American State and substituted career men who knew the language and the people of the countries to which they were delegated. The creation and inauguration of regular air service with Central and South America is discussed elsewhere.

In an address on April 13, 1929, Hoover repeated a declaration he had made many times on his South American trip:

"I mention one sinister notion as to policies of the United States upon our relationships with our Latin-American neighbors. That is, fear of an era of the mistakenly called dollar diplomacy. The implications that have been colored by that expression are not a part of my conception of inernational relations. I can say at once that it never has been and ought not to be the policy of the United States to intervene by force to secure or maintain contracts between our citizens and foreign States or their citizens. Confidence in that attitude is the only basis upon which the economic co-operation of our citizens can be welcomed abroad. It is the only basis that prevents cupidity encroaching upon the weakness of nations—but, far more than this, it is the true expression of the moral rectitude of the United States." [State Papers, Vol. I, pp. 29–30]

To give proof of his determination to end interventions, he gave directions to withdraw American Marines from Nicaragua. The withdrawal started on June 3, 1931.

December 7, 1929, he requested authority from the Congress for an official commission to examine the situation in Haiti and advise when and how we were to withdraw—in effect, how do we get out of the mess we had plunged into during the Great War. On receiving the report of the Commission he at once began the withdrawal of American forces and the building up of a local government.

As a result of these policies, carried on throughout the Hoover Administration, these interventions were ended. No friction has ensued in the Western Hemisphere; Hoover established a good will in South America not hitherto known in our history.

The Tacna-Arica dispute which had disturbed the relations of Chile and Peru for years was settled by a plan developed in Hoover's mind during his discussions with the officials of the governments concerned on his South American journey.

LIMITATION OF NAVAL ARMS

Naval limitation had been inaugurated under President Harding in 1921, covering mainly battleships. Coolidge in 1927 had inspired a conference to extend these limitations to other craft. That conference had failed. As President, Hoover took up the problem again. Starting on his campaign for international disarmament he stated in the Memorial Day address of May 30, 1929:

". . . since this day a year ago, a solemn declaration has been proposed by America to the world and has been signed by forty nations. It states that they

" 'Solemnly declare in the names of their respective peoples that they condemn recourse to war for the solution of international controversies, and renounce it as an instrument of national policy in their relations with one another.' "

"They

" 'Agree that the settlement or solution of all disputes or conflicts of whatever nature or of whatever origin they may be, which may arise among them, shall never be sought except by pacific means.' "

"That is a declaration that springs from the aspirations and hearts of men and women throughout the world. It is a solemn covenant to which the great nations of the world have bound themselves."

"But notwithstanding this noble assurance, preparedness for war still advances steadily in every land. As a result the pessimist calls this covenant a pious expression of foreign offices, a trick of statesmen on the hopes of humanity, for which we and other nations will be held responsible without reserve. With this view I cannot agree."

"But, if this agreement is to fulfill its high purpose, we and other nations must accept its consequences; we must clothe faith and idealism with action. That action must march with the inexorable tread of common sense and realism to accomplishment."

"Fear and suspicion will never slacken unless we can halt competitive construction of arms. They will never disappear unless we can turn this tide toward actual reduction."

". . . To say that such a measure cannot be found is the counsel of despair, it is a challenge to the naval authorities of the world, it is the condemnation of the world to the Sisyphean toil of competitive armaments."

"The present Administration of the United States has undertaken to approach this vital problem with a new program."

[*State Papers, Vol. I, p. 64*]

A month after the Inauguration, Ambassador Gibson, as the representative of the President and upon instructions from him, proposed to the European Arms Conference a new basis upon which to approach the naval question. While battleships had been limited in the Harding Administration rival building was under way in all other craft—which was the large majority of naval tonnage. Hoover followed this declaration with active personal negotiations with Premier MacDonald through Secretary Stimson and Ambassador Dawes. They reached a preliminary basis which seemed hopeful. This basis was communicated to the other governments and was tentatively accepted by Japan and rejected by France and Italy. Nevertheless, Hoover determined to proceed and invited Mr. MacDonald to visit the United States. At the Rapidan Camp, the President and MacDonald threshed out the problem and came to an agreement on October 9, 1929, on major questions, subject to the approval of Japan. The Japanese Government proved co-operative and they resolved to proceed even without France and Italy if necessary.

In a joint statement issued by Hoover and MacDonald on October 10, 1929, there is one especially pregnant paragraph on establishment of American-British good will:

"The part of each of our governments in the promotion of world peace will be different, as one will never consent to become entangled in European diplomacy and the other is resolved to pursue a policy of active co-operation with its European neighbors; but each of our governments will direct its thoughts and influence towards securing and maintaining the peace of the world."

"Our conversations have been largely confined to the mutual relations of the two countries in the light of the situation created by the signing of the Peace Pact. Therefore, in a new and reinforced sense the two governments not only declare that war between them is unthinkable, but that distrusts and suspicions arising from doubts and fears which may have been justified before the Peace Pact must now cease to influence national policy. We approach old historical problems from a new angle and in a new atmosphere. On the assumption that war between us is banished, and that conflicts between our military or naval forces cannot take place, these problems have changed their meaning and character; and their solution, in ways satisfactory to both countries, has become possible." [*State Papers, Vol. I, p. 108*]

The Naval Conference assembled in London in January, 1930. Treaties greatly limiting and reducing naval arms were settled in April, 1930. Secretary Stimson headed the American delegation of Secretary of the Navy Charles Adams, Ambassadors Charles Dawes and Hugh Gibson, Senators David Reed and Joseph Robinson, Mr. Dwight Morrow, and Admiral Wm. D. Pratt.

A sensational incident of this negotiation was the exposure by Hoover of a conspiracy of sabotage by American munitions manufacturers and shipbuilders of the unproductive conference held under the Coolidge Administration. After the admission of what they had done by the saboteurs, no further interference took place.

FRENCH DEMANDS OF GUARANTEES

During the Conference, the French demanded a guarantee of security as the price of co-operation in naval limitation. Some members of the American delegation were disposed to give certain assurances to France. Hoover refused to consider any such undertaking as no matter in what form they were phrased they would in case of war be insisted upon as an obligation. France and Italy joined in only immaterial parts of the treaty.

The President submitted the new Naval Limitation Treaty to the Senate on May 1, 1930. That body took no action and proposed to adjourn without doing so. In fact several members joined in a round robin demanding that the President delay ratification. His reply was to announce a special session of the Senate on July 7.

The President's Message to the Senate shows the magnitude of the accomplishment:

"In requesting the Senate to convene in session for the special purpose of dealing with the treaty for the limitation and reduction of naval armament signed at London April 22, 1930, it is desirable that I should present my views upon it. This is especially necessary because of misinformation and misrepresentation which have been widespread by those who in reality are opposed to all limitation and reduction in naval arms. We must naturally expect opposition from those groups who believe in unrestricted military strength as an objective of the American nation. Indeed, we find the same type of minds in Great Britain and Japan in parallel opposition to this treaty. Nevertheless, I am convinced that the overwhelming majority of the American people are opposed to the conception of these groups. Our people believe that military strength should be held in conformity with the sole purpose of national defense; they earnestly desire real progress in limitation and reduction of naval arms of the world, and their aspiration is for abolition of competition in the building of arms as a step toward world peace. Such a result can be obtained in no other way than by international agreement."

"The present treaty is one which holds these safeguards and advances these ideals. Its ratification is in the interest of the United States. It is fair to the other participating nations. It promotes the cause of good relations."

"The only alternative to this treaty is the competitive building of navies with all its flow of suspicion, hate, ill-will, and ultimate disaster. History supports those who hold to agreement as the path to peace. Every naval limitation treaty with which we are familiar, from the Rush-Bagot agreement of 1817, limiting vessels of war on the Great Lakes, to the Washington Arms Treaty of 1921, has resulted in a marked growth of good will and confidence between the nations which were parties to it."

"It is folly to think that because we are the richest nation in the world we can outbuild all other countries. Other nations will make any sacrifice to maintain their instruments of defense against us, and we shall eventually reap in their hostility and ill-will the full measure of the additional burden which we may thus impose upon them. The very entry of the United States into such courses as this would invite the consolidation of the rest of the world against us and bring our peace and independence into jeopardy. We have only to look at the state of Europe in 1914 to find ample evidence of the futility and danger of competition in arms."

"It will be remembered that in response to recommendations from the Senate a Conference between the United States, Great Britain and Japan, for limitation of those categories of naval arms not covered by the Washington Treaty of 1921 was held at Geneva in 1927. That Conference failed because the United States could not agree to the large size of fleets demanded by other governments. The standards set up at that time would have required an ultimate fleet of about 1,400,000 tons for the United States. As against this the total United States fleet set out under this treaty will be about 1,123,000 tons."

"Defense is the primary function of government, and therefore our first concern in examination of any act of this character is the test of its adequacy in defense. No critic has yet asserted that with the navies provided in this agreement together with our army, our aerial defense and our national resources, we cannot defend ourselves, and certainly we want no military establishment for the purpose of domination of other nations. Our naval defense position under this treaty is the more clear if we examine our present naval strength in comparison to the present strength of the other nations, and then examine the improvements in this proportion which will result from this treaty. This improvement arises from the anticipation of parity in battleships to be reached ten years hence under the Washington Arms Treaty and the fact that other nations have been building in the classes of ships not limited by that treaty, while we, until lately, lagged behind."

"On the first of January last the total naval tonnage, disregarding paper fleets, and taking only those ships actually built and building, was, for the United States 1,180,000 tons; for the British Empire 1,332,000 tons; for Japan 768,000 tons. That is, if the United States Navy be taken as 100, then the British Navy equals 113 and the Japanese Navy 65. Under this treaty the United States will have 1,123,000 tons; Great Britain 1,151,000 tons, and Japan 714,000 tons, or a ratio of 100 for the United States to 102.4 for Great Britain and 63.6 for Japan. The slightly larger tonnage ratio mentioned for Great Britain is due to the fact that her cruiser fleet will be constituted more largely of smaller vessels, weaker in gun power, but the United States has the option to duplicate the exact tonnage and gun calibre of the British cruiser fleet if we desire to exercise it."

"The relative improvement in the position of the United States under this treaty is even better than this statement would indicate. In the more important categories, battleships, aircraft carriers, 8-inch and 6-inch cruisers—that is, omitting the secondary arms of destroyers and submarines—the fleet built and actually building on January 1st of this year was 809,000 tons in the United States, 1,088,000 tons in Great Britain and 568,000 tons in Japan, or upon the basis of 100 for the United States it was 134 for Great Britain and 70 for Japan. Under this Treaty the United States will on January 1, 1937, possess completed 911,000 tons of these major units, Great Britain 948,000 tons and Japan 556,000 tons. In addition, the United States will have one 10,000 ton 8-inch cruiser two-thirds completed. This will give a ratio in these categories of 100 for the United States to 102.9 for Great Britain and 60.5 for Japan. The reason for the excess British tonnage is again as mentioned above. In other words, the United States, in these categories, increases by 102,-000 tons, Great Britain decreases by 140,000 tons and Japan decreases by 12,000 tons. These readjustments of units are to take place during the next six years. The treaty then comes to an end except for such arrangements as may be made then for its continuance."

"The major discussion has been directed almost wholly to the fact that the United States is to have 18 cruisers with 8-inch guns, with an aggregate tonnage of 180,000 tons, as against Great Britain's 15 such ships, with a tonnage of 146,800 tons and Japan's 12 such ships of a tonnage of 108,400 tons; the United States supplementing this tonnage with cruisers armed with 6-inch guns up to a total of 323,500 tons; Great Britain up to 339,000 tons and Japan to 208,800 tone. The larger gross tonnage to Great Britain as stated being compensation for the larger gun calibre of the American cruiser fleet, but as said the United States has the option to duplicate the British Fleet, if it so desires."

"Criticism of this arrangement arises from the fact that the General Board of the United States Navy recommended that to reach parity with Great Britain the United States should have three more of the 10,000 ton cruisers (21 instead of 18), with 8-inch guns, and a total of 315,000 tons or 8000 tons less total cruiser tonnage than this treaty provides. Thus this treaty provides that instead of this 30,000 tons more of 8-inch ships recommended by the General Board, we will have 38,000 tons of ships armed with 6-inch guns, there being no limitation upon the size of cruisers up to 10,000 tons. Therefore, criticism revolves around less than 3% of our whole fleet, and even within this 3% comes the lesser question of whether 30,000 tons of ships armed with 8-inch guns are better than 38,000 tons armed with 6-inch guns. The opinion of our high naval authorities is divided on the relative merits of these alternatives. Many earnestly believe that the larger tonnage of 6-inch ships is more advantageous and others vice versa. However, those who seek to make this the outstanding feature of criticism fail to mention that under the London Treaty the obligation of the Washington Arms Treaty of 1921 is so altered that Great Britain scraps 133,900 tons of battleships armed with 13½-inch guns, the United States scraps 70,000 tons of battleships armed with 12-inch guns, and Japan scraps 26,300 tons. These arrangements are made not only for reduction of arms but to anticipate the ultimate parity between the United States and Great Britain in battleships which would not otherwise be realized for several years."

"There is in this provision a relative gain in proportions compared with the British fleet of 63,900 tons of battleships with 13½-inch guns. This is of vastly more importance than the dispute as to the relative combatant strength of 38,000 tons of 6-inch cruisers against 30,000 tons of 8-inch cruisers. Indeed it would seem that such criticisms must be based upon an undisclosed desire to break down all limitation of arms."

"To those who seek earnestly and properly for reduction in warships, I would point out that as compared with January first of this year, the total aggregate navies of the three powers under this treaty will have been reduced by nearly 300,000 tons. Had a settlement been made at Geneva in 1927 upon the only proposal possible at that time, the fleets of the three powers would have been approximately 680,000 tons greater than under the treaty now in consideration."

"The economic burdens and the diversion of taxes from welfare purposes which would be imposed upon ourselves and other nations by failure of this treaty are worth consideration. Under its provisions the replacement of battleships required under the Washington Arms Treaty of 1921 is postponed for six years. The cost of replacing and maintaining the three scrapped battleships is saved. Likewise we make economies in construction and operation by the reduction in our submarine and destroyer fleets to 52,700 and 150,000 tons respectively. What the possible saving over an otherwise inevitable era of competitive building would be, no one can estimate."

"If we assume that our present naval program, except for this treaty, is to complete the ships authorized by Congress and those authorized and necessary to be replaced under the Washington Arms Treaty, and to maintain a destroyer fleet of about 225,000 tons and a submarine fleet of 90,000 tons, such a fleet will not reach parity with Great Britain, yet would cost in construction over $500,000,000 more during the next six years than the fleet provided under this treaty. But in addition to this, as stated, there is a very large saving by this treaty in annual operation of the fleet over what would be the case if we even built no more than the present programs."

"The more selfish-minded will give little credence to the argument that savings by other parties to the agreement in the limitation of naval construction are of interest to the American people, yet the fundamental economic fact is that if the resources of these other nations are freed for devotion to the welfare of their people and to pacific purposes of reproductive commerce, they will result in blessings to the world, including ourselves. If we were to accept the Geneva Conference base as the end of naval strength under competitive building for the three governments, the saving in construction and operation by the treaty is literally billions of dollars."

"The question before us now is not whether we shall have a treaty with either three more 8-inch cruisers or four less 6-inch cruisers, or whether we shall have a larger reduction in tonnage. It is whether we shall have this treaty or no treaty. It is a question as to whether we shall move strongly toward limitation and reduction in naval arms or whether we shall have no limitation or reduction and shall enter upon a disastrous period of competitive armament."

"This treaty does mark an important step in disarmament and in world peace. It is important for many reasons that it should be dealt with at once. The subject has been under discussion since the Geneva Conference three years ago. The lines of this treaty have been known and under discussion since last summer. The actual document has been before the American people and before the Senate for nearly three months. It has been favorably reported by the Senate Foreign Relations Committee. Every solitary fact which affects judgment upon the treaty is known, and the document itself comprises the sole obligation of the United States. If we fail now the world will be again plunged backward from its progress toward peace." "HERBERT HOOVER."

[*State Papers, Vol. I, pp. 351 ff.*]

The usual long wrangle took place in the Congress, but on July 22, 1930, when the Treaty was ratified and signed, the President said:

"With the ratification by the other governments the Treaty will translate an emotion deep in the hearts of millions of men and women into a practical fact of government and international relations. It will renew again the faith of the world in the moral forces of good will and patient negotiation as against the blind forces of suspicion and competitive armament. It will secure the full defense of the United States. It will mark a further long step toward lifting the burden of militarism from the backs of mankind and to speed the march forward of world peace. It will lay the foundations upon which further constructive reduction in world arms may be accomplished in the future. We should, by this act of willingness to join with others in limiting armament, have dismissed from the mind of the world any notion that the United States entertains ideas of aggression, imperial power or exploitation of foreign nations."[1]

[*State Papers, Vol. I, pp. 359–60*]

---

[1]Substantial naval limitation died after Hoover's Administration. We are now engaged in a world naval race. The Navy under Hoover cost an average of about $350,000,000 per annum. In the four years since, the cost has increased by over $300,000,000 per annum.

IMMUNITY OF FOOD SHIPS IN WAR

In 1929 President Hoover made a bold proposal to the world
that would go far to diminish war, to protect neutrals, and above
all, to lessen the horrors of war. In his Armistice Day address
on November 11, he made this suggestion:

"There is another of these age-old controversies which stir men's minds
and their fears. That is the so-called freedom of the seas. In reality in
our day it is simply the rights of private citizens to trade in time of
war, for there is today complete freedom of the seas in times of peace.
If the world succeeds in establishing peaceful methods of settlement of
controversies, the whole question of trading rights in time of war becomes
a purely academic discussion. Peace is its final solution."

"But I am going to have the temerity to put forward an idea which
might break through the involved legal questions and age-old interpretations of right and wrong by a practical step which would solve a large
part of the intrinsic problem. It would act as a preventive as well as a
limitation of war. I offer it only for the consideration of the world. I
have not made it a governmental proposition to any nation and do not
do so now. I know that any wide departure from accepted ideas requires
long and searching examination. No idea can be perfected except upon
the anvil of debate. This is not a proposition for the forthcoming naval
conference, as that session is for a definite purpose, and this proposal will
not be injected into it."

"For many years, and born of a poignant personal experience, I have
held that food ships should be made free of any interference in times of
war. I would place all vessels laden solely with food supplies on the same
footing as hospital ships. The time has come when we should remove
starvation of women and children from the weapons of warfare."

"The rapid growth of industrial civilization during the past half century has created in many countries populations far in excess of their
domestic food supply and thus steadily weakened their natural defenses.
As a consequence, protection for overseas or imported supplies has been
one of the most impelling causes of increasing naval armaments and military alliances. Again, in countries which produce surplus food their
economic stability is also to a considerable degree dependent upon keeping
open the avenues of their trade in the export of such surplus, and this
again stimulates armament on their part to protect such outlets."

"Thus the fear of an interruption in sea-borne food supplies has
powerfully tended toward naval development in both importing and ex-

porting nations. In all important wars of recent years, to cut off or to protect such supplies has formed a large element in the strategy of all combatants. We cannot condemn any one nation; almost all who have been engaged in war have participated in it. The world must sooner or later recognize this as one of the underlying causes of its armed situation, but, far beyond this, starvation should be rejected among the weapons of warfare."

"To those who doubt the practicability of the idea, and who insist that agreements are futile for the purpose of controlling conduct in war, I may point out that the Belgian Relief Commission delivered more than two thousand shiploads of food through two rings of blockade and did it under neutral guarantees continuously during the whole World War. The protection of food movements in time of war would constitute a most important contribution to the rights of all parties, whether neutrals or belligerents, and would greatly tend toward lessening the pressure for naval strength. Foodstuffs comprise about twenty-five per cent of the commerce of the world but would constitute a much more important portion of the trade likely to be interfered with by a blockade."

[State Papers, Vol. I, p. 125]

The proposal was welcomed with acclaim by all the South American States, by the former European neutrals, by Japan, and China, by Germany, Italy and Austria. Opposition came from France and the Admiralty groups in England. There was support in England from the more Liberal groups. Gilbert Murray said: "It is demanded by the conscience of the world." A French commentator said, "The proposal is bound to be condemned by diplomats as unspeakably humane." Our Administration inquiry at London and Paris found it would not be accepted. Hoover resolved it should be raised again when further opportunity offered.

THE JAPANESE INVASION OF MANCHURIA

A grave danger to the peace of America arose from the Japanese invasion of China in September, 1931. With the rise of the military dictatorship in Japan, that government abandoned its former co-operation in maintaining peace in the world. Its action in the invasion of Manchuria was a direct violation of the Nine-Power Treaty of 1921, by which all the powers in the Pacific undertook to respect the integrity of China. It was a gross violation of the Kellogg Pact and the John Hay Doctrine of "the Open Door in China."

The Japanese invasion of Manchuria was undertaken co-incident with the financial collapse in Europe and the disorders approaching mutiny in the British fleet. American feeling developed against Japan and there were the usual jingo outbreaks. A declaration of the attitude of our country was needed, for nations have gone to war for less justifiable causes.

It was the resolute action of Hoover that prevented our being drawn at least into a most dangerous situation.

Secretary Stimson's intimacy with the Philippines and the Orient made him a valuable adviser, but Hoover's life in the Orient gave him an unique power of discrimination and decision.

In a Cabinet meeting, the President said that he had given the matter deep consideration and would lay his analysis and conclusions before the members. In summary he stated:

"The whole transaction is immoral. The offense against the comity of nations and the affront to the United States is outrageous. But the Nine-Power Treaty and the Kellogg Pact are solely moral instruments based upon the hope that peace in the world can be held by the rectitude of nations and enforced solely by the moral reprobation of the world. We are not parties to the League of Nations, the covenant of which has also been violated."

"The problem lies in three parts:

"First, this is primarily a controversy between China and Japan. The United States has never set out to preserve peace among other nations by force and so far as this part is concerned we shall confine ourselves to friendly counsel. In this connection we must remember some essentials of Asiatic life. Time moves more slowly there; political movements are measured in decades or centuries not in days or in months; that while Japan has the military ascendancy today and no doubt could take over parts or all of China, yet the Chinese people possess transcendent cultural resistance; that the *mores* of the race have carried through a dozen foreign dynasties over three thousand years; that the Chinese are ten to one in population. No matter what Japan does in time they will not Japanify China and if they stay long enough they will be absorbed or expelled by the Chinese. For America to undertake this on behalf of China might expedite it but would not make it more inevitable."

"There is something on the side of Japan. Ours has been a long and deep-seated friendship with her and we should in friendship consider her side also. Suppose Japan had come out boldly and said:

" 'We can no longer endure these treaties and we must give notice that

China has failed to establish the internal order these treaties contemplated. Half her area is Bolshevist and co-operating with Russia, the government of Manchuria is in the hands of a military adventurer who ignores the Chinese Government, and China makes no effort to assert her will. That territory is in a state of anarchy that is intolerable. The whole living of our people depends upon expanding the sales of our manufactures in China and securing of raw materials from her. We are today almost economically prostrate because there is no order in China. Beyond this with Bolshevist Russia to the north and a possible Bolshevist China on our flank, our independence is in jeopardy. Either the signatories of the Nine-Power Pact must join with us to restore order in China or we must do it as an act of self-preservation. If you do not join we consider we cannot hold to an obligation around which the whole environment has changed.'"

"America certainly would not join in such a proposal and we could not raise much objection."

"Second, our whole policy in connection with controversies is to exhaust the processes of peaceful negotiation. But in contemplating these we must make up our minds whether we consider war as the ultimate if these efforts fail. Neither our obligations to China, nor our own interest, nor our dignity require us to go to war over these questions."

"These acts do not imperil the freedom of the American people, the economic or moral future of our people. I do not propose ever to sacrifice American life for anything short of this. If that were not enough reason, to go to war means a long struggle at a time when civilization is already weak enough. To win such a war is not solely a naval operation. We must arm and train Chinese. We would find ourselves involved in China in a fashion that would excite the suspicions of the whole world."

"Third, we have a moral obligation to use every influence short of war to have the treaties upheld or terminated by mutual agreement. We should co-operate with the rest of the world, we should do so as long as that co-operation remains in the field of moral pressures. As the League of Nations has already taken up the subject, we should co-operate with them in every field of negotiation or conciliation. But that is the limit. We will not go along on war or any of the sanctions either economic or military for those are the roads to war."

In the President's Message to the Congress on December 10, 1931, he said:

"We have been deeply concerned over the situation in Manchuria. As parties to the Kellogg-Briand Pact and to the Nine-Power Treaty, we have a responsibility in maintaining the integrity of China and a direct interest with other nations in maintaining peace there."

"When this controversy originated in September the League of Nations was in session and China appealed to the Council of that body which at once undertook measures of conciliation between China and Japan. Both China and Japan have participated in these proceedings before the Council ever since. Under the Kellogg-Briand Pact all of the signatories, including China and Japan, have covenanted to seek none but pacific means in the settlement of their disputes. Thus the ultimate purpose of proceedings under this section of the Kellogg-Briand Pact and of conciliation proceedings by the League Covenant coincide. It seemed, therefore, both wise and appropriate rather to aid and advise with the League and thus have unity of world effort to maintain peace than to take independent action. In all negotiations, however, the Department of State has maintained complete freedom of judgment and action as to participation in any measures which the League might finally be determined upon."

"Immediately after the outbreak of the trouble this government advised both Japan and China of its serious interest. Subsequently it communicated its views to both governments regarding their obligations under the Kellogg-Briand Pact. In this action we were joined by other nations signatory of the pact. This government has consistently and repeatedly by diplomatic representations indicated its unremitting solicitude that these treaty obligations be respected. In the recurring efforts of the nations to bring about a peaceful settlement this government has realized that the exercise of the utmost patience was desirable, and it is believed that public opinion in this country has appreciated the wisdom of this restraint."

"At present a resolution is pending before the meeting at Paris, with hopes of passage, under which Japan and China will agree to take no initiative which might lead to renewed conflict; in which Japan has reiterated its intention to withdraw the Japanese troops to the railway zone as soon as lives and property of Japanese nationals in Manchuria can be adequately protected; and under which both nations agree to a neutral commission to meet on the ground, to which commission all matters in dispute can be referred for investigation and report."

[*State Papers, Vol. II, pp. 76–77*]

It was known that the Japanese invasion was a *coup* by the military and that it was opposed by the more important civilian authorities. Our earlier negotiations therefore proceeded upon the hope that these more liberal elements might regain ascendancy. But with time, the military extended their action not only in Manchuria but in February, 1932, they attacked Shanghai.

The President at once ordered a strong contingent of American troops and naval forces to Shanghai to protect the lives of Americans. He re-inforced our Hawaiian and Philippine bases and gave orders that our forces should confine themselves rigidly to their task of protecting Americans, but no one could tell what incident might inflame the country. It was a period of added anxiety to the President for we were in the throes of the 1932 winter crisis.

During the spring of 1932, the smaller nation members of the League demanded the imposition of economic sanctions. The major members were not keen upon it. But to escape pressure their inspired press began blaming the United States for the inability of the League to act effectively unless we would join in the sanctions. Our State Department supported the idea that we should agree to participate in certain economic sanctions. The President, however, was adamant that this was simply the road to war itself and he would have none of it. It was at this moment that Hoover developed with Stimson the idea that we propose a great moral sanction. That was that all nations should agree that they would not recognize the acquisition of territory obtained in violation of the Kellogg Pact. That was agreed to by all principal nations and so far as the expressed reprobation of the nations can have effect, there it lies.

TRADE IN ARMS

An international treaty for control of Trade in Arms had been signed in the Coolidge Administration in June, 1925. The Senate had refused to ratify it. President Hoover in a special Message to the Congress on December 10, 1931, said:

"The Convention for the Supervision of the International Trade in Arms and Ammunition and in Implements of War, signed at Geneva, June 17, 1925, represents another of the steps taken in the general field of restriction of armament. It has been ratified unconditionally by some nations, conditionally by others. With the added impetus which ratification by the United States would lend to such a move, it is quite possible that the fourteen ratifications necessary by treaty sipulation would be received to bring the convention into force."

[State Papers, Vol. II, p. 81]

Again in a Message to the Congress, on January 10, 1933, the President said:

"To the Senate and House of Representatives:

"Recent events have emphasized the urgent need of more authority to the Executive in control of the shipment of arms from the United States for military purposes. There can be no doubt that the control of such shipments to areas of prospective and actual international conflict would greatly aid the earnest and unceasing efforts which all nations now make to prevent and lessen the dangers of such conflicts."

"However, for one nation alone to engage in such prohibitions while other nations continue to supply arms is a futility. Moreover it would tend to give advantage to one nation over another by increasing the war potentialities in manufacture and skill of non-co-operating nations."

"There is before the Senate an international convention for the suppression of international trade in arms and ammunition and implements of war signed at Geneva, June 17, 1925, awaiting ratification. This convention has been adhered to by a large number of the other important nations and is practically stopped through failure of the United States to adhere to it. Its ratification would contribute to the ends being sought by the entire world for the prevention and limitation of war. I earnestly urge that this convention should be ratified."

"If, however, it is impossible, as seems to be the case, for the Senate to now ratify this treaty it is urgent that legislation should be passed conferring upon the President authority in his discretion to limit or forbid shipment of arms for miilitary purposes in cases where special undertakings of co-operation can be secured with the principal arms manufacturing nations."

"While such a measure would not accomplish the whole of the purposes which the advance thought in the world requires, it would at least enable the Executive in special cases to place the United States in line with other nations who are willing to make such sacrifices in the prevention of military conflicts."

"I therefore urge that this convention should receive ratification of the Senate now, or alternatively that legislation to the purpose mentioned should be promptly enacted."

"I attach hereto the views of the Secretary of State upon this subject."

[*State Papers, Vol. II, pp. 565–6*]

On December 5, 1934, members of a committee of the Senate made some false statements as to Hoover's attitude on international trade in arms to which he replied:

"The full reports and details of the conference of sporting arms manufacturers which was called by myself as Secretary of Commerce in 1925 and yesterday referred to before a Senate Committee, are no doubt in the State Department. The conference was called at the request of the Secretary of State and for the purpose of giving a hearing to the manufacturers' views as to methods of discriminating between sporting arms on one hand and war arms on the other, and such other proper protections as might be necessary to the American industry at an international convention then about to be held in Europe. This convention was for the purpose of limiting the international traffic in war arms. As a result of the negotiations an international treaty was secured controlling that traffic. It was signed by the United States. During eight years from 1925 to 1933 its ratification was held up by the Senate and probably is yet. That ratification was incessantly advocated by President Coolidge, and myself, and by Secretaries Kellogg and Stimson. As late as January 10, 1933, I again urged its ratification and called the attention of the Senate to the fact that it had now been ratified by a large number of other nations and that its failure of adoption in the world was largely because of the failure of the United States. I further recommended that pending the ratification of the treaty they should give immediate and further authority to the President to control such traffic from the United States."

REDUCTION OF LAND ARMS

In an opening address on May 4, 1931, before the International Chamber of Commerce at Washington, President Hoover undertook a new drive on land arms:

Members of the International Chamber of Commerce:

"I bid you welcome to the United States. You have come from many lands and at a time of grave responsibilities at home."

"It is needless for me to emphasize the high degree of economic interdependence of the world—we require no more emphatic demonstration than the present world-wide depression."

"This is not an occasion for review of the action and interaction of such a multitude of forces, but I do wish to give emphasis to one of these war inheritances in which international co-operation can effect a major accomplishment in reducing the tax burdens of the world, removing a primary cause of unrest and establishing greater confidence for the long future. That is the limitation and reduction of armament. The world expenditure on all arms is now nearly five billions of dollars yearly, an increase of about 70 per cent over that previous to the Great War. We stand today with near 5,500,000 men actively under arms and 20,000,000 more in reserves. These vast forces greatly exceeding those of the pre-war period, still are to be demobilized, even though twelve years have passed since the Armistice was signed, because of fear and of inability of nations to co-operate in mutual reductions. Yet we are all signatories to the Kellogg-Briand Pact, by which we have renounced war as an instrument of national policy and agreed to settle all controversies by pacific means. Surely with this understanding, the self-defense of nations could be assured with proportionately far less military forces than these. This vast armament continues not only a burden upon the economic recuperation of the world but, of even more consequence, the constant threats and fears which arise from it are a serious contribution to all forms of instability, whether social, political, or economic."

"We must recognize that reduction of this gigantic waste of competition in military establishments is in the ultimate of an importance transcendent over all other forms of such economic effort."

"We have made considerable progress in the limitation and reduction of naval arms. We have laid the foundations for still further progress in the future. These agreements have contributed greatly to reduce the burden of taxes and to establish confidence and good will among the nations who have been signatory to them. Within a short time the principal nations of the world will meet to discuss the broad questions of reduction in land armament. The very calling of this conference is in itself not only proof of need but is an emphatic evidence of progress in the world demand for relief and for peace. Of all proposals for the economic rehabilitation of the world, I know of none which compares in necessity or importance with the successful result of that conference. The United States has a less direct interest in land armament reduction than any of the large nations because our forces have been already demobilized and reduced more than all others. We have, however, a vast indirect interest in greater assurance of peace, order and the increased economic prosperity of other nations."   [State Papers, Vol. I, p. 558]

In advancement of these ideas, our government joined in the World Disarmament Conference convened by the League of Nations at Geneva on February 2, 1932. Ambassador Hugh Gibson, whose experience and abilities were outstanding, headed the American delegation. Upon this subject, the President in a Message to the Congress on December 10, 1931, said:

". . . Up to the present time the record of achievement has been almost entirely in the field of naval disarmament. It is to be hoped that further progress can be made in reduction of naval arms and that limitation and reduction so urgently needed can be extended to land arms."

"The burden of taxes to support armament is greater today than before the Great War, and the economic instability of the world is definitely due in part to this cause and the fears which these huge armaments at all times create. No discouragements should be permitted to turn the world from sane and reasonable limitation of arms."

"With a view to establishing an atmosphere of confidence for the opening of this World Disarmament Conference, more than forty governments, including all the principal military and naval powers, have joined in accepting the principle of one-year armaments truce. This truce, which is the outgrowth of a proposal advanced last September by the Foreign Minister of Italy, is designed to prevent the expansion of armaments program during the coming months in the hope of removing the threat of a sudden revival of competition in arms before and during the conference. These steps were fully approved by our War and Navy Departments." [*State Papers, Vol. II, pp. 75–6*]

The conference engaged in futilities and oratory for over four months. The governments primarily concerned offered no constructive plans. Finally in order that it should stop dawdling and come to realities, Hoover through Secretary Stimson instructed Ambassador Gibson as to certain avenues of disarmament which he should first privately broach to the conference. These proposals were of a new order. They embraced the reduction of armies by one-third over the number required to preserve internal order and the abolition of "offensive" arms. They were the most practicable and far-reaching proposals made before or since that time. But while some members of the conference privately expressed their approval nothing resulted. Hoover then, despite protests from some of our delegation, instructed Ambassador Gibson to make the proposal public in order to summon world public opinion. This proposal was made in a note to the conference drafted in Hoover's handwriting:

"The delegations at the World Conference on Disarmament at Geneva are engaged in discussions as to methods by which a more comprehensive effort can be made toward disarmament."

"The following is the substance of instructions which have been given by the President to the American delegation for guidance in the discussions which are now occupying them."

" 'The time has come when we should cut through the brush and adopt some broad and definite method of reducing the overwhelming burden of armament which now lies upon the toilers of the world. This would be the most important world step that could be taken to expedite economic recovery. We must make headway against the mutual fear and friction arising out of war armament which kill human confidence throughout the world. We can still remain practical in maintaining an adequate self-defense among all nations; we can add to the assurances of peace and yet save the people of the world from ten to fifteen billions of wasted dollars during the next ten years.' "

" 'I propose that the following principles should be our guide:

" 'First: The Kellogg-Briand Pact, to which we are all signatories, can only mean that the nations of the world have agreed that they will use their arms solely for defense.' "

" 'Second: This reduction should be carried out not only by broad general cuts in armaments but by increasing the comparative power of defense through decreases in the power of the attack.' "

" 'Third: The armaments of the world have grown up in general mutual relation to each other. And, speaking generally, such relativity should be preserved in making reductions.' "

" 'Fourth: The reductions must be real and positive. They must effect economic relief.' "

" 'Fifth: There are three problems to deal with—land forces, air forces and naval forces. They are all interconnected. No part of the proposals which I make can be disassociated one from the other.' "

" 'Based on these principles, I propose that the arms of the world should be reduced by nearly one-third.' "

" '*Land Forces.* In order to reduce the offensive character of all land forces as distinguished from their defensive character, I propose the adoption of the presentation already made at the Geneva conference for the abolition of all tanks, all chemical warfare and all large mobile guns. This would not prevent the establishment or increase of fixed fortifications of any character for the defense of frontiers and sea-coasts. It would give an increased relative strength to such defenses as compared with the attack.' "

" 'I propose furthermore that there should be a reduction of one-third in strength of all land armies over and above the so-called police component.' "

" 'The land armaments of many nations are considered to have two functions. One is the maintenance of internal order in connection with the regular forces of the country. The strength required for this purpose has been called the "police component." The other function is defense against foreign attack. The additional strength required for this purpose has been called the "defense component." While it is not suggested that these different components should be separated, it is necessary to consider this contention as to functions in proposing a practical plan of reduction in land forces. Under the Treaty of Versailles and the other peace treaties, the armies of Germany, Austria, Hungary and Bulgaria were reduced to a size deemed appropriate for the maintenance of internal order, Germany being assigned 100,000 troops for a population of approximately 65,000,000 people. I propose that we should accept for all nations a basic police component of soldiers proportionate to the average which was thus allowed Germany and these other States. This formula, with necessary corrections for powers having colonial possessions, should be sufficient to provide for the maintenance of internal order by the nations of the world. Having analyzed these two components in this fashion, I propose as stated above that there should be a reduction of one-third in the strength of all land armies over and above the police component.' "

" '*Air Forces.* All bombing planes to be abolished. This will do away with the military possessions of types of planes capable of attacks upon civil populations and should be coupled with the total prohibition of all bombardment from the air.' "

" '*Naval Forces.* I propose that the treaty number and tonnage of battleships shall be reduced one-third; that the treaty tonnage of aircraft carriers, cruisers and destroyers shall be reduced by one-fourth; that the treaty tonnage of submarines shall be reduced by one-third, and that no nation shall retain a submarine tonnage greater than 35,000.' "

" 'The relative strength of naval arms in battleships and aircraft carriers, as between the five leading naval powers, was fixed by the Treaty of Washington. The relative strength in cruisers, destroyers and submarines was fixed, as between the United States, Great Britain and Japan, by the Treaty of London. For the purposes of this proposal, it is suggested that the French and Italian strength in cruisers and destroyers be calculated as though they had joined in the Treaty of London on a basis approximating the so-called accord of March 1, 1931. There are various technical considerations connected with these naval discussions which will be presented by the delegation.' "

" '*General.* The effect of this plan would be to effect an enormous saving in cost of new construction and replacements of naval vessels. It would also save large amounts in the operating expense in all nations of land, sea and air forces. It would greatly reduce offensive strength compared to defensive strength in all nations.' "

" 'These proposals are simple and direct. They call upon all nations to contribute something. The contribution here proposed will be relative and mutual. I know of nothing that would give more hope for humanity today than the acceptance of such a program with such minor changes as might be necessary. It is folly for the world to go on breaking its back over military expenditure and the United States is willing to take its share of responsibility by making definite proposals that will relieve the world.' "

[State Papers, Vol. II, pp. 211–213]

These proposals were declared workable by the technical staff of the Disarmament Conference. They were welcomed by the smaller nations and supported by some of the larger ones. The conference was in hopeful progress at the end of the Hoover Administration and Hoover proposed to keep it in conference until results were accomplished.[1] (See World War Debts, pages 498, 520.)

PHILIPPINE ISLANDS

President Hoover favored the independence of the Philippine Islands provided it was a complete and absolute separation which relieved the United States of all responsibility for their defense, and provided the economic stability of the islands had been assured after their divorce from the United States Customs Union. He did not approve of any conditional separation where we had responsibilities without authority. Nor did he believe that economic stability had yet been assured. Secretary Hurley was sent to the islands for a re-examination of the situation. Upon his return, the President said (October 27, 1931):

"With Secretary Hurley's return, the Cabinet this morning discussed the Philippine question at considerable length. . . . Independence of the Philippines at some time has been directly or indirectly promised by every President and by the Congress. In accord with those undertakings, the problem is one of time. In the interest of the Philippine people the time

---

[1]Without reference to actions of his predecessors, President Roosevelt on May 17, 1933, addressed a message to the sovereigns and presidents of fifty-four nations on this subject. His major suggestions were that they sign a pact of non-aggression and that they do away with offensive land weapons—bombing planes, mobile artillery, tanks, poison-gas. These proposals were less comprehensive than Hoover's.

element involves the necessity that independence must be assured of durability and the Government of the Philippines must be assured of stability. The economic independence of the Philippines must be attained before political independence can be successful. Independence tomorrow without assured economic stability would result in the collapse of Philippine Government revenues and the collapse of all economic life in the islands. We propose to give further consideration to the whole question during the immediate future." [*State Papers, Vol. II, p. 24*]

In December, 1932, the Democratic Congress passed a Philippine Independence Bill. Hoover vetoed it with this statement:

"The Philippine people have today as great a substance of ordered liberty and human freedom as any people in the world. They lack the form of separate nationality which is indeed their rightful spiritual aspiration. They have been encouraged in this aspiration by every President of the United States during the years of our association with the Philippines and by declaration of the Congress."

"But in securing this spiritual boon to the 13,000,000 people in these islands the United States has a triple responsibility. That is responsibility to the Philippine people, responsibility to the American people, and responsibility to the world at large. Our responsibility to the Philippine people is that in finding a method by which we consummate their aspiration we do not project them into economic and social chaos, with the probability of breakdown in government, with its consequences in degeneration of a rising liberty which has been so carefully nurtured by the United States at the cost of thousands of American lives and hundreds of millions of money. Our responsibility to the American people is that we shall see the fact of Philippine separation accomplished without endangering ourselves in military action hereafter to maintain internal order or to protect the Philippines from encroachment by others, and above all that this shall be accomplished so as to avoid the very grave dangers of future controversies and seeds of war with other nations. We have a responsibility to the world that having undertaken to develop and perfect freedom for these people we shall not by our course project more chaos into a world already sorely beset by instability. The present bill fails to fulfill these responsibilities. It invites all these dangers. It does not fulfill the idealism with which this task in human liberation was undertaken. . . ."

"During the period of intermediate government prior to complete independence, not alone the internal and external political relations of the Philippine people must be adjusted, but they must adjust their economic life to the complete abrogation of the present free-trade association with the United States. The period for such adjustment in this act is too short, too violent."

"A large part of the motivation for the passage of this bill is presumed relief to certain American agricultural industries from competition by Philippine products. We are trustees for these people and we must not let our selfish interest dominate that trust."

"The bill weakens our civil authority during the period of intermediate government to a point of practical impotence."

". . . During this period, however, the American flag will be flying and our army will be in occupation."

"The income of the Philippine Government has never in the past been sufficient to meet, in addition to other expenditures, the cost of supporting even the Filipino Scouts, much less an army or navy."

"If the American people consider that they have discharged their responsibilities to the Philippine people, have carried out the altruistic mission which we undertook, if we have no further national stake in the islands, if the Philippine people are now prepared for self-government, if they can maintain order and their institutions, if they can now defend their independence, we should say so frankly on both sides. I hold that this is not the case. Informed persons on neither side have made such declarations without many reservations. Nor can these conditions be solved by the evasions and proposals of this bill without national dishonor."

"In my view we must undertake further steps toward the liberation of the Philippine Islands, but they should be based upon a plebiscite to be taken 15 or 20 years hence. On such an occasion there would be a full impress upon the Filipinos of the consequences of their act. They should then have freedom to form their own constitution and government, both in the light of experience and the forces moving at that time. In the meantime we should develop steadily through an expansion of the organic act a larger importance to their own officials by extension of authority to Cabinet government, with a full reserve of powers to our representatives. Immigration should be restricted at once. We should co-operate with them to bring about their economic independence before the plebiscite by very gradual reduction of their free imports. We should, prior to such plebiscite, or any sooner date that the Philippine people propose, fix a mutual preference in trade similar to and on a wider scale than that with Cuba. The United States should plainly announce prior to the time of this plebiscite whether (*a*) it will make absolute and complete withdrawal from all military and naval bases, and from every moral or other commitment to maintain their independence, or (*b*) the conditions as to authority and rights within the islands under which we will continue that protection."

"These final steps can not be properly determined now by either the Philippine people or ourselves."

"We are here dealing with one of the most precious rights of man—national independence interpreted as separate nationality. It is the national independence of 13,000,000 human beings. We have here a specific duty. The ideals under which we undertook this responsibility, our own national instincts and our institutions which we have implanted on these islands, breathe with these desires. It is a goal not to be reached by yielding to selfish interests, to resentments, or to abstractions, but with full recognition of our responsibilities and all their implications and all the forces which would destroy the boon we seek to confer and the dangers to our own freedom from entanglements which our actions may bring. Neither our successors nor history will discharge us of responsibility for actions which diminish the liberty we seek to confer nor for dangers which we create for ourselves as a consequence of our acts. This legislation puts both our people and the Philippine people not on the road to liberty and safety, which we desire, but on the path leading to new and enlarged dangers to liberty and freedom itself."

[*State Papers, Vol. II, pp. 569 ff.*]

The Independence Act was passed over the President's veto.[1]

[1] Already the inadequacy of this Act has become evident and a clamor has arisen for its amendment.

NATIONAL DEFENSE

The military policies of the Hoover Administration were direct enough—complete preparedness, but solely for defense; and an earnest desire to reduce military strength in proportion with other nations.

In his Acceptance Speech at Palo Alto on August 11, 1928, he said:

"There are two factors in maintaining peace, the building of good will . . . and the adequate preparedness for defense. We must not only be just; we must be respected. . . ."

"We have been and we are particularly desirous of furthering the limitation of armaments. But in the meantime we know that in an armed world there is only one certain guarantee of freedom—and that is preparedness for defense. It is solely to defend ourselves, for the protection of our citizens, that we maintain armament. No clearer evidence of this can exist than the unique fact that we have fewer men in army uniform today than we have in police uniforms, and that we maintain a standing invitation to the world that we are always ready to limit our naval armament in proportion as the other naval nations will do likewise. We earnestly wish that the burdens and dangers of armament upon every home in the world might be lessened. But we must and shall maintain our naval defense and our merchant marine in the strength and efficiency which will yield to us at all times the primary assurance of liberty, that is, of national safety." [*The New Day*, Hoover, Stanford Press, *p. 40*]

In his Inaugural Address on March 4, 1929, he said:

"Peace can be contributed to by respect for our ability in defense."
[*State Papers, Vol. I, p. 15*]

Early in his administration, he put the question to the naval and army staffs: "Are our defenses strong enough to repel the landing of foreign soldiers on continental United States?" The reply was emphatically "yes."

Speaking on Armistice Day, November 11, 1929, he said:

"Until such time as nations can build the agencies of pacific settlements on stronger foundations . . . there will not have been established that confidence which warrants the abandonment of preparedness. . . ."

[*State Papers, Vol. I, p. 125*]

In his first Message to the Congress on December 3, 1929, President Hoover said:

"To preserve internal order and freedom from encroachment is the first purpose of government. Our Army and Navy are being maintained in a most efficient state under officers of high intelligence and zeal. The extent and expansion of their numbers and equipment as at present authorized are ample for this purpose."

"Under the Kellogg pact we have undertaken never to use war as an instrument of national policy. We have, therefore, undertaken by covenant to use these equipments solely for defensive purposes. From a defense point of view our forces should be proportioned to national need and should, therefore, to some extent be modified by the prospects of peace, which were never brighter than today."

"It should be borne in mind that the improvement in the National Guard by Federal support begun in 1920 has definitely strengthened our national security by rendering them far more effective than ever heretofore. The advance of aviation has also greatly increased our effectiveness in defense. In addition to the very large program of air forces which we are maintaining in the Army and Navy, there has been an enormous growth of commercial aviation. This has provided unanticipated reserves in manufacturing capacity and in industrial and air personnel, which again adds to our security."   [*State Papers, Vol. I, pp. 140–142*]

In an address from the White House on September 18, 1929, he said:

"Never has there been a President who did not pray that his administration might be one of peace, and that peace should be more assured to his successor. Yet these men have never hesitated when war became the duty of the nation . . . adequate preparedness is the assurance of peace. . . . Never have we had a President who was either a pacifist or a militarist."   [*State Papers, Vol. I, p. 100*]

In an effort to reduce world naval armament he inaugurated the Naval Conference of 1930 which has already been discussed. The effect of the results of this conference on our defense he explained in reply to a letter from the commander of the American Legion, on July 30, 1929.

"I am glad to have your assurance that the American Legion supports the policy of parity for our navy with that of Great Britain. This principle is enunciated by our naval authorities as a complete defense of the United States in any contingency and defense is all that we seek."

"The first step of the renewed consideration of reduction of the excessive world naval armament has been acceptance of that principle as a preliminary to discussion between Great Britain and the United States. This is a forward step of the first importance."

"It seems to me that every person of common sense will agree that it is far better to at least try to establish such a relation by agreement before we resign ourselves to continued attempts to establish it by rival construction programs on both sides of the Atlantic. We need not disguise the fact that (aside from the capital ship limitations under the Washington Treaty) competitive building has been in progress on both sides since the Great War, and we have arrived only at disparity, not parity. It creates burdensome expenditure, a constant stream of suspicion, ill-will and misunderstandings. Moreover, by constant expansion of naval strength we cannot fail to stimulate fear and ill-will throughout the rest of the world toward both of us, and thus defeat the very purposes which you have so well expressed as being the object of the Legion, when you say, 'The Legion stands uniformly for movements which will make permanent peace more certain and assure better understanding between nations.'"   [*State Papers, Vol. I, p. 84*]

In discussing the new Naval Limitation Treaty, in a Message to the Senate on July 7, 1930, Hoover said:

"Defense is the primary function of government, and therefore our first concern in examination of any act of this character is the test of its adequacy in defense. No critic has yet asserted that with the navies provided in this agreement together with our army, our aerial defense and our national resources, we cannot defend ourselves, and certainly we want no military establishment for the purpose of domination of other nations. Our naval defense position under this treaty is the more clear if we examine our present naval strength in comparison to the present strength of the other nations, and then examine the improvements in this proportion which will result from this treaty. This improvement arises from the anticipation of parity in battleships to be reached ten years hence under the Washington Arms Treaty and the fact that other nations have been building in the classes of ships not limited by that treaty, while we, until lately, lagged behind."

[State Papers, Vol. I, p. 352]

The President issued the following Navy Day statement on October 27, 1931:

"Navy Day offers a special opportunity for national consideration of our defense and an opportunity to express national appreciation to the body of men who give so high a service to the Nation."

"The first necessity of our government is the maintenance of a navy so efficient and strong that, in conjunction with our army, no enemy may ever invade our country. The commanding officers of our forces inform me that we are maintaining that strength and efficiency."

"Ours is a force of defense, not offense. To maintain forces less than that strength is to destroy national safety, to maintain greater forces is not only economic injury to our people but a threat against our neighbors and would be righteous cause for ill will amongst them. Our problem is to assure the adjustment of our forces to the minimum based upon the outlook in the world; to strive for lower armament throughout the whole world; to promote good will among nations; to conduct our military activities with rigid economy; to prevent extremists on one side from undermining the public will to support our necessary forces, and to prevent extremists on the other side from waste of public funds."

[State Papers, Vol. II, p. 23]

In the campaign of 1932, Hoover said on August 11, 1932:

"I insist upon an Army and Navy of a strength which guarantees that no foreign soldier will land on American soil. That strength is relative to other nations. I favor every arms reduction which preserves that relationship."

[State Papers, Vol. II, p. 257]

In maintaining the navy, and under the strong administration of Secretary of the Navy Adams, he completed the construction of 80,000 tons of new war vessels, largely completed 100,000 tons further, modernized four battleships wholly and three more partially.

Hoover believed in maintaining the efficiency of the army.

Under the able administrations of Secretaries of War James Good and Patrick Hurley, Hoover continued to build the Regular Army, the National Guard, and the Civilian Training Corps into strong skeleton organizations capable of quick expansion. During his administration, the mechanization of the army upon a thorough-going scale was carried out. The army posts were greatly improved in living quarters. The Coast Defense was greatly strengthened.

He increased the air forces of the army and navy by 40 per cent from 2000 planes to about 2800 planes with the necessary expansion of ground services. He reinforced the service potentially with the development of commercial aviation and its manufacturing equipment.

He preserved the complete defense of the United States with an expenditure upon the War and Navy Departments (excluding civilian activities) of about $650,000,000 per annum.[1]

[1]The present military expenditures exceed $1,000,000,000 per annum.

PRESERVING THE CONSTITUTION

Herbert Hoover's constitutional policy was single-minded and direct. That was to support the Constitution not only in letter but in spirit. More important legislation was passed in his administration than in any four previous peace time administrations in our history. Not a single law signed by him has been ruled unconstitutional by the courts. That was no accident, for it was his belief that it was his function as President to have every act of Congress rigidly scrutinized for constitutionality, and to advise that body thereon. He did not hesitate to veto all failures in this regard.

On three occasions he vetoed legislation on this ground—that is, on June 6, 1930, January 19, 1931, and January 24, 1933.

Hoover's approach to the Constitution was not legalistic. To him the center-point of the Constitution was the Bill of Rights with its safeguards of fundamental liberties. To him a large part of those safeguards were the independence of the Executive, Legislative and Judicial branches, and the division between Federal and State powers.

Vital problems of the relation of the Constitution to the people were rising more and more throughout Hoover's public life. His entire approach was that if necessary the Constitution should be amended by the people, but there should be no indirection.

As Secretary of Commerce, presiding at the national oratorical contest on the Constitution on May 26, 1928, he said:

". . . It is meet that the youth of our country should be enlisted in study and even in a rigid scrutiny of the Constitution and its consequences. We have no fears from its scrutiny. We can fear ignorance of it. More particularly do we require constant search into the consequences which have flowed from it, for the Constitution not only created a political system of self-government, but it set the framework for a new relation of man to man."

". . . Truly the Constitution has proved a brake upon ill-considered action, a check on storms of public passion, a curb on domination that would destroy equality of opportunity. Yet it has proved to have an adaptability to meet the shifting social needs . . . or changing ideas. And each new generation must find the changes in the activities of our Government which this increasing complexity of life brings."

Speaking in the Presidential campaign on August 10, 1928, he said:

". . . Change in the Constitution can and must be brought about only by the straightforward methods provided in the Constitution itself. There are those who do not believe in the purposes of several provisions of the Constitution. No one denies their right to seek to amend it. They are not subject to criticism for asserting that right. But the Republican Party does deny the right of any one to seek to destroy the purposes of the Constitution by indirection."

"Whoever is elected President takes an oath not only to faithfully execute the office of the President, but that oath provides still further that he will, to the best of his ability, preserve, protect, and defend the Constitution of the United States. I should be untrue to these great traditions, untrue to my oath of office, were I to declare otherwise."

He referred to the Constitution in many public addresses but not in the sense of debate.

"The founders of our Republic under Divine inspiration set up not alone a great political system of self-government, but they set up also a revolutionary social system in the relation of men towards men."

"Our political system is unique in the world. It is unique because of its decentralization of self-government and its checks and balances which safeguard ordered liberty and freedom to each individual."

One of the rising problems in American life was to make our economic system fit into our social requirements and do it under the Constitution. Secretary Hoover raised this question of the effect on our form of government in an address on October 14, 1925:

". . . Our Government was devised in spirit to sustain a dual purpose —to protect our people among nations by a great national power and to preserve individual freedom by local self-government. If we are to stretch the Interstate Commerce provision in the Constitution to regulate all those things that pass state lines whether there is necessity for it or not, we shall automatically absorb to Federal authority most of the government that lies within state lines, because our economic life has become so enmeshed that there is no longer that easy conception of our forefathers of what constituted interstate commerce. If we do not resist this extension, what becomes of that fundamental freedom and independence that can rise only from local self-government? Where the states can equally well solve these problems there is no remote reason for Federal invasion."

"Washington is already so overloaded with affairs that it cannot even now do justice to the great diversity of local interest. . . ."

"There is, indeed, a limit to theoretical efficiency which destroys more precious possession. I want to kick to local authority when the power rates are unjust; I want to kick where the searchlight of public opinion and local knowledge can be brought to bear. I don't want to deliver myself over to addressing the Interstate Power Commission at Washington, D. C., a thousand miles away, and have the letter referred to the Assistant Director in the Bureau of House Rates, and to be told that I should communicate in duplicate on form 311X to the Division of Rate Complaints of the Western District and be prepared to bring a lawyer and five expert witnesses to a town a thousand miles away to a preliminary hearing set eleven months hence, when their report has been received."

"But far more than all this I want to live in a community that governs itself, that neither wishes its responsibilities onto a centralized bureaucracy nor allows centralized bureaucracy to dictate to that local government. . . ."

Hoover gave this warning again in an address on September 7, 1926:

". . . But our real problem today is to prevent such a surrender of the sovereignty, dignity, independence, and responsibility of our state governments. We all know well enough of the time when we heard so much of 'States' Rights.' These forty-eight laboratories in government were born of States' Rights. At one time the states insisted on doing their own experimenting and carrying on their own responsibilities. But latterly many of our states are willing enough to pass difficult questions up to Washington, or allow other states to carry the burden of the solution. At all times we have to meet restless members of the community who rather than slowly develop a sense of state responsibility would rush to Washington for a mustard plaster for the whole Nation. Our Federal Government can carry this centralization of authority much less easily than can the European forms of government, and they have broken under it. Ours is ill-designed to carry such burdens; our population is too large and too diverse in its interest. Washington is already so overloaded with affairs that it cannot even now do justice to the great diversity of local interests in our country. The infinite energies of this great mass of humanity will be dulled and their progress stopped if we are to attempt more than a minor part of their government from Washington. So we have now come to the necessity of urging states to assume their responsibilities, and if they do not do so, then democracy has been indeed grievously weakened."

Speaking on February 3, 1931, President Hoover said:

"The moment responsibilities of any community, particularly in economic and social questions, are shifted from any part of the Nation to Washington, then that community has subjected itself to a remote bureaucracy with its minimum of understanding and of sympathy. It has lost a large part of its voice and its control of its own destiny. Under Federal control the varied conditions of life in our country are forced into standard molds, with all their limitations upon life, either of the individual or the community. Where people divest themselves of local government responsibilities they at once lay the foundation for the destruction of their liberties. . . ."   [State Papers, Vol. I, p. 502]

Speaking on this subject again on October 22, 1932, Hoover said:

". . . Today, perhaps as never before, our very form of government is on trial in the eyes of millions of our citizens. Economic stresses of unparalleled magnitude have racked our people, and in their distress some are tempted to lay the blame for their troubles upon the system of government under which they live. It is a not unnatural instinct, however mistaken it may be. . . . No man can foretell to what lengths the pressure of public clamor may at any time be brought to bear upon those charged with the processes of government to yield to changes which you know, before they are tried, would destroy personal liberty. . . ."
[State Papers, Vol. I, p. 330]

"Economic forces have spread business across state lines and have brought new strains upon our Federal system in its relationships with the state sovereignties. Laws that once were adequate to control private operations affecting the public interest proved unequal to these new conditions. Regulation and control were more than ever necessary."

"One of the great good fortunes of our form of government is that in the forty-eight states we have forty-eight laboratories of social and economic experimentation. . . . many of these activities—particularly those of banking and finance, of transportation, communications, and power— have expanded beyond state borders. It has become necessary during these years to develop gradually increasing burdens of Federal control. With growth and experience, these regulatory functions require constant revision. . . ."

"We must maintain on the one hand a sense of responsibility in the states. It is the local communities that can best safeguard their liberties. We must therefore impose upon the states the maximum responsibility in these regulatory powers over economic functions. On the other hand, we must be courageous in providing for extension of these regulatory powers when they run beyond the capacity of the states to protect their citizens."

"In the separation of responsibilities between the Federal and state Governments on matters outside of the economic field we have constantly to resist the well-meaning reformer who, witnessing the failure of local communities to discharge responsibilities of government, to extinguish crime, and to set up agencies of government free of corruption, to move apace with the thousand social and other advances which the country sorely needs, constantly advocates and agitates that the powers of the Federal Government be applied, that we may have a rigid uniformity of reform throughout the Nation. Yet even here it is better that we should witness some instances of failure of municipal and state governments to discharge responsibilities in protection and government of their people rather than that we should drive this Republic to a centralization which would mean the deadening of its great mainspring of progress, which is the discovery and experimentation and advancement by the local community."

"We must not believe that by guaranteeing the medium of perfection to all individuals, to all communities, to all municipalities and all states, through the deadening hand of centralization, we will secure progress."

Speaking to the American Bar Association on the occasion of the dedication of the new Supreme Court building on October 22, 1932, he took occasion to express his views as to the place of the Court in the scheme of government:

"It is your task to prove again what none knows better than you, that the very citadel of the rights of the poor against the oppression of rulers and against the extortions of the rapacious is the judicial system of the country, and that the impregnable apex of that system is the Supreme Court of the United States. It is impregnable because its membership in successive generations down to this moment has comprised the highest character of our land who preserving its great traditions have armored it with the moral support of the people, and thus, without physical power or the need of it, is able to stand equal and alone against legislative encroachment upon the people's rights or executive usurpation of them and, more precious than either, against private injustice and the enactment of public laws in violation of the fundamental protections of the Constitution." [State Papers, Vol. II, p. 331]

A statement of Hoover's in the campaign of 1932 has great significance today. On October 28, 1932, he said:

"In Governor Roosevelt's address delivered on October 25 he stated:"
" 'After March 4, 1929, the Republican Party was in complete control of all branches of the Government—Executive, Senate, and House, and I may add for good measure, the Supreme Court as well.' "
"I invite your attention to that statement about the Supreme Court. There are many things revealed by the campaign of our opponents which should give American citizens concern about the future. One of the gravest is the state of mind revealed by my opponent in that statement. He implies that it is the function of the party in power to control the Supreme Court. For generations Republican and Democratic Presidents alike have made it their most sacred duty to respect and maintain the independence of America's greatest tribunal. President Taft appointed a Democrat as Chief Justice; President Harding nominated a Democratic Justice; my last appointment was a Democrat from New York State whose appointment was applauded by Republicans and Democrats alike the Nation over. All appointees to the Supreme Court have been chosen solely on the basis of character and mental power. Not since the Civil War have the members of the court divided on political lines."
"Aside from the fact that the charge that the Supreme Court has been controlled by any political party is an atrocious one, there is a deeper implication in that statement. Does it disclose the Democratic candidate's conception of the functions of the Supreme Court? Does he expect the Supreme Court to be subservient to him and his party? Does that statement express his intention by his appointments or otherwise to attempt to

reduce that tribunal to an instrument of party policy and political action for sustaining such doctrines as he may bring with him?"

[State Papers, Vol. II, pp. 406–7]

The following statement in an address at Washington after his defeat in 1932 (December 10) has an ominous forecast:

"The life stream of this Nation is the generations of millions of human particles acting under impulses of advancing ideas and national ideals gathered from a thousand springs. These springs and rills have gathered into great streams which have nurtured and fertilized this great land over these centuries. Its dikes against dangerous floods are cemented with the blood of our fathers. Our children will strengthen these dikes, will create new channels, and the land will grow greater and richer with their lives."

"We are but transitory officials in Government whose duty is to keep these channels clear and to strengthen and extend their dikes. What counts toward the honor of public officials is that they sustain the national ideals upon which are patterned the design of these channels of progress and the construction of these dikes of safety. What is said in this or in that political campaign counts no more than the sound of the cheerful ripples or the angry whirls of the stream. What matters is— that God help the man or the group who breaks down these dikes, who diverts these channels to selfish ends. These waters will drown him or them in a tragedy that will spread over a thousand years."

Hoover had not often discussed the Constitution in his years of public service. Direct threats by government to the liberties of citizens and their safeguards only arose after his administration. The essence of his feeling in these subjects is concentrated in a speech given on Constitution Day (September 17, 1935), at San Diego:

"Our Constitution is not alone the working plan of a great federation of states under representative Government. There is embedded in it also the vital principles of the American system of liberty. That system is based upon certain inalienable freedoms and protections which not even the Government may infringe and which we call the Bill of Rights. It does not require a lawyer to interpret those provisions. They are as clear as the Ten Commandments. Among others the freedom of worship, freedom of speech and of the press, the right of peaceable assembly, equality before the law, just trial for crime, freedom from unreasonable search, and security from being deprived of life, liberty, or property without due process of law, are the principles which distinguish our civilization. Herein are the invisible sentinels which guard the door of every home from invasion of coercion, of intimidation and fear. Herein is the expression of the spirit of men who would be forever free."

"These rights were no sudden discovery, no overnight inspiration. They were established by centuries of struggle in which men died fighting bitterly for their recognition. . . . The Habeas Corpus, the 'Petition of Rights,' the 'Declaration of Rights,' the growth of the Common Law, marked their expansion security. Our forefathers migrated to America that they might attain them more fully. When they wrote the Declaration of Independence they boldly extended these rights. Before the Constitution could be ratified patriotic men . . . insisted that these hard-won rights should be incorporated in black and white. . . ."

"In the hurricane of revolutions which have swept the world since the Great War, men, struggling with the wreckage and poverty of that great catastrophe and the complications of the machine age, are in despair surrendering. . . . Whether it be Fascist Italy, Nazi Germany, Communist Russia, or their lesser followers. . . . Every day they repudiate every principle of the Bill of Rights. Freedom of worship is denied. Freedom of speech is suppressed. The press is censored and distorted with propaganda. The right of criticism is denied. Men go to jail or the gallows for honest opinion. They may not assemble for discussion. They speak of public affairs only in whispers. They are subject to search and seizure by spies and inquisitors who haunt the land. The safeguards of justice in trial or imprisonment are set aside. There is no right in one's savings or one's own home which the government need respect."

"Even in America, where liberty blazed brightest and by its glow shed light on all the others, it is besieged from without and challenged from within. Many, in honest belief, hold that we cannot longer accommodate the growth of science, technology, and mechanical power to the Bill of Rights and our form of government. With that I do not agree. Men's inventions cannot be of more value than men themselves. But it would be better that we sacrifice something of economic efficiency than to surrender these primary liberties. In them lies a spiritual right of men. Behind them is the conception which is the highest development of the Christian faith—the conception of individual freedom with brotherhood. From them is the fullest flowering of individual human personality."

"New invention and new ideas require the constant remolding of our civilization. The functions of government must be readjusted from time to time to restrain the strong and protect the weak. That is the preservation of liberty itself. . . ."

"Liberty never dies from direct attack. No one will dare rise tomorrow and say he is opposed to the Bill of Rights. Liberty dies from the encroachment and disregard of its safeguards. Its destruction can be no less potent from ignorance or desire to find short-cuts to jump over some immediate pressure. In our country, abdication of its responsibilities and powers by Congress to the Executive, the repudiation by the Government of its obligations, any alteration in the authority of the Supreme Court, the centralization of authority in the Federal Government at the expense of local government, the building up of huge bureaucracies, are the same first sapping of safeguards of human rights that have taken place in other lands. Here is the cause of anxiety and concern to the thinking citizens of the United States. George Washington in his Farewell Address warned:

" 'One method of assault may be to effect, in the form of the Constitution, alterations which may impair the energy of the system and thus to undermine that which cannot be directly overthrown.' "

Speaking upon legislative independence in its bearings upon liberty, Hoover said in an address on May 14, 1936:

"There is no fidelity higher than that owed by public officials to the Constitution and the safeguards of liberty in our Government. That extends far beyond the letter of the law. It must be supported in spirit. Anything less is betrayal of trust if this Republic is to live."

"When the New Dealers' Convention meets near Independence Hall they will no doubt summon with powerful oratory over a hundred broadcasting stations the shades of that heroic Continental Congress. I trust at that moment the American people will remember what the New Deal has done to the Congress of the United States in these recent years."

"The independences of Congress, the Executive, and the Supreme Court are the pillars at the door of liberty. For three years we have not had an independent Congress. We have not even had a good debating society. We have had a rubber stamp applied by presidentially-inspired gag rule. That is not fidelity to the spirit of the Constitution."

"For the first time in American history the word 'must' has been directed to an independent arm of the Government by the Executive. The NRA was enacted by the House of Representatives in six hours. The AAA was given eight hours."

"These measures would have gone far to transform the whole of

America into a Fascist state if they had not been set aside by the Supreme Court. Yet they had been operated for months in violation of the whole foundation precepts of democracy. Small business people have been penalized, people lost their jobs, and a thousand discouragements loosed in violation of the Constitution."

"Great groups of people receiving some special privilege have been built up. When this privilege is denied by the courts then the New Deal has sought to incite these people against the Court as a public enemy."

"The parliamentary principle of control of the purse has saved liberty a hundred times over these last three hundred years. It has saved the people from injustice in taxes many thousand times. So little is the New Deal Congress interested that it made only casual inquiry into what would be done with a whole $4,800,000,000 in one lump."

"We have worried much in our history over the independence of the Supreme Court. We have more cause to worry over the independence of Congress. Congress has delegated its conscience."

"If we examine the fate of wrecked republics the world over and through all history, we will find first comes a weakening of the legislative arm. It is in the legislative halls that liberty has committed suicide. For two hundred years the Roman Senate lingered on as a social distinction and as a scene of noisy prattle after it had surrendered its real responsibilities to personal government."

"Sea lawyers may argue that these things do not constitute a violation of oath of office. Right-thinking people will hold that they are a breach of public trust."

He again returned to the fundamental safeguards of liberty in speaking at Cleveland on June 10, 1936, to the Republican National Convention:

"There are principles which neither tricks of organization, nor the rigors of depression, nor the march of time, nor New Dealers, nor Socialists, nor Fascists can change. There are some principles which came into the universe along with the shooting stars of which worlds are made, and they have always been and ever will be true. Such are the laws of mathematics, the law of gravitation, the existence of God, and the ceaseless struggle of humankind to be free."

"Throughout the centuries of history, man's vigil and his quest have been to be free. For this, the best and bravest of earth have fought and died. To embody human liberty in workable government, America was born. Shall we keep that faith? Must we condemn the unborn generations to fight again and to die for the right to be free?"

"There are some principles that cannot be compromised. Either we shall have a society based upon ordered liberty and the initiative of the individual, or we shall have a planned society that means dictation, no matter what you call it or who does it. There is no half-way ground. They cannot be mixed. Government must either release the powers of the individual for honest achievement or the very forces it creates will drive it inexorably to lay its paralyzing hand more and more heavily upon individual effort."

"Less than twenty years ago we accepted those ideals as the air we breathed. We fought a great war for their protection. We took upon ourselves obligations of billions. We buried our sons in foreign soil. But in this score of years we have seen the advance of collectivism and its inevitable tyranny in more than half the civilized world. In this thundering era of world crisis distracted America stands confused and uncertain."

"The Whig party temporized, compromised upon the issue of slavery for the black man. That party disappeared. It deserved to disappear. Shall the Republican party deserve to receive any better fate if it compromises upon the issue of freedom for all men, white as well as black? . . ."

"Let us not blink the difficulties. Throughout the land there are multitudes of people who have listened to the songs of sirens. Thousands of men, if put to the choice, would willingly exchange liberty for fancied security even under dictatorship. Under their distress they doubt the value of their own rights and liberties. They do not see the Constitution as a fortress for their defense. They have been led to believe that it is an iron cage against which the wings of idealism beat in vain."

"They do not realize that their only relief and their hope of economic security can come only from the enterprise and initiative of free men."

"Let this convention declare without shrinking that the source of economic prosperity is freedom. Man must be free to use his own powers in his own way. Free to think, to speak, to worship. Free to plan his own life. Free to use his own initiative. Free to dare in his own adventure. It is the essence of true liberalism that these freedoms are limited by the rights of others."

"Freedom both requires and makes increased responsibilities. There is no freedom in exploitation of the weak or in the dead hand of bureaucracy."

"There's something vastly bigger than payrolls, than economics, than materialism at issue in this campaign. The free spirit of men is the source of self-respect, of sturdiness, of moral and spiritual progress.

With the inspirations of freedom come fidelity to public trust, honor and morals in government. The social order does not rest upon orderly economic freedom alone. It rests even more upon the ideals and character of a people. Governments must express those ideals in frugality, in justice, in courage, in decency, and in regard for the less fortunate, and, above all, in honor. Nations die when these weaken, no matter what their material prosperity."

"Fundamental American liberties are at stake. Is the Republican party ready for the issue? Are you willing to cast your all upon the issue, or would you falter and look back? Will you, for expediency's sake, also offer will-o'-the-wisps which beguile the people? Or have you determined to enter in a holy crusade for freedom which shall determine the future and the perpetuity of a Nation of free men? That star shell fired today over the no-man's-land of world despair would illuminate the world with hope."

Speaking in Denver on October 31, 1936, Hoover said:

"Through four years of experience this New Deal attack upon free institutions has emerged as the transcendent issue in America."

"All the men who are seeking for mastery in the world today are using the same weapons. They sing the same songs. They all promise the joys of Elysium without effort. But their philosophy is founded on the coercion and compulsory organization of men. True liberal government is founded on the emancipation of men. This is the issue upon which men are imprisoned and dying in Europe right now . . . centralized personal government disturbs only thinking men and women. But surely the NRA and the AAA alone, should prove what the New Deal philosophy of government means even to those who don't think."

"In these instances the Supreme Court, true to their oaths to support the Constitution, saved us temporarily. But Congress in obedience to their oaths should never have passed these acts. The President should never have signed them. But far more important than that, if these men were devoted to the American system of liberty they never would have proposed acts based on the coercion and compulsory organization of men."

"Fredeom does not die from frontal attack. It dies because men in power no longer believe in a system based upon Liberty. . . ."

"Does Mr. Roosevelt not admit all this in his last report on the state of the Union: 'We have built up new instruments of public power' which he admits could 'provide shackles for the liberties of the people.' Does freedom permit any man or any government any such power? Have the people ever voted for these shackles? . . ."

"The conviction of our fathers was that all these freedoms come from the Creator and that they can be denied by no man or no government or no New Deal. They were spiritual rights of men. The prime purpose of liberal government is to enlarge and not to destroy these freedoms. It was for that purpose that the Constitution of the United States was enacted. For that reason we demand that the safeguards of freedom shall be upheld. It is for this reason that we demand that this country should turn its direction from a system of personal centralized government to the ideals of liberty."

". . . will Mr. Roosevelt reply in plain words?"

"Does he propose to revive the nine acts which the Supreme Court has rejected as invasions of the safeguards of free men?"

"Has he abandoned his implied determination to change the Constitution? Why not tell the American people before election what change he proposes? Does he intend to stuff the Court itself? . . ."

Speaking upon President Roosevelt's proposals of February, 1937, to pack the Supreme Court, Hoover, after discussing the details of the proposal, said:

"That real issue is whether the President by the appointment of additional judges upon the Supreme Court shall revise the Constitution— or whether change in the Constitution shall be submitted to the people as the Constitution itself provides."

"This is no lawyers' dispute over legalisms. This is the people's problem. And it is the duty of every citizen to concern himself with this question. It reaches to the very center of his liberties."

"In the light of this background no one can conclude other than that the President seeks not to secure a Supreme Court that will find in accordance with the Constitution as it stands. He wants one that will revise the Constitution so it will mean what he wishes it to mean."

"And this is not a loose assertion. Mr. Roosevelt himself specifically confirms this purpose. In his Message to Congress he says that if these proposals be accepted then 'we may be relieved of the necessity of considering any fundamental changes in the powers of the Courts or the Constitution of our Government.'"

"Thus we are plainly told that Constitutional change is sought not by open and frank amendment of the Constitution but by judicial decision."

"If this is to be accomplished the new judges must necessarily be men who will ratify Mr. Roosevelt's projects. Unless they are pledged to Mr. Roosevelt's way of thinking he would not be, to use his own words, relieved of the necessity of considering fundamental changes in the Constitution. I am wondering what esteem these pledged judges would hold with the people."

"If Mr. Roosevelt can change the Constitution to suit his purposes by adding to the members of the Court any succeeding President can do it to suit his purposes. If a troop of 'President's judges' can be sent into the halls of justice to capture political power, then his successor with the same device can also send a troop of new 'President's judges' to capture some other power. That is not judicial process. That is force."

"The Court and the Constitution thus become the tool of the Executive and not the sword of the people. A leading newspaper which usually supports the President sums it up: 'It proposes to sanction a precedent which would make any President the master of the Supreme Court by the mere process of enlarging it.' Thus we are face to face with the proposition that the Supreme Court shall be made subjective to the Executive. Stripped to its bare bones that is the heart of this proposal. And that reaches to the very center of human liberty. The ultimate safeguard of liberty is the independence of the courts."

"In all the centuries of struggle for human freedom the independence of the judiciary from political domination has been the first battle against autocratic power."

"Our Constitution was not alone a statement of these rights. It was a framework of government for the safeguarding of these rights. Every schoolboy and girl knows that the very pillars of that temple are the independence of the Supreme Court, the Legislative branch, the Executive, and the division of powers within the states."

". . . And of these safeguards none is so final and so imperative as the independence of the courts. It is here alone where the humblest citizen and the weakest minority have their only sanctuary."

"No matter what his real intentions may be, no man will arise and say that he intends to suspend one atom of the rights guaranteed by the Constitution. Liberty dies from the encroachments and disregard of the safeguards of those rights. And unfortunately it is those whose purposes have often been good who have broken the levees of liberty to find a short-cut to their ends."

"These are serious times. Liberty is crumbling over two-thirds of the world. In less than a score of years the courts in a dozen nations have been made subjective to political power, and with this subjection the people's securities in those countries have gone out of the window. And, mark you this—in every instance the persuaders have professed to be acting for the people and in the name of progress. As we watch the parade of nations down that suicide road every American has cause to be anxious for our Republic."

"I have said this is the people's problem. It is the Supreme Court defending the people's rights and securities guaranteed by the Constitution which time and again has protected the people from those who seek for economic power or political power or to suppress free worship and free thought. It is the people's rights that are endangered. Once political power makes use of the Court, its strength, and its moral prestige are irretrievably weakened."

"It is not that our Constitution is a shackle on progress. It is a commonplace to repeat that the growth of social ideas and mechanical inventions and the ingenuity of wickedness force new problems in our national life. So far as they relate to government the vast majority of them are solvable within the Constitution. When specific problems arise which do require Constitutional amendment then the people have ever been willing to grant it. Such changes are not lightly to be undertaken. But the Constitution provides an open and aboveboard method by which they may be quickly accomplished."

"What is the hurry in all this? The Nation is recovering from depression. There is no emergency. Surely a year or two is no waste in the life of a great nation when its liberties are the stake of haste."

"If historic liberalism cannot be maintained under the present provisions of the Constitution, I shall be the first to support the President in amendment of it."

"But there are certain things that must not change. These things are the fundamental safeguards of human rights. We have already gone far on the road of personal government. The American people must halt when it is proposed to lay hands on the independence of the Supreme Court. That is the ultimate security of every cottage. It is the last safeguard of free men."

"Ladies and gentleman, I offer you a watchword—Hands off the Supreme Court."

INDEX